比较文学与文化丛书

蒋承勇 主编

高万隆　王爱琴
Frances Weightman
◎主编

中华文化语汇翻译

Chinese Cultural Terms and Phrases in English

中国社会科学出版社

图书在版编目（CIP）数据

中华文化语汇翻译／高万隆等主编．—北京：中国社会科学出版社，2015. 8

ISBN 978－7－5161－4469－5

Ⅰ. ①中…　Ⅱ. ①高…　Ⅲ. ①中华文化—词语—汉、英
Ⅳ. ①K203－61

中国版本图书馆 CIP 数据核字（2014）第 143671 号

出 版 人　赵剑英
责任编辑　罗　莉
责任校对　刘　娟
责任印制　戴　宽

出　　版　中国社会科学出版社
社　　址　北京鼓楼西大街甲 158 号
邮　　编　100720
网　　址　http://www. csspw. cn
发 行 部　010－84083685
门 市 部　010－84029450
经　　销　新华书店及其他书店

印刷装订　三河市君旺印务有限公司
版　　次　2015 年 8 月第 1 版
印　　次　2015 年 8 月第 1 次印刷

开　　本　880×1230　1/32
印　　张　14. 625
插　　页　2
字　　数　489 千字
定　　价　62. 00 元

主编　高万隆（浙江工商大学）
　　　王爱琴（台州学院）
　　　弗朗西丝·惠特曼（英国利兹大学）
译者　高万隆　王爱琴　李　勇　钱　虹
　　　戴连云　李彬彬　卓素玲　刘　芳
　　　张　琦　顾翠华

Editor-in-chief: Warren Gao (Zhejiang Gongshang University, China)
Anqin Wang (Taizhou University, China)
Frances Weightman (University of Leeds, UK)
Contributors: Warren Gao, Aiqin Wang, Yong Li, Hong Qian,
Lianyun Dai, Binbin Li, Suling Zhuo, Fang Liu,
Qi Zhang, Cuihua Gu

总　　序

“全球化”境遇与比较文学

蒋承勇

当今时代，不管从哪一个角度看，“全球化”已是客观存在的事实，是一种难以抗拒的时代潮流，人类的生存已处在全球化的境遇中。然而，“全球化”在人的不同的生存领域，其趋势和影响的程度是不同的，尤其在文化领域更有其复杂性。

“全球化”首先是在经济领域出现的，从这一层面看，全球化的过程是全球“市场化”的过程；“市场化”的过程，又往往是经济规则一体化的过程。人类“进入 80 年代以来，世界资本主义经历了一番结构性的调整和发展。在以高科技和信息技术为龙头的当代科学技术上升到一个新的台阶之后，商业资本的跨国运作，大型金融财团、企业集团和经贸集团的不断兼并，尤其是信息高速公路的开通，不仅使得经济、金融、科技的‘全球化’在物质技术层面成为可能，而且的确很大程度上变成了一种社会现实。越来越多的国家加入到一个联系越来越密切的世界经济体系之中，国际货币基金组织、世界贸易组织等世界性经贸联合体实行统一的政策目标，各国的税收政策、就业政策等逐步统一化，技术、金融、会计报表、国民统计、环境保护等，也都实行相对的标准”。[①] 这说明，全球化时代的人类经济生活，追求的是经济活动规则的一体化与统一化。所以，由于“全球化”的概念来自于经济领域，而经济领域的“全球化”又以一体化或统一化为追求目标和基本特征，因而，“全球化”这一概念与生俱来就与“一体化”连结在一起，或者说它一开始就隐含着“一体化”的意义。

在信息化的21世纪，伴随经济全球化而来的是金融全球化、科技全球化、传媒全球化，由此又必然产生人类价值观念的震荡与重构，这就是文化层面的全球化趋势。因此，经济的全球化必然会带来文化领域的变革，这是历史发展的规律。然而，文化的演变虽然受经济的制约，但它的变革方式与方向因其自身的独特性而不至于像经济等物质、技术形态那样呈一体化特征。因此，简单地说经济全球化必然带来文化全球化是不恰当的；或者说，笼统地讲文化全球化也像经济全球化那样走“一体化”之路，是不恰当的。在经济大浪潮的冲击下，西方经济强国的文化（主要是美国的）价值理念不同程度地渗透到经济弱国的社会文化机体中，使其本土文化在吸收外来文化因素后产生变革与重构。这从单向渗透的角度看，是经济强国的文化向经济弱国的文化的扩张，是后者向前者的趋同，其间有“一体化”的倾向。然而，文化之相对于经济的独特性在于：不同种类、不同质的文化形态的价值与性质并不取决于它所依存的经济形态的价值；文化价值的标准不像经济价值标准那样具有普适性，相反，它具有相对性。因此，在经济全球化、一体化的过程中，不同的文化形态在趋同的同时，依然呈多元共存的态势，文化的趋同性与多元

① 盛宁：《世纪末·“全球化”·文化操守》，《外国文学评论》2000年第1期。

性是统一的。在经济全球化的过程中，经济弱国的文化价值观念同时也反向渗透到经济强国的文化机体之中，这是文化趋同或“文化全球化”的另一层含义。所以，在谈论经济全球化背景下的文化全球化趋势时，我们既反对任何一种文化形态以超文化的姿态取代其他不同质文化的价值体系，也反对文化上的相对主义、民族主义和保守主义。我们认为，文化上的全球化，既不是抹煞异质文化的个性，也不能制造异质文化之间的彼此隔绝，而应当在不同文化形态保持个性的同时，对其他文化形态取开放认同的态度，使不同质的文化形态在对话、交流、认同的过程中，在趋同性与本土化的互动过程中既关注与重构人类文化的普适性价值理念，体现对人类自身的终极关怀，又尊重并重构各种异质文化的个性，从而创造一种普适性与相对性辩证统一、富有生命力而又丰富多彩的“世界文化”。在此，“世界文化”是一种包含了相对性的普适文化，是一种既包容了不同文化形态，同时又以人类普遍的、永恒的价值作为理想的人类新文化。因此，我们认为，经济和物质、技术领域的全球化，并不必然导致同等意义上的文化的“全球化”，即文化的“一体化”，而是文化的趋同化与本土化互动，普适性与多元化辩证统一的时代。所以，在严格的意义上，“全球化”仅限于经济领域。至少，在全球化的初期阶段是如此。

但是，不管怎么说，经济全球化的过程，人类文化无可抗拒地走向变革与重构，文学作为文化的一部分，也不可避免地处于变革与重构的境遇中。现实的情形是，在 20 世纪 90 年代以降，经济的全球化和文化的信息化、大众化，把文学逼入了边缘状态，使之失去了先前的轰动与辉煌，J. 希利斯 · 米勒则宣告了文学时代的“终结”。他说：“新的电信时代正在通过改变文学存在的前提和共生因素（concomitans）而把它引向终结。”[1] 相应地，“文学研究的时代已经过去。再也不会出现这样一个时代—为了文学自身的目的，撇开理论的或政治方面的思考而单纯地去研究文学。那样做不合时宜”。[2] 米勒的预言虽然在今天看来有些危言耸听，或者言过其实，但它也让人们注意到文学的衰退与沉落，文学工作者显然很有必要正视文学的这种现实和趋势。对文学的这种命运是否有可拯救之法，笔者无力解答，也无意于去解答。但我认为，在全球化的境遇中，文学研究者很有必要在研究的理论与方法上有所革新。也许，这样做无所谓是为了不让“文学研究的时代”成为“过去”，而是为了适应这个文化大变革的时代，适应这个“全球化”的时代。

文学的研究应该跳出本土文化的阈限，进而拥有世界的、全球的眼光，这样的呼声如果说以前一直就有，而且不少研究者早都已付诸实践，那么，在全球化境遇中，文学研究者对全球意识与世界眼光则更需有一种自觉意识。在这种意义上，比较文学及其方法有更值得文学研究者重视与借鉴的必要。比较文学本身就是站在世界文学的基点上对文学进行跨民族、跨文化、跨学科研究的，它与生俱来拥有一种世界的、全球的和人类的眼光与视野。正如美国耶鲁大学比较文学教授理查德·布劳德海德所说：“比较文学中获得的任何有趣的东西都来自外域思想的交流基于一种真正的开放式的、多边的理解之上，我们将拥有即将到来的交流的最珍贵的变体：如果我们愿意像坚持我们自己的概念是优秀的一样承认外国概念的力量的话，如果我们像乐于教授别人一

---

① J. 希利斯·米勒：《全球化时代文学研究还会继续吗?》，《文学评论》2001年第1期。

② 同上。

样地愿意去学习的话。”[1] 因此，在全球化境遇中，比较文学在文学研究中无疑拥有显著的功用和更强的生命力；比较文学的理论与方法应该是文学研究的基本理论与方法之一。

不仅如此，在全球化的境遇中，比较文学对文化的变革与重构，对促进异质文化间的交流、对话和互补、认同，对推动文化的趋同化与本土化的互动都有特殊的、积极的作用。比较文学之本质属性是文学的跨文化研究，这种研究至少在两种异质文化之间展开。比较文学的研究可以增进不同文化背景下的文学的理解与交流，促进异质文化环境中文学的发展，进而推动人类总体文学的发展。尤其是，比较文学可以通过异质文化背景下的文学的研究，促进异质文化的理解、对话与交流、认同。因此，比较文学不仅以异质文化视野为研究的前提，而且以异质文化的互认、互补为终极目的，它有助于异质文化间的交流，使之在互认的基础上达到互补共存，使人类文化处于普适性与多元化的良性生存状态。所以，比较文学在本质上又是一种文化的比较研究，比较文学与比较文化——也即比较文学与文化，是天然地联为一体的。也许，正是把比较文学置身于人类文化的大背景、大视野，正是把文学研究置身于人类文化的大背景、大视野，才有可能使全球化境遇中的文学研究找到一个新的生长点，使文学研究获得一种顺应文化变革与重构浪潮的生机，而且，文学和比较文学研究也就有可能在21世纪的全球化境遇中，在人类文化的变革与重构的大舞台里找到自己的用武之地。

正是基于上述一些想法，我们编撰这套“比较文学与文化”丛书。我们试图把文学置于人类文化的大背景中，从不同的层面

① ［美］理查德·布劳德海德：《比较文学的全球化》，王宁编《全球化与文化：西方与中国》，第235页。

展开研究，对异质文化背景下的文学做出新的阐释与体认，为中外文学的研究，为 21 世纪中外文化的交流与互补作点微薄的贡献。

2008 年春节

目　　录

体例说明

1. 本书语汇涵盖中华文化的各个方面，以尽可能对等的英译力求准确地传达中华文化语汇的丰富内涵，尤其集中翻译极具中华文化特色的用语词句、典籍名篇、文史事件、文学艺术、流派社团、风物遗迹、民俗风情等各个方面。选词的依据是具有鲜明的中国文化特色、中华民族特色和地方特色且具有影响的语汇。此书读者的定位既是中文读者，也是英文读者，目的是为这两类读者在中外文化交流和中英翻译方面提供有价值的参考和依据，为中国文化走出去的国家发展战略贡献绵薄之力。本书体例说明如下：

2. 每一词条按下列结构进行编排：汉语词条、汉语拼音、英语对应词、英语解释。

3. 本书所有词条均按照汉语拼音字母表顺序规则排列。第一个字母相同的，依照第二个字母排列；以下类推。

4. 词条的发音标识：以《汉语拼音方案》为基础，用汉语拼音字母和声调符号表示；发音以用本来的声调表示为原则，因音节的连续而产生的声调变化也不标示；适当使用隔音符号，使音节明白。如：

三国演义（sānguó yǎnyì）；大团结（dàtuánjié）；八拜之交（bā bài zhī jiāo）

5. 词条里的英译中多义项的释义用圈码①②③等分列；同

一义项的多个释义之间用“;”隔开。如:

阿斗(ādǒu)①Liu Shan(刘禅,207－271,the last emperor of the kingdom of Shu Han)②(fig.)a wimp;a feeble and incompetent person

6. 本书汉语词条的翻译尽量提供英语对应词,无对应词的提供英语解释性翻译。特别是有典故的语汇,译文中先提供比较精练的原意,再添加比喻意义或释义。如:

暗度陈仓(àn dù chéncāng)①(lit.)“to pretend to march along one route while sneaking along another route”－to do something in secret②(fig.)to have an illicit love affair;to commit adultery

程门立雪(chéngmén lìxuě)(lit.)“standing in snow to wait upon Master Cheng reverently”－to respect the teacher and learn from him with reverence

百家饭(bǎijiāfàn)(lit.)“the Hundred Family Meal”－begged leftovers

7. 涉及朝代起讫年限,公元后 AD 不标示,但涉及容易混淆时将其标出,如:汉朝(hàncháo)the Han Dynasty(206 BC－220 AD)

8. 涉及历史人物、历史事件的,括号里提供起讫年限。如:

慈禧太后(cíxǐ tàihòu)Empress Dowager Cixi(1835－1908)

鸦片战争(yāpiàn zhànzhēng)The Opium War;the Opium Wars [including The First Opium War(1840－1842)and The Second Opium War(1856－1860)]

辛亥革命(xīnhài gémìng)the Revolution of 1911;the 1911 Revolution

五卅运动(wǔsà yùndòng)the May 30th Movement(1925)

9. 涉及书名和各类作品名称，用书名号标示，英译名称为斜体，如：

《红楼梦》（hónglóumèng）*A Dream of Red Mansions*，*The Story of the Stone* – a novel by Cao Xueqin（曹雪芹，1715 – 1763）and Gao'E（高鹗，1758 – 1815）；an adaptation of this novel as a TV drama and film

语汇首字音序表

D

E

H

K

M

T

W

Y

Z

A

阿鼻地狱(ābídìyù)(Buddh.) the Avici Hell(the lowest level of hell)

阿昌族(āchāngzú) the Achang nationality

阿斗(ādǒu)①Liu Shan(刘禅,207－271,the last emperor of the kingdom of Shu Han)②(fig.)a wimp; a feeble and incompetent person

阿堵物(ādǔwù)① this; this thing ②money

阿飞(āfēi)a hooligan

阿訇(āhōng)an imam

阿罗汉(āluóhàn)(Buddh.)Arhat(a Buddhist who has gained a high level of spiritual attainment)

阿Q精神(Ā Q jīngshén)(lit.)"Ah Q-ism"－a spirit of self-deception in the face of defeat

《阿Q正传》(Ā Q zhèngzhuàn) *The True Story of Ah Q* － a short story by Lu Xun(鲁迅, 1881－1936) in 1921－1922

阿哥(àge)a Manchu prince

阿妈(àma)Father(Manchu term)

哀辞(āicí)an elegy;a lament

哀歌(āigē)a mourning song;an elegy;a dirge

哀祭(āijì) mourning; lamentation; to lament

哀家(āijiā)I, me(a self-appellation by the emperor)

哀荣(āiróng)①posthumous honor②an honorable funeral

艾灸(àijiǔ)moxibustion;to cauterize with moxa

艾卷儿(àijuǎnr)a moxa cigarette

艾柱灸(àizhùjiǔ) moxa-cone moxibustion

爱称(àichēng)a pet name

爱面子(àimiànzi)to be concerned about saving face

《爱情三部曲》(àiqíng sānbùqǔ) *Love Trilogy* － the three novels, *Fog*, *Rain*, *Lightning*, by Ba Jin(巴金, 1904－2005) in 1931

爱新觉罗(àixīnjuéluó) Aisin Gioro (the surname of the imperial dynasty of the Manchus)

碍面子(àimiànzi)to be unwilling to hurt somebody's feelings; to take somebody's sensibilities into consideration

安民告示(ānmín gàoshì) an official notice;an official announcement

安清帮(ānqīngbāng)the Green Gang (a Qing secret society which evolved into a criminal gang in Shanghai in the early 20th century)

安史之乱(ānshǐ zhī luàn)the An Shi Rebellion (which heralded the downfall of the Tang Dynasty)

庵堂(āntáng)a nunnery;a Buddhist convent

按察使(ànchásh ǐ) the provincial chief justice(in the Ming and Qing dynasties)

按语(ànyǔ)a note or comment(by an author or editor)

案牍(àndú)official documents or correspondence

案头(àntóu)on the desk

案头剧(àntóujù)a closet drama

案语(ànyǔ)a note or comment(by an author or editor)

暗娼(ànchāng)an unlicensed prostitute;a call girl

暗度陈仓(àn dù chéncāng)①(lit.)"to pretend to march along one route while sneaking along another route" – to do something in secret②(fig.)to have an illicit love affair;to commit adultery

暗楼子(ànloúzi)an attic storeroom

暗门子(ànménzi)an unlicensed whorehouse

暗香疏影(ànxiāng shūyǐng)①secret fragrance and dappled shadows(used as a description of the fragnance and posture of plum blossom)②plum blossom

暗转(ànzhuǎn)a blackout(in the middle of a scene or act of a play)

敖包(áobāo)Mongolian stone heaps(used for worship)

鳌头(áotóu)the head of a legendary turtle – used to mean the first place in a competition etc.

B

八百罗汉(bābǎiluóhàn)eight hundred Buddhist arhats

八百壮士(bābǎi zhuàngshì)the Eight Hundred Heroes

八拜之交(bā bài zhī jiāo)sworn brothers;sworn brotherhood

八宝菜(bābǎocài)eight-treasure pickles

八宝饭(bābǎofàn)eight-treasure Chinese rice pudding

八辈子(bābèizi)"eight lives" – for ages

八斗才(bādǒucái)a very gifted person;an extraordinary talent

八段锦(bāduànjǐn)eight trigram boxing;eight trigram exercise

八法(bāfǎ)the Eight Therapeutic Methods [proposed by Zhang Zhongjing(张仲景,150 – 219)]

八方桌(bāfāngzhuō)an octagonal table

八分(bāfēn)the Han clerical script(a style of Chinese calligraphy)

八纲(bāgāng)the eight principal syndromes;the eight principles(of traditional Chinese diagnostics)

八股文(bāgǔwén)①the eight-part essay;eight-legged essay②(fig.)a stereotyped piece of writing

八卦(bāguà)①the eight diagrams ②gossip

八卦教(bāguàjiào)the Eight Trigram Society;the Eight-Trigram sect

八卦炉(bāguàlú)the Eight-Trigram furnace

八卦婆(bāguàpó)a meddlesome woman

八卦拳(bāguàquán)Eight-Trigram Boxing

八卦掌(bāguàzhǎng)Eight-Trigram Palm

八卦阵(bāguàzhèn)Eight-Trigram Embattle

八极拳(bājíquán)Eight-Extremity Boxing

八角鼓(bājiǎogǔ)①an octagonal hand-held drum②the story-telling accompanied by such a drum

八节(bājié)the eight solar terms

八戒(bājiè)the Eight Commandments;the Eight Precepts

八苦(bākǔ)the Eight Sufferings

八难(bānàn)the Eight Impediments

八旗(bāqí)the"Eight Banners"(military-administrative organizations of the Man nationality in the Qing Dynasty)

八旗制度(bāqí zhìdù)the Banner System(of the Qing Dynasty)

八旗子弟(bāqí zǐdì)the bannermen

八识(bāshí)the eight kinds of perception

八抬大轿(bātái dàjiào)a big sedan chair

八体(bātǐ)the eight styles of calligraphy

八王之乱(bāwáng zhī luàn)the Internecine Wars of the Eight Princes

八仙(bāxiān)the Eight Celestials or Immortals

《八仙的传说》(bāxiān de chuánshuō)*The Legend of the Eight Immortals* – a film directed by Zhao Huanzhang(赵焕章)in 1985

八仙过海(bāxiān guò hǎi)①(lit.)the Eight Immortals crossing the sea ②(fig.)each one shows his or her special prowess

八仙桌(bāxiānzhuō)an square table (for eight people)

八相成道(bāxiàng chéng dào)the eight worldly incarnations of Buddha

八行书(bāhángshū)a formal eight line letter

八月节(bāyuèjié)the Mid-Autumn Festival

八珍(bāzhēn)the eight delicacies

八阵图(bāzhèntú)the Eightfold Maze;the Eight Battle Formation

八正道(bāzhèngdào)the Noble Eightfold Path

八字(bāzì)the Eight Characters(used for fortune-telling)

八字命理(bāzì mìnglǐ)the Four Pillars of Destiny

八字帖(bāzìtiě)eight character invitation(a written paper with the details of one's birthday used for a marriage proposal)

巴山蜀水(bā shānshǔ shuǐ)the mountains and rivers in Sichuan

巴蜀(bāshǔ)Sichuan

巴乌(bāwū)*bawu*(a bamboo flute)

芭蕉扇(bājiāoshàn)a palm-leaf fan

拔毒(bádú)to draw out poison(from a wound)

拔贡(bágòng)candidate for the imperial examinations

拔罐儿(báguànr)cupping(a method used in traditional Chinese medicine)

拔河(báhé)tug-of war

拔火罐(báhuǒguàn)①cupping glass ②cupping

跋文(báwén)an epilogue;a postscript(to a book)

把式(bǎshì)①kong fu;martial arts② a skilled person③skill

把兄弟(bǎxiōngdì)sworn brothers

把盏(bǎzhǎn)to raise a wine cup;to hold a drinking cup

把总(bǎzǒng)Commander in chief(of the capital military camp)

罢黜百家,独尊儒术(bàchù bǎijiā dúzūn rúshù)rejecting any schools of thought but Confucianism

霸王(bàwáng)①an overlord;a local tyrant;a despot②Xiang Yu(项羽,232－202 BC)

霸王鞭(bàwángbiān)①the Rattle Stick Dance(a folk dance)②a rattle stick(used in the folk dance)

《霸王别姬》(bàwáng bié jī)*Farewell to My Concubine*－a Bejing opera;a film directed by Chen Kaige(陈凯歌)in 1993

白册(báicè)the White Book(a tax levy book)

《白发魔女传》(báifà mónǚ zhuàn)*The Bride with the White Hair*－a kungfu novel by Liang Yusheng(梁羽生,1924－2009)in 1957－1958

白骨精(báigǔjīng)the White Bone Demon－a character from the novel *Journey to the West* by Wu Chengen(吴承恩,1501－1582)

白虎观(báihǔguān)the White Tiger Hall

《白虎通》(báihǔtōng)*Comprehensive Discussions in the White Tiger Hall*－a book compiled by Ban Gu(班固,32－92)

白话(báihuà) vernacular; colloquialism

白话诗(báihuàshī) free verse in the vernacular; vernacular poetry

白话文(báihuàwén) modern writings in the vernacular

白话文运动(báihuàwén yùndòng) the Vernacular Literature Movement (associated with the May Fourth Movement, 1919)

白话小说(báihuà xiǎoshuō) vernacular fiction; a vernacular novel

白剧(báijù) Bai opera

白口(báikǒu) ①a dramatic dialogue ② the blank-border format (of a kind of old Chinese book bound by stiches)

白莲教(báiliánjiào) the White Lotus Society

白莲宗(báiliánzōng) the White Lotus Sect; the White Lotus Society

白脸(báiliǎn) ① the "White Face" (one of the face paintings in Beijing opera) ②a harsh guy

白露(báilù) White Dew (one of the twenty-four Chinese solar terms)

白鹿洞书院(báilùdòng shūyuàn) White Deer Cave Academy; White Deer Hollow Academy (located in Lushan Mountain)

《白鹿原》(báilùyuán) *White Deer Plain* – a novel by Chen Zhongshi (陈忠实, 1942 –) in 1993

白马寺(báimǎsì) White Horse Temple

《白毛女》(báimáonǚ) *The White-Haired Girl* – an opera written by He Jingzhi (贺敬之) and Ding Yi (丁毅); a film directed by Wang Bin (王滨) in 1950

白面书生(báimiàn shūshēng) a pale-faced young scholar

白描(báimiáo) line drawing (one of the traditional techniques of Chinese painting)

白娘子(báiniángzǐ) Madam White Snake (in *The Tale of the White Snake*)

《白求恩大夫》(báiqiú'ēn dàifu) *Doctor Bethune* – a film directed by Li Shutian (李舒田) and Gao Zheng (高正) in 1964

白山黑水(báishān hēishuǐ) Changbai Mountain and Heilongjiang River (used to refer to northeast China)

《白蛇传》(báishé zhuàn) *The Tale of the White Snake*; *Madam White Snake* – one of the four great Chinese folklores, several films and TV dramas based on the folklore

白事(báishì) funeral

白陶(báitáo) white pottery

白头山天池(báitóushān tiānchí) the Heavenly Pool on top of Mount Baitou

白头翁(báitóuwēng) a Chinese bulbul

《白兔记》(báitù jì) *White Rabbit* - a southern drama of the Song and Yuan dynasties

白文(báiwén) ①the text of an annotated book②a book without annotation③the intagliated characters on a seal

白相(báixiàng) to play; to play with

白相人(báixiàngrén) a loafer; a trifler

白眼儿狼(báiyǎnrláng) (lit.) "white eyed wolf" - an ungrateful, heartless villain

《白洋淀纪事》(báiyángdiàn jìshì) *A Record of the Events at Baiyang Lake* - an anthology of prose by Sun Li(孙犁, 1913 - 2002) in 1958

白衣秀士(báiyī xiùshì) an untitled scholar

白云观(báiyúnguān) the White Cloud Monastery

白族(báizú) the Bai nationality

白族吹吹腔(báizú chuīchuīqiāng) the folk opera of the Bai nationality

百拜(bǎibài) ①to make many courtesy calls②too much polite

百工(bǎigōng) all sorts of craftsmen

百花奖(bǎihuājiǎng) the Hundred Flowers Award(for movies)

百花齐放,百家争鸣(bǎihuā qífàng, bǎijiā zhēngmíng) "let a hundred flowers blossom and a hundred schools of thought contend"

百花齐放,推陈出新(bǎihuā qífàng, tuīchén chūxīn) "let a hundred flowers blossom and let the new stand out from the old"

百家饭(bǎijiāfàn) (lit.) "the Hundred Family Meal" - begged leftovers

百家锁(bǎijiāsuǒ) (lit.) "the Hundred Family Padlock" - a kind of lock-shpaed gold and silver jewelry for children

《百家姓》(bǎijiāxìng) *Primer of One Hundred Family Names*

百家争鸣(bǎijiā zhēngmíng) the free contention of all schools of thought

《百骏图》(bǎijùn tú) *All the Pretty Horses* - a Chinese classical painting by Lang Shining [郎世宁(Giuseppe Castiglione), 1688 - 1766]

百里才(bǎilǐcái) a small talent; a person with less supervisory capability

《百炼成钢》(bǎiliàn chénggāng) *Tempered into Steel* - a novel by Ai Wu(艾芜, 1904 - 1992) in 1957

百衲本(bǎinàběn) a book in multiple-editions

百衲衣(bǎinàyī) ① a cassock; a

pat-chwork robe②a heavily patched garment

《百鸟朝凤》(bǎiniǎo cháofèng) *A Multitude of Birds Looking up to the Phoenix* - a suo-na(trumpet)solo

百濮(bǎipú)the Pu nationality

百日维新(bǎirì wéixīn)the Hundred-Day Political Reform; the Reform Movement of 1898; the Hundred Days Reform

百事通(bǎishìtōng)Jack of all trades;a knowledgeable person

百戏(bǎixì)acrobatics

摆份儿(bǎifènr)to go in for ostentation and extravagance

摆架子(bǎi jiàzi)to put on airs;to show off one's superiority;to assume an air of superiority

摆阔(bǎikuò)to flaunt one's wealth;to be ostentatious and extravagant

摆擂台(bǎi lèitái)to set up a stage for contest and challenges;to make open challenges

摆龙门阵(bǎi lóngménzhèn)①to embattle according to the "Dragongate" tactics ②to engage in idle talk

摆门面(bǎi ménmiàn)to keep up appearances;to put up a front

摆谱(bǎipǔ)①to keep up appearances;to show off②to put on airs;to throw one's weight about

摆手舞(bǎishǒuwǔ)the hand-swinging dance(the most representative of the Tujia ethnic sacrifice dance.)

摆摊(bǎi tān)to set up a vendor's stall

摆乌龙(bǎiwūlóng)(lit.)"to put down a black dragon" - to make a blunder

败北(bàiběi)to suffer defeat;to be a loser

败家子(bàijiāzǐ)a prodigal son;a wastrel

败走麦城(bàizǒu màichéng)(lit.)"to be defeated and retreat to Mai Town" - to suffer a major defeat

拜把兄弟(bài bǎxiōngdì)sworn brothers

拜把子(bài bǎzi)to become sworn brothers;to be blood brothers

拜佛(bàifó)to worship Buddha

拜年(bàinián)to pay a New Year call;to wish somebody a happy New Year

拜上(bàishàng)with my respectful bow;modestly yours;yours sincerely(a complimentary close to a letter)

拜师(bàishī)to be an apprentice or a disciple to a master

拜寿(bàishòu)to congratulate an elderly person on his or her birthday

拜堂(bàitáng)to perform a formal

wedding ceremony

拜天地(bài tiāndì) to kowtow to Heaven and Earth

拜谒(bàiyè) to pay a formal visit

《拜月亭》(bàiyuètíng) *The Pavilion of Moon-Worship* – a play by Guan Hanqing(关汉卿,1220 – 1300)

稗官野史(bàiguānyěshǐ) unofficial histories

稗史(bàishǐ) an unofficial history; a book of anecdotes

班禅(bānchán) Panchen; Panchen Lama

班禅喇嘛(bānchán lǎma) Panchen Lama

班底(bāndǐ) ①the members of a theatrical groupe ②the members of a group or an organization; group members

班房(bānfáng) a jail; a prison

班门弄斧(bānménnòngfǔ) (lit.) "to show off one's proficiency with an axe before Lu Ban (the master carpenter)" – to display one's skill before an expert; to teach fish to swim

班师(bānshī) to withdraw troops to the stations; to return after triumph

班师回朝(bānshī huícháo) to withdraw troops to the capital

班主(bānzhǔ) head of a theatrical troupe or a circus

《班主任》(bānzhǔrèn) *The Class Teacher* – a short story by Liu Xinwu (刘心武,1942 –) in 1977

搬兵(bānbīng) to maneuver reinforcements; to ask for help

板板六十四(bǎnbǎn liùshísì) (lit.) "a 64 – wen copper coin" – rigid; unaccommodating

板鼓(bǎngǔ) a troupe drum (in the traditional Chinese opera)

板胡(bǎnhú) *banhu* (a bowed stringed musical instrument)

板式(bǎnshì) the mode of drumming and clapping (for Chinese operas)

板眼(bǎnyǎn) the accented and unaccented beats (in traditional Chinese music and opera)

版口(bǎnkǒu) the blank-border format (of a traditional thread-bound book)

版心(bǎnxīn) the blank-border format (of a traditional thread-bound book)

办罪(bànzuì) to punish

半壁江山(bànbì jiāngshān) half of the country

半边天(bànbiāntiān) the "half of the sky" – referring to women in post – 1949 China

半坡村(bànpōcūn) Banpo Village

半部论语治天下(bànbù lúnyǔ zhì tiānxià) (lit.) "to rule the world using half of *The Analects of Confucius*" – to emphasize the importance of *The Analects of Confucius* to national governance

半路夫妻(bànlù fūqī)(lit.)"a halfway couple" – a couple married halfway through life

半路上杀出一个程咬金(bànlù shangshā chūyīgechéngyǎojīn)(lit.)"an unexpected intruder bouncing in half way" – someone appears out of nowhere

半律(bànlǜ) halftone; semitone (a term for ancient Chinese music)

半瓶醋(bànpíngcù)(lit.)"half a bottle of vinegar" – a dabbler

半晌(bànshǎng) half of the day; a long while

伴哥(bàngē) a rural teenager(in the operas of the Song and Yuan dynasties)

伴姑(bàngū) a rural young women(in the operas of the Song and Yuan dynasties)

伴君如伴虎(bànjūn rú bànhǔ)(lit.)"attending an emperor is like attending a tiger" – Nearest the king, nearest the gallow

伴郎(bànláng) the best man

伴娘(bànniáng) a bridesmaid

扮靓(bàn liàng) to beautify

扮酷(bàn kù) to play it cool

扮相(bànxiàng) the appearance of an actor or actress in costume and makeup

邦老(bānglǎo)(vulgarism) a thief; a rogue

帮办(bāngbàn) ①to assist in managing ②a deputy; an assistant

帮会(bānghuì) a secret society; a fraternity society; an underworld gang

帮腔(bāngqiāng) ①the vocal accompaniment(in traditional dramas) ② to speak for somebody; to back somebody up; to echo somebody

帮闲文人(bāngxián wénrén) a literary penster(who writes for the rich and powerful)

梆子(bāngzi) ①the watchman's clapper ②the wooden clappers(in traditional dramas) ③the "Clapper Drama"(a type of regional drama)

梆子腔(bāngziqiāng) the "Clapper Drama"

绑票(bǎngpiào) to kidnap (for ransom)

榜首(bǎngshǒu) the first place on a published list of successful candidates; No. 1 in a contest

榜书(bǎngshū) big characters(written on signboards, etc.)

榜文(bǎngwén) a proclamation; a public notice; an official announcement

榜眼(bǎngyǎn) "bangyan" – the scholar who won the second place in the highest imperial examinations

傍大款(bàng dàkuǎn) to be a mistress of a rich man

棒槌(bàngchui)①a washing wooden club(used to beat clothes in washing)②a clumsy and awkward man

包办婚姻(bāobàn hūnyīn) an arranged marriage

包打听(bāodǎtīng)①a detective②a snoop;a well-informed guy

包二奶(bāo èrnǎi) to keep a mistress or a concubine

包房(bāofáng)①to reserve a hotel room②a compartment(in a restaurant or a place of entertainment, etc.)

包袱底儿(bāofudǐr)①the long unused or valuable things of a family ②one's privacy③one's unique skill

包干到户(bāogān dàohù) to assign tasks or projects to households on a contract basis

包干儿(bāogānr) to assume a task until it is completed;to fulfil a task on a contract basis

包工头(bāogōngtóu) a labour contractor

包公(bāogōng)①Bao Zheng(a legendary upright offical of the Northern Song Dynasty)②an honest official

《包公案》(bāogōng àn) *The Cases by Judge Bao Gong* – a novel by An Yushi(安遇时)in the Ming dynasty

包饺子(bāo jiǎozi) to make *jiaozi* (Chinese dumplings)

包脚(bāojiǎo) to bind one's feet;footbinding

包票(bāopiào) to guarantee;warranty

包青天(bāoqīngtiān) Bao Zheng, the judge

《包青天》(bāo qīngtiān) *Bao Zheng, the Judge* – a film directed by Li Tie (李铁) in 1980;a TV drama directed by Sun Shupei(孙树培) in 1993

包身工(bāoshēngōng) an indentured labourer

包探(bāotàn) a police detective

包养(bāoyǎng) to keep(a mistress); to provide money or housing for(an extramarital partner)

包银(bāoyín)①remunerations(paid to troupe members or leading roles) ②taxes[levied in the Yuan Dynasty (1271 – 1368)]

包圆儿(bāoyuánr)①to buy the whole lot②to finish off

包拯(bāozhěng) Bao Zheng(an upright official of the Northern Song Dynasty)

包子(bāozi) steamed stuffed buns

宝岛(bǎodǎo) Taiwan

宝典(bǎodiǎn) a treasured book; a valuable book

宝货(bǎohuò)①baohuo(the ancient money)②valuable articles③a fool; an idiot

宝剑(bǎojiàn)a double-edged sword

宝卷(bǎojuàn)a literary type of storytelling and ballad singing

《宝莲灯》(bǎoliándēng) *Lotus Lantern* - a film adapted from a fairy tale and released in 1959

宝座(bǎozuò)a throne

饱学之士(bǎoxué zhī shì)a learned person;an erudite person

饱眼福(bǎo yǎnfú) to feast one's eyes;to enjoy what one sees

保镖(bǎobiāo)a bodyguard

保傅(bǎofù)a tutor for princes

保国会(bǎoguóhuì) the Society for Preserving the Nation (a political organization established in 1898)

保护伞(bǎohùsǎn)a protective umbrella;a shield;a protective power

保甲(bǎojiǎ)bao-jia(a neighborhood administrative system in old China)

保甲制度(bǎojiǎ zhìdù) the Baojia system

保驾(bǎojià)to escort the Emperor

保举(bǎojǔ)to recommend(somebody for the post of a high-ranking official)

保媒(bǎoméi) to serve as a match maker or a go-between

保人(bǎorén) a guarantor; a bondsman

《保卫延安》(bǎowèi yán'ān) *Defend Yan'an* - a novel by Du Pengcheng (杜鹏程,1921 - 1991) in 1954

保佑(bǎoyòu)to bless and protect

鸨母(bǎomǔ)a procuress

报告文学(bàogào wénxué)reportage

报馆(bàoguǎn)a newspaper office

报户口(bào hùkǒu) to apply for a permanent residence permit

报童(bàotóng) a newspaper delivery boy;a newsboy

报喜(bàoxǐ)to announce good news; to report success

报应(bàoyìng)retribution;due punishment

报章(bàozhāng)newspapers

抱不平(bàobùpíng)to be indignant at injustice

抱大腿(bào dàtuǐ)(lit.)"to embrace one's thighs"- to rely servilely on (the rich and powerful); to submit oneself under the protection of(an influential and powerful person)

抱佛脚(bào fójiǎo)(lit.)"to clasp Buddha's feet" - to make a hasty last-minute effort

《抱朴子》(bàopǔzǐ) *The Man Who Holds to Simplicity* - a theoretic book by Ge Hong (葛洪, 284 - 364)

抱团儿(bàotuánr)to hang together;to gang up

趵突泉(bàotūquán)Baotu Spring(in Jinan,rated as the finest spring under heaven)

鲍鱼之肆(bàoyú zhī sì)a salted fish shop - a bad environment

暴发户(bàofāhù)a new rich;an upstart

《暴风骤雨》(bàofēng zhòuyǔ)*Tempest* - a novel by Zhou Libo(周立波,1908 - 1979)in 1948

暴露文学(bàolù wénxúe)Literature of Exposure,which only reveals the dark side of the society

爆冷门(bàolěngmén)an unexpected winner turning up;a dark horse

爆竹(bàozhú)firecrackers

卑职(bēizhí)your humble servant

杯酒释兵权(bēijiǔ shì bīngquán)(lit.)"to relieve the generals of their commands at a compotation"- a stratagem used by Zhao Kuangyin(赵匡胤,927 - 976),founder of the Song Dynasty(960 - 1279)- to relieve the generals of their military leadership easily

杯中物(bēizhōngwù)the wine in the cup

悲歌(bēigē)a sad melody;a threnody

悲田院(bēitiányuàn)an asylum;an institution for relief of the poor

碑记(bēijì)a record of events inscribed on a stone tablet

碑碣(bēijié)a stone tablet;a stele

碑林(bēilín)the forest of steles

碑铭(bēimíng)an inscription on a stone tablet;a stone inscription

碑帖(bēitiè)rubbings from a stone inscription

碑亭(bēitíng)a pavilion sheltering stone tablets;a stone tablet pavilion

碑拓(bēità)rubbings from ancient stone tablets

碑文(bēiwén)an inscription on a stone tablet

碑阴(bēiyīn)the back of a stone tablet

碑志(bēizhì)a record of events inscribed on a tablet

背榜(bēibǎng)to be the last on the list of successful candidates

背包袱(bēi bāofu)to have a burden on one's mind; to take on mental burden

背黑锅(bēi hēiguō)to take the blame (for others); to become a scapegoat;to be unjustly blamed

背饥荒(bēi jīhuāng)to be in debt;to get into debt

北朝(běicháo)the Northern Dynasties (386 - 581)

北辰(běichén)the North Star

北大荒(běidàhuāng)the Great

Northern Wilderness

北斗(běidǒu) the Big Dipper; the Plough

北斗星(běidǒuxīng) the Big Dipper; the Plough

《北方的河》(běifāng de hé) *The River in the North* – a novel by Zhang Chengzhi(张承志,1948 –) in 1984

北方话(běifānghuà) northern dialects

北国(běiguó) the northern part of the country

北货(běihuò) delicacies from north China

北京烤鸭(běijīng kǎoyā) Beijing roast duck

《北京人》(běijīng rén) *Beijing Man* – a play by Cao Yu(曹禺,1910 – 1996) in 1941

北京猿人(běijīng yuánrén) the Beijing Apeman; Sinanthropus Pekinensis

北凉(běiliáng) the Northern Liang Dynasty

北漂(běipiāo) unsettled life in Beijing; an unsettled person in Beijing

北平(běipíng) Peiping(the old name for Beijing)

北齐(běiqí) the Northern Qi Dynasty (550 – 577)

北曲(běiqǔ) the northern operas

北宋(běisòng) the Northern Song Dynasty(960 – 1127)

北天师道(běitiānshīdào) the Way of Northern Celestial Masters in the Northern and Southern Dynasties (520 – 589)

北魏(běiwèi) the Northern Wei Dynasty(386 – 557)

北学(běixué) a study of Confucian classics undertaken during the Northern Dynasties

北燕(běiyàn) the Northern Yan Dynasty(407 – 436)

北洋军阀(běiyáng jūnfá) the Northern Warlords(1912 – 1927)

北洋水师(běiyáng shuǐshī) the Northern Fleet(established in 1888)

北岳(běiyuè) the Northern Sacred Mountain (referring to Hengshan Mountain,恒山)

北岳庙(běiyuèmiào) the Temple of Mount Heng

北杂剧(běizájù) the northern poetic drama

北周(běizhōu) the Northern Zhou Dynasty(557 – 581)

贝雕(bèidiāo) a shell carving

贝勒(bèilè) beile (a hereditary title for Manchu noblemen below the prince)

贝勒府(bèilèfǔ) the Beile House(the mansion where Beile lives in the Qing Dynasty)

贝勒爷(bèilèyé) Beile(a royal title in

the Qing Dynasty)

贝子(bèizǐ) Beise(a hereditary title for Manchu noblemen below beile)

背(被)搭子(bèidāzi) a cloth-bag

背躬(bèigōng) an aside(in traditional drama)

背时(bèishí) unlucky

背书(bèishū) endorsement

背水阵(bèishuǐzhèn) desperate situation

背运(bèiyùn) bad luck

背子(bèizi) a waistcoat; a sleeveless garment; a vest

倍律(bèilǜ) the lower octave notes

被窝儿(bèiwōr) a quilt(folded into a sleep bag)

辈分(bèifen) position in the family or clan hierarchy; family seniority

辈数儿(bèishùr) position in the family or clan hierarchy; family seniority

《奔马图》(bēnmǎ tú) *Running Horses* - a traditional painting by Xu Beihong (徐悲鸿, 1895 - 1953) in 1941

奔丧(bēnsāng) to make one's way home for the funeral of a parent or grandparent; to go and attend the funeral

奔小康(bēn xiǎokāng) to strive for a better-off life

《本草纲目》(běn cǎo gāngmù) *Compendium of Materia Medica* - a medical book by Li Shizhen(李时珍, 1518 - 1593) in 1578

本分(běnfèn) ①duty; obligation ②decent; honest

本行(běnháng) one's line; one's profession; one's trade

本号(běnhào) this shop; our shop

本惑(běnhuò)(Buddhism) fundamental delusion

本纪(běnjì) basic annals; biographies of prominent rulers and emperors

本家(běnjiā) a member of the same clan; a distant relative of the same surname

本命年(běnmìngnián) the animal year; the recurrent year in the 12 - year cycle of one's birth

《本命年》(běnmìngnián) *Animal Year* - a film directed by Xie Fei (谢飞) in 1989

本钱(běnqián) capital

本生灯(běnshēngdēng) the bunsen burner

畚箕(běnjī) ① a bamboo scoop ② a dustpan

笨伯(bènbó) a clumsy fellow; a fool

崩漏(bēnglòu) uterine bleeding

崩症(bēngzhèng) metrorrhagia

绷子(bēngzi) an embroidery frame; a tambour

蹦蹦儿戏(bèngbèngrxì) a predecessor of Pingju(northern regional opera)

逼供信(bīgòngxìn) confessions under duress

逼宫(bīgōng) to force the king or emperor to abdicate

逼和(bīhé) to be forced to accept a draw

逼上梁山(bī shàng liángshān) ①to be forced to join the Liangshan Marsh rebels – to be driven to revolt; be compelled to do something desperate ②*Driven to Revolt* (a Beijing opera adapted in 1943)

鼻烟(bíyān) snuff

鼻烟盒(bíyānhé) a snuffbox

鼻烟壶(bíyānhú) a snuff bottle; a snuffbox

比丘(bǐqiū) a Buddhist monk

比丘尼(bǐqiūní) a Buddhist nun

比翼鸟(bǐyìniǎo) a pair of lovebirds – a devoted couple

彼岸(bǐ'àn) ①Faramita; the paradise ②the other side (of the ocean, river, etc.)

秕糠(bǐkāng) chaff; worthless stuff

笔断意连(bǐ duàn yì lián) separate strokes and connected conation (in traditional painting and calligraphy)

笔杆子(bǐgǎnzi) ①the shaft of a pen or writing brush ②an effective writer

笔耕(bǐgēng) to engage in writing

笔划(点、横、竖、撇、捺、提、拐角、弯勾)(bǐhuà) strokes (of a Chinese character) (diǎn – a dot stroke; héng – a horizontal stroke; shù – a vertical stroke; piě – a left-falling stroke; nà – a right-falling stroke; tí –a rising stroke; guǎijiǎo – a turning stroke; wān'gōu – a hook stroke)

笔画(bǐhuà) the strokes of a Chinese character

笔会(bǐhuì) ①a forum for writing ②the association or society of writers

笔记小说(bǐjì xiǎoshuō) literary sketches

笔墨(bǐmò) ①pen and ink ②words; writing

笔墨官司(bǐmò guānsī) a battle of words

笔友(bǐyǒu) a pen-friend

笔札(bǐzhá) ①writing materials ②handwritten letters

笔战(bǐzhàn) written polemics and controversy

笔走龙蛇(bǐzǒu lóngshé) a vigorous and graceful calligraphic styles or strokes

鄙人(bǐrén) your humble servant; I

鄙意(bǐyì) my humble opinion; my idea

闭关锁国(bìguān suǒguó) to cut off contacts with other countries; to close the country to the rest of the world

闭关政策(bìguān zhèngcè)a closed-door policy

闭关自守(bìguān zìshǒu)to close the country to the outside world

闭门羹(bìméngēng)to be denied entrance;to given the cold-shoulder

闭门谢客(bìmén xièkè)to close one's door to visitors;to receive no guests

闭月羞花(bìyuè xiūhuā)(lit.)"(A woman's)beauty that obscures the moon and makes the flowers blush"– to be extremely beautiful

贲临(bìlín)to be present;to attend

陛见(bìjiàn)to have an audience with the emperor

陛下(bìxià)Your Majesty; His or Her Majesty

狴犴(bì'àn)①the image of a legendary beast(often painted on prison doors in ancient times)②a prison; a jail

婢女(bìnǚ)a servant-girl;a slave girl

弼马温(bìmǎwēn)①the Protector of Horses(an official title and post in the Heaven Palace)②the official title of Sun Wukong(the Monk King in *Journey to the West*)

筚篥(bìlì)an ancient bamboo pipe with a reed mouth piece

辟谷(bìgǔ)to refrain from eating grain(an ancient Taoist practice of asceticism for the purpose of becoming an immortal)

碧螺春(bìluóchūn)a special brand of green tea

碧落(bìluò)the blue sky

碧云寺(bìyúnsì)Temple of the Azure Clouds;Biyun Temple

壁龛(bìkān)a shrine

壁上观(bìshàngguān)to watch the fighting from the ramparts; be an onlooker

嬖人(bìrén)a monarch's favourite concubine

觱篥(bìlì)an ancient bamboo pipe with a reed mouth piece

避讳(bìhuì)to avoid a taboo

避暑山庄(bìshǔ shānzhuāng)the Imperial Mountain Summer Resort

《边城》(biānchéng)*Frontier City* – a novel by Shen Congwen(沈从文, 1902 – 1988); *Border Town*

边塞诗(biānsàishī)Frontier Poetry

边塞诗派(biānsài shīpài)the School of Frontier Poetry

边塞诗人(biānsài shīrén)the frontier poets

边寨(biānzhài)a borderland village

编镈(biānbó)an ancient Chinese carillon

《编辑部的故事》(biānjíbù de gùshì)*Stories from the Editorial Board* – a TV drama directed by Zhao Baog-ang(赵宝刚)in 1991

编磬(biānqìng) a set of musical stones

编钟(biānzhōng) a set of chimes or bells

篼舆(biānyú) a sedan chair

鞭笞(biānchī) to flog; to lash

贬黜(biǎnchù) to demote

扁担(biǎndan) a carrying pole; a shoulder pole

扁担舞(biǎndanwǔ) dancing with shoulder poles

扁食(biǎnshi) *jiaozi*; dumpling

匾额(biǎn'é) a horizontal inscribed board

弁言(biànyán) foreword; preface

汴京(biànjīng) Kaifeng (in Henan province)

汴梁(biànliáng) Bianliang (also Kaifeng in Henan province)

便函(biànhán) a short informal letter

便笺(biànjiān) a note; a memo

变把戏(biàn bǎxì) to perform conjuring tricks; to conjure

变法(biànfǎ) political reform; constitutional reform

变法维新(biànfǎ wéixīn) the Constitutional Reform and Modernization (of 1898)

变宫(biàngōng) the half tone lower than gong tone (in ancient musical notation)

变卦(biànguà) to change one's mind; to go back on one's word

变脸(biànliǎn) ①to turn hostile suddenly ②to change facial expression rapidly ③the Face Changes (in Sichuan Opera)

变天(biàntiān) ① to change (of weather) ②a comeback

变天账(biàntiānzhàng) the restoration records

变文(biànwén) *bianwen* (a popular genre of narrative literature prevailing in the Tang Dynasty, 618 – 907)

变戏法(biànxìfǎ) to perform conjuring tricks; conjure

变徵(biànzhǐ) a note corresponding to 4 in the numbered musical notation

辩士(biànshì) an orator; a sophist; a gifted debater

标兵(biāobīng) ①a parade guard ② an example; a model; a pacesetter

彪炳千古(biāobǐng qiāngǔ) to shine through the ages

镖局(biāojú) a commercial firm providing armed escort or bodyguards

镖客(biāokè) an armed escort

镖头(biāotóu) the head of escorts; the chief bodyguard

表亲(biǎoqīn) cousins; cousinship

表叔(biǎoshū) ①uncles ②the son of one's grandfather's sister; the son of one's grandmother's sister or brother; one's father's younger male cousin

表意文字(biǎoyì wénzì) ideograph; ideogram

表字(biǎozì) a old courtesy name

婊子(biǎozi) a prostitute; a whore; a harlot

裱褙(biǎobèi) to mount (a picture, etc.)

裱糊(biǎohú) to paper; to paste paper on

裱装(biǎozhuāng) to mount (a picture, etc.)

瘪三(biēsān) a bum; a loafer

别传(biézhuàn) an anecdotal biography

别号(biéhào) another name; alias; nickname

别集(biéjí) a collection of individual works

别名(biémíng) another name; nickname; alias

别史(biéshǐ) a privately compiled history

别字(biézì) ①an informal name②a wrongly written character

宾白(bīnbái) the spoken parts in Chinese operas

傧相(bīnxiàng) an attendant of the bride or the bridegroom at a wedding; a bridesmaid or a best man

殡殓(bìnliàn) to encoffin the dead and carry it to the grave; a funeral

冰雕(bīngdiāo) ice sculpture; ice carving

冰轮(bīnglún) the moon

冰人(bīngrén) a go-between; a match maker

《冰山上的来客》(bīngshān shàng de láikè) *The Visitor on Ice Mountain* − a film directed by Zhao Xinshui(赵心水) in 1963

冰糖葫芦(bīngtáng húlu) a stick of sugar-coated haws

冰嬉(bīngxī) the ice-sports

冰心(bīngxīn) a pure and innocent soul; chastity; virtuous

兵部(bīngbù) the Ministry of War

兵法(bīngfǎ) the art of war; military strategy and tactics

兵符(bīngfú) ①a commander's tally; a military tally②a book on the art of warfare

兵家(bīngjiā) the military strategists; military commanders; soldiers

兵家必争之地(bīngjiā bìzhēng zhī dì) a place of strategic significance; a strategic point

兵谏(bīngjiàn) armed remonstrance; exhortations backed up by force of arms

兵马俑(bīngmǎyǒng) the terra cotta warriors

兵痞(bīngpǐ) army riffraff; an army

ruffian;a wicked seasoned soldier

兵戎(bīngróng)arms;weapons

兵书(bīngshū)a book on the art of warfare

兵卒(bīngzú)soldiers

丙部(bǐngbù)the philosophical or historical works(one of the Chinese ancient book four-branch classification)

柄臣(bǐngchén)a powerful courtier or official

炳灵(bǐnglíng)God of Fire

炳灵寺石窟(bǐnglíngsì shíkū)the grottoes at Bingling Temple

禀帖(bǐngtiě)a petition or a report (to government authorities)

并蒂莲(bìngdìlián)(lit.)"twin lotus flowers on one stalk"(a devoted married couple)

病笃(bìngdǔ)to be critically ill

病脉(bìngmài)an abnormal pulse

病榻(bìngtà)a sickbed

拨浪鼓(bōlanggǔ)a rattle drum

拨子(bōzi)a plectrum

波霸(bōbà)a busty woman

波浪鼓(bōlanggǔ)a rattle drum

波罗蜜多(bōluómìduō)paramita(a Buddhist term)

钵盂(bōyú)an alms bowl

饽饽(bōbo)a steamed bun

伯乐(bólè)a good judge of talent;a talent scout

伯仲(bózhòng)①brothers②almost the same;not much difference

伯仲叔季(bózhòngshūjì)the eldest, second, third and youngest of brothers; the order of seniority among brothers

孛老(bèilǎo/bólǎo)a middle-age or old character in the ancient drama

驳面子(bómiànzǐ)to make somebody lose face

帛画(bóhuà)a painting on silk

帛书(bóshū)a silk manuscript; a book copied on silk

舶来品(bóláipǐn)imported goods;foreign goods

博客(bókè)a blog

博士(bóshì)an erudite

博士弟子(bóshì dìzi)①a student of the court academician②a student (in feudal China)

博弈(bóyì)gambling;to play chess

薄酒(bójiǔ)light wine

薄礼(bólǐ)a modest gift; a meagre present

薄面(bómiàn)for my sake

薄命(bómìng)to be born unlucky; ill-fated

薄幸(bóxìng)inconstant in love;fickle;heartless and unfaithful

簸箕(bòji)①a dustpan②a winnowing fan

簸箩(bǒluo)a winnowing basket; a

wicker basket

擘画(bòhuà)to arrange;to plan

擘窠书(bòkēshū)big character

卜儿(bǔr)an old women

卜骨(bǔgǔ)oracle bone

卜卦(bǔguà)divination; to tell fortune

卜课(bǔkè)divination;fortune-telling

卜千秋壁画(bǔqiānqiū bìhuà)the Buqianqiu Paintings in Fresco

卜筮(bǔshì)divination by tortoise shell;fortune-telling

卜算子(bǔsuànzǐ)the Song of Divination(one of the names of the *ci*'s tune)

卜问(bǔwèn)to pray and consult the oracle

卜宅(bǔzhái)①to choose the location of the capital by geomancy②to choose the location of a house or tomb by geomancy

补服(bǔfú)the ceremonial gown

补元气(bǔ yuánqì)to tonify primordial qi

捕快(bǔkuài)a yamen captor

《捕蛇者说》(bǔshézhě shuō)*Discourse of a Snake-catcher* - an essay by Liu Zongyuan(柳宗元,773 - 819)

捕头(bǔtóu)the head captor

不白之冤(bùbái zhī yuān)unredressed injustice

《不差钱》(bù chāqián)*Got the Money Anyway* - a famous skit in Spring Festival Gala in 2009;*Money Is Not A Problem*

不揣冒昧(bùchuǎimàomèi)may I take the liberty to;I venture to

不打不成器(bùdǎ bù chéngqì)no punishment,no good boys

不打不相识(bùdǎ bù xiāngshí)friendship grows out of fighting;no discord,no concord

不倒翁(bùdǎowēng)a tumbler; a roly-poly

不到长城非好汉(bù dào chángchéng fēi hǎohàn)one who has never been to the Great Wall is not a true man

不到黄河心不死(bù dào huánghé xīn bù sǐ)(lit.)"never stop until reaching the Yellow River"(to pursue one course to the bitter end)

不二法门(bùèrfǎmén)the only way;the only proper course to take

《不见不散》(bùjiànbú sàn)*Be There or Be Square* - a film directed by Feng Xiaogang(冯小刚)in 1998

不见经传(bùjiàn jīngzhuàn)not to be found in the classical canon;unauthoritative;unknown

不靠谱(bùkàopǔ)not accurate or reliable(in speech and action)

不佞(bùnìng)(humbly)your dull-witted servant;I

不识相(bùshíxiàng)to have no sense of propriety;to lack judgment

不祧之祖(bùtiāo zhī zǔ)the revered earliest ancestor

不孝有三,无后为大(bùxiào yǒu sān,wúhòu wéi dà)In the three aspects of being an unfilial son, the most serious is to have no heir. (Mencius)

不肖子孙(bùxiào zǐsūn)unworthy descendants

不在其位,不谋其政(bùzài qíwèi, bùmóu qízhèng)One who holds no official position does not discuss official affairs

不正之风(bùzhèng zhīfēng)unhealthy social trends; evil social practices;social malpractices

不抓辫子,不打棍子(bùzhuā biànzi, bùdǎ gùnzi)without having sb by the braid, without beating sb with a stick – not to capitalize on somebody's mistakes, not to chastise somebody

布白(bùbái)the intentional blankness in the layout of Chinese calligraphy and painting

布帛(bùbó)cloth and silk

布达拉宫(bùdálāgōng)the Potala Palace

布袋和尚(bùdàihéshang)the Clothbag Monk

布朗族(bùlǎngzú)the Bulang nationality

布票(bùpiào)a cloth coupon

布萨(bùsà)a retreat for spiritual refreshment

布施(bùshī)alms giving;donation

布鞋(bùxié)cloth shoes

布衣(bùyī)ordinary people; a commoner

布衣之交(bùyī zhī jiāo)the friendship between ordinary people; the friends in days of simple living

布依戏(bùyīxì)the opera of the Buyei nationality

布依族(bùyīzú)the Buyi or Buyi nationality

布庄(bùzhuāng)a cloth store

《步辇图》(bùniǎn tú)*The Royal Sedan Chair Borne by Attendants* – a painting by Yan Liben(阎立本, 601 – 673)

《步天歌》(bùtiāngē)*Song of Pacing the Heavens* – an astronomical poem by Wang Ximing(王希明), an official of the Tang Dynasty

步行街(bùxíngjiē)a pedestrian street

步韵(bùyùn)to write a poem by following another poem's rhyme-scheme

部首(bùshǒu)radicals(by which

characters are arranged in traditional Chinese dictionaries)

C

擦边球(cābiānqiú)①an edge ball;a touch ball②to take advantage of the loopholes in policies or laws

擦屁股(cāpìgu)to clear up a messy situation(left by someone);to settle an impasse

猜谜(cāimí)a guessing game; to guess a riddle

猜拳(cāiquán) a finger-guessing game

才高八斗(cáigāobādǒu) extremely ta-lented;to have profound learning

才人(cáirén)①a gifted scholar②an imperial concubine③a lady serving at the imperial court

才子佳人(cáizǐ jiārén)a gifted scholarand a beautiful lady

才子佳人小说(cáizǐ jiārén xiǎoshuō)the novel of the gifted scholar and beautiful lady (a kind of romance fiction turning up in the transitional period of the Ming and Qing Dynasties)

财帛(cáibó)money;wealth

财东(cáidōng)①a shop owner; a businessman②a moneybags

财迷(cáimí)a money-grubber;a miser

财神(cáishén)the God of Wealth;an extremely rich person

财神爷(cáishényé)the God of Wealth

财运(cáiyùn)a luck in making money

财主(cáizhu) a rich man; a moneybags

采茶灯(cǎichádēng)①the folk song and dance of tea-picking ② *Tea-picking Girls Chasing Butterflies* – a world-famous folk melody of tea-picking

采茶戏(cǎicháxì) the tea-plucking opera;the Caicha opera

采地(cǎidì)fief

采风(cǎifēng)to collect folk songs

采莲船(cǎiliánchuán) the lotus gathering boat dance (a popular folk dance in Hubei province)

采莲队舞(cǎiliánduìwǔ)the lotus-picking team dance(a royal dance in the Song Dynasty)

采邑(cǎiyì)feoff;fief

彩车(cǎichē)a float;a specially decoratedcart or car

彩瓷(cǎicí)decorative porcelain

彩旦(cǎidàn)a female comedian; a female clown role (in opera); the role of an shrewd or evil woman(in Chinese classical operas)

彩调(cǎidiào)the colored-tone opera (a local opera)

彩坊(cǎifāng)a decorated archway

彩轿(cǎijiào)a bridal sedan chair

彩礼(cǎilǐ)betrothal gifts

彩门(cǎimén)a decorated archway

彩民(cǎimín)a lottery ticket buyer

彩排(cǎipái)a rehearsal;to rehearse

彩牌楼(cǎipáilóu)a decorated archway

彩票(cǎipiào)a lottery ticket;lottery

彩塑(cǎisù)a painted sculpture

彩陶(cǎitáo)painted pottery

彩陶文化(cǎitáo wénhuà) the Painted-Pottery Culture(of the Neolithic Age)

彩头(cǎitóu)good luck(in business, gambling,etc.)

彩选(cǎixuǎn)a dice game(for nominating officials)

彩釉陶(cǎiyòutáo)glazed colour pottery

《彩云追月》(cǎiyún zhuīyuè) *Silver Cloud Running after the Moon* – a folk melody

踩道(cǎidào)to spy out the place before taking action

踩点(cǎidiǎn) to spy out the place before taking action

踩高跷(cǎigāoqiāo) stilt-walking; to walk on stilts

踩藕(cǎi'ǒu) to stand and walk unsteadily

菜场(càichǎng)a food market

菜馆(càiguǎn)a restaurant

菜篮子(càilánzi) a basket for carrying vegetables and foods;a shopping basket

菜篮子工程(càilánzi gōngchéng) the shopping basket project(solving the short supply of fresh vegetables, put forward in 1988)

菜鸟(càiniǎo)(dialect)a new hand; a rookie;a greenhorn

菜色(càisè)a famished look;an emaciated look

《蔡文姬》(càiwénjī) *Cai Wenji the Poetess* – a historical play by Guo Moruo(郭沫若, 1892 – 1978) in 1959

参拜(cānbài) to call formally on; to pay one's respects to;to pay a courtesy call

参禅(cānchán)to sit in deep meditation for penetration of truth

参劾(cānhé)to impeach

参见(cānjiàn)to pay one's respect to

参事(cānshì)a counsellor ;an adviser

参他一本(cāntāyīběn) to submit a written statement to a higher authority to inform against somebody

参谒(cānyè)①to pay one's respects to(a superior, etc.)②to pay homage to(a dead person or a deadee)

残本(cánběn) an incomplete ancient text ;a book with missing pages

残花败柳(cánhuā bàiliǔ) faded flowers and withered willow (a faded beauty); a fallen women

残局(cánjú) ①the final phase (of a chess match) ②the last stage

残篇断简(cánpiān duànjiǎn) the fragments of an ancient text; a book with missing pages

残棋(cánqí) the last phase of a chess match; an endgame

残阳(cányáng) the setting sun

残月(cányuè) the waning moon; the fading moon

蚕食(cánshí) to nibble

孱头(càntou) a weakling; a coward

仓颉造字(cāngjié zàozì) Cangjie inventing Chinese characters (a legend during the reign of the Yellow Emperor)

仓廪(cānglǐn) a granary

仓廪实而知礼节(cānglǐnshí ér zhīlǐjié) when the granaries are full, people think much of observing etiquette

伧父(cāngfù) a boor; a bumpkin; a vulgar person

沧海(cānghǎi) the vast sea

沧海桑田(cānghǎi sāngtián) time brings great changes to the world

沧海一粟(cānghǎi yīsù) a drop in the ocean

沧浪亭(cānglàngtíng) the Blue-Wave Pavilion (in Suzhou)

沧桑(cāngsāng) the vicissitudes of life

苍龙(cānglóng) ①the Black Dragon ②the eastern constellations in the lunar mansions③a fiend

苍穹(cāngqióng) the vault of heaven; the firmament

《苍穹之昴》(cāngqíong zhī mǎo) *Firmamental Pleiades* – a TV drama co-produced by China and Japan in 2009

苍生(cāngshēng) common people

藏经阁(cángjīnggé) the depository of Buddhist scriptures

藏经楼(cángjīnglóu) the depository of Buddhist scriptures

藏猫儿(cángmāor) to play hide-and-seek

藏书票(cángshūpiào) a bookplate; a book label; an Ex Libris

藏头诗(cángtóushī) a head-hidden verse (in which the first character of each line, put together, forms a phrase or sentence that expresses the intended idea)

操琴(cāoqín) to play a Chinese fiddle (huqin)

操守(cāoshǒu) personal integrity

漕船(cáochuán) a boat for carrying grain in ancient times

漕粮(cáoliáng) grain transported by

water to the capital; tribute grain

漕运(cáoyùn) water transport of grain to the capital (in the imperial period)

槽坊(cáofang) a traditional brewery or distillery

草庵(cǎoān) a thatched hut

草包(cǎobāo) ①a straw bag or sack ②an idiot

草编(cǎobiān) straw weaving; straw plaiting; straw woven articles

草鸡(cǎojī) ①a hen ②a coward; a timid person

草芥(cǎojiè) trifle; a worthless thing

草寇(cǎokòu) bandits

草隶(cǎolì) ①clerical script (calligraphy) ②cursive script (calligraphy)

草莽(cǎomǎng) ①a thick growth of grass ②wilderness

草莽英雄(cǎomǎng yīngxióng) a greenwood hero

草莓族(cǎoméizú) (lit.) "the strawberry generation" (the individualisticand flimsy younger generation)

草民(cǎomín) ①common people; vulgar people ②I; me (as a commoner)

草木皆兵(cǎomù jiēbīng) (lit.) "every bush and tree looks like an enemy soldier" (to be in a state of imaginary fear; to be paranoid)

草市(cǎoshì) a country fair

草书(cǎoshū) the cursive script (calligraphy)

草台班子(cǎotái bānzi) a small, scantily-equipped theatrical troupe

草堂(cǎotáng) a thatched hut; a cottage

草体(cǎotǐ) ①the cursive script ②the running handwriting of a phonetic alphabet

草头王(cǎotóuwáng) a bandit chief

草药(cǎoyào) medicinal herbs; herbal medicine

草药医生(cǎoyào yīshēng) a herbalist

草野(cǎoyě) among the common people; common people

草医(cǎoyī) a village doctor

草字(cǎozì) a Chinese character written in the cursive script

册封(cèfēng) to confer a title of nobility on; to bestow on somebody the title of

册立(cèlì) to make a crown prince or empress

侧室(cèshì) ①a side room; a side chamber ②a concubine

侧卫(cèwèi) a flank guard

厕身(cèshēn) to occupy an important position in; to be an unqualified member of

厕身士林(cèshēn shìlín) to be a member of the scholar class

测字(cèzì) the fortune-telling by analyzing the component parts of a Chinese character; to divine by means of characters; glyphomancy

测字先生(cèzì xiānsheng) a fortune-teller; a glyphomancer

策论(cèlùn) a discourse on politics; an essay on current affairs

策士(cèshì) a strategist; a tactician; a schemer

策试(cèshì) an examination on Confucian canonical writings

策问(cèwèn) to ask the examinees questions on Confucian canonical writings and state affairs (at imperialexaminations)

蹭车(cèngchē) to steal a lift; to take a bus or train without paying the fare

蹭饭(cèngfàn) to get a free meal

插队(chāduì) ①to jump a queue②to go or be sent to live and work as a member of a production team in the countryside (in the 1960s and 1970s)

插队落户(chāduì luòhù) to go and live as a member of a production team in the countryside

插队知青(chāduì zhīqīng) a high-school graduate living and working as a member of a rural production team

插杠子(chāgàngzi) to poke one's nose into somebody's business; to meddle; to butt in

插花(chāhuā) ikebana; flower arranging

插科打诨(chākē dǎhùn) to make impromptu comic gestures and remarks; buffoonery; jesting

插曲(chāqǔ) ①an interlude②a song in a movie or play③an episode

插足(chāzú) ①to gain a foothold②to get involved

查抄(cháchāo) to confiscate; to inspect and confiscate

查封(cháfēng) to seal up; to close down

查户口(cháhùkǒu) to check residence cards

查铺(chápù) to make a bed check

查夜(cháyè) to make a night patrol

茬口(chákǒu) ①crops for rotation② the soil on which crops are planted and harvested ③ an opportune moment; a juncture; an opportunity

茶博士(chábóshì) ①a waiter in the teahouse; a tea waiter②an expert in tea production or tasting

茶场(cháchǎng) a tea farm; a tea plantation

茶道(chádào) the tea ceremony; the way of tea; sado

茶点(chádiǎn) tea and pastries; refreshments

茶房(cháfáng)①a teahouse waiter②a boiler room

茶缸子(chágāngzi)a mug;a tea mug

茶倌(cháguān)a teahouse waiter

茶馆(cháguǎn)a teahouse

《茶馆》(cháguǎn) *The Teahouse* - a modern Chinese play by Lao She (老舍,1899 - 1966) in 1958

茶话会(cháhuàhuì) a tea party; a tea forum

茶几(chájī) a tea table; a teapoy; a coffee table

茶具(chájù) the tea set

茶寮酒肆(cháliáo jiǔsì) teahouse and wineshop

茶陵诗派(chálíng shīpài) the School of Chaling Poetry - a poetic school represented by Li Dongyang(李东阳,1447 - 1516) lived in Chaling, Hunan province

茶楼(chálóu) a teahouse

茶钱(cháqián) ①the payment for tea ②a tip

茶肆(chásì) a teahouse

茶摊(chátān) a roadside tea-stall

茶亭(chátíng) a tea booth;a tea kiosk

茶托(chátuō) a saucer

茶文化(cháwénhuà) tea culture; tea etiquette

茶叶蛋(cháyèdàn) a tea egg(an egg boiled in tea)

茶艺(cháyì) the skill of making tea; the art of tea;the tea ceremony

茶役(cháyì) a teahouse waiter

茶栈(cházhàn) a business house trading all kinds of Chinese tea; a tea shop

茶砖(cházhuān) a tea brick; compressed tea

茶座(cházuò) ① a teahouse; a tea stall ②the seats in a teahouse or at a tea stall

察举(chájǔ) to recommend by local administrative executives (the system of recommendation of able and virtuous men as officials in the Han Dynasty)

岔曲儿(chàqǔr) a lyrical song or ditty

岔子(chàzi) ①a branch road; a side road ②an accident

差遣(chāiqiǎn) to send somebody on an errand

差使(chāishǐ) ①an errand; a job ② to assign

差事(chāishi) an errand

差役(chāiyì) ① corvee ② a yamen runner

拆白党(chāibáidǎng) a gang of swindlers; swindlers

拆墙脚(chāiqiángjiǎo) to undermine; to pull the rug from under somebody

拆台(chāitái) to cut the ground from under somebody's feet; to pull away a prop; to undermine

拆字(chāizì)to tell the fortune by analyzing the component parts of a Chinese character; to divine by means of characters;glyphomancy

侪辈(cháibèi)the people of the same generation;peers

柴扉(cháifēi)a wicker gate;a brushwood door

柴火(cháihuo)firewood

柴米夫妻(cháimǐ fūqī)an impoverished couple

单于(chányú)the king or chief of the Xiongnu(Huns)

婵娟(chánjuān)①a lovely and graceful woman②the moon

婵媛(chányuán)①a beautiful lady②to be implicated;to be involved③to be linked together

禅房(chánfáng)a Buddhist temple;a room for meditation; Buddhist monks' living quarters

禅画(chánhuà)a Zen brush painting

禅机(chánjī)a Buddhist allegorical word or gesture

禅偈(chánjì)a Zen Gatha or a Zen verse

禅经(chánjīng)the Buddhist scripture

禅理(chánlǐ)Buddhist doctrines; Buddhist tenets

禅林(chánlín)a Buddhist temple

禅门(chánmén)Buddhism

禅师(chánshī)a Buddhist monk; a Zen master

禅堂(chántáng)a meditation room

禅悟(chánwù)the realization of truth;awakening to truth

禅心(chánxīn)a meditative mind; a peaceful mind

禅学(chánxué)the doctrine of Zen; Zen Buddhism

禅院(chányuàn)a Buddhist temple or monastery

禅杖(chánzhàng)a Buddhist monk's staff

禅宗(chánzōng)Zen Buddhism; the Zen sect;the Zen school

缠足(chánzú)foot-binding

澶渊之盟(chányuān zhī méng)the Treaty of Chanyuan (signed in 1004)

蟾蜍(chánchú)①a toad②the moon ③the fabled toad in the moon

蟾宫(chángōng)the moon

蟾宫折桂(chángōng zhéguì)(lit.) "to pluck the laurel bough in the palace of the moon" – to obtain a jinshi degree in the imperial examination

产婆(chǎnpó)a midwife

忏法(chànfǎ)a way or rite of confession

伥鬼(chāngguǐ)a ghost who helps tigers to devour men

娼妇(chāngfù)(swearword) a bitch; a whore

娼门(chāngmén) a brothel; a whorehouse

阊阖(chānghé) the gate of heaven; a palatial entrance; the front gate of a palace

长安(cháng'ān) Chang'an (the ancient capital of China)

长城(chángchéng) the Great Wall

长虫(chángchong) a snake

长短句(chángduǎnjù) ① lyrical poetry (composed of long and short lines) ② the ci genre of poetry

长庚(chánggēng) Venus; Hesperus

长鼓(chánggǔ) a long drum

长鼓舞(chánggǔwǔ) a long-drum dance

《长恨歌》(chánghèngē) *A Song of Everlasting Sorrow* – a long poem by Bai Juyi (白居易,772 – 846) in 806; a TV drama adapted from the novel by Wang Anyi (王安忆,1954 –)

《长恨歌传》(chánghèngē zhuàn) *A Song of Everlasting Sorrow* – a long poem by Chen Hong (陈鸿) in the Tang Dynasty

长江(chángjiāng) the Changjiang river; the Yangtze river

《长江三日》(chángjiāng sānrì) *Three Days on the Yangtze River* – a prose article by Liu Baiyu (刘白羽,1916 – 2005)

长江三峡(chángjiāng sānxiá) The Three Gorges of the Yangtze River

长卷(chángjuàn) a long scroll (of painting or calligraphy)

长龙(chánglóng) a long queue

长眠(chángmián) an eternal sleep; death

长明灯(chángmíngdēng) an altar lamp; an ever-burning lamp

长命百岁(chángmìng baǐsuì) a long life; "many happy returns of the day"

长命锁(chángmìngsuǒ) a "long-life lock" (a mascot for longevity worn by a child)

长年(chángnián)(dialect) long-term labourer

长袍马褂(chángpáo mǎguà) traditional Chinese long gowns and mandarin jackets

长拳(chángquán) the long punch boxing (a style of Chinese boxing)

长衫(chángshān) a long gown

长勺之战(chángsháo zhī zhàn) the Battle of Changshao (648 BC)

长舌妇(chángshéfù) a big mouth; a gossipy woman; a yenta

长蛇阵(chángshézhèn) single-line battle formation

长生不老(chángshēng bùlǎo) immortality; living forever; agelessness

长生不老药(chángshēngbùlǎo yào) the elixir of life

《长生殿》(chángshēngdiàn) *The Palace of Eternal Life* – a play by Hong Sheng(洪昇, 1645 – 1704); *The Immortal Hall*

长生果(chángshēngguǒ) a longevity nut; peanuts; groundnuts

长寿灌顶(chángshòu guàndǐng) tshe-dbang(an annual ceremony to pray for long life in Tibetan Buddhism)

长寿面(chángshòumiàn) longevity noodles

长亭(chángtíng) a road-side pavilion

长物(chángwù) a superfluous thing

长阳人(chángyángrén) the Changyang Man(a type of primitive man of about 100,000 years ago)

长揖(chángyī) to make a deep bow

长斋(chángzhāi) a long abstention from meat, fish, etc; a vegetarian diet

《长征》(chángzhēng) *The Long March* – a TV drama directed by Tang Guoqiang(唐国强) in 2001

长征(chángzhēng) ①an expedition; a long march②the Long March

长治久安(chángzhì jiǔān) long political stability

常平仓(chángpíngcāng) the ever-normal granary (in Hebei) (in ancient China)

常胜将军(chángshèng jiāngjūn) an ever-victorious general

常言道(chángyándào) as the saying goes; it is well said that

常州词派(chángzhōucípài) the Changzhou School of *Ci* Poetry

嫦娥(cháng'é) the goddess in the moon; the Lady in the Moon; the Moon Lady

《嫦娥奔月》(cháng'é bènyuè) *The Story of Chang'E, the Goddess of the Moon* – a Chinese myth

场面话(chǎngmiànhuà) a polite platitudefor the occasion

场面人(chǎngmiànrén) ① a man about town; a very sociable person ②a person of prestige; a celebrity

倡寮(chàngliáo) a brothel; a whorehouse

倡优(chāngyōu) ①a singer, dancer or entertainer②a prostitute and actor or actress

唱白脸(chàngbáiliǎn) ①to play the villan ② to pretend to be harsh and severe

唱本(chàngběn) the libretto (script) of a ballad singer

唱酬(chàngchóu) an exchange of poems between friends; to write and reply in regulated verse between friends

唱独角戏(chàng dújiǎoxì) to play a monodrama; to put on a one-man show; to go it alone

唱段(chàngduàn) an aria (from an opera)

唱对台戏(chàng duìtáixì) to stage a rival show; to enter into rivalry; to voice opposing views; to say or do the opposite

唱反调(chàng fǎndiào) to sing a different tune; to speak or act deliberately contrary to

唱高调(chàng gāodiào) to make high-sounding statements; to say fine-sounding things; to indulge in high-flown rhetoric

唱工(chànggōng) the art of singing; the skill of singing

唱功(chànggōng) the art of singing

唱功戏(chànggōngxì) the singing-based Chinese opera (featuring singing rather than acting or acrobatics)

唱红脸(chàng hóngliǎn) to wear the red makeup of the stage hero; to play the hero; to pretend to be amicable and generous

唱空城计(chàng kōngchéngjì) (lit.) "to apply the Empty-City stratagem" – to present a bold front so as to hold back a weak defence

唱老调(chàng lǎodiào) to sing the same song; to harp on the same old theme

唱念做打(chàngniànzuòdǎ) singing, recitation, acting and acrobatics

唱票(chàngpiào) to count votes aloud; to call out the names of voters

唱腔(chàngqiāng) vocal music (in a Chinese opera)

唱诗(chàngshī) to recite a poem

唱双簧(chàng shuānghuáng) ① to give a two-man comic show ② to echo each other

唱戏(chàngxì) to sing and act in an opera; to put on a theatrical performance

唱主角(chàngzhǔjué) to play the leading role

抄本(chāoběn) a transcript; a copy; a hand-copied book; a manuscript

抄后路(chāohòulù) to outflank and attack from the rear

抄家(chāojiā) to ransack somebody's home and confiscate their property

抄家问斩(chāojiā wènzhǎn) to confiscate somebody's property and execute him

抄手(chāoshǒu) ① wontons ② to fold one's arms ③ a copyist

抄斩(chāozhǎn) to confiscate somebody's property and execute him

钞票(chāopiào) a banknote; paper

money

超度(chāodù) to release souls from purgatory; to expiate the sins of the dead; deliverance from hell

超凡入圣(chāofán rùshèng) to overcome all worldly thoughts and enter sainthood; to ascend to transcendence; self-perfection

超升(chāoshēng) the ascension (of a man's soul) to the paradise

超生(chāoshēng) ①reincarnation②to give unplanned births

《超生游击队》(chāoshēng yóujīduì) *More Children Guerrilla* - a comic skit starring Huang Hong(黄宏) and Song Dandan(宋丹丹) in 1990; *Anti-family plan Guerilla*

朝拜(cháobài) to pay respects to (a sovereign); to pay homage to; to worship

朝参(cháocān) a court counsel

朝臣(cháochén) a courtier; a government official

朝顶(cháodǐng) to make a pilgrimage to a Buddhist mountain temple

朝房(cháofáng) a waiting room for courtiers

朝奉(cháofèng) ①a middle-ranking official in court ②a rich man ③a pawnbroker

朝服(cháofú) court dress

朝纲(cháogāng) court discipline

朝贡(cháogòng) to pay tribute (to an imperial court); to present tribute to an emperor

朝见(cháojiàn) to have an audience with (a king, an emperor, etc.)

朝觐(cháojìn) ①to have an audience with②to go on a pilgrimage

朝山(cháoshān) to make a pilgrimage to a temple on a mountain

朝审(cháoshěn) a court assize

朝鲜族(cháoxiǎnzú) the Chaoxian (Korean) nationality; Chinese Koreans

朝香(cháoxiāng) to visit a temple to burn joss-sticks

《朝阳沟》(cháoyánggōu) *Facing Sun Ravine* - an Yu opera directed by Yang Lanchun(杨兰春) in 1958

朝野(cháoyě) ①the court and the commonality; the government and the populace②the ruling party and the opposition

朝中有人好做官(cháozhōng yǒurén hǎo zuòguān) You will have a bright official career if you have powerful backing in the government.

朝珠(cháozhū) long string of beads (made of coral or agate, and worn by senior officials of the Qing Dynasty)

潮剧(cháojù) Chaozhou opera

潮绣(cháoxiù)Chaozhou embroidery

潮语(cháoyǔ)a catchword; a buzz word

炒更(chǎogēng)to be engaged in a second occupation in one's sparetime;moonlighting

炒家(chǎojiā)a skillful broker or speculator;profiteer

炒冷饭(chǎo lěngfàn)(lit.)"to heat leftover rice"– to say or do the old same thing;to rehash

炒青(chǎoqīng)to parch tea-leaves in a special pot

炒什锦(chǎo shíjǐn)a stir-fried assorted dish

炒鱿鱼(chǎo yóuyú)to dismiss somebody from office;to fire somebody

炒友(chǎoyǒu)a speculator

炒杂烩(chǎo záhuì)to fry assorted ingredients;chop suey

炒作(chǎozuò)to promote;to publicize

炒作(chǎozuò)①speculation;hype;②to hype

车把式(chēbǎshi)a cart driver

车夫(chēfū)a cart driver;a chauffeur

车轱辘(chēgūlu)(dialect)a wheel; a felloe

车轱辘话(chēgūlu huà)repetitious talk;the same old stuff

车轱辘会(chēgūlu huì)a regular dinner party(with each member taking turns to host)

车驾(chējià)an imperial carriage

车裂(chēliè)tearing a man's body into pieces using five carts(a cruel punishment in ancient China)

车轮战术(chēlún zhànshù)the tactic of several men fighting one opponent in turn to exhaust him

车马坑(chēmǎkēng)a chariot pit

扯淡(chědàn)to talk nonsense;nonsense

扯后腿(chě hòutuǐ)to hold somebody back;to be a drag on somebody;to be a hindrance to somebody

扯家常(chě jiācháng)to chat about domestic trivia;to engage in small talk

扯皮(chěpí)①to dispute over trifles;to argue back and forth;to wrangle ②to pass the buck to each other

抻面(chēnmiàn)to make hand-pulled noodles;hand-pulled noodles

尘世(chénshì)this world;this mortal life;the mundane world

尘缘(chényuán)the predestined bond;the earthly bond

臣服(chénfú)①to submit oneself to the rule of;to acknowledge allegiance to ② to serve a ruler as his subject

臣工(chéngōng)all the officials at the imperial court

臣僚(chénliáo) officials (in imperial times)

臣民(chénmín) the subjects of a feudal ruler

臣子(chénzǐ) officials (in imperial times)

沉脉(chénmài) the deep pulse

沉香(chénxiāng) eaglewood

沉鱼落雁(chényú luòyàn) (lit.) "so beautiful she would make wild geese alight and fish sink" – a very beautiful woman

辰时(chénshí) the period of the day from 7 a. m. to 9 a. m.

陈谷子烂芝麻(chén gǔzi làn zhīma) (lit.) "old millet and stale sesame" – repetitious bygones

《陈奂生上城》(chénhuànshēng shàng chéng) *Chen Huansheng Goes to Town* – a short story by Gao Xiaosheng(高晓声, 1928 – 1999) in 1980

陈年老账(chénnián lǎozhàng) a longstanding debt; the things that happened a long time ago

陈桥兵变(chénqiáo bīngbiàn) the Mutiny in Chenqiao [engineered by Zhao Kuangyin (赵匡胤, 927 – 976) in 960]

陈胜吴广起义(chénshèng wúguǎng qǐyì) the Chen Sheng-Wu Guang Uprising (in 209 BC) (the first large-scale peasant uprising in China's history)

陈世美(chénshìměi) ①Chen Shimei (a notorious character in traditional Chinese opera) ②a heartless husband

陈式太极拳(chénshì tàijíquán) the Chen-style shadowboxing; Chen-style tai-chi chuan

宸断(chénduàn) the verdict of the monarch

宸翰(chénhàn) the monarch's calligraphy

宸垣(chényuán) the national capital

宸衷(chénzhōng) the emperor's wishes

晨钟暮鼓(chénzhōng mùgǔ) (lit.) "the morning bell and the evening drum" – to exhort people to lead a life of virtue and purity

衬钱(chènqián) religious donation

衬字(chènzì) an inserted character or word (in a line of verse for balance or euphony)

趁钱(chènqián) to be rich in money; to have pots of money

谶纬(chènwěi) divination (by mystical interpretation of Confucianist belief)

谶纬之学(chènwěi zhī xué) divination (combined with mythical Confucian belief)

谶语(chènyǔ)a prophecy

称兵(chēngbīng)to launch a military attack;to start a war

称大(chēngdà)to vaunt one's seniority;to put on airs

称孤道寡(chēnggū dàoguǎ)to look upon oneself as the supreme leader

称兄道弟(chēngxiōng dàodì)to call each other brothers;to be on intimate terms

撑场面(chēng chǎngmiàn)to keep up appearances

撑门面(chēng ménmiàn)to keep up appearances

撑腰(chēngyāo)to support;to back up;to bolster up

丞相(chéngxiàng)Prime Minister;Premier

成道节(chéngdàojié)the Buddha's Enlightenment Day

成方(chéngfāng)a set prescription

成皋之战(chénggāo zhī zhàn)the Battle of Chenggao(from 205－203 BC)

成吉思汗(chéngjísīhán)Genghis Khan

《成吉思汗》(chéngjísīhán)*Genghis Khan* － a TV drama directed by Wang Wenjie(王文杰)in 2002

成家(chéngjiā)①to get married②to become a recognized authority

成劫(chéngjié)the epoch of formation

成礼(chénglǐ)a prescriptive etiquette and ceremony;to get married

成年式(chéngniánshì)an initiation ritual

成气候(chéng qìhòu)to be promising;to be something

成器(chéngqì)to grow up to be a useful person

成亲(chéngqīn)to get married

成仁(chéngrén)to die for a righteous cause

成药(chéngyào)patent medicine

成也萧何,败也萧何(chéngyěxiāohé,bàiyěxiāohé)the same person can contribute to both your success and downfall

成则为王,败则为寇(chéngzéwéiwáng,bàizéwéikòu)legitimacy belongs to the winner,the losers are always in the wrong

呈文(chéngwén)the official document submitted to a superior;a petition

呈正(chéngzhèng)to submit a piece of writing(to a friend)for criticism and correction

承尘(chéngchén)a canopy(over one's seat in ancient times)

承乏(chéngfá)to take up a post(for lack of a better candidate)

承蒙(chéngméng)to be granted a favor;to be indebted(to somebody for a kindness)

承题(chéngtí)the second part of the eight-part essay; an exposition of the theme

承祧(chéngtiāo)to become a heir to one's uncle who has no son

承运(chéngyùn)to be ordained by Heaven

城府(chéngfǔ)subtle thinking; a shrewd, sophisticated mind

城郭(chéngguō)inner or outer city walls; city walls

城壕(chénghāo)a moat; a city trench

城隍(chénghuáng)the town god; the city god

城隍庙(chénghuángmiào)the temple of the town god

城楼(chénglóu)a gate tower

《城南旧事》(chéngnán jiùshì) *My Memories of Old Beijing* – a film directed by Wu Yigong(吴贻弓) in 1983

城濮之战(chéngpú zhī zhàn)the Battle of Chengpu(633 BC)

城阙(chéngquè)the imperial palace; the watch tower on either side of a city gate

城下之盟(chéngxià zhī méng)the treaty signed under coercion

《乘风破浪》(chéngfēng pòlàng) *Plough Through; Braving Wind and Waves* – a TV drama released in 1975

乘龙快婿(chénglóng kuàixù)an ideal son-in-law

盛殓(chéngliàn)to encoffin

惩前毖后(chéngqián bìhòu)to learn from past mistakes to avoid future ones

程门立雪(chéngmén lìxuě)(lit.) "standing in snow to wait upon Master Cheng respectfully" – to respect the teacher and learn from him with reverence

程派演员(chéngpài yǎnyuán)the Cheng school performers

程朱理学(chéngzhū lǐxué)Cheng-Zhu Neo-Confucianism

程朱学派(chéngzhū xuépài)the Cheng-Zhu School

秤砣(chèngtuó)①a sliding weight of a steelyard②a fatty or heavy weight

吃白饭(chī báifàn)①to have meals at others' expense; to have free meals②to sponge off sb; to live off others.

吃白食(chī báishí)①to have a free meal; to eat at others' expense②to live idly without work

吃白眼(chī báiyǎn)to be looked down upon

吃饱了撑的(chībǎole chēngde)(lit.) "to be restless from overeating" – to do something silly or otiose

吃闭门羹(chī bìméngēng)to be denied entrance at the door; to be refused

吃瘪子(chībiězi) to stand to lose; to get the worst of it; to be embarrassed

吃不开(chībukāi) to be unpopular; to fail to gain public favour

吃不了兜着走(chībuliǎo dōuzhezǒu) to bear all consequences; to land oneself in serious trouble

吃不消(chībuxiāo) unable to stand; cannot bear or endure

吃不住(chībuzhù) unable to bear or support

吃长斋(chī chángzhāi) to be on a vegetarian diet all the year round

吃醋(chīcù) to be jealous

吃错药(chī cuò yào) (lit.) "to take the wrong medicine" - (a person's) behavior is strange and impolite

吃错药了(chī cuò yào le) (lit.) "to take wrong medicine" - to be abnormal

吃大锅饭(chī dàguōfàn) (lit.) "to eat from the same big pot" - to get an equal share regardless of the work done

吃大户(chī dàhù) ①to eat free meals or seize grain in landlords' homes② to make somebody who can afford it stand treat

吃得开(chīdekāi) to be popular; to get along all right

吃得苦中苦,方为人上人(chī de kǔzhōngkǔ, fāng wéi rénshàngrén) the man who can bear the bitterness of hardship can then stand above others; No cross, no crown.

吃等食(chī děngshí) to lead an idle life

吃豆腐(chī dòufu) (lit.) "to eat beancurd" - to flirt with women; to engage in minor sexual harassment

吃独食(chī dúshí) to refuse to share with others

吃粉笔灰(chī fěnbǐhuī) to live off chalk dust - to live by teaching

吃干醋(chī gāncù) to be jealous without reason; to be green with envy

吃干饭(chī gānfàn) to hold down a position without doing the work

吃功夫(chī gōngfu) to require great effort; to be strenuous

吃官粮(chī guānliáng) to live on a salary from the government

吃官司(chī guānsi) to be prosecuted or sued; to be punished by law; to be involved in a legal action

吃馆子(chīguǎnzi) to eat at a restaurant; to dine out

吃喝风(chīhē fēng) the unhealthy practice of feasting on public money

吃喝嫖赌(chī hē piáo dǔ) to go feasting, wining, gambling and whoring -

to lead a dissipated life

吃黑枣儿(chī hēizǎor)to be executed

吃后悔药(chī hòuhuǐyào)to cry over spilt milk;to feel remorse

吃花酒(chī huājiǔ)to carouse in the company of flirtatious girls;to enjoy a dinner party with flirtatious girls in attendance

吃花生米(chī huāshēngmǐ)to be shot dead

吃皇粮(chī huángliáng)to live on the wages paid by government

吃回扣(chī huíkòu)to get commission;to receive a kickback

吃货(chīhuò)①a chowhound;a gastronome②to stock with goods;to lay in merchandise③to buy at the bottom of the shares

吃讲茶(chī jiǎngchá)"drink dispute-solving tea"- an custom in old China-to go to a teahouse to settle dispute

吃开口饭(chī kāikǒufàn)to make a living as an entertainer

吃老本(chī lǎoběn)to live off one's past gains or achievements

吃里扒外(chīlǐ páwài)to live off one person while secretly serving another

吃零嘴(chī língzuǐ)to take snacks;to eat between meals

《吃面条》(chī miàntiáo) *Eating Noodles* - a Chinese skit starring Chen Peisi(陈佩斯)and Zhu Shimao(朱时茂)in 1984

吃偏饭(chī piānfàn)to enjoy special privilege; to enjoy favorable treatment

吃枪药(chī qiāngyào)to be in a bad temper;to be irritable

吃枪子(chī qiāngzǐ)to be hit by a bullet;to be shot dead

吃请(chīqǐng)to accept an invitation to dinner

吃软饭(chī ruǎnfàn)to live off women rather than work for a living

吃素(chīsù)①to be a vegetarian②to be incompetent or weak

吃瓦片(chī wǎpiàn)to make a living on rental property;to live on rent

吃闲饭(chī xiánfàn)to be a loafer;to lead an idle life;to remain idle

吃相(chīxiàng)table manners

吃香(chīxiāng)to be very popular;to be in great demand

吃小灶(chī xiǎozào)to have a special meal; to receive special treatment; to give someone individual tuition and training,etc.

吃斋(chīzhāi)to practice abstinence from meat and fish;to eat vegetarian food

蚩尤(chīyóu)Chiyou(a legendary warrior who fought with the Yellow

Emperor)

笞刑(chīxíng)whipping;flogging

痴长(chīzhǎng)to be older; to be somebody's senior

弛禁(chíjìn)to rescind a prohibition; to lift a ban

《池偶谈》(chíǒután) *Occasional Talks at the North of the Pond* – an collection of literary sketches by Wang Shizhen(王士祯,1634 – 1711)

池鱼之殃(chíyúzhīyāng)(lit.)"a disaster for the fish in the pond"– a disaster that one is unfortunately invovled in;an unexpected calamity

池中物(chízhōngwù)(lit.)"a fish in a pond"– a person without any ambition

驰书(chíshū)to send an urgent message;to send a letter in haste

持节(chíjíe)to hold the imperial insignia(as credentials)

持久战(chíjiǔ zhàn)a protracted war

持斋(chízhāi)to keep to a vegetarian diet

尺牍(chǐdú)①correspondence②a model of epistolary art

尺蠖之屈(chǐhuò zhī qū)a temporary setback

尺素(chǐsù)①a small painting②correspondence

齿录(chǐlù)to employ;to hire;to take somebody on the staff

斥革(chìgé)to dismiss from office

《赤壁》(chìbì) *Red Cliff* – a film directed by Wu Yusen(吴宇森) in 2008

《赤壁怀古》(chìbì huáigǔ) *Recalling Antiquity at the Red Cliff* – a *ci* poem by Su Shi(苏轼,1037 – 1101)

赤壁之战(chìbì zhī zhàn)the Battle of Chibi(208 AD)

赤脚医生(chìjiǎo yīshēng)a barefoot doctor

赤佬(chìlǎo)a ghost;a devil

赤眉起义(chìméi qǐyì)the Chimei Uprising(18 – 25 AD)

赤嵌之战(chìqiàn zhī zhàn)the Battle of Chiqian(1661)

赤色分子(chìsè fènzǐ)the members and followers of the communist party; the people who believe in communism;the Reds

赤色宣传(chìsè xuānchuán)the Red propaganda; the communist propaganda

赤陶(chìtáo)terra-cotta

赤卫队(chìwèiduì)the Red Armed Escorts(the local armed units in the revolutionary base areas in the Second Revolutionary Civil War from 1927 to 1937)

赤县(chìxiàn)China

赤县神州(chìxiàn shénzhōu)China

赤子(chìzǐ)①a newborn baby②a simple-hearted person

赤子之心(chìzǐ zhī xīn)(lit.)"the heart of a newborn baby"-utter innocence

饬令(chìlìng)①to order②a document giving orders to subordinates

敕封(chìfēng)to appoint somebody to a post;to confer a title on somebody (by imperial order)

敕建(chìjiàn)to build by imperial edict

《敕勒歌》(chìlè gē) *The Chile Ballad* - a ballad of the Northern Dynasty (386-581)

敕令(chìlìng)an imperial order;an edict;a decree

敕书(chìshū)an imperial edict to court officials

敕造(chìzào)to be built by imperial edict

充大个儿(chōng dàgèr)to pretend to be an able man(to insist on doing something beyond one's ability)

充军(chōngjūn)to be banished to a distant place for penal servitude

充壳子(chōng kézi)to pretend to be an expert

冲龄(chōnglíng)a tender age;very young

冲喜(chōngxǐ)the"warding-off"wedding(which was used to ward off evils or bad influence)

《冲虚经》(chōngxūjīng) *The Classic of Perfect Emptiness* - a Daoist classic by Liezi(列子)from 450 to 375BC;*Liezi*

重九(chóngjiǔ)the Double Ninth Festival

重庆谈判(chóngqìng tánpàn)the Chongqing Negotiations(1945)

重适(chóngshì)to remarry

重文(chóngwén)the variant form of a character

重五(chóngwǔ)the Dragon Boat Festival

重午(chóngwǔ)the Dragon Boat Festival

重霄(chóngxiāo)the highest heaven

重阳(chóngyáng)the Double Ninth Festival

重阳节(chóngyángjié)the Double Ninth Festival

重整旗鼓(chóngzhěng qígǔ)to rally one's forces(after a defeat)

崇文馆(chóngwénguǎn)Chongwen Pavilion(set up in 639)

崇洋媚外(chóngyáng mèiwài)to worship foreign things and fawn on foreigners

崇祯(chóngzhēn)Chongzhen(the title of the reign,1627-1644)

《崇祯历书》(chóngzhēn lìshū) *The Calendar of Emperor Chongzhen* -

the calendar series compiled chiefly by Xu Guangqi (徐光启, 1562 - 1633) from 1629 to 1634

抽工夫(chōugōngfu) to manage to find time

抽签(chōuqiān) to draw or cast lots

抽头(chōutóu) to take a percentage or cut of (the winnings in gambling, etc.)

抽陀螺(chōu tuóluó) to whip a spinning top

抽绣(chōuxiù) drawnwork

抽壮丁(chōu zhuàngdīng) to press-gang

俦类(chóulèi) people of the same generation; people of similar tastes or inclinations; class

俦侣(chóulǚ) a companion; a partner

绸舞(chóuwǔ) a silk dance

《畴人传》(chóurén zhuàn) *The Biographies of Astronomers and Mathematicians* - an arithmetic book compiled chiefly by Ruan Yun (阮元, 1764 - 1849) from 1795 to 1799

畴日(chóurì) formerly; in the old days

畴昔(chóuxī) in former times

酬唱(chóuchàng) to respond to a poem with a poem

酬酢(chóuzuò) ①an exchange of toasts②to socialise with

酬答(chóudá) ①to reward somebody for his kindness②to respond with a poem or speech

酬劳(chóuláo) ①to thank somebody with a gift; to reward; to remunerate ②reward; remuneration

丑八怪(chǒubāguài) a very ugly guy

丑表功(chǒubiǎogōng) to brag shamelessly about one's deeds; to claim undeserved merit

丑旦(chǒudàn) a female clown in Chinese opera

丑角(chǒujué) ①a clown; a buffoon; a comic character; a jester②an ignoble role

《丑陋的中国人》(chǒulòu de zhōng guórén) *The Ugly Chinaman* - a book by Boyang (柏杨, 1920 - 2008) in 1985; *The Ugly Chinaman and the Crisis of Chinese Culture*

丑婆子(chǒupózi) a female clown on stage; an old comedienne

丑时(chǒushí) the period of the day from 1 a. m. to 3 a. m.

臭街了(chòujiēle) to be a fad or a craze

臭老九(chòulǎojiǔ) "the stinking number nine" - a term of abuse by ultra-Leftists for teachers and other educated people during the Cultural Revolution in China

臭美(chòuměi) to flatter oneself

臭皮囊(chòupínáng) (lit.) "a vile skin-bag" - the human body (Buddhism)

臭棋(chòuqí) a lousy chess move; a blunder(in chess)

臭棋篓子(chòuqílǒuzi) an unskilled chess player

出榜(chūbǎng) ①to issue a list of successful candidates or examinees ②to put up a notice

出殡(chūbìn) to carry a coffin to the cemetery; to hold a funeral procession; funeral

出彩(chūcǎi) ①a red liquid(used as blood to indicate injury in traditional Chinese drama) ②to make a fool of somebody or oneself; to embarrass somebody

出场费(chūchǎngfèi) an appearance fee; a performance fee

出丑(chūchǒu) to make a fool of somebody or oneself; to be disgraced

出道(chūdào) to start a job or a new career; to embark on one's career

出典(chūdiǎn) ①the source of a quotation or allusion ②mortgage; pawn

出份子(chū fènzi) to club together

出风头(chū fēngtou) to seek the limelight; to get a lot of publicity

出伏(chūfú) to end the hot season

出阁(chūgé) to get married to; to marry

出更(chūgēng) to go on a tour of inspection; to go on patrol

出恭(chūgōng) to have a bowel movement; (slang) to take a dump

出号(chūhào) to quit a job

出继(chūjì) to be adopted as a son or daughter

出家(chūjiā) to become a monk or a nun

出家人(chūjiārén) a Buddhist or a Taoist priest

出嫁(chūjià) (of a woman) to get married; to marry

出将入相(chūjiàngrùxiàng) to be qualified to be either a general or a chief minister

出九(chū jiǔ) the end of the cold season

出科(chū kē) to graduate from a professional theatrical school

出娄子(chū lóuzi) to get into trouble

出乱子(chū luànzi) to go wrong; to get into trouble

出梅(chū méi) to emerge from the rainy season

出门(chūmén) ①to be away from home; to go on a journey ②to get married; to marry

出门子(chūménzi) to get married; to marry

出聘(chūpìn) ①to get married ②to take on a diplomatic mission abroad; to serve as an envoy abroad

出气筒(chūqìtǒng) a punch bag; a whipping boy

出塞(chūsài) ① to go beyond the Great Wall (the northwest border) ②*On the Frontier* - a famouse poem by Wang Changling(王昌龄,698 - 757)

出丧(chūsāng) to carry a coffin to the cemetery; to hold a funeral procession; funeral

出山(chūshān) to take up a official post or task

出身(chūshēn) ①family background; class origin②previous experience or occupation

出师(chūshī) ①to complete one's apprenticeship ② to launch a campaign; to dispatch troops to fight; to send out an army

出世间(chūshìjiān) (Buddhism) beyond life and death

出世作(chūshìzuò) a virgin work; a maiden work; first effort

出仕(chūshì) to serve as an official; to take up an official career

出台(chūtái) ① to appear on the stage; enter②to come out from behind the scenes; to come into the open③ to make something public; to publicize

出挑(chūtiāo) ①to grow prettier; to grow into ② to develop (in skill, etc.)

出头(chūtóu) ①to free oneself from miserable circumstances②to appear personally; to take the lead; to come forward

出徒(chūtú) to complete one's apprenticeship

出污泥而不染(chū yūní ér bùrǎn) (lit.) "to come out of the dirty mud unsoiled" - to remain undefiled in spite of general corruption; to emerge unstained

出息(chūxi) ①promise; prospects; a bright future②to make progress

出虚恭(chūxūgōng) to break wind; (slang) to fart

出血(chūxiě) to pay up; to cough up

出洋相(chūyángxiàng) to make an exhibition of oneself; to cut a sorry figure; to make a fool of onself; to play the fool

出月子(chūyuèzi) to complete one's confinement month after giving birth to a baby

出蛰(chūzhé) to come out of hibernation

初潮(chūcháo) menophania; first menses; first period

初出茅庐(chūchū máolú) at the beginning of one's career; completely inexperienced in society; young and inexperienced

初伏(chūfú)the first of the three ten-day periods of the hot season

初岁(chūsuì)the beginning of a year

初唐四杰(chūtáng sìjié) the Four Preeminent Poets of the Early Tang Dynasty [Wang Bo(王勃,650 - 676), Yang Jiong(杨炯,650 - 693?), Lu Zhaolin(卢照邻, about 637 - 689) and Luo Binwang(骆宾王,619? - 687)]

初文(chūwén) the earliest written form of a Chinese character

初夜(chūyè)the wedding night

摴蒱(chūpú)a dice-throwing game

刍议(chúyì)my humble opinion

除服(chúfú) to emerge from a period of mourning

除丧(chúsāng)to take off the mourning apparel; to emerge from a period of mourning

除四害(chú sìhài) to eliminate the four pests (rats, bedbugs, flies and mosquitos)

除夕(chúxī) the Chinese New Year's Eve

雏儿(chúr)①a young bird②an inexperienced young person; a fledgling

雏妓(chújì) a child prostitute

储君(chǔjūn) a crown prince

楮墨(chǔmò) ①paper and ink-stick ②poetry, painting and calligraphy

楚帛书(chǔbóshū) the silk book of the State of Chu (unearthed in Changsha, Hunan province in 1942)

楚辞(chǔcí) the Chu verse

《楚辞》(chǔcí) *The Songs of Chu* - a collection of the Chu verse by Liu Xiang(刘向, about 77 - 6 BC); *The Elegies of Chu*

楚国(chǔguó) Chu Kingdom or the State of Chu(1042 - 223 BC)

楚汉战争(chǔhàn zhànzhēng) the War between the Chu and Han (206 - 203 BC)

楚河汉界(chǔhé hànjiè) the borderline on the Chinese chessboard; the border of two opposing countries

楚剧(chǔjù) the Chu opera

楚囚(chǔqiú) ① the native of the State of Chu captured and imprisoned in the State of Jin ② a man caught in a predicament

楚天(chǔtiān) the skies above the middle and lower reaches of the Yangtze River

楚腰(chǔyāo) a slender waist

处女作(chǔnǚzuò) the first work (of an author)

处士(chǔshì) a man of virtue and wisdom (who leads the life of a hermit); a scholarly recluse

处暑(chǔshǔ) the Limit of Heat (the 14th of the 24 Chinese solar terms, usually falling on the 23rd of August)

处子(chǔzǐ)a virgin;a maiden

畜生道(chùshēngdào)the Path of the Animal (a Buddhist term which means that an evil man would become a beast after his death)

黜免(chùmiǎn)to depose;to dismiss

黜退(chùtuì) to dismiss somebody from office

啜茗(chuòmíng)to sip tea

川菜(chuāncài) Sichuan food; Sichuan cuisine

川剧(chuānjù)Sichuan opera

川军(chuānjūn)Sichuan troops

川妹子(chuānmèizi)a Sichuan girl

穿廊(chuānláng)a covered corridor; a breezeway

穿堂儿(chuāntángr)a hallway

穿堂风(chuāntángfēng)draught

穿堂门(chuāntángmén) a passageway;a alley gate

穿小鞋(chuān xiǎoxié)(lit.)"to give somebody tight shoes to wear"–to get somebody into trouble on purpose; to make things difficult for somebody

穿孝(chuānxiào)to be in mourning; to wear mouring clothes

穿靴戴帽(chuānxuē dàimào)(lit.) "to wear boots and hats"–a cliché

穿窬(chuānyú)to cut through a wall and climb over it

穿窬之辈(chuānyú zhī bèi)burglars and thieves

传帮带(chuánbāngdài)to pass on experience,help and guide(novices)

传本(chuánběn) a circulating edition;an extant book

传抄(chuánchāo)to copy and circulate

传抄本(chuánchāoběn) a hand-copied book

传袋(chuándài)to walk over bags(an old marriage custom)

传灯(chuándēng)to teach the Buddhist doctrine

传家宝(chuánjiābǎo) a family heirloom;a hereditary treasure

传戒(chuánjiè)to initiate somebody into Buddhist monkhood or nunhood

传经送宝(chuánjīng sòngbǎo) to pass on one's valuable experience

传奇(chuánqí) ① the tales of the Tang and Song dynasties; marvel tales ② the poetic dramas of the Ming and Qing dynasties ③ a prose romance

传奇剧(chuánqíjù)a romantic play

传人(chuánrén)a person who inherits and passes on a certain scholarship or craft

传舌头(chuán shétou)to pass on a misrepresented message

传世(chuánshì) to be handed down from ancient times

传世之作(chuánshì zhī zuò) a work from ancient times

传为佳话(chuán wéi jiāhuà) to become a favourite topic; to be handed down as a popular tale

传为美谈(chuán wéi měitán) to pass from mouth to mouth with approbation

《传习录》(chuánxílù) *Records of the Teaching of the Master* – the analects of Wang Shouren (王守仁, 1472 – 1529)

传檄(chuánxí) to promulgate an official denunciation; to set out a war proclamation

传薪(chuánxīn) to impart knowledge (to students)

传艺(chuányì) to impart skills

传召大法会(chuánzhào dàfǎhuì) the Monlam or Grand Summons Ceremony (a tradition in Tibetan Buddhism)

传旨(chuánzhǐ) to deliver an imperial order

传宗接代(chuánzōng jiēdài) to have a son to carry on one's family name

船帮(chuánbāng) a merchant fleet

船家(chuánjiā) a boatman

船老大(chuánlǎodà) ① the chief boatman ② a boatman

椽笔(chuánbǐ) (lit.) "a writing brush as big as a rafter" – your magnificent writing

椽子(chuánzi) a rafter

串联(chuànlián) to link one by one; to establish contacts

串铃(chuànlíng) ① a hollow metal ring ② a string of bells

串门(chuàn mén) to call on somebody; to drop in

串亲戚(chuàn qīnqi) to visit one's relatives

串戏(chuànxì) to act in a play or opera (especially where amateurs perform with a professional troupe)

串演(chuànyǎn) to play or act the role of

钏子(chuànzi) a bracelet

窗格子(chuānggézi) a window lattice

窗花(chuānghuā) a paper-cut for window decoration; a paper-cutting pasted on panes

窗棂子(chuānglíngzi) window lattice; window bars; windowpane

窗友(chuāngyǒu) a fellow student; a schoolmate

窗纸(chuāngzhǐ) the window paper (for lattice windows)

床榻(chuángtà) a bed; a couch

床帏(chuángwéi) a curtain over the bed; (fig.) sexual relations or affairs

床笫(chuángzǐ) the bed for lovemaking

床笫之欢(chuángzǐ zhī huān) the intimacies between man and woman in bed; sexual intercourse

闯关东(chuǎng guāndōng) (lit.) "to brave a risky journey to the Northeast" – to earn a living

《闯关东》(chuǎng guāndōng) *Brave Journey to the Northeast* – a TV drama directed by Kong Sheng(孔笙) in 2008

《闯关东前传》(chuǎng guāndōng qiánzhuàn) *Prequel to Brave Journey to the Northeast* – a TV drama directed by Wang Bin (王滨) in 2013

闯江湖(chuǎng jiānghú) to make a living wandering from place to place

闯王(chuǎngwáng) Chuang Wang or Daring King – a title for Gao Yingxiang(高迎祥,? – 1636) and then Li Zicheng(李自成,1606 – 1645)

《闯王进京》(chuǎngwáng jìn jīng) *Chuangwang Li Entering the Capital* – a Beijing opera libretto by Ma Shaobo (马少波, 1918 – 2009) in 1944

创牌子(chuàngpáizi) to produce and establish a brand name

创收(chuàngshōu) extra-moneymaking; extra-earning; to increase income by providing paid services

《创业》(chuàngyè) *Carve Out* – a film directed by Yu Yanfu (于彦夫) in 1974

《创业史》(chuàngyè shǐ) *A History of Pioneers* – a novel by Liu Qing(柳青,1916 – 1978) in 1960

创造社(chuàngzàoshè) the Creation Society [the earliest and the most influential literary group initiated by Guo Moruo (郭沫若, 1892 – 1978), Yu Dafu (郁达夫, 1896 – 1945), Tian Han (田汉, 1898 – 1968), Cheng Fangwu (成仿吾, 1987 – 1984) and Zhang Ziping(张资平,1893 – 1959) in 1926]

吹边哨(chuī biānshào) (lit.) "to blow a whistle to the side" – to create a disturbance; to inflame or agitate people

吹打乐(chuīdǎyuè) Chinese wind and percussion instruments

吹灯(chuīdēng) (lit.) "to blow out a lamp" – ①to die ②to fail; to collapse; to break down

吹灯拔蜡(chuīdēng bálà) to die; (slang) to kick the bucket

吹法螺(chuī fǎluó) to brag; to boast

吹风(chuīfēng) ①to be in a draught; to catch a chill ②to fill somebody in on something in advance

吹鼓手(chuīgǔshǒu) ①a trumpeter; a

bugler②a eulogist

吹火筒(chuīhuǒtǒng) a blowtube; a stove pipe

吹拉弹唱(chuīlātánchàng)(lit.)"to blow, bow, pluck and sing" - to sing and perform various kinds of instruments

吹喇叭(chuī lǎbā)(lit.)"to blow the trumpet" - to praise extensively; to flatter somebody

吹冷风(chuī lěngfēng)(lit.)"to blow a cold wind" - to throw cold water on

吹牛(chuīniú) to boast; to brag; to talk big

吹牛大王(chuīniú dàwáng) a braggart; a braggadocio; a boaster

吹牛皮(chuīniúpí) to boast; to brag; to talk big

炊饼(chuībǐng) a steamed round flat cake

炊烟(chuīyān) cooking smoke

炊帚(chuīzhou) a kitchen brush; a pot-scouring brush

垂爱(chuíài) your kind concern (used to express modest gratitude in correspondence)

垂范(chuífàn) to set an example

垂拱而治(chuígǒng ér zhì) to rule with ease; to rule in a laissez-faire manner

垂花门(chuíhuāmén) an ornamental inner gate

垂帘(chuílián)(lit.)"to let down the curtain" - to act on behalf of the legitimate sovereign

垂帘听政(chuílián tīngzhèng) to attend to state affairs from behind a screen

《垂帘听政》(chuílián tīngzhèng) *Reign behind the Curtain* - a film directed by Hon Cheung Lee(李翰祥) in 1983

垂暮(chuímù) dusk

垂暮之年(chuímù zhī nián) old age

垂青(chuíqīng) to lavish one's attention on somebody

垂髫(chuítiáo) early childhood

《春》(chūn) *Spring* - one of the trilogy entitled *Turbulent Currents* by Ba Jin(巴金, 1904 - 2005) in 1938

春饼(chūnbǐng) a spring pancake

《春蚕》(chūncán) *Spring Silkworms* - a novel by Mao Dun(茅盾, 1896 - 1981) in 1933

春城(chūnchéng) the City of Spring (Kunming, provincial capital of Yunnan)

春分(chūnfēn) the Vernal Equinox or Spring Equinox

春分点(chūnfēn diǎn) the vernal equinox point

春宫(chūngōng) ①the official residence of a crown prince②a pornographic picture

春画（chūnhuà）a pornographic picture

《春江花月夜》（chūnjiānghuāyuèyè）*Moonlight and Flowers in the Spring River* – a famous poem by Zhang Ruoxu（张若虚，about 660 – 720）；a famous traditional *pipa* melody

春节（chūnjié）the Spring Festival

春节联欢晚会（chūnjié liánhuān wǎnhuì）the Spring Festival Gala

春卷（chūnjuǎn）spring rolls

春兰秋菊（chūnlán qiūjú）（lit.）"spring orchids and autumn chrysanthemums" – everything has its own beauty; everyone has their strong points

春蕾计划（chūnléi jìhuà）the Spring Buds Project（helping children in poor areas to attend schools, launched in 1989）

春联（chūnlián）Spring Festival couplets

春梦（chūnmèng）a spring dream – a transient joy

《春苗》（chūn miáo）*Spring Seedlings* – a film directed by Xie Jin（谢晋，1923 – 2008）in 1975

《春秋》（chūnqiū）*The Spring and Autumn Annals* – a Confucian classic attributed to Confucius（551 – 479 BC）

春秋笔法（chūnqiū bǐfǎ）the writing style of *The Spring and Autumn Annals*

《春秋繁露》（chūnqiūfánlù）*Rich Dew of Spring and Autumn* – a political and philosophical work by Dong Zhongshu（董仲舒，179 – 104 BC）

《春秋公羊传》（chūnqiū gōngyáng zhuàn）*Gongyang's Commentaries on the Spring and Autumn Annals* – a Confucian classic by Gongyang Gao（公羊高）in the Warring States Period 475 – 221 BC

春秋三传（chūnqiū sānzhuàn）The Three Commentaries on Spring and Autumn Annals

《春秋释例》（chūnqiū shìlì）*Interpretation of The Spring and Autumn Annals* – an ancient works by Du Yu（杜预，222 – 284）

春秋五霸（chūnqiūwǔbà）The Five Feudal Lords in the Spring and Autumn Period［Duke Huan of Qi（齐桓公，? – 643 BC），Duke Wen of Jin（晋文公，671 – 628 BC），Duke Mu of Qin（秦穆公，? – 621 BC），Duke Xiang of Song（宋襄公，650 – 637 BC）and King Zhuang of Chu（楚庄王，? – 591 BC）］

春秋战国（chūnqiū zhànguó）the Spring and Autumn and the Warring States

春社(chūnshè)the Day of Sacrifice to the God of the Land

春试(chūnshì)the imperial examinations in spring

春条(chūntiáo)a strip of red paper on which auspicious words are written

春晚(chūnwǎn)the Spring Festival Gala Evening; the CCTV New Year's Gala

《春望》(chūnwàng)*A Spring View* - a poem by Du Fu(杜甫,712 - 770) in 757

春闱(chūnwéi)the imperial examinations in spring

春宵(chūnxiāo)a spring night; a night of sexual bliss

春药(chūnyào)aphrodisiac; love potion

《春夜宴桃李园图》(chūnyè yàn táolǐ yuán tú)*Painting of a Banquet with Friends on a Spring Night* - a painting by Chou Ying(仇英, 1509? - 1551)

椿萱(chūnxuān)parents; father and mother

椿萱并茂(chūnxuān bìngmào)both parents are alive and well; both parents are in good health.

唇吻(chúnwěn)eloquence; speech talent

鹑衣(chúnyī)ragged clothes

錞于(chúnyú)a bronze musical instrument in ancient times

蠢货(chǔnhuò)a blockhead; a dunce; an idiot

戳脊梁骨(chuō jǐlianggǔ)to criticize somebody behind his back

戳记(chuōjì)an official seal

绰号(chuòhào)nickname

辍笔(chuòbǐ)to give up writing or painting midway

词臣(cíchén)an official in charge of imperial edicts and mandates, etc.

词调(cídiào)the tonal patterns and rhyme schemes of *ci* poetry

词赋(cífù)*cifu*(a genre of classic Chinese poetry as represented by *The Poetry of Chu*)

词话(cíhuà)①annotations on *ci* poetry ②storytelling(interspersed with songs and ballads)③a novel with parts in verse

词令(cílìng)the words or speech(appropriate to the occasion)

词牌(cípái)the names of tunes(to which *ci* poems are composed); the verse patterns

词谱(cípǔ)a collection of tunes of ci poems

词曲(cíqǔ)ci poetry and *qu* poetry

词人(círén)a *ci* writer; a man of literary poetry

词余(cíyú)*qu* poetry

词韵(cíyùn)the rhymes of ci poetry

词章(cízhāng)poetry and prose; the art of writing; rhetoric

祠庙(címiào)an ancestral temple; a memorial temple

祠堂(cítáng)an ancestral hall; an ancestral temple; a memorial hall

瓷公鸡(cígōngjī)(lit.)"a porcelain rooster" - a skinflint; a miser

瓷婚(cíhūn)porcelain wedding anniversary(the 20th wedding anniversary)

瓷窑(cíyáo)a porcelain kiln

慈航(cíháng)the journey of salvation

慈命(címìng)a mother's wish or instruction

慈禧(cíxǐ)Empress Dowager Cixi

慈禧太后(cíxǐ tàihòu)Empress Dowager Cixi(1835 - 1908)

辞赋(cífù)*cifu*; poetic prose

辞旧迎新(cíjiù yíngxīn)to ring out the Old Year and ring in the New Year

辞灵(cílíng)to bow before a coffin (before it is carried to the grave)

辞令(cílìng)the words or speech(appropriate to the occasion)

辞书(císhū)a dictionary; a lexicographical work

辞岁(císuì)to bid farewell to the outgoing year; to celebrate the lunar New Year's Eve

辞灶(cízào)to bid farewell to the kitchen god

辞章(cízhāng)poetry and prose; the art of writing; rhetoric

此岸(cǐàn)this shore; temporality

次韵(cìyùn)to write and reply in poems according to original poem's rhyming words

刺儿话(cìrhuà)sarcastic remarks

刺儿头(cìrtóu)a nit-picker; a fault-finder

刺客(cìkè)an assassin

刺配(cìpèi)to tattoo the face of a criminal and send him into exile

刺史(cìshǐ)Regional Inspector; Prefect

刺绣(cìxiù)① embroider ② embroidery

刺字(cìzì)①to tattoo the skin with characters ② to brand a criminal by tattooing

赐死(cìsǐ)to order somebody to commit suicide

从残(cóngcán)multifarious anecdotes

从父(cóngfù)a paternal uncle

从良(cóngliáng)to give up being a prostitute and get married

从母(cóngmǔ)a maternal aunt

从戎(cóngróng)to enlist

从叔(cóngshū)father's younger male cousin

从兄(cóngxiōng)an elder male cousin(on the paternal side)

从一而终(cóng yī ér zhōng) to be faithful to one's husband to the very end

从子(cóngzǐ) brother's son; nephew

从坐(cóngzuò) to be punished for being related to an offender

从集(cóngjí) ①to crowd together; to pile up②collected writings; a series of books; a collection

丛刊(cóngkān) a series of books; a collection; collected writings

丛刻(cóngkè) a series of block-printed books

丛书(cóngshū) a series of books; series; a collection

丛谈(cóngtán) collected writings; an essay or a book composed of many similar parts

丛葬(cóngzàng) a multiple burial; a multiple grave

丛冢(cóngzhǒng) a group of usually unkept graves

凑胆子(còudǎnzi) to muster up one's courage by gathering people together

凑份子(còu fènzi) ①to club together; to pool money (to buy a present for somebody) ②to add trouble (especially by interfering in somebody else's business)

凑合事儿(còuhe shìr) to go through the motions

凑趣儿(còuqùr) ①to join in (an activity) to please others②to make a joke about

凑热闹(còu rènào) ①to join in the fun②to add trouble to

凑数(còushù) ①to make up the number or amount②to serve as a stopgap

凑整儿(còuzhěngr) to make up a round number

粗茶淡饭(cū chá dàn fàn) ① a homely meal; plain food; a simple diet②a simple life

粗话(cūhuà) a vulgar language; coarse words

粗人(cūrén) a boor; a rough person

殂谢(cúxiè) to die; to pass away

醋罐子(cùguànzi) a jealous person

醋海生波(cùhǎi shēngbō) a storm of jealousy; complications caused by jealousy

醋劲儿(cùjìnr) jealousy; very jealous

醋溜儿小生(cùliūr xiǎoshēng) a sentimental wimp; a young man easily moved by emotion

醋坛子(cùtánzi) a jealous person

蹙金(cùjīn) to be embroidered with golden thread

蹴鞠(cùjū) an ancient football

氽丸子(cuān wánzi) soup with meat balls

蹿个儿(cuāngèr) to grow taller rapidly

蹿火(cuānhuǒ) to flare up; get angry; to burn with anger

篡国(cuànguó) to usurp the state political power

催命鬼(cuīmìng guǐ) a person who keeps pressing or urging another for something

《翠湖春晓》(cuìhú chūnxiǎo) *A Spring Morning on the Emerald Lake* – a piece of national orchestral music by Nie Er (聂耳, 1912 – 1935) in 1934

村长(cūnzhǎng) a village head

村夫(cūnfū) a villager; a countryman; an uncouth rustic; a country bumpkin

村夫俗子(cūnfū súzǐ) a boorish and vulgar man; an uneducated persons

村妇(cūnfù) a country woman; a vulgar woman

村公所(cūngōngsuǒ) a village office

村姑(cūngū) a village girl; a farmer's daughter; a young country woman

村塾(cūnshú) an old-style private school in a village; a village school

村寨(cūnzhài) a fortified village; a village

皴法(cūnfǎ)(art) the wrinkle method; texture strokes

踆乌(cūnwū) a legendary three-legged bird; the sun

存古学堂(cúngǔ xúetáng) a school for ancient learning

存天理,灭人欲(cún tiānlǐ, miè rényù) Eliminating human desires and preserving the principles of heaven

寸草春晖(cùncǎo chūnhuī) one can never adequately repay one's parents' love

寸金难买寸光阴(cùn jīn nán mǎi cùn guāngyīn) money can not buy time; time is more precious than gold

寸劲儿(cùnjìnr) ①an explosive force ②coincidence

寸楷(cùnkǎi) one-square-inch block character

寸楷羊毫(cùnkǎi yángháo) a small-sized writing brush

寸口(cùnkǒu) the *cunkou* pulse (one of the three pulses on the wrist)

寸口脉(cùnkǒumài) the *cunkou* pulse (one of the three pulses on the wrist)

寸头(cùntóu) a crew cut (a style of haircut); short spiky hair

寸心(cùnxīn) feelings; heart; mind

寸阴(cùnyīn) a very short time

搓板(cuōbǎn) a washboard

搓火(cuōhuǒ) to get angry; to worry; to feel impatient

搓麻将(cuō májiàng) to play mahjong

撮合(cuōhé) to make a match; to act as a match-maker or go-between; to bring together

矬子(cuózi) a short person; a dwarf

错简(cuòjiǎn) a textual error

错银(cuòyín) an article handicrafted with inlaid silver filigree; to inlay with silver; silver-inlaid

《错斩崔宁》(cuòzhǎn cuīníng) *The Erroneous Execution of Cui Ning* – a script for story-telling in Song and Yuan folk literature

D

搭班(dābān) to join a troupe to perform temporarily; to join in a group's work temporarily

搭班唱戏(dābān chàngxì) to put a theatrical troupe together to stage an opera

搭帮(dābāng) to travel together; to join somebody on a trip

搭便车(dā biànchē) to hitchhike

搭档(dādàng) ①to pair up; to cooperate; to work together ②to team up with ③a partner

搭话(dāhuà) to accost; to strike up a conversation

搭伙(dāhuǒ) ①to join as a partner ② to eat regularly in (a cafeteria, etc.)

搭末班车(dā mòbānchē) (lit.) "to catch the last bus" – to seize the last opportunity

达官贵人(dáguān guìrén) a high ranking official; a VIP

达赖(dálài) Dalai Lama

达赖喇嘛(dálài lǎma) Dalai Lama

达士(dáshì) a great scholar

达斡尔族(dáwòěrzú) the Daur nationality; Daur

妲己(dájǐ) Daji [a concubine of King Zhou of the Shang Dynasty (1600 – 1046 BC)]; a seductress

答拜(dábài) a return call; to pay a return call

答访(dáfǎng) to pay a return visit

答礼(dálǐ) a gift in return

鞑靼(dádá) Tartar

打把势(dǎ bǎshi) to dance for joy; to practice martial arts

打白条(dǎbáitiáo) to issue an IOU

打摆子(dǎbǎizi) to suffer from malaria

打板子(dǎ bǎnzi) to flog with bamboo or cane

打边鼓(dǎ biāngǔ) to act, assist or speak up for somebody from the sidelines

打擦边球(dǎ cābiānqiú) to play on the touchline with; to play the edge ball with

打禅(dǎchán)to sit in meditation

打长工(dǎ chánggōng)to work as a long term hired hand

打场子(dǎchǎngzi)to attract an audience by singing, drumming and yelling

打出手(dǎchūshǒu)to throw weapons back and forth (in traditional opera)

打春(dǎchūn) the Beginning of Spring;Spring begins

打当面鼓(dǎ dāngmiàngǔ)to speak in somebody's presence

打道回府(dǎdàohuífǔ)to return to one's residence with the pawns leading the procession and clearing the way;to go home

打灯笼(dǎ dēnglong)to carry or hold a lighted lantern

打灯谜(dǎ dēngmí)to guess a riddle;to solve a riddle

打底子(dǎdǐzi)①to eat before drinking②to lay a foundation

打地铺(dǎ dìpù)to make a bed on the ground

打点(dǎdiǎn)①to bribe②to get ready

打赌(dǎdǔ)to bet

打短工(dǎ duǎngōng)to work as a casual laborer; to be a temporary worker

打翻身仗(dǎ fānshēnzhàng)to work hard to bring about an uprising

打更(dǎgēng)to patrol in the streets at night;to sound the night watches

打工(dǎgōng)to work to earn a living;to do manual work

打工妹(dǎgōngmèi)a working girl

《打工奇遇》(dǎgōng qíyù)*Fortuitous Meeting at Work* - a Chinese skit starringby Zhao Lirong(赵丽蓉) and Gong Hanlin(巩汉林)in 1996

打工仔(dǎgōngzǎi)a migrant boy; a working boy

打工族(dǎgōngzú)migrant workers

打躬作揖(dǎgōng zuōyī)to salute with folded hands and make deep bows;to cup one hand in the other before the chest to show respect

打拱(dǎgǒng)to salute with one's hands folded

打拱作揖(dǎgǒng zuòyī)to salute with folded hands and make deep bows;to cup one hand in the other before the chest to show respect

打谷场(dǎgǔchǎng)a threshing floor

打鼓(dǎgǔ)(lit.)"to beat a drum"-to feel uncertain;to feel nervous

打卦(dǎguà)to cast lots

打官腔(dǎ guānqiāng)to talk like a bureaucrat;to assume official airs in speech

打官司(dǎ guānsi)to go to law; to

file a lawsuit; to go to court; to engage in a lawsuit

打光棍儿(dǎ guānggùnr) to remain a bachelor, to stay single

打哈哈(dǎ hāha) ①to make fun; to crack a joke ② to assume official airs in speech and action

打号子(dǎ hàozi) to sing a work song

打黑枪(dǎ hēiqiāng) to take a sniper's shot at, to fire from behind

打诨(dǎhùn) to make ad-lib comic gestures and remarks; buffoonery

打饥荒(dǎ jīhuāng) to have financial difficulty; to be in debt

打价儿(dǎjiàr) to bargain; to haggle

打尖(dǎjiān) to stop for refreshment

打江山(dǎ jiāngshān) to fight to win state power

打交道(dǎ jiāodào) to make contact with; to make dealings with

打擂台(dǎ lèitái) to join a contest in martial arts on stage; to accept a challenge; to take up a challenge

打冷枪(dǎ lěngqiāng) to take a sniper's shot at

打冷战(dǎ lěngzhàn) to shiver; to launch a cold war

打离婚(dǎ líhūn) to divorce; to go through formalities for the divorce

打里打外(dǎlǐ dǎwài) to take care of everything both inside the home and out

打麻将(dǎ májiàng) to play mahjong

打马虎眼儿(dǎ mǎhuyǎnr) to exploit others' carelessness; to act dumb; to pretend to be ignorant

打埋伏(dǎ máifu) to lie in ambush; to hold something back for one's own purpose

打闷棍(dǎ mèngùn) to rob a victim after stunning him/her with a club; to give a stunning blow

打炮(dǎpào) to shine in one's opening performance

打炮戏(dǎpàoxì) one's specialty

打屁股(dǎ pìgu) to be punished

打平手(dǎ píngshǒu) to end in a draw

《打扑克》(dǎ pūkè) *Playing Poker* – a famous skit starring by Huang Hong(黄宏) and Hou Yaowen(侯耀文) in 1994

打气(dǎqì) (lit.) "to pump up" – to encourage

打千儿(dǎqiānr) to go down on one's left knee

打前站(dǎ qiánzhàn) to set out in advance; to make preparations and arrangements

打秋风(dǎqiūfēng) to sponge off somebody

打拳(dǎquán) to practice shadow boxing

打如意算盘(dǎ rúyì suànpān) to expect things to turn out as one wishes;to indulge in wishful thinking

打入冷宫(dǎrù lěnggōng)to leave sb out in the cold; to consign to the back shelf;to relegate to limbo

打手(dǎshǒu)a goon;a hired roughneck;a hatchet man

打通关(dǎ tōngguān)to triumph over others by a finger-guessing game(so as not to knock over a drink at the feast)

打头炮(dǎ tóupào)(lit.)"to fire the first shot"-to be the first to speak or act

打头阵(dǎ tóuzhèn)①to lead the attack;to fight in van②to be the vanguard

打退堂鼓(dǎ tuìtánggǔ)to back out; to beat a retreat; to draw in one's horns

打陀螺(dǎ tuóluó)to spin a top;to whip a spinning top

打下手(dǎ xiàshǒu)to act as an assistant

打先锋(dǎ xiānfēng)to be a pioneer; to be the vanguard

打小报告(dǎ xiǎobàogào)to inform secretly on a colleague, etc. ; to snitch

打小算盘(dǎ xiǎosuànpán)to show petty shrewdness;to be niggling

打牙祭(dǎ yájì)to have a rare sumptuous meal;to have a special dinner

打哑谜(dǎ yǎmí)to make puzzling remarks

打烊(dǎyàng)to close the store for the night;to put up the shutters

打野鸡(dǎ yějī)to visit low class brothels

打油诗(dǎyóushī)a doggerel

打游击(dǎ yóujī)①to engage In guerrilla warfare;join the guerrillas ②to make a living by doing odd jobs③to work(eat, sleep, etc.)at no fixed place

《打渔杀家》(dǎ yú shā jiā)*Revolt of the Fishing Folks*-a famous Beijing opera

打圆场(dǎ yuánchǎng)to mediate a dispute;to smooth things over

打杂儿(dǎzár)to do odd jobs

打折扣(dǎzhékòu)①to fall short of a requirement②to discount

打嘴仗(dǎzuǐzhàng)to quarrel;to argue

打坐(dǎzuò)to sit in meditation

大阿哥(dààge)the eldest prince(in the Qing Dynasty)

大班(dàbān)①taipan; the manager of a foreign firm in old China②the senior group(in kindergarten)

大包干(dàbāogān)to fix a plot of land for each household; all-round responsibility or contract system

大部头(dàbùtóu) a monumental work;a thick book

大乘(dàchéng)(Buddhism) the Great Vehicle;Mahayana

大虫(dàchóng) a tiger

大吹法螺(dà chuī fǎluó) ①to expound the doctrines of Buddhism② to blow one's own trumpet; to talk big;to brag

大刀会(dàdāohuì) the Big Sword Society (a folk clandestine mass organization in Shandong, Jiangsu Henan and Anhui provinces in the Qing Dynasty)

大帝(dàdì) the heavenly emperor

大典(dàdiǎn) ①a collection of great classics;a body of the classic documents of the nation②a grand ceremony

大殿(dàdiàn) an audience hall; the main hall of a Buddhist Temple

大法(dàfǎ) the fundamental laws and principles(of a state);constitution; an important law

《大风歌》(dàfēnggē) *A song of a Strong Wind* – a poem by Liu Bang (刘邦,256 – 195 BC) in 195 BC

大夫(dàfū) Grand Master(an official title in imperial China); Great Officer

大腹贾(dàfùgǔ) a potbellied merchant;a rich merchant

大恭(dàgōng) excrement

大姑子(dàgūzi) husband's elder sister;a sister-in-law

大鼓(dàgǔ) dagu (folk tale sung in verse accompanied by a small drum, clappers, a three-stringed plucked instrument,etc.)

大褂(dàguà) an unlined long Chinese gown

大锅饭(dàguōfàn)(lit.)"the big pot rice" – extreme equalitarianism;the food prepared in a communal kitchen

大寒(dàhán) the Great Cold(the 24th of the 24 Chinese solar terms, usually falling on around the 20th of January)

大号(dàhào) a given name

《大红灯笼高高挂》(dàhóng dēnglong gāo gāo guà) *Raise the Red Lantern* – a film directed by Zhang Yimou(张艺谋) in 1991

大户(dàhù) ①a large family;a rich and influential family ② important customers

大花脸(dàhuāliǎn) the painted face (a male role of dignified type in Chinese opera)

大换血(dà huàn xiě) (lit.) " to change blood " – to change completely;a complete change

大吉大利(dàjí dàlì) unusually lucky

大家风范(dàjiā fēngfàn)noble manners

大家闺秀(dàjiā guīxiù)a daughter of an eminent family; a lady; a lady from cultured family

大驾(dàjià)①a carriage for a sovereign or emperor ② Emperor; your gracious presence;you

大驾光临(dàjià guānglín)a visit; coming(to honour someone with a visit)

大将军(dàjiāngjūn)Great General

大节(dàjié)political integrity;loyalty

大襟(dàjīn)the front of a Chinese garment

大舅子(dàjiùzi)wife's elder brother; brother-in-law

大楷(dàkǎi)a regular script in big Chinese characters

大款(dàkuǎn)the rich; a moneyed man

大魁(dàkuí)Number One Scholar (the title conferred on the one who came first in the highest imperial examination);head of bandits

《大浪淘沙》(dàlàng táoshā) *Great Waves Wash Away the Sand* – a film directed by Yi Lin(伊琳)in 1966

大牢(dàláo)a jail;a prison

大老粗(dàlǎocū)an uneducated person

大老婆(dà lǎopo)the wife of a man with one or more concubines

大老爷(dàlǎoye)your Lordship

大礼(dàlǐ)solemn ceremonies or etiquette

大礼包(dà lǐbāo)a gift package

大理(dàlǐ)Dali(an ancient City in Yunnan province)

大吏(dàlì)the local governor(in imperial China)

大殓(dàliàn)to encoffin

《大路》(dàlù) *The Big Road* – a film directed by Zhou Xiaowen(周晓文)in 1993

大路货(dàlùhuò) staple goods; cheap,ordinary goods

大妈(dàmā)①father's elder brother's wife;aunt②aunt(an affectionate or respectful form of address for an elderly woman)

大卖场(dàmàichǎng) a warehouse market

大帽子(dàmàozi)a political label;an unwarranted charge

大媒(dàméi)a go-between;a matchmaker

《大米,红高粱》(dàmǐ, hóng gāoliáng) *Rice, Red Sorghum* – a Chinese skit starring by Guo Da(郭达)in 1991

大面儿(dàmiànr) general appearance;surface

大名(dàmíng) ① a formal personal

name②great reputation

《大明宫词》(dàmínggōngcí) *Palace of Desire* – a TV drama directed by Li Shaohong(李少红) in 1998

大鸣大放(dàmíngdàfàng) to speak out freely and air one's views fully; to air one's views freely

大内(dànèi) the imperial palace

大男大女(dànán dànǚ) unmarried adult men and women

大年(dànián) the Spring Festival, a good year; a great year

大年夜(dàniányè) the Chinese New Year's Eve; the lunar New Year's eve

大娘(dàniáng) ① Aunt (wife of father's elder brother) ②Aunt (a respectful appellation for an elderly woman) ③wife (of a man with one or more concubines)

大娘子(dàniángzǐ) wife (of a man with one or more concubines); a lady

大批判(dàpīpàn) mass criticism

大批判运动(dàpīpàn yùndòng) the mass criticism campaign

大辟(dàpì) capital punishment (in imperial China)

大墙文学(dàqiáng wénxué) Prison Literature

《大墙下的红玉兰》(dàqiáng xià de hóngyùlán) *The Red Magnolia within the Tall Walls* – a novelette by Cong Weixi (从维熙, 1933 –) in 1979

《大秦帝国纵横》(dàqín dìguó zònghéng) *The Qin Empire II Alliance* – a TV drama directed by Ding Hei (丁黑) in 2013

大庆(dàqìng) a grand celebration; a great occasion

大秋(dàqiū) the harvest season in autumn; autumn crops; the autumn harvest

大曲(dàqū) ①yeast (for making hard liquor) ②a hard liquor

大去(dàqù) to leave forever; to pass away

大全(dàquán) a complete collection

大人(dàrén) ① your Excellency ② parents or other elders

大儒(dàrú) a distinguished learned scholar

大嫂(dàsǎo) sister-in-law (elder brother's wife)

大少爷(dàshàoye) your eldest son; the young master (of the house); a spoilt boy

大婶儿(dàshěnr) aunt (wife of father's younger brother)

大师(dàshī) a master; Master; Great Master

大师傅(dàshīfu) a senior cook; Great Master; a Buddhist monk

大手笔(dàshǒubǐ) the calligraphy of an authority; the work of a well known writer

大叔(dàshū) uncle

大暑(dàshǔ) the Great Heat(the 12th of the 24 Chinese solar terms, usually falling on the 23rd of July)

大帅(dàshuài) commander in chief; generalissimo

大司马(dàsīmǎ) Grand Minister of War

大司徒(dàsītú) Grand Minister of Civil Administration

《大宋提刑官》(dàsòng tíxíngguān) *The Song Dynasty Justice* - a TV drama directed by Han Weiping(阚卫平) in 2005

《大宋宣和遗事》(dàsòng xuānhé yíshì) *The Stories from the Reign of Song Emperor Huizong*; *The Tales of the Xuanhe Period of the Great Song* - a novel simulating the script for story-telling, the prototype of *Outlaws of the Marsh*

《大唐西域记》(dà táng xīyù jì) *Great Tang Records on the Western Regions* - a book compiled by Bianji (辩机,? -649) in 646

《大唐狄公案》(dàtáng dígōng àn) *Judge Dee Mysteries* - a classic work by Netherlandish Sinologist Robert Hans van Gulik(罗伯特·汉斯·范·古利克, namely 高罗佩, 1910 -1967)

大堂(dàtáng) ①the courtroom in a *yamen* (magistrate's court) ②the lobby of a hotel

大同(dàtóng) Great Unity

大团结(dàtuánjié) (slang) a ten-yuan banknote; Renminbi

《大腕》(dàwàn) *Top Notch* - a film directed by Feng Xiaogang(冯小刚) in 2001

大腕(dàwàn) a distinguished personage; a big name; a star(in literature or art)

大王(dàwáng) ①Great King(a term of address for a king or a bandit chief, used in traditional operas and novels) ② a tycoon ③ a highly-skilled person

大媳妇(dàxífu) ① daughter-in-law (the wife of one's eldest son) ② wife(of a man with one or more concubines)

大喜(dàxǐ) great rejoicing; wedding

大戏(dàxì) full-length Chinese opera; Beijing opera

大仙(dàxiān) ①a celestial; an immortal ②a sorcerer; a wizard

大贤(dàxián) a sage; a man of great talent and great virtue

大限(dàxiàn) one's last moment of life; the day of one's doom

大小姐(dàxiǎojiě)the eldest daughter

大姓(dàxìng)①a celebrated family ②a very common family name

大雄宝殿(dàxióngbǎodiàn)Great Buddha Hall;Grand Hall(in a Buddhist temple)

《大学》(dàxué)*The Great Learning* - a Chinese classic

大雪(dàxuě)the Great Snow(the 21st of the 24 Chinese solar terms, usually falling on the 7th of December)

大雅之堂(dàyǎzhītáng)①an elegant place②a refined taste

大烟(dàyān)opium

大烟鬼(dàyānguǐ)an opium addict

《大堰河——我的保姆》(dàyànhé—wǒde bǎomǔ)*The Dayan River, My Nursemaid* - a long poem by Ai Qing(艾青,1910 - 1996)in 1933

大洋(dàyáng)a silver dollar

大爷(dàyé)①a lazy, arrogant and wilful man ②uncle(father's elder brother)

大姨(dàyí)aunt(mother's eldest sister)

大姨子(dàyízi)wife's elder sister; sister-in-law

大禹治水(dàyǔzhìshuǐ)DaYu's Flood Control(an ancient legend)

大员(dàyuán)a high-ranking official

大月(dàyuè)a solar month of 31 days;a lunar month of 30 days

大跃进(dàyuèjìn)the Great Leap Forward

大运河(dàyùnhé)the Grand Canal

大杂烩(dàzáhuì)①mishmash②hotchpotch

大杂院(dàzáyuàn)a courtyard or compound(occupied by a number of households)

大泽乡起义(dàzéxiāng qǐyì)the Dazexiang Uprising(209 BC)

《大宅门》(dàzháimén)*The Grand Mansion Gate* - a Chinese TV drama directed by Guo Baochang(郭宝昌)in 2001

大丈夫(dàzhàngfu)a real man;a true man;a strong man

大中丞(dàzhōngchéng)the official in charge of personnel affairs(in imperial China)

大众化(dàzhònghuà)popularization

大轴子(dàzhóuzi)the last item on a theatrical programme

大篆(dàzhuàn)the great seal script

大字报(dàzìbào)Big Character Poster(which is popular during the Cultural Revolution)

傣剧(dǎijù)opera of the Dai minority

傣族(dǎizú)the Dai nationality

代茶(dàichá)a betrothal gift(an old practice in China)

大夫(dàifu)a doctor;a physician

大王(dàiwang)the great king

带刺儿(dàicìr)to be sarcastic

带徒弟(dài túdi)to train an apprentice; to take on an apprentice; to train a novice

戴孝(dàixiào)to be in mourning(for a parent, relative, etc.)

待茶(dàichá)to receive(a guest)with tea

待业(dàiyè)to wait for a job; to wait for employment

待字(dàizì)to be not yet betrothed(to a man)

戴高帽(dài gāomào)to make compliments; to flatter

戴绿帽子(dài lǜmàozi)to have an unfaithful wife; to be a cuckold

戴孝(dàixiào)to be in mourning

丹方(dānfāng)①a folk prescription ②alchemy; the skill of making magical pellets

丹凤眼(dānfèngyǎn)slanting eyes; almond-shaped eyes

丹青(dānqīng)①a painting②historical records

丹田(dāntián)(lit.)"the elixir field"-the pubic region

丹心(dānxīn)a loyal heart

单帮(dānbāng)a trader(travelling by oneself)

单传(dānchuán)①to have only one son for several generations②to impart a skill from a single master to a single apprentice

单打一(dāndǎyī)①to concentrate on one thing only②to have a one-track mind

单刀(dāndāo)a short-hilted broadsword

《单刀会》(dāndāohuì)*Lord Guan Goes to the Feast*-a play by Guan Hanqing(关汉卿,1220-1300)

单丁(dāndīng)a young man without brothers

单寒(dānhán)to be from a humble family and low in social status

单口相声(dānkǒu xiàngsheng)comic monolog; cross talk performed by one actor only

单亲(dānqīn)a single parent

单亲家庭(dānqīn jiātíng)a single-parent family

单人锣鼓(dānrén luógǔ)a solo performance of gongs and drums

单身贵族(dānshēn guìzú)a"single aristocrat"-a single well-off person

单弦儿(dānxiánr)danxianr(storytelling to musical accompaniment)

单相思(dānxiāngsī)unrequited love

担名(dānmíng)to be associated with a certain name; to bear a certain reputation

赕佛(dǎnfó)to donate money or tribute to a temple

担担面(dàndanmiàn)hot spicy noodles;Sichuan noodles

担子(dànzi)a carrying pole and the load on it;a load;a burden

旦角(dànjué)the Dan role(a female role in traditional opera)

弹弓(dàngōng)a catapult;a slingshot

弹丸之地(dànwánzhīdì)a tiny area;a very small bit of land

淡泊明志(dànbó míngzhì)to live a simple life with clear goals;to live simply to express one's ambition

淡季(dànjì)an offseason;a dead month;a slack season

当差(dāngchāi)to be a low ranking official;to be a servant in a government office or in someone's home

当家(dāngjiā)to run a household;housekeeping

当家的(dāngjiāde)the head of a family;a housekeeper;a husband

当局者迷(dāngjúzhě mí)those deeply involved cannot see clearly

当面锣,对面鼓(dāngmiàn luó, duìmiàn gǔ)to argue face to face;to say something to somebody's face

当权(dāngquán)to be in power;regime

当政(dāngzhèng)to be in office;to be in power

挡驾(dǎngjià)to turn away a visitor with some excuse;to decline to receive a guest

挡箭牌(dǎngjiànpái)a pretext;an excuse

党八股(dǎngbāgǔ)stereotyped party writing;Party jargon

党锢(dǎnggù)an autocratic rule;one-party dictatorship

党棍(dǎnggùn)a dirty politician(who abuses his power to promote self-interest)

党国(dǎngguó)the Kuomintang and its government

党徒(dǎngtú)①a member of a clique or a reactionary political party ②a henchman

党羽(dǎngyǔ)an adherent, a henchman;a follower of a party or clan chief

谠言(dǎng yán)candid remarks

当票(dàngpiào)a pawn receipt

当铺(dàngpù)a pawnshop

荡妇(dàngfù)a dissolute woman;a fallen woman;a vamp

《荡寇志》(dàngkòuzhì)*Account of Driving Away Bandits* - a novel by Yu Wanchun(俞万春, 1794 - 1849)in 1847

刀笔(dāobǐ)the writing of indictments;pettifoggery

刀笔吏(dāobǐlì)①a pettifogger②a petty official(who draws up indictments)

刀马旦(dāomǎdàn)*daomadan* (an

actress with martial arts skills in Chinese opera)

刀枪不入(dāoqiāng bùrù)(lit.) "neither swords nor spears can penetrate" - ① invulnerability ② being unable to make an impression on sb/something

刀枪剑戟(dāoqiāngjiànjǐ)(lit.) "broadsword, two-edged swords and halberts" - all the ancient weapons

刀枪入库,马放南山(dāoqiāng rù kù, mǎfàng nánshān)(lit.) "to put the weapons back in the arsenal and graze the war horses on the hillside" - to relax vigilance against war

刀削面(dāoxiāomiàn) *daoxiao* noodles(made by slicing dough directly into boiling water)

刀子嘴(dāozizuǐ) a sharp tongue; to speak sarcastically and bitterly

刀俎(dāozǔ)(lit.) "a knife and a chopping board" - an oppressor; a persecutor

倒板(dǎobǎn) a stylized tune (preceding an integrated singing part in traditional Chinese opera)

倒戈(dǎogē) to change sides in a war; to transfer one's allegiance

倒戈卸甲(dǎogē xièjiǎ) to lay down arms

倒买倒卖(dǎomǎi dǎomài) to buy low and sell high; to scalp

倒嗓(dǎosǎng) to lose one's voice

倒胃口(dǎo wèikou) ①to spoil one's appetite; to lose one's appetite ②to dampen one's spirit

倒爷(dǎoyé) a scalper; a profiteer; a speculator

捣蛋(dǎodàn) to make (or cause) trouble

捣蛋鬼儿(dǎodànguǐr) a trouble maker

倒插门(dàochāmén) to marry into and reside with the bride's family

倒打一耙(dàodǎ yīpá) to make false countercharges; to put the blame on the victim

倒剪(dàojiǎn) with one's hands clasped or tied behind one's back

倒苦水(dào kǔshuǐ) to pour out one's grievances

倒栽葱(dàozāicōng) to fall headlong; to fall head over heels

悼词(悼辞)(dàocí) a memorial speech

盗寇(dàokòu) a bandit; a robber

盗墓(dào mù) to excavate and rob a grave; grave looting

道白(dàobái) spoken parts in an opera

道藏(dàozàng) the collected Taoist scriptures; the Taoist Canon

道场(dàochǎng) Taoist or Buddhist rites; a place where Taoist or Buddhist rites are performed

《道德经》(dàodéjīng) *Tao-Te Ching* – a Chinese classic by Lao-zi (老子, about 571 – 471 BC); *The Classic of the Virtue of the Tao*; *The Classic of the Way and Its Virtue*

道高一尺，魔高一丈(dàogāo yīchǐ, mógāo yīzhàng) (lit.) "as virtue grows by one foot, vice rises by ten" – goodness is strong, but evil is ten times stronger

道姑(dàogū) a Taoist nun

道观(dàoguàn) a Taoist temple

道光(dàoguāng) the Reign (1821 – 1850) of Emperor Aisin Gioro Minning (1782 – 1850)

道行(dàohang) moral conduct; spiritual character; supernatural skill; ability

道家(dàojiā) Taoism; Daoism; Taoist school

道家经典(dàojiā jīngdiǎn) the classics of Taoism

道教(dàojiào) Taoism; Daoism

道教名山(dàojiào míngshān) a Taoist mountain; the sacred Taoist mounta-ins

道门(dàomén) ① Daoism; Taoism ② superstitious sects and secret societies

道袍(dàopáo) a Taoist priest's robe

道人(dàorén) a Taoist priest

道士(dàoshi) a Taoist priest

道术(dàoshù) Taoist magic arts; methods; tricks

道统(dàotǒng) Confucian orthodoxy; the orthodox teaching of Confucianism

道学(dàoxué) ① the School of the Study of the Way (a Confucian school of philosophy) ② affectedly moral

道学先生(dàoxué xiānshēng) a pedant; a pedantic scholar

道院(dàoyuàn) Taoist residence; a Taoist temple

得道多助，失道寡助(dédào duōzhù, shīdào guǎzhù) a just cause gains much support while a unjust cause finds little support

得陇望蜀(délǒng wàngshǔ) appetite comes with eating; avarice knows no bounds

得势(déshì) to be in power; to get ahead; to get the upper hand

得鱼忘筌(déyú wàngquán) (lit.) "to forget the trap as soon as the fish is caught" – to forget the means by which the end is attained

德育(déyù) moral education; education in ethics

德政(dézhèng) a good government; good political measures or policies

灯彩(dēngcǎi) ① decorative lanternmaking②festoon lighting; decorative coloured lanterns

灯虎(dēnghǔ) a lantern riddle

灯会(dēnghuì) ①the Chinese Lantern Festival②a lantern show

灯笼(dēnglong) a lantern

灯笼裤(dēnglongkù) knee-length or ankle-length sports trousers; knickerbockers

灯谜(dēngmí) lantern riddles

灯市(dēngshì) a lantern fair

灯盏(dēngzhǎn) an oil lamp

登第(dēngdì) to pass the top-level imperial examination

登基(dēngjī) to ascend the throne

登科(dēngkē) to pass the civil-service examination; to receive a government degree

登台拜将(dēngtái bàijiàng) to appoint a military leader

登堂入室(dēngtáng rùshì) (lit.) "to pass through the hall into the inner chamber" - to reach a higher level in one's studies or to become more proficient in one's profession

登徒子(dēngtúzǐ) a playboy; a lecher

登位(dēngwèi) to ascend the throne

《登幽州台歌》(dēng yōuzhōutái gē) *The Song to the Youzhou Platform* - a poem by Chen Ziang(陈子昂, about 661 - 702)

等第(děngdì) rank or grade (of people)

等闲之辈(děngxián zhī bèi) quite ordinary

的哥(dīgē) a male taxi driver

的士(dīshì) a taxi

《狄公案》(dígōng'àn) *The Cases of Judge Di* - a novel by Wu Jianren (吴趼人, 1866 - 1910)

敌后(díhòu) the enemy's rear area

敌后根据地(díhòu gēnjùdì) the base areas behind the enemy lines

《敌后武工队》(díhòu wǔgōngduì) *The Armed Working Teams behind the Enemy Lines* - a novel by Feng Zhi(冯志, 1923 - 1968) in 1963

敌伪(díwěi) the enemy and their puppet regime

笛子(dízi) a bamboo flute

嫡出(díchū) to be born of the legal wife

嫡传(díchuán) to be handed down directly from the master

嫡传弟子(díchuán dìzǐ) a disciple personally instructed by the master

嫡母(dímǔ) Mother (of the direct line)

嫡派(dípài) the direct line of descent; a disciple taught by the master

嫡派真传(dípài zhēnchuán) to be personally instructed by a master;

嫡派子孙(dípài zǐsūn) the children of

the direct line of descent

嫡亲(díqīn)close paternal relations; blood relations; by the same father; of the paternal grandfather

嫡堂(dítáng)the relationship between cousins of the same paternal grandfather

嫡系(díxì)the direct line of descent; one's own clique

嫡子(dízǐ)the son, especially the eldest son, of the legal wife in premodern times

底本(dǐběn)a master copy; the original text

底工(dǐgōng)basic skills(for a theatrical performer) the essentials of basic training; basic training

底襟儿(dǐjīnr)the smaller or inner piece(on the right side of a Chinese garment which buttons on the right)

底牌(dǐpái)①a hidden card; the last card②the inside story③the last resort

底气(dǐqì)physical strength; basic strength and confidence

底下人(dǐxiàrén)servants in general

底线(dǐxiàn)①a spy(in the enemy's camp)②the baseline

底样(dǐyàng)a master copy; a copy of something for the record or for reproduction; a text against which other texts are checked

底蕴(dǐyùn)①hidden wisdom and insight ② detailed content; an inside story

底子(dǐzi)a foundation; a rough draft or sketch; a copy kept as a record; remnant; a base

抵命(dǐ mìng)a life for a life; to pay with one's life

抵账(dǐ zhàng)to pay a debt in kind or by laboring

抵罪(dǐ zuì)to be punished for a crime

地保(dìbǎo)a town crier; an errand man(for a local government)

《地道战》(dìdàozhàn) *Tunnel Warfare* – a film directed by Ren Xudong(任旭东)in 1965

地动仪(dìdòngyí)the seismograph

地方戏(dìfāngxì)a local drama(opera); a regional opera

地方志(dìfāngzhì)local chronicles; the annals of local history

地府(dìfǔ)the nether world; the underworld

地宫(dìgōng)an underground palace; a terrestrial palace

地窖(dìjiào)a cellar; a storage pit; a subterranean cell

地牢(dìláo)a dungeon

《地雷战》(dìléizhàn) *Mine Warfare* – a film directed by Tang Yingqi(唐英奇,1912–1999)in 1962

地利(dìlì)a favourable geographical position;topographical advantages

地利人和(dìlì rénhé)Terrain is favourable and people are friendly

地盘(dìpán)①a domain;the territory under one's control ② the sphere of influence

地痞(dìpǐ)a bad egg;a local ruffian

地契(dìqì)the title deed for land

《地球,我的母亲》(dìqiú,wǒde mǔqīn) *The Earth, My Mother* – a poem by Guo Moruo(郭沫若,1892 – 1978) in 1919

地煞(dìshà)the handle of the Big Dipper

地摊(dìtān)a vender's roadside stand;a wayside stall

地头蛇(dìtóushé)a local villain or bully

地下党(dìxiàdǎng)an underground party(an organization of the Communist Party)

地下宫殿(dìxià gōngdiàn)an underground palace

地窨子(dìyìnzi)a cellar;a basement

地支(dìzhī)the Twelve Earthly Branches

地主(dìzhǔ)a landlord;a landowner;a host

地主阶级(dìzhǔjiējí)landocracy;the landlord class

地主之谊(dìzhǔzhīyì)the friendship or hospitality of a host

弟妹(dìmèi)sister-in-law(younger brother's wife)

弟子(dìzǐ)a disciple;a student;a follower

帝号(dìhào)the title of an emperor;an imperial title

帝王将相(dìwángjiàngxiàng)kings, princes, generals and ministers

递解(dìjiè)to be escorted from one place to another;to deport

递条子(dì tiáozi)to send a brief informal note

递眼色(dì yǎnsè)to wink meaningfully at somebody

第三者(dìsānzhě)①a third party;the other one②a mistress

第三者插足(dìsānzhě chāzú)the involvement of a third party

第五代中国导演(dìwǔdài zhōngguó dǎoyǎn)the fifth generation of Chinese film directors

第一把手(dìyībǎshǒu)the first in command;a person holding primary responsibility

嗲声嗲气(diǎshēng diǎqì)to be affectedly sweet;to talk and act like a spoiled child;in a coquettish voice

滇红(diānhóng)black tea from Yunnan

滇剧(diānjù)Yunnan opera

典故(diǎngù)a literary quotation;a

classical allusion;a cultural or literary reference

典籍(diǎnjí) ancient books and records

典借(diǎnjiè) pawn;mortgage

典礼(diǎnlǐ) a ceremony; a celebration

典身钱(diǎnshēnqián) money from selling oneself or a family member

典宪(diǎnxiàn) an institution;decrees and regulations

典刑(diǎnxíng) ①the standard penalty②to enforce punishment;to wield a penalty③to face capital punishment

典押(diǎnyā) to mortgage;to pawn

典狱(diǎnyù) a prison warden

典章(diǎnzhāng) decrees and regulations

典章制度(diǎnzhāng zhìdù) ancient laws and regulations

典制(diǎnzhì) decrees and regulations

典质(diǎnzhì) to mortgage;to pawn

典租(diǎnzū) to rent mortgaged land; a lien tenancy

点兵(diǎnbīng) to gather soldiers for a roll call or inspection

点拨(diǎnbo) to give advice;to show how (to do something); to give a hint

点播(diǎnbō) to make a request(for a song etc.) on a radio station

点菜(diǎncài) to order dishes

点唱(diǎnchàng) to request a song

点厾(diǎndū) to add casual touches (a technique used in Chinese ink painting)

点鬼火(diǎn guǐhuǒ) to stir up trouble secretly

点化(diǎnhuà) ①to reveal ②to be transformed by a Buddhist (or Taoist) monk

点将(diǎnjiàng) to appoint a person for an important mission;to name sb for a particular post

点金石(diǎnjīnshí) the philosophers' stone

点卯(diǎnmǎo) to call the roll in the morning;to sign in

点染(diǎnrǎn) ①to add details to a painting②to touch up (or polish) a piece of writing

点头之交(diǎntóu zhījiāo) a nodding acquaintance

点戏(diǎnxì) to choose a theatrical programme from the list

点穴(diǎnxué) (martial arts) to hit one's opponent at a vital point

点子(diǎnzi) an idea;a key point

点子大王(diǎnzi dàwáng) King of Ideas (a person who always has great ideas)

点子公司(diǎnzi gōngsī) a consultancy company

电大(diàndà)a Radio & TV university(similar to the UK's Open University)

电视大学(diànshìdàxué)a TV university

佃东(diàndōng)the owner of the land;a landowner

佃户(diànhù)a tenant

佃农(diànnóng)a tenant farmer

佃契(diànqì)a tenancy contract

佃租(diànzū)land rent

店东(diàndōng)a shop owner

店面(diànmiàn)the facade or front of a shop,hotel or restaurant

店铺(diànpù)a shop;a store

店堂(diàntáng)the business quarter of a shop

店小二(diànxiǎo'èr)a waiter;a boy servant

垫背(diànbèi)(lit.)"to act as a cushion" - to bear the blame for others;to become a scapegoat

垫话(diànhuà)①a prologue in cross-talk or storytelling②to let somebody know in advance

垫脚石(diànjiǎoshí)a stepping-stone

奠都(diàndū)to establish a capital

奠祭(diànjì)to offer libation;to hold a memorial ceremony for;to offer sacrifice to

奠酒(diànjiǔ)to pour wine on the ground in sacrifice;libation

奠仪(diànyí)a gift of money made for a funeral or a memorial ceremony

殿后(diànhòu)to bring up the rear

殿军(diànjūn)a rearguard

殿试(diànshì)the palace examination;the final imperial examination

殿堂(diàntáng)a palace;a palace hall;a great hall

殿下(diànxià)Your Highness;His or Her Highness

殿元(diànyuán)the first-place winner in the highest imperial examination

刁风弄月(diāofēng nòngyuè)to carry on a clandestine love affair

刁民(diāomín)unruly people

貂蝉(diāochán)Diaochan(one of the four great Chinese beauties in history);a great beauty

碉堡(diāobǎo)a blockhouse;a pillbox

碉楼(diāolóu)a military watchtower

雕版(diāobǎn)the cut a block for painting;the wood block for printing

雕版印刷(diāobǎn yìnshuā)block printing

雕虫篆刻(diāochóng zhuànkè)insignificant or mediocre craftsmanship

雕舫(diāofǎng)a richly ornamented boat

雕花(diāohuā)to carve patterns or designs on woodwork;carving

雕栏玉砌(diāolán yùqì)(lit.)

"carved balustrades and marble steps" - richly ornamented palace buildings

雕梁画栋(diāoliáng huàdòng)(lit.) "carved beams and painted rafters" - a richly ornamented building

屌丝(diǎosī) a cock wire - a self-mocking term referring to a man who is in adversity or in a position of inferiority; an underdog

吊膀子(diàobàngzi) to flirt with

吊儿郎当(diào'er lángdāng) to be careless and casual; to dally slovenly; to loiter away

吊古(diàogǔ) to visit a historical relic and ponder over the past

吊祭(diàojì) to offer libation to; to hold a memorial for; to condole with sb; condolences

吊楼(diàolóu) a house projecting over the water

吊毛(diàomáo) to turn a backward somersault and fall on one's back (the action of an opera actor or actress)

吊桥(diàoqiáo) a suspension bridge; a drawbridge

吊嗓子(diào sǎngzi) to exercise one's voice

吊丧(diàosāng) to pay condolences to (the bereaved)

吊审(diàoshěn) to bring up for trial; to renote the case for trial

吊死鬼(diàosǐguǐ) the ghost of a hanged person (usu by suicide)

吊死问疾(diàosǐwènjí) to show great concern for the dead and ill

吊胃口(diàowèikǒu) to whet somebody's appetite; to tempt somebody with something; to tantalize

吊孝(diàoxiào) to pay one's condolences to (the bereaved)

调包(diàobāo) to substitute stealthily

调兵遣将(diàobīng qiǎnjiàng) to move troops; to deploy forces

调档(diàodàng) to ask for an applicant's dossier

调干(diàogàn) to be enrolled as cadres (from among workers)

调干生(diàogànshēng) a college student (enrolled from among cadres); a cadre student

调虎离山(diàohǔlíshān)(lit.) "to lure the tiger out of the mountains" - to lure the enemy away from his base

调侃儿(diàokǎnr) to talk in professional jargon

调令(diàolìng) a transfer order

调门儿(diàoménr) pitch; the tone of speech

调演(diàoyǎn) to promote an organized performance; to organize a joint performance

掉包(diàobāo)to substitute one thing for another stealthily

掉膘(diàobiāo)to lose weight

掉队(diàoduì)to drop off;to fall behind

掉价(diàojià)to come down in price;to lose social status;to degrade oneself

掉书袋(diàoshūdài)to pepper one's speech with quotations and allusions;to show off one's erudition by citing literary quotations or historical allusions

跌份(diēfèn)to lose face,to be humiliated

叠罗汉(diéluóhàn)a human pyramid (an acrobatic performance)

叠韵(diéyùn)vowel rhyme;assonance;rhyming compound

叠字(diézì)a reduplicated word

《蝶恋花》(diéliànhuā) Butterfly Loves Flowers - a ci poetry tune

蹀躞(diéxiè)①to walk in small steps ②to pace about

丁册(dīngcè)a residence booklet or a household certificate [in the Qing Dynasty(1636 - 1912)]

丁丑(dīng chǒu)Ding Chou(the fourteenth year of the cycle of sixty in the Chinese calendar)

丁村人(dīngcūnrén) the Dingcun Man(one of the fossils of Homo sapiens found in Xiangfen, Shanxi province in 1953)

丁亥(dīng hài)Ding Hai(the twenty fourth year of the cycle of sixty in the Chinese calendar)

丁卯(dīngmǎo)Ding Mao(the fourth year of the cycle of sixty in the Chinese Calendar)

丁是丁,卯是卯(dīng shì dīng,mǎo shì mǎo)to be strict;to be conscientious and meticulous;to be fastidiously accurate

丁税(dīngshuì)a poll tax

丁未(dīngwèi) Ding Wei (the forty fourth year of the cycle of sixty in Chinese calendar)

钉子户(dīngzihù) a nail household (who are reluctant to relocate)

顶班(dǐngbān)to substitute for somebody absent; to work for somebody absent

顶戴(dǐngdài)official cap button(in the Qing Dynasty);to salute

顶缸(dǐnggāng) to take blame for others

顶岗(dǐnggǎng)to take over somebody's shift(while they are absent)

顶刮刮(dǐngguāguā)great,fabulous,excellent

顶礼膜拜(dǐnglǐ móbài)①to kneel and worship;to prostrate oneself in worship②to make a fetish of

顶梁柱(dǐngliángzhù) a pillar; a backbone

顶牛儿(dǐngniúr) to be at loggerheads with

顶事(dǐngshì) to be useful; to serve the purpose

顶头上司(dǐngtóu shàngsi) one's direct superior; one's boss

顶珠(dǐngzhū) bead embedded in the centre of a Qing official's hat

顶嘴(dǐngzuǐ) to answer back; to reply defiantly; to talk back

鼎食(dǐngshí) extravagant and luxurious

鼎峙(dǐngzhì) a tripartite confrontation

鼎足之势(dǐngzú zhī shì) a situation of tripartite confrontation

订婚(dìnghūn) to be engaged; to be betrothed

定场白(dìngchǎngbái) a soliloquy to introduce oneself (when making one's first appearance)

定场诗(dìngchǎngshī) poem to set the scene (on a character's first appearance in Chinese opera)

定鼎(dìngdǐng) to establish a capital

定都(dìngdū) to choose a site for the capital; to establish a capital

定金(dìngjīn) front money; deposit

定局(dìngjú) a foregone conclusion; a final conclusion; an inevitable outcome; to settle

《定军山》(dìngjūnshān) *The Battle of Dingjunshan* – a Beijing opera

定礼(dìnglǐ) the bride price; a betrothal gift

定钱(dìngqián) the earnest (paid to the parents of the prospective bride at a betrothal)

定亲(dìngqīn) to be betrothed; to be engaged; engagement; betrothal

定情(dìngqíng) to pledge love

定情戒指(dìngqíng jièzhi) a pre-engagement ring

定情之物(dìngqíng zhī wù) a token of love

定弦(dìngxián) ①to tune a stringed instrument ②to make up one's mind

定心丸(dìngxīnwán) assurance; mind relief

定音鼓(dìngyīngǔ) a kettledrum; a timpani

丢车保帅(diūjū bǎoshuài) to sacrifice the knight to save the king

丢丑(diūchǒu) to lose face; to be disgraced; to be left with egg on one's face

丢份儿(diūfènr) to lose face

丢盔卸甲(diūkuī xièjiǎ) to flee empty-handed; to throw away everything when escaping

丢脸(diūliǎn) to lose face; shame

丢人现眼(diūrén xiànyǎn) to lose

face(in public)

丢眼色(diūyǎnsè) to wink at somebody

丢卒保车(diūzú bǎojū)(lit.)"to give up a pawn to save the chariot" – to sacrifice minor things to save major ones

东北大鼓(dōngběi dàgǔ) the Big Drum of the Northeast(story telling with a drum accompaniment, from Manchuria)

东北二人转(dōngběi èrrénzhuàn) a song and dance duet from the Northeast

《东北一家人》(dōngběi yījiārén) *A Family in the Northeast* – a TV drama directed by Ying Da(英达) in 2001

东厂(dōngchǎng) the Eastern Depot (the emperor's secret service during the Ming Dynasty); espionage agency(in the Ming Dynasty)

东床(dōngchuáng) a son-in-law

东床快婿(dōngchuáng kuàixù) a good son-in-law

东床坦腹(dōngchuáng tǎnfù) a son-in-law

东道主(dōngdàozhǔ) the host

《东方红》(dōngfāng hóng) *The East Is Red* – a revolutionary song; a large-scale singing and dancing epic

东风(dōngfēng)(lit.)"the east wind" – the drivingforce of revolution

东风射马耳(dōngfēng shè mǎ'ěr)(lit.)"the east wind shoots the ear of a horse" – to go in one ear and out the other

东风压倒西风(dōngfēng yādǎo xīfēng)(lit.)"the East Wind prevails over the West Wind" – justice force prevails over evil

东宫(dōnggōng) ①the East Palace (the residence of the crown prince) ②the crown prince

东郭先生(dōngguō xiānsheng) ① Master Dongguo(a legendary softhearted scholar) ② a naive person who is kind to evil people

东汉(dōng hàn) the Eastern Han Dynasty(25 – 220)

东胡(dōnghú) the Eastern barbarians

东家(dōng jia) the master; the landlord

东晋(dōngjìn) the Eastern Jin Dynasty(317 – 420)

《东京梦华录》(dōngjīng mèng huálù) *The Townscape and Scenery in the Capital* – a book by Meng Yuanlao(孟元老) in 1147

《东京审判》(dōngjīng shěnpàn) *The Tokyo Trial* – a film directed by Gao Qunshu(高群书) in 2006

东君(dōngjūn) the Chinese Apollo;

the sun-god

东坡肉(dōngpōròu)the Dongpo pork

东三省(dōngsānshěng)the three provinces in the northeast of China (Heilongjiang,Jilin,Liaoning)

东施效颦(dōngshī xiàopín)to play the ape;a blind imitation with ludicrous effect;to look all the uglier by mimicking the beauty

东魏(dōng wèi)the Eastern Wei Dynasty(534-550)

东洋(dōngyáng)Japan

东洋人(dōngyángrén)a Japanese; Japanese people

东瀛(dōngyíng)the East Sea;Japan

东岳(dōngyuè)Mount Tai

东周(dōng zhōu)the Eastern Zhou Dynasty(770-256 BC)

《东周列国志》(dōngzhōu lièguó zhì) *Annals of the Kingdoms in the Eastern Zhou Dynasty* - a novel by Feng Menglong(冯梦龙,1574-1646); *The Romance of the Eastern Zhou*

冬不拉(dōngbùlā)Dobro;Dombra(a Kazakh plucked string instrument)

冬烘先生(dōnghōng xiānsheng) a pedant

冬至(dōngzhì)the Winter Solstice

《董永和七仙女》(dǒngyǒng hé qīxiānnǚ)*Dong Yong and the Seventh Fairy Maiden* - a legendary love story

懂行(dǒngháng)to know the ropes;to know the business

动粗(dòngcū)to beat somebody;to be violent

动肝火(dòng gānhuǒ)to get angry;to lose one's temper;to flare up

动漫(dòngmàn)a cartoon; an animated film

动土(dòngtǔ)to break ground;to start building

动刑(dòngxíng)to subject somebody to torture

侗剧(dòngjù)the opera of the Dong Nationality

侗族(dòngzú)the Dong Nationality

栋梁(dòngliáng)(lit.)"ridgepoles and beams"- a pillar of the state

栋梁之材(dòngliáng zhī cái)a person of tremendous promise

洞房(dòngfáng)a bridal or nuptial chamber

洞房花烛(dòngfáng huāzhú)wedding festivities;the wedding night

洞房花烛夜(dòngfáng huāzhú yè) the wedding night

洞府(dòngfǔ)the abode of fairies and immortals

洞天(dòngtiān)a cave heaven(a fairyland; paradise; a heavenly abode)

洞天福地(dòngtiān fúdì)cave heavens and sanctuaries(paradise; a

heavenly abode)

洞箫(dòngxiāo) a vertical bamboo flute

兜兜(dōudou) an undershirt; a vest (underwear covering the chest and abdomen)

兜肚(dōudu) an undershirt; a vest (covering the chest and abdomen)

兜风(dōufēng) to go for a drive

兜老底(dōu lǎodǐ) to show up one's past

兜圈子(dōu quānzi) ①to go around in circles②to beat about the bush

斗方(dǒufāng) ①a square sheet of paper(for painting and calligraphy) ②a painting or calligraphy(done on a square sheet of paper)

斗方名士(dǒufāng míngshì) a pretender to culture and refinement; a self-styled scholar

斗拱(dǒugǒng) brackets between pillar and crossbeam(in a building)

斗箕(dǒuji) fingerprints

斗筐(dǒukuāng) a bamboo basket

斗笠(dǒulì) a bamboo hat

斗筲(dǒushāo) a rice basket; an ancient bamboo container

斗筲之辈(dǒushāozhībèi) a person of shallow understanding

斗筲之材(dǒushāozhīcái) a person of limited capacity

斗筲之器(dǒushāozhīqì) a person of shallow understanding

斗室(dǒushì) a small room

斗笔(dǒubǐ) a big paint brush

斗地主(dòudìzhǔ) Fight the Landlord (a card game)

斗法(dòufǎ) contest in secret; match magical powers

斗鸡(dòujī) cockfighting; gamecock

斗蟋蟀(dòuxīshuài) cricket fighting

斗嘴(dòuzuǐ) to quarrel; to exchange banter

豆瓣酱(dòubànjiàng) a thick broad-bean sauce

豆豉(dòuchǐ) fermented soya beans

豆腐脑儿(dòufunǎor) tofu jelly; beancurd jelly

豆腐乳(dòufurǔ) fermented beancurd

豆腐西施(dòufu xīshī) a beautiful woman; a beauty

豆腐渣工程(dòufuzhā gōngchéng) a jerry-built project; a badly structured project; a shoddy construction

豆蔻年华(dòukòu niánhuá) teenage; in one's early teens

豆芽儿(dòuyár) (lit.) "a bean sprout" - small and thin

逗乐儿(dòulèr) to amuse others; to clown around

逗趣儿(dòuqùr) to amuse; raillery

逗笑儿(dòuxiàor) amusing; to amuse

饾版(dòu bǎn) a multi-color wood-block printing

《窦娥冤》(dòué yuān) *The Injustice to Dou E* – a play by Guan Hanqing (关汉卿,1220 – 1300)

都督(dūdu) a commander-in-chief; a provincial military governor

都督府(dūdufǔ) Chief Military Commission

都尉(dūwèi) Commandery Defender

督办(dūbàn) ①to supervise and handle ② the highest official (in a supervising institution set up in the Qing Dynasty)

督抚(dūfǔ) a civil and military governor (in the Ming and Qing Dynasties)

督府(dūfǔ) a military or government office; an official residence

督军(dūjūn) a provincial military governor (in the early days of the Republic of China)

督学(dūxué) an educational inspector or supervisor

督战(dūzhàn) to supervise operations; to direct a campaign

毒草(dúcǎo) (lit.) "poisonous weeds" – ideologically harmful writing, speech, etc.

读本(dúběn) a textbook; a reader

读后感(dúhòugǎn) reflections after reading a book or an article

读经(dújīng) to study the Confucian classics

读书破万卷(dúshū pò wànjuàn) (lit.) "to have read ten thousand volumes" – to be well read

读书人(dúshūrén) a scholar; an intellectual

渎职(dúzhí) malpractice; malfeasant

独夫民贼(dúfū mínzéi) the autocrat and traitor to the people

独角戏(dújiǎoxì) a one-man show; a monodrama

独立自主,自力更生(dúlì zìzhǔ, zìlì gēngshēng) to maintain one's independence and self-reliance; independence and self-reliance

独龙族(dúlóngzú) the Dulong nationality

独轮车(dúlúnchē) a wheelbarrow

独门独院(dúmén dúyuàn) a quadrangle courtyard (occupied by one family)

独苗儿(dúmiáor) the only child, the only heir

独木桥(dúmùqiáo) a single-plank bridge; a difficult path

独善其身(dúshàn qíshēn) to preserve one's personal integrity

独生女(dúshēngnǚ) an only daughter

独生子(dúshēngzǐ) an only son

独生子女(dúshēngzǐnǚ) an only child

独生子女政策(dúshēngzǐnǚ zhèngcè) the One Child Policy

独眼龙(dúyǎnlóng) a one-eyed person

独占鳌头(dúzhàn áotóu) to be the champion; to come out first

独子(dúzǐ) the only son

笃信(dǔxìn) to be a devout believer in; to ardently believe in

笃学(dǔxué) to be diligent in study; to be devoted to study

笃志(dǔzhì) to devote oneself to

堵心(dǔxīn) mentally uncomfortable

堵嘴(dǔzuǐ) to gag somebody; to silence somebody

赌场(dǔchǎng) a gambling house; a casino

赌棍(dǔgùn) a professional gambler; a hardened gambler

赌局(dǔjú) a gambling party

赌具(dǔjù) gambling devices

赌窟(dǔkū) a gambling-den

《赌神》(dǔshén) *The God of Gamblers* – a film directed by Wang Jing(王晶) in 1989

赌徒(dǔtú) a gambler

《杜鹃山》(dùjuānshān) *Azalea Mountain* – a modern Beijing opera

杜康(dù kāng) ①Du Kang(according to legend, the first winemaker in China) ②wine or liquor

《杜拉拉升职记》(dùlālā shēngzhí jì) *Du Lala Go* – a film directed by Xu Jinglei(徐静蕾) in 2010; *A Story of Lala's Promotion* – a TV drama directed by Chen Mingzhang(陈铭章) in 2010

杜门谢客(dùménxièkè) to shut one's door to visitors; to decline to receive visitors

度牒(dùdié) an official permit to become a monk(nun) and join a monastery; a clerical certificate; the qualification of a monk

度假村(dùjiàcūn) a resort; a holiday village

度蜜月(dù mìyuè) to honeymoon; to be on one's honeymoon

度曲(dùqǔ) to compose; to write music

《渡江侦察记》(dùjiāng zhēnchájì) *Reconnaissance across the Yangtze* – a film directed by Tang Xiaodan(汤晓丹) in 1954

镀金(dùjīn) to get gilded; gold-plated

蠹弊(dùbì) a corrupt practice; an abuse

端架子(duān jiàzi) to put on airs

端节(duānjié) the Dragon Boat Festival

端午节(duānwǔjié) the Dragon Boat Festival

端砚(duānyàn) an ink slab of high quality

端阳(duānyáng) the Dragon Boat Festival

端月(duānyuè) the first lunar month

短打(duǎndǎ)①a hand-to-hand fight (opera)②to be dressed in a Chinese-style jacket and trousers

《短歌行》(duǎngēxíng) *A Brief Cantus* – a poem by Cao Cao(曹操,155 –220)

短见(duǎnjiàn) a shortsighted view; suicide

短命鬼(duǎnmìngguǐ)(curse) a short-lived guy; to die young

短拳(duǎnquán) the short jab(a Chinese boxing style); Short Boxing

断案(duàn'àn) to settle a lawsuit

断背(duànbèi)(lit.)"Brokeback" – gay, homosexual

断背婚姻(duànbèi hūnyīn) a gay marriage

断编残简(duànbiān cánjiǎn) the stray fragments of text

断肠(duàncháng) heartbroken

断炊(duànchuī) to run out of rice and fuel

断档(duàndàng) to be sold out

断顿(duàndùn) to be unable to afford the next meal; to go hungry

断发文身(duàn fà wénshēn) to cut one's hair short and tattoo one's body(a custom in Jiangsu and Zhejiang in ancient times)

《断鸿零雁记》(duànhóng língyàn jì) *The Lone Swan* – a novel by Su Manshu(苏曼殊, 1884 – 1918) in 1912

断后(duànhòu)①to bring up the rear ②to have no progeny

断魂(duànhún) to be overwhelmed with sorrow or joy; to feel like a lost soul

断简残编(duànjiǎn cánbiān) the stray fragments of text

断井颓垣(duànjǐng tuíyuán)(lit.)"dry wells and dilapidated fences" – a scene of devastation

断句(duànjù) to make pauses in reading unpunctuated ancient writings; to punctuate

断粮(duànliáng) to run out of grain or food

断七(duànqī) to conduct a service on the 49th day after one's death

断弦(duànxián) to lose one's wife

断狱(duànyù) to try and decide a case

断种(duànzhǒng) to have no offspring; to become extinct

断子绝孙(duànzǐ juésūn) to have no male heir; may you die without offspring!

堆栈(duīzhàn) a storehouse; a warehouse

对簿(duìbù) confront the accused with his accuser

对簿公堂(duìbù gōngtáng) to be interrogated in court; to check facts according to the requests of the court; to go to a court

对对子(duì duìzi) to supply the antithesis to a given phrase

对歌(duìgē) to sing in an antiphonal style

对号入座(duìhào rùzuò)(lit.)"to take one's seat according to the number on the ticket" - to put somebody or something in its rightful place

《对花枪》(duìhuāqiāng) *Silver Spear* - a Beijing opera

对襟(duìjīn) a Chinese-style jacket with buttons down the front

对酒当歌，人生几何？(duìjiǔ dānggē, rénshēng jǐhé?) Sing while drinking and enjoy life when one can.

对局(duìjú) to play a game of chess, etc.

对口词(duìkǒucí) rhymed dialogue (a form of folk art)

对口径(duì kǒujìng) to give the same account by arrangement; to arrange to give the same story

对口相声(duìkǒu xiàngsheng) cross talk; comic dialogue

对联(duìlián) couplet; antithetical couplet

对门(duìmén) the opposite door; the neighbour opposite

对牛弹琴(duìniú tánqín)(lit.)"to play the lute to a cow" - to cast pearls before swine; to choose the wrong audience; to preach to deaf ears

对偶(duì'ǒu) antithesis; dual

对亲(duìqīn) to establish a marital relationship; the blind date for intended marriage

对台戏(duìtáixì) a rival show

对头(duìtóu) an enemy; a rival; an opponent

对胃口(duìwèikǒu) to be to one's taste; to be agreeable

对象(duìxiàng) ①a target; an object ②a boy or girl friend; partner

对眼(duìyǎn) to one's liking

对弈(duìyì) to play chess

对仗(duìzhàng) antithesis; parallel couplets

对症下药(duìzhèng xiàyào)(lit.)"to suit the medicine to the illness" - to suit the remedy to the case

对酌(duìzhuó) to drink face to face; to drink together

对着干(duìzhegàn) to adopt a confrontational approach; to set oneself against

对子(duìzi) a pair of antithetical phrases, etc; antithetical couplet

兑换券(duìhuànquàn) a bank draft; a money order; a coupon

敦煌石窟(dūnhuáng shíkū)the Dunhuang Grottoes(in Gansu province, dating from 366 AD, containing Buddhist statues, frescoes and valuable manuscripts)

蹲班房(dūn bānfáng)to be in jail

蹲点(dūndiǎn)to work on site; to stay in selected primary units (to improve overall work); to choose a place at which to gain experience at the grassroots

蹲坑(dūnkēng)a latrine pit

顿号(dùnhào)a slight-pause mark, used in lists; a half-comma

顿开茅塞(dùnkāi máosè)to suddenly see the light; to become enlightened at once

顿首(dùnshǒu)to kowtow(used after one's signature at the end of a letter to show one's respect)

顿悟(dùnwù)insight; satori (Buddhism)

遁词(dùncí)an evasive answer; a subterfuge; a quibble

遁迹(dùnjì)to live in seclusion

遁入空门(dùnrù kōngmén)to follow Buddhism; to become a monk or nun

遁世(dùnshì)reclusion

多宝槅(duōbǎogé)a curios shelf

多尔衮(duō'ěrgǔn)Dorgon – the fourteenth son of the founding emperor (Nurhachi) in the Qing Dynasty, (1612 – 1651)

多口相声(duōkǒu xiàngsheng)cross talk performed by more than two persons

多劳多得(duōláo duōdé)more pay for more work

多面手(duōmiànshǒu)a generalist; an all rounder; Jack of all trades

多难兴邦(duōnàn xīngbāng)great tribulation regenerates a nation

多事之秋(duōshì zhī qiū)an eventful period; a period of turbulence

多文为富(duōwén wéifù)Learning is wealth

多咱(duōzan)whenever; when

多嘴(duōzuǐ)talkative; to speak out of turn; to shoot off one's mouth

多嘴多舌(duōzuǐ duōshé)gossipy and meddlesome; to be long-tongued

咄嗟(duōjiē)to tut-tut; to cry out; in an instant

咄嗟立办(duōjiēlìbàn)to get something done straight away

夺标(duóbiāo)to win the first prize; to receive a tender

夺冠(duóguàn)to gain the championship

夺魁(duókuí)to win the first prize; to win the title

夺命(duómìng)to kill; to murder

夺权(duóquán)to seize power; seizure of state power; to take over power

夺印(duóyìn)(lit.)"to seize the seal"－to seize power

垛口(duòkǒu)crenels

躲年(duǒnián)to avoid creditors on the Lunar New Year's Eve

躲清闲(duǒ qīngxian)to find a place to avoid external disturb

E

阿弥陀佛(ēmítuófó)(Buddh)①Amitabha②May Buddha preserve us

阿房宫(ēpánggōng)Epang Palace

《阿房宫赋》(ēpánggōng fù)*Rhapsody on Epang Palace* － an essay by Du Mu(杜牧,803－852)

讹舛(é chuǎn)an error in a text

娥眉(éméi)(lit.)"delicate eyebrows"－a beautiful woman

娥眉月(éméiyuè)crescent moon

峨冠博带(éguān bódài)(lit.)"a high cap and a wide belt"－official scholars

峨眉山(éméishān)Mount Emei;Emei Mountain(in Sichuan province)

鹅蛋脸(édànliǎn)an oval face

额鲁特(élǔtè)Mongolian tribes

额娘(éniáng)mother

恶霸(èbà)a local tyrant

恶补(èbǔ)①to take too much tonic ②to take too many supplementary lessons

恶鬼(èguǐ)an evil spirit;a devil

恶煞(èshà)a demon; an atrocious man

恶少(èshào)a young ruffian

恶岁(èsuì)a bad harvest year

恶相(èxiàng)an evil or angry countenance

恶作剧(èzuòjù)a practical joke; a prank;mischief

饿殍(èpiǎo)the corpse of the starved

鄂伦春族(èlúnchūnzú)the Elunchun nationality

鄂温克族(èwēnkèzú)the Ewenke nationality

噩耗(èhào)devastating news

恩宠(ēnchǒng) imperial favor; to show special favor to(a minister, etc.)

恩赐(ēncì)①to bestow(favors,charity,etc.)②a favor;a bounty

恩典(ēndiǎn)a favor;a grace

恩公(ēngōng)a benefactor

恩师(ēnshī)a loving teacher

恩同再造(ēntóng zàizào) kindness tantamount to giving somebody a new lease of life

恩泽(ēnzé)a bounty; a benefit bestowed from above

恩重如山(ēnzhòng rúshān)(lit.) "grace as weighty as a mountain"－

a great debt of gratitude

恩准(ēnzhǔn) to be approved by His Majesty

儿辈(érbèi) children; young generation

儿曹(ércáo) children

儿妇(érfù) a daughter-in-law

儿皇帝(érhuángdì) a boy emperor; a puppet emperor

儿郎(érláng) ①a youth; a son ②a man③the rank-and-file soldiers

儿男(érnán) a man; a boy

儿女情长(érnǚ qíngcháng) to be immersed in love; affection between man and woman

儿女债(érnǚzhài) the burden of raising children to maturity

儿童团(értóngtuán) the Children's Corps

儿媳妇(érxífu) daughter-in-law

儿戏(érxì) a trifling matter

儿韵(éryùn) r-ending retroflexion

而立之年(érlìzhīnián) thirty years of age

尔曹(ěrcáo) you people

《尔雅》(ěryǎ) *The Erya* – a Confucian classic

耳巴(ěrba) a slap on the face; a clip around the ear

耳报神(ěrbàoshén) a spy

耳背(ěrbèi) to be hard of hearing

耳边风(ěrbiānfēng) (lit.) "a puff of wind passing the ear" – unheeded advice

耳鬓厮磨(ěrbìn sīmó) to have a close childhood friendship with; very intimate

耳朵软(ěrduo ruǎn) to be susceptible to flattery; credulous

耳风(ěrfēng) the news on the street

耳福(ěrfú) the good fortune of hearing something rare or beautiful

耳刮子(ěrguāzi) a slap in the face; a box on the ear

耳光(ěrguāng) a slap in the face

耳环(ěrhuán) earrings

耳门(ěrmén) a side door

耳目(ěrmù) ①well-informed; information②one who spies for someone else

耳旁风(ěrpángfēng) unheeded advice

耳热(ěrrè) (somebody's) "ears are burning" – too excited; too shy

耳软心活(ěrruǎn xīnhuó) to be credulous and pliable

耳生(ěrshēng) to sound unfamiliar

耳熟(ěrshú) familiar

耳顺(ěrshùn) ①the age of sixty ②pleasing to the ear

耳顺之年(ěrshùn zhī nián) the age of sixty

耳提面命(ěrtí miànmìng) to give earnest exhortations;

耳听八方(ěrtīng bāfāng) to have

keen ears; to be alert

耳针(ěrzhēn) ear acupuncture

耳坠子(ěrzhuìzi) eardrops

二八(èrbā) sixteen

二把刀(èrbǎdāo) to have a smattering of something; a dabbler

二把手(èrbǎshǒu) the second chief

二百五(èrbǎiwǔ) a stupid person

二道贩子(èrdàofànzi) a two way dealer; a person who resells at inflated prices

二房(èrfáng) ①the second branch of a big family ②a concubine

二房东(èrfángdōng) a sublessor (of a room or house); a sub-landlord

二伏(èrfú) the second of the three 10 day periods of the hot season

二锅头(èrguōtóu) erguotou (a strong, colourless liquor distilled from sorghum)

二胡(èrhú) erhu; urheen; a two stringed Chinese fiddle

二花脸(èrhuāliǎn) the Er Painted Face (a male role in traditional Chinese opera)

二黄(èrhuáng) erhuang (one of the tunes in traditional Chinese opera)

二婚(èrhūn) ①a woman who marries for the second time ②to marry for the second time

二婚头(èrhūntóu) a woman who marries twice

二进宫(èrjìngōng) to be imprisoned again

二赖子(èrlàizi) a shameless loafer

二郎腿(èrlángtuǐ) a cross-legged sitting position

二愣子(èrlèngzi) a rash fellow

二流子(èrlíuzi) an idler, a loafer, a bum

二奶(èrnǎi) a kept woman; a mistress (lover)

《二刻拍案惊奇》(èrkè pāi'àn jīngqí) *The Second Striking the Table in Amazement at the Wondrous Stories* – a collection of short stories by Ling Mengchu (凌濛初, 1580 – 1644)

二乔(èrqiáo) the Qiao sisters (famous beauties during the period of Three Kingdoms)

《二泉映月》(èrquán yìngyuè) *Two Springs Reflect the Moon* – an erhu melody; *Moonlight on the Pond*

二人台(èrréntái) song and dance duet

二人转(èrrénzhuàn) song and dance duet

二十八宿(èrshíbāxiù) 28 constellations

《二十年目睹之怪现状》(èrshínián mùdǔ zhī guài xiànzhuàng) *The Strange Events for the Last Twenty Years* – a novel by Wu Jianren (吴趼人, 1866 – 1910) in 1903 – 1905

二十四节气(èrshísì jiéqì) the twenty four solar terms

二十四史(èrshísì shǐ) *The Twenty Four Histories*

二踢脚(èrtījiǎo) ①a double-kick ②a cannon cracker; double-bang firecracker

二万五千里长征(èrwàn wǔqiān lǐ chángzhēng) the Long March of 25000 Li (by the Chinese Red Army from 1934 to 1936)

二线(èrxiàn) ①the second line (of defense in a war) ②to be not in charge of actual work; to take indirect responsibilities for leadership

贰臣(èrchén) a turncoat official

F

发榜(fābǎng) to publish a list of successful candidates

发飙(fābiāo) to fly off the handle, to flip out; to act violently

发痴(fāchī) to stare blankly; to be in a daze

发嗲(fādiǎ) to be affectedly sweet; to talk and act like a spoiled child

发福(fāfú) to grow stout; to gather flesh; to get fat

发话(fāhuà) to give an oral instruction

发迹(fājì) to gain fame and fortune; to rise to power and position

发家(fājiā) to build up a family fortune

发家致富(fājiāzhìfù) to build up a family fortune

发牢骚(fā láosao) to mutter; to grumble; to complain

发落(fāluò) to deal with (an offender)

发蒙(fāmēng) to get confused; to be at a loss

发墨(fāmò) to get ink from an ink stone

发难(fānàn) to launch an attack; to rise in revolt

发疟子(fāyàozi) to have an attack of malaria; to suffer from malarial fever

发配(fāpèi) to banish; to be exiled for penal servitude

发轫(fārèn) to set something in motion; the start of one's career

发丧(fāsāng) ①to declare the death of somebody; to send out an obituary ②to deal with the funeral affairs; to arrange a funeral

发痧(fāshā) to have heatstroke

发烧友(fāshāoyǒu) a fancier; a zealot; an enthusiastic fan

发神经(fāshénjīng) to go mad; to go crazy; to lose one's mind

发思古之幽情(fā sīgǔ zhī yōuqíng) to muse over the things of the remote past

发帖子(fā tiězi) to post something on the web

发文(fāwén) to issue an official document

发文簿(fāwénbù) register of out-going official documents etc.

发祥地(fāxiángdì) the place of origin; birthplace

发饷(fāxiǎng) to issue pay (to soldiers)

发噱(fāxué) to laugh; to make people laugh

发洋财(fāyángcái) (lit.) "to earn money from foreigners" – to gain unexpected wealth

乏嗣(fásì) to have no descendants

罚酒(fájiǔ) to be made to drink as a forfeit

罚一劝百(fáyī quànbǎi) to punish one as a warning to a hundred; to make an example of

阀阅(fáyuè) ①meritorious deeds ②a family noted for meritorious deeds

法宝(fǎbǎo) a magic weapon

法场(fǎchǎng) an execution ground; a place of execution

法出多门(fǎchū duōmén) Laws come from multiple administrati-ve departments

法号(fǎhào) a religious name (Buddhism)

法家(fǎjiā) Legalism; Legalist School

《法华经》(fǎhuájīng) *The Lotus Sutra* – one of important cannons of Mahayanan Buddhism

法华宗(fǎhuázōng) the Lotus Sect; the Lotus School

《法经》(fǎjīng) *The Book of Laws* – a statute book by Li Kui (李悝, 455 – 395 BC)

法门(fǎmén) an initial approach or way to become a Buddhist believer

法名(fǎmíng) a religious name (Buddhism)

法器(fǎqì) musical instruments (used in a Buddhist or Taoist mass); religious tools

法师(fǎshī) Master (a title of respect for a Buddhist or Taoist priest)

法事(fǎshì) a religious ceremony or service

法书(fǎshū) model calligraphy; your honorable penmanship

法术(fǎshù) magic arts

法坛(fǎtán) a sacrificial altar

法堂(fǎtáng) ①a court of law ②a family hall for worshipping Buddha

法帖(fǎtiè) a calligraphy model for practice

法王(fǎwáng) the prince of dharma; dharmaraja

法眼(fǎyǎn) discerning eyes; insight

发髻(fàjì) hair worn in a bun or coil

发廊(fàláng)a barbershop;a hair salon

发妻(fàqī)the first wife

发小(fàxiǎo) a close childhood friend;a friend from childhood

番邦(fānbāng)foreign countries

番号(fānhào) the designation of a military unit

幡子(fānzi)a flag

翻案(fān' àn)to reverse a verdict;to reverse a sentence;to revoke a decision

翻本(fānběn)to win back the money (lost in gambling); to earn back the capital(lost in business)

翻车(fānchē)(lit.)"to turn over a cart"- to run into difficulties

翻跟头(fāngēntou)to turn a somersault;to loop the loop

翻筋斗(fānjīndǒu)to turn a somersault;to loop the loop

翻旧账(fān jiùzhàng)to bring up old scores again;to rekindle old grievances

翻老账(fān lǎozhàng)bring up old scores again; to rekindle old grievances

翻脸(fānliǎn)to fall out;to turn hostile suddenly

翻脸不认人(fānliǎn bù rènrén) to turn against a friend; to break an old friendship;to turn one's back on old friends

翻身(fānshēn)to free oneself; to be emancipated; to stand up and win one's emancipation

翻身仗(fānshēnzhàng)a battle which transforms a backward state or a difficult situation.

翻手为云,覆手为雨(fānshǒuwéi yún,fùshǒuwéiyǔ)to be as changeable as the moon; to blow hot and cold

翻天(fāntiān)①(lit.)"to overturn the heavens"- overturn the government②to behave wildly

藩国(fānguó)a vassal state

藩镇(fānzhèn)a military governor(of the Tang Dynasty in control of outlying prefectures)

藩属(fānshǔ)a vassal state

凡尘(fánchén)this world;this mortal life

凡夫俗子(fánfū súzǐ)ordinary people;a mortal;everyman

凡人(fánrén)an ordinary person

凡心(fánxīn)worldly fancies and attachments

繁体字(fántǐzì) traditional Chinese characters; complex Chinese characters

繁文缛节(fánwén rùjié)mumbo jumbo; prolix style and hackneyed rites; unnecessary and over-elaborate formalities

反串(fǎnchuàn) to play a reversed role temporarily(in opera)

反帝反修(fǎndì fǎn xiū) Anti-imperialist and Anti-revisionist

反动文人(fǎndòng wénrén) a reactionary man of letters

反动学术权威(fǎndòng xuéshù quánwēi) a reactionary academic authority

反戈一击(fǎngē yījī) to hit back at somebody; to deal a counterblow

反革命(fǎngémìng) counterrevolution; a counterrevolutionary

反革命分子(fǎngémìng fènzǐ) a counterrevolutionary

反攻大陆(fǎngōng dàlù) to counterattack against mainland China

反攻倒算(fǎngōng dàosuàn) the counterattack to settle old scores; to launch a vindictive counterattack; to retaliate

反剪(fǎnjiǎn) to have one's hands tied behind one's back ② to hold one's hands behind one's back

反精神污染运动(fǎn jīngshén wūrǎn yùndòng) The Anti-Spiritual Pollution campaign(a political campaign spanning from October 1983 to December 1983 by the Communist Party that was aimed to prevent the spreading of capitalist ideas among the Chinese populace)

反面角色(fǎnmiàn juésè) ① the villain of the piece ② a negative character

反面教材(fǎnmiàn jiàocái) a negative example(serving as a lesson)

反面教员(fǎnmiàn jiàoyuán) a teacher by negative example

反面人物(fǎnmiàn rénwù) a villain (in drama, etc.); a negative character

反目(fǎnmù) to fall out(esp. between husband and wife or friends)

反派(fǎnpài) a villain (in drama, etc.); a negative character

反其道而行之(fǎnqídào ér xíng zhī) to act in a diametrically opposite way

反切(fǎnqiè) a traditional way to note tones of a Chinese character

反诗(fǎnshī) ironic verse

反水(fǎnshuǐ) to be a turncoat; to go over to the enemy; to defect

反思小说(fǎnsī xiǎoshuō) Introspective Fiction; Re-thinking Fiction

反围剿(fǎn wéijiǎo) to counter encircle and suppress

反咬一口(fǎnyǎo yīkǒu) to trump up a countercharge against one's accuser; to make a false countercharge

反右派运动(fǎnyòupài yùndòng) the Anti-Rightist Campaign (a political campaign launched by the Communist Party in 1957)

反右运动(fǎnyòu yùndòng)the Anti-Rightist Campaign(a political campaign launched by the Communist Party in 1957)

返场(fǎnchǎng)to come back to the stage;to do an encore

返里(fǎnlǐ)to return to one's hometown

犯不上(fànbushàng)not worthwhile

犯不着(fànbuzháo)not worthwhile

犯得上(fàndeshàng)worthwhile(often used in rhetorical questions)

犯得着(fàndezháo)worthwhile(often used in rhetorical questions)

犯嘀咕(fàn dígu)to have doubts;to feel uneasy

犯讳(fànhuì)to violate a taboo

犯浑(fànhún)to be not sober in one's mind, and to ignore the consequences of speech or actions

犯忌(fànjì)to break a taboo

犯贱(fànjiàn)to lack self-respect

犯节气(fàn jiéqi)to contract seasonal illness

犯科(fànkē)to violate the law

犯傻(fànshǎ)to do something stupid;to stare blankly

犯上(fànshàng)to go against the king or emperor(in former times);to defy one's elders,superiors,etc.

犯上作乱(fànshàng zuòluàn)to defy one's superiors and start a rebellion;rebel

犯事(fànshì)to commit a crime;to commit an offence;to be discovered when doing something wrong

泛舟(fànzhōu)to drift about on a boat

饭局(fànjú)a banquet;a dinner party

饭坑酒囊(fànkēng jiǔnáng)"a wine skin and rice bag"- a good-for-nothing

饭票(fànpiào)a meal ticket;a meal coupon

饭铺(fànpù)a(small)restaurant;an eating house

饭桶(fàntǒng)①(lit.)"a rice bucket"- a big eater;a piggish eater②a fathead;a good-for-nothing

饭庄(fànzhuāng)a restaurant

贩夫(fànfū)a pedlar;a hawker

贩夫走卒(fànfū zǒuzú)pedlars and menial servants;small tradesmen and potters

贩子(fànzi)a dealer;a seller

梵呗(fànbài)a Buddhist chant or eulogy

梵典(fàndiǎn)a Buddhist book

梵宫(fàngōng)a Buddhist temple

梵刹(fànchà)a Buddhist temple

梵天(fàntiān)Brahma;Brahma the creator

梵文(fànwén)Sanskrit

梵语(fànyǔ)Sanskrit

梵字(fànzì)①Ancient Indian characters②Buddhist classics

方步(fāngbù)measured steps

方寸(fāngcùn)heart;mind

方技(fāngjì)the art of seeking immortality or making pills of immortality;skills in divination,astrology,medicine,physiognomy,etc.

方剂(fāngjì)a prescription;a recipe

方家(fāngjiā)a person who is well versed in a certain skill;a master

方巾气(fāngjīnqì)pedantic behavior and ideas;conservative

方块字(fāngkuàizì)Chinese characters

方腊起义(fānglà qǐyì)Fang La's Uprising(1120 - 1121)

方枘圆凿(fāngruì yuánzáo)(lit.)"a square tenon doesn't fit a round mortice" - to be incompatible with each other; a square peg in a round hole

方士(fāngshì)a necromancer;an alchemist

方世玉(Fāngshìyù)①Fang Shiyu;Fong Sai-Yuk(a legendary *kung fu* master)② *Fong Sai-Yuk* - a modern film starring Jet Li(李连杰)directed by Corey Yuen(元奎)in 1993

方书(fāngshū)a medical book; a book for alchemy

方术(fāngshù)the arts of necromancy,astrology,medicine,etc.

方外(fāngwài)①Buddhist, Taoist monks②the territories beyond China

方药(fāngyào)a prescription

方丈(fāngzhàng)a Buddhist abbot

方志(fāngzhì)local chronicles;local records

方子(fāngzi)a prescription;a formula

坊本(fāngběn)a block-printed edition

坊间(fāngjiān)in the streets; in the bookshops

芳邻(fānglín)a good neighbor

芳龄(fānglíng)the age(of a young woman)

芳名(fāngmíng)①the name(of a young woman)②good reputation

芳心(fāngxīn)the heart(of a young woman)

防空洞(fángkōngdòng)a air-raid shelter;a bomb shelter

防空警报(fángkōng jǐngbào)air-raid warning;air-raid siren

房奴(fángnú)a"house slave"- a person under the pressure of home loan

房契(fángqì)the title deed for a house

房山(fángshān)gable

房事(fángshì)sexual intercourse(between a married couple)

房帖(fángtiē)a rent advertisement on the wall

仿宋(fǎngsòng)the imitation of the Song-Dynasty-style typeface

仿纸(fǎngzhǐ)a sheet for practicing calligraphy

访贫问苦(fǎngpín wènkǔ)to visit the poor and the suffering

纺车(fǎngchē)a spinning wheel

放暗箭(fàng ànjiàn)to stab in the back;to make an underhand attack

放榜(fàng bǎng)to publish a list of successful candidates

放包袱(fàngbāofu)to unload a mental burden

放黜(fàng chù)to dismiss

放风(fàngfēng)to let prisoners out for exercise or to relieve themselves;to leak certain information;to spread news

放高利贷(fàng gāolìdài)to be a loan shark;to practice usury

放歌(fànggē)to sing aloud

放虎归山(fànghǔ guīshān)(lit.)"to set free the tiger back to the mountains"- to store up trouble for the future

放空炮(fàng kōngpào)to talk big;to spout hot air

放冷箭(fàng lěngjiàn)to stab(somebody) in the back; to snipe (at somebody)

放马后炮(fàng mǎhòupào)(lit.)"to start firing after the enemy has gone" - Monday morning quarterbacking;to close the stable door after the horse has bolted

放炮(fàngpào)①to fire a gun②to blast③to shoot off one's mouth

放屁(fàngpì)to break wind;to fart;to talk nonsense

放权(fàngquán)to transfer power(to a lower level)

放哨(fàngshào)to be on sentry duty;to stand guard

放生(fàngshēng)to set free captive animals;to set the animals free

放下包袱(fàngxià bāofu)(lit.)"to lay down the burden" - to take a load off one's mind

放下架子(fàngxià jiàzi)to drop all pretentiousness;to pocket one's dignity

放下屠刀,立地成佛(fàngxià túdāo, lìdì chéngfó)(lit.)"to lay down one's cleaver and become a Buddha"- to achieve salvation as soon as one gives up evil

放洋(fàngyáng)to go abroad for further education;to sail on the sea

放印子(fàngyìnzi)to give a loan

放债(fàngzhài)to lend money with interest

放赈(fàngzhèn)to give money or food (to help those suffering from a disaster)

放赈救灾(fàngzhèn jiùzāi)to give relief and avert calamity

放之四海而皆准(fàng zhī sìhǎi ér jiē zhǔn) universally applicable; valid everywhere

飞白(fēibái)hollow brush strokes(a special technique in calligraphy or drawing)

飞镖(fēibiāo) a dartlike weapon; a dart

飞车走壁(fēichēzǒubì)cycling, driving or motorcycling on the inner surface of a cylindrical wall(an acrobatics stunt)

飞归(fēiguī)to calculate double-digit division using an abacus

飞鸿(fēihóng)(lit.)"a swan goose" – letters; correspondence

飞鸿传情(fēihóngchuánqíng)to convey one's love by correspondence or letters

飞黄腾达(fēihuáng téngdá) to be successful in one's career; to climb up the social ladder rapidly; to have a meteoric rise

飞毛腿(fēimáotuǐ)a fleet footed runner; fleet of foot

飞天(fēitiān) the flying Apsaras(in the frescoes of the Dunhuang Caves)

飞檐走壁(fēiyán zǒubì) to fly over the eaves and run on the walls; to fly over walls and walk over defenses; to leap onto roofs and vault over walls

妃子(fēizi) ①an imperial concubine ②the wife of a prince

《非诚勿扰》(fēichéngwùrǎo) *If You Are the One* – a film directed by Feng Xiaogang(冯小刚)in 2008

非礼(fēilǐ)a sexual assault

非命(fēimìng) an abnormal death; a violent death

绯闻(fēiwén)a rumor about an abnormal relationship between a man and a woman

扉画(fēihuà)the pictorial frontispiece to a book

扉页(fēiyè)the title page

蜚声文坛(fēishēng wéntán) to be famous in literary circles

肥差(féichāi) a well-paid job; a plum job

肥缺(féiquē)a lucrative post

匪帮(fěibāng)a bandit gang

匪巢(fěicháo)a bandit lair

匪患(fěihuàn) the evil of banditry; banditry

匪窟(fěikū)a bandit lair

匪首(fěishǒu) bandit chieftain(or chief)

匪穴(fěixué)a bandits' lair

菲敬(fěijìng)my small gift(a self-depreciatory expression)

菲仪(fěiyí)my small gift

菲酌(fěizhuó)a humble meal

吠形吠声(fèixíng fèishēng)(lit.) "when one dog barks at a shadow all the others join in" - to echo others slavishly

废黜(fèichù)to depose;to dethrone

废帝(fèidì)a dethroned emperor

《废都》(fèidū) *The Abandoned Capital* - a novel by Jia Pingwa(贾平凹,1952 -)in 1993

《沸腾的群山》(fèiténg de qúnshān) *Mountains in Impulse* - a film directed by Gan Xuewei(干学伟)in 1976

肺腑之言(fèifǔ zhī yán)words from the bottom of one's heart;true sentiments

肺痨(fèiláo) consumption; tuberculosis

费口舌(fèi kǒushé) to waste one's words;to do a lot of explaining

分兵把守(fēnbīng bǎshǒu)to defend by dividing forces

分爨(fēn cuàn) to divide the extended family and make a living individually;to live apart

分寸(fēncùn)proper limits for speech or action;a sense of propriety

分号(fēnhào) a semicolon; a branch (of a firm,etc.)

分红(fēnhóng)to share out bonuses; to draw extra dividends; to receive extra profits

分家(fēnjiā)to divide up family property and live apart

分节歌(fēnjiégē)a strophic

分袂(fēnmèi)to leave each other; to part company;to part

分娩(fēnmiǎn)childbirth;parturition

分片包干(fēnpiàn bāogān)to divide up the work and assign a part to each

分水岭(fēnshuǐlǐng) a watershed; a divide; a boundary; a demarcation line

分庭抗礼(fēntíng kànglǐ)to stand up to somebody as an equal; act independently and defiantly

分头(fēntóu) parted hair; to have a parting

分赃(fēnzāng)to share the loot;to divide the spoils

坟包(fénbāo)a grave mound

坟丘(fénqīu)a grave mound

坟山(fénshān) a hillside with many tombs;a high tomb

坟头(féntóu)a grave mound

坟茔(fényíng) ①a grave; a tomb ② a graveyard

汾酒(fénjiǔ)Fenyang liquor(distilled

in Shanxi Province)

焚膏继晷(féngāo jìguǐ)(lit.)"to light a lamp or a candle to replace daylight"– to study or work hard day and night

焚琴煮鹤(fénqín zhǔhè)(lit.)"to burn musical instruments as firewood and cook cranes as food"– to fool with exquisite and fine things; to act like a philistine

焚书坑儒(fénshū kēngrú) burning books and burying scholars alive (an event carried out by First Emperor Qin in 213 and 212 BC)

焚香(fénxiāng) to burn joss sticks; to light up joss sticks; to burn incense

焚香拜佛(fénxiāng bàifó) to burn joss sticks and prostrate oneself before the image of Buddha; to light up joss sticks and worship Buddha

焚香操琴(fénxiāng cāoqín)(lit.)"to play a Chinese zither while burning incense"– to face danger in a composed manner

《焚香记》(fénxiāng jì) *Burning Incense* – a play by Wang Yufeng(王玉峰) in the Ming Dynasty

粉黛(fěndài) a beauty

粉坊(fěnfáng) a bean-noodle factory

粉墨登场(fěnmò dēngchǎng)(lit.)"to ascend the stage with powder and rouge make-up"– to embark upon a political venture

粉饰太平(fěnshì tàipíng) to present a false picture of peace and prosperity; to whitewash an odious situation

粉丝(fěnsī) ① Chinese vermicelli ②fans

粉头(fěntóu) a prostitute

份饭(fènfàn) a table d'hote; a set meal

忿詈(fènlì) to curse furiously

偾事(fènshì) to spoil something; to make things worse

粪箕子(fènjīzi) a manure basket

粪土(fèntǔ) dung and dirt; muck; rubbish

丰碑(fēngbēi) a monument

丰功伟绩(fēnggōng wěijì) great achievements; significant contributions

《丰乳肥臀》(fēngrǔ féitún) *Big Breasts and Wide Hips* – a novel by Mo Yan(莫言,1955 –) in 1995

《风》、《雅》、《颂》(fēng, yǎ, sòng) *Songs*, *Odes*, *Hymns* – the three parts of *The Book of Songs*

风波(fēngbō)(lit.)"wind and waves"– disturbance

风伯(fēngbó) the God of Wind

风潮(fēngcháo) agitation; unrest

风尘(fēngchén) ①travel weariness ② an unstable society ③prostitution

风尘女子(fēngchén nǚzǐ) a prostitute

风尘侠士(fēngchén xiáshì)a chivalrous person

风范(fēngfàn)①demeanour;bearing ②a style;a manner

风骨(fēnggǔ)strength of character;a vigorous style(of writing,painting or calligraphy)

风戽(fēnghù)a wind-powered waterwheel

风花雪月(fēnghuā xuěyuè)(lit.)"wind,flowers,snow and moon"-romantic themes

风化(fēnghuà)morals and manners;decency

风凉话(fēngliánghuà)irresponsible and sarcastic remarks

风流(fēngliú)①refined and tasteful ②unconventional in spirit and life style③romantic;amorous;licentious

风流才子(fēngliú cáizǐ)a talented and romantic scholar

风流人物(fēngliú rénwù)①a remarkable man;a truly great and noble hearted man②a romantic person

风流倜傥(fēngliú tìtǎng)a casual and elegant bearing

风流韵事(fēngliú yùnshì)a love affair;a romantic escapade

风派人物(fēngpài rénwù)an opportunist;a timeserver;a chameleon

风骚(fēngsāo)①literary excellence ②coquettish;flirtatious

风水(fēngshuǐ)*fengshui*;geomancy;geomantic theories

风水宝地(fēngshuǐ bǎodì)a place with many advantages;a valuable land with good fengshui

风水先生(fēngshuǐ xiānsheng)a geomancer

风头(fēngtóu)the trend of development of something.(affecting a person);changes in circumstances

风味小吃(fēngwèi xiǎochī)local delicacies

风箱(fēngxiāng)an air bellows

风雅(fēngyǎ)①elegant;refined②literary interests

风谣(fēngyáo)a popular ballad

风月(fēngyuè)①(lit.)"wind and moon"— the scene;the view②romantic affairs;the seductive arts of a woman

风月场(fēngyuèchǎng)the arena of love

《风云初记》(fēngyún chū jì)①*Recorded at the Beginning of Wind and cloud* - a novel by Sun Li(孙犁,1913 - 2002)in1951 ②*Beginning of the Changeable* - a film directed by Luo Tai(罗泰)in1983

《风云儿女》(fēngyún érnǚ)*Children of Troubled Times* - a film directed by Xu Xingzhi(许幸之)in 1935

风云人物(fēngyún rénwù)an influential man; hero of the hour

风韵(fēngyùn) charm

风筝(fēngzheng) a kite

风中之烛(fēngzhōng zhī zhú)(lit.) "a candle in the wind"— to die or perish at any moment

风烛残年(fēngzhú cánnián) in one's declining years; to have one foot in the grave

封禅(fēngshàn) a grand sacrifice made on a mountain top

封官许愿(fēngguān xǔyuàn) to promise official posts and other favours

封建残余(fēngjiàn cányú) the remnant of feudalism

《封建论》(fēngjiàn lùn) *On Feudalism* - an essay by Liu Zongyuan(柳宗元,773 - 819)

封疆大吏(fēngjiāng dàlì) the high officer of the frontier; the governor of a border province

封门(fēngmén) to seal up a door with a strip of paper

封妻荫子(fēngqī yìnzǐ) to grant titles to the wives and children of heroes

《封神榜》(fēngshénbǎng) *Granting Titles to Gods* - a novel by Xu Zhongli(许仲琳,1567 -?); *The Investiture of the Gods*

《封神演义》(fēngshén yǎnyì) *Granting Titles to Gods* - a novel by Xu Zhongli(许仲琳,1567 -?); *The Investiture of the Gods*

封条(fēngtiáo) a strip of paper (used for sealing up the door)

疯子(fēngzi) a madman; a lunatic

烽火(fēnghuǒ) a beacon-fire

烽火台(fēnghuǒtái) a beacon tower

烽燧(fēngsuì) a beacon tower

蜂窝炉(fēngwōlú) a honeycomb briquet stove

蜂窝煤(fēngwōméi) honeycomb briquets

酆都城(fēngdūchéng) the Capital of Hell

逢凶化吉(féngxiōng huàjí) to turn ill luck into good; to tide over a crisis

凤阁龙楼(fènggé lónglóu) phoenix towers and dragon towers (imperial palace)

凤冠(fèngguān) ①a phoenix coronet (worn by empresses or imperial concubines) ②a bride's headdress

凤凰(fènghuáng) a Chinese phoenix

《凤凰涅槃》(fènghuáng nièpán) *Phoenix Nirvana* - a poem by Guo Moruo(郭沫若, 1892 - 1978) in 1920

《凤凰琴》(fènghuángqín) *Country Teachers* - a film directed by He Qun(何群) in 1994

凤求凰(fèng qiú huáng) a man courting a woman

凤眼(fèngyǎn)phoenix eyes; eyes which slant upwards delicately

凤阳花鼓(fèngyáng huāgǔ) the Fengyang Flower Drum in Anhui province

奉安(fèng'ān)①the burial of an emperor; burial of somebody's father② to emplace the statue of a god or the Buddha or their memorial tablets

奉若神明(fèngruò shénmíng)to worship someone. or something. ; to make a fetish of something.

奉天承运(fèngtiān chéngyùn)to be subjected to the order of Heaven; under the order of Heaven

奉为圭臬(fèngwéi guīniè)to look up to as a standard; to hold up as a model

奉召(fèngzhào)to receive orders

奉旨(fèngzhǐ)by the order of the emperor; by imperial order

俸禄(fènglù)an official's salary

佛地(fódì)Buddhist temples

佛典(fódiǎn)Buddhist classics; Buddhist scriptures

佛法(fófǎ)Buddhist doctrine; the power of the Buddha

佛光(fóguāng)the light around the head of the Buddha; a Brock-en bow

佛光寺(fóguāngsì)Halo Monastery (located in Shanxi province and built in 857)

佛号(fóhào)the name of Buddha

佛家(fójiā)Buddhists

佛教(fójiào)Buddhism

佛教名山(fójiào míngshān)a famous Buddhist mountain; a sacred mountain associated with Buddhism

佛经(fójīng)Buddhist books; Buddhist scriptures

佛龛(fókān)a niche for a statue of the Buddha

佛口蛇心(fókǒu shéxīn)(lit.) "a Buddha's mouth but a viper's heart"–honeyed words but an evil intent

佛老(fólǎo)Buddhism and Taoism

佛门(fómén)Buddhism

佛门弟子(fómén dìzǐ)the followers of Buddhism; a Buddhist

佛事(fóshì)a Buddhist ceremony or service

佛寺(fósì)a Buddhist temple

佛陀(fótuó)the Buddha

佛香阁(fóxiānggé)the Pavilion of the Fragrance of the Buddha (in the Summer Palace)

佛像(fóxiàng)statue of the Buddha; the figure of the Buddha

佛学(fóxué)Buddhist studies

佛眼相看(fóyǎn xiāngkàn)to regard with mercy

佛爷(fóye)the Buddha; the emperor

佛珠(fózhū)Buddhist beads; a rosary

佛祖(fózǔ)Buddhist patriarch; the

founder of a Buddhist sect

夫唱妇随(fūchàng fùsuí)(lit.)"the husband sings and the wife follows"-(a traditional ideal of) domestic harmony or marital harmony

夫妻店(fūqīdiàn)a small shop run by a couple

夫权(fūquán)(law) manus; authority of the husband

夫婿(fūxù)husband

夫子庙(fūzǐmiào)the Temple of Confucius; the Confucian Temple

趺坐(fūzuò) to sit cross-legged in meditation

伏笔(fúbǐ)a hint of what is to come (in a novel etc.); foreshadowing

伏羲(fúxī) Fuxi (one of the earliest legendary rulers)

伏诛(fúzhū) to be executed

扶乩(fújī) planchette writing; spirit writing; sciomancy

扶鸾(fúluán) planchette writing; spirit writing; sciomancy

扶贫(fúpín) to support the poor; poverty alleviation program

扶桑(fúsāng) a legendary mulberry tree; Japan

扶正(fúzhèng) ①to give a concubine the status of legitimate wife ② to strengthen the body's resistance

芙蓉国(fúróngguó)(lit.)"the land of hibiscus" - a poetic reference to Hunan

《芙蓉镇》(fúróngzhèn) *Hibiscus Town* - a film directed by Xie Jin (谢晋) in 1986

服丧(fúsāng) to be in mourning

服刑(fúxíng) to serve a sentence; to serve one's term of imprisonment

服膺(fúyīng) ①to bear in mind ②to feel deeply convinced

服膺长叹(fúyīng chángtàn) to beat one's chest and heave a deep sigh

浮财(fúcái) movable property

浮夸风(fúkuā fēng) a tendency to exaggerate achievements; a tendency toward boasting and exaggeration; boastfulness

浮名(fúmíng) an empty name

浮生(fúshēng) a short and unstable life; a floating life

浮图(fútú) the Buddha; a Buddhist stupa

浮屠(fútú) the Buddha; a Buddhist stupa

符节(fújié) a tally issued by the Emperor to be used as credentials or as a warrant

符咒(fúzhòu) magic figures or incantations

福地(fúdì) paradise; a Happy Land

福分(fúfen) good fortune

福晋(fújìn) a prince's wife; Madam (an appellation for the prince's wife

or concubines)
福气(fúqì)good luck;good fortune
福如东海(fú rú dōnghǎi)vast happiness
福无双至(fú wú shuāng zhì) Lucky things do not occur in succession
福相(fúxiàng) a face showing good fortune
福星(fúxīng)a lucky star;a mascot; God of Blessings
福音(fúyīn)gospel;glad tidings;good news
福祉(fúzhǐ)happiness;blessedness
抚今追昔(fǔjīn zhuīxī) to evoke memories of the past on seeing something
抚恤(fǔxù)to give relief to;to comfort or compensate a bereaved family
府邸(fǔdǐ) a mansion; a mansion house
府第(fǔdì) a mansion; a mansion house
府上(fǔshàng)your home;your family;your native place
府尹(fǔyǐn)a prefectural magistrate; the governor of a prefecture
斧正(fǔzhèng) to make corrections and improvements
俯就(fǔjiù)to condescend to take or accept(a post,job,etc.)
俯念(fǔ niàn)to condescend to consider;to miss(somebody)
俯首(fǔshǒu) to bow one's head(in submission)
俯首就范(fǔshǒu jiùfàn) to submit meekly;to surrender without struggle
俯首听命(fǔshǒu tīngmìng) to bow down to obey submissively
釜底抽薪(fǔdǐ chōuxīn)(lit.)"to take away the firewood from under the cauldron" - to take drastic measures to deal with a situation
腐儒(fǔrú) a pedantic scholar; a pedant
腐乳(fǔrǔ)fermented beancurd
《腐蚀》(fǔshí)*Corrosion* - a novel by Mao Dun(茅盾, 1896 - 1981) in 1941
腐刑(fǔxíng)castration(as a punishment)
父老(fùlǎo) the elders(of a country or district)
父老乡亲(fùlǎo xiāngqīn) fellow countrymen
父母官(fùmǔguān)a local magistrate
父母之邦(fùmǔ zhī bāng)motherland
父母之命,媒妁之言(fùmǔ zhī mìng,méishuò zhī yán)(lit.)"the dictates of parents and the words of matchmakers" - the proper way of contracting an arranged marriage
父执(fùzhí)father's friends
讣告(fùgào) to announce a death;

an obituary

讣文(fùwén)a notice of death

讣闻(fùwén)an obituary

付丙(fùbǐng)to burn(a letter,a manuscript,etc.)

付讫(fùqì)to have been paid;to settle one's account

付梓(fùzǐ)to have a manuscript published;to send to the press;to put into print

妇道(fùdao)female virtues

妇道人家(fùdaorénjiā)women;womenfolk

妇联(fùlián)the Women's Federation

妇孺(fùrú)women and children

负案(fùàn)to be investigated(by the police after committing a crime)

负笈(fùjí)(lit.)"to carry a case of books"-to leave home to study

负笈从师(fùjí cóngshī)to leave home to study under a master or a teacher

负笈求学(fùjí qíuxué)to leave home to pursue one's study

负荆请罪(fùjīng qǐngzuì)(lit.)"to carry a rod on one's back and ask to be punished"-to apologise for wrong doing;to be contrite and ask for pardon;to proffer a birch and ask for a flogging

负心(fùxīn)to transfer one's love(to somebody else);to fail one's beloved

负心汉(fùxīnhàn)a man who betrays his lover;a perfidia

附白(fùbái)①to explain by way of parenthesis②the words of explanation in parenthesis

附笔(fùbǐ)additional remarks(in a letter,document,etc.)

附凤攀龙(fùfèngpānlóng)to court favour with famous people;to put oneself under the patronage of a bigwig

附骥(fùjì)to be famous on the strength of famous people;to follow one's lead;to ride to success on one's coat-tails

附言(fùyán)a postscript(P. S)

附庸(fùyōng)vassals;a small state attached to a large neighbor;a dependency

附庸风雅(fùyōng fēngyǎ)to mingle with men of letters and pose as a lover of culture

附注(fùzhù)the notes(appended to a book,etc.)

驸马(fùmǎ)the emperor's son-in-law

复方(fùfāng)medicine made of many ingredients

复古(fùgǔ)to restore ancient ways;to return to the ancients

复命(fùmìng)to report back after carrying out an order

复姓(fùxìng)a compound surname;a two character surname

副刊(fùkān)a supplement

副敛(fùliǎn)to levy taxes

副业(fùyè)a sideline;a side occupation

《富春山居图》(fùchūn shānjū tú)*Residing in the Fuchun Mountai-ns* - a painting by Huang Gongwang(黄公望,1269 - 1354)

富贵病(fùguìbìng) the rich man's disease

富贵不能淫(fùguì bùnéng yín)incorruptible by riches and honors

富豪(fùháo)a rich and powerful person

富农(fùnóng)a rich peasant

富婆(fùpó) a rich woman; a wealthy woman

富态(fùtai)portly;stout

富翁(fùwēng)a wealthy man;a rich man;a moneybags

富裕中农(fùyù zhōngnóng)an upper-middle peasant

赋(fù)verse(a prose poem);a rhapsody

赋课(fùkè)taxes

赋闲(fùxián)to be out of work

赋役(fùyì)taxes and corvée

腹地(fùdì)a hinterland

腹稿(fùgǎo)a draft worked out in one's mind;a mental note

腹心之患(fùxīn zhī huàn)(lit.)"disease in one's vital organs" - danger from within;a serious hidden trouble

赙金(fùjīn)money given to a bereaved family

赙仪(fùyí)a gift to a bereaved family

覆车之鉴(fùchē zhī jiàn)a lesson drawn from another's mistake

覆辙(fùzhé)the track of an overturned cart

G

旮旯(gālá)a corner;a nook

轧朋友(gápéngyou)to make friends with

轧姘头(gápīntou)to live illicitly with;to cohabit

噶伦(gálún)bkav-blon(high official of the former local government of Tibet)

噶厦(gáxià)Kashag(the former local government of Tibet before 1959)

《嘎达梅林》(gǎdá méilín)*Gada Meilin* - a Chinese film directed by Feng Xiaoning(冯小宁)in 2002

垓下之战(gāixià zhīzhàn)the Battle of Gaixia(202 BC)

改朝换代(gǎicháo huàndài)dynastic changes;to replace an old regime or dynasty with a new one

改革开放(gǎigé kāifàng)reform and openness;to reform and open

改革小说(gǎigé xiǎoshuō) Reform Fiction

改嫁(gǎijià) to remarry(of a woman)

改醮(gǎijiào) to remarry (of a woman)

改良主义(gǎiliáng zhǔyì) reformism

改土归流(gǎitǔ guīliú) the bureaucratization of native officers; the nomination of magistrates over minority groups(in the Ming and Qing dynasties)

改元(gǎiyuán) to change the designation of an imperial reign; to change the title of a reign

改制(gǎizhì) to change a system; to reform

丐帮(gàibāng) a gang of beggars

盖戳(gàichuō) to affix one's seal; to put a stamp on

盖棺论定(gàiguān lùndìng) a final judgment can be passed on a person only when he is in his coffin; to pass a final judgment on; to pronounce a final verdict on(somebody)

盖世(gàishì) unparalleled; matchless

盖世英雄(gàishì yīngxióng) a peerless hero

盖头(gàitou) a bridal veil

干爸(gānbà) a godfather; an adoptive father

干杯(gānbēi) bottoms up; to drink a toast; cheers

干柴烈火(gānchái lièhuǒ) (lit.) "dry wood and a blazing fire" – to be burning with passion and love

干爹(gāndiē) a godfather; an adoptive father

干儿子(gān'érzi) an adopted son

干闺女(gānguīnü) an adopted daughter

干妈(gānmā) a godmother; an adoptive mother

干娘(gānniáng) a godmother; an adoptive mother

干女儿(gānnǚr) an adopted daughter

干亲(gānqīn) an adoptive kinship

干预生活小说(gānyù shēnghuó xiǎoshuō) the Intervention-in-life Novel

干政(gānzhèng) to intervene in government affairs

干支(gānzhī) the Heavenly Stems and Earthly Branches(a way of numbering the hour, the day or the year in ancient Chinese calendar)

甘拜下风(gānbài xiàfēng) to bow to one's superiority; to acknowledge one's inferiority candidly

肝胆相照(gāndǎn xiāngzhào) to treat each other sincerely and openly

赶场(gǎnchǎng) ①to go to a village market or fair ②to hurry from one place to another to give performances

赶潮流(gǎn cháoliú) to follow the fashion and trend

赶车(gǎnchē) ①to drive a cart②to catch a bus

《赶车传》(gǎnchē zhuàn) *The Story of the Cart Driver* – a long narrative poem by Tian Jian (田间, 1916 – 1985) in 1946

赶道(gǎndào) to hurry on with one's journey

赶集(gǎnjí) go to a market or fair

赶脚(gǎnjiǎo) to lead a donkey or mule for hire

赶考(gǎnkǎo) to go for an imperial examination

赶路(gǎnlù) to hurry on with one's journey

赶庙会(gǎn miàohuì) to go to a temple fair

赶明儿(gǎnmíngr) one of these days; another day

赶时髦(gǎn shímáo) to follow the fashion

赶趟儿(gǎntàngr) to be in time for

赶圩(gǎnxū) to go to a village market or fair

感怀(gǎnhuái) ①to recall with emotion②reflections; thoughts

感怀往事(gǎnhuái wǎngshì) to recall past events with emotion

感世(gǎnshì) to sigh with emotion at the lack of morality in the world

感言(gǎnyán) a speech (made on some occasion to express one's feelings)

擀面杖(gǎnmiànzhàng) a rolling pin

干架(gànjià) to quarrel or fight with

干将(gànjiàng) a capable person; a go-getter

干群关系(gàn qún guānxì) the relations between cadres and masses

干事(gànshì) a secretary or a person in charge of something.

干校(gànxiào) a cadre school

干仗(gànzhàng) to quarrel or fight with

赣剧(gànjù) the Gan opera (a local opera in Jiangxi province)

《冈底斯的诱惑》(gāngdǐsī de yòuhuò) *Enticement of Kailash* – a novel by Ma Yuan (马原, 1953 –) in 1985

岗子(gāngzi) a hillock, a mound

纲常(gāngcháng) the feudal ethical codes; the three cardinal guides (i. e. ruler guides subject, father guides son and husband guides wife) and the five constant virtues (i. e. benevolence, righteousness, propriety, wisdom and fidelity)

纲纪(gāngjì) rules and regulations

纲举目张(gāngjǔ mùzhāng) (lit.) "once the headrope of a fishing net is pulled up, all its meshes open" –

once the key link is grasped, everything will turn out to be right

钢镚儿(gāngbèngr) a coin

钢铁长城(gāngtiě chángchéng) (lit.) "the great wall of steel" – the Chinese People's Liberation Army

《钢铁战士》(gāngtiě zhànshì) *Steel Soldiers*; *Iron Warriors* – a Chinese film directed by Cheng Yin(成荫) in 1950

罡风(gāngfēng) the winds in the Empyrean(Daoism)

港澳(gǎng'ào) Hong Kong and Macao

港澳台同胞(gǎng'àotái tóngbāo) compatriots from(in) Hong Kong, Macao and Taiwan

杠房(gàngfáng) an undertake-r's premises

杠夫(gàngfū) a professional coff-in bearer

杠头(gàngtóu) ① the chief coffin bearer ② a person who likes to argue for the sake of arguing ③ a hard baked cake

戆头(gàngtóu) a fool; an idiot

高才生(gāocáishēng) a brilliant student

高参(gāocān) a competent counsellor

高调(gāodiào) high-sounding words; big talk

高风亮节(gāofēng liàngjié) noble character and sterling integity

高富帅(gāofùshuài) a tall, rich, handsome man

高干(gāogàn) a high-ranking official

高阁(gāogé) ① a high building ② high shelves

高官厚禄(gāoguān hòulù) a high position with high pay

高见(gāojiàn) a great idea

高就(gāojiù) to be employed

高考(gāokǎo) a university entrance examination

高帽子(gāomàozi) ① flattery; insincere compliments ② a tall paper hat

高密东北乡(gāomì dōngběixiāng) The Northeast Hometown in Gaomi (a place name under the pen of Mo Yan)

高腔(gāoqiāng) high-pitched singing (a style of opera)

高人(gāorén) ① a man of noble character ② a man of superior attainments; a past master

高僧(gāosēng) an eminent monk

高山景行(gāoshān jǐngxíng) (lit.) "high mountain and broad road" – noble morality and respectable behavior

高山流水(gāoshān liúshuǐ) (lit.) "high mountains and flowing water" – ① sublime music ② a rare bosom friend

《高山流水》(gāoshān liúshuǐ) *High*

Mountain and Flowing Water - one of the most famous Chinese zither melodies

《高山下的花环》(gāoshānxià de huāhuán) *Wreaths at the Foot of the Mountain* - a novel by Li Cunbao (李存葆,1946 -) in 1983; a film directed by Xie Jin(谢晋) in 1984

高山族(gāoshānzú) the Gaoshan nationality; the Gaohans

高手(gāoshǒu) a past master; an expert

高寿(gāoshòu) ①longevity; long life ②your venerable age

高抬贵手(gāotái guìshǒu) to be generous; not to be too hard on (somebody)

高汤(gāotāng) a soup-stock (made with chicken or meat

高堂(gāotáng) ①a big hall②parents

高徒(gāotú) an outstanding student or discipline

高招(gāozhāo) a clever idea

高枕无忧(gāozhěn wúyōu) to rest easy; to be carefree

高枝儿(gāozhīr) (lit.) "high branches" - a person with high social status

高足(gāozú) a brilliant student or discipline

高祖(gāozǔ) a great-great-grandfather; forefather

高祖母(gāozǔmǔ) a great-great-grandmother

膏肓(gāohuāng) the vital organs of a human body

膏粱子弟(gāoliáng zǐdì) the children of rich and powerful families

膏药(gāoyào) plaster

搞对象(gǎoduìxiàng) to date somebody; to go together; to be in love

搞鬼(gǎoguǐ) to play a trick; to be up to some mischief

搞笑(gǎoxiào) funny; to do something funny to amuse other people

告白(gàobái) ①to confess one's love (to somebody) ②a public notice

告便(gàobiàn) to ask for permission to absent for a moment

告禀(gàobǐng) to report (to one's superior)

告捷(gàojié) ①to win victory②to report a victory

告老(gàolǎo) to retire on the account of age; to retire in old age

告老还乡(gàolǎo huáanxiāng) to retire and return to one's native place

告罄(gàoqìng) to run out; to be exhausted

告示(gàoshi) an official notice, a bulletin

告御状(gào yùzhuàng) to accuse somebody before the emperor or higher authorities

告状(gàozhuàng)①to bring a lawsuit against (somebody) ② to make a complaint against (somebody with one's superior)

诰封(gàofēng) to confer honorary by imperial mandate

诰命(gàomìng) an imperial mandate

诰命夫人(gàomìng fūrén) a titled lady (a lady with an honorary title conferred by imperial mandate)

膏笔(gàobǐ) to smooth a writing brush on the edge of inkstone

戈壁(gēbì) Gobi; the Gobi desert

戈壁滩(gēbìtān) the Gobi desert

哥儿们(gērmen) brothers; buddies

哥老会(gēlǎohuì) the Society of Brothers (a secret society in the late Qing Dynasty)

哥们义气(gēmen yìqì) brotherhood loyalty; a gang spirit

袼褙(gēbei) pieces of old cloth or rags (pasted together to make cloth shoes)

割爱(gē'ài) to give up one's cherished lover or possession

割臂之盟(gēbìzhīméng) to make a cut on the arm as a sign of the oath of alliance; to be blood brothers

割袍断义(gēpáo duànyì) (lit.) "to cut the robe and break off friendly relations with somebody" - to break off friendship

割尾巴(gē wěiba) to do away with old practices

割席断交(gēxí duànjiāo) (lit.) "to cut the mat and break off friendly relations with somebody" - to break up an old friendship

歌功颂德(gēgōng sòngdé) to eulogize oen virtues and achievements; to sing the praises of somebody

歌诀(gējué) an intonable formulas (in verse)

歌女(gēnǚ) a singing-girl

歌台舞榭(gētái wǔxiè) halls for the performance of songs and dances

歌坛(gētán) the circle of singers

歌坛新秀(gētán xīnxiù) a new singing star

歌舞升平(gēwǔ shēngpíng) to sing and dance to extol good times; to celebrate peace by singing and dancing

歌仔戏(gēzǎixì) the Gezai opera (a popular local opera in Taiwan and Fujian provinces)

革故鼎新(gégù dǐngxīn) to discard the old and introduce the new; to make general reforms

革履(gélǚ) leather shoes

《革命家庭》(gémìng jiātíng) *A Revolutionary Family* - a film directed by Shui Hua(水华) in 1960

《革命军》(gémìngjūn) *Revolutionary*

Army - a pamphlet by Zou Rong(邹容,1885 - 1905) in 1903

革职(gézhí) to be removed from office; to be dismissed from one's post

格调(gédiào) ①a literary or artistic style②moral quality; taste

格格(gége) a Manchu princess; a Manchu lady

格律(gélǜ) the rules and forms of classical poetic composition (with respect to tonal pattern, rhyme scheme, etc.)

格物(géwù) science; to investigate things

格物致知(géwù zhìzhī) to attain knowledge by investigating things

格致(gézhì) science

格子窗(gézichuāng) a lattice window

胳肢(gézhi) to tickle(somebody)

隔岸观火(gé'àn guānhuǒ) (lit.) "to watch a fire from the other side of the river" - to look on indifferently at the suffering of others

隔年皇历(génián huánglì) (lit.) "the calendar of the past year" - old rules and practices

隔扇(géshàn) a partition board

槅门(gémén) a latticed door

槅扇(géshàn) a partition board

个体户(gètǐhù) a privately-owed small enterprise; a self-employed worker

个中人(gèzhōngrén) a person in the know; an insider

各打五十大板(gè dǎ wǔshí dà bǎn) to punish the innocent and the guilty alike; to blame both sides

给脸(gěiliǎn) to save another's face; to avoid embarrassing somebody else; to be nice and considerate to somebody else

给面子(gěi miànzi) to save one's face; to give sb dignity

给小鞋穿(gěi xiǎoxié chuān) (lit.) "to give somebody tight shoes to wear" - to bully somebody or treat somebody unfairly on purpose

给颜色看(gěi yánsè kàn) to threaten to teach somebody a lesson

《给战斗者》(gěi zhàndòuzhě) *To the Fighters* - a poem by Tian Jian(田间,1916 - 1985) in 1943

根雕(gēndiāo) tree-root carving

根儿硬(gēnr yìng) to be of good origin(usu. from a lower class family background)

根儿正(gēnr zhèng) to be of good origin(usu. from a lower class family background)

根据地(gēnjùdì) a base area

跟班(gēnbān) a servant; an attendant

跟包(gēnbāo) the attendant of a stage actor

跟差(gēnchāi) a servant; an attendant

跟风(gēnfēng) to follow the trend; to do as others do

跟屁虫(gēnpìchóng) a yes-man; a copycat

跟着感觉走(gēnzhe gǎnjué zǒu) to follow one's feeling; to follow one's instincts

更次(gēngcì) the period of a night watch

更夫(gēngfū) a night watchman

更鼓(gēnggǔ) a night watchman's drum

更楼(gēnglóu) a night watch tower

更衣(gēngyī) to change one's clothes

庚齿(gēngchǐ) age

庚日(gēngrì) the 7th of the Ten Heavenly Stems

庚帖(gēngtiě) a card containing one's horoscope (used for a betrothal)

工笔(gōngbǐ) meticulous brushwork

工笔画(gōngbǐhuà) a meticulous-style painting

工读(gōngdú) to work one's way through school; a part-time job while studying

工读教育(gōngdú jiàoyù) education for juvenile offenders

工读学校(gōngdú xuéxiào) a reformatory school

工分(gōngfēn) workpoint

工夫(gōngfu) time

工龄(gōnglíng) length of employment

工农(gōngnóng) workers and peasants

工农兵(gōngnóngbīng) workers, peasants and soldiers

工农联盟(gōngnóng liánméng) the alliance of workers and peasants

工薪族(gōngxīnzú) wage-earners

工友(gōngyǒu) a fellow worker

工贼(gōngzéi) a scab; a blackleg

公安派三袁(gōng'ānpài sānyuán) the Three Yuans of the late Ming Gong'an School, (the three brothers-Yuan Zongdao, Yuan Hongdao and Yuan Zhongdao)

公案(gōngàn) ①a table in a courtroom②a legal case③a controversial issue

公案小说(gōngàn xiǎoshuō) detective fiction

公车上书(gōngchē shàngshū) the Joint Petition of the Imperial Examination Candidates to the Emperor (led by Kang Youwei in 1895)

公敌(gōngdí) a public enemy

公爹(gōngdiē) father-in-law; the husband's father

公牍(gōngdú) official documents

公干(gōnggàn) official business

公公(gōnggong) ① father-in-law; husband's father②a eunuch

公馆(gōngguǎn) the mansion of a wealthy or important person

公会(gōnghuì)a trade council; a trade association; a guild

公祭(gōngjì)a public memorial ceremony

公家(gōngjia)the state; the public

公开信(gōngkāixìn)an open letter

公款(gōngkuǎn)public funds

公历(gōnglì)Gregorian calendar

公了(gōngliǎo)to settle a dispute in the courts(rather than in private)

公婆(gōngpó)parents-in-law; the husband's parents

公仆(gōngpú)public servants

公社(gōngshè)a commune

公说公有理,婆说婆有理(gōng shuō gōng yǒulǐ, pó shuō pó yǒulǐ)everyone says he is right

公私合营(gōngsī héyíng)joint state-private ownership

公堂(gōngtáng)①a law court②an ancestral hall; a memorial temple

公务员(gōngwùyuán)a public servant; a governmental functionary

《公羊传》(gōngyáng zhuàn)*The Commentaries of Gongyang* – a Confucian classic by Gongyang Gao(公羊高)

公羊学派(gōngyáng xuépài)the Gongyang School

公主(gōngzhǔ)a princess

公子(gōngzǐ)a prince; son of a wealthy person or a high official

公子哥(gōngzǐgē)a dandy; a playboy; the sons of wealthy persons or high officials

公子王孙(gōngzǐ wángsūn)the sons of princes and nobles

功夫(gōngfu)①Kungfu②a skill

功夫茶(gōngfuchá)the gongfu tea(a kind of tea-making skill and tea-drinking etiquette)

功夫片(gōngfu piàn)a Kungfu film

功劳簿(gōngláobù)a record of one's merits

功名(gōngmíng)a scholarly honor or an official rank

功名富贵(gōngmíng fùguì)fame and fortune

功名利禄(gōngmíng lìlù)fame and fortune

攻城略地(gōngchéng lüèdì)to attach cities and seize territories

攻讦(gōngjié)to rake up one's past and use it to attack him

宫灯(gōngdēng)a palace lantern

宫殿(gōngdiàn)an imperial palace

宫调(gōngdiào)the modes of ancient Chinese music

宫娥(gōng é)a maid in the imperial palace

宫禁(gōngjìn)①the emperor's living quarters②palace prohibitions

宫女(gōngnǚ)a maid in the imperial palace

宫阙(gōngquè) an imperial palace

宫体诗(gōngtǐshī) palace-style poetry

宫廷画(gōngtínghuà) court-style painting

宫闱(gōngwéi) ①an imperial palace ②palace chambers

宫闱秘事(gōngwéi mìshì) a palace secret

宫刑(gōngxíng) castration

恭敬不如从命(gōngjìng bùrú cóngmìng) it is better to accept willingly than refuse politely; obedience is worth more than respect

觥筹交错(gōngchóu jiāocuò) to toast each other; to wine and dine freely; a drink-fuelled party

拱门(gǒngmén) an arched door

拱桥(gǒngqiáo) an arch bridge

共产党(gòngchǎndǎng) Communist Party

共产主义(gòngchǎn zhǔyì) Communism

共青团(gòngqīngtuán) Communist Youth League

贡品(gòngpǐn) a tribute

贡生(gòngshēng) a gongsheng (a scholar recommended by the provincial government to go to the Imperial College in the capital city for further studies in the Ming and Qing dynasties)

贡税(gòngshuì) tribute and taxes

贡院(gòngyuàn) a provincial examination center in Imperial China

供奉(gòngfèng) to enshrine and worship; to consecrate

供品(gòngpǐn) offerings

供桌(gòngzhuō) an altar table

勾魂(gōuhún) to captivate one's soul; to enchant; to bewitch

勾栏(gōulán) a theatre; a brothel

勾阑(gōulán) a theatre; a brothel

勾脸(gōuliǎn) to make up the face (in traditional Chinese operas)

狗皮膏药(gǒupí gāoyào) (lit.) "a dogskin plaster" – quack medicine; a fraud

狗屁(gǒupì) nonsense; bullshit

狗头军师(gǒutóu jūnshī) an scheming adviser; a villainous adviser

狗腿子(gǒutuǐzi) a henchman; a hired thug; a lackey

狗熊(gǒuxióng) a black bear; a coward

狗眼看人低(gǒuyǎn kàn rén dī) to be snobbish; to act like a snob

狗咬吕洞宾(gǒu yǎo lǚdòngbīn) (lit.) "to snarl and snap at Lu Dongbin" – to wrong a kind-hearted person; to mistake a good person for a bad one

苟合(gǒuhé) illicit sexual relations

诟病(gòubìng) to denounce; to castigate

够交情(gòu jiāoqing)to be a true friend

够朋友(gòu péngyou)to be a true friend

够呛(gòuqiàng)terrible; difficult to handle

够意思(gòu yìsi)①great②to be a true friend

媾和(gòuhé)to make peace

姑夫(gūfu)uncle(father's sister's husband)

姑父(gūfu)uncle(father's sister's husband)

姑姑(gūgu)aunt(father's sister)

姑老(姥)爷(gūlǎoye)son-in-law(used to address a man by his wife's family members)

姑姥姥(gūlǎolao)the paternal aunt of one's mother

姑妈(gūmā)aunt(father's sister)

姑母(gūmǔ)aunt(father's sister)

姑奶奶(gūnǎinai)①a married daughter(used to address a married woman by her family members)②the sister of one's paternal grandfather; a great aunt③a young girl

姑婆(gūpó)①grandfather's sister; great-aunt②husband's paternal aunt

姑嫂(gūsǎo)sisters-in-law(a woman and her brother's wife)

《姑苏行》(gūsūxíng)*Journey to Suzhou* – a Chinese flute solo

姑爷(gūyé)son-in-law(used to address a man by his wife's family members)

姑爷爷(gūyéye)great-uncle; paternal great-aunt's husband

姑丈(gūzhàng)uncle(father's sister's husband)

姑子(gūzi)a Buddhist nun

孤哀子(gū'āizǐ)a son bereaved of both parents

孤本(gūběn)the only extant copy

孤臣孽子(gūchén nièzǐ)a supporter of a doomed dynasty or a lost cause

孤胆英雄(gūdǎn yīngxióong)a solitary warrior

孤岛文学(gūdǎo wénxué)Literature in the Isolated Island(in the concession in Shanghai from 1934 to 1941); the Solitary Island Literature

孤芳自赏(gūfāng zìshǎng)to indulge in self-admiration

孤家寡人(gūjiā guǎrén)a person who is completely alone

古刹(gǔchà)an ancient temple

《古船》(gǔchuán)*Ancient Boat* – a novel by Zhang Wei(张炜,1956 –) in 1986

古道热肠(gǔdào rècháng)warm-hearted and considerate

《古画品录》(gǔhuà pǐnlù)*The Record of the Classification of Old Paintings* – an ancient work on the theory of painting by Xie He(谢赫,479－502)

古琴(gǔqín)a seven-stringed plucked instrument

古色古香(gǔsè gǔxiāng)antique

古诗(gǔshī) old poetry; classical poetry;classical poems;ancient poems

《古诗十九首》(gǔshī shíjiǔ shǒu) *Nineteen Ancient-Style Poems* – a group of Chinese poems compiled by Xiao Tong(萧统,501－531)

古体诗(gǔtǐshī)classical poetry written in the ancient style

古为今用(gǔwéijīnyòng)to make the past serve the present

古文(gǔwén) ancient Chinese prose or essay;classical Chinese writings

《古文观止》(gǔwén guānzhǐ) *Collected Ancient Prose* – a book compiled by Wu Chucai(吴楚材)and Wu Diaohou(吴调侯)in 1694; *Gems From Chinese Culture*;*Best of Classical Prose*

古文运动(gǔwén yùndòng)the Classical Prose Movement; Ancient Literature Movement

古稀之年(gǔxī zhī nián) seventy years of age

古训(gǔxùn)an old maxim

古筝(gǔzhēng) *guzheng* (a plucked musical instrument made of wood, with 21or 25 strings)

古装(gǔzhuāng)an ancient costume

《谷梁传》(gǔliáng zhuàn) *The Commentaries of Guliang* – a Confucian classic by Guliang-zi

古装剧(gǔzhuāngjù) a costume drama

谷雨(gǔyǔ)Grain Rain(the 6th of the 24 Chinese solar terms,usually falling on the 19th, 20th or 21st of April)

股肱(gǔgōng)(lit.)"thigh and upper arm"– a right-hand man

股肱之臣(gǔgōng zhīchén) a trustworthy minister

骨雕(gǔdiāo)a bone sculpture

骨干(gǔgàn) ①a mainstay or backbone②a key member; a core member

骨干分子(gǔgàn fènzǐ) a key member;a core member

骨刻(gǔkè)a bone carving

骨气(gǔqì) ① moral integrity ② strength(calligraphy)

骨肉(gǔròu)flesh and blood;kindred

骨肉兄弟(gǔròu xiōngdì) flesh-and-blood brothers;blood relations

骨肉之情(gǔròu zhī qíng) kindred feelings;blood ties

骨头轻(gǔtou qīng)to be of no moral integrity

骨血(gǔxuè)(lit.)"flesh and blood"– offspring

贾祸(gǔhuò)to incur disaster
鼓板(gǔbǎn)clappers
鼓词(gǔcí)the lyrics to dagu (a versified story which is sung accompanied by a small drum and other instruments)
鼓乐(gǔyuè) music accompanied by drumbeats; drum music; percussion music
鼓楼(gǔlóu)a drum tower
鼓书(gǔshū) a versified song accompanied by a small drum and other musical instruments
鼓子词(gǔzǐcí)the drum-song
固若金汤(gùruòjīntāng) as strong as iron; strongly fortified; to be secure against assault
故地(gùdì)an old haunt; former home
故都(gùdū)a former capital
故宫(gùgōng) ①the palace of a former Dynasty②the Imperial Palace; the Forbidden City
故宫博物院(gùgōng bówùyuàn) the National Palace Museum
故交(gùjiāo)an old friend
故居(gùjū)a former residence
故里(gùlǐ)native place
故去(gùqù)to pass away; to die
故人(gùrén) ① an old friend ② the dead
故土(gùtǔ)hometown; native land
《故乡》(gùxiāng) *Hometown* – a short story by Lu Xun (鲁迅, 1881 – 1936) in 1921
故友(gùgyǒu)a departed friend
故园(gùyuán) a hometown; a native land
顾家(gùjiā) to look after one's family; to have one's family always in mind
顾面子(gù miànzi) to save face
顾命(gùmìng) ①to cherish life; to be concerned about one's safety ② the emperor's will and testament
顾命大臣(gùmìng dàchén) a minister regent
顾命之恩(gùmìng zhī ēn) the favor of being nominated as the minister regent
顾绣(gùxiù) Gu embroidery (handed down from the Ming Dynasty in Shanghai)
雇农(gùnóng) a farm laborer; a farmhand
瓜葛(guāgé) association; connection
瓜皮帽(guāpímào) a skullcap
瓜子脸(guāzǐ liǎn) an oval face
刮鼻子(guā bízi) to scrape one's nose (as a kind of punishment in the game)
刮脸皮(guā liǎnpí) to rub one's cheek – point the finger of scorn at somebody
刮痧(guāshā) scraping the neck,

chest or back (an ancient folk treatment for illnesses)

呱呱叫 (guāguājiào) great; terrific; gorgeous

寡人 (guǎrén) I; me (self-appellation for the Emperor)

挂彩 (guàcǎi) ①to decorate with colored silk for celebration②to be injured on the battlefield

挂冠 (guàguān) (lit.) "to hang up one's official hat" – to resign from office

挂花 (guàhuā) to be injured in battle

挂历 (guàlì) a wall calendar

挂名 (guàmíng) titular; to be only nominal; only in name

挂牌 (guàpái) (lit.) "to put up a shop sign" – to open for business

挂帅 (guàshuài) to be in command; to assume leadership; to take charge of

挂职 (guàzhí) to take up a temporary post

挂轴 (guàzhóu) a hanging scroll

褂子 (guàzi) a short gown; a Chinese-style upper garment

拐子 (guǎizi) ①a cripple②a swindler

怪话 (guàihuà) grumbles; cynical remarks; complaints

怪罪 (guàizuì) to blame (someone)

关帝 (guāndì) Guan Yu (160 – 220) (a famous general in the period of the Three Kingdoms, 220 – 280)

关帝庙 (guāndì miào) the Temple of Guan Yu

关东 (guāndōng) northeast China;

关公 (guāngōng) Guan Yu (a famous general in the period of the Three Kingdoms)

《关雎》(guānjū) *A Fair Maiden* – the first poem of *The Book of Songs*

关里 (guānlǐ) inside the Pass; the areas inside the Great Wall

关门大吉 (guānmén dàjí) to close down for good

关内 (guānnèi) inside the Pass; the areas inside the Great Wall

关牛棚 (guān niúpéng) to put people in a cowshed

关塞 (guānsài) a fortress

关山 (guānshān) mountains and passes

关外 (guānwài) outside the Pass; the areas outside the Great Wall

关系 (guānxì) relatives or close friends in power

关系户 (guānxì hù) a well-connected individual or group

关系网 (guānxì wǎng) a social network; a well-connected network

关中 (guānzhōng) within the Pass; the central Shaanxi plain

关子 (guānzi) the climax or the most interesting part (in a novel, story or play)

观(世)音[guān(shì)yīn] Avalokitesvara; Guanyin; goddess of mercy

观音会(guānyīnhuì) the religious festival to celebrate the birthday of Guanyin

纶巾(guānjīn) a blue-ribboned silk kerchief

纶巾羽扇(guānjīn yǔshàn)(lit.)"to have a feather fan and wear a blue silk ribbon scarf" - to be handsome and graceful in behavior

官差(guānchāi) a public errand

官场(guānchǎng) officialdom; official circles

《官场现形记》(guānchǎng xiànxíng jì) *The Bureaucrat: A Revelation* - an exposure novel by Li Baojia(李宝嘉, 1867 - 1906) in 1903 - 1905; *Exposure of the Official World*

官邸(guāndǐ) an official residence; an official mansion

官府(guānfǔ) a local government

官官相护(guānguān xiānghù) officials protect each other

官话(guānhuà)①official dialect - Mandarin②official jargon

官宦之家(guānhuàn zhī jiā) the family of a government official

官家(guānjiā)①government②official③the emperor

官架子(guānjiàzi) the airs of an official

官吏(guānlì) government officials

官了(guānliǎo) to settle a dispute in the courts rather than in private

官迷(guānmí) an office seeker

官气十足(guānqì shízú) to be full of bureaucratic airs

官腔(guānqiāng) a bureaucratic tone

官人(guānrén)①an official②Sir(a respectful way to address a man in ancient times)③husband(a term of address a woman used to call her husband)

官样文章(guānyàng wénzhāng) official jargon; mere formalities

冠盖(guān'gài)(lit.)"official hats and canopies" - officials

冠盖如云(guān'gài rú yún) many officials and dignitaries

冠冕(guānmiǎn)①a royal crown②an official hat

馆子(guǎnzi) a restaurant

管家(guǎnjiā) a butler; a chief servant; a housekeeper

管家婆(guǎnjiāpó)①a chief woman servant②a housewife; a woman housekeeper

管见(guǎnjiàn) my humble opinion

管事(guǎnshì)①to be in charge②a manager; a steward③effective

《管子》(guǎnzǐ) *Guanzi* - a collected

papers of Guanzi(723 - 645 BC)

灌迷魂汤(guàn míhúntāng) to say honeyed words to somebody to flatter him; to be bewitched by means of flattery

灌米汤(guàn mǐtāng) to say honeyed words to someone to flatter him; to be bewitched by means of flattery

灌水(guàn shuǐ) to fill a webpage with one's articles or comments

光复(guāngfù) to regain (a lost territory, regime etc.); to restore

光杆司令(guānggǎn sīlìng) a commander without an army; a leader without followers

光棍儿(guānggùnr) a bachelor; an unmarried man; a man who has lost his wife

光荣榜(guāngróngbǎng) an honor roll (containing the names and deeds of outstanding people)

光荣之家(guāngróng zhī jiā) an honorable family

光绪(guāngxù) Emperor Guangxu [the 9th emperor of the Qing Dynasty(1636 - 1912)]

光阴(guāngyīn) time

光阴荏苒(guāngyīn rěnrǎn) Time flies; time slipped away

光宗耀祖(guāngzōng yàozǔ) to bring honor to one's family and ancestors

广播剧(guǎngbōjù) a radio drama

广播体操(guǎngbō tǐcāo) setting-up exercises to radio music

广东戏(guǎngdōng xì) Cantonese Opera

广寒宫(guǎnghángōng) the Moon Palace (the mythical palace in the moon)

《广陵散》(guǎng líng sǎn) *Music from Guangling* - a Chinese classical melody

广式月饼(guǎngshì yuèbǐng) Cantonese mooncakes

广绣(guǎngxiù) the Guangdong embroidery

广州起义(guǎngzhōu qǐyì) the Guangzhou Uprising(1927)

逛灯(guàngdēng) to go to enjoy the lantern displays

逛街(guàngjiē) to take a walk in the street

逛窑子(guàng yáozi) to visit prostitutes

归根(guīgēn) to return to one's own native land

归国华侨(guīguó huáqiáo) a returned overseas Chinese

归宁(guīníng) to visit her own parents (after marriage)

《归潜志》(guīqiánzhì) *Reminiscence* - a book by Liu Qi (刘祁, 1203 - 1250)

归侨(guīqiáo) a returned overseas

Chinese
《归去来辞兮》(guī qù lái cí xi) *On Returning Home* - an essay by Tao Yuanming(陶渊明,365 - 427)
归天(guītiān)to pass away;to die
归田(guītián)to resign and return to one's native land
归西(guīxī)to pass away;to die
归隐(guīyǐn)to withdraw from society and live in solitude; to retire from the world
圭表(guībiǎo)a sundial
圭臬(guīniè)a criterion;a standard
龟卜(guībǔ) to divine by a tortoise shell;divination using a turtle shell
龟趺(guīfū)the turtle base(of a stone tablet)
龟鉴(guījiàn)a lesson for the future
闺范(guīfàn) the moral norms for women
闺房(guīfáng)a young lady's chamber;a boudoir
闺阁(guīgé)a young lady's chamber;a boudoir
闺门旦(guīméndàn)a female role of the maidenly type(in Chinese opera)
闺女(guīnü) ① an unmarried girl ②daughter
闺秀(guīxiù)the daughter of a rich or powerful family
闺怨(guīyuàn)boudoir sorrows
鬼把戏(guǐ bǎxì) mischief; a dirty trick
鬼才(guǐcái) a person of special talent
鬼点子(guǐ diǎnzi) a wicked idea; a trick;a bright idea
鬼画符(guǐhuàfú) ① scrawly handwriting②hypocritical talk
鬼混(guǐhùn) to fool around; to do nothing meaningful
鬼节(guǐjié)the Ghosts' Festival
鬼灵精(guǐlíngjīng)a smart person
鬼门关(guǐménguān) the gate of Hell;the jaws of death;a dangerous place
鬼主意(guǐ zhǔyi) a bright idea; a wicked idea
鬼子(guǐzi) a foreign invader, a foreigner;a foreign devil
刽子手(guìzishǒu)①an executioner ②a slaughterer
柜房(guìfáng)the cashier's office(in a shop)
柜子上(guìzishàng)the cashier's office(in a shop)
贵妃(guìfēi)an imperial concubine
《贵妃醉酒》(guìfēi zuìjiǔ) *The Drunken Concubine* - a Beijing opera; *The Drunken Beauty*
贵庚(guìgēng)your age
贵人(guìrén)①a man of eminence② an imperial concubine

贵姓(guìxìng)your surname

贵胄(guìzhòu)a descendant of the feudal ruler or aristocrat

贵子(guìzǐ)your son

桂花酒(guìhuājiǔ)osmathus-flavored wine

桂剧(guìjù)the Gui opera

跪拜(guìbài)to kowtow to somebody (to show your respect)

跪叩(guìkòu)to kowtow

衮服(gǔnfú)an imperial robe; the robe worn by the emperor

衮衮诸公(gǔngǔn zhūgōng)high-ranking government officials

滚刀肉(gǔndāoròu)an unreasonable trouble-maker

磙子(gǔnzi)a stone roller

棍棒政策(gùnbàng zhèngcè)a crack-down policy

锅贴(guōtiē)fried dumplings

锅庄(guōzhuāng)a Tibetan folk dance

蝈蝈儿(guōguor)a katydid; a long-horned grasshopper

国宝(guóbǎo)national treasure

国宾(guóbīn)a state guest

国柄(guóbǐng)state power; the political power of a nation

国粹(guócuì)the quintessence or best of Chinese culture

国父(guófù)Father of the Country

国格(guógé)national dignity; national prestige

国共合作(guógòng hézuò)the Kuomintang-Communist cooperation; the cooperation between Chinese Nationalist Party and Chinese Communist Party

国号(guóhào)the title of a reigning dynasty

国花(guóhuā)the national flower

国画(guóhuà)traditional Chinese painting; a Chinese painting

国画家(guóhuàjiā)a painter in the traditional Chinese style

国家兴亡,匹夫有责(guójiā xīngwáng, pǐfū yǒu zé)every common man has the obligation for the fate of his country

国脚(guójiǎo)a football player in the national team

国舅(guójiù)the brother of a queen or empress

国库券(guókùquàn)a treasury bill

国乐(guóyuè)traditional Chinese music

国民党(guómíngdǎng)Chinese Nationalist Party; KMT; Kuomintang

国民性(guómínxìng)national character; national traits

国母(guómǔ)Mother of the Country; First Lady

国难(guónàn)a national crisis

国难当头(guónàn dāngtóu)The

country is faced with a crisis; a national crisis is imminent.

国破家亡(guópò jiāwáng) the country is conquered and the home is lost

国戚(guóqì) the relatives of the emperor or queen

国庆(guóqìng) National Day

国庆节(guóqìngjié) National Day

国人(guórén) compatriots; countrymen

国丧(guósāng) national mourning

国色天香(guósè tiānxiāng) a woman of great beauty; a great beauty

国殇(guóshāng) a national martyr

国手(guóshǒu) a national champion; a great master

国术(guóshù) traditional Chinese martial arts

国统区(guótǒngqū) the areas under the control of KMT(Kuomintang)

国统区文学(guótǒngqū wénxué) Literature in the Guomindang-controlled areas

国玺(guóxǐ) the imperial seal; the national seal

国学(guóxué) ① studies of Chinese national culture; sinology; studies of ancient Chinese civilization ② the Imperial College

国学大师(guóxué dàshī) master of Chinese culture

国语(guóyǔ) Mandarin; a national language

国子监(guózǐjiàn) Directorate of the Imperial Academy; the Imperial Institute; the Highest Educational Administrative Bureau; the Palace Building of Education

果腹(guǒfù) to satisfy one's hunger

裹脚(guǒjiǎo) foot-binding; to have a girl's feet bound

裹脚布(guǒjiǎobù) the bandages for binding women's feet

裹腿(guǒtuǐ) leggings; puttee

过房(guòfáng) to adopt a child from relatives

过关斩将(guòguān zhǎnjiàng) to beat opponents one by one to go into the next round of competition; to overcome various difficulties one by one

《过河》(guò hé) *Over the River* - a skit starring Pan Changjiang(潘长江) and Yan Shuping(阎淑萍) in the Spring Festival Gala in 1996

过继(guòjì) to have one's child adopted by a relative

过家伙(guò jiāhuo) to fight with somebody

过家家(guò jiājiā) to play house

过街楼(guòjiēlóu) an overhead building projection(spanning a lane); a bridge gallery; an arcade

过客(guòkè)a passing traveler; a passer-by

过来人(guòláirén)an old hand; a peron with sufficient experience

过劳死(guòláosǐ)death from overwork;to die from overwork

过礼(guòlǐ)①to deliver betrothal gifts to the bride's family②to greet; to salute

过门(guòmén)①to marry into a family; to move into her husband's house on the wedding day②a short interlude(in music)

过年(guònián)to celebrate the Lunar New Year

《过秦论》(guòqínlùn)*On the Faults of the Qin* – an article by Jia Yi(贾谊,200 – 168 BC)

过世(guòshì)to pass away;to die

过堂(guòtáng)to be interrogated in the court;to be tried in the court

过堂风(guòtángfēng)the wind through a passageway

过午(guòwǔ)in the afternoon

过眼云烟(guò yǎn yúnyān)to be as transient as a fleeting cloud

过瘾(guòyǐn)to satisfy a craving; to enjoy oneself to the full;very enjoyable

H

哈韩族(hāhánzú)young fans of Korean pop culture

哈喇子(hālázi)dribble;drivel

《哈罗,黄土坡》(hāluo, huángtǔpō) *Hello, Huangtupo* – a skit starring Guo Da(郭达)and Cai Ming(蔡明)in 1993

哈尼族(hānízú)the Hani nationality

哈萨克族(hāsākèzú)the Kazak nationality

哈巴狗(hǎbagǒu)①a Pekinese (dog)②a sycophant

哈达(hǎdá)*hada*;hatha(a long piece of silk used as greeting gift among Tibetan and Mongolian nationalities)

海报(hǎibào)a playbill;a poster

《海港》(hǎigǎng)*Harbour* – a modern Beijing opera

海归(hǎiguī)an overseas returnee; a returned student from abroad

海龟(hǎiguī)①a sea turtle;a green turtle②an overseas returnee; a returned student from abroad

《海国图志》(hǎiguó túzhì)*Illustrated Records of the Maritime Nations* – a book by Wei Yuan(魏源,1794 – 1857)in 1841 – 1851

海涵(hǎihán)to be magnanimous enough to forgive

《海角七号》(hǎijiǎo qīhào)*Cape No. 7* – a film directed by Wei Desheng(魏德圣)in 2008

海角天涯(hǎijiǎo tiānyá)(lit.)"the corners of the sea and ends of the sky" – the remotest corner of the world; a far-off region

海禁(hǎijìn)a ban on maritime trade or contact with foreign countries

海枯石烂(hǎikū shílàn)(lit.)"till the sea dries up and the rocks turn to dust" – in love forever

海量(hǎiliàng)①to be magnanimous ②a enormous capacity for alcoholic drinks

海内(hǎinèi) throughout the land; throughout the country

海南戏(hǎinánxì)Hainan Opera

海派(hǎipài)Shanghai style

海派文化(hǎipài wénhuà)Shanghai culture

《海瑞罢官》(hǎiruì bàguān)*Hai Rui Dismissed from Office* – a Beijing opera

海誓山盟(hǎishì shānméng) a solemn pledge of love; an oath of eternal love

《海霞》(hǎixiá)*Rosy Clouds on the Sea* – a film directed by Qian Jiang (钱江) in 1975

《海鹰》(hǎiyīng)*The Eagles of the Sea* – a film directed by Yan Jizhou (严寄洲) in 1959

海选(hǎixuǎn)extensive audition; select from an extremely large range

害群之马(hàiqún zhīmǎ) a black sheep; a pest who harms society; a rotten apple

害喜(hàixǐ)to have morning sickness

憨子(hānzi)idiot; simpleton

含沙射影(hánshā shèyǐng)to attack by innuendo; to point at one but abuse another

含笑九泉(hánxiào jiǔquán)to smile in the grave; to die happy

含饴弄孙(hányí nòngsūn)(lit.)"to play with one's grandchildren while chewing maltose" – to lead a happy old life

《邯郸梦》(hándān mèng)*The Dream of Handan* – a play by Tang Xianzu (汤显祖,1550 – 1616)

邯郸学步(hándān xuébù)(lit.)"to try to learn to walk like the people of Handan, but to forget one's own style of walking in the process" – blind imitation of others will make one lose one's individuality.

函授(hánshòu) a correspondence course

函授教育(hánshòu jiàoyù)education by correspondence courses; distance learning

涵养(hányǎng)self-restraint; the virtue of patience; the ability to control oneself

寒碜(hánchen)ugly; shabby; shameful

寒窗(hánchuāng)(lit.)"a cold window" – the hardship of a poor student

寒露(hánlù)Cold Dew(the 17th of the 24 solar terms, usually falling on the 8th or 9th of October)

寒门(hánmén)a poor family; a humble family

寒舍(hánshè)my humble home

寒食(hánshí)the Cold Food Festival

寒士(hánshì)a poor scholar

寒酸(hánsuān)shabby and miserable

寒暄(hánxuān)a conventional greeting; to exchange greetings

寒鸦(hányā)a jackdaw

《寒鸦戏水》(hányā xìshuǐ) *Jackdaw Playing in the Water* – a piece of Chinese zither music

《寒夜》(hányè) *Cold Night* – a novel by Ba Jin(巴金, 1904 – 2005) in 1944 – 1946

《韩非子》(hánfēizǐ) *The Book of Master Han Fei* – a book by Han Fei(韩非, 280 – 233 BC)

《韩熙载夜宴图》(hánxīzài yèyàn tú) *Han Xizai's Evening Feast* – a painting by Gu Hongzhong(顾闳中, 910 – 980)

喊魂(hǎnhún)to call one's soul back

汉朝(hàncháo)the Han Dynasty(206 BC – 220 AD)

汉代(hàndài)the Han Dynasty(206 BC – 220 AD)

汉赋(hànfù) *hanfu*; rhyme prose(a literary genre originating in the Han Dynasty)

《汉宫春晓图》(hàngōng chūnxiǎo tú) *Spring Dawn in the Han Palace* – a painting by Chou Ying(仇英, 1498 – 1552)

《汉宫秋》(hàngōngqiū) *Autumn in the Han Palace* – a historical play by Ma Zhiyuan(马致远, 1250 – 1324)

《汉宫秋月》(hàngōng qiūyuè) *The Moon over the Han Palace* – a piece of lute music

汉奸(hànjiān)a traitor(to China)

汉剧(hànjù)Hubei opera

汉隶(hànlì)the Han script(a written form of the Chinese language, used in the Han dynasty)

汉人(hànrén)the Hans; the Han people

《汉书》(hànshū) *The History of the Han* – a historical work by Ban Gu(班固, 32 – 92)

汉文(hànwén)①Chinese language②Chinese characters

《汉武大帝》(hànwǔ dàdì) *Great Emperor Wu of the Han Dynasty* – a TV drama directed by Hu Mei(胡玫) in 2005

汉学(hànxué)①Sinology ②the School of Han Learning

汉语拼音方案(hànyǔ pīnyīn fāng'àn)Scheme for the Chinese Phonetic Alphabet

汉子(hànzi)①a man;a fellow②husband

汉字(hànzì)Chinese characters

汉族(hànzú)the Han nationality;the Han people

汗马功劳(hànmǎ gōngláo)great contributions;war efforts;exploits and achievements in battle

汗青(hànqīng)historical records

旱船(hànchuán)a land boat(a folk artistic form in Shanxi province)

旱鸭子(hànyāzi)a non-swimmer

旱烟(hànyān)tobacco

旱烟袋(hànyāndài)a long-stemmed Chinese tobacco pipe

颔联(hànlián)the third and fourth line of a Tang poem(of Regulated Verse)

颔首(hànshǒu)to nod

颔首致意(hànshǒu zhìyì)to nod in greeting

翰林(hànlín)a member of the Imperial Academy[from the Tang Dynasty(618-907)onward]

翰林院(hànlínyuàn)the Imperial Academy;the Hanlin Academy

翰墨(hànmò)(lit.)"brush and ink"-writing,painting or calligraphy

行行出状元(hángháng chū zhuàngyuán)every profession has its top expert;every trade has its master;one may distinguish oneself in any trade

行情(hángqíng)quotations(on the market)

行市(hángshì)quotations(on the market)

行伍(hángwǔ)the ranks

行伍出身(hángwǔ chūshēn)to be originally in the army;to have a military background

行院(hángyuàn)house of prostitutes or actresses

行栈(hángzhàn)a broker's storehouse

豪放词派(háofàng cípài)the Powerful and Unrestrained School of *ci* poetry

豪杰(háojié)a hero;a person of exceptional ability

豪客(háokè)a robber;a bandit

豪门(háomén)a wealthy and influential family

豪绅(háoshēn)despotic gentry

豪侠(háoxiá)a gallant man

号丧(háosāng)①to wail in mourning;to howl at a funeral②to howl(as if at a funeral)

好处费(hǎochùfèi)the reward for being a go-between or middleman;a kickback;pickings

好汉(hǎohàn)a brave man;a hero

好好先生(hǎohǎo xiānshēng) Mr. Please-all;a yes-man

好来宝(hǎoláibǎo)haolaibao(a kind of folk singing, popular in Inner Mongolian)

好男不跟女斗(hǎonán bù gēn nǚ dòu)a gentleman never fights with a woman

好戏(hǎoxì)①a good play②a great fun

好走(hǎozǒu)goodbye

好大喜功(hàodà xǐgōng) to desire greatness and success

好色(hàosè)to lust for women;to be fond of women;flirtatious

好色之徒(hàosè zhītú) a lecher; a libertine

好为人师(hàowéi rénshī)to be fond of teaching other people

好逸恶劳(hàoyì wùláo)to love comfort and hate work;indolence

号脉(hàomài) to feel somebody's pulse

号外(hàowài) an extra edition of a newspaper

号子(hàozi) a work song; a chant sung while working

浩劫(hàojié)a great calamity;a catastrophe

皓首(hàoshǒu) a hoary head; grey hair

皓首穷经(hàoshǒu qióngjīng)to continue one's study in old age

喝闷酒(hē mènjiǔ)to drink alone;to drown one's sorrows

喝墨水(hē mòshuǐ)(lit.)"to drink ink"– to go to school

喝西北风(hē xīběifēng)(lit.)"to drink the northwest wind"– to have nothing to eat;to live on air

合家欢(héjiāhuān) a family group photo

合卺(héjǐn) to go through the marriage ceremony

合十(héshí) to put one's palms together before one's chest(Buddhist greeting)

合同工(hétónggōng)a contract worker

合葬(hézàng) to be buried in the same grave

合掌(hézhǎng) to join one's palms before one's chest(Buddhist greeting)

《何日君再来》(hérì jūn zàilái) *When Will You Come Again* – a song sung by singers such as Zhou Xuan(周璇),Li Xianlan(李香兰)and Deng Lijun(邓丽君)from 1937

何仙姑(héxiāngū) He Xiangu; Ho Hsien-Ku(one of the Eight Immortals in ancient mythology)

和会(héhùi)a peace conference
《和平年代》(hépíng niándài) *Times of Peace* - a TV drama directed by Li Shu(李舒)and Zhang Qian(张前)in 1996
和棋(héqí) a draw in chess or other board games
和气生财(héqì shēngcái) harmony brings wealth
和亲(héqīn) to make peace with the rulers of minorities in the border areas by marriage;a political marriage
和尚(héshang)a Buddhist monk
和尚头(héshangtóu)a shaven head
和事老(héshìlǎo)a peacemaker
和谐社会(héxié shèhuì) a harmonious society
河伯(hébó) River Uncle(the god of the Yellow River)
河汉(héhàn)galaxy
河姆渡文化(hémǔdù wénhuà) Hemudu Culture(Neolithic culture in Zhejiang)
河南梆子(hénán bāngzi) Henan Clapper opera;Henan opera
河清海晏(héqīng hǎiyàn)(lit.) "The sea is calm and the Yellow River is clear." - What a peaceful world!
《河殇》(héshāng) *River Elegy* - a modern documentary by Su Xiaokang(苏晓康)et al. in 1989
河套(hétào) ①the bend of a river ② the Great Bend of the Huanghe River
河西走廊(héxī zǒuláng) the Hexi Corridor(in Gansu province)
荷包(hébāo)a pouch;a small bag
荷包蛋(hébāodàn)a fried egg
《荷花淀》(héhuādiàn) *Lotus Lake* - a short story by Sun Li(孙犁,1913-2002)in 1944
荷花淀派(héhuādiàn pài) the Lotus Lake School(a school of literature in the 1950s)
荷花生日(héhuāshēngrì) the Lotus Festival
阖府(héfǔ)your whole family
阖家(héjiā)your whole family
喝彩(hècǎi)to acclaim;to cheer
喝道(hèdào)to shout to the crowd to make way for somebody or something
喝倒彩(hè dàocǎi) to boo; to make catcalls
贺匾(hèbiǎn)a congratulatory plaque
贺礼(hèlǐ)a congratulatory gift
贺联(hèlián)congratulatory couplets
贺年片(hèniánpiàn)a New Year card
贺岁片(hèsuìpiàn) the New Year Film(a film issued for the Chinese Spring Festival)
贺仪(hèyí)a congratulatory gift
贺幛(hèzhāng) a congratulatory silk

scroll

赫哲族(hèzhézú) the Hezhe nationality

鹤发童颜(hèfà tóngyán)(lit.) "white hair and youthful complexion" - being healthy in old age

鹤立鸡群(hèlì jīqún)(lit.) "A crane stands among chickens" - to be the pick of the bunch; to be an outstanding person

黑帮(hēibāng) gangsters; a sinister gang

《黑冰》(hēibīng) *Black Ice* - a TV drama directed byWang Jixing(王冀邢) in 2001

黑车(hēichē) ①an unlicensed taxi ②a car without registration

黑道(hēidào) ①illegal activities ②the underworld

黑店(hēidiàn) a gangster inn; a tourist trap

《黑洞》(hēidòng) *The Black Hole* - a TV drama directed by Guan Hu(管虎) in 2002

黑户(hēihù) ①an unregistered family or resident ②an illegal shop without a business license

黑话(hēihuà) secret language or in-house language(of thieves or bandits)

黑货(hēihuò) smuggled goods

《黑骏马》(hēi jùnmǎ) *The Black Steed* - a novelette by Zhang Chengzhi(张承志,1948 -) in 1981

黑马(hēimǎ) a dark horse; an unexpected winner

黑名单(hēimíngdān) a blacklist

《黑炮事件》(hēipào shìjiàn) *The Black Cannon Incident* - a film directed by Huang Jianxin(黄建新) in 1986

黑人(hēirén) an unregistered resident

黑色收入(hēisè shōurù) illegal income; illicit gains

黑哨(hēishào) unfair refereeing

黑社会(hēishèhuì) an underworld

黑陶文化(hēitáo wénhuà) black-pottery culture(mainly in Shandong province)

黑箱操作(hēixiāng cāozuò) a black-box operation; a closed-box operation; undercover activities

《黑旋风李逵》(hēixuànfēng lǐkuí) *Li Kui, the Black Whirlwind* - a Beijing opera starring Yuan Shihai(袁世海) in 1953

亨通(hēngtōng) prosper

哼哈二将(hēnghā èr jiàng) the marshals Heng and Ha(two fierce-looking divinities guarding a temple gate); a pair of fierce men(serving one master)

姮娥(héng'é) Chang'e; the Goddess in the moon

恒山(héngshān)Hengshan Mountain; Mt Hengshan

横幅(héngfú)a horizontal scroll(of painting or calligraphy)

横批(héngpī)a horizontal scroll (bearing an inscription, usu. hung over a door and flanked by two vertical scrolls forming a couplet)

横行霸道(héngxíng bàdào) to play the tyrant; to tyrannize; to domineer

横着出来(héngzhe chūlái) to die

横财(hèngcái) a windfall; illegally-gotten money

横祸(hènghuò) an unexpected disaster or misfortune

横死(hèngsǐ) a sudden or unexpected death

烘托(hōngtuō) ①to set off(eg. one color against another) ② to add shading around an object to make it stand out(in Chinese painting)

薨逝(hōngshì) to die; to pass away

弘治(hóngzhì) the Hongzhi Emperor (r. 1488 - 1505)

红白喜事(hóngbái xǐshì) weddings and funerals

红榜(hóngbǎng) an honor roll

红包(hóngbāo) red money, a red envelope(containing money, usu. given as a present, tip, bonus or bribe)

红宝书(hóngbǎoshū) the Little Red Book; *Quotations from Chairman Mao*

红茶(hóngchá) black tea

红尘(hóngchén) the mortal world; vanity fair; human society

红蛋(hóngdàn) a red egg (used to celebrate the birth of a child or a wedding)

《红灯记》(hóngdēng jì) *The Legend of the Red Lantern* - a modern Beijing opera

《红豆》(hóngdòu) *Red Bean* - a short story by Zong Pu(宗璞, 1928 -) in 1957

红豆(hóngdòu) red beans; jequirity

红粉佳人(hóngfěn jiārén) a beautiful young woman

红粉知己(hóngfěn zhījǐ) a beautiful young woman and soulmate

《红高粱》(hóng gāoliang) *Red Sorghum* - a novel by Mo Yan(莫言); a film adapted from the novel and directed by Zhang Yimou(张艺谋) in 1987

《红高粱模特队》(hóng gāoliang mótèduì) *Red Sorghum Model Team* - a skit starring Zhao Benshan(赵本山) and Fan Wei(范伟) in the Spring Festival Gala in 2007

《红河谷》(hónghégǔ) *Red River Valley* - a film directed by Feng Xiaoning(冯小宁) in 1999

红巾起义(hóngjīn qǐyì) the Red Turbans Uprising(in 1351)

红净(hóngjìng) a red-face role (in traditional Chinese opera)

红军(hóngjūn) the Red Army

红领巾(hónglǐngjīn) ①a red scarf (worn by Young Pioneers) ②the Young Pioneers

《红楼二尤》(hónglóu èryóu) *The You Sisters in the Red Chamber* – a traditional Beijing opera

《红楼梦》(hónglóumèng) *A Dream of Red Mansions*, *The Story of the Stone* – a novel by Cao Xueqin(曹雪芹, 1715 – 1763) and Gao'E (高鹗, 1758 – 1815); an adaptation of this novel as a TV drama and film

红媒(hóngméi) a matchmaker

红男绿女(hóngnán lǜnǚ) gaily dressed young men and women; fashionably dressed men and women

红娘(hóngniáng) ①a matchmaker ②Hongniang[a maid in *The Romance of the West Chamber* – a classical poetic opera by Wang Shifu(王实甫, 1260 – 1336)]

《红娘》(hóngniáng) *Hongniang*, *Red Maid* – a Beijing opera

《红旗谱》(hóngqípǔ) *Keep the Red Flag Flying* – a novel by Liang Bin (梁斌, 1914 – 1996) in 1958; *Song of the Red Flag*

红旗手(hóngqíshǒu) a red-banner pacesetter; a model worker

红区(hóngqū) Red Area (i. e. controlled by the Chinese Communist Party)

红人(hóngrén) a favourite with someone in power; a blue-eyed boy

《红日》(hóngrì) *The Red Sun* – a film directed by Tang Xiaodan (汤晓丹) in 1963; a novel by Wu Qiang (吴强, 1910 – 1990) in 1958

《红嫂》(hóngsǎo) *The Red Sister*; *The Red Wife of Our Brother* – a dance drama

《红色娘子军》(hóngsè niángzǐjūn) *The Red Detachment of Women* – a modern dance drama directed by Pan Wenzhan(潘文展) in 1970; a film directed by Xie Jin (谢晋) in 1961

红山文化(hóngshān wénhuà) the Culture of Hongshan(Neolithic culture in Inner Mongolia)

红双喜(hóng shuāng xǐ) Double Happiness(a brand)

红头文件(hóngtóu wénjiàn) an official document

红卫兵(hóngwèibīng) the Red Guards

红小兵(hóngxiǎobīng) the Little Red Guards

红学(hóngxué) studies of *A Dream of*

Red Mansions; Redology

红学家(hóngxuéjiā) a scholar of *A Dream of Red Mansions*; a Red-ologist

《红岩》(hóngyán) *Red Rock* – a novel by Luo Guangbin(罗广斌, 1924–1967) and Yang Yiyan(杨益言, 1925 –) in 1962

红颜薄命(hóngyán bómìng) beautiful women often suffer ill fates and die at an early age

红眼病(hóngyǎnbìng) envy; jealousy

红缨枪(hóngyīngqiāng) a red-tasselled spear

《红樱桃》(hóngyīngtáo) *Red Cherry* – a film directed by Ye Daying(叶大鹰) in 1995

红妆(hóngzhuāng) ①feminine attire ②a young woman

红装(hóngzhuāng) ①feminine attire ②a young woman

洪帮(hóngbāng) The Hong Society(a popular secret society in 19th century China)

洪福(hóngfú) a great blessing

《洪湖赤卫队》(hónghú chìwèiduì) *The Red Guards on Honghu Lake* – a film directed by Xie Tian(谢添) in 1961

洪家拳(hóngjiāquán) Hung Gar Boxing[founded by Hong Xiguan(洪熙官) in Fujian province]

洪拳(hóngquán) Hung Boxing(in Guangdong province)

洪武(hóngwǔ) Emperor Hongwu(r. 1368 – 1398)

洪熙(hóngxī) Emperor Hongxi(1424 – 1425)

鸿福(hóngfú) a great blessing

鸿鹄(hónghú) ①a swan ②a person with lofty ambitions

鸿鹄之志(hónghú zhī zhì) lofty ambitions; high aspirations

鸿毛(hóngmáo)(lit.)"a goose feather" – an unimportant thing, insignificant or trivial thing

鸿门宴(hóngmén yàn) ①the Dinner at Hongmen; the Banquet at Hongmen between Liu Bang(刘邦, 256 – 195 BC) and Xiang Yu(项羽, 232 –202 BC) in 206 BC ②a malicious dinner party(intended to murder the guests)

鸿儒(hóngrú) a man of great learning

鸿雁传书(hóngyàn chuánshū)(lit.) "a letter delivered by a swan goose" – a letter from afar

黉门(hóngmén) a school; an academy

黉门秀才(hóngmén xiùcai) a scholar (who passed the imperial examination at the county level)

黉门学子(hóngmén xuézǐ) students in the school

哄场(hòngchǎng) to make catcalls;

to boo

猴精(hóujīng)①smart, clever, shrewd ② a mischief-maker; a clever and mischievous person

猴年马月(hóuniánmǎyuè)(lit.)"the year of the monkey and the month of the horse" – an impossible date; "God knows when"

猴皮筋(hóupíjīn)a rubber band

猴拳(hóuquán) Monkey Boxing (a form of martial arts)

猴戏(hóuxì) a performing monkey show

后宫(hòugōng)①the palaces for the queen and other imperial concubines; the imperial harem ② the queen and imperial concubines

《后宫甄嬛传》(hòugōng zhēnhuán zhuàn) *Empresses in Palace; A Legend of Concubine Zhen Huan* – a Chinese TV drama

后汉(hòuhàn)①the Eastern Han Dynasty (25 – 220) ②the Later Han Dynasty(947 – 950)

《后汉书》(hòuhàn shū) *The History of Eastern Han* – a historical work by Fanye(范晔,398 – 445)

后悔药(hòuhuǐyào)(lit.)"medicine for remorse" – regret

后晋(hòujìn) the Later Jin Dynasty (936 – 947)

后梁(hòuliáng) the Later Liang Dynasty(907 – 923)

后妈(hòumā)a stepmother

后门(hòumén) ① a backdoor ② a backdoor deal

后母(hòumǔ)a stepmother

后娘(hòuniáng)a stepmother

后七子(hòuqīzǐ) the Latter Seven Masters(a school of literature from 1520 to 1570)

后起之秀(hòuqǐ zhī xiù)a promising young person; a rising star

后生可畏(hòushēng kěwèi)the young may surpass the old; youth should not be looked down on

后事(hòushì)①what happened afterwards②funeral affairs

后台老板(hòutái lǎobǎn)a backstage boss

后羿射日(hòuyì shèrì)"Hou Yi shot down the suns" – an ancient Chinese myth of shooting down nine of the ten suns by a man named Hou Yi

后周(hòuzhōu) the Later Zhou Dynasty(951 – 960)

候教(hòujiào) to await your instructions

忽必烈(hūbìliè) Kublai Khan (the first emperor of the Yuan Dynasty)

忽悠(hūyou) to persuade someone to believe something; to coax; to sweet-talk

狐狸精(húli jīng)(lit.)"a fox spirit"-a seductive woman

狐仙(húxiān)a fox spirit;a fox fairy

胡匪(húfěi)a bandit

胡笳(hújiā)a reed pipe

《胡笳十八拍》(hújiā shíbāpāi) *Eighteen Songs Accompanied by the Tartar Reed Flute* - an eighteen-stanza ancient suite by Cai Wenji (蔡文姬,177-?)

《胡椒面》(hújiāomiàn) *Pepper* - a skit starring Chen Peisi(陈佩斯) and Zhu Shimao(朱时茂)in 1989

胡琴(húqín) *huqin* (a two-stringed bowed instrument)

胡人(húrén) the northern barbarian tribes(in ancient China)

胡同(hútòng)a lane;an alley

胡同串子(hútòng chuànzi)a lane; an alley

胡子工程(húzi gōngchéng) a slow, delayed project or engineering work

湖笔(húbǐ) the Huzhou pen brush (made in Huzhou, Zhejiang province)

湖广总督(húguǎng zǒngdū)the governor of Hunan, Hubei, Guangdong and Guangxi during the Qing Dynasty

湖心亭(húxīntíng) a mid-lake pavilion; a pavilion in the middle of a lake

糊口(húkǒu) to make a living; to get by

糊涂虫(hútuchóng) a blunderer; a bungler;a nitwit

糊涂账(hútuzhàng)chaotic accounts; a mess

虎符(hǔfú) a tiger-shaped tally (issued to generals as imperial authorization for troop movement)

虎将(hǔjiàng)a brave general

虎落平阳被犬欺(hǔ luò píngyáng bèi quǎn qī) (lit.) "a tiger on level ground may be bullied by a dog" - A person who has lost his power or wealth may be bullied by lowlife

虎门条约(hǔmén tiáoyuē)the Treaty of Humen(1843)

《虎妞、阿Q逛厂甸》(hǔniū, ā Q guàng chǎngdiàn) *Huniur and A Q Wander in Changdian* - a skit starring Siqingaowa(斯琴高娃) and Yan Shunkai(严顺开)in

虎头牌(hǔtóupái) tiger-head tablet (erected in front of a magistrate's court)

虎穴龙潭(hǔxuè lóngtán)(lit.)"the tiger's den and the dragon's lair"-a dangerous place

户部(hùbù)the Ministry of Revenue

户部尚书(hùbù shàngshū) Minister of Revenue

户籍(hùjí)a household registration

户口(hùkǒu)a registered permanent residence; residence registration; *hukou*

户口本(hùkǒuběn)a permanent residence booklet

户口簿(hùkǒubù)a permanent residence booklet

户枢不蠹(hùshū bùdù)(lit.)"A door hinge is never eaten by worms"- constant activity staves off decay

户头(hùtóu)a bank account

户牖(hùyǒu)door and window

护城河(hùchénghé)a city moat; a moat

护犊子(hù dúzi)to shield one's child;to be biased in favour of one's own children

护短(hùduǎn)to shield one's shortcomings or errors; to conceal one's faults

护法(hùfǎ)①the protector of Buddhist doctrine②an almsgiver who donates his property to temples③to protect the constitution

护驾(hùjià)to protect the emperor

护身符(hùshēnfú)①an amulet②a protective talisman

沪剧(hùjù)Shanghai opera

扈从(hùcóng)a retainer; retinue; an attendant

花茶(huāchá)scented tea

花旦(huādàn)*huadan*(the painted female role in traditional opera)

花灯(huādēng)a festive lantern

花灯戏(huādēngxì)Huadeng opera(a folk opera in Hunan province)

花雕(huādiāo)Shaoxing rice wine

花鼓(huāgǔ)a flower-drum dance

花鼓戏(huāgǔxì)the flower-drum opera(in Hunan, Hubei, Anhui and Guangdong provinces)

花冠(huāguàn)a wedding hat

花棍舞(huāgùnwǔ)a rattle stick dance

花果山(huāguǒshān)the Mountain of Flowers and Fruit

花好月圆(huāhǎo yuèyuán)(lit.)"blooming flowers and full moon"- a perfect marriage

花和尚(huāhéshàng)①a non-observant monk②Lu Zhishen[鲁智深(a monk in the novel *The Water Margin*)]

花红(huāhóng)a bonus; an extra dividend

花花公子(huāhuā gōngzǐ)a playboy; a dandy

花花世界(huāhuā shìjiè)the dazzling human world with many temptations

花会(huāhuì)a flower market;a fair; a flower exhibition

花甲(huājiǎ)sixty years of age

花架子(huājiàzi)①showy but useless martial arts②mere form

花间词派(huājiān cípài)the Among-the-Flowers School of ci poetry(appeared in the late Tang Dynasty and the Five Dynasties)

花轿(huājiào)a bridal sedan chair

花街柳巷(huājiē liǔxiàng)the red-light district;a street of brothels

花卷(huājuǎn)steamed twisted rolls

花魁(huākuí)①the queen of flowers ②the leading courtesan

花脸(huāliǎn)a painted face role(in a traditional Chinese opera)

花翎(huālíng)a peacock tail feather on the hat of an official

《花木兰》(huāmùlán)*The Story of Hua Mulan* - a legend;a Yu opera

花鸟画(huāniǎohuà)the bird-and-flower painting(a kind of Chinese painting)

花拳绣腿(huāquán xiùtuǐ)showy martial arts with no practical usage

花容月貌(huāróng yuèmào)extremely beautiful and pretty

花天酒地(huā tiān jiǔ dì)to lead a life of debauchery

花烛夫妻(huāzhú fūqī)legally married husband and wife

华表(huábiǎo)ornamental pillars(erected in front of a palace or tomb)

华诞(huádàn)your birthday

华灯(huádēng)colorfully decorated lanterns

华发(huáfà)gray hair

华盖(huágài)a canopy;an umbrella-like cover over an imperial carriage

华侨(huáqiáo)overseas Chinese

华清池(huáqīngchí)Huaqing Pool(a hotspring in Xi'an, Shannxi province)

华人(huárén)Chinese

华文(huáwén)Chinese;Chinese language

华西(huáxī)the West of China

华夏(huáxià)China

华夏子孙(huáxià zǐsūn)the descendants of Chinese ancestry

华兴会(huáxīnghuì)the Society for the Revival of China(established in 1904)

华严宗(huáyánzōng)the Huayan Sect(of Buddhism)

《华严经》(huáyánjīng)*The Avatamsaka Sutra*; *The Flowery Splendor Sutra*

华严寺(huáyánsì)the Huayan Temple(in Guangzhou)

华裔(huáyì)an ethnic Chinese;a foreign citizen of Chinese origin

华语(huáyǔ)Chinese;Chinese language

华章(huázhāng)your brilliant writing or work

华胄(huázhòu)①the descendants of a noble family②Chinese people

滑稽戏(huájī xì)a situation comedy; a farce

划拳(huáquán) a finger-guessing drinking game

化干戈为玉帛(huà gān'gē wéi yùbó)to make peace; to turn hostility into friendship; to bury the hatchet

化境(huàjìng) sublimity; perfection; virtuosity

化缘(huàyuán)to beg alms

化斋(huàzhāi)to beg for food from door to door

华山(huàshān)Mount Hua

华佗(huàtuó) Hua Tuo (a famous doctor in the Han Dynasty)

画舫(huàfǎng) a barge; a colorful pleasure boat

画舫斋(huàfǎng zhāi)the Garden of the Painted Boat (an imperial palace for short stays in the Qing Dynasty)

画家村(huàjiā cūn)an artist village

画卷(huàjuàn)①a picture scroll; a handscroll of painting ② splendid scenery or a stirring scene

画龙点睛(huà lóng diǎn jīng)(lit.) "bring a dragon to life by painting in the pupils of the eyes" – to add the finishing touch; to put a cherry on the top

画皮(huàpí)(lit.)"a painted skin" – the disguise or mask of an evildoer

《画皮》(huàpí) *Painted Skin* – a story in *Strange Tales of Liaozhai* by Pu Songling(蒲松龄,1640 – 1715); a film directed by Chen Jiashang(陈嘉上)in 2008

画屏(huàpíng)a painted screen

画押(huàyā) to put a signature on; to sign

画院(huàyuàn) ① the imperial art academy②an art academy

画轴(huàzhóu) a scroll painting; a painting scroll

话白(huàbái) ① dialogues; monologues (in a play) ② the opening words(in traditional story telling)

话本(huàběn) a script for storytelling; storytellers' scripts

话柄(huàbǐng)a subject for ridicule; a laughing stock

话家常(huàjiācháng)to have a chitchat

话旧(huàjiù) to reminisce; to chat about the old days

《话说陶然亭》(huàshuō táorántíng) *Talking about Taoranting Park* – a short story by Deng Youmei (邓友梅,1931 –) in 1980

话匣子(huàxiázi)①a chatterbox②a gramaphone; a radio

怀才不遇(huáicái bùyù)to have no chance to show one's talents

怀春(huái chūn)to be anxious for love;to be in love

怀古(huáigǔ)to reflect on an ancient event;to meditate on the past

怀古伤今(huáigǔ shāngjīn)to meditate on the past and feel sad about the present

怀鬼胎(huái guǐtāi)to have an evil motive;to harbor an evil intention

怀柔政策(huáiróu zhèngcè)the policy of pacification

淮剧(huáijù)Huai opera

《淮南子》(huáinánzǐ)*The Book of Master Huainan* – a classical work compiled by Liu An(刘安,179 – 122 BC)

坏水(huàishuǐ)wicked ideas

坏心眼(huài xīnyǎn)evil intentions

还魂(huánhún)to revive(from death)

还俗(huánsú)to resume secular life;secularization

还阳(huányáng)to revive(from death)

还愿(huányuàn)①to fulfill a vow to a god②to keep one's promise

《还珠格格》(huánzhū gége)*Princess Pearl* – a TV drama directed by Sun Shupei(孙树培)in 1998

寰宇(huányǔ)the Earth;the whole world

缓兵之计(huǎnbīng zhī jì)a strategy to gain time in battle;a stalling tactic

宦官(huànguān)a eunuch

宦海(huànhǎi)the official circles;officialdom

宦海沉浮(huànhǎi chénfú)the ups and downs of officialdom;the vicissitudes of an official career

宦途(huàntú)an official career

宦游(huànyóu)to go around in pursuit of an official post

《浣溪沙》(huànxīshā)*Sand of Silk-washing Stream* – the name of the tune of a ci poem

换妻(huàn qī)wife swap;to swap wives

换亲(huàn qīn)to exchange daughters(in marriage to each other's sons)

换帖(huàntiě)to exchange cards bearing personal and family details and thereby become sworn brothers

换帖兄弟(huàntiěxiōngdì)a sworn brother;sworn brotherhood

患难之交(huànnàn zhī jiāo)friends in adversity

《荒山泪》(huāngshānglèi)*Tears of Barren Mountain* – a Bejing opera

荒冢(huāngzhǒng)a nameless grave;a derelict grave

皇储(huángchǔ) a crown prince; a designated heir(to the throne)

皇历(huánglì) the lunar almanac

皇粮(huángliáng) ①grain tax in imperial times②the salary paid by the government

皇上(huángshàng) the emperor; Your Majesty; His Majesty

皇太后(huángtàihòu) the empress dowager; the mother of the emperor

皇太子(huángtàizǐ) a crown prince

皇天(huángtiān) Heaven; Great Heaven

皇天后土(huángtiān hòutǔ) Heaven and Earth; the god of justice

皇位(huángwèi) throne

皇子(huángzǐ) a prince; a son of the emperor

皇族(huángzú) the imperial clan

黄包车(huángbāochē) a rickshaw

黄白之术(huángbái zhī shù) the art of the "yellow and white" (the Taoist alchemy)

黄巢起义(huángcháo qǐyì) the Huangchao Uprising(875 – 884)

黄道(huángdào) ecliptic

黄道吉日(huángdào jírì) a propitious date

黄道婆(huángdàopó) Huang Daopo (a female innovator of textile techniques in the Yuan Dynasty)

黄道十二宫(huángdào shíèrgōng) the 12 signs of the zodiac

黄帝(huángdì) the Yellow Emperor or Emperor Huang (the legendary ancestor of the Chinese nation)

《黄帝内经》(huángdì nèijīng) *The Yellow Emperor's Canon of Internal Medicine* – a Chinese classical treatise on medicine; *Classic of Internal Medicine*

《黄飞鸿》(huángfēihóng) *Once Upon a Time in China* – a film directed by Xu Ke(徐克) in 1991

黄河(huánghé) the Yellow River

《黄河大合唱》(huánghé dàhéchàng) *Yellow River Cantata* – a cantata by Xian Xinghai (冼星海,1904 – 1945)

黄鹤楼(huánghèlóu) Yellow Crane Pavilion; Yellow Crane Tower; Yellow Crane Pagoda (located in Wuhan, Hubei province)

黄花闺女(huánghuā guīnü) a virgin; a virgin girl

黄花后生(huánghuā hòushēng) a virgin boy

黄花女儿(huánghuā nǚ'r) a virgin girl

黄昏恋(huánghūn liàn) love between old people; love in the twilight years

黄教(huángjiào) Shamanism; theYellow Hat Sect

黄巾起义(Huángjīnqǐyì) the Yellow

Turbans Uprising(184 - 192)

黄金周(huángjīnzhōu) the golden week(the National Day Holidays or May Day holidays)

黄口小儿(huángkǒu xiǎo'ér) an ignorant young fellow

黄老君(huánglǎojūn) Lord Huanglao (one of the five legendary gods)

黄老哲学(huánglǎo zhéxué) Emperor Huang and Lao Tzu's philosophical teachings

黄历(huánglì) the lunar almanac

黄粱美梦(huángliáng měimèng) (lit.) "golden millet dream" - a daydream; a pipe dream

黄粱梦(huángliáng mèng) (lit.) "golden millet dream" - a daydream; a pipe dream

黄龙(huánglóng) ① Yellow Dragon [the capital of the Kingdom of Jin (1115 - 1234)] ② the enemy's den; the enemy's capital

黄毛丫头(huángmáo yātou) (derog.) an ignorant little girl

黄梅季(huángméijì) the rainy season

黄梅戏(huángméixì) Huangmei opera

《黄泥街》(huángní jiē) *Yellow Mud Street* - a novel by Canxue(残雪, 1953 -)

黄牛(huángniú) a ticket scalper

黄袍加身(huángpáo jiāshēn) to drape an imperial yellow robe over one's shoulder and acclaim him emperor; to be made emperor

黄片(huángpiàn)) an erotic and obscene film or TV program; a pornographic movie

黄埔军校(huángpǔ jūnxiào) Huangpu(or Whampoa) Military Academy

黄埔条约(huángpǔ tiáoyuē) the Treaty of Huangpu(or the Treaty of Whampoa signed in 1844)

黄浦江(huángpǔjiāng) the Huangpu River(in Shanghai)

黄泉(huángquán) the underworld; the netherworld

黄山(huángshān) Huangshan Mountain; Mount Huang

《黄石公三略》(huángshígōng sān luè) *The Three Strategies of Huang Shigong* - a book on the art of war written in the late period of Western Han dynasty

《黄土地》(huángtǔdì) *Yellow Earth* - a film directed by Chen Kaige(陈凯歌) in 1984

黄账(huángzhàng) a bad debt

黄种(huángzhǒng) yellow-skinned race

幌子(huǎngzi) ①a shop sign ②a pretence

灰色收入(huīsè shōurù) gray income; semi-overt income; off-the-book income

徽菜(huīcài)Anhui cuisine

徽调(huīdiào)the tune of Anhui opera

徽剧(huījù)Anhui opera

徽墨(huīmò)a Huizhou inkstick

回拜(huíbài)to pay a return visit

回禀(huíbǐng)to report back to

回春(huíchūn)①the return of spring ②to revive from death; to bring back to life

回光返照(huíguāng fǎnzhào)(lit.)"the last glow of the setting sun"-a momentary recovery of consciousness before death

回教(huíjiào)Islam;Muslim

回老家(huílǎojiā)①to die; to be dead ②to return to one's native place

回历(huílì)the Islamic calendar

回笼觉(huílóngjiào)to sleep again after getting up

回马枪(huímǎqiāng)a back thrust;to turn back to attack one suddenly

回门(huímén)to return to the bride's home(after the wedding)

回民(huímín)Hui;the Hui people;a Chinese Muslim

回师(huíshī)(of an army)to move troops back to;to move back to

回天乏术(huítiān fáshù)to have no power to save a desperate situation

回头客(huítóukè)a regular customer;a regular;a frequenter

回头率(huítóulǜ)a head-turning glance;attraction

回头人(huítóurén)a remarri-ed woman

回头是岸(huítóu shì àn)(lit.)"turn around and the shore is at hand"-it's never too late to repent

回文诗(huíwénshī)a palindromic poem;a poem in palindromic sequence;palindrome poetry

《回延安》(huí yán'ān)*Back to Yan'an*-a poem by He Jingzhī(贺敬之,1924-)

回音壁(huíyīnbì)the Echo Wall(in the Temple of Heaven in Bejing)

回族(huízú)the Hui nationality

悔婚(huǐhūn)to break an engagement

悔棋(huǐqí)to retract a move in a chess game

汇报演出(huìbào yǎnchū)a performance(for special audience)

汇演(huìyǎn)a joint performance

会道门(huìdàomén)superstitious sects and secret societies

会馆(huìguǎn)a provincial or county guild;a guild hall

会师(huìshī)to join forces

会试(huìshì)the imperial examination(held in the capital);the metropolitan examination

会演(huìyǎn)a joint performance

会意字(huìyìzì) an associative compound character

会元(huìyuán) the first in the imperial examination

会战(huìzhàn) to meet in a decisive battle; a battle

讳词(huìcí) a taboo word

讳疾忌医(huìjí jìyī) (lit.) "to refuse to receive medical treatment for fear that other people will know one's illness" – to refuse to face one's troubles or mistakes

讳字(huìzì) a taboo character

绘画六法(huìhuà liùfǎ) The Six Principles of Chinese Painting (viz., spiritual resonance, bone method, correspondence to the object, color suitability to type, planning and locating, transmission by copying)

荟萃(huìcuì) to assemble; to gather together

晦气(huìqì) bad luck

惠存(huìcún) please keep something as a souvenir

惠顾(huìgù) your patronage; to patronize

惠临(huìlín) your gracious presence

惠书(huìshū) your kind letter

惠赠(huìzèng) your kind help, gift or money

慧根(huìgēn) innate intelligence

慧心(huìxīn) wisdom

慧眼(huìyǎn) sharp eyes; discerning eyes

昏君(hūnjūn) a fatuous and self-indulgent ruler

婚联(hūnlián) a wedding couplet

《婚姻变奏曲》(hūnyīn biànzòuqǔ) *Marriage Variations* – a skit starring Guo Da (郭达) and Cai Ming (蔡明) in 1990

阍者(hūnzhě) a gatekeeper; a janitor

浑蛋(húndàn) a wretch; a bastard; son of a bitch

浑家(húnjiā) wife

浑球儿(húnqiúr) a wretch; a scoundrel

浑天仪(húntiānyí) a celestial globe

馄饨(húntun) wonton (a kind of dumpling)

混混儿(hùnhunr) a loafer; scoundrel

混世魔王(hùnshì mówáng) an evil monster; a human fiend

混账(hùnzhàng) a wretch; a bastard; the son of a bitch

混子(hùnzi) a hooligan; a quack

豁出去(huō chūqù) to risk everything for; to do something at any price

豁子(huōzi) ①a breach; an opening ②a harelipped person

活版(huóbǎn) typography

活宝(huóbǎo) a funny person; a bit of clown

活地图(huó dìtú)a walking map

活地狱(huó dìyù)a living hell

活佛(huófó)the Living Buddha

活计(huóji)a piece of handicraft; handiwork

活见鬼(huó jiànguǐ)nonsense; ridiculous

活教材(huó jiàocái)a living textbook

活口(huókǒu)① the survivor of an attempted murder ② a captive

活络(huóluò)smart; clever

活菩萨(huó púsà)a living Buddha; an extremely kind and generous person

活神仙(huó shénxiān)a living immortal; a supernatural being; a celestial being

活受罪(huó shòuzuì)to live a miserable life; to suffer greatly

活阎王(huó yánwang)the devil incarnate; a tyrant

《活着》(huózhe)*To Live* – a film directed by Zhang Yimou(张艺谋) in 1994

活字典(huó zìdiǎn)a walking dictionary

活字印刷(huózì yìnshuā)movable-type printing

活罪(huózuì)great hardships; bitter suffering

火把节(huǒbǎjié)the Torchlight Festival(a key traditional one for the Yi and Bai nationalities in Yunnan province)

《火车头》(huǒchētóu)*Locomotive* – a novel by Cao Ming(草明, 1913 – 2002) in 1950

火夫(huǒfū)①a stoker②a cook③a fireman

火罐儿(huǒ guànr)a cupping jar

火锅(huǒguō)a hotpot; a chaffy dish

《火红的年代》(huǒhóng de niándài) *The Fiery Years* – a film directed by Fu Chaowu(傅超武)et al. in 1974

火居道士(huǒjū dàoshi)a Taoist priest at home

火坑(huǒkēng)a living hell; an abyss of misery and suffering

火头军(huǒtóujūn)an army cook

伙房(huǒfáng)a kitchen

伙夫(huǒfū)a cook

伙计(huǒji)a partner; a fellow; a salesman; a shop assistant; a farm labourer

和稀泥(huò xīní)to mediate differences; to smooth things over(without consideration of principles)

货郎(huòláng)a walking vendor; an itinerant pedlar

货郎担(huòlángdàn)an itinerant pedlar's load

货郎鼓(huònlánggǔ)a rattle-drum

祸起萧墙(huò qǐ xiāoqiáng)(lit.) " troubles starting in one's own walls"– internal strife

祸水(huòshuǐ) the cause of a disaster;someone who brings trouble

《霍小玉传》(huòxiǎoyù zhuàn) *The Story of Huo Xiaoyu* – a Tang legend by Jiang Fang(蒋防,792 –?)

《霍元甲》(huòyuánjiǎ) ①*Fearless* – a film directed by Yuan Heping(袁和平) in 1982; or directed by Yu Rentai(于仁泰) in 2006 ② *Huo Yuanjia* – a TV drama directed by Xu Xiaoming(徐小明) in 1981

J

《击鼓骂曹》(jīgǔ màcáo) *Beat the Drum and Condemn Cao Cao* – a Beijing opera

机关(jīguān) government departments

机关干部(jīguān gànbù) a government functionary;an office worker

机灵鬼(jīlingguǐ) a smart person

机宜(jīyí) the principle of action; guidelines

机缘(jīyuán) a lucky chance; good luck

肌肤之亲(jīfū zhī qīn) to have sex

鸡肋(jīlèi) things of little value or interest

鸡毛蒜皮(jīmáo suànpí) trivial things

《鸡毛信》(jīmáoxìn) *The Letter with Feathers* – a film directed by Shi Hui(石挥) in 1954

鸡毛信(jīmáoxìn) (lit.) "a feathered letter"– an urgent letter

鸡鸣狗盗(jīmíng gǒudào) small tricks

鸡犬升天(jīquǎn shēngtiān) (lit.) "Even the chickens and the dogs rise up to the heavens"– the relatives and followers of a high official get promotion along with him

姬妾(jīqiè) concubines

屐履(jīlǚ) shoes

积德(jīdé) to do good deeds; to be philanthropic

积极分子(jījí fènzǐ) an activtist; an enthusiast

积阴德(jīyīndé) to do good deeds for one's next life;to accumulate merits for the afterlife

笄礼(jīlǐ) an ancient ceremony for a girl's coming of age

基诺族(jīnuòzú) the Jinuo nationality

赍志而殁(jīzhìérmò) to die without fulfilling one's ambitions

箕斗(jīdǒu) loops and whorls on a finger

箕踞(jījù) to sit with one's legs stretched out in an uncouth manner

畿辅(jīfǔ) the surrounding area of the capital of a state

稽考(jīkǎo) to ascertain;to verify

稽延(jīyán) to delay

稽延时日(jīyán shírì)to be considerably delayed

《激流三部曲》(jīliú sānbùqǔ) *The Torrents Trilogy* – the three novels, *The Family*, *Spring*, *Autumn*, by Ba Jin(巴金,1904 – 2005); *The Trilogy of the Turbulent Currents*

羁旅(jīlǚ) to stay long in a strange place; to live in a strange land

及第(jídì) to pass an imperial examination

及冠(jíguàn) to be of age; to grow into manhood

及笄(jíjī) to be of age; to grow into womanhood

及时雨(jíshíyǔ)(lit.) "timely rain" – timely assistance

吉剧(jíjù) Jilin opera

吉人天相(jírén tiānxiàng) a good person is blessed by Heaven; Heaven looks after a good man

吉日(jírì) an auspicious day; a lucky day

吉日良辰(jírì liángchén) an auspicious day

吉祥(jíxiáng) lucky; auspicious

吉祥物(jíxiángwù) a mascot

吉星(jíxīng) a lucky star

吉星高照(jíxīnggāo zhào) the lucky star shines brightly; to be blessed by a lucky star

吉凶(jí xiōng) good luck and bad luck

吉凶未卜(jí xiōngwèi bǔ) an unknown fate; fate is in the balance

吉兆(jízhào) the signs of good luck; a good omen

即景诗(jíjǐngshī) an extempore poem (inspired by what one sees)

即位(jíwèi) enthronement; to ascend to the throne

即兴诗(jíxìngshī) an extempore poem

极乐世界(jílèshìjiè) ①the Elysium; paradise②the final resting place

急递铺(jídìpù) express postal service

急就章(jíjiùzhāng) a hurriedly-completed work

急来抱佛脚(jí lái bào fójiǎo)(lit.) "to clasp Buddha's feet when in trouble" – to seek help in time of emergency

急先锋(jíxiānfēng) a daring vanguard

《集结号》(jíjiéhào) *The Assembly* – a film directed by Feng Xiaogang(冯小刚) in 2007

辑录(jílù) to compile

辑要(jíyào) a summary; an abstract

辑佚(jíyì) to edit

籍贯(jíguàn) the ancestral home; native place

《几度夕阳红》(jǐdù xīyánghóng) *The Last Sunset* – a novel by Qiong Yao (琼瑶,1938 –); a film directed by Li Hanxiang(李翰祥) in 1966

挤牙膏(jǐyágāo)(lit.)"to squeeze toothpaste out of a tube"- to be forced to tell or give something bit by bit

脊梁骨(jǐliáng gǔ)backbone

伎俩(jìliǎng)a trick

纪传体(jìzhuàntǐ)the history presented in a series of biographies

纪年(jìnián)a way of recording the years;annals;a chronological record of events

纪事(jìshì)recorded events;annals

纪事本末体(jìshì běnmòtǐ)a genre of the historical records of important events

纪要(jìyào)a summary

纪元(jìyuán)the beginning of an era

妓院(jìyuàn)a whorehouse;a brothel

忌辰(jìchén)the anniversary of somebody's death

忌讳(jìhuì)a taboo

忌口(jìkǒu)to avoid certain food

忌日(jìrì)the anniversary of somebody's death

继父(jìfù)a stepfather

继母(jìmǔ)a stepmother

继女(jìnǚ)a stepdaughter

继嗣(jìsì)to adopt a young heir

继位(jì wèi)to succeed to the throne

继子(jìzǐ)a stepson

寄父(jìfù)a foster father

寄名(jìmíng)to have a baby named by a monk or a Taoist

寄母(jìmǔ)a foster mother

祭奠(jìdiàn)to hold a memorial ceremony for

祭酒(jìjiǔ)sacrificial wine

祭礼(jìlǐ)①sacrificial rites②a memorial ceremony③sacrificial offerings

祭品(jìpǐn)sacrificial offerings

祭日(jìrì)the date for offering sacrifices to gods or ancestors;a fete-day

祭扫(jìsǎo)to offer sacrifice at and sweep the ancestral tomb

祭祀(jìsì)to offer sacrifice to(the deceased)

祭文(jìwén)a funeral oration

祭灶(jìzào)to offer sacrifices to the kitchen god

加官晋爵(jiāguān jìnjué)to be promoted to a higher office and rank

加塞儿(jiāsāir)to jump the queue

夹棍(jiāgùn)clamping rods(a penalty for criminals)

夹生饭(jiāshēngfàn)①half-cooked rice②a task not thoroughly performed

佳话(jiāhuà)a much-told story; a story on everybody's lips

佳境(jiājìng)an enjoyable and pleasant stage

佳丽(jiālì)a beauty

佳偶(jiā'ǒu)a happily married couple

佳期(jiāqī)a wedding day;a date

佳音(jiāyīn)good news

《家》(jiā) *The Family* – one of the *Torrents Trilogy* by Ba Jin(巴金)in 1933

家长里短(jiācháng lǐduǎn)domestic trivia

家常便饭(jiācháng biànfàn)(lit.) "homely food" – a common occurrence

家常话(jiāchánghuà)chitchat;small talk

家丑(jiāchǒu)a family scandal; dirty linen

家传秘方(jiāchuán mìfāng)a secret family recipe

家祠(jiācí)an ancestral temple or shrine

家慈(jiācí)my mother

家当(jiādàng)family belongings; property

家道(jiādào)the household finances

家道中落(jiādào zhōngluò)The family fortunes declined;the family is in straitened circumstances

家法(jiāfǎ)domestic discipline

家风(jiāfēng)family traits;the family tradition

家馆(jiāguǎn)a family school

家规(jiāguī)the domestic discipline; the family rules

家教(jiā jiào)family education

家眷(jiājuàn)①wife and children; family②wife

家里的(jiālǐde)my wife

家门(jiāmén)family

家庙(jiāmiào)an ancestral temple or shrine

家谱(jiāpǔ)genealogy;a family tree

家世(jiāshì)a family's social standing

家室(jiāshì)wife

家书(jiāshū)a letter from home; a home letter

家塾(jiāshú)a family school

家乡话(jiāxiānghuà)one's native dialect

家训(jiāxùn)family precepts

《家有儿女》(jiā yǒu érnǚ)*Home with Kids* – a TV drama directed by Lin Cong(林丛)in 2004

袈裟(jiāshā)a cassock

跏趺(jiāfū)to sit cross-legged

嘉靖(jiājìng)Jiajing(the reign title of Zhu Houcong, the 11th emperor of the Ming Dynasty)

嘉庆(jiāqìng)Jiaqing(the reign title of Yongyan,the 12th emperor of the Qing Dynasty)

嘉峪关(jiāyùguān)the Jiayu Pass (located in northwest of Gansu province)

甲第(jiǎdì)the highest rank in the imperial examinations

甲骨文(jiǎgǔwén)inscriptions on oracle bones;oracle bone inscriptions

甲科(jiǎkē) the list of those passed the imperial examination

《甲方乙方》(jiǎfāng yǐfāng) *The Dream Factory* – a film directed by Feng Xiaogang(冯小刚)in 1997

《甲午风云》(jiǎwǔ fēngyún) *The Naval Battle of* 1894 – a film directed by Lin Nong(林农)in 1962

甲午战争(jiǎwǔ zhànzhēng) the Sino-Japanese War of 1894 – 1895

甲胄(jiǎzhòu) armour

甲子(jiǎzǐ) a cycle of sixty years

假传圣旨(jiǎ chuán shèngzhǐ) to deliver a false imperial edict; to deliver a false order

假道学(jiǎ dàoxué) a hypocrite

假公济私(jiǎgōng jìsī) to use public office for private gain; jobbery

假借(jiǎjiè) a phonetic loan character

假仁假义(jiǎ rén jiǎ yì) to pretend to be a paragon of virtue; hypocrisy

假山(jiǎshān) a rockery

假小子(jiǎ xiǎozi) a tomboy

假洋鬼子(jiǎ yángguǐzi) a fake foreigner

假正经(jiǎ zhèngjing) to be hypocritical; to pretend to be a virtuous saint

价值连城(jiàzhí liánchéng) very precious; priceless

驾崩(jià bēng) demise; death; to die

架秧子(jià yāngzi) to make trouble; to create a disturbance

架子(jiàzi) ①airs; a haughty manner ③a stance

架子花(jiàzihuā) male character with a mask(in Chinese opera)

嫁出去的女儿,泼出去的水(jiàchūqù de nǚ'er, pōchūqù de shuǐ) girls who are married off are seen as water poured out on the ground

嫁鸡随鸡(jià jī suí jī) to follow the man you marry, no matter what he is

嫁奁(jiàlián) dowry; trousseau

嫁妆(jiàzhuang) dowry

稼穑(jiàsè) sowing and reaping; farm work

奸臣(jiānchén) a treacherous court official; a minister who is a traitor

奸夫(jiānfū) an adulterer

奸妇(jiānfù) an adultress

奸雄(jiānxióng) an arch-careerist

坚甲利兵(jiānjiǎ lìbīng) (lit.) "strong armour and sharp weapons" – a strong armed force

肩舆(jiānyú) a sedan chair

兼爱(jiān'ài) universal love

监察御史(jiānchá yùshǐ) Investigating Censor

监军(jiānjūn) a military inspector; a military supervisor

监司(jiānsī) an Imperial Inspector

笺牍(jiāndú) letters; correspondence

笺札(jiānzhá)letters;correspondence

笺注(jiānzhù)notes and commentary

剪彩(jiǎncǎi)to cut the ribbon at an opening ceremony

《剪灯新话》(jiǎndēng xīnhuà)*New Stories by the Oil Light* – a collection of short stories by Qu You(瞿佑,1347 – 1433)

《剪灯余话》(jiǎn dēng yú huà)*Complementary Stories by the Oil Light* – a collection of short stories by Li Zhen(李祯,1376 – 1451)

剪纸(jiǎnzhǐ)paper-cutting;a paper-cut

简化字(jiǎnhuàzì)simplified Chinese characters

简体字(jiǎntǐzì)simplified Chinese characters

见背(jiànbèi)to pass away

见鬼(jiànguǐ)①fantastic;absurd②to go to hell

见教(jiànjiào)your advice or suggestion

见面礼(jiànmiànlǐ)a gift given at one's first meeting with somebody

见识(jiànshi)①to experience;to undergo;to enrich one's experience②experience;knowledge;sensibleness

见世面(jiàn shìmiàn)to see the world;to enrich one's experience

见笑(jiànxiào)to laugh at;to incur ridicule

建安(jiàn'ān)Jian'an[the reign title of Liuxie,one of the emperors of the East Han Dynasty(25 – 220)]

建安风骨(jiàn'ān fēnggǔ)the lively spirit and style of Jian'an Literature;the thematic and stylistic features of Jian'an literature

建安七子(jiàn'ān qī zǐ)the "Seven Masters of the Jian'an Period"[Kong Rong(孔融,153 – 208),Chen Lin(陈琳,? – 217),Wang Can(王粲,177 – 217),Xu Gan(徐干,170 – 217),Ruan Yu(阮瑀,? – 212),Ying Yang(应玚,? – 217),Liu Zhen(刘桢,? – 217)];the seven outstanding literary figures during the Jian'an Period

建安文学(jiàn'ān wénxué)Jian'an Literature

建都(jiàndū)to found a capital

《建国大业》(jiànguó dàyè)*The Founding of A Republic* – a film directed by Han Sanping(韩三平)in 2009

建康(jiànkāng)Nanjing, Jiang-su provinte

建文(jiànwén)Jianwen,the reign title of Zhe Yunwen(the second emperor of the Ming Dynasty)

建元(jiàn yuán)Jianyuan(a reign title used by the first Chinese emperor of each dynasty)

饯行(jiànxíng)to give a farewell dinner

剑门关(jiànménguān) the Jianmen Pass(known as the most precipitous pass, located in Sichuan province)

剑侠(jiànxiá)a swordman

贱骨头(jiàngǔtou) a contemptible wretch

贱民(jiànmín)underclass; ragtag; untouchables

贱内(jiànnèi)my wife

贱人(jiànrén)a slut; a bitch

监生(jiànshēng) an Imperial Academy student; a student of the Imperial College

健锐营(jiànruìyíng)the Jianrui Army [set up by the Emperor Qianlong (乾隆,1711 - 1799)]

谏议大夫(jiànyì dàfū)the senior expostulative official

毽子(jiànzi)a shuttlecock

僭越(jiànyuè) to overstep one's authority

槛车(jiànchē) enclosed vehicle for transporting prisoners (in ancient China)

箭楼(jiànlóu) an embrasured watchtower

江北(jiāngběi) north of the Changjiang River(Yangtze River)

江东父老(jiāngdōng fùlǎo)the elders of one's hometown

《江河水》(jiāng hé shuǐ) *The Flowing River* - a urheen solo adapted by Huang Haihuai (黄海怀, 1935 - 1967) in 1962; *The River of Sorrow*

江湖(jiānghú) ①every corner of the country②wandering people

江湖好汉(jiānghú hǎohàn) a wild buddy; a brave man; a hero

江湖骗子(jiānghú piànzi) a swindler; a charlatan

江湖医生(jiānghú yīshēng) a mountebank; a quack

江湖义气(jiānghú yìqì) personal loyalty

江湖艺人(jiānghú yìrén) a wandering performer; an itinerant entertainer

江南(jiāngnán) south of the Changjiang River(Yangtze River)

江山(jiāngshān) ①the country; state power②landscape

江西诗派(jiāngxī shīpài) the Jiangxi School of Poetry [represented by Huang Tingjian (黄庭坚, 1045 - 1105) in the Northern Song Dynasty]

江洋大盗(jiāng yáng dà dào) a great robber; an infamous robber

江左(jiāngzuǒ) south of the Yangtze River

姜太公钓鱼(jiāngtàigōng diàoyú) (lit.) "Master Jiang casts a (hookless and baitless) line for the fish (that wanted to be caught)" - to be willing to fall into a trap

将军肚(jiāngjūndù) a beer belly; a potbelly

《将军令》(jiāngjūnlìng) *The General's Mandate* - a folk music started from the Tang Dynasty

将作大匠(jiāngzuò dàjiàng) an official in charge of civil engineering (in the West Han dynasties)

讲唱文学(jiǎngchàng wénxué) spoken and sung literature (popular oral literature)

讲排场(jiǎng páichǎng) to go in for pomp; to hanker after vainglory

讲义气(jiǎng yìqi) to be loyal to one's friends; to remain faithful to one's friends

奖掖(jiǎngyè) to reward and promote

蒋宋孔陈(jiǎng sòng kǒng chén) the Four Great Families[the families of Jiang Jieshi (蒋介石, 1887 - 1975), Song Ziwen(宋子文,1894 - 1971), Kong Xiangxi (孔祥熙, 1880 - 1967), Chen Guofu (陈果夫,1892 - 1951) and Chen Lifu(陈立夫,1900 - 2001)]

将门(jiàngmén) the family of a general

《将相和》(jiàngxiàng hé) *The General and the Minister Are Reconciled* - a Beijing Opera

交白卷(jiāo báijuàn) ①to hand in a blank examination paper②to fail to achieve anything

交拜(jiāobài) to exchange bows at a wedding ceremony

交杯酒(jiāobēijiǔ) the wedding wine (for a couple)

交恶(jiāowù) to become enemies

交情(jiāoqing) fellowship

郊寒岛瘦(jiāohán dǎoshòu) the poetic style of Meng Jiao(孟郊,751 - 814) and Jia Dao(贾岛,779 - 843)

娇嗔(jiāochēn) to grumble flirtingly or coquettishly; to pretend to be angry, in a flirtatious way

娇娘(jiāoniáng) a beautiful young woman

浇冷水(jiāolěngshuǐ) to pour cold water on; to discourage

骄子(jiāozǐ) a favourite child

教书匠(jiāoshūjiàng) a pedagogue; a teacher

教书先生(jiāoshū xiānsheng) a school teacher

《焦氏易林》(jiāoshì yìlín) *The Forest of Changes by Jiao* - a book by Jiao Yanshou(焦延寿) in the Han Dynasty

蛟龙(jiāolóng) ①a flood dragon②a person with great capability

嚼舌(jiáoshé) to gossip; to wag one's tongue

角楼(jiǎolóu) a turret

角门(jiǎomén) a side gate

佼佼者(jiǎojiǎozhě) an outstanding figure; a strong performer

绞脑汁(jiǎonǎozhī) to rack one's brain

饺子(jiǎozi) jiaozi; dumplings

饺子皮(jiǎozi pí) a dumpling wrapper

饺子馅(jiǎozi xiàn) the filling or stuffing for dumplings

脚本(jiǎoběn) a script

脚夫(jiǎofū) a porter; a man leading a pack horse or donkey

脚力(jiǎolì) footwork; strong legs

搅局(jiǎojú) to ruin a scheme or plan

剿饷(jiǎoxiǎng) taxation (imposed by the Ming government to suppress peasant uprisings)

叫板(jiàobǎn) ①to introduce a musical interlude (in traditional opera) ②to challenge

叫魂(jiàohún) to make a shocked child come to himself by calling his soul back; to call back one's soul (from a coma)

叫门(jiàomén) to call at the door

叫座(jiàozuò) a box-office success; to draw a large audience; to appeal to the audience

校雠(jiàochóu) (very formal) to collate

校勘(jiàokān) to collate

轿夫(jiàofū) a sedan-chair bearer

轿子(jiàozi) a sedan-chair

较劲儿(jiàojìnr) to challenge; to be at loggerheads

较真儿(jiàozhēnr) serious; to take to heart; to take seriously

教鞭(jiàobiān) a teacher's pointer

教师节(jiàoshījié) Teacher's Day

教头(jiàotou) a chief military instructor; a coach; a trainer

教正(jiàozhèng) to give comments and criticisms

接驾(jiējià) to welcome the emperor

接客(jiēkè) ①to receive a guest; to meet a guest ②to receive a brothel visitor or whoremaker

接亲(jiēqīn) ①to get married ②to meet the bride

接旨(jiēzhǐ) to receive an imperial edict

揭榜(jiēbǎng) to announce the results of an examination

揭短(jiēduǎn) to reveal a weakness; to show up one's shortcomings

揭盖子(jiē gàizi) (lit.) "to take the lid off" - to bring something. into the open; to expose the truth

揭竿而起(jiēgānérqǐ) to rise up in rebellion

揭老底(jiēlǎodǐ) to reveal the inside story; to disclose a buried secret; to dredge up the past

街坊四邻(jiēfang sìlín) neighbours;neighbourhood

街谈巷议(jiētán xiàngyì) street gossip;the word on the street;the talk of the town

街头剧(jiētoujù) a street performance;a street opera

街头卖艺(jiētou màiyì) to perform in the streets;to be a busker

街头诗(jiētoushī) a street poem(distributed in the street or posted on the street walls)

节本(jiéběn) an abridged edition

节操(jiécāo) moral integrity

节度使(jié dù shǐ) the provincial governor;Military Commisioner

节妇(jiéfù) a widow of moral integrity;a chaste widow

节骨眼(jiéguyǎn) a vital moment

节烈(jiéliè) rigorously chaste

节气(jiéqì) solar terms or periods

节译(jiéyì) an abridged translation

《节振国》(jiézhènguó) *Jie Zhenguo, the National Hero* – a Beijing opera

劫数(jiéshù) inexorable doom; predestined fate

洁身自好(jiéshēn zìhào) to preserve one's purity;to maintain one's moral integrity

结巴(jiēba) ①to stammer ②a stammerer

结拜(jiébài) to become sworn brothers or sisters

结拜兄弟(jiébài xiōngdì) sworn brothers

结党营私(jiédǎng yíngsī) to form a clique to pursue selfish interest

结发(jiéfà) marriage

结发夫妻(jiéfà fūqī) husband and wife(by first marriage)

结亲(jiéqīn) ①to marry;to get married ② to become related by marriage

结社(jiéshè) to form an association

结社自由(jiéshè zìyóu) freedom of association

结绳记事(jiéshéng jìshì) to keep records by tying knots

结义(jiéyì) to become sworn brothers or sisters

结义兄弟(jiéyì xiōngdì) sworn brothers

桀纣(jiézhòu) ①King Jie and King Zhou [the most ferocious kings in Chinese history:the last king of the Xia Dynasty(2070 – 1600 BC) and the last king of the Shang Dynasty (1600 – 1046 BC)] ② ferocious rulers

婕妤(jiéyú) Jieyu;a favoured beauty (title of an accomplished imperial concubine)

羯鼓(jiégǔ) the Jie drum(a kind of drum stemmed from the Jie nationality)

姐丈(jiězhàng) brother-in-law; the elder sister's husband

解放脚(jiěfàngjiǎo) unbound feet

解放军(jiěfàngjūn) the Liberation Army

解放区(jiěfàngqū) the liberated areas

解放区文学(jiěfàngqū wénxué) the literature in the liberated areas

《解放日报》(jiěfàng rìbào) *Liberation Daily*; *Jiefang Daily*

解放鞋(jiěfàngxié) the training shoes worn by liberation army soldiers

解放战争(jiěfàng zhànzhēng) the War of Liberation(1945 - 1949)

解甲归田(jiějiǎ guītián)(lit.)"to take off one's armor and return to the fields" - to be demobilized; to retire from office

解试(jiěshì) the qualifying examination

解手(jiěshǒu)(euphemism) to wash one's hands; to go to toilet; to relieve oneself

解差(jièchāi) an escort officer; a guard escorting prisoners

解首(jièshǒu) the scholar who won the first place in the provincial imperial examinations

解元(jièyuán) the scholar who won the first place in the provincial imperial examinations (in Ming-Qing dynasties)

介胄之士(jièzhòu zhī shì) men in armor; ancient warriors

戒尺(jièchǐ) a ferule; a ruler used for classroom discipline

戒刀(jièdāo) a Buddhist monk's knife

戒碟(jièdié) a monk or nun's certificate issued by the government

《借东风》(jiè dōngfēng) *By Means of the East Wind* - a Beijing opera

借古讽今(jiègǔ fěngjīn) to use the past to satirize the present

借光(jièguāng) excuse me (usu. before asking a question)

借花献佛(jièhuā xiàn fó) to offer presents provided by someone else; to offer somebody favors at the expense of another

借字(jiè zì) a borrowed word (a term in Chinese folk music)

巾帼(jīnguó) women

巾帼英雄(jīnguó yīngxióng) a heroic woman; a heroine

今草(jīncǎo)(calligraphy) one of the three styles of Caoshu script

《今古奇观》(jīngǔ qíguān) *The Wonders of the Present and the Past* - a collection of the scripts for storytelling compiled by the Aged Baoweng(抱瓮老人) in the late Ming Dynasty (1368 - 1644); *Wonderful Tales New and Old*

今文(jīnwén) the modern script

金榜(jīnbǎng) a list of successful candidates in the imperial examination

金榜题名(jīnbǎng tímíng) ①to pass the final imperial examination ②to succeed in the government examination

《金钗记》(jīnchāi jì) *Gold Hairpin* - a drama copied in 1431 -1432

金朝(jīncháo) the Jin Dynasty

金城汤池(jīnchéng tāngchí) an impregnable fortress; a strongly fortified city

金丹(jīndān) the gold elixir

金丹道(jīndāndào) the Inner Elixir Tao(a Taoist sect)

《金粉世家》(jīnfěn shìjiā) *The Story of A Noble Family* - a novel by Zhang Henshui(张恨水, 1895 - 1967) in the 1920s - 1930s

金刚(jīn'gāng) the Buddha's warrior attendant; a temple door god

金刚怒目(jīn'gāng nùmù) (lit.) "to glare like a temple door god" - to be fierce of visage; to look fierce like a temple door god; to have a ferocious expression

金戈铁马(jīngē tiěmǎ) (lit.) "shining spears and armoured horses" - the war or warriors

金箍棒(jīngūbàng) the golden cudgel (the weapon of the Monkey King in the novel *Journey to the West*)

《金光大道》(jīnguāng dàdào) *The Golden Road* - a novel by Hao Ran (浩然, 1932 - 2008) in 1970

金龟婿(jīnguīxù) a rich husband

《金婚》(jīnhūn) *Golden Wedding* - a TV drama directed by Zheng Xiaolong(郑晓龙) in 2006

金鸡独立(jīnjī dúlì) standing on one leg like a rooster(a position in Chinese boxing)

金鸡奖(jīnjījiǎng) the Golden Rooster Award(one of the top awards for movies in mainland China)

金交椅(jīnjiāoyǐ) an extremely powerful post

金科玉律(jīnkē yùlǜ) an infallible law

金口玉言(jīnkǒu yùyán) ①the emperor's utterances ② authoritative sta-tements or utterances

《金匮要略》(jīnkuì yàoluè) *Synopsis of Prescriptions of the Golden Chamber* - a book on Chinese medicine by Zhang Zhongjing(张仲景, ? 150 -? 219)

金兰(jīnlán) friendship; sworn brothers or sisters

金兰谱(jīnlánpǔ) a friendship card (with their names, birthday, birthplace etc. as a promise for sworn brothers or sisters)

金兰之交(jīnlán zhī jiāo) intimate friendship; sworn brotherhood

金莲(jīnlián) the bound feet

金陵(jīnlíng) Nanjing

金陵八家(jīnlíng bājiā) the Eight Well-known Painters of Nanjing [Gong Xian(龚贤), Fan Qi(樊圻), Wu Hong(吴宏), Zou Zhe(邹喆), Xie Sun(谢荪), Ye Xin(叶欣), Gao Chen(高岑) and Hu(胡)]

《金陵十三钗》(jīnlíng shísānchāi) *The Flowers Of War* - a novel by Yan Geling(严歌苓, 1957 -) in 2011; a film directed by Zhang Yimou(张艺谋) in 2011

金缕玉衣(jīn lǚ yùyī) jade burial suit sewn with fine gold thread

金銮殿(jīnluándiàn) Throne Hall; stately hall for an audience with the Emperor

金马奖(jīnmǎjiǎng) the Golden Horse Award(in Taiwan)

《金瓶梅》(jīnpíngméi) *The Golden Lotus* - a novel by Xiaoxiaosheng(笑笑生); *The Plum in The Golden Vase*

金嗓子(jīnsǎngzi) a beautiful voice

《金沙江畔》(jīnshājiāng pàn) *Along the Jinsha River* - a film directed by Fu Chaowu(傅超武) in 1963

《金蛇狂舞》(jīnshé kuáng wǔ) *Wild Dancing of the Golden Snake* - a piece of music composed by Nie Er(聂耳, 1912 - 1935) in 1934

金水河(jīnshuǐhé) the Golden Water Moat(flowing through the Imperial Palace and the Tiananmen Square)

金水桥(jīnshuǐqiáo) the Golden Water Bridge(the five bridges across the Golden Water Moat)

金童玉女(jīntóng yùnǚ) the boy and girl attendants of immortals

金文(jīnwén) the inscriptions on ancient bronze objects; bronze inscriptions

金屋藏娇(jīnwū cángjiāo) ①to keep a mistress in a splendid abode ②to take a concubine

金玉良言(jīnyù liángyán) invaluable advice

金枝玉叶(jīn zhī yù yè) the descendants of a royal family

金字招牌(jīnzì zhāopái) ①a gold-lettered signboard ②a vainglorious title

紧箍咒(jǐngūzhòu)(lit.) "the incantation of the golden hoop"(from the novel *Journey to the West*) - inhibition; trammel(used to keep somebody under control)

锦囊(jǐnnáng) an small embroidered bag

锦囊妙计(jǐnnáng miàojì) a stratagem(to deal with an emergency);a secret master plan (to tackle an emergency)

锦衣卫(jǐnyīwèi) a guard with embroidered uniform; the Secret Service of the Imperial Court

《锦衣卫》(jǐnyīwèi) *Secret Service of the Imperial Court* – a film directed by Lu Jungu(鲁俊谷) in 1984; *14 Blades* – a film directed by Li Rengang(李仁港) in 2010

尽孝(jìnxiào) to fulfil one's duty to one's parents; to treat parents with filial piety

尽忠(jìnzhōng) to be loyal to

妗母(jìnmǔ) aunt (the wife of one's mother's brother); maternal uncle's wife

妗子(jìnzi) aunt (the wife of one's mother's brother); maternal uncle's wife

近水楼台(jìnshuǐ lóutái) ①a waterfront pavilion②a favored position

近体诗(jìntǐshī) the modern style poetry

近朱者赤,近墨者黑(jìn zhū zhěchì, jìn mòzhě hēi) a person who keeps company with wolves will learn to howl; to be influenced by close association

进宫(jìngōng) to be put in prison; to be sent to jail

进贡(jìngòng) to pay tribute to

进谏(jìnjiàn) to remonstrate with

进局子(jìnjúzi) to be put in prison; to be sent to jail; to be taken into custody

进身之阶(jìnshēn zhī jiè) a stepping-stone(in one's official career)

进士(jìnshì) the Presented Scholar(a successful candidate in the highest level of imperial examination)

进香(jìnxiāng) a pilgrimage; to worship in a temple

进香客(jìnxiāngkè) a Buddhist pilgrim

晋朝(jìncháo) the Jin Dynasty(265 – 420)

晋祠(jìncí) Jin Temple (located in Taiyuan)

晋见(jìnjiàn) to call on (somebody holding high office); to have an audience with

晋剧(jìnjù) Shanxi opera

晋谒(jìnyè) to call on (somebody holding high office); to have an audience with

禁军(jìnjūn) the palace guards; the imperial guards

禁苑(jìnyuàn) the imperial park

觐见(jìnjiàn) to present oneself before(a monarch); to go to court; to have an audience with

京白(jīngbái)Beijing dialect in Beijing opera

京官(jīngguān)an official in the capital;a Beijing official

京胡(jīnghú)a Beijing opera fiddle(a small two-stringed bowed instrument used for the accompaniment in Beijing opera)

京华(jīnghuá)the capital

《京华烟云》(jīnghuá yānyún) *Moment in Beijing* – a Chinese novel by Lin Yutang(林语堂,1895 – 1976) in 1938 – 1939

京畿(jīngjī)the national capital and its neighborhood

京剧(jīngjù)the Beijing opera; the Beijing opera

京剧票友(jīngjù piàoyǒu)a Beijing opera fan

京剧艺术大师(jīngjù yìshù dàshī)a Beijing Opera master

京锣(jīngluó)a Beijing opera gong

京派(jīngpài)the Bejing school of Bejing opera

京腔(jīngqiāng)the Beijing accent

京师(jīngshī)the capital of a country

京师大学堂(jīngshī dàxuétáng)Capital Imperial University;the Imperial University of Beijing

京师同文馆(jīngshī tóngwénguǎn) Tongwen College of Beijing; the School of Combined Learning in the Capital

京戏(jīngxì)Beijing opera; Beijing opera

京绣(jīngxiù)Beijing embroidery (popular in Beijing)

京油子(jīngyóuzi)a cunning person from Beijing

京韵大鼓(jīngyùn dàgǔ)the Drum Song of Beijing(story-telling in Beijing dialect with drum accompaniment)

京兆尹(jīngzhàoyǐn)the chief executive of the national capital

京族(jīngzú)the Jing nationality(located in Guangxi Zhuang Autonomous Region)

经籍(jīngjí)the Confucian classics

经纶(jīnglún)statecraft; statesmanship

经络(jīngluò)(medicine) main and collateral channels;meridians

经脉(jīngmài)(medicine)meridians; channels

经师(jīngshī)the masters of Chinese Islam

经史子集(jīngshǐzǐjí)Confucian classics, history, philosophy and literature

经世之才(jīngshì zhī cái)a great ability to administrate the country

经书(jīngshū)Confucian classics

经学(jīngxué)the study of the Confucian classics

经义(jīngyì) the meaning of Confucian classics

《荆钗记》(jīngchāi jì) *Romance of A Hairpin* – a traditional drama in South China

荆轲刺秦王(Jīngkē cì qínwáng) ① Jingke attempted to assassinate the Qin Emperor② *The Emperor and the Assassin* – a film directed by Chen Kaige(陈凯歌) in 1999

惊堂木(jīngtángmù) a wooden block (used by a magistrate to strike the table to call for attention or order)

惊蛰(jīngzhé) the Awakening of Insects(the 3rd of the 24 Chinese solar terms, usually falling on 5th, 6th, or 7th of March)

旌表(jīngbiǎo) to confer honors on the virtuous and the worthy

精兵简政(jīngbīng jiǎnzhèng) better troops and simpler administration; to cut out dead wood in the administration; to streamline administration

精神文明(jīngshén wénmíng) spiritual civilization

精神污染(jīngshén wūrǎn) spiritual contamination; ideological pollution

精卫填海(jīngwèi tián hǎi) (lit.) "Jingwei, a mythical bird, tries to fill up the sea with pebbles" – a dogged determination to achieve one's purpose; to be adamant

《精武门》(jīngwǔmén) *The Fist of Fury* – a film directed by Chen Musheng(陈木胜) in 1995

精忠报国(jīngzhōng bàoguó) to serve one's country with unreserved loyalty; to repay one's country with supreme loyalty

井底之蛙(jǐngdǐ zhī wā) (lit.) "A frog in a well" – a person with a very limited outlook

井冈山(jǐnggāngshān) Jinggang Mountains(located in Jiangxi province)

景德镇(jǐngdézhèn) Jingdezhen (a town in Jiangxi Province, known for its pottery and porcelain)

景教(jǐngjiào) Nestorianism

景颇族(jǐngpōzú) the Jingpo nationality(located in Yunnan province)

景泰蓝(jǐngtàilán) cloisonne; cloisonne enamel

儆戒(jǐngjiè) to warn; to admonish

《警察故事》(jǐngchá gùshì) *Two Jolly Cops* – a film directed by Jackie Chan(成龙) in 1985

《警察与小偷》(jǐngchá yǔ xiǎotōu) *Cops and Robbers* – a skit starring Chen Peisi(陈佩斯) and Zhu Shimao(朱时茂) in 1991

警花(jǐnghuā) a young and beautiful policewoman

警世(jǐngshì) to warn or admonish the world

《警世通言》(jǐngshì tōngyán) *Comprehensive Stories to Admonish the World* – a collection of short stories by Feng Menglong(冯梦龙,1574 – 1646) in 1624

净地(jìngdì)(Buddhism) the Pure Land

净角(jìngjué) jing(painted-face role in traditional opera)

净土(jìngtǔ)(Buddhism) the Pure Land

净土宗(jìngtǔzōng)(Buddhism) the Pure Land Sect

竞渡(jìngdù) a boat race

敬酒(jìngjiǔ) to propose a toast

敬启者(jìngqǐzhě) To whom it may concern; Dear Sir/Madam

敬上(jìngshàng) Yours respectfully; Yours sincerely

靓妆(jìngzhuāng) to be gorgeously dressed

靖边(jìngbiān) to pacify the border region

靖康(jìngkāng) the reign title of Zhaohuan(1126 – 1127) [the emperor of the Northern Song Dynasty(960 – 1127)]

靖康之乱(jìngkāng zhī luàn) the Catastrophe of Jingkang(1127)

靖乱(jìngluàn) to put down a rebellion

《静夜思》(jìngyè sī) *Thinking in the Silent Night* – a poem by Li Bai(李白,701 – 762)

镜花水月(jìnghuā shuǐyuè)(lit.) "the flowers in the mirror and the moon in the water" – an illusion

《镜花缘》(jìnghuāyuán) *Flowers in a Mirror* – a novel by Li Ruzhen(李汝珍,1763 – 1830)

赳赳武夫(jiūjiū wǔfū) a stalwart; a martial man

揪辫子(jiū biànzi) to seize upon one's faults

揪痧(jiūshā) to pinch the patient's neck (a folk treatment for sunstroke)

九重天(jiǔchóngtiān) the highest heavens

九重霄(jiǔchóngxiāo) the highest heavens

九鼎(jiǔdǐng)(lit.) "the nine tripods" – something of great importance

《九辩》(jiǔbiàn) *Nine Arguments* – a poem by Song Yu(宋玉,301 – 240 BC) in 249 BC

《九歌》(jiǔgē) *Nine Songs* – the poems by Qu Yuan(屈原,339 – 278 BC)

九宫格(jiǔgōnggé) squared paper for practicing Chinese calligraphy

九华山(jiǔhuáshān)Jiuhua Mountain

九节鞭(jiǔjiébiān) a nine-section iron chain; a nine-section whip; cat of nine tails

九九表(jiǔjiǔbiǎo) multiplication table

九龙壁(jiǔlóngbì) the Nine-dragon Wall (built opposite to the main gate of palaces and temples)

九门提督(jiǔmén tídū) the chief commander of the infantry

九品(jiǔpǐn) the nine grades of rank in imperial China

九卿(jiǔqīng) the nine ministers of the central government

九衢(jiǔqú) bustling downtown streets

九泉(jiǔquán) the nether world

九泉之下(jiǔquán zhī xià) after death; in the nether world

九三学社(jiǔsānxuéshè) the Jiu San Society (a democratic party in China)

九天(jiǔtiān) the highest heavens

九头鸟(jiǔtóuniǎo) ①a nine-headed bird - a bad omen②a crafty fellow

九尾狐(jiǔwěihú) a nine-tailed fox - a crafty and villainous person

九五之尊(jiǔwǔzhīzūn) the stateliness of the emperor; the royal prerogative; the imperial throne

九霄(jiǔxiāo) the highest heavens

九叶诗派(jiǔyè shīpài) the Nine Leaves Poets

九一八事变(jiǔyībā shìbiàn) the September 18 Incident; the Mukden Incident(1931)

九译令(jiǔyìlìng) official in charge of the minority affairs

九寨沟(jiǔzhàigōu) Jiuzhaigou (a well-known scenic spot in Sichuan province)

《九章》(jiǔzhāng) *Nine Elegies* - the poems by Qu Yuan (屈原, 339 - 278 BC)

《九章算术》(jiǔzhāng suànshù) *Nine Chapters on the Mathematical Art*; *Nine Chapters on Arithmetic* - the first China's writings on mathematics, completed in 1st century

九州(jiǔzhōu) China

九族(jiǔzú) the nine clans; the nine agnates; one's family and direct relatives

久病床前无孝子(jiǔbìng chuángqián wú xiàozǐ) no dutiful children can endure attending their bedridden parent at the bedside for so long

久仰(jiǔyǎng) to admire or worship (somebody) for a long time; to have long desired to know (somebody)

酒保(jiǔbǎo) a bartender; a barkeeper

酒鳖子(jiǔbiēzi) a wine container

酒鬼(jiǔguǐ) a drunkard, a sot

《酒国》(jiǔ guó) *The Republic of Wine - a novel by Mo Yan*(莫言, 1955 -) in 1989

酒后吐真言(jiǔhòu tǔ zhēnyán) when wine is in, truth is out

酒家(jiǔjiā) ①a wineshop; a tavern ② a restaurant

酒帘(jiǔlián) a wineshop sign

酒令(jiǔlìng) a drinking game

酒楼(jiǔlóu) a restaurant

酒囊饭袋(jiǔnáng fàndài) a good-for-nothing

酒肉朋友(jiǔròu péngyǒu) a mercenary friend; a fair-weather friend

酒色之徒(jiǔsè zhī tú) a voluptuary; a debauchee; a libertine

酒肆(jiǔsì) a wineshop; a public house

旧部(jiùbù) former subordinates

旧历(jiùlì) the lunar calendar

旧历年(jiùlìnián) the lunar new year

旧学(jiùxué) the old Chinese learning

旧雨(jiùyǔ) a former friend; an old friend

旧雨新知(jiùyǔ xīnzhī) old and new friends

柩车(jiùchē) a hearse

救驾(jiùjià) ①to rescue the emperor ②to come to the rescue

救亡(jiùwáng) to save the nation; national salvation

救亡图存(jiùwáng túcún) to save the nation from subjugation and ensure its survival

救亡运动(jiùwáng yúndòng) the national salvation movement

救星(jiùxīng) a liberator; a savior

舅父(jiùfù) uncle(mother's brother); a maternal uncle

舅妈(jiùmā) aunt(mother's brother's wife); a maternal uncle's wife

舅母(jiùmǔ) aunt(mother's brother's wife); a maternal uncle's wife

舅嫂(jiùsǎo) sister-in-law(wife's brother's wife)

舅子(jiùzi) brother-in-law(wife's brother)

居民委员会(jūmín wěiyuánhuì) a neighborhood committee

居丧(jūsāng) bereavement and mourning

居士(jūshì) ①a lay Buddhist ②a retired scholar

居孀(jūshuāng) to remain a widow; to live in widowhood

拘礼(jūlǐ) to be punctilious; to stand on ceremony

拘票(jūpiào) an arrest warrant

鞠躬尽瘁,死而后已(jūgōng jìncuì, sǐér hòuyǐ) to spare no effort in the performance of one's duty until one's death

局子(júzi) a police station

《菊豆》(júdòu) *Ju Dou* - a film directed by Yang Fengliang(杨凤良) in 1990

举案齐眉(jǔ'àn qíméi)(husband and wife) to treat each other with respect

举国上下(jǔguó shàngxià) the whole nation from top to bottom

举人(jǔrén) juren(the Recommended Man)(a successful candidate in the provincial imperial examination)

举业(jǔyè) to take the imperial examination

举子(jǔzi) a candidate for the imperial examination

句读(jùdòu) pauses in a sentence; the period and the comma; sentences and phrases

巨擘(jùbò) an authority(in a certain field)

巨匠(jùjiàng) a great master; a consummate craftsman; a giant

剧坛(jùtán) theatrical circles

惧内(jùnèi) to be henpecked; to fear one's wife

聚宝盆(jùbǎopén)(lit.)"a treasure bowl" - a place rich in natural resources; a cornucopia

聚赌(jùdǔ) to get together to gamble; to gamble in group

聚首(jùshǒu) to meet; to gather

《捐款》(juānkuǎn) *Donation* - a skit starring Zhao Benshan(赵本山) in 2010

卷铺盖(juǎn pūgai) to pack up and get out; to get the sack; to be dismissed

卷帙(juànzhì) books; volumes

卷轴画(juànzhóuhuà) a scroll painting

卷宗(juànzōng) ①folder ②dossier; file

绢本(juànběn) a silk scroll

绢花(juànhuā) a silk flower

绢画(juànhuà) a classical Chinese painting on silk; a silk painting

眷村(juàncūn) army village; military dependents' village(in Taiwan)

角力(juélì) wrestle

《决裂》(juéliè) *Breaking with Old Ideas* - a film directed by Li Wenhua(李文化) in 1975

决一雌雄(jué yī cíxióng) to fight it out; to have it out with

决一死战(jué yī sǐzhàn) to fight to the death; to do or die; to fight with a rope round one's neck

诀别(juébié) to bid farewell; to part

绝笔(juébǐ) ①the last words(written before somebody's death) ②the last work(of an author or painter)

绝唱(juéchàng) the peak of poetic perfection; a perfect masterpiece

绝代佳人(juédài jiārén) a matchless beauty; a peerless beauty

《绝代双娇》(juédài shuāngjiāo) *Pretty Twins* – a TV drama directed by Hua Jianmeng(华践盟) in 2000

绝户(juéhù) ①without offspring ②a childless person

绝活(juéhuó) a unique technique

绝句(juéjù) a *jueju* poem; a curtailed verse; a poem of four lines

《绝望中诞生》(juéwàng zhōng dànshēng) *Emerge from Despair* – a novelette by Zhu Sujin (朱苏进, 1953 –) in 1989

绝招(juézhāo) ①a unique skill ②an unexpected tactic

倔驴(juèlǘ) a very stubborn person

军阀(jūnfá) a warlord

军阀混战(jūnfá hùnzhàn) the tangled warfare between warlords

军阀作风(jūnfá zuòfēng) a warlord style

军赋(jūnfù) military taxation

军机处(jūnjīchù) Council of Military Plan (under Manchu government)

军机大臣(jūnjī dàchén) Grand Minister of State

军令(jūnlìng) a military order

军令状(jūnlìngzhuàng) a military pledge

军旅小说(jūnlǚ xiǎoshuō) a military novel

军旅作家(jūnlǚ zuòjiā) military wri ters

军棋(jūnqí) military chess; army chess (a Chinese stratego game)

军嫂(jūnsǎo) a soldier's wife; a military spouse

军师(jūnshī) a war counsellor; a military counsellor

军统(jūntǒng) the Bureau of Investigation and Statistics of the Military Council (BIS) (founded in 1938)

军饷(jūnxiǎng) a soldier's pay and provisions

军宣队(jūnxuānduì) a military team to promote Maoism; Mao Zedong Thought Propaganda team of the PLA

军属(jūnshǔ) the soldier's dependant; military family

君侧(jūn cè) a monarch's trusted followers

君子(jūnzǐ) a nobleman; a person of noble character; a gentleman

君子三戒(jūnzǐ sānjiè) the gentleman's three commandments (a gentleman should not be fond of sex when he is young, not be aggressive when he is middle-aged and not seek ease and comfort when he is old)

君子协议(jūnzǐ xiéyì) a gentlemen's agreement

君子之交(jūnzǐ zhī jiāo) the evergreen friendship between gentlemen

钧座(jūnzuò) Your Excellency; Your Honour

郡县制(jùnxiànzhì) the system of prefectures and counties; the administrative system of commanderies and counties

郡守(jùnshǒu) Commandery Governor

郡主(jùnzhǔ) the daughter of a prince

K

开春(kāichūn) the beginning of spring

开裆裤(kāidāngkù) open crotch underpants; split pants

开倒车(kāi dàochē) (lit.) "to reverse the car" – to turn back the clock

开方子(kāi fāngzi) to write out a prescription; to prescribe

开光(kāiguāng) consecration

开国大典(kāiguó dàdiǎn) ① founding ceremony (of a new state) ② *The Founding Ceremony of New China* – a film directed by Li Qiankuan(李前宽) in 1989

开国元勋(kāiguó yuánxūn) founder of a state; a founding father

开后门(kāi hòumén) (lit.) "to open the back door" – to make an under-the-counter deal; to offer advantages to one's friends or relatives by underhand means; to abuse one's power to secure advantages for others

开化(kāihuà) to be civilized

开荤(kāihūn) to begin or resume a meat diet; to end a meatless diet

开戒(kāijiè) to break an abstinence

开局(kāijú) the opening (of a chess, game, etc.)

开卷有益(kāijuàn yǒuyì) To open a book is always beneficial; reading enriches the soul

开脸(kāiliǎn) to remove fine hair from a bride's face (on the girl's wedding day)

开路先锋(kāilù xiānfēng) a pathbreaker; a pioneer

开绿灯(kāi lǜdēng) to give the green light to; to give somebody permission (to do something)

开锣(kāiluó) to begin a project

开门红(kāiménhóng) a good start

开门七件事(kāimén qījiànshì) the daily necessities of life (viz., firewood, rice, oil, salt, soy, vinegar and tea)

开明绅士(kāimíng shēnshì) enlightened gentry

开山祖师(kāishān zǔshī) the founder of a religious sect or a school of thought

开涮(kāishuàn) (slang) to make a fool of (somebody)

开台锣鼓(kāitái luógǔ)a flourish of gongs and drums indicating the beginning of a theatrical performance; a prelude

开天辟地(kāitiān pìdì)the creation of heaven and earth; the beginning of history

开天窗(kāi tiānchuāng)the empty space(left on a newspaper because a certain article has been deleted by the authority and the substitute does not fill the space perfectly); to leave a blank on a publication

开小差(kāi xiǎochāi)①to be absent without leave②to be absent-minded

开小灶(kāi xiǎozào)to give special favor

开洋荤(kāi yánghūn)①to have a taste of exotic food the first time② to experience or have a taste of something new

开夜车(kāi yèchē)to work late into the night; to work at night

开元(kāiyuán)Kaiyuan[the reign title of Li Longji(李隆基, 685 - 762), an emperor of the Tang Dynasty 618 - 907)]

《开元占经》(kāiyuán zhànjīng) *The Treatise on Astrology of the Kaiyuan Era* - an astrological work compiled by Gautama Siddha(瞿昙悉达)in 718 - 726

开斋(kāizhāi)to resume a meat diet

开张(kāizhāng)①to open a business ②to open for business; to start; to begin

揩油(kāiyóu)to get petty advantages at expense of other people or the state

楷模(kǎimó)a model; an example; a paragon

楷书(kǎishū)(calligraphy)the regular script

楷体(kǎitǐ)(calligraphy)the regular script

看家本领(kānjiā běnlǐng)an unique skill; an ace up one's sleeve; a stock-in-trade

看家狗(kānjiāgǒu)a watch dog; a house dog; a loyal servant

戡乱(kānluàn)to suppress a rebellion

侃大山(kǎndàshān)to shoot the breeze; to chew the fat; to engage in idle gossip

侃爷(kǎnyé)a big talker

看茶(kànchá)to serve tea

看风水(kàn fēngshuǐ)to practice geomancy(for selecting a site for a tomb, house, etc.)

看破红尘(kànpò hóngchén)to see through the vanity of the world; to be disillusioned with the mortal world

看手相(kàn shǒuxiàng)to practise

palmistry; read palms (as a means of fortune-telling); palm reading

看相(kànxiàng) to tell one's fortune; to practise physiognomy

看笑话(kàn xiàohuà) to watch the fun; to have a good laugh at somebody

康熙(kāngxī) Kangxi [the reign title of XuanYe(玄烨), the second emperor of the Qing Dynasty 1644 – 1912)]

《康熙大帝》(kāngxī dàdì) *Kangxi the Great* – a TV drama directed by Chen Jialin(陈家林) in 2001

《康熙王朝》(kāngxī wángcháo) *Kangxi Dynasty* – a TV drama directed by Chen Jialin(陈家林) in 2001

《康熙微服私访记》(kāngxī wēifú sīfǎngjì) *Emperor Kangxi's Inspection Trip incognito* – a TV drama directed by Zhang Guoli (张国立) in 1997

《康熙字典》(kāngxī zìdiǎn) *The Great Kangxi Dictionary*; *Dictionary of the Kangxi Emperor*

康庄大道(kāngzhuāng dàdào) a broad road

慷慨悲歌(kāngkǎi bēigē) to chant in a heroic but mournful tone; to sing with solemn fervor

扛长工(káng chánggōng) to work as a full-time farm laborer; to be a full time laborer (in old China)

扛长活(káng chánghuó) to work as a full-time farm laborer; to be a full time farm laborer (in old China)

扛大个儿(káng dàgèr) to work as a porter

扛大梁(káng dàliáng) to take up the main task; to become the mainstay (of a family, etc.)

扛活(ránghuó) to work as a farm laborer

伉俪(kànglì) a married couple; husband and wife

抗大(kàngdà) the Chinese People's Anti-Japanese Military and Political College

抗洪救灾(kànghóng jiùzāi) to fight flooding and provide disaster relief

抗美援朝(kàngměi yuáncháo) the War to Resist US Aggression and Aid Korea (1950 – 1953); the Korean War

抗日民族统一战线(kàngrì mínzú tǒngyī zhànxiàn) the anti-Japanese national united front; the Second United Front (1936 – 1941)

抗日战争(kàngrì zhànzhēng) the War of Resistance Against Japan (1937 – 1945); the Anti-Japanese War (1937 – 1945)

抗战(kàngzhàn) the Anti-Japanese War

炕头(kàngtóu) the edge of a *kang*

炕桌(kàngzhuō) a *kang* table

考妣(kǎobǐ) deceased parents

考试院(kǎoshìyuàn) the Department of Examinations of the Republic of China

烤鸭(kǎoyā) roast duck

烤烟(kǎoyān) flue-cured tobacco

烤羊肉串(kǎo yángròuchuàn) kebab

犒赏三军(kàoshǎng sānjūn) to to reward soldiers with a feast; to reward the soldiers

靠边儿站(kàobiānr zhàn) to stand aside; to be dismissed from one's post; to be deprived of authority

靠盘儿(kàopánr) reliable

靠谱(kàopǔ) reliable; reasonable

靠旗(kàoqí) armor flags or pennants (worn in traditional opera)

靠山(kàoshān) a patron; a backer

苛捐杂税(kējuān záshuì) exorbitant taxes and levies

苛政(kēzhèng) a harsh government; a tyrannical government

苛政猛于虎(kēzhèng měng yú hǔ) tyranny is fiercer than a tiger; a bad government is more dreaded than tigers

科白(kēbái) the actions and spoken parts in classical Chinese drama

科班(kēbān) ① an old-style opera school ② regular professional training

科班出身(kēbān chūshēn) to be professional by training; to be professionally trained

科场(kēchǎng) an imperial examination hall

科第(kēdì) to grade the candidates in the imperial examinations

科诨(kēhùn) to make impromptu comic gestures and remarks

科甲(kējiǎ) the top grade in the imperial examination

科举(kējǔ) the imperial examination

科举制度(kējǔ zhìdù) the imperial examination system; the civil service examination system

科考(kēkǎo) the preliminary examination (prior to the provincial examinations in the Qing Dynasty)

窠臼(kējiù) a set pattern; stereotype

磕巴(kēba) to stammer; a stutter

磕蜜(kēmì) to strike up a conversation with a strange girl

磕头(kētóu) to kowtow

蝌蚪文(kēdǒuwén) the tadpole script (an ancient form of Chinese script)

《可可西里》(kěkěxīlǐ) *Mountain Patrol* - a film directed by Lu Chuan (陆川) in 2004

可圈可点(kěquān kědiǎn) brilliant; remarkable

《渴望》(kěwàng) *Aspiration* - a TV

drama directed by Lu Xiaowei(鲁晓威)in 1990

可汗(kèhán)Khan

克夫(kèfū)to bring bad luck to one's husband

克己复礼(kèjǐ fùlǐ)to deny self and return to propriety;to restrain oneself and abide by the rites

克绍箕裘(kèshào jīqiú)to follow in one's father's footsteps

克星(kèxīng)①a powerful remedy②an invincible opponent

刻本(kèběn)a block-printed edition

刻花(kèhuā)engraved designs; a carved design

客帮(kèbāng)groups of merchants

客串(kèchuàn)to be a guest performer; to play a part in a professional performance

客官(kèguān)a customer or guest

客家(kèjiā)the Hakkas

客家话(kèjiāhuà)Hakka dialect

客家土楼(kèjiā tǔlóu)a Hakka castle (dwellings)

客卿(kèqīng)keqing(a guest official from one's feudal state serving in the court of another)

客商(kèshāng)a traveling trader

客死他乡(kèsǐ tāxiāng)to die in a strange land

客岁(kèsuì)last year

客套(kètào)polite formulae

客套话(kètàohuà)polite formulae or expressions

客姓(kèxìng)a foreign surname(in a village where a clan lives)

客栈(kèzhàn)an inn

课税(kèshuì)to levy texes;taxes

溘然长逝(kèrán chángshì)to pass away;to die

啃骨头(kěn gǔtou)(lit.)"to gnaw a bone"-to do a hard job;to fulfill a difficult task;to get over a difficulty

坑爹(kēngdiē)cheating

空巢家庭(kōngcháo jiātíng)an "empty nest"family(a family where the old parents live alone after their children have grown up and left home)

空城计(kōngchéngjì)the empty-fortress stratagem(presenting a bold front to conceal a weak defense)

《空城计》(kōngchéngjì)*The Empty-fortress Stratagem*;*The Empty Town Ruse*-a traditional drama

空门(kōngmén)Buddhism

《空山鸟语》(kōngshān niǎoyǔ)*Birdsong in the Quiet Valley*-an urheen solo

空头支票(kōngtóu zhīpiào)a rubber check;an empty promise

空心萝卜(kōngxīn luóbo)a person without genuine talent

空穴来风(kōngxué láifēng)a groundless rumour

空中楼阁(kōngzhōng lóugé) castles in the air

箜篌(kōnghóu) the Chinese standing harp(a 23-stringed traditional Chinese musical instrument)

孔方兄(kǒngfāngxiōng) money

孔夫子(kǒngfūzǐ) Confucius; Master Kong

孔府(kǒngfǔ) Confucius Family Mansion

孔家店(kǒngjiādiàn) Confucius and Sons; the School of Confucius

孔教(kǒngjiào) Confucianism

孔林(kǒnglín) Confucius Forest; Confucius Cemetery (located in Qufu, Shangdong province)

孔孟之道(kǒngmèng zhī dào) the doctrines of Confucius and Mencius; Confucianism

孔庙(kǒngmiào) Confucius Temple

孔明灯(kǒngmíngdēng) a Kongming lantern[invented by Kong Ming(孔明,181 - 234)]

《孔雀东南飞》(kǒngquè dōngnán fēi) *The Peacock Flies to the Southeast* - one of the music-bureau poems of the Han Dynasty; *Southeast the Peacock Flies*

孔武有力(kǒngwǔ yǒulì) to have great physical strength and courage; full of energy; very strong

《孔乙己》(kǒngyǐjǐ) *Kong Yiji*; *A Pedantic Scholar* - a short story by Lu Xun(鲁迅,1881 - 1936) in 1919

孔子(kǒngzǐ) Confucius

《孔子》(kǒngzǐ) *Confucius* - a film directed by Hu Mei(胡玫) in 2010

抠门儿(kōuménr) stingy; to be a scrooge

抠字眼儿(kōu zìyǎnr) to find fault with the choice of words; to pay too much attention to the shades of meaning of words

口碑(kǒubēi) public praise

口北(kǒuběi) to the north of the Great Wall

口耳之学(kǒuěr zhī xué) second-hand knowledge

口风(kǒufēng) one's intention as revealed in what one says

口福(kǒufú) the good fortune to eat something delicious; the gourmet's luck

口赋(kǒufù) a poll tax on children

口腹之欲(kǒufù zhī yù) an appetite for food and drink

口技(kǒujì) oral stunts; ventriloquism

口角(kǒujué) a quarrel; a bicker; to quarrel; to bicker

口诀(kǒujué) a pithy formula

口粮(kǒuliáng) grain ration

口头禅(kǒutóuchán) a pet phrase

口头文学(kǒutóu wénxué) oral literature

口头语(kǒutóuyǔ)a pet phrase

口诛笔伐(kǒuzhū bǐfá)to condem both in speech and in writing

叩拜(kòubài)to *kowtow*; to pay one's respect

叩阍(kòuhūn)to lodge a complaint with the imperial court

叩见(kòujiàn)to visit; to call on (one's superior)

叩首(kòushǒu)to kowtow

叩头(kòutóu)to kowtow

叩谢(kòuxiè)to kowtow in thanks; to offer earnest thanks

扣帽子(kòu màozi)to put a label on; to give somebody a label; name-calling

扣屎盆子(kòu shǐpénzi)to insult; to bring disgrace

哭鼻子(kūbízi)to weep

哭穷(kūqióng)to complain about impoverishment; to pretend to be poor

哭丧(kūsāng)to wail at funeral; keening

哭丧棒(kūsāngbàng)the keening stick (used by the son of the deceased in a funeral procession)

《哭祖庙》(kū zǔmiào)*Crying in the Ancestral Temple* – a Beijing opera

窟宅(kūzhái)the bandits' lair

《苦菜花》(kǔcàihuā)*Bitter Herb* – a novel by Feng Deying (冯德英, 1935 –) in 1954 – 1957; a film directed by Li Ang(李昂)in 1965

苦果(kǔguǒ)a bitter pill; something unpleasant as a result of some action

苦海(kǔhǎi)the abyss of misery; the sea of sorrow

苦海无边,回头是岸(kǔhǎi wúbiān, huítóu shì'àn)(lit.)"the bitter sea of life is boundless, repent and the shore is near" – it is never too late to stop doing something bad

苦酒(kǔjiǔ)① bitter liquid ② sadness; suffering

苦力(kǔlì)a coolie

苦命(kǔmìng)a cruel fate; an ill-fated life

苦命人(kǔmìngrén)a luckless person

《苦恼人的笑》(kǔnǎorén de xiào) *Troubled Laughter* – a film directed by Deng Yimin(邓一民)in 1979

苦肉计(kǔròujì)the ruse of self-injury (to win somebody's confidence)

苦行僧(kǔxíngsēng)①a saddhu②a person who lives a life of self-denial and mortification

酷吏(kùlì)an oppressive official

夸父(kuāfù)Kuafu (a mythical Chinese giant)

夸父逐日(kuāfù zhúrì)(lit.)"Kuafu tries to overtake the sun" – to misjudge one's strength; to do something beyond one's ability

夸海口(kuāhǎikǒu)to brag about;to talk big

侉子(kuǎzi)the "northern barbarians";the northern people

胯下之辱(kuàxià zhī rǔ)(lit.)"the disgrace of crawling through between someone's legs" – extremely deep humiliation

跨院儿(kuàyuànr)a side courtyard

跨灶(kuàzào)(of a son)to surpass his father

快板儿(kuàibǎnr) clapper talk (rhythmic talk or monologue to the accompaniment of bamboo clappers)

快书(kuàishū)quick-patter(rhythmic storytelling accompanied by bamboo or copper clappers)

快婿(kuàixù)a good son-in-law

《快嘴李翠莲记》(kuàizuǐ lǐcuìlián jì) *The Story of Quick-tongued Li Cuilian* – a story-telling script in the Ming dynasty

脍炙人口(kuàizhìrénkǒu)to enjoy great popularity

筷子(kuàizi)chopsticks

宽宏大量(kuānhóng dàliàng)large-minded;magnanimous

宽衣(kuānyī)to take off one's coat

宽衣解带(kuānyī jiědài)to undress oneself

款哥(kuǎngē)a rich young man

款姐(kuǎnjiě)a rich young lady

款曲(kuǎnqū)heartfelt feelings

款爷(kuǎnyé)a moneybags; a rich man

款识(kuǎnzhì)an inscription

匡扶(kuāngfú)to assist;to support

匡正时弊(kuāngzhèng shíbì)to correct the maladies of the times

狂草(kuángcǎo)the excessively free cursive script(one of the three categories of the cursive script)

《狂流》(kuángliú)*Raging Waves* – a film directed by Cheng Bugao(程步高)in 1933

《狂人日记》(kuángrén rìjì)*A Madman's Diary* or *Diary of a Madman* – a short story by Lu Xun(鲁迅, 1881 – 1936)in 1918

旷夫(kuàngfū)an unmarried man

旷夫怨女(kuàngfū yuànnǚ)an unmarried man and an unmarried woman;bachelors and spinsters

旷世之才(kuàngshì zhī cái)an rare talent; a man of brilliance unequalled in his time

魁首(kuíshǒu)the first;the best

魁元(kuíyuán)the brightest and best

傀儡(kuǐlěi)a puppet

傀儡戏(kuǐlěixì)a marionette show;a puppet play

坤角儿(kūnjué'r)an actress

坤宅(kūn zhái)bride's side;the wife's family

昆弟(kūndì)brothers;elder and younger brothers

昆仑(kūnlún)the Kunlun Mountains (stretching across Uygur Autonomous Region,Tibet en Autonomous Region and Qinghai province)

昆明湖(kūnmínghú)Kunming Lake (located in the Summer Palace)

昆腔(kūnqiāng)the melodies for Kunqu opera

昆曲(kūnqǔ)Kunqu opera

昆仲(kūnzhòng)elder and younger brothers

鲲鹏(kūnpéng)①a roc;a mythical giant bird②a greatly ambitious person

阔别(kuòbié)to part for a long time; to have not seen each other for a long time

阔佬(kuòlǎo)a rich man

阔少(kuòshào)a richling; a rich young man

L

拉帮结伙(lābāng jiéhuǒ)to gang up; to band together

拉场子(lā chǎngzi)to perform in the open at fairs or in marketplaces

拉队伍(lā duìwu)to raise a force;to form a band

拉风箱(lā fēngxiāng)to work the bellows

拉钩(lāgōu)a pinky swear;a fingers-hooked covenant)

拉呱儿(lāguǎr)to chat

拉关系(lā guānxi)to try to establish a relationship with somebody;to try to curry favour with

拉后腿(lā hòutuǐ)to hinder somebody;to be a drag on;to hold somebody back

拉祜族(lāhùzú)the Lahu nationality (in Yunnan province)

拉魂腔(lāhúnqiāng)the Sizhou opera [stemmed from Qianlong reign (1736－1795)in Xuzhou]

拉家常(lā jiācháng)to chitchat; to engage in small talk

拉近乎(lā jìnhu)to try to be friendly with

拉客(lākè)①to solicit guests or diners②to solicit patrions

拉郎配(lā láng pèi)to make an arbitrary arrangement for one to marry another

拉面(lāmiàn)stretched noodles; hand-pulled noodles

拉皮条(lā pítiáo)to act as a procurer;to procure;to pimp

拉山头(lā shāntóu)to form a faction

拉下马(lā xiàmǎ)to bring somebody

down; to knock somebody down

拉下水(lā xiàshuǐ) to drag somebody into the mire; to make an accomplice of someone; to corrupt somebody

喇叭(lǎba) a trumpet

喇嘛(lǎma) Lama

喇嘛教(lǎmajiào) Lamaism; Tibetan Buddhism

腊八(节)[Làbā(jié)] the Laba Festival(falling on December 8 of the lunar Chinese Calender)

腊八粥(làbāzhōu) Laba Rice Porridge; Eight-treasure Porridge

腊日(làrì) the day of winter sacrifice

腊肉(làròu) preserved ham

腊月(làyuè) the 12th month of the Lunar Chinese Calendar

蜡染(làrǎn) Batik or wax printing

辣妹子(làmèizi) a spicy girl

来鸿(láihóng) a letter from faraway

来龙去脉(láilóng qùmài) ins and outs; cause and effect

来生(láishēng) the afterlife; the other life; the life beyond

来世(láishì) the next life; the afterlife

癞皮狗(làipígǒu) ①a mangy dog②a loathsome creature

兰花指(lánhuāzhǐ) the orchid-shaped fingers(a lady's hand gesture)

兰谱(lánpǔ) the genealogical records

《兰亭集序》(lántíngjí xù) *The Preface to the Orchid Pavllion Collection* - an essay by Wang Xizhi(王羲之, 303 - 361)

兰章(lánzhāng) your beautiful writings

拦路虎(lánlùhǔ) (lit.) "a tiger in the way" - an obstacle; a stumbling block

《蓝风筝》(lán fēngzheng) *The Blue Kite* - a film directed by Tian Zhuangzhuang(田壮壮) in 1993

蓝青官话(lánqīng guānhuà) non-standard Mandarin

蓝田人(lántiánrén) Lantian Man (a primitive tribe living in early Palaeolithic Age)

蓝田文化(lántián wénhuà) the Culture of Lantian Man

览胜(lǎnshèng) to visit scenic spots

揽笔(lǎnbǐ) to take up one's pen; to write

揽活(lǎnhuó) to take on work

揽爷(lǎnyé) a person who gets commision by soliciting business for a hotel or restaurant

《懒汉相亲》(lǎnhàn xiāngqīn) *The Sluggard's Blind Date* - a skit starring Lei Kesheng(雷恪生), Zhao Lianjia(赵连甲) and Song Dangdang(宋丹丹) in 1989

烂摊子(làntānzi) an awful mess

烂尾(lànwěi) unfinished

烂尾楼(lànwěilóu) an unfinished building

烂账(lànzhàng)①accounts in a mess ②a bad debt;bad accounts

滥好人(làn hǎorén) a bleeding heart; a soft touch (a person who always gives what anyone asks for)

滥觞(lànshāng) origin;beginning

滥竽充数(lànyú chōngshù) to be there just to make up the numbers

郎才女貌(lángcái nǚmào) (lit.) "a brilliant young scholar and a beautiful woman" – the traditional ideal of a perfect match between a man and a girl;a fine couple

郎舅(lángjiù) a man and his wife's brother

郎君(lángjūn) my husband

郎中(lángzhōng) a hakeem;a doctor; a physician trained in herbal medicine

狼毫(lángháo) a writing brush (made from the hair of the tail of weasels)

狼牙棒(lángyábàng) a wolf-teeth club (an ancient weapon)

《狼山喋血记》(lángshān diéxuè jì) *Bloodshed on Wolf Mountain* – a film directed by Fei Mu (费穆) in 1936

狼烟(lángyān) a fire beacon

狼烟四起(lángyān sìqǐ) fire beacons lit on all sides; war alarms raised everywhere

狼主(lángzhǔ) the monarch of a nomadic minority regime in northern China

廊庙(lángmiào) the imperial court

廊檐(lángyán) the eaves of a veranda

廊子(lángzi) a veranda; a porch; a corridor

浪船(làngchuán) a swingboat

《浪淘沙》(làngtáoshā) *Ripples Sifting Sand* – one of the tune patterns of *ci* poetry

浪子(làngzǐ) a prodigal son;a loafer; a wastrel

浪子回头金不换(làngzǐ huítóu jīn bù huàn) a prodigal who returns is more precious than gold

捞稻草(lāo dàocǎo) (lit.) "to try to catch at a straw" – to try to take advantage of

捞外快(lāo wàikuài) to make extra money

捞油水(lāo yóushuǐ) to line one's pocket;to make a side profit;to get a squeeze

劳动号子(láodòng hàozi) a work song

劳驾(láojià) excuse me;may I trouble you

劳苦功高(láokǔ gōnggāo) to have worked hard and performed a valuable service

劳民伤财(láomín shāngcái)to waste man-power and money

劳模(láomó)a model worker

劳师动众(láoshī dòngzhòng)to drag in lots of people

劳燕分飞(láo yàn fēn fēi)to go in separate ways; to part from each other

牢笼(láolóng)①a cage; bonds ②a trap; a snare

牢头(láotóu)a jailer

崂山(láoshān)Laoshan Mountain; Mt. Lao(located in Shandong province)

《崂山道士》(láoshān dàoshì)*A Taoist from Laoshan Mountain* – a story in *Strange Stories from a Scholar's Studio* by Pu Songling(蒲松龄, 1640 – 1715)

老八板儿(lǎobābǎnr)conservative; old-fashioned

老白干(lǎobáigān)white spirit(a spirit distilled from sorghum or maize)

老鸨(lǎobǎo)a procuress

老鼻子(lǎobízi)plenty of; a great number of; an awful lot

老表(lǎobiǎo)①a male cousin ②a male stranger

《老兵新传》(lǎobīng xīn zhuàn)*New Story of An Old Soldier* – a film directed by Shen Fu(沈浮)in 1959

《老残游记》(lǎocán yóujì)*The Travels of Lao Can* – a novel by Liu E(刘鹗, 1857 – 1909)in 1903; *The Travel Records of Lao Can*

老搭档(lǎodādàng)an old workmate or partner

《老大的幸福》(lǎodà de xìngfú)*The Eldest Brother's Happiness* – a TV drama directed by Fan Wei(范伟)in 2009

老大难(lǎodànán)a long-standing difficulty

老旦(lǎodàn)*laodan*(an elderly female role in traditional opera)

老道(lǎodào)a senior Taoist priest

老掉牙(lǎodiàoyá)very old; out of date; obsolete

老东西(lǎodōngxī)①an old thing ②an old guy; an old woman

老佛爷(lǎofóye)①an old Buddha ②the queen mother or the emperor's father ③the Empress Dowager

老夫子(lǎofūzǐ)a tutor in a private school; a pedantic scholar

老公(lǎogōng)(informal)husband

老姑娘(lǎogūniang)①an old spinster; an old maid ②the youngest daughter

老古董(lǎogǔdǒng)①an old-fashioned article; an antique ②an old fogey

老关系(lǎoguānxì)an old acquaintance

老虎凳(lǎohǔdèng) the Tiger Bench (a torture rack); a cucking stool

老皇历(lǎohuánglì) an old history; an obsolete practice

老黄牛(lǎohuángniú) an honest and industrious worker

老江湖(lǎojiānghú) a man of the world; an old traveller; a man of rich experience

老交情(lǎojiāoqing) a long-standing friendship; an old friend

《老井》(lǎo jǐng) *Old Well* – a film directed by Wu Tianming(吴天明) in 1986

老来俏(lǎoláiqiào) mutton dressed as lamb

老衲(lǎonà) ①an old monk ②I; me (self-appellation for an old monk)

老娘(lǎoniáng) ①an old mother ②I; me (self-appellation for a woman)

老奴(lǎonú) an old lackey (self-appellation for a servant)

老三届(lǎosānjiè) the high school graduates of 1966 – 1968; the school leavers of 1966 – 1968

老三篇(lǎosānpiān) the Three Old Articles [*Serve the People* (1944), *In Memory of Norman Bethune* (1939) and *The Foolish Old Man Removed the Mountains* (1945)] by Mao Zedong (毛泽东, 1893 – 1976)

老少爷们儿(lǎo shào yémenr) elders and brethren

老生(lǎoshēng) *laosheng* (an elderly male role in traditional opera)

老寿星(lǎoshòuxīng) ①god of longevity ②an elderly person

老乡(lǎoxiāng) a fellow-townsman; a fellow-villager

老学究(lǎoxuéjīu) an old pedant

老爷子(lǎoyézi) ①an old man ②old father

老油条(lǎoyóutiáo) a wily old bird; an old slicker; a sophisticate

老妪(lǎoyù) an old woman

老丈人(lǎozhàngrén) father-in-law

老庄学派(lǎozhuāng xuépài) the school of Taoism [of Laozi (老子) and Zhuangzi (庄子)]

老子(lǎozi) ①father ②I; me

《老子》(lǎozǐ) *the Lao-tse*; *the Laozi*; *the Dao De Jing* – a Taoist scripture

老子(lǎozǐ) Lao-tse; Lao-tzu; Laozi (an ancient Chinese philosopher, one of the founders of Taoism)

老字号(lǎozìhào) an old and famous shop or enterprise; a time-honoured brand

姥姥(lǎolao) mother's mother; maternal grandmother

姥爷(lǎoye) mother's father; maternal grandfather

唠嗑(làokē)to have a chat

《烙印》(làoyìn) *Brand* - a collection of poems by Zang Kejia(臧克家, 1905 - 2004) in 1933

落不是(làobùshì) to get blamed

肋腻(lēte) sloppy; slovenly; untidy

乐不思蜀(lèbùsīshǔ) to be too happy as to forget one's home and duty; to be too delighted to be homesick

乐极生悲(lèjíshēngbēi) extreme joy begets sorrow; excessive joy tur-ns to sorrow

乐平腔(lèpíngqiāng) Leping opera (one of traditional Chinese operas)

乐卿(lèqīng) ①Leqing (the 8th rank of nobility in martial arts) ②an alternative for Taichang qing(太常卿) an official title

乐山大佛(lèshān dàfó) the Leshan Giant Buddha (in Sichuan province)

乐善好施(lèshàn hàoshī) ready to do charity; philanthropic

乐天派(lètīanpài) an optimist

乐天知命(lètīan zhīmìng) to be content with one's lot; to be easily contented

乐土(lètǔ) the land of happiness; the land of promise

雷池(léichí) a forbidden area

雷倒(léi dǎo) to be shocked

雷峰塔(léifēngtǎ) the Leifeng Pagoda (near the West Lake in Hangzhou, Zhejiang province)

雷锋(léifēng) ①Lei Feng (1940 - 1962), a soldier who was always ready to help others and has been regarded as an example for others② anyone who is ready to help others

雷公(léigōng) Thunder God

雷人(léirén) very shocking

《雷雨》(léiyǔ) *Thunderstorm* - a play by Cao Yu(曹禺, 1910 - 1996) in 1929 - 1933

雷子(léizi) a policeman

擂台(lèitái) a ring (for martial arts contests); an arena

冷板凳(lěngbǎndèng) ①an insignificant post②a cold reception

冷场(lěngchǎng) ①a stage wait; an awkward silence on the stage (when an actor enters late or forgets his lines) ②an awkward silence during a meeting

冷宫(lěnggōng) the cold palace (a place where disfavored queens and comcubines were banished)

冷箭(lěngjiàn) an arrow shot from hiding; a sniper's shot

冷脸子(lěngliǎnzi) severe expression; indifference

冷门(lěngmén) ①an unexpected winner②a dark horse

冷面(lěngmiàn) ①cold noodles ②

stern-faced

愣神儿(lèngshénr) to stare blankly; to be in a daze

愣头青(lèngtóuqīng) a rash fellow; a hothead

梨花大鼓(líhuā dàgǔ) the Pear Blossom Drumming (a unique *quyi* in Xingtai, Hebei province)

梨园(líyuán) the Pear Garden (operatic circles; the world of theatre)

梨园弟子(líyuán dìzǐ) the disciples of the Pear Garden (operatic professionals)

梨园戏(líyuánxì) the Pear Garden Opera

梨园子弟(líyuán zǐdì) an operatic actor or actress

离愁别绪(líchóu biéxù) the sorrow of parting

离宫(lígōng) an imperial palace for short stays away from the capital; a temporary dwelling palace of an emperor when away from the capital

离经叛道(líjīng pàndào) to rebel against orthodoxy

离谱(lípǔ) improper; unreasonable

离情别绪(líqíng biéxù) the sad feeling of parting

《离骚》(lísāo) *Sorrowful to Bid Farewell* – a Chu poem by Qu Yuan (屈原, 340 – 278 BC); *Sorrow after Departure*; *Lament on Encountering Sorrow*

离弦走板(líxián zǒubǎn) to deviate from the accepted norm; to be non-standard

漓江(líjiāng) Lijiang; the Lijiang River (in Guangxi Autonomous Region)

黎民百姓(límín bǎixìng) the common people

《黎明的河边》(límíng de hébiān) *Dawn of the River Bank* – a short story by Jun Qing (峻青, 1922 –) in 1955

黎庶(líshù) the common people

黎族(lízú) the Li nationality (located mainly in Hainan province)

篱笆(líba) a bamboo fence

《篱笆、女人和狗》(líba, nǚrén hé gǒu) *The Fence, Women and Dog* – a TV drama directed by Chen Yuzhong (陈雨中) in 1989

篱笆墙(líbaqiáng) a wattled wall

罹难(línàn) to die in a disaster or an accident

礼拜六派(lǐbàiliùpài) the Saturday School (a school of literature in the early Republic of China, 1912 – 1949)

礼部(lǐbù) the Board of Rites and Ceremonies

礼部尚书(lǐbù shàngshū) Director of the Board of Rites

《礼记》(lǐjì) *The Book of Rites*; *The Classic of Rites*; *The Record of Rites* - a Confucian classic compiled by Dai Sheng(戴圣) in the Western Han Dynasty(206 BC - 8 AD)

礼教(lǐjiào) the feudal code of ethics; feudal ethics and rites

礼尚往来(lǐshàng wǎnglái) courtesy demands reciprocity

礼数(lǐshù) courtesy; etiquette

礼贤下士(lǐxián xiàshì) to treat worthy men with courtesy; to be considerate and kind to men of talent

礼仪之邦(lǐyí zhībāng) a land of ceremony and propriety

礼义廉耻(lǐyí liánchǐ) propriety, righteousness, honesty and the sense of shame (the four cardinal virtues)

礼治(lǐzhì) to rule by propriety

李杜(lǐdù) ①Li Bai(李白, 701 - 762) and Du Fu(杜甫, 712 - 770) ②Li Shangyin(李商隐, 812 - 858) and Du Mu(杜牧, 803 - 852)

《李慧娘》(lǐhuìniáng) *Lady Li Huiniang* - a drama by Zhou Chaojun (周朝俊, 1573 -?); a film directed by Deng Yimin(邓逸民) in 1981

《李家庄的变迁》(lǐjiāzhuāng de biànqiān) *The Changes of Lijia Village*- a novel by Zhao Shuli(赵树理, 1906 - 1970) in 1945

《李靖与唐太宗问对》(lǐjìng yǔ táng tàizōng wènduì) *The Dialogues between Li Jing and Tang Taizong* - a military book by Ruan Yi(阮逸) in the Song Dynasty

李逵(lǐ kuí) Li Kui[a character in *All Men Are Brothers* by Shi Naian(施耐庵, 1296 - 1371)]

《李师师外传》(lǐshīshī wàizhuàn) *The Legend of Li Shishi* - a romance between Li Shishi and Emperor Huizong in the Song Dynasty(960 - 1279)

《李双双》(lǐshuāngshuāng) *Li Shuangshuang* - a novel by Li Zhun(李凖, 1928 - 2000); a film directed by Lu Ren(鲁韧) in 1962

李铁拐(lǐtiěguǎi) Li Tieguai; Iron-crutch Li(one of the legendary Chinese Eight Immortals)

《李娃传》(lǐwá zhuàn) *The Story of Li Wa* - a romance by Bai Xingjian (白行简, 776 - 826)

李下之嫌(lǐxià zhī xián) to be found in a suspicious position; to be suspected of a theft

《李小龙传奇》(lǐxiǎolóng chuánqí) *The Legend of Bruce Lee* - a TV drama directed by Li Wenqi(李文岐) in 2007

《李有才板话》(lǐyǒucái bǎnhuà) *A Story of Li Youcai* - a novel by Zhao

Shuli (赵树理, 1906 - 1970) in 1943

《李自成》(lǐzìchéng) *Li Zicheng* - a five-volume novel by Yao Xueyin (姚雪垠,1910 - 1999) in 1957 -1999

李自成起义(lǐzìchéng qǐyì) the Li Zicheng Rebellion (1630 - 1645)

里弄(lǐnòng) lanes and alleys; neighborhood

理气(lǐqì) to regulate the flow of Qi (vital energy)

理学(lǐxué) Neo-Confucianism; the Confucian school of rationalistic philosophy; the School of Principle

鲤鱼跳龙门(lǐyú tiào lóngmén) (lit.) "A Carp jumps over the Dragon Gate" - to rise from rags to riches; to become someone with a very promising future

力役(lìyì) a corvee (in feudal China)

《历史的天空》(lìshǐ de tiānkōng) *The Sky of History* - a novel by Xu Guixiang (徐贵祥,1959 -)

历史散文(lìshǐ sǎnwén) historical prose

历史小说(lìshǐ xiǎoshuō) the historical novel

历史演义小说(lìshǐ yǎnyì xiǎoshuō) the historical romances

历书(lìshū) an almanac

历物十事(lìwù shíshì) the Ten Paradoxical Propositions (important part of the thoughts of the Pre-Qin School of Names)

《历象考成》(lìxiàng kǎochéng) *Calendar Reckoning* - a classic on astronomy compiled in 1713

历元(lìyuán) an epoch

厉兵秣马(lìbīng mòmǎ) to get ready to take military action

立春(lìchūn) the Beginning of Spring (the 1st of the 24 Chinese solar terms, usually falling on the 4th of February)

立嫡(lì dí) to legitimate a son of the empress as a heir to the throne

立冬(lìdōng) the Beginning of Winter (the 19th of the 24 Chinese solar terms, usually falling on the 7th or 8th of November)

立门户(lì ménhù) ① to establish one's own school of thought ② to set up one's own organization ③ to maintain an independent house

立秋(lìqiū) the Beginning of Autumn (the 13th of the 24 Chinese solar terms, usually falling on the 8th or 9th of August)

立身处世(lìshēn chǔshì) the ways of conducting oneself in society; to get on in the world

立夏(lìxià) the Beginning of Summer (the 7th of the 24 Chinese solar terms, usually falling on the 5th or

6th of May)

吏部(lìbù)the Board of Civil Office; the Ministry of Personnel Affairs

吏治(lìzhì)local administration

丽江古城(lìjiāng gǔchéng)the old town of Lijiang(in Yunnan province)

丽人(lìrén)a beautiful woman; a beauty

《丽人行》(lìrén xíng)*The Ballad of Beauties* - a poem by Du Fu(杜甫,712 - 770);*Two for the Road*

利禄(lìlù)rank and wealth; wealth and position

励精图治(lìjīngtúzhì)to exert one's efforts to make the country prosperous

例言(lìyán)introductory remarks

隶书(lìshū)the Clerical script; the official script(calligraphy)

俪辞(lìcí)antithetical words and phrases; antithetical literary writings

俪句(lìjù)parallel sentences; antithetical sentences

《荔枝蜜》(lìzhī mì)*The Honey of Lychee flowers* - a prose by Yang Shuo(杨朔,1913 - 1968);*The Lychee Honey*

傈僳族(lìsùzú)the Lisu nationality(living mainly in Yunnan province)

詈骂(lìmà)to scold; to abuse

连裆裤(liándāngkù)underpants with no slit in the seat

连锅端(liánguōduān)to get rid of, or remove, the whole lot

连环保(liánhuánbǎo)collective responsibility

连环计(liánhuánjì)a set of interlocking stratagems

连环套(liánhuántào)a chain of rings

连襟(liánjīn)the husbands of sisters; brothers-in-law

连理(liánlǐ)marriage

连理枝(liánlǐzhī)(lit.)"two trees with branches interlocked" - a loving couple

连篇累牍(liánpiān lěidú)lengthy and tedious; at great length

连中三元(lián zhòng sānyuán)come first in all three levels of the imperial examinations.

连珠炮(liánzhūpào)①continuous firing②to speak in a quick and continuous way

连坐(liánzuò)to be punished for being related to an offender

怜香惜玉(liánxiāng xīyù)to show pity and tenderness to a woman

莲步(liánbù)graceful way of walking(of a lady)

莲花落(liánhuālào)the Lotus Rhyme(a folk art form popular in the Ming Dynasty,1368 - 1644)

莲台(liántái) the seat of a Buddha; a lotus throne

莲座(liánzuò) the seat of a Buddha; a lotus throne

联欢(liánhuān) to have a get-together; to get together

联欢会(liánhuānhuì) a get-together

联欢晚会(liánhuān wǎnhuì) an evening party; an evening get-together

an euening Ponty

联句(liánjù) linking verses; to do linking verses

联袂(liánmèi) to go or come together (to do something)

联谊会(liányìhuì) ①a get-together party②a fellowship society

联姻(liányīn) to have connections through marriage; to be related by marriage

脸谱(liǎnpǔ) the types of facial makeup (in opera)

脸谱化(liǎnpǔhuà) lacking individuality

练功(liàngōng) to do exercises (in gymnastics, *kongfu*, acrobatics, etc); to practice one's skill

练武(liànwǔ) ①to learn or to practice martial arts②to practice one's military skills

炼丹(liàndān) to make pills of immortality

炼丹术(liàndānshù) alchemy

恋栈(liànzhàn) to be loath to give up one's post

殓衣(liànyī) grave clothes

良辰吉日(liángchén jírì) an auspicious day

良辰美景(liángchén měijǐng) the beautiful scene in a good day

良娣(liángdì) one of the imperial concubines

良家妇女(liángjiā fùnǚ) a woman from a respectable family; a respectable woman

《良家妇女》(liángjiā fùnǚ) *A Good Woman* - a film directed by Huang Jianzhong(黄健中) in 1985

良民(liángmín) a good citizen; a law-abiding person

良师益友(liángshī yìyǒu) a good teacher and helpful friend

《良宵》(liángxiāo) *Beautiful Night* - a piece of music for the urheen

良药苦口(liángyào kǔkǒu) good medicine is hard to swallow; bitter pills have a wholesome effect; unpalatable advice benefits one's conduct

良缘(liángyuán) a good match; a happy match

良渚文化(liángzhǔ wénhuà) Liangzhu Culture (of the Neolithic Age, located in Liangzhu, Zhejiang province)

凉棚(liángpéng)a mat shelter;a mat-awning

《梁山伯与祝英台》(liángshānbó yǔ zhùyīngtái)*Liang Shanbo and Zhu Yingtai*;*The Butterfly's Love*;*The Butterfly Lovers*:*Leon and Jo* – a legend;a violin concerto by Chen Gang(陈刚)and He Zhanhao(何占豪)in 1958;a film directed by Sang Hu(桑弧)and Huang Sha(黄沙)in 1953

梁上君子(liángshàng jūnzǐ)a burglar;a thief

《梁祝》(liáng zhù)*The Butterfly Lovers*– a Chinese violin concerto

粮秣(liángmò)army provisions

粮票(liángpiào)a food coupon;a grain coupon

粮饷(liángxiǎng)provisions and funds for troops

粮栈(liángzhàn)a wholesale grain store;a grain depot

两岸关系(liǎng'àn guānxì)the relations across the Taiwan Straits;cross-straits relations

两广(liǎngguǎng)the areas of Guangdong and Guangxi

两汉(liǎnghàn)the Western Han Dynasty(202 BC – 8 AD)and the Eastern Han Dynasty(25 – 220)

两湖(liǎnghú)the areas of Hunan and Hubei

两口子(liǎngkǒuzi)(dialect)husband and wife;a couple

两肋插刀(liǎnglèi chādāo)to do anything for a friend

两面光(liǎngmiànguāng)to please both parties;to try to keep the favour of both sides

两面派(liǎngmiànpài)a double-dealer

两小无猜(liǎngxiǎo wúcāi)to be innocent childhood playmates

两袖清风(liǎngxiù qīngfēng)to have clean hands;to remain uncorrupted

《亮剑》(liàng jiàn)*Drawing Sword* – a TV drama directed by Zhang Qian(张前)in 2005

亮相(liàng xiàng)①to strike a pose on the stage;to make a stage pose ②to declare one's position

靓女(liàngnǚ)a pretty young girl

靓仔(liàngzǎi)a handsome young boy

辽宁大鼓(liáoníng dàgǔ)Liaoning Drumming(a folk art form)

《聊斋志异》(liáozhāi zhìyì)*Strange Tales of Liaozhai* – an anthology of classical tales by Pu Songling(蒲松龄,1640 – 1715)in 1680;*Strange Stories from a Scholar's Studio*

僚婿(liáoxù)the husbands of sisters;brothers-in-law

僚属(liáoshǔ)the officials under somebody in authority;subordinates

寮房(liáofáng)①a humble house②a boudoir(of the Li nationality in Hainan Province)③a Buddhist or Taoist house(where monks or Taoists live)

了悟(liǎowù)to understand;to realize

料酒(liàojiǔ)cooking wine

撂地(liàodì)to show acrobatic skill in open spaces;to give a street performance

撂挑子(liào tiāozi)to give up one's job;to refuse to work

列传(lièzhuàn)biographies(of important figures)

列国(lièguó)various states or nations

列强(lièqiáng)the great powers

《列子》(lièzǐ) *The Book of Master Lie*;*Liezi*;*The Classic of the Perfect Emptiness* – a Taoist classic by Lie Yukou(列御寇)

列祖列宗(lièzǔ lièzōng)successive generations of ancestors;all the ancestors

劣根性(liègēnxìng)deep-rooted bad habits;scoundrelism

《烈火金刚》(lièhuǒ jīngāng) *Steel Meets Fire* – a novel by Liu Liu(刘流)in 1958;a TV drama directed by Wang Yikai(王奕开)in 2002;a film directed by He Qun(何群) in 1991

烈女(liènǚ)a paragon of chastity

烈士(lièshì)a martyr

烈士暮年,壮心不已(lièshì mùnián, zhuàngxīn bùyǐ)an old noble-hearted person still retains his high aspirations

烈属(lièshǔ)the family members of a revolutionary martyr; the family of a martyr

猎艳(lièyàn) to chase after pretty women

邻邦(línbāng)a neighboring country

《林海雪原》(línhǎi xuěyuán) *Immense Forest and Snow Field* – a novel by Qu Bo(曲波, 1923 – 2002)in 1952 – 1956;*Tracks in the Snowy Forest* – a film directed by Liu Peiran(刘沛然)in 1960

《林家铺子》(línjiā pùzi) *The Shop of the Lin Family* – a novel by Mao Dun(茅盾, 1896 – 1981); a film directed by Shui Hua(水华) in 1959

林苑(línyuàn)a hunting park

临池(línchí)①at the pond②to practice calligraphy

临川四梦(línchuān sìmèng)the Four Dreams of Linchuan[it refers to the four plays by Tang Xianzu(汤显祖,1550 – 1616)]

临盆(línpén)to be in labour; to be giving birth

临时抱佛脚(línshí bào fójiǎo) to

make an effort at the last moment; to seek last-minute help

临时工(línshígōng) a casual labourer; a temporary worker

临帖(líntiè) to practice calligraphy after a model

临幸(línxìng) to visit a place(used of an emperor)

廪生(lǐn shēng) linsheng (a scholar who lived on government stipend in the Ming and Qing Dynasties)

伶俜(língpīng) lonely

伶人(língrén) an actor or actress

灵车(língchē) a hearse

灵榇(língchèn) a coffin(containing a corpse); a bier

灵床(língchuáng) a bier

灵丹妙药(língdān miàoyào) a remedy for all problems; a cure-all

灵幡(língfān) a white band of mourning(held by son of deceased); a funeral banner

灵柩(língjiù) a coffin (containing a corpse); a bier

灵牌(língpái) a spirit tablet (for the deceased)

灵寝(língqǐn) a place where a coffin is kept; the seat of a bier

灵山(língshān) Vulture Peak (where Lord Buddha resided)

灵堂(língtáng) a mourning hall

灵位(língwèi) a spirit tablet (for the deceased); a temporary memorial tablet

《灵宪》(língxiàn) *The Origin of the Universe* - a book by Zhang Heng (张衡,78 - 139)

灵隐寺(língyǐnsì) Temple of Soul's Retreat; Lingyin Temple (located in Hangzhou, Zhejiang Province)

囹圄(língyǔ) a jail; a prison

岭南画派(lǐngnán huàpài) the Lingnan School of Painting (formed by Guangdong painters and founded in the late Qing Dynasty, 1636 - 1912)

岭南学派(lǐngnán xuépài) the Lingnan School of Thought (shaped in the middle and late Ming Dynasty, 1368 - 1644)

《凌波曲》(língbōqǔ) *Walking over Ripples* - a piece of dance music composed by Li Longji (李隆基, 685 - 762)

凌迟(língchí) to put to death by dismembering the body

陵寝(língqǐn) the resting place (of an emperor or a king); a mausoleum

陵替(língtì) (of law and order) to break down; to decline

翎子(língzi) ① peacock feathers (worn at the back of a mandarin's hat); hat feathers ② the long pheasant tail feathers (worn on a warrior's helmet in traditional opera)

领班(lǐngbān) a gaffer; a foreman

领头羊(lǐngtóuyáng) a bellwether

令爱(lìng'ài) your daughter

令嫒(lìngài) your daughter

令箭(lìngjiàn) an arrow(used as a token of authority); an arrow-shaped token

令阃(lìngkǔn) your wife

令郎(lìngláng) your son

令亲(lìngqīn) your relative

令史(lìngshǐ) the cabinet secretariat

令堂(lìngtáng) your mother

令尹(lìngyǐn) lingyin (the highest official who was in charge of the army and government in the state of Chu in the Spring and Autumn and the Warring States Periods, 770 – 221 BC)

令尊(lìngzūn) your father

溜号(liūhào) to sneak away; to slink off

溜须拍马(liūxū pāimǎ) to fawn on; to lick somebody's boots

《刘老根》(liúlǎogēn) *Liu Laogen* – a TV drama directed by Zhao Benshan(赵本山) in 2002

《刘巧儿》(liúqiǎo'er) *Liu Qiaoer* – a Ping opera by Wang Yan(王雁) in the 1950s; a film directed by Yi Lin (伊琳) in 1956

《刘三姐》(liúsānjiě) *Third Sister Liu* – a film directed by Su Li(苏里) in 1960

流芳百世(liúfāng bǎishì) to leave a good name for generations; to gain immortal fame

流寇(liúkòu) roving bandits; roving rebel bands

流落江湖(liúluò jiānghú) to live a vagabond life

流眄(liúmiǎn) to give a sidelong glance; to ogle

流年(liúnián) fleeting time

流年不利(liúnián bùlì) to have an unlucky year

流盼(liúpàn) to cast amorous glances at

流觞(liúshāng) flowing wine cups

流水席(liúshuǐxí) an open-air banquet; a feast at which guests are served as they come

流水账(liúshuǐzhàng) a day-to-day account

流刑(liúxíng) the punishment of banishment

流贼(liúzéi) roving bandits

留后路(liú hòulù) to leave a way out

留后手(liú hòushǒu) to leave room for maneuver; to leave oneself a loop-hole

留面子(liú miànzi) to save one's face

留一手(liú yīshǒu) to keep a card up one's sleeve

留园(liúyuán)the Lingering Garden (in Suzhou)

琉璃瓦(líuliwǎ)glazed tiles

柳暗花明(liǔ'àn huāmíng)hard times take a turn for the better; every cloud has a silver lining

柳眉(liǔméi)beautiful eyebrows

柳腔(liǔqiāng)Qingdao opera

柳琴(liǔqín)① liuqin (a plucked stringed musical instrument) ② Liuqin opera; the Liuzi opera

柳体(liǔtǐ)the calligraphic style of Liu Gongquan(柳公权,778-865)

柳下惠(liǔxiàhuì)a virtuous man who resists temptation even with a lady in his arms

柳腰(liǔyāo)a wasp waist; a slender and fine waist

《柳毅传》(liǔyì zhuàn)*The Story of Liu Yi* - a romance by Li Chaowei (李朝威,766-820)

柳子戏(liǔzixì)the Liuzi opera

六部(liùbù)the Six Boards (Board of Personnel, Board of Revenues, Board of Rites and Ceremony, Board of Defence, Board of Justice, Board of Works)

六察(liùchá)the six aspects (of inspecting an official in the Tang Dynasty, 618-907)

六长(liùcháng)the six techniques of traditional Chinese painting

六朝(liùcháo)the Six Dynasties (from the third to sixth century)

六朝金粉(liùcháo jīnfěn)the gaiety and splendour of aristocratic life in the Six Dynasties (from the third to sixth century)

六朝三杰(lìucháo sān jié)the three master painters of the Six Dynasties [Gu Kaizi(顾恺之,344? -405), Zhang Sengyao(张僧繇,in the 6th centery) and Lu Tanwei(陆探微, unknown birth year)]

六尘(lìuchén)the six roots of desires (sight, sound, smell, taste, touch and thought)

六尺之孤(liùchǐ zhī gū)a young orphan

六道轮回(liùdào lúnhuí)karma; a circle of guilt

六法(liùfǎ)the six standards of appreciating traditional Chinese figure drawing

六根(liùgēn)the six "roots" (senses); the six sensory organs of human beings

六根清静(liùgēn qīngjìng)free from worries

六官(liùguān)the six head officials of the six Boards

六合(liùhé)① the six directions (east, west, north, south, heaven and earth) ② the whole world;

the universe

六和塔(liùhétǎ) Pagoda of Six Harmonies

六甲(liùjiǎ) pregnancy

六经(liùjīng)(medicine) the six meridians

六礼(liùlǐ) the six ceremonies (of betrothal and marriage)

六律(liùlǜ) the six pitches

六气(liùqì) the six factors in nature (wind, cold, summer heat, humidity, dryness and fire)

六亲(liùqīn) ①parents, brothers, wife and children ②(one's) relatives

六亲不认(liùqīn bùrèn) ①to disown all one's relatives and friends ②very indifferent; stone-hearted

六卿(liùqīng) the Six Ministers

六书(liùshū) the six categories of Chinese character; the six types of writings

六畜(liùchù) domestic animals

《六幺》(liùyāo) *Six One* – a piece of music from the Tang Dynasty, 618 – 907

六艺(liùyì) the six classical arts (rites, music, archery, riding, writing, arithmetic)

六院(liùyuàn) the imperial concubines' residential palaces

遛弯儿(liùwān'r) to take a walk; to go for a stroll

龙船(lóngchuán) a dragon boat

龙的传人(lóng de chuánrén) ①the descendants of the dragon ② the Chinese people

龙灯(lóngdēng) a dragon lantern

龙凤呈祥(lóngfèng chéngxiáng) an auspicious spectacle; extremely good fortune; a happy reunion

龙凤帖(lóngfèngtiě) a marriage certificate

龙宫(lónggōng) the Dragon King's palace; the Dragon palace

龙虎相争(lónghǔ xiāngzhēng) a fierce fight between well-matched opponents

龙江剧(lóngjiāngjù) Longjiang opera (the local opera in Heilongjiang province)

龙井茶(lóngjǐngchá) Longjing tea; Dragon Well tea

龙门石窟(lóngmén shíkū) the Longmen grottoes (in Luoyang, He'nan province)

龙门阵(lóngménzhèn) ①the Dragon Gate Deployment ②a chat

龙袍(lóngpáo) the imperial robe; the emperor or king's robe

龙泉瓷(lóngquáncí) Longquan porcelain; Longquan celadon (hailed as one of the five famous porcelains in China, and produced in Longquan County, Zhejiang, in the Song Dynasty)

龙山文化(lóngshān wénhuà) the Longshan culture (first found in Shandong province in 1928)

龙生九子(lóng shēng jiǔzǐ)(lit.) "the dragon had nine different sons" – the brothers of the same parents differ from each other

龙套(lóngtào) an actor playing a walk-on part

龙王(lóngwáng) Dragon King (a legendary king ruling the sea)

《龙须沟》(lóngxūgōu) *Dragon Beard Ditch* – a play by Lao She (老舍, 1899 – 1966) in 1951

龙颜(lóngyán) the emperor's countenance; the mood of the king

龙颜大怒(lóngyán dànù) the anger of the emperor

龙舟(lóngzhōu) a dragon boat

龙舟竞渡(lóngzhōu jìngdù) a dragon-boat race

龙爪书(lóngzhǎoshū) the Dragon Claw script – a kind of chirography invented by Wang Xizhi (王羲之, 303 –361)

笼屉(lóngtì) a food steamer

隆庆(lóngqìng) Longqing [the reign title of Zhu Zaihou (朱载垕, 1537 – 1572), one of the emperors of the Ming Dynasty]

陇剧(lǒngjù) Gansu opera

喽啰(lóuluó) ①a band of outlaws ②an underling; a lackey

楼阁(lóugé) a pavilion

楼台亭阁(lóutái tínggé) towers and pavilions

陋室(lòushì) a humble room

陋习(lòuxí) a corrupt custom; a bad habit

漏壶(lòuhú) a clepsydra; a water clock

镂花(lòuhuā) ornamental engraving

露白(lòubái) to show one's money and valuables unintentionally

露丑(lòuchǒu) to make a fool of oneself in public

露马脚(lòu mǎjiǎo) to give oneself away; to reveal oneself; to let the cat out of the bag

露馅儿(lòu xiàn'r) to give the game away; to give oneself away

露一手(lòu yīshǒu) to exhibit one's abilities or skills; to show off

庐剧(lújù) Lu opera (prevalent in Anhui province)

庐山(lúshān) Lushan Mountain (in Jiangxi province)

《庐山恋》(lúshān liàn) *Romance on Lushan Mountain* – a film directed by Huang Zumo (黄祖模) in 1980

庐山真面目(lúshān zhēn miànmù) one's true self; the truth of something

卢沟桥事变(lúgōuqiáo shìbiàn)The Lugou Bridge Incident(1937);The Marco Polo Bridge Incident

《芦花荡》(lúhuādàng)*Reed Marshes* – a novel by Sun Li(孙犁,1913 – 2002)in 1944

芦苇荡(lúwěidàng)reed marshes

鲁班(lǔbān)Lu Ban(a legendary master carpenter)

《鲁班的传说》(lǔbān de chuánshuō)*Lu Ban,the Skillful Craftsman* – a film directed by Sun Yu(孙瑜)in 1958

鲁班尺(lǔbānchǐ)the carpenter's square

鲁菜(lǔcài)Shandong cuisine;Shandong food

录白(lùbái)official to whom the emperor gave instructions in person

录囚(lùqiú)interrogation of prisoners

录遗(lùyí)the make-up examination (in the imperial examination system)

《鹿鼎记》(lùdǐngjì)*The Deer and the Cauldron* – a novel by Jin Yong(金庸,1924 –)in 1969 – 1972;a TV drama directed by Ou Yaoxing(欧耀兴)in 1998 and by Yu Min(于敏)in 2008;*Royal Tramp* – a film directed by Cheng Xiaodong(程小东)and Wang Jing(王晶)in 1992

路祭(lùjì)to offer sacrifices on the route of a funeral procession

路见不平,拔刀相助(lù jiàn bù píng,bá dāo xiāng zhù)(lit.)"to see injustice on the road and draw one's sword to help the victim" – to come to the rescue of someone in distress

路柳墙花(lùliǔ qiánghuā)a woman of the street;a prostitute

路遥知马力(lùyáo zhī mǎlì)(lit.)"A long road tests a horse's strength" – to judge people after a period of time

路子(lùzi)a method;a way

戮尸(lùshī)to excruciate the corpse of a dead convict(punitive damage to a corpse)

辘轳(lùlu)a well-pulley;a windlass;a winch

绿林好汉(lùlín hǎohàn)(lit.)"a greenwood hero" – a brigand;forest outlaws

绿林起义(lùlín qǐyì)the Lulin Uprising(17 AD)

绿营(lùyíng)the Green Standard Army;the green camp;the army of the Han soldiers(in the Qin Dynasty)

露水夫妻(lùshuǐ fūqī)illicit lovers;man and woman living together witho-ut being married

露天剧场(lùtiān jùchǎng)an open-air theatre

露头角(lù tóujiǎo) to make a name for oneself; to begin to show ability or talent; to cut a conspicuous figure

驴打滚(lúdǎgǔn) "the rolling donkey" ①snowballing usury; high-interest debt ②a glutinous rice rolls with sweet bean flour

驴年马月(lúnián mǎyuè) an impossible date; a time that will never come

驴皮影(lúpíyǐng) a leather-silhouette show; a shadow play

闾里(lúlǐ) a home town; a native village

闾巷(lúxiàng) an alley; a lane

闾阎(lúyán) ①the district inhabited by the common people ②the common people

闾左(lúzuǒ) ①the district inhabited by the poor; a poor neighbourhood ②poor people

吕洞宾(lǚdòngbīn) Lü Dongbin (one of the Eight Immortals in Chinese legend)

吕剧(lǚjù) Lü opera (a local opera in Shangdong province)

《吕氏春秋》(lǚshì chūnqiū) *The Spring and Autumn Annals of Mr Lü* - an encyclopedic work by Lü Buwei (吕不韦, 290 - 235 BC)

律诗(lǜshī) regulated verse

律学(lǜxué) the study of temperament

律宗(lǜzōng) the Ritsugaku Sect (Buddhism)

《绿化树》(lǜ huà shù) *The Horse Tassel Flower* - a novelette by Zhang Xianliang (张贤亮, 1936 -) in 1984

绿帽子(lǜmàozi) to cuckold; a cuckold

绿腰(lǜyāo) luyao (a female solo dance, popular in the Tang Dynasty)

娈童(luántóng) ①a handsome boy ②a catamite; a gigolo

鸾凤(luánfèng) a married couple

銮驾(luánjià) ①the imperial carriage ②the emperor

銮舆(luányú) the imperial carriage

乱臣贼子(luànchén zéizǐ) rebellious subjects and undutiful sons; traitors and usupers

乱弹(luàntán) the Strum opera (a local opera arising in the Qing Dynasty, 1636 - 1912)

乱弹琴(luàn tánqín) to act or talk like a fool; to talk nonsense

乱坟岗(luànfén'gǎng) unmarked burial mounds; unmarked common graves

乱世(luànshì) troubled times; turbulent days

乱世英雄(luànshì yīngxióng) heroes in times of trouble

乱葬岗子(luànzànggǎngzi) unmarked common graves; unmarked burial-mounds

抡圆了(lūnyuánle) to one's heart's content; as much as one likes

伦常(lúncháng) the feudal order of human relationships

沦陷区(lúnxiànqū) the enemy-occupied areas

沦陷区文学(lúnxiànqū wénxué) literature of the enemy-occupied areas

轮回(lúnhuí) metempsychosis; samsara; transmigration

《论语》(lúnyǔ) *The Analects of Confucius*; *The Analects*; *The Confucian Analects*

论语派(lúnyǔpài) the School of *The Analects*

《论衡》(lùnhéng) *Balanced Inquiries* – a philosophical work by Wang Chong(王充,27 – 97) in 86

《罗成叫关》(luóchéng jiàoguān) *Luo Cheng at the Gate* – a traditional story-telling script in Beijing dialect with drum accompaniment

罗锅儿(luóguō'r) ① hunchbacked; humpbacked ② a hunchback; a humpback

罗汉(luóhàn) a Buddhist arhat

罗圈腿(luóquāntuǐ) ① bowlegs; bandy legs ② bowlegged; bandy-legged

罗帏(luówéi) a gauze curtain

罗衣(luóyī) a garment of thin silk

逻卒(luózú) soldiers on patrol; patrolmen

锣鼓(luógǔ) the gong and drum

骡马店(luómǎdiàn) an inn (with sheds for carts and animals)

《洛神赋》(luòshénfù) *Goddess of the Luo River* – a poem by Cao Zhi(曹植,192 – 232) in 230

《洛神赋图》(luòshénfù tú) *Goddess of the Luo River* – a classical painting by Gu Kaizhi(顾恺之,344 – 405)

洛阳纸贵(luòyáng zhǐ guì) (lit.) "paper becomes expensive in Luoyang" – a best seller

《骆驼祥子》(luòtuo xiángzi) *The Rickshaw Boy*; *Camel Xiangzi* – a novel by Lao She(老舍,1899 – 1966) in 1936; a film directed by Ling Zifeng(凌子风) in1982

珞巴族(luòbāzú) the Luoba nationality (living in Tibet)

落榜(luòbǎng) to fail in an entrance examination

落草(luòcǎo) to take to the bush (heather); to take to the greenwood; to become an outlaw

落草为寇(luòcǎo wéi kòu) to take to the greenwood and become an outlaw

落第(luòdì) to fail in an imperial examination

落发(luòfà)to become a monk or a nun

落后分子(luòhòu fènzǐ)a slow coach

落脚(luòjiǎo)to stop over;to put up

落井下石(luòjǐng xiàshí)to take mean advantage of someone when he is disadvantaged;to kick somebody when he is down

落款(luòkuǎn)to inscribe names, time, verse and a postscript, etc.(in a painting or a calligraphic work)

落马(luòmǎ)to fall from horseback; to fall down(from office);to be defeated

落水狗(luòshuǐgǒu)(lit.)"a drowning dog"- a villain who is down

落汤鸡(luòtāngjī)a person who is soaked through

落套(luòtào)to have bad luck

M

妈祖(māzǔ)Mazu;Matsu(goddess of the sea)

妈祖庙(māzǔmiào)Mazu Temple

麻花(máhuā)a Chinese doughnut;a fried dough twist

麻将(májiàng)Mah-jong

麻将牌(májiàngpái)Mah-jong tiles

麻酱(májiàng)sesame paste

麻辣烫(málàtàng)hotpot

麻雀战(máquèzhàn)the sparrow warfare(guerilla warfare during the Anti-Japanese War)

麻子(mázi)①pockmarks;a pitted face②a pockmarked person

马帮(mǎbāng)a caravan;a train of horses carrying goods

马弁(mǎbiàn)a bodyguard

马褡子(mǎdāzi)saddle-bags

马大哈(mǎdàhā)①careless②a scatterbrain;a careless person

《马大姐外传》(mǎdàjiě wàizhuàn) *Anecdotes of Sister Ma* - a Chinese skit starring by Cai Ming(蔡明) and Guo Da(郭达)in 2006

《马大帅》(mǎdàshuài)*Ma Dashuai* - a Chinese TV drama directed by Zhao Benshan(赵本山)in 2004

马灯(mǎdēng)a barn lantern;a lantern

马夫(mǎfū)a groom;a horsekeeper

马革裹尸(mǎgé guǒshī)(lit.)"to be wrapped in horsehide after death"- to die on the battle field

马褂(mǎguà)a mandarin's jacket;a Chinese jacket

马关条约(mǎguān tiáoyuē)the Treaty of Shimonoseki(1895)

马倌(mǎguān)a groom;a stableboy

马后炮(mǎhòupào)action taken or advice given after the event;suggestions offered retrospectively

马家浜文化(mǎjiābāng wénhuà)Majiabang culture(Neolithic culture in the Lower Yangtze Region)

《马路天使》(mǎlù tiānshǐ) *The Street Angel* – a film directed by Yuan Muzhi(袁牧之, 1909 – 1978) in 1937

马路新闻(mǎlù xīnwén) hearsay; gossip; the word on the street

马屁精(mǎpìjīng) a flatterer; a bootlicker; an apple-polisher; an ass-kisser

马前卒(mǎqiánzú) a pawn; a cat's paw; catspaw; a puppet

《马桥词典》(mǎqiáo cídiǎn) *A Dictionary of Maqiao* – a novel by Han Shaogong(韩少功, 1953 –) in 1996

马桶(mǎtǒng) a nightstool; a commode; a toilet bowl

马头琴(mǎtóuqín) a stringed instrument with a carved horse head at one end

马王堆(mǎwángduī) the Mawangdui Han tombs (in Changsha, Hunan province)

马爷(mǎyé) a policeman

马扎(mǎzhá) a campstool, a folding stool

马子(mǎzi)(dialect) ①a nightstool; a commode②a bandit; a brigand

码长城(mǎ chángchéng)(lit.) "to build the Great Wall" – to play mahjong

骂街(màjiē) to shout abuse in the street

骂娘(màniáng) to abuse; to curse

买办(mǎibàn) a comprador

买单(mǎidān) to pay a bill

买好(mǎihǎo) to try to win one's favour; to ingratiate oneself with; to play up to

买路钱(mǎilùqián) the toll money; money paid to bandits for passage

买卖婚姻(mǎimài hūnyīn) a mercenary marriage

买面子(mǎi miànzi) to have regard for one's face; to defer to somebody

买通(mǎitōng) to bribe; to buy over; to buy off

买通官府(mǎitōng guānfǔ) to bribe the local authorities

麦积山石窟(màijīshān shíkū) the Maijishan Grottoes (in Gansu province)

卖唱(màichàng) to sing for a living

《卖车》(mǎi chē) *Selling a Wheelchair* – a skit starring by Zhao Benshan(赵本山) and Fan Wei(范伟) in 2002

卖儿鬻女(mài'ér yùnǚ) to sell one's children

《卖柑者言》(màigānzhě yán) *The Orange Vendor* – an essay by Liu Ji (刘基, 1311 – 1375)

卖狗皮膏药(mài gǒupí gāoyào) to

sell quack remedies

卖乖(màiguāi) to show off one's cleverness

《卖拐》(mài guǎi) *Selling the Crutches* – a skit starring by Zhao Benshan(赵本山) and Fan Wei(范伟) in 2001

卖关子(màiguānzi) to keep one's audience in suspense

卖官鬻爵(màiguān yùjué) to sell official posts and titles

卖国求荣(màiguó qiúróng) to seek power and wealth by betraying one's country; to turn traitor for personal gain

卖老(màilǎo) to flaunt one's seniority; to put on the airs of a veteran

卖萌(màiméng) to act cute

卖俏(màiqiào) to play the coquette; to flirt

卖青苗(mài qīngmiáo)(lit.) "to sell young crops" – to sell book manuscripts

卖人情(mài rénqíng) to show favors to somebody for one's own ends; to win gratitude by favors

卖身(màishēn) ①to sell oneself or a member of one's family ② to sell one's body; to prostitute oneself for a living

卖身契(màishēnqì) an indenture by which one sells oneself or a family member

卖笑(màixiào) to show a smiling face and flirt; to be forced to earn a living by prostitution or singing

卖淫(màiyín) to be a prostitute

卖座(màizuò) to draw large audiences; to attract large numbers of customers

脉络(màiluò) ①arteries and veins; venation②train of thought

脉门(màimén) the most important part

脉息(màixī) pulse

脉象(mài xiàng) the condition of one's pulse

脉诊(mài zhěn) to diagnose by feeling the pulse

蛮子(mánzi) the "southern barbarians"; southerners

馒头(mántou) a steamed bun

《满城尽带黄金甲》(mǎnchéng jìn dài huángjīnjiǎ) *Curse of The Golden Flower* – a film directed by Zhang Yimou(张艺谋) in 2006)

满腹经纶(mǎnfù jīnglún) to be possessed of learning and ability; full of learning; profoundly learned

《满江红》(mǎnjiānghóng) *The Whole River is Red* – a poem by Yue Fei (岳飞, 1103 – 1142); the name of a *ci* poetry tunes

满师(mǎnshī) to serve out one's apprenticeship; to finish serving one's time

满堂红(mǎntánghóng) an all-round victory

满月(mǎnyuè) ①the full moon ②to complete the first month of one's (baby's) life

满招损,谦受益(mǎn zhāosǔn, qiān shòuyì) haughtiness invites disaster, and humility benefits; pride comes before a fall

满洲(mǎnzhōu) Manchuria

满族(mǎnzú) the Manchu nationality

慢待(màndài) to fail to treat somebody properly; to neglect somebody; to coldshoulder somebody

慢词(màncí) a long slow *ci* poem

芒种(mángzhòng) the Grain in Ear (9th of the 24 Chinese solar terms, usually falling on the 5th of June)

盲流(mánglíu) unemployed migrant people; floating population

蟒袍(mǎngpáo) the official robe (worn by ministers in the Ming and Qing dynasties); ceremonial robe

猫腻(māonì) an illegal deal; a trick

毛笔(máobǐ) a brush; a writing brush; a brush pen; a pen brush

毛边纸(máobiānzhǐ) deckle-edged paper; writing paper made from bamboo

毛孩子(máoháizi) a little child

毛毛雨(máomaoyǔ) drizzle; something not very important or serious

毛南族(máonánzú) the Maonan nationality (in Guangxi Zhuang Autonomous Region)

毛遂自荐(máosuí zì jiàn) (lit.) "to offer one's service as Maosui did" – to volunteer one's services

《毛选》(máo xuǎn) *The Selected Works of Mao Zedong*

毛丫头(máoyātou) a little girl

毛泽东(máozédōng) Mao Zedong (1893 – 1976) (one of the founders of the People's Republic of China)

毛泽东思想(máozédōng sīxiǎng) Mao Zedong Thought

《毛泽东选集》(máozédōng xuǎnjí) *The Selected Works of Mao Zedong*

《毛主席语录》(máozhǔxí yǔlù) *Quotations from Chairman Mao*

毛子(máozi) ①a westerner; a white person ②a bandit

茅草棚(máocǎo péng) a thatched shed or shack

茅庐(máolú) a thatched cottage

茅山(máoshān) Mount Mao (one of major Taoist mountains in Jiangsu province)

茅山派(máoshānpài) the Maoshan school (Taoism)

茅台酒(máotáijǐu) Maotai (spirit)

卯时(mǎoshí) the period of the day

from 5 a. m. to 7 a. m.

冒渎(màodú)to bother or annoy a superior

冒儿爷(mào'eryé)a stupid person

冒失鬼(màoshiguǐ)an imprudent and obstrusive person

冒天下之大不韪(mào tiānxià zhī dà bùwěi)to defy universal opinion; to risk everyone's condemnation

耄耋之年(màodié zhīnián)old age (between seventy and ninety)

貌合神离(màohé shénlí)to be seemingly in harmony but actually at variance

没骨头(méi gǔtóu)spineless; weak-kneed

没好气(méi hǎoqì)impolite; sulky

没门儿(méiménr)no way; impossible

没谱(méipǔ)(informal)to be unsure

没趣(méiqù)to feel put out; to feel snubbed

没日子(méi rìzi)to have no hope

没商量(méi shāngliang)to have no room to reconsider

没戏(méixì)hopeless

没辙(méizhé)to have no other way out

没咒念(méi zhòuniàn)to have no solution

没主见(méi zhǔjiàn)to have no personal views on(something)

眉批(méipī)notes and commentaries at the top margin of a page; a top margin note

《梅花三弄》(méihuā sānnòng) *The Plum-blossom in Three Movements* – a flute melody; *Plum blossom Melodies*

梅兰芳(méilánfāng)①Mei Lanfang (1894 – 1961, a famous Beijing opera master)②*Forever Enthralled* – a film directed by Chen Kaige(陈凯歌)in 2008

梅派大师(méipài dàshī)the great master of Mei school

梅派经典剧目(méipài jīngdiǎn jùmù)the classic Beijing operas of Mei school

梅派男旦(méipài nándàn)a Mei school's female impersonator; an Mei school's actor(disguised in female attire)

梅雨(méiyǔ)the plum rains; the rainy season

媒婆(méipó)a femaleo matchmaker

媒人(méirén)a matchmaker

媒妁之言(méishuò zhī yán)the good advice of a matchmaker

煤窑(méiyáo)a coalpit

煤油灯(méiyóudēng)a kerosene lamp; a kerosene burner

美猴王(měihóuwáng) Handsome Monkey King

美妞(měiniū)a beautiful girl

美人计(měirénjì)a beauty trap;a honeytrap

美言(měiyán)to put in a good word for(somebody)

妹夫(mèifu)brother-in-law(younger sister's husband)

昧良心(mèiliángxīn)against one's conscience

昧心钱(mèixīnqián)ill-gotten gains;filthy lucre

媚骨(mèigǔ)obsequiousness;sycophancy

媚世(mèishì)to try to please the public

媚眼(mèiyǎn)seductive eyes;a soft glance

门巴族(ménbāzú)the Monba nationality(in Tibet)

门当户对(méndāng hùduì)to be well-matched in social and economic status

门道(méndào)①know-how②a gateway;a doorway

门第(méndì)family status

门丁(méndīng)a gatekeeper;a porter

门房(ménfáng)①a gate house;the porter's lodge ②a gatekeeper;a doorman;a porter

门风(ménfēng)the ethics and moral standards of a family or a clan;a family's customary moral standards

门户(ménhù)①the door②sect;faction③family

门户之见(ménhù zhī jiàn)sectarian bias

门客(ménkè)a hanger-on of an aristocrat

门联(ménlián)door or gate couplet

门楼(ménlóu)the gate house;the gate tower;an arch over a gateway

门楣(ménméi)①the lintel of a door ②family status

门面(ménmiàn)①the facade of a shop;shop front ②appearance;facade

门面话(ménmiànhuà)a kind of lip service;formal remarks in social intercourse which are not necessarily sincere

门神(ménshén)the door-god

门生(ménshēng)a pupil;a disciple;a follower

门徒(méntú)a disciple

门外汉(ménwàihàn)a layman

闷葫芦(mènhúlu)①a puzzle②a man of few words

盟兄弟(méngxiōngdì)sworn brothers

盟主(méngzhǔ)the leader or chief of an alliance

朦胧诗(ménglóngshī)Misty Poetry;Obscure Poetry

蒙馆(méngguǎn)a private school

蒙汗药(ménghànyào)sleeping pills;knockout drops

蒙冤(méngyuān) to be wronged; to suffer an injustice

蒙古包(měnggǔbāo) a Mongolian yurt

《蒙古秘史》(měnggǔ mìshǐ) *The Secret History of Mongolia*; *The Confidential History of Mongolia* - an anonymous historical book finished around the 13th century

蒙古语(měnggǔyǔ) Mongolian

蒙古族(měnggǔzú) the Mongolian nationality

孟春(mèngchūn) the first month of spring

孟冬(mèngdōng) the first month of winter

孟姜女(mèngjiāngnǚ) Meng Jiangnu (a legendary woman whose flow of tears caused the Great Wall to crack)

《孟姜女》(mèngjiāngnǚ) *The Story of the Woman Seeking Her Husband* - one of the four great love legends

孟庙(mèngmiào) Temple of Mencius; Meng Temple

孟母三迁(mèngmǔ sānqiān) the three moves by Mencius' mother (for a preferable environment to better his education)

孟秋(mèngqīu) the first month of autumn

孟夏(mèngxià) the first month of summer

孟子(mèngzǐ) Mencius (372 - 289 BC)

《孟子》(mèngzǐ) *The Book of Master Meng*; *The Works of Menciu*; *Mencius*

《梦游天姥吟》(mèngyóu tiānmǔ yín) *Dreaming of Sightseeing in the Tianmu Mountains* - a poem by Li Bai (李白, 701 - 762)

弥勒(mílè) Maitreya (Buddhism)

弥勒佛(mílèfó) Maitreya; the Laughing Buddha

弥陀(mítuó) Amitabha (Buddhism)

迷魂汤(míhúntāng) magic potion; an enticing spell; honeyed words

迷魂阵(míhúnzhèn) a scheme for confusing or bewildering somebody; a maze; a trap

迷津(míjīn) (lit.) "to miss the ferry" - deviation from the correct path; being on the wrong track a maze; a wild-goose chase

《迷途的羔羊》(mítú de gāoyáng) *A Lamb Astray*; *The Lost Lamb* - a film directed by Cai Chusheng (蔡楚生) in 1936

谜底(mídǐ) the answer to a riddle

米醋(mǐcù) rice vinegar

米酒(mǐjiǔ) rice wine

米粮川(mǐliángchuān) a rich rice-producing area

弭谤(mǐbàng) to put an end to slander

弭兵(mǐbīng) to stop a war; to have a truce

弭患(mǐhuàn) to remove a trouble or danger

弭乱(mǐluàn) to put down a rebellion; to stop a civil war

汨罗江(mìluójiāng) the Miluo river (running through Jiangxi, Hu'nan and Hubei provinces)

秘方(mìfāng) a secret recipe

秘笈(mìjí) tips

秘籍(mìjí) a rarely seen and expensive book; esoterica

秘史(mìshǐ) ①a secret history ②an inside story

密教(mìjiào) Tantrism

密宗(mìzōng) Esoteric Buddhism

蜜月(mìyuè) honeymoon

棉袄(mián'ǎo) a cotton-padded jacket

棉裤(miánkù) cotton-padded trousers

棉鞋(miánxié) cotton-padded shoes

棉衣(miányī) cotton-padded clothes

免战牌(miǎnzhàn pái) a truce sign

眄视(miànshì) to give a sidelong glance

面呈(miànchéng) to submit in person

面的(miàndí) a taxi mini-van

面罄(miànqìng) to explain in detail in person

面首(miànshǒu) a noblewoman's gigolo or kept man

面授机宜(miànshòu jīyí) to give confidential instruction

面子(miànzi) ①outside ②face ③feelings

苗剧(miáojù) Miao opera

苗绣(miáoxiù) Miao embroidery; the embroidery of the Miao Minority

苗族(miáozú) the Miao nationality

妙手回春(miàoshǒu huíchūn) to effect a miraculous cure and bring back the dying to life; the magic touch

庙号(miàohào) (lit.) the posthumous title of an emperor

庙会(miàohuì) a fair; a temple fair

庙堂(miàotáng) ①the imperial ancestral temple ②the imperial court

庙祝(miàozhù) a temple attendant in charge of incense and religious service

灭佛(mièfó) the suppression of Buddhism

灭门(mièmén) to exterminate an entire family

灭族(mièzú) to exterminate an entire family

民办(mínbàn) to be run by the local people

民兵(mínbīng) ①people's militia ②a militiaman

民风(mínfēng) folk customs; local

traits

民国(mínguó)the Republic of China

民康物阜(mín kāng wù fù)products abound and people live in peace

民权主义(mínquán zhǔyì)the Principle of Democracy(one of the Three Principles of the People by Sun Yat-sen)

民生主义(mínshēng zhǔyì)the Principle of the People's Livelihood(one of the Three Principles of the People by Sun Yat-sen)

民团(míntuán)the civil corps

民营(mínyíng)run privately

民乐(mínyuè)folk music;Chinese national music;traditional Chinese instruments

民乐队(mínyuèduì)a traditional orchestra

民乐合奏(mínyuè hézòu)an ensemble of traditional instruments

民脂民膏(mínzhī míngāo)the flesh and blood of the people

民族文化宫(mínzú wénhuàgōng)Cultural Palace of Nationalities

民族主义(mínzú zhǔyì)the Principle of Nationalism(one of the Three Principles of the People by Sun Yat-sen)

岷山(mínshān)Minshan Mountain(in Gansu and Sichuan provinces);Mt. Min

闽菜(mǐncài)Fujian Cuisine

闽剧(mǐnjù)Min opera(popular in Fujian province)

名垂青史(míngchuí qīngshǐ)to go down in the annals of history;to be on the scroll of fame

名分(míngfèn)a person's status

名讳(mínghuì)name taboo

名家(míngjiā)①the school of Logicians;the Logicians ②a person of academic or artistic distinction;a virtuoso

名教(míngjiào)the Confucian ethical code

名落孙山(míngluò sūnshān)(lit.)"to fall behind Sun Shan"－to fail in a competitive examination

名门(míng mén)a famous family

名门闺秀(míngmén guīxiù)a daughter of an illustrious,glorious,or eminent family

名山(míngshān)famous mountains

名胜古迹(míngshèng gǔjì)scenic spots and historical sites

名师(míngshī)a great master;a prominent teacher

名师出高徒(míngshī chū gāotú)a great teacher produces a brilliant student.

名士(míngshì)a personage;a celebrity

明朝(míngchāo)the Ming Dynasty

(1368 - 1644)

明代后七子(míngdài hòu qīzǐ) the "Later Seven Gifted Poets" of the Ming Dynasty(a school of literature from 1520 to 1570)

《明会典》(mínghuìdiǎn) *The Laws and Regulations of the Ming Dynasty* - a officially-compiled book in 1587

明镜高悬(míngjìng gāoxuán)(lit.) "a clear mirror hangs on high" - impartial and perspicacious judge

明媒正娶(míngméi zhèngqǔ) to be legally and formally married; a formal wedding

明末清初(míngmò qīngchū) the transitional period from late Ming (1368 -1644) to early Qing(1636 - 1912)

明眸皓齿(míngmóu hàochǐ) to have bright eyes and white teeth; to have beautiful features

明器(míngqì) funerary wares; burial objects

明清小说(míngqīng xiǎoshuō) the novels of the Ming & Qing Dynasties; the fiction of the Ming and Qing Dynasties

明孝陵(míngxiàolíng) the Tomb of Emperor Zhu Yuanzhang; the Ming Xiaoling Mausoleum

明修栈道,暗度陈仓(míngxīu zhàndào, àndù chéncāng) to do one thing under cover of another

《明月几时有》(míngyuè jǐshí yǒu) *When Will the Moon Be Clear and Bright* - a *ci* poem by Su Shi(苏轼,1037 - 1101)

明正典刑(míngzhèng diǎnxíng) to carry out a death sentence according to the law

鸣不平(míng bùpíng) to voice one's discontent; to cry out against injustice

《鸣凤记》(míng fèng jì) *Phoenix Warbling* - a romance of the Ming Dynasty(1368 - 1644)

鸣鼓而攻之(mínggǔ ér gōngzhī) to make a scathing indictment of someone; to publicly denoun-ce someone

鸣金收兵(míngjīn shōubīng) to beat the gong and recall the troops; to call off a battle

鸣锣开道(míngluó kāidào)(lit.) "to beat gongs to clear the way" - to prepare the public for a coming event; to pave the way for

冥府(míngfǔ) the nether world

冥寿(míngshòu) the birth anniversary of a deceased person

铭文(míngwén) an epigraph

瞑目(míngmù) to die content; to close one's eyes in death

命案(mìng'àn) a homicide case; a murder case

命根子(mìnggēnzi) lifehood; life

命门(mìngmén) the gate of vitality

命途多舛(mìngtú duōchuǎn) to suffer many setbacks and frustrations in one's life

命相(mìngxiàng) fortune and appearance; eight Chinese characters and animal signs (used to foretell a person's destiny and a prospective couple's suitability)

谬种(miùzhǒng) ①error; fallacy ②a scoundrel

摸黑儿(mōhēir) to grope one's way in the dark; to grope one's way on a dark night

摹刻(mókè) ①to copy by carving ②a carved reproduction of an inscription or painting

模仿秀(mófǎngxiù) an act of mimicry; an imitation show

摩利支天(mólìzhītiān) Marici (Buddhism)

磨洋工(mó yánggōng) to lie down on the job; to dawdle along

磨嘴皮子(mó zuǐpízi) to do a lot of talking; to jabber; to indulge in idle talk

嬷嬷(mómo) ①an elderly woman ②a wet nurse

魔法(mófǎ) witchcraft

魔王(mówáng) ①Prince of the Devils ②a fiend; a tyrant; a despot

抹脖子(mǒ bózi) to cut one's own throat; to commit suicide

抹黑(mǒhēi) to blacken somebody's name; to throw mud at

抹杀(mǒshā) to blot out; to write off; to obliterate

抹稀泥(mǒ xīní) to try to gloss things over; to try to mediate differences at the sacrifice of principle

抹胸(mǒxiōng) an undergarment (covering the chest and abdomen)

末代皇帝(mòdài huángdì) The last emperor; Aisin Gioro Pu Yi

《末代皇帝》(mòdài huángdì) *The Last Emperor* - a film directed by Bernardo Bertolucci (贝纳尔多·贝托鲁奇) in 1987

《茉莉花》(mòlìhuā) *A Jasmine Flower* - a popular folk song stemmed from Anhui and Jiangsu provinces

陌路(mòlù) a stranger

陌路人(mòlùrén) a stranger

陌头(mòtóu) roadside

秣马厉兵(mòmǎ lìbīng) (lit.) "to feed the horses and sharpen the weapons" - to prepare for battle

莫高窟(mògāokū) the Mogao grottoes (in Dunhuang, Gansu province)

莫逆之交(mònì zhī jiāo) bosom

friends

莫须有(mòxūyǒu) groundless; fabricated

墨宝(mòbǎo) ①your beautiful handwriting②a treasured piece of calligraphy or painting

《墨攻》(mògōng) *Battle of Wits* – a film directed by Zhang Zhiliang(张之亮) in 2006

墨家(mòjiā) the Mohist school; Mohism; Moism

墨客(mòkè) literary men; men of letters

墨吏(mòlì) corrupt officials

墨守成规(mòshǒu chéngguī) to stick to convention; routinism; scholasticism

墨刑(mòxíng) the punishment of tattooing the face

墨汁(mòzhī) prepared Chinese ink

墨子(mòzǐ) Mozi; Motse(around 468 – 381 BC)

《墨子》(mòzǐ) *Mozi*; *Mo-tsu* – a Chinese classic

谋臣(móuchén) a counsellor (of the imperial court)

谋士(móushì) an adviser; a counsellor; an ideas man

母老虎(mǔlǎohǔ) (lit.) "a tigress" – a termagant

母夜叉(mǔyèchā) an ugly shrew

《牡丹亭》(mǔdāntíng) *The Peony Pavilion* – a play by Tang Xianzu (汤显祖,1550 – 1616)

木版画(mùbǎnhuà) a woodcut; a wood engraving

木版年画(mùbǎn niánhuà) a block-printed Chinese New Year picture

木匾(mùbiǎn) a wooden plaque

木雕(mùdiāo) a wooden sculpture; a wood carving

木椟(mùdú) an inscribed wooden tablet

木刻版画(mùkè bǎnhuà) a wood-cut block print

木刻印刷(mùkè yìnshuā) woodblock printing

《木兰从军》(mùlán cóngjūn) *Mulan Joins the Army* – a folk legend in the later Northern Wei Dynasty (386 – 534)

《木兰诗》(mùlánshī) *The Ballad of Mulan* – a folk song of the Northern Dynasties

木讷(mùnè) simple and slow in speech

木牛流马(mùniú liúmǎ) (lit.) "the wooden ox and gliding horse" – a vehicle for transporting supplies

木偶戏(mùǒuxì) a puppet show

木头疙瘩(mùtóu gēda) ①a wooden knot②a blockhead

木头人(mùtóurén) a blockhead

木俑(mùyǒng) a wooden figurine

木鱼(mùyú) a wooden fish(usded by Buddhist monks to beat rhythm when chanting scriptures)

仫佬族(mùlǎozú) the Mulao nationality(distributed mainly in Guangxi Zhuang Autonomous Region)

目不识丁(mùbùshídīng) to be completely illiterate

《牧马人》(mùmǎrén) *The Herdsman* - a film directed by Xie Jin(谢晋) in 1982

《牧羊记》(mùyángjì) *Herding Sheep* - a traditional southern drama, anonymous in the Song and Yuan Dynasties

墓祭(mùjì) to pay respects to a deceased person at his or her grave

墓志(mùzhì) an epitaph; an inscription on a memorial tablet

墓志铭(mùzhìmíng) an epitaph

幕府(mùfǔ) the office of a commanding general

幕僚(mùliáo) aides and staff; an assistant(to a ranking official or general)

睦邻(mùlín) good-neighborliness

暮春(mùchūn) the late spring

暮鼓晨钟(mùgǔ chénzhōng)(lit.) "the evening drum and morning bell" - the daily call to religious life; the timely exhortations to virtue and piety

暮年(mùnián) one's later life

暮秋(mùqīu) the late autumn

暮生儿(mùshengr) a posthumous child

暮云春树(mùyún chūnshù)(lit.) "sunset, clouds and spring trees" - to long for a friend who is far away

《穆桂英挂帅》(mùguìyīng guàshuài) *Lady Mu Guiying Assumes Command* - a traditional Yu opera adapted in 1954

穆斯林(mùsīlín) Muslim

N

拿大顶(nádàdǐng) to stand on one's hands; to do a handstand

拿架子(ná jiàzi) to put on airs; to be haughty

拿来主义(nálái zhǔyì) the doctrine of "taking"; grabbism - a term created by Lu Xun(鲁迅) in 1934

拿腔拿调(náqiāng nádiào) to speak affectedly

拿手(náshǒu) expert in, good at

拿手好戏(náshǒu hǎoxì) ①the part that an actor does best ②(one's) speciality ③a masterpiece

拿主意(ná zhǔyì) to make a decision; to decide

那达慕(nàdámù) the Nadam Fair(a Mongolian traditional fair)

那摩温(nàmówēn)①number one(an early transliteration)②a taskmaster

《那五》(nàwǔ) *Nawu* – a novelette by Deng Youmei(邓友梅,1931 –);a TV drama directed by Xie Tian(谢添)in 1989

纳彩(nàcǎi)to present betrothal gifts (to the bride's family)

纳呆(nàdāi) indigestion or the loss of appetite

纳福(nàfú)to enjoy a life of ease and comfort

纳贡(nàgòng)to pay tribute

纳谏(nàjiàn)to accept an admonition

纳降(nàxiáng)to accept the enemy's surrender

纳凉(nàliáng)to enjoy the cool

纳聘(nàpìn)to present betrothal gifts (to the bride's family);to pay the bride-price

纳妾(nàqiè)to take a concubine

纳西族(nàxīzú) the Naxi nationality (distributed mainly in Yunnan province)

纳鞋底(nà xiédǐ)to stitch the sole of a cloth shoe

奶妈(nǎimā)a wet nurse

奶娘(nǎiniáng)a wet nurse

奶油小生(nǎiyóu xiǎoshēng)(lit.) "a 'cream boy'" – a good looking young man with feminine traits

奶子酒(nǎizijiǔ)fermented milk

囡囡(nānnān)little darling

男扮女装(nánbàn nǚzhuāng) a man disguised as a woman;a man dressed like a woman;a man in drag

男扮女装的流行歌手(nánbàn nǚzhuāng de liúxíng gēshǒu) a cross-dressing pop singer

男傧相(nán bīnxiàng)the best man; the groomsman;the bridesman

男旦(nándàn) a female impersonator (in traditional Chinese opera)

男旦演员(nándàn yǎnyuán)a female impersonator

男盗女娼(nándào nǚchāng)(lit.) "to behave like thieves and whores" – to be full of greed and lust;to be out-and-out scoundrels

男耕女织(nángēng nǚzhī)(lit.) "men plough the fields and women weave" – an agricultural community's ideal of ease and order

《男人的一半是女人》(nánrén de yībàn shì nǚrén) *Half of Man Is Woman* – a novelette by Zhang Xianliang(张贤亮,1936 –)in 1985

男尊女卑(nánzūn nǚbēi) the notion that men are superior to women

南梆子(nánbāngzi)the southern wooden clappers (a percussion instrument used in traditional Chinese operas)

南北朝(nánběicháo) the Northern

and Southern Dynasties(420－589)

南昌起义(nánchāng qǐyì) the Nanchang Uprising(1927)

南朝(náncháo) the Southern Dynasties(420－589)

《南村辍耕录》(náncūn chuògēng lù) *Talks in the Intervals between Ploughing* － a literary sketches by Tao Zongyi(陶宗仪,1321－1407)

《南渡记》(nándùjì) *Go toward the South*;*Move in the South* － a Chinese novel by Zong Pu(宗璞,1928－) in 1988

南国(nánguó) South China;the South

南汉(nánhàn) the Southern Han Dynasty(917－971)

南洪北孔(nánhóng běikǒng) Hong Sheng(洪昇,1645－1704, the dramatist of *The Palace of Eternal Life*) in the South and Kong Shangren(孔尚任,1648－1718, the dramatist of *The Peach-Blossom Fan*) in the North

南胡(nánhú) the "southern fiddle"; erhu(a two-stringed Chinese fiddle)

南京大屠杀(nánjīng dàtúshā) the Nanjing massacre(1937);the Rape of Nanjing;the Rape of Nanking

南京条约(nánjīng tiáoyuē) the Treaty of Nanjing(signed in 1842)

《南柯梦》(nánkē mèng) *The Dream of Nanke* － a play by Tang Xianzu(汤显祖,1550－1616)

《南柯太守传》(nánkē tàishǒu zhuàn) *The Governor of the Soutern Tributary State* － a Tang legend by Li Gongzuo(李公佐) in the Tang Dynasty(618－907); *the Prefecture Chief*

南乐(nányuè) southern classical music

南凉(nánliáng) the Southern Liang(397－414)

南泥湾精神(nánníwān jīngshén) the Nanniwan spirit(the spirit of hard work of the 359th brigade of the Eighth Route Army)

南齐(nánqí) the Southern Qi Dynasty(479－502)

南腔北调(nánqiāng běidiào) a mixed accent

南曲(nánqǔ) ① southern tunes ② opera sung to southern tunes

南拳(nánquán) southern-style boxing

南社(nánshè) the Southern Society(the first modern revolutionary literary society established in 1909)

南施北宋(nánshī běisòng) Shi Runzhang(施闰章,1618－1683) in the south and Song Wan(宋琬,1614－1673) in the north(two famouse poets of the Qing Dynasty)

南宋(nánsòng) the Southern Song

Dynasty(1127 - 1276)

南唐二主(nántáng èrzhǔ) the two emperors of the Southern Tang - Li Jing(李璟,916 - 961) and Li Yu (李煜,937 - 978)

南戏(nánxì) southern opera; southern drama

《南行记》(nán xíng jì) *Heading South* - short stories by Ai Wu(艾芜,1904 - 1992) in 1935

南岳(nányuè) the Southern Sacred Mountain; Hengshan; Mr. Heng

南诏(nánzhào) Nanzhao, a local regime in Yunnan province during the Tang Dynasty

《南征北战》(nánzhēng běizhàn) *Fighting North and South* - a film directed by Cheng Yin(成荫) and Tang Xiaodan(汤晓丹) in 1952

难得糊涂(nándé hútu) ignorance is bliss

《难夫难妻》(nànfū nànqī) *The Difficult Couple* - a film directed by Zhang Shichuan(张石川) in 1913

难兄难弟(nànxiōng nàndì) fellow sufferers

囊中物(nángzhōngwù) something certain of attainment; something already in the bag; to be easily got at

孬种(nāozhǒng) a coward

铙钹(náobó) big cymbals

闹别扭(nào bièniu) ①to fall out②to be at loggerheads with; to be at odds with

闹洞房(nào dòngfáng) to tease the newlywed on their wedding night

闹翻身(nào fānshēn) to fight for emancipation; to struggle for liberation

闹风潮(nào fēngcháo) to stage strikes or demonstration; to incite unrest

闹革命(nào gémìng) to make revolution; to rise up in revolution

闹鬼(nàoguǐ) ①to be haunted②to play tricks behind somebody's back

闹花灯(nào huādēng) the lantern show(in the Lantern Festival)

闹脾气(nào píqì) to vent one's spleen; to lose one's temper

闹情绪(nào qíngxù) to be disgruntled; to be in a fit of pique

闹市(nàoshì) busy streets; the downtown area

闹笑话(nào xiàohuà) to make a stupid mistake; to make a fool of oneself

《呐喊》(nàhǎn) *Cry Out* - a collection of short stories by Lu Xun(鲁迅,1881 - 1936) in 1923

内白(nèibái) the words spoken by an actor from off-stage

内臣(nèichén) a chamberlain

内当家(nèidāngjiā) the wife; a capable wife

内弟(nèidì) brother-in-law (wife's younger brother)

内封(nèifēng) title page

内功(nèigōng) internal qigong; the inner power; internal energy

内讧(nèihòng) the internal conflict; the internal strife

内画壶(nèihuàhú) an intermally decorated bottle or pot

内家拳(nèijiāquán) the internal boxing[founded by Zhang Sanfeng(张三丰,1247 - 1458)]

内奸(nèijiān) a secret enemy agent; a hidden traitor

《内经》(nèijīng) *The Internal Canon of Medicine*; *The Classic of Internal Medicine* - a Chinese medical work

内眷(nèijuàn) the female members of a family

内亲(nèiqīn) the relatives on one's wife's side

内人(nèirén) my wife

内务府(nèiwùfǔ) the Royal Household Bureau; the Ministry of Internal Affairs

内线(nèixiàn) a tipster; a planted agent

内兄(nèixiōng) brother-in-law (wife's elder brother)

内忧外患(nèiyōu wàihuàn) domestic trouble and foreign invasion

内掌柜(nèizhǎngguì) wife of a shopkeeper

内侄(nèizhí) a nephew (on wife's side)

内侄女(nèizhínǚ) a niece (on wife's side)

能掐会算(néngqiā huìsuàn) to be able to tell fortunes; to be able to predict the future course of events

能文能武(néngwén néngwǔ) to be skilled in using both pen and the rifle; to be versed in both literary and martial arts

尼庵(ní' ān) (Buddhism) a Buddhist convent; a Buddhist nunnery

尼布楚条约(níbùchǔ tiáoyuē) the Sino-Russian Treaty of Nerchinsk (1689)

尼姑(nígū) a Buddhist nun

泥塑(nísù) clay sculpture

泥腿子(nítuǐzi) (dated) a bumpkin; a clodhopper

泥俑(níyǒng) a clay figurine used at funerals; earthen figurine

《霓虹灯下的哨兵》(níhóngdēng-xià de shàobīng) *The Guards in the Neon Lights* - a film directed by Wang Ping(王苹) in 1964; *Sentinels under the Neon Lights*

《霓裳羽衣歌》(níshàng yǔyī gē) *The Song of Rainbow-Coloured and Feathered Costumes* - a poem by Bai

Juyi(白居易,772－846)

《你在高原》(nǐ zài gāoyuán) *You are on the Plateau* － a novel by Zhang Wei(张炜,1956－) in 2010

逆流(nìliú) ①to go against the current②an adverse current

逆旅(nìlǚ) a hotel;an inn

逆伦(nìlún) the violation of proper human relationships

逆子(nìzǐ) (dated) an unfilial son

匿名信(nìmíngxìn) an anomymo-us letter

拈花惹草(niānhuā rěcǎo) (lit.) "to toy with flowers and grass"－to dally with women

拈阄儿(niān jiūr) to draw lots

年表(niánbiǎo) a chronological table

年齿(niánchǐ) (formal) age

年饭(niánfàn) the family dinner on lunar New Year's Eve

年高德劭(niángāo déshào) of venerable age and eminent virtue

年庚(niángēng) the time (year, month, day and hour) of a person's birth;the date of birth

年关(niánguān) the end of the year

年号(niánhào) a reign title;the title of an emperor's reign

年画(niánhuà) a New Year picture;a Chinese Spring Festival picture

年货(niánhuò) the special purchases for the Spring Festival

年鉴(niánjiàn) a yearbook;an almanac;annals

年景(niánjǐng) the year's harvest

年谱(niánpǔ) the chronicle of somebody's life

年三十(niánsānshí) the eve of the Chinese new year

年夜(niányè) the lunar New Year's Eve

年夜饭(niányè fàn) the family reunion dinner on the lunar New Year's Eve

捻军(niǎnjūn) the Nian army(1853－1868)

捻军起义(niǎnjūn qǐyì) the Nian Uprising;the Nien Rebellion (1851－1868)

碾磙子(niǎngǔnzi) a stone roller

碾盘(niǎnpán) a millstone (upon which a stone roller is used)

《碾玉观音》(niǎnyù guānyīn) *Goddess of Grinding Jade* － a script for story-telling from the Song Dynasty (960－1279);*The Jade Avalokitesvara*

碾子(niǎnzi) the roller and millstone;a roller

念白(niànbái) the spoken part of a Chinese opera

念佛(niànfó) to pray to Buddha

念经(niànjīng) to recite or chant scriptures

念旧(niànjiù)to keep old friendships in mind;to think of one's old friends or the past

《念奴娇》(niànnújiāo) *Charm of a Maiden Singer* - a verse pattern

念珠(niànzhū)prayer beads;beads

念兹在兹(niànzī zàizī) to bear in mind always; to be constantly on one's mind

娘家(niángjia)the home of a married woman's parents

娘舅(niángjìu) uncle (mother's brother)

娘娘腔(niángniangqiāng) a sissy tone;an effeminate voice

娘姨(niángyí)aunt(mother's sister)

娘子(niángzi) ① madam; ma'am ② one's wife

娘子军(niángzǐjūn) a detachment of women

《鸟朦胧月朦胧》(niǎo ménglóng yuè ménglóng) *Hazy Birds and Dim Moonlight* - a novel by Qiong Yao (琼瑶,1938 -) in 1977;a film directed by Chen Yaoqi(陈耀圻) in 1978

鸟篆(niǎo zhuàn)the bird script(an ancient form of Chinese writing)

袅袅婷婷(niǎoniǎo tíngtíng)graceful in manner

捏把汗(niē bǎ hàn)to be on edge;to be keyed up

涅槃(nièpán)(Buddhism) nirvana; extinction of all desire and pain

《孽海花》(nièhǎihuā)*A Flower in an Ocean of Sin* - a novel by Zeng Pu (曾朴,1872 - 1935)

孽障(nièzhàng)①a sin that will lead to retribution②the evil creature

孽种(nièzhǒng)an undutiful child

《孽子》(niè zǐ) *The Crystal Boys* - a novel by Bai Xianyong(白先勇, 1937 -) in 1977 - 1981;a TV drama directed by Cao Ruiyuan(曹瑞原)in 2003;*Outcasts / The Outsiders* - a film by Yu Kanping(虞戡平)in 1986

宁馨儿(níng xīn'er)a lovely child

宁为玉碎,不为瓦全(nìngwèi yùsuì, bùwèi wǎquán)It is better to die in glory than live in dishonor

佞臣(nìngchén)an obsequious official or courtier

妞妞(niūniu)a little girl

牛鬼蛇神(níu guǐ shé shén)monsters and demons; the forces of evil; all sorts of bad people

牛角挂书(níujiǎo guàshū)(lit.)"to hang the History of the Han Dynasty on an ox horn" - to be assiduous in one's studies

牛角尖(niújiǎojiān)(lit.)"the tip of a horn" - an insignificant or insoluble problem; a problem not worth the effort of attempting to solve

牛郎(niúláng) the Cowherd (a figure of a folk tale); the cow boy

《牛郎织女》(niúláng zhīnǚ) *The Cowherd and the Weaving Maid* – a folk tale; a film directed by Cen Fan (岑范) in 1964; *The Herd-boy and the Weaving-girl*

牛郎织女(niúláng zhīnǚ) the Cowherd and the Weaving Maid; husband and wife who live far apart

牛皮大王(niúpí dàwáng) a braggart

牛气(niúqì) very proud and arrogant; conceited; overbearing

牛头马面(niútóu mǎmiàn) (lit.) "ox head and horse face" – hideous lackeys

扭秧歌(niǔ yānggē) to perform a yangko dance (a popular folk dance in the north)

扭转乾坤(niǔzhuǎn qiánkūn) to bring about a radical change in the situation; to turn things around; to turn the tide

农会(nónghuì) peasant association

农家(nóngjiā) ①the Agriculturalists (a school of thoughts in the period of Eastern Zhou, 770 – 256 BC) ②a farmhouse; a peasant family

农家乐(nóngjiālè) agritainment; agri-tourism; to go on agri-tourism

农历(nónglì) the Chinese lunar calendar

农贸市场(nóngmào shìchǎng) a market of farm produce; a farmers' market

农民运动讲习所(nóngmín yùndòng jiǎngxísuǒ) the Peasant Movement Institute

《农奴》(nóngnú) *Serfs* – a film directed by Li Jun (李俊) in 1964

农奴(nóngnú) a serf

农奴制(nóngnúzhì) the serf system; serfdom

农奴主(nóngnúzhǔ) serf-owner

《农政全书》(nóngzhèng quánshū) *Complete Treatise on Agriculture* – a book compiled by Xu Guangqi (徐光启, 1562 – 1633)

弄潮儿(nòngcháo'er) (lit.) "a tide player" – a current leader; a tastemaker; a pioneer

弄臣(nòngchén) (dated) a favorite courtier

弄权(nòng quán) to manipulate power for personal ends

奴婢(núbì) slave girls and maidservants

奴才(núcai) a flunkey; a lackey

奴家(nújiā) I, me (a girl's or young woman's self-depreciating way of referring to herself)

奴颜媚骨(núyán mèigǔ) sycophancy and obsequiousness

驽胎(nútāi)①an inferior horse②a mediocre person

弩弓(nǔgōng)a crossbow

弩箭(nǔjiàn)a crossbow arrow

怒发冲冠(nùfà chōngguān)to bristle with anger;to be in a towering rage

怒族(nùzú)the Nu nationality(distributed mainly in Yunnan and Tibet)

女扮男装(nǚbàn nánzhuāng)a woman disguised as a man

女傧相(nǚ bīnxiàng)a bridesmaid

女儿酒(nǚérjiǔ)the daughter's wine(a kind of wine brewed after a daughter is born, buried underground and taken out to entertain guests when the daughter gets married)

《女驸马》(nǚ fùmǎ)*The Female Son-in-Law of the Emperor* – a famous Huangmei opera

女工(nǚgōng)①woman worker; female employee ②needlework

女红(nǚhóng)(dated)needlework – a woman of brilliant ability

《女诫》(nǚ jiè)*Lessons for Women* – a book by Ban Zhao(班昭,49 – 117)

女伶(nǚlíng)an actress

女强人(nǚ qiángrén)a strong woman

女色(nǚsè)feminine charms

《女神》(nǚshén)*The Goddess* – an anthology of poetry by Guo Moruo(郭沫若,1892 – 1978)in 1921

女史(nǚshǐ)(dated)①a female official②a female intellectual

《女史箴图》(nǚshǐ zhēntú)*Admonitions of the Court Ladies* – a painting by Gu Kaizhi(顾恺之,348 – 409)

女书(nǚshū)women's script(stemmed from Hunan province)

女娲(nǚwā)Nuwa(a creator-goddess in Chinese mythology)

女娲补天(nǚwā bǔtiān)Nuwa repairing the sky(a fairy tale)

女娲造人(nǚwā zào rén)Nuwa creating man(a fairy tale)

女性文学(nǚxìng wénxué)women's literature;women's writing

女优(nǚyōu)an actress(in traditional opera)

女真(nǚzhēn)Nuzhen(the ancestors of the Manchus)

暖房(nuǎnfáng)①to go to the bridal chamber(to extend one's congratulations on the eve of a wedding)②to pay a house-warming visit ③a greenhouse

暖寿(nuǎnshòu)the celebrations on the eve of a birthday

傩神(nuóshén)a god who drives out pestilence

傩戏(nuóxì)the Nuo opera(a regional opera popular in Sichuan,Guizhou, Anhui and Hubei provinces)

搦战(nuòzhàn) to provoke one into fighting; to challenge one to a fight

O

欧体(ōutǐ) the Ouyang style – a style of calligraphy represented by Ouyang Xun(欧阳询,557 – 641)

瓯剧(ōujù) Wenzhou opera

瓯绣(ōuxiù) Wenzhou embroidery

呕心沥血(ǒuxīn lìxuè) to take great pains over something; to work one's heart out

怄气(òu qì) to be sulky

P

扒手(páshǒu) thief; pickpocket

爬格子(pá gézi) to engage in writing

爬灰(páhuī)(lit.) "to scratch in ashes" – to commit adultery with one's daughter-in-law

怕老婆(pà lǎopo) to be henpecked; to be under the thumb

怕生(pà shēng) to be timid or shy of strangers

拍案叫绝(pāi'àn jiàojué) to strike the table and shout bravo; to applaud madly

《拍案惊奇》(pāi'àn jīngqí) *Striking the Table in Amazement at the Wondrous Stories* – a collection of short stories by Feng Menglong(冯梦龙, 1574 – 1646)

拍板(pāibǎn)(lit.) "to slap the board" – to make a final decision

《拍电影》(pāi diǎnyǐng) *Making A Film* – a skit starring by Chen Peisi (陈佩斯) and Zhu Shimao(朱时茂) in 1985

拍马屁(pāimǎpì) to flatter; to toady; to bootlick

拍拖(pāituō) to date; to go on a date with; to have a love affair with

俳谐文(páixiéwén) a satiric essay; satire

俳优(páiyōu) an actor or actress who performs in a low comedy

排比(páibǐ) parallelism

排场(páichǎng) ① ostentation and extravagance; pomp and ceremony ②lavish; sumptuous

排行(páiháng) to rank brothers and sisters(according to seniority); seniority; ranking

排律(páilǜ) a long poem in regulated verse(usu. five-characters per line)

排笙(páishēng) a reed pipe wind instrument with a keyboard

排戏(páixì) to rehearse a play

排箫(páixiāo) a panpipe

排钟(páizhōng) chimes

牌匾(páibiǎn) an inscribed board; a tablet; a plaque

牌坊(páifāng)a memorial archway or gateway

牌号(páihào)①the name of a shop ②a trademark

牌九(páijiǔ)Chinese dominoes

牌楼(páilou)a decorated archway

牌位(páiwèi)a memorial wooden tablet

牌子曲(páiziqǔ)the singing of a succession of lyrics or stories to the tunes of various ballads(a folk art form)

派头(pàitóu)an impressive manner or style

攀高枝(pān gāozhī)to be friends with or be married to somebody of a higher social status

攀龙附凤(pānlóng fùfèng)(lit.)"to attempt to be attached to dragons and phoenixes"- to butter up people of power and influence;to curry favor with those in power

攀亲(pānqīn)①to claim to be the relative or kin of someone;to establish friendly relationships with other units or organizations ②to arrange a marriage

盘缠(pánchan)traveling expenses

盘古(pángǔ)Pangu(the creator of the universe)

盘账(pánzhàng)to check accounts

磐石之安(pánshí zhī ān)as solid as a rock

蟠桃(pántáo)the sacred peach;the immortal peach(Based on a mythology,having such a peach,a mortal being can become immortal)

蟠桃会(pántáohuì)the Sacred Peach Feast[According to Taoist mythology,on the Birthday of Queen Mother of Heaven(王母娘娘),fairies are invited for a feast of sacred peaches]

判官(pànguān)①the assistant of a local government official [in the Tang(618 - 907) and Song(960 - 1279) Dynasties] ②a judge in the nether world

判教(pànjiào)the different sects of Buddhist teaching

盼头(pàntou)hope;good prospects

《彷徨》(pánghuáng)*Hover* - a collection of short stories by Lu Xun's(鲁迅,1881 - 1936) in 1924 - 1925;*Hesitation*

旁白(pángbái)an aside(in a play)

旁观者清(pángguānzhě qīng)onlookers see clearly;the onlooker is clear-headed

旁门左道(pángmén zuǒdào)a heretical scheme;a heterodox school

抛头露面(pāotóu lùmiàn)to show one's face in public; to appear in public

抛头颅,洒热血(pāo tóulú,sǎ rèxuè) to shed one's blood and lay down one's life;to sacrifice oneself

抛绣球(pāo xiùqiú) to throw coloured silk balls (often as a means to choose a husband)

抛砖引玉(pāozhuān yǐnyù)(lit.)"to throw a brick in order to get a gem"-to make crude remarks in the hope of gaining valuable opinions

庖厨(páochú)①a kitchen②a chef

庖代(páodài) to exceed one's remit and interfere in somebody else's affairs;to act in somebody's place

庖正(páozhèng) the court official in charge of the king's food

炮烙(páoluò) the hot pillar(a cruel form of torture)

袍笏登场(páohù dēngchǎng) ① to dress up and go on stage ② to assume an official post

袍泽(páozé) fellow officers(in the army)

袍泽故旧(páozé gùjiù) old friends (who used to be comrades in the army)

袍子(páozi) a robe;a gown

跑单帮(pǎo dānbāng) to travel long distance while doing retail business alone; to travel around trading on one's own

跑官(pǎoguān) to seek official position by dishonest methods

跑旱船(pǎohànchuán) to perform the boat dance(a folk dance)

跑合儿(pǎohér) to act as go-between in a business deal

跑江湖(pǎo jiānghú) ①to rove the country②to make a living by traveling around

跑龙套(pǎo lóngtào) ① to play a walk-on part in a drama or opera on stage②to do something insignificant under someone;to play a minor role

跑龙套的演员(pǎo lóngtào de yǎnyán) a walk-on performer

跑马卖解(pǎomǎ màixiè) to make a living by performing acrobatics on horseback

跑码头(pǎo mǎtou) to travel from port to port as a trader;to be a traveling merchant

跑买卖(pǎo mǎimai) to do business by traveling from one place to another;to be a commercial traveller

跑堂儿的(pǎotángrde) a waiter or waitress(in a restaurant)

跑腿的(pǎotuǐde) an errand

跑腿儿(pǎotuǐr) to run errands

跑圆场(pǎo yuánchǎng) to walk around the stage to indicate scene change or traveling a long distance in a traditional drama or opera

跑账(pǎozhàng) to run around to collect bills or debts

泡吧(pàobā) to hang around in bars (such as internet bars)

泡菜(pàocài) pickles; salted vegetables

泡蘑菇(pào mógu) ①to play for time; to use delaying tactics ②to idle about; to dawdle

泡妞(pàoniū)(dialect) to chase girls

泡汤(pàotāng) to fall through; to fail

炮筒子(pào tǒngzi) ①a gun barrel② a loudmouth; a blunt person

炮仗(pàozhang) a firecracker

陪吊(péidiào) a person who is employed to receive guests at a funeral

陪都(péidū) an alternate or secondary capital; an provisional capital

陪房(péifang) a maiden servant accompanying the bride to the bridegroom's home

陪嫁(péijià) a dowry

陪奁(péilián) a dowry

陪葬(péizàng) to be buried with the dead

陪葬品(péizàngpǐn) funerary objects; objects to be buried with somebody

赔不是(péi bùshi) to apologize; to say sorry

赔小心(péi xiǎoxīn) to try to appease someone humbly

赔笑脸(péi xiàoliǎn) to show a smiling face to appease someone; to smile obsequiously or apologetically

赔罪(péizuì) to apologize (for a wrong done to somebody); to make an apology (for one's wrongdoing)

配殿(pèidiàn) a side hall (in a palace or temple)

配房(pèifáng) a side room or wing room; an apprentice

朋侪(péngchái) friends; companions

朋俦(péngchóu) friends; companions

朋党(péngdǎng) a clique; a faction

蓬荜生辉(péngbì shēnghuī) you bring radiance to my humble house

蓬莱仙岛(pénglái xiāndǎo) the Penglai fairy island

蓬莱仙境(pénglái xiānjìng) the Penglai fairyland

蓬门荜户(péngmén bìhù) a humble house

篷车(péngchē) a covered carriage

捧场(pěngchǎng) to boost somebody in a performance; to flatter

捧角(pěngjué) to try to boost an actor or actress; to applaud to show high praise on a particular actor or actress

碰钉子(pèng dīngzi) to hit a snag; to be completely rejected

碰头会(pèngtóuhuì) a very brief meeting

碰运气(pèng yùnqì) to try one's luck; to take a chance

批斗(pīdòu)to criticize and denounce (at a public meeting)

批斗大会(pīdòu dàhuì) a public meeting of criticism and denouncement; a public interrogation assembly; a struggle session

批判会(pīpànhuì) a criticism meeting; a struggle session

批条(pītiáo) a note bearing a superior's instructions or comments; a superior's note

批文(pīwén) written instructions

披挂上阵(pīguà shàngzhèn) to put on one's armor and go to fight; to go into action

披红戴花(pīhóng dàihuā) to drape a band of red silk over one's shoulder and pin a big red flower on one's chest (as a token of honor or on a festive occasion)

披麻戴孝(pīmá dàixiào) to wear the coarse hempen cloth of mourning

皮包公司(píbāo gōngsī) a briefcase company; a fly-by-night company; a bubble company; a speculation company

皮簧(píhuáng) xipi and erhuang (two key vocal motifs in traditional operas)

皮影戏(píyǐngxì) a shadow play

啤酒肚(píjiǔdù) a beer belly; a big belly

琵琶(pípá) the *pipa* (a Chinese four-stringed musical instrument); the four-stringed Chinese lute

《琵琶记》(pípájì) *A Legendary Pipa* – a play by Gao Ming (高明, 1305 – 1359); *The Story of a Pipa Lute*

《琵琶行》(pípáxíng) *Song of a Pipa Player* – a poem by Bai Juyi (白居易, 772 – 846) in 816

裨将(píjiàng) the subordinate general

貔虎(píhǔ) brave troops; brave warriors

貔貅(píxiū) ①pixiu (a mythical wild animal) ②brave troops; fierce warriors

鼙鼓(pígǔ) the war drum; the battle drum

匹夫(pǐfū) an ordinary man; an ignorant man

匹夫之勇(pǐfū zhī yǒng) fool-hardy courage; reckless courage

否极泰来(pǐjí tàilái) good luck comes after extremely bad luck; out of the depth of misfortune comes bliss

痞子(pǐzi) a rascal; a hooligan

痞子文学(pǐzi wénxué) hooligan literature

屁颠儿(pìdiānr) happy and gay

屁话(pìhuà) rubbish, nonsense

辟谣(pìyáo) to deny a rumour; to refute a rumour

偏安一隅(piān'ān yīyú) to be fully

content to rule over only a small part of a country

偏殿(piāndiàn)side hall(in a palace or a temple)

偏方(piānfāng)a folk prescription;a folk remedy

偏房(piānfáng)①a wing of a building②a concubine

偏旁(piānpáng)the basic components of Chinese characters;a radical on one side of a character

偏裨(piānpí)deputy military commander

偏心眼儿(piānxīnyǎnr)partiality;bias

骈俪(piánlì)antithesis;the art of parallelism

骈体(piántǐ)the parallel style of writing

骈体文(piántǐwén)rhyming prose

骈文(piánwén)parallel prose

片警(piànjǐng)a local policeman in charge of a certain area

嫖客(piáokè)a whoremonger;a whoremaster

《漂亮妈妈》(piàoliang māma) *Breaking the Silence* – a film directed by Sun Zhou(孙周)in 2000

票法(piàofǎ)a system of transporting and selling tea and salt by the credences(from the late Ming Dynasty to 1866)

票贩子(piàofànzi)a ticket scalper

票号(piàohào)an exchange shop

票商(piàoshāng)salt dealers[engaged in salt business in the Ming (1368 – 1644) and Qing (1636 – 1912) Dynasties];salt barons

票友(piàoyǒu)an amateur opera performer;a guest player

票庄(piàozhuāng)an exchange shop

骠骑将军(piàoqí jiāngjūn)cavalry general

姘居(pīnjū)extramarital cohabitation

姘头(pīntou)a paramour;a lover

拼盘(pīnpán)assorted cold dishes

拼音(pīnyīn)①to phoneticize②Pinyin(the phonetic system for the transcription of Chinese characters)

拼音文字(pīnyīn wénzì)alphabetic writing;phonetic writing

拼音字母(pīnyīn zìmǔ)①phonetic alphabet②Chinese phonetic letters

贫道(píndào)I(humble self-appellation by a poor cleric)

贫贱之交(pínjiàn zhī jiāo)friends in times of poverty;a friend in need

贫农(pínnóng)a poor peasant

贫僧(pínsēng)I(humble self-appellation by a poor cleric)

贫下中农(pínxiàzhōngnóng)poor and lower-middle peasants

贫嘴(pínzuǐ)garrulous;loquacious

贫嘴贱舌(pínzuǐ jiànshé)to be

sharp-tongued and opinionated; to be spiteful and talkative

嫔妃(pínfēi) ①a concubine of the emperor ②a female attendant at court

嫔嫱(pínqiáng) a female court official

品第(pǐndì) status, rank

品服(pǐnfú) official costume; official dress (showing difference in rank)

品鉴(pǐnjiàn) to judge; to appraise

品茗(pǐnmíng) ①to taste tea (to judge its quality) ②to sample tea

品头论足(pǐntóu lùnzú) ①to make frivolous remarks about a woman's appearance ②to find fault with minor details

聘金(pìnjīn) ①betrothal money ②commission; hiring fee

聘礼(pìnlǐ) betrothal gifts

乒乓球(pīngpāngqiú) ①table tennis or ping-pong ②a table tennis ball

平板车(píngbǎnchē) a flatbed tricycle; a flatbed rickshaw

平辈(píngbèi) people of the same generation; peers

平步青云(píngbù qīngyún) to have a meteoric rise (in one's position, fame or career)

《平凡的世界》(píngfán de shìjiè) *The Ordinary World* – a novel by Lu Yao(路遥, 1949 – 1992) in 1988

平反(píngfǎn) to rehabilitate; to reverse an unjust verdict on somebdy; rehabilitation

平话(pínghuà) popular tales; storytelling

平康(píngkāng) ①peaceful and prosperous ②a brothel

平康坊(píngkāngfǎng) the Pingkang Lanes (a district inhabited mostly by prostitutes); a red-light district

平民艺术(píngmín yìshù) a folk art

《平沙落雁》(píngshā luòyàn) *Wild Geese over the Clam Sands* – a piece of music published in 1634

《平山冷燕》(píngshān lěngyàn) *The Story of the Four Gifted Scholars* – a novel in the Qing Dynasty (1636 – 1912) with the extant earliest version in 1658

平身(píngshēn) ①to get up after genuflection ②"Rise!" (said by an emperor to a kowtowing subject)

平声(píngshēng) an even tone; a level tone

平粜(píngtiào) to sell grain from public granaries during a famine

平遥古城(píngyáo gǔchéng) The Ancient City of Pingyao (a well-persevered traditional Chinese county town in Shanxi)

平一(píngyī) to put down rebellions and unify the land

《平原游击队》(píngyuán yóujīduì)

The Guerrillas Sweep the Plains – a film directed by Su Li (苏里) in 1955

平仄(píngzè) ①level and oblique tones; even and uneven ②the tonal patterns (in classical Chinese poetry)

评弹(píngtán) *pingtan* (a form of storytelling with singing in the Suzhou dialect)

评话(pínghuà) pinghua (a type of folk art form, with a narrator telling a story in his or her local dialect)

评剧(píngjù) Pingju opera (a local opera of north China and northeast China)

评书(píngshū) ①pingshu (a Chinese folk art form in which the performer tells a long story by using a folding fan, a handkerchief, and a gavel as props) ② storytelling

凭吊(píngdiào) to pay a visit to (a historical site or tomb etc.)

屏风(píngfēng) a folding screen

屏门(píngmén) a screen door

萍水相逢(píngshuǐ xiāngféng) to meet by chance

《萍踪侠影录》(píngzōng xiáyǐng lù) *Stories of the Wandering Hero* – a novel by Liang Yusheng (梁羽生, 1924–2009) in 1959–1960

泼妇(pōfù) a termagant; a shrew; a virago; a vixen

泼辣旦(pōladàn) a shrewish role (in traditional Chinese opera)

泼冷水(pō lěngshuǐ) to pour cold water on; to dampen somebody's spirits or enthusiasm

泼墨(pōmò) to splash ink on a piece of paper (a Chinese painting technique)

泼皮(pōpí) a rogue; a hooligan; a ruffian; a scoundrel

泼水节(pōshuǐjié) the Water-Splashing Festival [a festival of Dai Minority (傣族) in mid-April in Yunnan Province]

婆家(pójia) the husband's family

婆娘(póniáng) ①a married woman ②wife

婆婆妈妈(pópo māmā) garrulous; fussy and sentimental like an old woman

婆婆嘴(pópozuǐ) (lit.) "an old woman's mouth" – a garrulous person; a chatterbox

笸箩(pǒluo) a shallow osier or bamboo basket

破财消灾(pòcái xiāozāi) unexpected financial loss might free one from trouble and disaster

破釜沉舟(pòfǔ chénzhōu) (lit.) "to smash the pots and pans and sink the boats (after crossing the river)" – to cut off all means of retreat; to never retreat; to burn one's bridges

破关斩将(pòguān zhǎnjiàng) (lit.) "to cross many passes and vanquish generals in battle" – to overcome a lot of difficulties

破镜重圆(pòjìng chóngyuán) (lit.) "a broken mirror joined together" – the reunion of husband and wife after separation

破落户(pòluòhù) an impoverished family

破身(pòshēn) to lose one's virginity; to have sex for the first time

破四旧,立四新(pò sìjiù, lì sìxīn) to cast away the Four Olds(old ideas, old culture, old customs and old habits) and introduce the Four News (new ideas, new culture, new customs and new habits) (a slogan used during the Cultural Revolution in the 1960s and 1970s)

破题(pòtí) topic sentences; to state one's theme in the first few sentences

破天荒(pòtiānhuāng) to occur for the first time; to be unprecedented

破五(pòwǔ) the fifth day of the first lunar month

破鞋(pòxié) (lit.) "shabby and worn-out shoes" – a loose woman; a promiscuous woman

《破窑记》(pòyáo jì) *Poor Cave Dwelling* – a romance by Wang Shifu (王实甫,1260 – 1336)

铺盖卷儿(pūgàijuǎnr) a bedding roll; a luggage roll

莆仙戏(púxiānxì) Puxian opera (a Fujian local opera)

菩萨(púsà) ① Bodhisattva ② a kind-hearted person

《菩萨蛮》(púsàmán) *Buddhist Dancers* – a verse pattern

菩萨心肠(púsà xīncháng) kind-heartedness

菩提(pútí) Bodhi(supreme wisdom or enlightenment in Buddhism)

菩提树(pútíshù) Bodhi tree(the Buddhist tree of wisdom or enlightenment)

脯脩(púxiū) ① dried meat ② a teacher's wage(in ancient China)

蒲包(púbāo) a cattail bag, a rush bag

蒲墩儿(púdūnr) a cattail hassock

蒲节(pújié) the Calamus Festival; the Dragon Boat Festival(falling on the fifth day of the fifth lunar month)

蒲剧(pújù) Pu opera(a local opera in south Shanxi Province)

蒲扇(púshàn) a palm leaf fan

蒲团(pútuán) a cattail hassock; a cattail mattress

朴学(pǔxué) textual criticism

普度(pǔdù) to deliver all from torment;to release(Buddhism)

普度众生(pǔdù zhòngshēng) to deliver all living creatures from torment(Buddhism)

普洱茶(pǔ'ěrchá) Pu'er Tea

普罗文学(pǔluó wénxué) Proletarian Literature

普米族(pǔmǐzú) the Pumi nationality (distributed mainly in Yunnan province)

普通话(pǔtōnghuà) Putonghua; Mandarin

普陀山(pǔtuóshān) Putuo Mountain; Mount Putuo (one of the four famous Buddhism mountains in China,located in Zhejiang province)

普照寺(pǔzhàosì) Monastery of Omnipresent Light (on Mount Tai in Shandong province)

溥仪(pǔyí) Aisin Gioro Pu Yi(溥仪, 1906 – 1967) the last emperor of the Qing Dynasty

氆氇(pǔlu) the Tibetan woollen fabric

铺保(pùbǎo) a shopkeeper as a guarantor

铺房(pùfáng) to decorate the bridal chamber

铺面(pùmiàn) ①the front or façade of a shop②the sales area

Q

七步成诗(qībùchéngshī) (lit.) "composing a poem within seven paces" – to be skilled at creating spontaneous poetry [referring to the talent of Cao Zhi (曹植, 192 – 232)]

《七步诗》(qībùshī) *Seven-Pace Poem* – a poem by Cao Zhi (曹植,192 – 232)

七步之才(qībù zhī cái) (lit.) "a seven-pace talent" – an amazing talent of spontaneous literary creation

七大古都(qī dà gǔdū) the seven great ancient capitals (Xi'an, Luoyang, Nanjing, Beijing, Kaifeng, Hangzhou and Anyang)

《七剑下天山》(qījiàn xià tiānshān) *Seven Swords of Mount Heaven* – a film directed by Xu Ke (徐克) in 2005

七律(qīlǜ) seven-syllable regulated verse(an eight-line poem with seven characters in each line, written by following rigorous prosodic rules)

七闽(qīmǐn) Fujian

七品芝麻官(qīpǐn zhīmaguān) a minor or petty official; a junior official;a county magistrate

《七品芝麻官》(qīpǐn zhīmaguān) *The Seventh-grade Petty Official* – a Yu opera; a film directed by Xie Tian(谢添) in 1979; *The Presump-*

tuous Mr. Nobody

七七(qīqī) the seventh-day memorial ceremony(held on the 49th day after somebody's death)

七七事变(qīqī shìbiàn) the July 7 Incident of 1937

七窍(qīqiào) the seven apertures in the human head(eyes, ears, nostrils and mouth)

七擒七纵(qīqín qīzòng) to capture seven times and release seven times – a strategy from the 14th century novel *The Romance of the Three Kingdoms*

七情(qīqíng) the seven human emotions (joy, anger, worry, missing, sadness ,terror and surprise)

七声(qīshēng) the seven notes of the ancient Chinese musical scale (gong, shang, jue, bianzhi, zhi, yu and biangong);(equivalent to) do, re, me, fa, so, la, te

七十二变(qīshí'èr biàn) the seventy-two metamorphoses – one of the abilities of Monkey King in the 16th century novel *Journey to the West*

七十二行(qīshí'èr háng) (lit.) "seventy-two industries" – all walks of life

七夕(qīxī) the seventh evening of the seventh moon; the Chinese Valentine's Day; the Chinese Double Seventh Festival

七弦琴(qīxiánqín) a heptachord; a seven-stringed zither

七言绝句(qīyán juéjù) seven-syllable quatrain(a four-line poem with seven characters in each line)

七言诗(qīyánshī) seven-syllable poem

七音(qīyīn) the seven notes of the ancient Chinese musical scale (gong, shang, jue, bianzhi, zhi, yu and biangong);(equivalent to) do, re, me, fa, so, la, te

七月诗派(qīyuè shīpài) the July Poets(who published their poems in the magazine named July initiated in 1937)

《七子之歌》(qīzǐ zhī gē) *The Songs of the Seven Sons* – poems by Wen Yiduo(闻一多, 1899 – 1946) in 1925; the theme song of the TV documentary *Days of Macau* (1998)

妻孥(qīnú) wife and children

妻室(qīshì) wife

期颐(qīyí) ①a 100-year-old person; a centenarian ② one hundred years of age

漆画(qīhuà) a lacquer painting

祁剧(qíjù) Qi opera – a local opera of Qiyang(祁阳), Hunan province

齐东野语(qídōng yěyǔ) hearsay; gossip

齐家文化(qíjiā wénhuà) the Qijia culture(the Neolithic Culture found in Gansu province in 1923)

齐鲁文化(qílǔ wénhuà) Shandong culture

齐民(qímín) the common people; the populace

《齐民要术》(qímín yàoshù) *Important Arts for the People's Welfare* – an agricultural encyclopedia by Jia Sixie(贾思勰) in 533 – 544

齐天大圣(qítiān dàshèng) the Saint in Heaven; Monkey King(a hero in the novel *Journey to the West*)

岐黄(qíhuáng) ① Qibo(岐伯) and Huangdi(黄帝)(the legendary founders of Chinese medicine) ② Chinese medicine

岐黄之术(qíhuáng zhī shù) traditional Chinese medical science

奇门遁甲(qímén dùnjiǎ) the art of becoming invisible(Taoist magic)

《奇袭白虎团》(qíxí báihǔtuán) *Raid on the White-Tiger Regiment* – a modern Beijing opera and a model one first performed in 1955

祈福(qífú) to pray for blessings

祈年(qínián) to pray for a good harvest in the coming year; to pray for a year of abundance

祈年殿(qíniándiàn) Hall of Prayer for Good Harvests(the main architecture of the Temple of Heaven in Beijing established in 1420)

耆艾(qí'ài) an elderly person; an aged person

耆老(qílǎo) ① an aged person; an elderly person ② a founder

耆年硕德(qínián shuòdé) of advanced years and noble character

耆绅(qíshēn)(formal) an elderly gentleman

耆宿(qísù)(formal) a renowned senior citizen; a venerable old person; an elderly sage

骐骥(qíjì) a thoroughbred horse; a steed

骑楼(qílóu) a overhead terrace; an arcade

棋逢对手(qíféng duìshǒu) to meet one's match in a game of chess; to meet one's match in a contest

棋路(qílù) chess tactics

棋谱(qípǔ) a chess manual

棋圣(qíshèng) a champion chess player; a chess grandmaster

棋手(qíshǒu) a chess player

棋坛(qítán) chess circles

棋坛高手(qítán gāoshǒu) a grandmaster in chess circles; a chess grandmaster

棋坛新秀(qítán xīnxiù) a rising star in the chess circles; a new chess talent

《棋王》(qíwáng) *Chess King* - a novelette by A Cheng(阿城,1949 -) in 1984;a film directed by Yan Hao (严浩)in 1991;*King of Chess*

棋艺(qíyì)skill in playing chess

棋友(qíyǒu) a fellow chess player; a chess friend

旗鼓相当(qígǔ xiāngdāng)to be well matched

旗号(qíhào)①the banner②an excuse;a pretext

旗开得胜(qíkāi déshèng)to win victory in the first round

旗袍(qípáo) a Chinese cheongsam; a qipao;a mandarin gown

旗人(qírén)a Manchu

旗手(qíshǒu)a standard-bearer

旗装(qízhuāng) Manchu dress; Manchu attire

麒麟(qílín)①a kylin;a Chinese unicorn②a symbol of luck and happiness

乞巧(qǐqiǎo) the Double Seventh Festival(on the seventh evening of the 7th lunar month)

乞巧节(qǐqiǎojié)the Double Seventh Festival(on the seventh evening of 7th lunar month)

启禀(qǐbǐng)to report(to one's superior)

启奏(qǐzòu)to present a memorial(to the emperor)

杞人忧天(qǐrén yōutiān)(lit.)"to act like the man of the Qi State who feared that the sky might fall" - to be haunted by imaginary fears

起笔(qǐbǐ)①the first stroke of a Chinese character;to begin to write the first stroke of a Chinese character② to begin to write

起兵(qǐbīng) to send off troops; to dispatch troops

起草(qǐcǎo)to make a draft;to draw up

起承转合(qǐchéngzhuǎnhé)introduction, development, transition, conclusion(the four steps in composing a Chinese classical essay)

起更(qǐgēng) to sound the the first night watch

起哄(qǐhòng) to gather together to create a disturbance; to kick up a fuss

起讲(qǐjiǎng)to give a brief summary of the whole argument in an essay (the third part of a traditional Chinese"eight-legged essay")

起解(qǐjiè) to send a prisoner away under guard

起居室(qǐjūshì) a living room; a sitting room

起课(qǐkè)to start to divine;to start a session in divination

起灵(qǐlíng) to move somebody's coffin; to move somebody's ashes (to the burial place)

起事(qǐshì) to start armed struggle; to rise in rebellion

起夜(qǐyè) to get up during the night (to urinate)

起坐间(qǐzuòjiān) a living room; a sitting room

稽首(qǐshǒu) to kowtow

气包子(qìbāozi) a person who is easily offended

气功(qìgōng) qigong, the Chinese breathing exercise; breathing technique

气功师(qìgōngshī) a qigong master

气节(qìjié) integrity

气量(qìliàng) tolerance; forbearance

气数(qìshù) destiny

气虚(qìxū) the deficiency of vital energy

气血(qìxuè) vital energy and state of blood

气韵(qìyùn) the spirit, character, tone or style

气滞(qìzhì) the stagnation of the circulation of vital energy

弃妇(qìfù) an abandoned wife

弃甲曳兵(qìjiǎ yèbīng) (lit.) "to throw away armour and trail weapons behind one" – to flee in defeat

契丹(qìdān) Qidan; Khitan (an ancient nationality in northern China)

契刀(qìdāo) qidao (an ancient coin, one qidao equals to five hundred coin)

契文(qìwén) the oracle bone script; oracle bone writing

契友(qìyǒu) a close friend; a bosom buddy

掐诀(qiājué) to calculate on one's fingers; to make finger gestures during religious incantations

掐算(qiāsuàn) to count; to reckon (usually on one's fingers)

袷袢(qiāpàn) a Uygur or Tajik robe

千层饼(qiāncéngbǐng) multi-layer steamed bread

千层底(qiāncéngdǐ) multi-layer soles; strong cloth soles

千古(qiāngǔ) through the ages; eternal; for all time

千古绝唱(qiāngǔ juéchàng) to rank as a masterpiece throughout the ages; a masterpiece for all time

千古罪人(qiāngǔ zuìrén) to stand condemned through the ages; a man of eternal guilt; a traitor through the ages

《千家诗》(qiānjiāshī) *An Anthology of Popular Ancient Chinese Poems* – an poetry anthology of the Tang and Song Dynasties

千金(qiānjīn)①a lot of money②your precious daughter

《千金方》(qiānjīnfāng) *Priceless Vital Prescriptions* – a medical book by Sun Simiao(孙思邈,581 – 682) in 652

千军易得,一将难求(qiānjūn yìdé, yījiàng nánqiú)(lit.)"it is easier to recruit a thousand soldiers than to find one general to lead them" – it is very difficult to hire professional and talented person;good leaders are hard to come by

《千里江山图》(qiānlǐ jiāngshān tú) *Long Undulating Mountains and Rivers* – a traditional Chinese painting by Wang Ximeng(王希孟,1096 –?)

千里驹(qiānlǐjū)(lit.)"a thousand-li colt" – a promising youngster

千里马(qiānlǐmǎ)(lit.)"a swift horse" – a person of great talent

千里眼(qiānlǐyǎn)①a far-sighted person②a telescope or field glasses ③a Taoist patron saint

千里姻缘(qiānlǐ yīnyuán) marriage is preordained; a preordained marriage.

千秋(qiānqiū)(lit.)"a thousand autumns" – centuries;ages

千秋大业(qiānqiū dàyè) a great undertaking or cause with everlasting significance; an everlasting enterprise

千秋万代(qiānqiū wàndài) throughout the ages;generation after generation;everlasting

千手观音(qiānshǒu guānyīn)(Buddhism) Avalokitesvara(the Goddess of Mercy with a thousand arms)

千岁(爷)[qiānsuì(yé)] Your/His Royal Highness(used to address the brother of the king or other nobles of similar rank)

《千万不要忘记》(qiānwàn bùyào wàngjì) *Never Forget* – a film directed by Xie Tieli(谢铁骊) in 1964

《千字文》(qiānzìwén) *One Thousand Character Primer* – a book compiled by Zhou Xingsi(周兴嗣,469 – 521)

阡陌(qiānmò) crisscross footpaths between fields

迁都(qiāndū) to move the capital to another place

迁户口(qiān hùkǒu) to change one's residence registration

牵线搭桥(qiānxiàn dāqiáo) to bring somebody into contact with somebody else;to act as a go-between for

谦谦君子(qiānqiān jūnzǐ) a modest and self-disciplined gentleman

签呈(qiānchéng) a brief document (submitted to a superior);a memorial

签押(qiānyā) to put one's signature or seal on an official document

前辈(qiánbèi) a senior; an older person; the older generation

前车之鉴(qiánchē zhī jiàn)(lit.) "the warning of the overturned cart ahead" - one should learn lessons from one's previous mistakes and from those of others

前房(qiánfáng) deceased wife; late wife

前汉(qiánhàn) the Western Han Dynasty(206 BC - 8AD)

前后脚儿(qiánhòujiǎor) almost simultaneously

前记(qiánjì) preface; foreword; introduction

前襟(qiánjīn) the front part(of a traditional Chinese robe or jacket)

前七子(qiánqīzǐ) the Former Seven Masters; the Former Seven Scholars (a school of literature from 1480 to 1520)

前清(qiánqīng) the Early Qing Dynasty

前事不忘,后事之师(qiánshì búwàng, hòushì zhī shī) past experience, if not forgotten, is a guide for the future

前缘(qiányuán) a preordained affinity

钤印(qiányìn) to affix a seal to

虔婆(qiánpó) a procuress; an old hag

钱褡裢(qiándālian) a money bag (carried over the shoulder)

钱褡子(qiándāzi) a money bag(carried over the shoulder)

钱谷(qiángǔ) magistrate's assistant in charge of revenue(in the Qing Dynasty, 1636 - 1912)

钱谷师爷(qiángǔ shīyé) revenue clerk(in the Qing Dynast, 1636 - 1912)

钱柜(qiánguì) a money locker; a money-box

钱龙(qiánlóng) a string of coins; a string of cash

钱票(qiánpiào) paper money

钱塘潮(qiántángcháo) the tide of the Qiantang River; the Qiantang tide (in Zhejiang province, the most spectacular tide in China)

钱塘江(qiántángjiāng) the Qiantang River(in Zhejiang province)

钱庄(qiánzhuāng) a private bank

乾坤(qiánkūn) ① the universe; the cosmos; the course of events ② heaven and earth; *yin* and *yang*; male and female

乾陵(qiánlíng) the Qianling Mausoleum[the tomb of Emperor Li Zhi(李治, 628 - 683) and his wife Empress Wu Zetian(武则天, 624 - 705) of the Tang Dynasty, 618 -

907]

乾隆(qiánlóng) Qianlong(the reign title of Emperor *Hongli*, the 4th emperor of the Qing Dynasty)

乾隆皇帝(qiánlóng huángdì) the Qianlong Emperor

乾清宫(qiánqīnggōng) Palace of Heavenly Purity(inside The Forbidden City in Beijing)

乾宅(qiánzhái) husband's family and house

掮客(qiánkè) a broker; a commission merchant

《潜伏》(qiánfú) *Lurk* – a TV drama directed by Jiang Wei(姜伟) in 2008

潜规则(qiánguīzé) an unspoken rule; a hidden rules

黔剧(qiánjù) Guizhou opera

黔首(qiánshǒu) the common people; ordinary folk

浅斟低唱(qiǎnzhēn dīchàng)(lit.) "to sip wine slowly and hum a tune" – to enjoy oneself by drinking leisurely and singing softly

遣戍(qiǎnshù) to banish; to send into exile

遣唐使(qiǎntángshǐ) Japanese envoys to China(in the Tang Dynasty, 618 – 907)

谴责小说(qiǎnzé xiǎoshuō) the Novels of Indictment(a school of literature bloomed in the late Qing Dynasty after 1900)

谴谪(qiǎnzhé) to be demoted and sent into exile

欠安(qiàn'ān) to feel unwell; to be indisposed

倩男倩女(qiànnán qiànnǚ) smartly dressed men and women

《倩女离魂》(qiànnǚ líhún) *The Young Girl who died for Love* – a play by Zheng Guangzu(郑光祖) in the Yuan Dynasty

《倩女幽魂》(qiànnǚ yōuhún) *A Chinese Ghost Story* – a film directed by Cheng Xiaodong(程小东) in 1987; a film directed by Ye Weixin(叶伟信) in 2011; *Enchanting Shadow*

歉年(qiànnián) a bad year; a year of poor harvest; a lean year

歉收(qiànshōu) ①to have a bad harvest; to yield poorly ② a bad harvest; a poor harvest

歉岁(qiànsuì) a bad year; a year of poor harvest; a lean year

羌族(qiāngzú) the Qiang nationality (distributed mainly in Sichuan province)

《将进酒》(qiāngjìnjiǔ) *Invitation to Wine* – a poem by Li Bai(李白, 701 – 762)

强梁(qiángliáng) brutal; tyrannical

强弩之末(qiángnǔ zhī mò)(lit.)"an arrow at the end of its flight"–a spent force

强学会(qiángxuéhuì)the Society for the Study of National Strengthening (established in 1895)

墙报(qiángbào)a wall newspaper

墙头草,随风倒(qiángtóucǎo, suífēngdǎo)(lit.)"the grass on the top of a wall sways with the wind"–a fence-sitter; a weather cock

《墙头马上》(qiángtou mǎshang) *Pei Shaojun and Li Qianjun* – a play by Bai Pu(白朴,1226–1306?)

抢饭碗(qiǎng fànwǎn)to fight for a job

抢风头(qiǎng fēngtou)to steal the show

抢婚(qiǎnghūn)to carry off a woman and marry her by force(a traditional wedding custom)

抢镜头(qiǎng jìngtóu)to steal the show; to seek the limelight

抢亲(qiǎngqīn)①to pretend to kidnap one's bride(a traditional wedding custom)②to kidnap or force a woman to be one's wife

抢手(qiǎngshǒu)①to be in great demand; to sell well; to sell like hot cakes ② popular; to attract many suitors

强颜欢笑(qiǎngyán huānxiào)to put on an air of cheerfulness; to try to look happy

襁褓(qiǎngbǎo)swaddling clothes

敲边鼓(qiāo biāngǔ)(lit.)"to beat drums from the sidelines"–to back somebody up

敲警钟(qiāo jǐngzhōng)to sound the alarm bell; to warn someone beforehand

敲锣打鼓(qiāoluó dǎgǔ)to beat drums and gongs

敲门砖(qiāoménzhuān)(lit.)"a brick used to knock on the door"–a stepping stone to progress

敲竹杠(qiāozhúgàng)daylight robbery; blackmail; to fleece somebody

《乔厂长上任记》(qiáochǎngzhǎng shàngrèn jì) *Qiao, New Director of the Factory* – a short story by Jiang Zilong(蒋子龙,1941–)in 1979

《乔家大院》(qiáojiā dàyuàn) *Qiao's Grand Courtyard* – a TV drama directed by Hu Mei(胡玫)in 2006

乔迁(qiáoqiān)①to move to a better place②to get a promotion

乔迁之喜(qiáoqiān zhī xǐ)congratulations offered on entering a new house; a housewarming

桥楼室(qiáolóushì)a bridge house (nautical)

桥牌(qiáopái)bridge(a card game)

桥头堡(qiáotóubǎo)a bridgehead; a

bridge tower

翘楚(qiáochǔ)an outstanding person

谯楼(qiáolóu)a watchtower;a drum tower

樵夫(qiáofū)a woodcutter;a woodman

巧夺天工(qiǎoduó tiāngōng)something so exquisite it surpasses Nature

俏皮话(qiàopíhuà)a witty remark;paronomasia;witticism

翘辫子(qiàobiànzi)(lit.)"to stick one's pigtail up"-to kick the bucket;to pop one's clogs

翘尾巴(qiàowěiba)(lit.)"to stick one's tail up"-to be haughty or cocky

切磋(qiēcuō)to learn from each other by exchanging views, experience or skills

伽蓝(qiélán)a Buddhist temple

切脉(qièmài)to feel somebody's pulse

切音(qièyīn)to indicate the sound of a Chinese character(by confluent consonants and vowel of two Chinese characters)

切诊(qièzhěn)(Chinese medicine) pulse feeling and palpation as a means of diagonosis

妾身(qièshēn)I;me(a modest self-appellation for a woman in premodern China)

窃钩者诛,窃国者侯(qiègōuzhě zhū, qièguózhě hóu)petty thieves are hanged but great thieves are honored

窃国大盗(qièguó dàdào)an arch usurper of state power

窃喜(qièxǐ)to chuckle to oneself

亲兵(qīnbīng)a bodyguard

亲丁(qīndīng)a blood relation

亲贵(qīnguì)the emperor's close relatives or trusted courtiers

亲朋故旧(qīnpéng gùjiù)relatives and old acquaintances

亲事(qīnshì)marriage

亲王(qīnwáng)a prince

亲征(qīnzhēng)to lead a military expedition in person(of an emperor)

亲政(qīnzhèng)to take over the reign of government(when the heir is old enough)

亲族(qīnzú)members of the same clan

钦差(qīnchāi)an imperial envoy

钦差大臣(qīnchāi dàchén)①an imperial envoy;a government inspector ②a high official with full power

钦赐(qīncì)granted by the emperor

钦定(qīndìng)to be authorized by the emperor

钦命(qīnmìng)①an imperial order② ordered by the emperor

衾冷枕寒(qīnlěng zhěnhán)(lit.)"both the quilt and the pillow are cold"– to feel lonely in bed(when one's beloved is far away); cold bedding

秦朝(qíncháo) the Qin Dynasty (221 – 206 BC)

秦川(qínchuān)the plains to north of Qinling mountains(in Shaanxi and Gansu provinces)

秦晋之好(qínjìn zhī hǎo)(lit.)"the amity between the states of Qin and Jin" – the alliance formed between two families by marriage

秦楼楚馆(qínlóu chǔguǎn)the towers of Qin and the inns of Chu – brothels

秦腔(qínqiāng)Shaanxi opera

秦始皇(qínshǐhuáng)Emperor Qin; Emperor Qinshihuang; the First Emperor of the Qin Dynasty(221 – 206 BC)

《秦始皇》(qínshǐhuáng) *The First Emperor* – a TV drama directed byYan Jiangang(阎建钢)in 2002; *The First Qin Emperor*

《秦俑》(qínyǒng) *A Terracotta Warrior*– a film directed by Cheng Xiaodong(程小东)in 1989

秦俑(qínyǒng) the Terracotta Warriors of the Qin Dynasty(221 – 206 BC); a Terracotta Warrior

秦篆(qínzhuàn)the Qin Dynasty seal (an ancient style of calligraphy)

琴剑飘零(qínjiàn piāolíng)to wander from place to place

琴棋书画(qínqíshūhuà) music, chess, calligraphy and painting

琴瑟不调(qínsè bùtiáo)discord between husband and wife; marital discord

琴瑟和谐(qínsè héxié)husband and wife in harmony; a happy marriage life

琴书(qínshū)storysinging(with musical accompaniment)

勤工俭学(qíngōng jiǎnxué) part-time-work and part-time-study

勤王(qínwáng)①to save or rescue the throne②to serve the throne; to do one's best to serve the king

寝宫(qǐngōng)①the sleeping quarters of the emperor and empress② the coffin chamber inside an imperial tomb; the imperial mausoleum; the imperial burial place

《沁园春·雪》(qìnyuánchūn xuě) *Spring in a Pleasure Garden-Snow* – a poem by Mao Zedong(毛泽东, 1893 – 1976)in 1936

青帮(qīngbāng) the Qing Gang (a Qing secret society which evolved into a criminal gang in Shanghai in the early 20th century)

青藏高原(qīngzàng gāoyuán) the Qinghai-Tibet plateau

青春饭(qīngchūnfàn) a young person's profession; a profession for young persons only

《青春万岁》(qīngchūn wànsuì) *Forever Young* – a film directed by Huang Shuqin(黄蜀芹) in 1983; *Hurrah for Youth* – a novel by Wang Meng(王蒙,1934 –) in 1957

《青春之歌》(qīngchūn zhī gē) *The Song of Youth* – a novel by Yang Mo (杨沫,1914 – 1995) in 1958

青灯黄卷(qīngdēng huángjuàn)(lit.) "green light and yellow book" – to study at night

青瓜头(qīngguātóu)(lit.)"the cap of a green melon" – inexperienced and unsophisticated impetuous youth

青红帮(qīnghóngbāng) the Qing gang and the Hong gang (a Qing secret society)

青花瓷(qīnghuācí) blue-and-white Chinese porcelain

青衿(襟)(qīngjīn) ①a scholar or intellectual's dress ② a scholar; an intellectual

青龙(qīnglóng) the Green Dragon (the guardian spirit of the East in Taoism)

青楼(qīnglóu) a whorehouse; a brothel

青梅竹马(qīngméi zhúmǎ)(lit.) "green plums and a bamboo horse" – to have had an affection for each other since childhood

青鸟(qīngniǎo) ①the bird messenger of the Queen Mother of the West②a messenger

青纱帐(qīngshāzhàng) a green curtain of tall crops

青史(qīngshǐ) the annals of history

《青松岭》(qīngsōnglǐng) *Pine Ridge* – a film directed by Liu Guoquan(刘国权) in 1965

青天(qīngtiān) the clear sky; an upright official

青天白日(qīngtiānbáirì) the blue sky and the bright sun; bright and sunny; the party flag of the Kuomingtang(KMT)

青衣(qīngyī) ①a housemaid; a woman servant②*qingyi* (the role of a quiet and gentle lady in traditional Chinese opera)

青云(qīngyún) a high official position

青云直上(qīngyún zhíshàng) to advance rapidly in one's career

青云志(qīngyúnzhì) high aspirations or high ambitions

轻车简从(qīngchē jiǎncóng)(lit.) "a light carriage and few attendants" – to travel light

轻裘缓带(qīngqiú huǎndài)(lit.)"light furs and loose girdles" - to live a comfortable and leisurely life, free from pressure

倾城倾国(qīngchéng qīngguó) so beautiful as to cause the fall of a city or a state; exceedingly beautiful (of a woman)

《倾城之恋》(qīngchéng zhī liàn) *Love in A Fallen City* - a novel by Zhang Ailing [Eileen Chang (张爱玲, 1920 - 1995)] in 1943; a film directed by Xu Anhua (许鞍华) in 1984

卿卿我我(qīngqīng wǒwǒ) to bill and coo (between lovers); to be very much in love

清帮(qīngbāng) the Qing gang (a Qing secret society)

清唱(qīngchàng) to sing opera arias (without makeup and acting)

清朝(qīngcháo) the Qing Dynasty (1636 - 1912)

清道夫(qīngdàofū) a street cleaner; a street sweeper

清福(qīngfú) a happy and leisurely life; a life of ease

清官(qīngguān) a just and upright official

清君侧(qīng jūncè) ①to rid the emperor of his "evil" ministers ② to purge the emperor's court

清客(qīngkè) the hangers-on of rich and powerful families; the protégés of powerful families

清流(qīngliú) an upright group of scholars

清明(qīngmíng) Pure Brightness (the name of the 5th of the 24 Chinese solar terms)

清明节(qīngmíngjié) Tomb-sweeping Day; Tomb-sweeping Festival; the Qingming Festival

《清明上河图》(qīngmíng shàng hé tú) *A Riverside Scene at Qingming Festival* - a Chinese painting by Zhang Zeduan (张择端, 1085 - 1145)

《清平山堂话本》(qīngpíng shāntáng huàběn) *The Story Scripts of Qingping Shantang* - a script for storytelling by Hong Pian (洪楩) in the Ming Dynasty

清讫(qīngqì) the payment is received; the account is settled

清水脸(qīngshuǐliǎn) an unmade-up face; a face without makeup

清水衙门(qīngshuǐ yámen)(lit.) "the plain water *yamen*" -①a government office without outside income②an organization or institution with very limited funds and welfare facilities

清谈(qīngtán) idle or empty talk

清心寡欲(qīngxīn guǎyù)to have a pure heart and very few worldly desires

清一色(qīngyīsè)①all of one suit; all of the same suit(in mah-jong or card games)②all of the same colour, style, etc.

清音(qīngyīn)①voiceless sound②Jiangxi-style ditty-singing(a type of folk art popular in Jiangxi)③surd; voiceless consonant ④ wind music played at weddings or funerals

清印(qīngyìn)the official seals of the Qing Dynasty(1636–1912)

清真寺(qīngzhēnsì)a mosque

《清忠谱》(qīng zhōng pǔ) *In Praise of Honesty and Uprightness* – a play by Li Yu(李玉,1610–1620)et al.

情场(qíngchǎng)the arena of love; the tournaments of love

情场得意(qíngchǎng déyì)to be lucky in love

情场老手(qíngchǎng lǎoshǒu)a womanizer

情场失意(qíngchǎng shīyì)to be frustrated in love

情痴(qíngchī)a love maniac; obsessed with desire for somebody

情分(qíngfèn)mutual affection

情夫(qíngfū)an illicit lover(of a married woman)

情妇(qíngfù)an illicit lover(of a married man)

情郎(qíngláng)a(male)lover; a sweetheart

情侣(qínglǚ)sweethearts; lovers

情面(qíngmiàn)feelings; sensibilities; face-saving

情人(qíngrén)a sweetheart; a lover

晴雨表(qíngyǔbiǎo)①a weatherglass ② a barometer ③ an indicator of change

擎天柱(qíngtiānzhù)a mainstay; a person who shoulders heavy responsibility

请安(qǐng'ān)①to wish somebody good health ②to pay respects(to somebody)

请春客(qǐng chūnkè)to entertain relatives and friends after the Spring Festival

请功(qǐnggōng)to ask the higher authorities to record or reward somebody's praiseworthy deeds

请命(qǐngmìng)①to plead on somebody's behalf②to ask(one's superiors)for instruction

请缨(qǐngyīng)to submit a request for a military assignment

庆父不死,鲁难未已(qìngfǔ bùsǐ, lǔ nàn wèiyǐ)(lit.)"the civil strife in the state of Lu will not end until Qingfu dies" – there will always be trouble until the one who causes it is removed

庆功会(qìnggōnghuì)a victory meeting

庆历(qìnglì)Qingli(1041 - 1048), the reign title of Emperor Song Renzong(宋仁宗赵祯,1010 - 1063)

庆祝大会(qìngzhù dàhuì)a celebration meeting

亲家(qìngjia)①relatives by marriage ②the parents-in-law of one's son or daughter

亲家公(qìngjiagōng)the father-in-law of one's son or daughter

亲家母(qìngjiamǔ)the mother-in-law of one's son or daughter

罄竹难书(qìngzhú nánshū)to be too numerous to be listed; to have too many to record; innumerable

穷棒子(qióngbàngzi)①a pauper②a poor peasant(with high spirit)

穷棒子精神(qióngbàngzi jīngshén) the spirit of the poor peasant(used to describe a spirit of self-reliance, hard-work and adherence to the socialist road under difficult conditions)

穷兵黩武(qióngbīng dúwǔ)to use all one's armed power to wage aggressive wars; to be wantonly aggressive

穷骨头(qiónggǔtou)a poor wretch; a pauper

穷光蛋(qióngguāngdàn)a pauper

穷酸(qióngsuān)poor and pedantic

穷秀才(qióngxiùcai)an impoverished scholar

穷则思变(qióngzésībiàn) poverty gives a person the desire for change

琼浆(qióngjiāng)a jade-like wine; nectar; top-class wine

琼剧(qióngjù)Hainan opera

琼林宴(qiónglínyàn)a special banquet granted by the emperor

琼楼玉宇(qiónglóu yùyǔ)(lit.) "marble towers and jade halls" - a richly decorated magnificent house or building complex

丘八(qiūbā)a soldier

《秋》(qiū)*Autumn* - one of the *Trilogy of Turbulent Currents* by Ba Jin (巴金,1904 - 2005)in 1940

秋波(qiūbō)the charming glances of a beautiful girl

秋分(qiūfēn)the Autumnal Equinox (the 16th of the 24 Chinese solar terms, usually falling on the 22nd or 23rd or 24th of September)

《秋菊打官司》(qiūjú dǎguānsi)*The Story of Qiu Ju* - a film directed by Zhang Yimou(张艺谋)in 1992

秋老虎(qiūlǎohǔ)a hot spell after the beginning of Autumn

秋审(qiūshěn)a judicial review of all death sentences in autumn[a practice in the Ming(1368 - 1644)and

Qing(1636 - 1912) dynasties]

秋试(qiūshì) the imperial provincial examinations (which took place in autumn)

秋收起义(qiūshōu qǐyì) The Autumn Harvest Uprising(1927)

秋水(qiūshuǐ) bright eyes

秋水伊人(qiūshuǐ yīrén) the friend one is longing for

秋闱(qiūwéi) the imperial provincial examinations (which took place in autumn)

囚笼(qiúlóng) a cage used for prisoners

求偶(qiúǒu) to seek a spouse

求签(qiúqiān) to divine by drawing lots in a temple; to pray and draw divination sticks at a temple

求亲(qiúqīn) to seek a marital alliance

求仁得仁(qiúrén dérén) (lit.) "to seek perfect virtue and have it" - to achieve what one seeks

求神拜佛(qiúshén bàifó) (lit.) "to plead with immortals and kneel down before Buddha" - to pray for help; to ask for help

求田问舍(qiútián wènshè) to have no high aspirations and pursuit in life

求仙(qiúxiān) ①to seek immortality ②to seek advice from divinities

求雨(qiúyǔ) to pray for rain

虬髯(qiúrán) curly sideburns; curly beard

《虬髯客传》(qiúránkè zhuàn) *The Story of the Curly Beard* - a romance by Du Guangting(杜光庭, 850 - 933)

曲笔(qūbǐ) distortion of facts (to hide the truth)

曲意逢迎(qūyì féngyíng) to do everything to fawn on somebody; to be completely sycophantic

驱邪(qū xié) to exorcise evil spirits

屈才(qūcái) to underuse one's talent; to waste one's skills

屈驾(qūjià) to honor somebody with one's presence; to be so kind as to come

屈就(qūjiù) to condescend to accept a post

屈宋(qūsòng) Qu Yuan(屈原, 340 - 278 BC) and Song Yu(宋玉, 298 - 222 BC)

屈原(qūyuán) Qu Yuan (a famous poet and patriot in the Warring States Period, 475 - 221 BC)

《屈原》(qūyuán) *Qu Yuan the Poet* - a play by Guo Moruo(郭沫若, 1892 - 1978) in 1942

屈尊(qūzūn) to condescend; to deign; to stoop

祛除邪魔(qūchú xiémó) to drive out evil spirits

祛瘀活血(qūyū huóxuè) to remove blood stasis and promote blood circulation

趋附权贵(qūfù quánguì) to curry favour with bigwigs

趋炎附势(qūyán fùshì) to curry favour with the powerful; to suck up to those in power

渠魁(qúkuí) enemy chief; head of an armed rebellious group or a hostile party

曲高和寡 (qǔgāo hèguǎ) (lit.) "highbrow songs find few singers" - to be so highbrow that common people can hardly enjoy nor understand; too high to be popular; culturally elitist

曲剧(qǔjù) the Ballad-Singing opera (a local opera in Henan)

曲牌(qǔpái) name of a tune; title of a melody

曲坛(qǔtán) the circles of *quyi* performers

曲艺(qǔyì) *quyi* (Chinese folk vocal art forms)

曲终人散(qǔzhōng rénsàn) (lit.) "When the tune ends, the audience disperses" - the sadness of separation follows a joyful reunion

取经(qǔjīng) ①to go on a pilgrimage to India to acquire Buddhist scriptures②to learn experience from

娶亲(qǔqīn) to get married

去火(qùhuǒ) ①to cool down; to be mollified②to relieve inflammation

去声(qùshēng) the falling tone (of Chinese intonation)

去势(qùshì) to emasculate; to castrate

去梯之言(qùtī zhī yán) (lit.) "to talk upstairs after removing the ladder" - a confidential discussion; a secret conversation

趣剧(qùjù) farce; slapstick

圈定(quāndìng) to draw a circle around something to show approval or selection

圈阅(quānyuè) (lit.) "to read and circle" - to readcircle; to circle one's name listed on a document after reading it

全家福(quánjiāfú) a photograph of the whole family

全民皆兵(quánmín jiēbīng) an entire nation in arms; to turn every man into a soldier

《全唐诗》(quán tángshī) *The Complete Anthology of Tang Poetry* - a collection of poems compiled by Cao Yin (曹寅, 1658 - 1712) et al.; *The Complete Poetry of the Tang Dynasty*

《全唐文》(quán tángwén) *The Complete Collection of Tang Prose* - a collection of articles compiled by

Dong Gao (董诰, 1740 – 1818) et al. in 1808 – 1814

《全相平话五种》(quán xiāng pínghuà wǔzhǒng) *Five Illustrated Popular Stories* (published in the Yuan Dynasty, 1271 – 1368)

全真道(quánzhēndào) the Pefect Realization sect – a main sect of Taoism established by Wang Chongyang (王重阳, 1112 – 1170)

权臣(quánchén) powerful and domineering ministers or officials

权贵(quánguì) dignitaries; bigwigs

权奸(quánjiān) powerful and treacherous officials

权门(quánmén) the families of influential officials

权术(quánshù) political trickery; power tactics

权欲熏心(quányù xūnxīn) to be blinded by a lust for power

泉台(quántái) the nether world

泉下(quánxià) ①the nether world ② in the nether world; after one dies

拳不离手, 曲不离口 (quán bù lí shǒu, qǔ bù lí kǒu) (lit.) "a boxer must keep practicing boxing and a singer must keep practicing singing" – practice makes perfect.

拳法(quánfǎ) the fist principles; the principles of boxing

拳谱(quánpǔ) training manual (for boxing)

拳师(quánshī) a boxing coach; a boxing master

拳术(quánshù) the skill of Chinese boxing

铨叙(quánxù) to examine the records and qualifications of officials while making appointments

犬马之劳(quǎnmǎ zhī láo) (lit.) "to serve like a dog or a horse" – to be of service to somebody; to serve somebody faithfully

犬子(quǎnzǐ) my son (modest address)

劝谏(quànjiàn) to advise; to admonish; to exhort

缺德(quēdé) mean; wicked

缺心眼儿(quē xīnyǎnr) simple-minded; slow-witted; mentally deficient

阙文(quēwén) omissions or missing parts (in a book or text)

鹊报(quèbào) (lit.) "the cry of the magpie" – a good omen

鹊桥(quèqiáo) the Magpie Bridge – formed by magpies enabling the Weaving-girl [Zhinv (织女)] to go across to meet the Cowherd [Niulang (牛郎)] on the 7th evening of the 7th lunar month

《鹊桥仙》(quèqiáoxiān) *Immortals Meeting on the Magpie Bridge* – the name of a tune for *qu* or *ci* poetry

鹊桥相会(quèqiáo xiānghuì)(lit.) "to meet each other on the magpie bridge" – the reunion of husband and wife or lovers after a long separation

裙钗(qúnchāi)women

裙带风(qúndàifēng) petticoat influence;nepotism

裙带关系(qúndài guānxi)a network gained from family connections;petticoat influence

群芳(qúnfāng) ① many beautiful flowers ② a great many beautiful women

群芳之冠(qúnfāng zhī guàn)(lit.) "the queen of flowers" – the reigning beauty;beauty queen

群口铄金(qúnkǒu shuòjīn)(lit.) "words from mouths of many people can melt gold" – public opinion has great or fatal power

群龙无首(qúnlóng wúshǒu)(lit.) "a host of dragons without a head" – a group of brave men without a leader

群言堂(qúnyántáng)(lit.) "the conference hall where everyone is allowed to have a say" – to air one's views freely

群英(qúnyīng)many talented people; many heroes

《群英会》(qún yīng huì) *Gathering of the Heroes* – a Beijing opera(based on some chapters of *The Romance of the Three Kingdoms*;a TV drama directed by[Frankie Chan(陈勋奇) in 2003]

群英会(qúnyīnghuì) a gathering of many heroes

R

髯口(ránkou)artificial beard or whiskers(worn by traditional opera performers)

染坊(rǎnfáng) a dye-house; a dye-works

染指(rǎnzhǐ)to encroach on;to have a finger in

禳解(rángjiě) to avert (disaster or misfortune) by prayers

让位(ràngwèi)to abdicate;to give up one's position to

让贤(ràngxián)to yield one's position to a virtuous and talented person

饶舌(ráoshé) to be talkative; to be garrulous

绕佛(ràofó) ① to walk around the Buddha(to show respect to it) ②to walk slowly

绕口(ràokǒu)①hard to articulate②a tongue twister

绕口令(ràokǒulìng)a tongue twister

绕弯子(rào wānzi)to talk in a roundabout way;to beat about the bush

绕嘴(ràozuǐ)hard to articulate

惹乱子(rě luànzi)to stir up trouble; to make trouble

热潮(rècháo)a great mass fervour; a upsurge

热门货(rèménhuò)goods in great demand; a hot item

热丧(rèsàng)to be in mourning(for the recent death of one's father or mother)

热孝(rèxiào)to wear the mourning gown(over the recent death of one's grandparents, parents, husband, etc.)

人臣(rénchén)a minister; a subject

《人到中年》(rén dào zhōngnián) *At Middle Age* – a film directed by Wang Qimin(王启民)in 1982

人贩子(rénfànzi)a trader in human beings; a human trafficker

人非圣贤,孰能无过(rén fēi shèngxián, shúnéng wúguò)Human beings are no saints, how can they be free from errors and mistakes?; to err is human

人尖子(rénjiānzi)a distinguished person

《人间词话》(rénjiān cíhuà) *Prosody of Ci Poetry* – a critical work by Wang Guowei(王国维, 1877 – 1927)in 1908; *Poetic Remarks in the Human World*

《人间正道是沧桑》(rénjiān zhèngdào shì cāngsāng) *The Vicissitudes of Life Is the Right Way in the World* – a TV drama directed by Zhang Li(张黎)in 2009

人精(rénjīng)①a shrewd person②an extremely clever person

人君(rénjūn)a prince; a ruler

人来疯(rénláifēng)to show off one's liveliness in the presence of visitors; childish pranks in the presence of guests

人伦(rénlún)human relations

人脉(rénmài)interpersonal relationship; relationship

《人面桃花》(rénmiàn táohuā) *Charming Face among Peach Blossoms* – a novel by Ge Fei(格非,1964 –)

《人民日报》(rénmín rìbào) *People's Daily*

人气(rénqì)①popularity②character; personality

人情练达(rénqíng liàndá)experienced in the ways of the world

人情世故(rénqíng shìgù)worldly wisdom; the ways of the world

人情味(rénqíngwèi)human kindness

人情小说(rénqíng xiǎoshuō)the Novels of Manners(a school of realistic novels)

人情债(rénqíngzhài)a debt of gratitude

人日(rénrì)(lit.)"the man-day" - the seventh day of the first lunar month of the Chinese lunar calendar

人瑞(rénruì)①the propitious omen in the man's world②a venerable old man or woman

人蛇(rénshé)(lit.)"a human snake" - an illegal human trader; a human trafficker

《人生》(rénshēng) *The Road of Life* - a novel by Lu Yao(路遥,1949 - 1992) in 1982; a film directed by Wu Tianming(吴天明) in 1984

人烟(rényān) a sign of human habitation

《人在囧途》(rén zài jiǒngtú) *Lost on Journey* - a film directed by Ye Weimin(叶伟民) in 2010

《人在囧途之泰囧》(rén zài jiǒngtú zhi tàijiǒng) *Lost in Thailand* - a sequel of the Chinese film *Lost on Journey*, directed by Xu Zheng(徐峥) in 2012

人渣(rénzhā)(dialect) dregs of society; social trash; scum

人治(rénzhì) the rule by man(rather than by law)

仁弟(réndì) my benevolent younger brother; my dear friend

仁人君子(rénrén jūnzǐ) a benevolent gentleman

仁兄(rénxiōng) my benevolent elder brother; my dear friend

仁义道德(rényì dàodé) humanity, justice and virtue; virtue and morality

仁政(rénzhèng) the policy of benevolence; a benevolent government

仁至义尽(rénzhì yìjìn) to do one's best to help others; to treat someone with the utmost kindness

稔知(rěnzhī) to know somebody very well

认命(rènmìng) to accept one's fate; to resign oneself to one's fate

认亲(rènqīn)①to become related by marriage② to claim a family connection

认生(rènshēng) to feel shy with strangers

《日出》(rìchū) *The Sun Rises*; *Sunrise* - a modern play by Cao Yu(曹禺, 1910 - 1996) in 1936

日晷(rìguǐ) a sundial

《日知录》(rìzhīlù) *The Record of Everyday knowledge* - a book by Gu Yanwu(顾炎武,1613 - 1682); *Record of Daily Learning*

戎机(róngjī)① military affairs ② a good chance for a victory in a battle

戎马生涯(róngmǎ shēngyá) a military life; an army life

荣军(róngjūn) a disabled soldier (wounded in the revolutionary war)

冗官(rǒngguān)an idle official;a redundant official

冗员(rǒngyuán)redundant personnel

肉票(ròupiào)a hostage

《肉蒲团》(ròu pǔtuán) *The Carnal Prayer Mat* – a novel by Li Yu(李渔,1611 – 1680)

《如此包装》(rúcǐ bāozhuāng) *Such Packaging* – a skit starring Zhao Lirong(赵丽蓉)and Gong Hanlin(巩汉林)in 1995

如弟(rúdì)a sworn brother(younger)

如夫人(rúfūrén)a concubine

如来(rúlái)Tathagata(Buddhism)

如来佛(rúláifó) Tathagata (Buddhism)

如丧考妣(rú sàng kǎobǐ) to be grieved as if one had lost one's parents;to be distraught

如意(rúyì) ruyi (an S-shaped jade sceptre)

如意算盘(rúyì suànpán) wishful thinking;an optimistic plan

儒道(rúdào)Confucianism and Taoism

儒家(rújiā) the Confucian school;Confucianism

儒家思想(rújiā sīxiǎng)Confucianism;Confucian ideology

儒教(rújiào)Confucianism

儒林(rúlín) ①Confucian scholars ②academic circles

《儒林外史》(rúlín wàishǐ) *The Scholars* – a novel by Wu Jingzi(吴敬梓,1701 – 1754)in 1750

儒生(rúshēng) ①a Confucian scholar ②an ordinary scholar

儒术(rúshù) Confucian thought and teachings;Confucianism

儒学(rúxué) Confucian teachings;Confucianism

儒雅(rúyǎ)scholarly and refined

儒宗(rúzōng) the learned Confucian masters

孺人(rúrén) ①a doctor's wife ②the mother or wife of an official (a county magistrate in the Ming and Qing dynasties) ③a lady

孺子(rúzǐ)a child

孺子不可教(rúzǐ bùkějiào)a foolish kid is not teachable.

孺子可教(rúzǐ kějiào) a smart kid has a bright future.

孺子牛(rúzǐniú)(lit.)"the herdboy's willing ox" – a faithful servant of the people

汝辈(rǔbèi)you;you people

汝窑(rǔyáo) the Ruzhou Kiln (in Henan province)

乳名(rǔmíng)an infant name;a pet name for a child

乳母(rǔmǔ)a wet nurse

乳娘(rǔniáng)a wet nurse

入定(rùdìng)to sit in meditation

入伏(rùfú)the beginning of the hottest days of the year

入彀(rùgòu)(lit.)"to come within an arrow's range"-①to fall under somebody's control②to conform to general formalities and requirements ③to be absorbed

入国问禁(rùguó wènjìn)when entering a foreign country, one needs to ask about its prohibitions and taboos; when in Rome, do as the Romans do

入画(rùhuà)to be suitable for a painting; to be picturesque

入静(rùjìng)to sit in meditation and achieve absolute mental tranquility

入闱(rùwéi)①to enter the imperial examination place②to be selected after taking the examination

入药(rùyào)to be used as medicine

入蛰(rùzhé)to enter hibernation

入赘(rùzhuì)to be married into and live with the bride's family

软刀子(ruǎndāozi)(lit.)"a soft knife"- a velvet dagger; something imperceptibly harmful

软钉子(ruǎndīngzi)(lit.)"a soft nail"- an indirect refusal; a polite rebuttal

软耳朵(ruǎn ěrduo)(lit.)"soft ears"- a credulous, indecisive person

软骨头(ruǎn gǔtou)(lit.)"soft bones"- a weak-kneed person

软话(ruǎnhuà)appeasing words

软玉温香(ruǎnyù wēnxiāng)feminine charms

瑞雪兆丰年(ruìxuě zhào fēngnián)a timely snowfall augurs a good harvest for the coming year; a fall of seasonable snow gives promise of a fruitful year

闰年(rùnnián)a leap year; an intercalary year

闰日(rùnrì)a leap day; an intercalary day

闰月(rùnyuè)a leap month; an intercalary month

润笔(rùnbǐ)①to dip a writing brush in ink②the remuneration for a writer, painter, or calligrapher

弱冠(ruòguàn)①to enter adulthood; to come of age(at 20 years old)② the ritual of crowning a young man at the age of 20

箬帽(ruòmào)a broad-rimmed conical bamboo hat

S

撒对儿(sāduìr)to challenge one's opponent by striking a pose

撒酒疯(sā jiǔfēng)to be roaring drunk; to be drunk and act crazily

撒拉族(sālāzú) the Salar nationality (mainly distributed in Qinghai province)

撒手归西(sāshǒu guīxī) to pass away; to die

撒手锏(sāshǒujiǎn) (lit.) "an unexpected thrust with the mace" – a trump card

撒丫子(sāyāzi) to take to one's heels

撒野(sāyě) to act wildly

撒帐(sǎzhàng) to spread nuts and fruits on the wedding bed (a custom praying for an offspring)

洒狗血(sǎ gǒuxiě) to overact

洒家(sǎjiā) I (used by men in early vernacular)

萨满教(sàmǎnjiào) shamanism

塞北(sàiběi) North of the Great Wall

塞外(sàiwài) North of the Great Wall

塞翁失马，安知非福(sàiwēng shīmǎ, ānzhī fēifú) (lit.) "just like when the old man on the frontier lost his mare, who could have known it was a blessing" – misfortune may turn out to be a blessing in disguise

赛龙舟(sài lóngzhōu) the dragon boat race

三八红旗手(sānbā hóngqíshǒu) a female pace-setter

三百六十行(sānbǎiliùshí háng) all walks of life; all trades and professions

三班六房(sānbān liùfáng) all the officials in the *yamen*; all the people working in the county magistrate's office

三宝(sānbǎo) Triratna – the triad of the Buddha, the dharma, and the sanyha

三保太监下西洋 (sānbǎo tàijiàn xiàxīyáng) the expeditions to the Western Ocean led by Zheng He (郑和, 1371 – 1433) during 1405 –1433

三才(sāncái) (Taoism) the Cosmic Triad (heaven, earth and human)

三彩(sāncǎi) three-color glazed pottery

三曹(sāncáo) The "Three Caos" [Cao Cao (曹操, 155 – 220), Cao Pi (曹丕, 187 – 226) and Cao Zhi (曹植, 192 – 232)]

三叉戟(sānchājǐ) a three-pronged spear; a trident

三长两短(sāncháng liǎngduǎn) unexpected misfortune; something unfortunate

三从四德(sāncóng sìdé) the three obediences and four virtues of the Confucian ideal of womanhood (obedience to father before marriage, to husband after marriage and to son after being widowed, with virtues of morality, proper speech, modesty and diligence)

三寸不烂之舌(sāncùn bùlàn zhī shé)a silver tongue

三寸金莲(sāncùn jīnlián)the three-inch lotus feet(referring to women's bound feet)

《三打祝家庄》(sāndǎ zhùjiāzhuāng)*The Three Sieges of Zhujia Village* – a Beijing opera selected from *The Romance of the Three Kingdoms*

三大殿(sāndàdiàn)the Three Great Halls(the Hall of Supreme Harmony, the Hall of Middle Harmony, and the Hall of Protecting Harmony in the Imperial Palace)

三代(sāndài)the three earliest dynasties[Xia(夏,21st century – 16th century BC), Shang(商, 1600 – 1046 BC) and Zhou(周,1046 – 256 BC)]

三道(sāndào)the three stages of self-cultivation

三法(sānfǎ)the three therapeutic methods (of traditional Chinese medicine)

三法印(sānfǎyìn)the Three Seals of Buddhist Truth

三藩之乱(sānfān zhī luàn)the Rebellion of the Three Vassal Princes (1673 – 1681)

三反运动(sānfǎn yùndòng)the Three Antis Campaign(1951 – 1954)

三伏(sānfú)①the three ten-day periods of the hot season ②the last of the three periods of the hot season

三纲五常(sāngāng wǔcháng)the three cardinal bonds (ruler over subject, father over son, and husband over wife) and the five constant virtues (benevolence, righteousness, propriety wisdom and fidelity)

《三个摩登女性》(sānge módēng nǚxìng)*Three Modern Ladies* – a film directed by Bu Wancang(卜万苍)in 1933

三宫六院(sāngōng liùyuàn)(lit.) "three palaces and six chambers" – the imperial harem

三顾茅庐(sāngù máolú)(lit.) "three personal calls at the thatched cottage" – repeated and sincere invitations

三光政策(sānguāng zhèngcè)the policy of "burn all, kill all, loot all" (employed by the Japanese invaders in China)

三国(sānguó)the Three Kingdoms [the Wei(220 – 265), the Shu(221 – 263) and the Wu (222 – 280)]

《三国演义》(sānguó yǎnyì)*The Romance of the Three Kingdoms* – a

novel by Luo Guanzhong(罗贯中, 1330 – 1400?)

《三国志》(sānguó zhì) *The History of the Three Kingdoms* – a historical book by Chen Shou(陈寿, 233 – 297)

三合房(sānhéfáng) a three-section compound(with houses surrounding a courtyard on three sides)

三皇五帝(sānhuáng wǔdì) The Three Sovereigns and Five Emperors [the Three Sovereigns: Fu Xi(伏羲), Shennong(神农) and Suiren(燧人) or Zhurong(祝融); the Five emperors: Yellow Emperor(黄帝), Zhuanxu(颛顼), Di Ku(帝喾), Di Yao(帝尧) and Di Shun(帝舜)]

三角债(sānjiǎo zhài) tripartite debts

三脚猫(sānjiǎo māo) a jack of all trades, but master of none

三教九流(sānjiào jiǔliú)(lit.) "the three religions and nine schools of thought" – ① various religious sects and academic schools ② people of all walks of life

三节棍(sānjié gùn) a three-section cudgel

《三进山城》(sānjìn shānchéng) *Three Attacks on A Mountain Town* – a film directed by Zhang Fengxiang(张凤翔) in 1965

三九天(sānjiǔ tiān) the third nine-day period after the winter solstice; deep winter

三礼(sānlǐ) The Three Classics on Rites(*The Rites of Zhou*, *The Record of Rites* and *Etiquette and Rites*)

《三里湾》(sānlǐwān) *Three Mile Bay* – a novel by Zhao Shuli(赵树理, 1906 – 1970) in 1955; *Three Li Bay*

三六九等(sānliùjiǔ děng) of all grades and ranks

三茅真君(sānmáo zhēnjūn)(Daoism) the Mao brothers(the founders of the Mao school of Taoism/Daoism)

三昧(sānmèi)(Buddhism) samadhi

三面红旗(sānmiàn hóngqí) the Three Red Banners(the General Line of socialist Construction, the Great Leap Forward and the People's Commune, formulated in 1958, calling Chinese people to build a socialist state)

三民主义(sānmín zhǔyì) the Three Principles of the People(advocated by Sun Yat-sen)

三千世间(sānqiān shìjiān) all things

三清天(sānqīngtiān) the Three Pure Heavens(the highest heavens where reside the supreme deities of Taoism)

三青子(sānqīngzi) a rude person

三秋(sānqiū) three autumns; three years

三髯(sānrǎn) full whiskers

三生(sānshēng) the three incarnations(the present life, the past life and the future life)

三生石(sānshēng shí) the Rock of Lives(a symbol of predestined relationship of a person's existence)

三牲(sānshēng) the three sacrifices (pig, sheep and ox)

三尸三恶门(sānshī sān'è mén) evil desires

三尸五道门(sānshī wǔdào mén) the burden of worldly desires

三师七证(sānshī qīzhèng)(Buddhism) three superior monks and seven witnesses

三十而立(sānshí ér lì) to be independent at the age of 30

三十二相(sānshí'èr xiàng)(Buddhism) the thirty-two physical features

《三十六计》(sānshíliù jì) *Thirty-Six Stratagems* - an ancient Chinese military book originated in the Northern and Southern dynasties (420 - 589)

三十六计,走为上计(sānshíliù jì, zǒu wéi shàngjì) of the thirty-six stratagems, the best is running away; the best thing to do now is to quit

三十六天(sānshíliù tiān) the Thirty-Six Heavens(Taoism)

三世佛(sānshìfó) the Buddhas of the past, present and future

三苏(sānsū) The "Three Sus" [Su Shi (苏轼, 1037 - 1101), Su Xun (苏洵, 1009 - 1066) and Su Zhe (苏辙, 1039 - 1112)]

三孙子(sānsūnzi) a yes-man

三潭印月(sāntányìnyuè) the Three Pools Mirroring the Moon (located in Hangzhou)

三天尊(sāntiānzūn) the Three Celestial Worthies

三头六臂(sāntóu liùbì)(lit.) "with three heads and six arms" - superhuman powers

三下五除二(sān xiá wǔ chú èr) (lit.) "three-down-five-reject-two" - neat and quick

三弦(sānxián) the Chinese three-stringed fiddle; the three-stringed lute

三贤位(sānxiánwèi)(Buddhism) the three virtuous positions

三性(sānxìng)(Buddhism) trilaksana; three types of character (good, bad and undefinable)

三玄(sānxuán) the three works of profound learning - *Laozi* (《老子》), *Zhaungzi*(《庄子》) and *The*

Book of Changes(《周易》)

三学(sānxué)①the three imperial educational instituitions ②(Buddhism)trisiksa

三言二拍(sānyán'èrpāi)*Three Collections of Short Stories and Two Volumes of Amazing Stories – Stories to Enlighten the World*(《喻世明言》), *Stories to Warn the World*(《警世通言》), *Stories to Awaken the World*(《醒世恒言》)edited by Feng Menglong(冯梦龙,1574 – 1646)and two volumes Amazing Stories(《初刻拍案惊奇》and《再刻拍案惊奇》)edited by Ling Mengchu(凌蒙初,1580 – 1644)

三元(sānyuán)the lunar New Year's day

三藏(sānzàng)Tripitaka(Buddhist sutras)

三藏法师(sānzàng fǎshī)Master of Tripitaka

三障(sānzhàng)(Buddhism)the three barriers

三支两军(sānzhī liǎngjūn)three supports(support to the Left, industry and agriculture)and two military actions(military regulation and training)

三只手(sānzhī shǒu)a pickpocket

《三字经》(sānzì jīng)*Three-Character Textbook* – one of the three enlightened readings by Wang Yinglin(王应麟,1223 – 1296); *Three Character Classic*; *Verse in Three Characters*

三自爱国运动(sānzì' àiguó yùndòng)the Three-Self Patriotic Movement(of the Protestant Church in China)

三座大山(sānzuò dàshān)the three big mountains(imperialism, feudalism and bureaucrat-capitalism)

散板(sǎnbǎn)free rhythm(the type of music in Beijing opera)

散兵(sǎnbīng)skirmisher

散打(sǎndǎ)free sparring(in martial arts)

散工(sǎngōng)①odd jobs②an odd-job man;a casual laborer

散曲(sǎnqǔ)sanqu(the type of opera with tonal patterns modelled on tunes drawn from folk music);sanqu songs;non-dramatic songs

散套(sǎntào)a sequence of *sanqu* songs with a particular musical mode

散文诗(sǎnwén shī)a prose poem

散寒(sànhán)to take the chill out of the house

散摊子(sàn tānzi)to dissolve;to disband;to break up

丧棒(sāngbàng)a funeral stick(held by the son of the deceased in a funeral procession)

丧服(sāngfú)mourning apparel

丧门星(sāngmén xīng)①a woman who brings ill luck to her husband's family②anyone who brings ill luck

丧家之犬(sàngjiā zhī quǎn) a stray cur

丧尽天良(sàngjìn tiānliáng) to be utterly devoid of conscience; conscienceless;heartless

丧权辱国(sàngquán rǔguó) to humiliate the nation and forfeit its sovereignty; to surrender a country's sovereign rights under humiliating terms

丧心病狂(sàngxīn bìngkuáng) frenzied;frantic;perverse

骚货(sāohuò)a loose woman

骚客(sāokè)a poet

骚人(sāorén)a poet

骚人墨客(sāorén mòkè)literary men; men of letters;literati

骚体(sāotǐ)the Sao style(the poetic style of"Li Sao")

骚体诗(sāotǐ shī)Sao-style poetry; the poetic prose of the Kingdom of Chu

扫边(sǎobiān)(opera)to play a minor role

扫地出门(sǎodì chūmén)(lit.)"to sweep the garbage out" - to drive somebody out of their home; to sweep the floor

扫黄打非(sǎohuáng dǎfēi) to eliminate pornography and illegal publications;the campaign against porn

扫祭(sǎojì) to clean and offer sacrifices at a tomb

扫脸(sǎoliǎn)to lose face

扫盲(sǎománg)to eliminate illiteracy

扫眉才子(sǎoméi cáizi) a female poet or scholar

扫墓(sǎomù)to sweep a grave;to pay respect to the dead

扫堂腿(sǎotángtuǐ)a sweep kick

嫂夫人(sǎofūren)your wife(respectful term of address)

嫂嫂(sǎosao) sister-in-law (elder brother's wife)

嫂子(sǎozi)sister-in-law(elder brother's wife)

扫帚星(sàozhouxīng)①comet②a person who brings ill luck

《色·戒》(sè jiè)*Lust, Caution* - a short story by Zhang Ailing[Eileen Chang(张爱玲,1920 - 1995) in 1978; a film directed by Ang Lee (李安)in 2007]

色胆(sèdǎn)to be sex-crazed

色鬼(sèguǐ)a lecher;a sex maniac

色拉寺(sèlāsì) Sera Monastery (in Lhasa,Tibet)

色魔(sèmó)a sex maniac

色相(sèxiàng)①(Buddhism)the external appearance of something; form and aspect②feminine charms ③the colors of the spectrum - red, orange, yellow, green, blue, indigo and violet

森罗殿(sēnluódiàn)the Hall of Darkness (in Pingyuan county, Shangdong)

僧多粥少(sēngduō zhōushǎo)(lit.) "little gruel and many monks" - not enough to go round

僧自恣日(sēng zì zīrì)the day of unreserved criticisms(on the 15th day of the 7th lunar month)

杀风景(shā fēngjǐng) to spoil the fun; to be a wet blanket

《杀狗记》(shāgǒu jì)*Kill the Dog* - a traditional drama by Xu Zhongyou (徐仲由)in the Yuan Dynasty

杀回马枪(shā huímǎqiāng) to make a backward thrust at one's pursuer; to wheel around and hit back at somebody

杀戒(shājiè)(Buddhism) the prohibition against taking life

杀青(shāqīng) ① to heat bamboo strips to prepare them for writing② to finalize a manuscript; to wrap a film, etc. ③ the process of baking green tea

杀人越货(shārén yuèhuò) to kill a person and seize his goods; to rob and kill

杀身成仁(shāshēn chéngrén)(lit.) "to die to achieve virtue" - to die for a just cause

杀手锏(shāshǒujiǎn)a trump card

杀一儆百(shāyi jǐngbǎi) to execute one as a warning to a hundred

沙和尚(shāhéshàng) Monk Sha (a character in the novel *Journey to the West*)

《沙家浜》(shājiābāng)*Shajia Creek* - a modern Beijing opera; *Shajiabang*

沙弥(shāmí)a Buddhist novice

沙弥尼(shāmíní)a female novice

沙燕儿(shāyànr)a swallow kite

纱帽(shāmào)①a black gauze hat② an official post

《莎菲女士的日记》(shāfēi nǚshì de rìjì)*Miss Sophie's Diaries* - a novelette by Ding Ling(丁玲, 1904 - 1986)in 1928

傻帽儿(shǎmàor)a fool

傻青儿(shǎqīngr)a naive young person

歃血为盟(shàxuè wéiméng)to smear blood on the mouth as a sign of an oath; to swear with one's blood

色子(shǎizi)dice; a die

山不转水转(shānbùzhuàn shuǐzhuàn) (lit.) "even if the mountain doesn't move, the water does" - change is bound to happen

山顶洞人(shāndǐngdòngrén) the Upper Cave Man (a type of primitive man whose fossil remains were found in 1933 at Zhoukoudian near Beijing)

山东梆子(shāndōng bāngzi) Shandong clapper opera

山东大鼓(shāndōng dàgǔ) the Shandong Big Drum(a local style of story-telling)

山东快书(shāndōng kuàishū) Shandong clapper ballad

山高皇帝远(shāngāo huángdì yuǎn) remote areas where laws are not strictly enforced

山歌(shān'gē) a mountain song; a folk song

《山海经》(shānhǎijīng) *The Classic of Mountains and Seas* – a Chinese classic; *Book of Mountains and Seas*

山门(shānmén) the gate to the temple ①the gate of a Buddhist temple ②Buddhism

山盟海誓(shānméng hǎishì) a solemn pledge of love

山人(shānrén) a hermit

《山上的小屋》(shānshàng de xiǎowū) *The Hut on the Mountain* – a short story by Can Xue (残雪, 1953 –)

山水画(shānshuǐ huà) landscape painting

山水画家(shānshuǐ huàjiā) a landscape painter

山水田园诗派(shānshuǐ tiányuán shīpài) the Pastoral Landscape Poetry Genre [developed in the Tang Dynasty(618 – 907) and represented by Wang Wei (王维, 701 – 761) and Meng Haoran (孟浩然, 689 – 740). So it is also called "Wang Meng Poetry Genre" (王孟诗派)]

山头主义(shāntóu zhǔyì) mountain-stronghold mentality (a type of sectarianism)

山外有山(shānwài yǒushān) (lit.) "there is always a mountain beyond a mountain" – there is always something or someone better; nothing or nobody can be perfect

山西梆子(shānxī bāngzi) Shanxi clapper opera

《山乡巨变》(shānxiāng jùbiàn) *Great Changes in the Mountain Village* – a novel by Zhou Libo(周立波, 1908 – 1979) in 1958 – 1960

山药蛋派(shānyaodàn pài) the Potato School of Literature; the Shanxi School

山雨欲来风满楼(shānyǔ yùlái fēngmǎnlóu) (lit.) "the wind sweeping through the tower heralds a rising storm in the mountains" –

the indications are that a storm is imminent

山寨(shānzhài) a fortified mountain village

山珍海味(shānzhēn hǎiwèi) delicacies from land and sea

煽风点火(shānfēng diǎnhuǒ) to fan the flames; to stir up trouble

潸然(shānrán) in tears; tearful

《闪闪的红星》(shǎnshǎn de hóngxīng) *Sparkling Red Star* – a film directed by Li Ang(李昂) in 1974

陕西梆子(shǎnxī bāngzi) Shaanxi clapper opera

扇风耳(shānfēng'ěr) flappy ears

扇阴风,点鬼火(shān yīnfēng, diǎn guǐhuǒ) to fan the winds of evil and spread the fires of turmoil; to foment trouble

善报(shànbào) to reward the good

善本(shànběn) a reliable text; a trustworthy edition

善才(shàncái) a skilled and renowned *pipa* player

善刀而藏(shàn dāo'ér cáng) (lit.) "to store a good sword" – to know where or when to stop

善果(shànguǒ) good results; good rewards

善后(shànhòu) to deal with problems arising from an accident; to deal with the aftermath of an event

善男信女(shànnán xìnnǚ) Buddhist devotees

善始善终(shànshǐ shànzhōng) to start well and end well; to do well from start to finish

善有善报,恶有恶报(shànyǒushàn bào, èyǒuèbào) Good is rewarded with good, and evil with evil

禅让(shànràng) to abdicate and hand over the crown to

骟马(shànmǎ) a castrated horse; a gelding

伤风败俗(shāngfēng bàisú) to offend public morality; to violate common decency; to corrupt public morals

伤寒(shānghán) typhoid fever

《伤寒杂病论》(shānghán zábìng lùn) *Febrile and Other Diseases* – a medical book by Zhang Zhongjing (张仲景, 150 – 215) in 205

伤痕文学(shānghén wénxué) the Scar Literature (in the late 1970s and the 1980s)

伤脑筋(shāng nǎojīn) troublesome

伤食(shāngshí) dyspepsia caused by excessive eating or improper diet

《伤逝》(shāngshì) *Regret for the Past* – a short story by Lu Xun (鲁迅, 1881 – 1936) in 1925; a film directed by Shui Hua(水华) in 1981

商埠(shāngbù) a commercial port

商朝(shāngcháo) the Shang Dynasty

(1600 – 1046 BC)

商贾(shānggǔ) a merchant

商行(shāngháng) a business, commercial firm

《商君书》(shāngjūn shū) *The Book of Lord Shang* – a legalist classic by Shang Yang(商鞅, 395 – 338 BC)

商鞅变法(shāngyāng biànfǎ) the Shangyang Reforms(359 – 350 BC)

商鞅量(shāngyāng liàng) the Shang Yang measure (made during the Shangyang Reforms, 359 – 350 BC)

觞咏(shāngyǒng) to compose or chant poems while drinking

晌饭(shǎngfàn) lunch

晌觉(shǎngjiào) an afternoon nap

晌午(shǎngwǔ) noon; midday

赏赐(shǎngcì) to grant, to reward

赏光(shǎngguāng) to request the pleasure of somebody's company

赏脸(shǎngliǎn) to honor somebody with one's presence; to honor somebody by accepting something

赏识(shǎngshí) to think highly of; to appreciate

赏月(shǎngyuè) to enjoy the full moon

上班族(shàngbānzú) office workers

上辈子(shàngbèizi) one's previous existence

上不着天,下不着地(shàng bùzháo tiān, xià bùzháo dì) (lit.) "to touch neither the sky nor the ground" – to be suspended in midair; stranded mid-way

上朝(shàngcháo) to go to court

上党梆子(shàngdǎng bāngzi) Shangdang clapper opera (popular in Southeast Shanxi)

上都(shàngdū) the summer capital of the Yuan Dynasty(1271 – 1368)

尚方宝剑(shàngfāng bǎojiàn) the emperor's sword (a symbol of delegated power)

上房(shàngfáng) the main rooms

上坟(shàngfén) to visit a grave (to honor the memory of the dead)

《上甘岭》(shànggānlǐng) *Battle on Shangganling Mountain* – a film directed by Lin Shan(林杉) in 1956

上甘岭战役(shàngānlǐng zhànyì) the Battle of Shangganling (1952); the Battle of Sanggamyong Ridge

上纲上线(shànggāng shàngxiàn) to magnify a person's flaws or mistakes with the intention of fixing a political label on him

《上海滩》(shànghǎitān) *Shanghai Bund* – a TV drama directed by Zhao Zhenqiang(招振强) in 1980

上界(shàngjiè) the world above; heav-en

上九流(shàngjiǔliú) professional people in good standing; people with high social status

上联(shànglián) the first line or the upper line of a couplet

上梁不正下梁歪(shàngliáng bùzhèng xiàliáng wāi) (lit.) "if the upper beam is not straight, the lower ones will go aslant" – when those above behave unworthily, those below will do the same

上门女婿(shàngmén nǚxù) a live-in son-in-law

上逆天道,下违人常(shàng nì tiān dào, xià wéi rénchánɡ) to run counter to the ways of both Heaven and man; to be grossly unjust

上山下乡(shàngshān xiàxiāng) to go to work or live in the countryside or mountain areas; (of Educated Youth during the Cultural Revolution) to be sent down to the countryside

上声(shàngshēng) the rising tone

上疏(shàngshū) to submit a memorial (to the emperor)

上西天(shàngxītiān) (lit.) "to go to the Western Paradise" – to die

上香(shàngxiāng) to burn joss sticks

上相(shàngxiàng) to come out well in a photograph; to be photogenic

上心(shàngxīn) to set one's heart on (something)

上谕(shàngyù) an imperial edict

上元节(shàngyuánjié) the Lantern Festival

上奏(shàngzòu) to memorialize or petition the emperor; to report to the throne

上座(shàngzuò) the seat of honor

尚方宝剑(shàngfāng bǎojiàn) the emperor's sword (a symbol of delegated power)

尚派演员(shàngpài yǎnyán) a performer from the Shang school (playing a martial role in Chinese operas)

《尚书》(shàngshū) *The Book of History* – attributed to Confucius

尚书(shàngshū) Imperial Secretary

尚飨(shàngxiǎng) I beg you to partake of this sacrifice (used at the end of an elegiac address)

捎搭(shāodā) conveniently; without making a special effort

捎带脚儿(shāodàijiǎor) incidentally; in passing

烧包(shāobāo) to have a swollen head; to be too big for one's boots

烧刀子(shāodāozi) the spirit distilled from sorghum or maize

烧高香(shāogāoxiāng) to burn joss sticks in worship of Buddha or a god

烧香(shāoxiāng) to burn joss sticks

烧纸(shāozhǐ) to burn paper money

(for the dead); paper money burnt as an offering to the dead

艄公(shāogōng) a boatman

芍药(sháoyào) Chinese herbaceous peony

韶华(sháohuá) ①beautiful springtime ②glorious youth

少艾(shào'ài) young and handsome; young and beautiful

少白头(shàobáitóu) to be prematurely grey

少东家(shàodōngjiā) the young master

少府(shàofǔ) Minister for the Palace Revenues

少妇(shàofù) a young married woman

少牢(shàoláo) sacrificial sheep and pigs

少林拳(shàolínquán) Shaolin boxing

少林寺(shàolínsì) Shaolin Monastery

《少林寺》(shàolínsì) *Shaolin Monastery* – a film directed by Zhang Xinyan(张鑫炎,1934) in 1982

《少林足球》(shàolín zúqiú) *Shaolin Soccer* – a film directed by Zhou Xingchi(周星驰) in 2001

少奶奶(shàonǎinai) ①young mistress ②daughter-in-law

少年宫(shàoniángōng) Children's Palace

少年先锋队(少先队)(shàonián xiānfēngduì) the Young Pioneers

少年之家(shàonián zhī jiā) a children's centre; a children's club

少爷(shàoye) ①young master ②your or somebody else's son

少爷脾气(shàoye píqì) the behavior of a spoilt boy

少壮(shàozhuàng) young and vigorous

少壮不努力,老大徒伤悲(shàozhuàng bù nǔlì, lǎodà tú shāngbēi) if one does not exert himself in youth, regrets in old age will be in vain

绍剧(shàojù) Shaoxing opera

绍兴酒(shàoxīng jiǔ) Shaoxing wine

畲族(shēzú) the She nationality (mainly distributed in Zhejiang)

舌耕(shégēng) to make a living by teaching

舌人(shérén) officials acting as interpreters

舌战(shézhàn) to have a verbal battle with; to argue heatedly with

蛇郎中(shélángzhōng) a specialist in healing snake bites

蛇拳(shéquán) snake boxing (martial arts)

舍命陪君子(shěmìng péi jūnzi) to accompany somebody at the risk of one's life

舍间(shèjiān) my humble abode; my house

舍监(shèjiān) the warden of a school

dormitory

舍利(shèlì)(Buddhism) sarira (sacred relics, consisting of a saint's ashes)

舍利塔(shèlìtǎ) sarira stupa (a pagoda for Buddist relics)

舍亲(shèqīn) my relative; a relative of mine

舍下(shèxià) my humble abode; my house

社稷(shèjì) the country; the state

社稷坛(shèjì tán) altar to the god of land and grain

社稷之臣(shèjìzhī chén)(lit.)"a loyal servant of the dynasty's sacred altars" - a bulwark of the state; a pillar of the state

社神(shèshén) the god of the land

社戏(shèxì) a village theatrical performance

社学(shèxué) a village school

《射雕英雄传》(shèdiāo yīngxíong zhuàn) *The Eagle Shooting Heroes* - a novel by Jin Yong(金庸,1924 -) in 1959; a TV drama directed by Wang Rui(王瑞) et al. in 2003; *The Legend of the Condor Heroes* - a TV drama directed by Wang Tianlin (王天林) in 1983

摄政(shèzhèng) to act as regent

摄政王(shèzhèngwáng) the regent; the prince regent

摄篆(shèzhuàn) to act as deputy

申时(shēnshí) the period of the day from 3 p. m. to 5 p. m.

身怀六甲(shēn huái liùjiǎ) to be with child; to be pregnant

身家(shēnjiā) ① oneself and one's family ② family background

身教胜于言教(shēnjiào shèng yú yánjiào) example is better than precept; actions speak louder than words

身世(shēnshì) life experience

身手(shēnshǒu) skill; talent

身在曹营心在汉(shēn zài cáoyíng xīn zài hàn)"to live in the Cao camp but with one's heart in the Han camp" - to be half-hearted

身子骨儿(shēnzigǔr) one's health; physique

深闺(shēnguī) the women's living quarters

深宅大院(shēnzhái dàyuàn) imposing dwellings and spacious courtyards

《神笔马良》(shénbǐ mǎliáng) *The Story of the Magic Painbrush* - a story by Hong Xuntao(洪汛涛, 1928 - 2001) in the 1950s; a film directed by Jin Xi(靳夕) et al. in 1955

《神鞭》(shén biān) *Magic Braid* - a film directed by Zhang Zien(张子

恩)in 1986

神道碑(shéndào bēi)①a stone tablet guarding a tomb passage②the inscription on such a stone tablet

神道社教(shéndào shèjiào)to teach and rule(the people)by imitating the way of deities

《神雕侠侣》(shéndiāo xiálǚ)*The legend of the Condor Hero* – a novel by Jin Yong(金庸, 1924 –) in 1959;a TV drama directed by Wang Tianlin(王天林)in 1983 and by Yu Min(于敏)in 2006

《神话》(shénhuà)*The Myth* – a film directed by Tang Jili(唐季礼)in 2005;a TV drama directed by Jeffrey Chiang(蒋家俊)in 2009

神龛(shénkān)a shrine;an ancestral tablet

《神灭论》(shénmiè lùn)*On the Extinction of Spirit* – a famous article by Fan Chen(范缜,450 –515);*On the Destructibility of the Soul*

神魔小说(shénmó xiǎoshuō)tales about gods and demons;supernatural fiction

神农(shénnóng)the God of Agriculture

《神农本草经》(shénnóng běncǎo jīng)*Shen Nong Materia Medica* – attributed to Shen Nong(神农)in the Eastern Han Dynasty,25 –220

神婆(shénpó)a sorceress;a witch

神哨(shénshào)talkative

神神道道(shénshen dāodāo)odd;fantastic;bizarre

《神探狄仁杰》(shéntàn dírénjié)*Detective Di Renjie* – a TV drama directed by Qian Yanqiu(钱雁秋)in 2004 –2010

神童(shéntóng)a child prodigy

神武门(shénwǔmén)the Gate of Divine Prowess(the Northern Gate of the Forbidden City,namely the Gate of the Palace Museum,Beijing)

神仙(shénxiān)a supernatural being;a celestial being;an immortal

神仙会(shénxiānhuì)the“meeting of immortals”– a meeting at which the participants express their views freely

神州(shénzhōu)the Divine Land;China

沈诗任笔(shěnshī rénbǐ)prose

沈阳事变(shěnyáng shìbiàn)the Shenyang Incident(in 1937);the Mukden Incident

婶母(shěnmǔ)aunt(wife of father's younger brother)

婶娘(shěnniáng)aunt(wife of father's younger brother)

婶婆(shěnpó)the wife of one's husband's uncle

婶婶(shěnshen)aunt(wife of father's

younger brother)

婶子(shěnzi)aunt(wife of father's younger brother)

蜃景(shènjǐng)a mirage

升官发财(shēngguān fācái)to win promotion and get rich;to be out for power and money

升平(shēngpíng)peace

升天(shēngtiān)to ascend to Heaven;to die

生产建设兵团(shēngchǎn jiànshè bīngtuán)production and construction corps

生辰八字(shēngchén bāzì)the eight characters(four Celestial Stems and four Terrestrial Branches, generated from a person's date of birth and hour of birth)

生齿(shēngchǐ)population;the members of a family

生祠(shēngcí)a memorial hall set up for a living official

生旦净末丑(shēngdànjìngmòchǒu)sheng(the chief male), dan(the chief female), jing(a comic role), mo(the second male)and chou(the clown)(the main operatic role categories)

生地黄(shēngdìhuáng)①(Chinese medicine)rehmannia glutinosa ② virgin soil;uncultivated land

生分(shēngfēn)estranged; not as close as before

生角(shēngjué)a male role(in traditional Chinese opera)

生灵(shēnglíng)the people

生事(shēngshì)to make trouble; to create a disturbance

生手(shēngshǒu)a newbie;a novice

生肖(shēngxiào)any of the 12 symbolic animals of the Chinese horoscope

生障(shēngzhàng)the affairs of life

声调(shēngdiào)tone

声东击西(shēngdōng jīxī)to employ decoy tactics

声母(shēngmǔ)initial consonant

《声声慢·寻寻觅觅》(shēngshēng màn, xúnxún mìmì) *Slow Slow Song:Repeated Seeking* - a *ci* poem by Li Qingzhao(李清照, 1084 - 1155)

牲口棚(shēngkou péng)a barn; a livestock shed

胜败乃兵家常事(shèngbài nǎi bīng jiā chángshì)for a military commander, winning or losing a battle is a common occurrence

胜不骄,败不馁(shèng bùjiāo, bài bùněi)neither be smug with success nor discouraged by failure

胜朝(shèngcháo)the defunct dynasty;the previous dynasty

笙(shēng)a Chinese reed pipe

笙歌(shēnggē) playing instruments and singing songs

笙管乐(shēngguǎnyuè) the music produced with traditional Chinese wind instruments

笙磐同音(shēngpán tóngyīn) to work together in perfect harmony

绳鞭技(shéngbiān jì) (to perform) tricks with a whip

绳耳(shéng'ěr) (lit.) "rope-fixing ears" - the two ends of a carrying pole where the ropes are fixed

绳技(shéngjì) rope juggling; tight-rope walking

绳之以法(shéngzhīyǐfǎ) to prosecute and punish somebody by law; to bring to justice

省港大罢工(shěnggǎng dà bàgōng) the Strike of the Workers of Guangzhou and Hong Kong(1925 - 1926)

省试(shěngshì) the provincial imperial examination; the metropolitan exa-mination

圣躬(shènggōng) the emperor's health

圣经贤传(shèngjīng xiánzhuàn) Confucian classics

圣庙(shèngmiào) a Confucian temple

圣明(shèngmíng) august wisdom

圣人(shèngrén) a sage

圣人无常师(shèngrén wú chángshī) sages have no constant teachers; a sage has more than one teacher

圣上(shèngshàng) Your Majesty

圣贤(shèngxián) sages and men of virtue

圣药(shèngyào) imperial medicine

圣谕(shèngyù) an imperial decree

圣旨(shèngzhǐ) an imperial edict

盛夏(shèngxià) midsummer

剩女(shèngnǚ) a spinster; a girl who's been left on the shelf; an old maid

尸位素餐(shīwèisùcān) to get paid without doing a stroke of work; to neglect one's duties while in office

失聪(shīcōng) to go deaf; deafness

失道寡助(shīdào guǎzhù) an unjust cause finds scant support

失礼(shīlǐ) to commit a breach of etiquette

失恃(shīshì) to lose one's mother in the childhood

失之东隅,收之桑榆(shī zhī dōngyú, shōu zhī sāngyú) (lit.) "to lose in the east and gain in the west" - to make up on the roundabouts what one loses on the swings

失之毫厘,谬以千里(shī zhī háolí, miù yǐ qiānlǐ) a tiny error can lead you far astray; a minor discrepancy can set you way off course

师承(shīchéng) ①to have studied under (a teacher); to be a disciple of ②transmission from master to disciple

师傅领进门，修行在个人(shīfu lǐng jìnmén，xiūxíng zài gèrén) the master initiates the apprentice in a certain trade, but their improvement of the skill depends on their own efforts

师公(shīgōng) the master of one's master

师姑(shīgū) a nun

师姐(shījiě) ①a senior(female) fellow apprentice ② the daughter of one's master(older than oneself)

师妹(shīmèi) ①a junior(female) fellow apprentice ② the daughter of one's master(younger than oneself)

师母(shīmǔ) the wife of the teacher or master

师娘(shīniáng) the wife of the teacher or master

师兄(shīxiōng) ①a senior(male) fellow apprentice ② the son of one's master(older than oneself)

师爷(shīyé) a private adviser

虱多不痒，债多不愁(shī duō bùyǎng，zhài duō bùchóu) when one is covered with lice, one doesn't feel an itch, when one is submerged in debt, one will not bc worried

诗才(shīcái) a poetic genius

诗话(shīhuà) notes on poets and poetry; stories interspersed with poems

诗集(shījí) an anthology of poems

诗界革命(shījiè gémìng) the Revolution in the Circles of Poetry(a poetry-improving movement around 1898)

《诗经》(shījīng) *The Book of Songs* – an ancient collection of poems from 1100 BC to 600 BC; *The Book of Odes*

诗律(shīlǜ) prosody

《诗品》(shīpǐn) *Grades of Poetry* – a critical work on poetry by Zhong Rong(钟嵘, 468 – 518) of the Southern Dynasties or by Sikong Tu (司空图, 837 – 908) in the Tang Dynasty

《诗三百》(shī sānbǎi) *Three-hundred Poems* (also known as *The Book of Songs*)

诗圣(shīshèng) a poet-sage; a sage poet

诗史(shīshǐ) the history of poetry

诗书(shīshū) the Confucian classics

诗书门第(shīshū méndì) a scholarly family

《诗薮》(shīsǒu) *Collection of Poems* – a poetry anthology by Hu Yinglin (胡应麟, 1551 – 1602) in the Ming Dynasty

诗坛(shītán) poetic circles

诗仙(shīxiān) a poet-immortal; the "Celestial Poet" – an epithet for Li

Bai(李白,701 –762)

诗选(shīxuǎn) an anthology of poems;a poetry anthology

诗余(shīyú) ci poetry

诗韵(shīyùn) rhyme(in poetry)

诗钟(shīzhōng) timed verse composition (a game of composing verses within a time limit)

《施公案》(shīgōng àn) *The Cases of Judge Shi* – a novel written in Qianlong(乾隆,reign:1736 – 1795) and Jinqing (嘉庆, reign: 1796 – 1820) years

施食会(shīshíhuì) the Feeding Hungry Ghosts (on the 15th day of the 7th lunar month)

施斋(shīzhāi) to provide (itinerant monks) with free food

施粥(shīzhōu) to provide free porridge(for the poor)

施主(shīzhǔ) (monk's or nun's form of address for a layman) a patron

狮子大开口(shīzi dà kāikǒu) ①to make an excessive demand ② to talk big

狮子林(shīzilín) Lion Woods (in the northeast of Suzhou)

狮子耍绣球(shīzi shuǎ xiùqiú) a lion playing with a colored silk ball (a folk dance)

狮子舞(shīziwǔ) the lion dance

十八般兵器(shíbābān bīngqì) the 18 traditional weapons of Chinese martial arts

十八般武艺(shíbābān wǔyì) (lit.) "the skill in wielding the 18 kinds of weapons" – skill in various types of combat;versatile skills

十八层地狱(shíbācéng dìyù) (lit.) "the eighteenth hell" – the lowest depths of hell

十八界(shíbājiè) (Buddhism) the eighteen realms

十八罗汉(shíbāluóhàn) the Eighteen Arhats; the Eighteen Disciples of the Buddha

十重戒(shíchóngjiè) (Buddhism) the Ten Unpardonable Sins

十地(shídì) (Buddhism) the ten stages

十冬腊月(shídōng làyuè) the cold months of the year

十恶(shí'è) the Ten Evil Things (established officially in the Sui Dynasty,581 –618)

十恶不赦(shí'è bùshè) to be guilty of unpardonable evil; unpardonably wicked

十二部经(shí'èr bù jīng) the twelve Conffucian classics

十二分(shí'èr fēn) more than 100 percent;extremely

十二律(shí'èr lǜ) the twelve tones of ancient Chinese music

十二生肖(shí'èr shēngxiào) the 12 symbolic animals associated with a 12 - year cycle; the Chinese horoscope

十二行相(shí'èr xíngxiàng)(Buddhism) the twelve processes

十二因缘(shí'èr yīnyuán)(Buddhism) the Twelve Nidanas

十方(shífāng)(Buddhism) the ten directions (i. e. the four cardinal points, the intermediate points and above and below)

十个手指有长短(shíge shǒuzhǐ yǒu chángduǎn)(lit.) "all ten fingers are different in length" - you can't expect everybody to be the same

十戒(shíjiè)(Buddhism) the Ten Prohibitions

十力(shílì)(Buddhism) the ten intelligent powers

十六国(shíliù guó) the Sixteen Kingdoms(304 - 439)

《十六国春秋》(shíliùguó chūnqiū) *The Spring and Autumn Annals of the Sixteen Kingdoms* - a historical book by Cui Hong(崔鸿, 470 - 520)

十六罗汉(shíliù luóhàn) the Sixteen Arhats

十六小地狱(shíliù xiǎo dìyù) the Sixteen Minor Hells

十六心(shíliù xīn) the sixteen mental conditions

《十面埋伏》(shímiàn máifú) *House of Flying Daggers* - a film directed by Zhang Yimou(张艺谋) in 2004; *Ambush on All Sides* - a piece of music for the lute

十年动乱(shínián dòngluàn) the decade of disturbance; the ten-years of upheaval; the ten chaotic years of the Cultural Revolution (1966 - 1976)

十年寒窗(shínián hánchuāng) "ten years' study at a cold window" - a student's long years of hard study

十年内战(shínián nèizhàn) the Ten-Year Civil War(the Second Revolutionary Civil War 1927 - 1937)

十年树木,百年育人(shínián shùmù, bǎinián yùrén) It takes ten years to grow trees, but a hundred to rear people.

十三点(shísāndiǎn) a simple-minded person; an eccentric

十三经(shísānjīng) the Thirteen Classics of Confucianism

十三陵(shísānlíng) the Thirteen Tombs, or the Ming Tombs

十三虚无(shísān xūwú)(Taoism) the Thirteen Rules for Health

十三辙(shísānzhé) the thirteen rhyme schemes

十善(shíshàn)(Buddhism) the Ten

Virtues

十事(shíshì)(Buddhism) the Ten Things Forbidden

《十五贯》(shíwǔ guàn) *Fifteen Strings of Cash* – a play by Zhu Suchen(朱素臣) in the Qing Dynast

《十月围城》(shíyuè wéichéng) *Bodyguards and Assassins* – a film directed by Chen Desen(陈德森) in 2009

《十字街头》(shízì jiētou) *Crossroads* – a film directed by Shen Xiling(沈西苓) in 1937

十字绣(shízìxìu) cross-stitched embroidery

什不闲儿(shíbùxiánr) shibuxianr (a folk art form of ballad-singing accompanied by percussion instruments)

石舫(shífǎng) a stone boat (as a garden ornament); a boat-shaped stone pavilion

石鼓文(shígǔwén) ①the inscriptions on drumshaped stone blocks ② the script used for such inscriptions

《石壕吏》(shíháo lì) *The Shihao Official* – a poem by Du Fu(杜甫, 712 –770)

石经(shíjīng) ①the Confucian classics engraved on stone tablets ②the Buddist sutras engraved on stone tablets

石刻(shíkè) ① a carved stone ② a stone inscription

石窟(shíkū) a stone cave; a grotto

石榴裙(shíliúqún) (lit.) "a pomegranate-red skirt" – feminine charms

《石头记》(shítoujì) *The Story of the Stone*; *The Dream of Red Mansions* – a novel by Cao Xueqin(曹雪芹, 1715 – 1763)

石钟山石窟(shízhōngshān shíkū) Mount Shizhong Grottoes; the Grottoes of Mount Shizhong (located in Dali, Yunnan province)

时辰(shíchén) one of the 12 two-hour periods

时穷节乃见(shíqióng jié nǎixiàn) integrity shines out in times of woe

时势造英雄(shíshì zào yīngxióng) heroes are products of their times

识时务者为俊杰(shí shíwù zhě wéi jùnjié) a person who understands the signs of the times is wise; whosoever understands the current reality is a great man.

识相(shíxiàng) to show good sense; to be sensible

实践出真知(shíjiàn chū zhēnzhī) genuine knowledge comes from practice.

实名制(shímíngzhì) a real-name system (in which one's identity card is obliged to present)

实心眼儿(shíxīnyǎnr) honest and serious-minded

拾遗(shíyí) gleanings; to pocket what one finds

蚀本(shíběn) to lose one's business capital

食古不化(shígǔbùhuà) to swallow ancient learning without digesting it

食客(shíkè) ①a person sponging off an aristocrat; a hanger-on of an aristocrat②a customer in a restaurant

史部(shǐbù) the history as the second of the four divisions of an ancient Chinese library collection

史乘(shǐshèng) a history; annals

史官(shǐguān) an official historian; a historiographer

史馆(shǐguǎn) a historiographer's office

史话(shǐhuà) the stories about historical events

《史记》(shǐjì) *The Records of the Great Historian* – a historical book by Sima Qian(司马迁, 145 – 87 BC)

《史通》(shǐtōng) *The Generality of Historiography* – a monograph on historical theory by Liu Zhiji(刘知几, 661 – 721) in 710

使绊儿(shǐbànr) ①to trip somebody up in wrestling②to injure somebody by underhand methods

使出浑身解数(shǐchū húnshēn xièshù) to use all one's skill; to do all one is capable of

使坏水儿(shǐhuàishuǐr) to play a dirty trick

使唤(shǐhuan) ①to order about②to use; to handle

使唤丫头(shǐhuanyātou) a slave girl; a young maidservant

使女(shǐnǚ) a maidservant; a housemaid

使性子(shǐ xìngzi) to get angry; to lose one's temper

使眼色(shǐ yǎnsè) to wink

始作俑者(shǐzuòyǒngzhě) (lit.) "the man who first made tomb figures" – the creator of a bad precedent

士别三日,刮目相看(shìbié sānrì, guāmù xiāngkàn) A scholar who has been away for three days must be seen in a different light

《士兵突击》(shìbīng tūjī) *Soldiers' Sortie* – a TV drama directed by Kang Honglei(康洪雷) in 2006

士大夫(shìdàfū) scholar-officials or scholar-bureaucrats

士可杀不可辱(shì kěshā bùkě rǔ) A scholar may be killed but may not be insulted.

士为知己者用,女为悦己者容(shì wéi zhījǐzhě yòng, nǚ wéi yuèjǐzhě róng) a gentleman dies for his true friend, as a woman makes herself beautiful for her lover

士族(shìzú) the influential and privileged family of scholar-officials

世家(shìjiā) ①a noble family ②the hereditary house of a noble ③the biographies of noble rulers, nobility and bureaucrats

世交(shìjiāo) ①friendship spanning two or more generations ②old family friends

世面(shìmiàn) the various aspects of society; the world; society at large

世情小说(shìqíng xiǎoshuō) the Human-feeling Fiction [one school of fiction in the Ming(1368 - 1644) and Qing(1636 - 1912) Dynasties]

《世说新语》(shìshuōxīnyǔ) *New Collection of Anecdotes of Famous Personages* - a scatchbook by Liu Yiqing(刘义庆,403 - 444); *A New Account of Tales of the World*; *A New Account of Social Talk*

世态炎凉(shìtài yánliáng) (lit.) "warmth or coldness is the way of the world" - people are friendly or unfriendly, depending on whether one is successful or not

世外桃源(shìwài táoyuán) the Land of Peach Blossoms - a fictitious land of peace, away from the turmoil of the world; a Shangri-La

世袭(shìxí) hereditary

世系(shìxì) pedigree; genealogy

世兄(shìxiōng) the student of one's father; the son of one's teacher; the son of one's friend

世医(shìyī) a physician descended from generations of medical practitioners; a hereditary physician

世子(shìzi) the feudal prince's son and legal heir

世族(shìzú) an old and great family

世尊(shìzūn) Bhagavat (a respectful appellation for Buddha)

仕宦(shìhuàn) to be an official; to be in government service

仕女(shìnǚ) ①a maid in the imperial palace ②a genre of traditional Chinese painting with the subject matter of beautiful women

市曹(shìcáo) ①a market place ②the officials in charge of shops and stores ③a public square

市井风俗小说(shìjǐng fēngsú xiǎoshuō) the Fiction of Townpeople's Life

市井之徒(shìjǐng zhī tú) a philistine

事必躬亲(shìbì gōngqīn) to attend to everything oneself; to take care of every single thing personally; to micromanage

事儿妈(shìrmā) a meddler

事后诸葛亮 (shìhòu zhūgěliàng)

(lit.)"to be a Zhuge Liang only after something unpleasant has happened"-to be wise after the event

侍从(shìcóng)an attendant

侍从官(shìcóngguān)an attendant

侍奉(shìfèng)to look after;to serve

侍郎(shìláng)the vice-president - of one of the Six Boards of Ministries in the Ming(1368-1644)and Qing(1636-1912)dynasties

侍女(shìnǚ)a maidservant

侍卫(shìwèi)①a guard②an imperial bodyguard

侍者(shìzhě)an attendant;a servant

是可忍,孰不可忍(shì·kěrěn, shú bùkěrěn)if this can be tolerated, what cannot be

贳器店(shìqìdiàn)a rental shop

舐犊情深(shìdúqíngshēn)(lit.)"a cow fondly licking her calf"-parental love

舐痔(shìzhì)(lit.)"to lick somebody's piles"-to debase oneself in trying to please somebody important or powerful

逝世(shìshì)to pass away

逝者如斯(shìzhě rúsī)time passes by as water flows along a stream

逝者如斯,不舍昼夜(shìzhě rúsī, bùshě zhòuyè)Thus do things pass away,by day and by night

谥号(shìhào)a posthumous title

释藏(shìzàng)the Buddhist Canon

释典(shìdiǎn)the Buddhist Scripture

释迦牟尼(shìjiāmóuní)(Buddhism) Sakyamuni(c. 565-486 BC);Gautama

释迦子(shìjiāzǐ)Buddhist adherents: Buddhists

释教(shìjiào)Buddhism

释老(shìlǎo)Buddhism and Taoism

《释名》(shìmíng)*The Explanation of Names*-an ancient book by Liu Xi(刘熙,160-?)

收工(shōugōng)to stop work for the day

收回成命(shōuhuí chéngmìng)to countermand an order; to revoke an order

收买(shōumǎi)①to purchase②to bribe

收生婆(shōushēngpó)a midwife

收心(shōuxīn)①to get into the frame of mind for work or study; to concentrate on more serious things②to have a change of heart

手把手(shǒubǎshǒu)to instruct personally;to pass on one's own knowledge and skills.

手笔(shǒubǐ)①handwriting②a literary skill

手鼓(shǒugǔ)a tabor

《手机》(shǒujī)*Cell Phone* - a film directed by Feng Xiaogang(冯小

刚）in 2003；a TV drama directed by Shen Yan（沈严）et al. in 2010

手脚不干净（shǒujiǎo bùgānjìng）sticky-fingered；dishonest in money matters

手紧（shǒujǐn）①hard-up②stingy

手令（shǒulìng）an order personally issued by somebody in command

手面（shǒumiàn）the extent of one's spending；the level of one's expenditure

手拿把掐（shǒuná bǎqiā）a sure thing；it's in the bag

手气（shǒuqì）luck

手书（shǒushū）①to write in one's own hand②a personal letter

手无寸铁（shǒuwú cùntiě）unarmed

手无缚鸡之力（shǒuwú fùjī zhīlì）（lit.）"to lack the strength to truss a chicken"－to be weak physically

手下（shǒuxià）①under the leadership of②at hand

手下败将（shǒuxià bàijiàng）one's vanquished foe；one's defeated opponent

手下留情（shǒuxià liúqíng）to show mercy；to be lenient

手下人（shǒuxiàrén）①one's subordinate②a servant

手相（shǒuxiàng）palmistry

手眼（shǒuyǎn）tricks；artifices

手谕（shǒuyù）personally written orders or instructions；a handwritten directive

手泽（shǒuzé）manuscripts from a previous generation；the handwriting or articles left by one's forefathers

手诏（shǒuzhào）an imperial edict written by the emperor

守财奴（shǒucáinú）a miser

守服（shǒufú）to observe mourning for one's deceased parent

守寡（shǒuguǎ）to remain a widow；to live in widowhood

守活寡（shǒu huóguǎ）to live apart from one's husband；to be a grass widow

守节（shǒujié）to remain unmarried after the death of one's husband or betrothed

守旧派（shǒujiùpài）conservatives；old fogeys

守空房（shǒu kōngfáng）to stay home alone

守灵（shǒulíng）to stand as guards at the bier；to keep vigil beside the coffin

守身如玉（shǒushēn rúyù）（lit.）"to keep oneself as pure as jade"－to preserve one's chastity

守岁（shǒusuì）to stay up late or all night on New Year's Eve；to see the New Year in

守孝（shǒuxiào）to observe a period of

mourning for one's deceased parent

首七(shǒuqī)the seventh day after a person's death

首日戳(shǒurì chuō)(stamp-collecting)a first-day issue postmark

首日封(shǒurì fēng)(stamp-collecting)a first-day cover

寿比南山,福如东海 (shòubǐ nán shān,fúrú dōnghǎi)may you live to be as old as Zhongnan Mountain and may your happiness be as deep as the Eastern Sea

寿材(shòucái)a coffin(prepared before one's death)

寿诞(shòudàn)one's birthday

寿联(shòulián)a birthday couplet; birthday scrolls;a longevity couplet

寿眉(shòuméi)long full eyebrows(indicating age and health)

寿面(shòumiàn)birthday noodles

寿星(shòuxīng)①the god of longevity②an elderly person(whose birthday is being celebrated)

寿衣(shòuyī)graveclothes

寿幛(shòuzhàng)a birthday banner

寿终正寝(shòuzhōng zhèngqǐn)to die a natural death

受宠若惊(shòuchǒng ruòjīng)to be overwhelmed(by an unexpected favor);to feel extremely flattered

受夹板气(shòu jiābǎnqì)to be blamed by both sides

受戒(shòujiè)to be initiated into monkhood or nunhood

《受戒》(shòujiè)*Ordination* - a short story by Wang Zengqi(汪曾祺, 1920 - 1997)in 1980

受气包(shòuqìbāo)one who always gets blamed;a whipping boy

绶带(shòudài)a silk ribbon attatched to an official seal or a medal

瘦金体(shòujīntǐ)the thin-tendon style(a style of Chinese calligraphy)

瘦西湖(shòuxīhú)Slender West Lake (located in Yangzhou)

书案(shū'àn)a writing desk

书茶馆儿(shūcháguǎnr)a storytelling teahouse

书场(shūchǎng)a place of quyi performances

书呆子(shūdāizi)a bookish man

书蠹(shūdù)①a bookworm②a pedant

书法(shūfǎ)calligraphy

书法风格(shūfǎ fēnggé)a calligraphic style

书法家(shūfǎjiā)a calligrapher

书法艺术(shūfá yìshù)the calligraphic art

书法艺术家(shūfǎ yìshùjiā)a calligraphic artist

书坊(shūfāng)a bookshop with printing works

书鼓(shūgǔ)a small drum(used as an accompanying instruments in story-telling)

书馆(shūguǎn)a storytelling teahouse

书翰(shūhàn)①calligraphy②letters

书贾(shūjiǎ)a bookseller

书简(shūjiǎn)letters

《书经》(shūjīng)*The Classic of History*;*The Book of History* – attributed to Confucius

书局(shūjú)a publishing house; a bookshop

书卷气(shūjuànqì)bookishness;scholarliness;cultivation

书口(shūkǒu)a book margin

书吏(shūlì)a government clerk

书林(shūlín)(lit.)"a forest of books"– a treasury of books

书面语(shūmiànyǔ)the written language;literary language

书契(shūqì)a written contract

书生(shūshēng)an intellectual; a scholar

书生之见(shūshēng zhī jiàn)a bookish approach;a pedantic view

书圣(shūshèng)the"sage of Chinese calligraphy" – Wang Xizhi(王羲之,303 –361)

书塾(shūshú)an old-style private school

书肆(shūsì)a bookshop;a bookstore

书体(shūtǐ)a style of calligraphy

书童(shūtóng)a page boy

书香门第(shūxiāng méndì)a literary family;a family of scholars

书院(shūyuàn)an academy of classical learning

书斋(shūzhāi)a study

书中自有黄金屋,书中自有颜如玉(shūzhōng zìyǒu huángjīnwū, shūzhōng zìyǒu yánrúyù)golden houses and beautiful wives can be found through study

叔父(shūfù)uncle(father's younger brother)

叔公(shūgōng)one's husband's uncle(his father's younger brother)

叔母(shūmǔ)aunt(wife of father's younger brother)

叔叔(shūshu)uncle

叔祖(shūzǔ)great-uncle(paternal grandfather's younger brother)

叔祖母(shūzǔmǔ)great-aunt(wife of paternal granfather's younger brother)

枢密院(shūmìyuàn)the Privy Council;the Council of Military Affairs;the Supreme Military Council

殊途同归(shūtú tóngguī)to reach the same goal by different routes

梳篦(shūbì)thick and fine-toothed combs

淑女(shūnǚ)an elegant lady;a fair maiden

输嘴(shūzuǐ) to admit mistake or defeat in argument

赎身(shúshēn) to redeem oneself; to buy back one's freedom

赎刑(shúxíng) to redeem one from punishment by paying a ransom

塾师(shúshī) a tutor of a private school

熟客(shúkè) a frequent visitor

熟年(shúnián) a year of good harvests; a good year; a year of abundance

熟语(shúyǔ) an idiom; an idiomatic expression

属国(shǔguó) a vassal state; a dependent state

属相(shǔxiàng) any of the 12 symbolic animals used to denote the year of one's birth

鼠辈(shǔbèi) rascals; scoundrels

鼠胆(shǔdǎn) to be as timid as a mouse; to be cowardly

鼠目寸光(shǔmù cùnguāng) (lit.) "a mouse can see only an inch" – to be short-sighted; to lack vision or foresight

数典忘祖(shǔdiǎn wàngzǔ) (lit.) "to give all the historical facts except those about one's own ancestors" – to forget one's own origins

数冬瓜道茄子(shǔdōngguā dào qiézi) to chatter

数伏(shǔfú) the beginning of the three hottest ten-day periods of the year

数九(shǔjiǔ) the beginning of the nine-day periods following the Winter Solstice; the beginning of the coldest days of the year

数九寒天(shǔjiǔ hántiān) the coldest days of the year

数来宝(shǔláibǎo) rhythmic storytelling

数一数二(shǔyī shǔ'èr) to count as one of the very best; to rank very high

《蜀道难》(shǔdàonán) *Hard is the Road to Shu* – a poem by Li Bai(李白,701 – 762)

蜀汉(shǔhàn) the Kingdom of Shu Han(221 – 263)

蜀锦(shǔjǐn) Sichuan brocade

蜀黍(shǔshǔ) Chinese sorghum; Gaoliang

蜀绣(shǔxiù) Sichuan embroidery

蜀中无大将,廖化作先锋(shǔzhōng wú dàjiàng, liàohuà zuò xiānfēng) in the land of the blind, the one-eyed man is king

术士(shùshì) ①a Confucian scholar ②a magician

戍边(shùbiān) to defend the frontiers; to guard the frontiers

戍守(shùshǒu) to defend; to guard

束脩(shùxiū)the gift for one's teacher (on his first meeting with his teacher in old time)

束之高阁(shùzhī gāogé)(lit.)"to tie something up and place it on the top shelf"- to lay aside and neglect;to shelve something

述怀(shùhuái)to pour out one's feelings

树欲静而风不止(shù yù jìng' ér fēng bùzhǐ)(lit.)"the tree may crave calm, but the wind will not drop"- things take their own course regardless of one's desires

竖臣(shùchén)a small palace attendant

竖琴(shùqín)a harp

竖蜻蜓(shùqīngtíng)(lit.)"a vertical dragonfly"- a handstand; head-balancing

竖子(shùzi)a mean fellow;a lad

恕不奉陪(shù bù fèngpéi)please excuse me(for not keeping you company)

庶出(shùchū)to be born of a concubine

庶民(shùmín)the common people

庶母(shùmǔ)one's father's concubine

庶人(shùrén)the common people

庶室(shùshì)a concubine

庶子(shùzǐ)the son of a concubine

数位艺术(shùwèi yìshù)a digital art

刷课(shuākè)to skip school; to play truant

刷夜(shuāyè)to stay away from home all night

耍把戏(shuǎbǎxì)to give an acrobatic performance;to play tricks

耍刺儿(shuǎcìr)to find fault with

耍单儿(shuǎdānr)to wear fewer clothes for the sake of looking good;to flaunt good health in cold weather

耍刀枪(shuǎdāoqiāng)to play swords and spears;to brandish swords and spears

耍骨头(shuǎgǔtóu)naughty;to make trouble

耍猴儿(shuǎhóur)(lit.)"to put on a monkey show"- to tease; to make fun of somebody

耍花腔(shuǎhuāqiāng)to cheat somebody by glib talk; to sweet-talk somebody

耍花招(shuǎhuāzhāo)to display showy movements in martial arts; to play tricks

耍滑头(shuǎhuátóu)to try to shirk work or responsibility; to act in a slick way

耍赖(shuǎlài)to act shamelessly

耍赖皮(shuǎlàipí)to act shamelessly

耍流氓(shuǎliúmáng)to behave like a hoodlum;to take liberties with women

耍龙灯(shuǎlóngdēng)the dragon lantern dance;the dragon dance

耍排场(shuǎpáichǎng)to parade one's wealth;to be ostentatious

耍盘子(shuǎpánzi) plate-spinning; disc-spinning;to juggle plates

耍脾气(shuǎpíqì)to put on a show of bad temper;to go into a huff;to sulk

耍贫嘴(shuǎpínzuǐ)to be garrulous

耍人(shuǎrén)to make fun of somebody

耍手段(shuǎshǒuduàn)to use artifices;to play tricks

耍手艺(shuǎshǒuyì)to make a living as a craftman

耍死狗(shuǎsǐgǒu)to try to brazen it out

耍坛子(shuǎtánzi) to juggle with jars;a jar balancing act

耍威风(shuǎwēifēng)to make a show of authority;to throw one's weight about;to be overbearing

耍无赖(shuǎwúlài)to act shamelessly

耍心眼儿(shuǎxīnyǎnr) to exercise one's wits for personal gain

耍嘴皮子(shuǎzuǐpízi)to talk glibly; to pay lip service to something; mere empty words

摔跟头(shuāi gēntou)to fall;to tumble;to make a blunder

摔耙子(shuāi pázi) to pack in one's job

甩脸子(shuǎiliǎnzi) to pull a long face;to sulk

甩卖(shuǎimài)the disposal of goods at reduced prices; to dispose of goods at a reduced price

甩手掌柜(shuǎishǒu zhǎngguì) a handsoff boss (a boss who merely gives general instructions but keeps his hands off any practical work)

甩袖子(shuǎi xiùzi)(lit.)"to swing one's sleeves"–to wash one's hands of(work or other matters)

帅才(shuàicái) a talent for military command; a born military commander

帅旗(shuàiqí) the flag of a commander in chief

帅印(shuàiyìn) the seal of a commander in chief

涮羊肉(shuàn yángròu) mutton hot-pot;lamb hot-pot

双百方针(shuāngbǎi fāngzhēn) the policy of letting a hundred flowers blossom and a hundred schools of thought contend

双规(shuāngguī) to demand a relevant officeholder to confess their problems at the prescribed time and place(a disciplinary measure outside the regular legal system under which the Party members are detained and interrogated); to put (an official) under detention and interrogation

双簧(shuānghuáng) a two-person act; a two-man comic show; a double act

双肩挑(shuāngjiān tiāo) to shoulder responsibility for both professional and administration work (in the same department)

双面绣(shuāngmiàn xiù) double-sided embroidery

双身子(shuāngshēnzi) a pregnant woman

双十二事变(shuāngshí'èr shìbiàn) the Xi'an Incident of 12 December 1936

双喜(shuāngxǐ) double happiness

双喜临门(shuāngxǐ línmén) a double blessing has descended upon the house

霜降(shuāngjiàng) the Frost's Descent (the 18th of the 24 Chinese solar terms, usually falling on 23rd of October)

孀妇(shuāngfù) a widow

孀居(shuāngjū) to be a widow

《谁是最可爱的人》(shuí shì zuì kě'àide rén) *Who is the Most Loveable Person?* – a piece of prose by Wei Wei (魏巍, 1920 – 2008) in 1951

水车(shuǐchē) a waterwheel

《水调歌头》(shuǐdiàogētóu) *Prelude to Water Melody* – one of the patterns of the ci poem in the Sui, Tang and Song Dynasties

水分(shuǐfèn) moisture content; exaggeration

《水浒》(shuǐhǔ) *Outlaws of the Marsh* – a novel by Shi Nai'an (施耐庵, 1296 – 1371); *The Water Margin*

《水浒传》(shuǐhǔzhuàn) *Outlaws of the Marsh* – a novel by Shi Nai'an (施耐庵, 1296 – 1371); *The Water Margin*

水货(shuǐhuò) ① smuggled goods ② inferior goods

水饺(shuǐjiǎo) boiled dumplings; *jiaozi*

《水经注》(shuǐjīngzhù) *A Commentary on the Classic of Waterways* – a geographical treatise by Li Daoyuan (郦道元, 466 – 527)

水晶灯笼(shuǐjīng dēnglóng) very shrewd and discerning

水晶宫(shuǐjīnggōng) the Crystal Palace (of the Dragon King)

水帘洞(shuǐliándòng) Water Curtain Cave

水磨工夫(shuǐmógōngfū) patient and precise work

水墨画(shuǐmòhuà) an ink-wash painting; a freehand painting

水能载舟，亦能覆舟（shuǐ néng zàizhōu，yì néng fùzhōu）while the waters can keep a boat afloat，they can also overturn it

水师提督（shuǐshī tídū）the commander-in-chief of the navy

水榭（shuǐxiè）a waterside pavilion

水性杨花（shuǐxìngyánghuā）（of a woman）of easy virtue；wanton

水袖（shuǐxiù）long wide sleeves

水烟袋（shuǐyāndài）a shisha pipe；a hookah pipe

水印（shuǐyìn）a watermark

水中捞月（shuǐzhōng lāoyuè）（lit.）"to fish for the moon"－to make impractical or vain efforts

水中月镜中花（shuǐzhōng yuè jìng zhōng huā）（lit.）"the moon in the water，the flowers reflected in the mirror"－something within sight but beyond reach；an illusion

水族（shuǐzú）①the Shui nationality（distributed mainly in Guizhou）②aquatic animals

说客（shuìkè）a persuasive talker

顺风耳（shùnfēng'ěr）①a clairaudient；a psychic who can hear distant voices②a well-informed person

顺杆儿爬（shùngānr pá）to take one's cue from somebody else and say everything to please them

顺口溜（shùnkǒuliū）a jingle；a doggerel

顺我者昌，逆我者亡（shùnwǒzhě chāng，nìwǒzhě wáng）those who submit will prosper，while those who resist shall perish

顺治（shùnzhì）the title of the reign of Fulin（福临，1638－1661，the first emperor of the Qing Dynasty）

说白（shuōbái）the spoken parts in an opera

说部（shuōbù）the novels consisting of anecdotes；anecdotal fiction

说曹操曹操到（shuō cáocāo cáocāo dào）talk of the devil（and the devil is sure to appear）；speak of the angels and you will hear their wings

说长道短（shuōcháng dàoduǎn）to indulge in idle gossip

说唱（shuōchàng）①musical dialogue（a form of popular entertainment）②rap

说唱文学（shuōchàng wénxué）storytelling and ballad singing（a genre of popular literature）

说话（shuōhuà）storytelling in the Tang and Song Dynasties

说漏嘴（shuōlòuzuǐ）to let slip a remark；a slip of the tongue

说媒（shuōméi）to act as a matchmaker

说胖就喘（shuōpàng jiùchuǎn）（lit.）

"to puff and blow when others say you are fat" – a person who cannot stand praise from others

说破嘴(shuōpòzuǐ) to talk till one is hoarse

说亲(shuōqīn) to act as a matchmaker

说情(shuōqíng) to plead for mercy for somebody else; to intercede for somebody

说三道四(shuōsān dàosì) to make irresponsible remarks; to gossip

说书(shuōshū) extended form of story-singing or story-telling

说书场(shuōshū chǎng) a storytelling salon; a place of *quyi* performances

《说文解字》(shuōwén jiězì) *The Explanation of the Script and Elucidation of Characters* – a Chinese dictionary by Xu Shen(许慎, 58 – 147) in 100 – 121; *The Origin of Chinese Characters*

说戏(shuōxì) to explain (to one or more actors) how a part or a scene is to be acted

说闲话(shuō xiánhuà) to gossip

说学逗唱(shūoxuédòuchàng) talking, imitation, fun-making and singing (basic skills for cross talk)

说一不二(shuōyī bù'èr) to mean what one says; to stand by one's word

朔方(shuòfāng) north

朔日(shuòrì) the first day of the lunar month

朔望(shuòwàng) the first and the fifteenth day of the lunar month

朔望月(shuòwàng yuè) lunar month

数脉(shuòmài) rapid pulse

丝绸之路(sīchóu zhī lù) the Silk Road; the Silk Trading Routes

丝弦(sīxián) ① a silk string (for a musical instrument) ② Hebei provincial opera

丝竹(sīzhú) ① traditional stringed and woodwind instruments ② music

司空(sīkōng) Minister of Works; Minister of Public Works

司空见惯(sīkōng jiànguàn) a common occurence; commonly seen

司寇(sīkòu) Minister of Justice

司马(sīmǎ) Minister of War; Minister of Defence

《司马法》(sīmǎ fǎ) *The Methods of Sima* – a military book by Sima Rangju(司马穰苴) in the Spring and Autumn Period

司马光砸缸(sīmǎguāng zágāng) (lit.) "Sima Guang smashed the vat wittily" – to save the drowning child

司马昭之心,路人皆知(sīmǎzhāo zhīxīn, lùrén jiēzhī) (lit.) "every man in the street is aware of Sima Zhao's intent" – the villain's design is obvious to all

司南(sīnán)a southward-pointing instrument;an early compass

司徒(sītú)Minister of Civil Administration

司仪(sīyí)master of ceremonies;an MC

私房钱(sīfángqián)pin money;the private savings of a family member

私交(sījiāo)personal friendship

私了(sīliǎo)to settle or solve a dispute privately;to settle out of court

《私人生活》(sīrén shēnghuó)*Private Life* – a novel by Chen Ran(陈染,1962 –)in 2001

私淑弟子(sīshū dìzǐ)a self-styled disciple;a self-proclaimed follower of somebody

私塾(sīshú)an old-style private school

私刑(sīxíng)illegal punishment

私有化(sīyǒuhuà)privatization

私有制(sīyǒuzhì)private ownership

思凡(sīfán)(of monks or immortals) to long for the world;to yearn for the company of the opposite sex

思如泉涌(sīrú quányǒng)ideas teeming in one's mind;a head bursting with ideas

思想包袱(sīxiǎng bāofu)mental load;something weighing on one's mind

思想斗争(sīxiǎng dòuzhēng)ideological struggle

思想工作(sīxiǎng gōngzuò)ideological work

思想作风(sīxiǎng zuòfēng)the way of thinking

斯文(sīwén)gentle;refined;cultured;polite

斯文扫地(sīwén sǎodì)(lit.)"scholarly dignity swept into the dust" – to disgrace one's scholarly dignity

撕票(sīpiào)to kill the hostage

撕破脸(sīpòliǎn)to put aside all considerations of face;to argue openly

死不瞑目(sǐ bù míngmù)(lit.)"not to be able to close one's eyes when one dies" – to die with everlasting regret

死党(sǐdǎng)sworn followers;sworn supporters;die-hard followers

死读书(sǐdúshū)to study mechanically

死对头(sǐduìtou)a deadly enemy

死鬼(sǐguǐ)a devil

死角(sǐjiǎo)an untouched area

死扛(sǐkáng)to go all out to support or shoulder responsibility

死老虎(sǐlǎohǔ)(lit.)"a dead tiger" – a person who has lost their power and influence

死脑筋(sǐnǎojīn)one-track mind;an inflexible thinker

死棋(sǐqí)①a dead piece in a game of chess②a hopeless case

死契(sǐqì)an irrevocable title deed or contract

死生有命,富贵在天(sǐshēng yǒu mìng,fùguì zàitiān)life and death are a matter of destiny,while wealth and honour are decreed by Heaven

死无葬身之地(sǐwú zàngshēn zhīdì) to die without a proper place for burial;to come to a bad end

死心眼儿(sǐxīnyǎnr)stubborn;obstinate;pig-headed;a person with a one-track mind

死于非命(sǐyú fēimìng)to die an unnatural or violent death

巳(sì)the sixth of the twelve Earthly Branches

四不像(sìbùxiàng)(Zoology)Père David's deer;a milu

四部(sìbù)the four categories of ancient books(classics,history,philosophy and belles-letters)

四禅(sìchán)four-stage meditation

四禅天(sìchántiān)(Buddhism)the four *dhyana* heavens

四大(sìdà)(Buddhism)the four elements(earth,water,fire and wind)

四大部洲(sìdà bùzhōu)(Buddhism) the four inhabited continents

四大传奇(sìdà chuánqí)the four great romance plays(in the Ming Dynasty,1368 - 1644)

四大发明(sìdà fāmíng)ancient China's four great inventions(the compass,gunpowder,paper-making and printing)

四大皆空(sìdà jiēkōng)(Buddhism) the sensual world is illusory;all physical existence is vanity

四大金刚(sìdà jīn'gāng)(Buddhism)the four diamond kings(in Mount Wutai,Emei,Meru and Kunlun respectively)

四大名旦(sìdà míngdàn)the four famous *dan* performers in Beijing opera[Mei Lanfang(梅兰芳,1894 - 1961),Cheng Yanqiu(程砚秋,1904 - 1958),Xun Huisheng(荀慧生,1900 - 1968)and Shang Xiaoyun(尚小云,1900 - 1976)]

四大天王(sìdà tiānwáng)(Buddhism)the four Heavenly Kings;the four immortal temple guardians

四谛(sìdì)(Buddhism)the Four Noble Truths

四法印(sìfǎyìn)the Four Seals of Buddhist Truth

四皈依(sìguīyī)(Buddhism)the four refuges;the four convertions

四海(sìhǎi)the four seas;the whole country;the whole world

四海升平(sìhǎi shēngpíng)world peace

四海之内皆兄弟(sìhǎi zhīnèi jiē xiōngdì) within the four seas, all men are brothers

四合院(sìhéyuàn) a quadrangle dwelling; a quadrangle courtyard; a siheyuan

四呼(sìhū) the four categories of rhyming syllables

四胡(sìhú) a four-stringed Chinese fiddle

四化(sìhuà) the Four Modernizations (of agriculture, industry, national defense and science and technology)

四劫(sìjié) the four quarters of a kalpa

《四进士》(sì jìnshì) *Four Successful Candidates in the Imperial Exams* – a traditional Beijing opera

四旧(sìjiù) the four "olds" (old ideas, old culture, old customs and old habits)

四空天(sìkōngtiān) (Buddhism) the immaterial heavens

四库(sìkù) four bibliographic categories (the four traditional divisions of a Chinese library – classics, history, philosophy and belles-lettres)

《四库全书》(sìkùquánshū) *The Complete Collection in Four Treasuries*; *The Complete Books of the Four Imperial Repositories* – the series of the collections of ancient books compiled in 1773 – 1782

《四郎探母》(sìláng tàn mǔ) *The Fourth Son Returning to Visit His Mother* – a Beijing opera about Yang Yanhui (杨延辉), one of the Generals of the Yang family in the Northern Song Dynasty, 960 – 1127

四六体(sìliùtǐ) the four-six literary style (a euphuistic style of parallel constructions, known for pairs of sentences of four and six characters)

四六文(sìliùwén) four-six prose (a kind of rhythmical prose with parallel constructions consisting of pairs of sentences of four and six characters)

四面楚歌(sìmiàn chǔgē) (lit.) "the folk songs of the Chu State were heard on all sides" – to be besieged on all sides; to be utterly isolated

四清运动(sìqīng yùndòng) the "four clean-ups" movement (a political movement in countryside launched in 1962)

四人帮(sìrénbāng) the Gang of Four [the ringleaders of the ultra-leftists during the Cultural Revolution, who are Jiang Qing (江青, 1914 – 1991), Yao Wenyuan (姚文元, 1931 – 2005), Wang Hongwen (王

洪文,1935 - 1992), Zhang Chunqiao(张春桥,1917 - 2005)]

四摄(sìshè)(Buddhism) the four virtues

四声(sìshēng) the four tones(of Chinese pronunciation)

四圣谛(sìshèngdí)(Buddhism) the Four Noble Truths

四时八节(sìshí bājié) four seasons and eight solar terms(generally refer to the solar terms)

四世同堂(sìshì tóngtáng) four generations living under the same roof

《四世同堂》(sìshì tóngtáng) *Four Generations Living Together* - a novel by Lao She(老舍,1899 - 1966) in 1949; a TV drama directed by Lin Ruwei(林汝为) et al. in 1985); *Four Generations under One Roof*

四书(sìshū) The Four Books(*The Great Learning*, *The Doctrine of the Mean*, *The Analects of Confucius* and *The Mencius*)

《四书集注》(sìshū jízhù) *Collected Commentaries on the Four Books* - a book by Zhu Xi(朱熹,1130 - 1200)

四书五经(sìshū wǔjīng) The Four Books and The Five Classics [with the former referring to *The Great Learning*, *The Doctrine of the Mean*, *Confucian Analects* and *The the Works of Mencius*, and the latter including *The Book of Poetry*(*The Book of Songs*), *The Book of History*, *The Book of Rites*, *The Book of Changes* and *The Spring and Autumn Annals*]

四体书(sìtǐshū)(calligraphy) the four scripts(the regular script, the cursive script, the official script and the seal character)

四王天(sìwángtiān)(Buddhism) the Heaven of the Four Deva-Kings

四无量(sìwúliàng)(Buddhism) the four boundless qualities

四言诗(sìyán shī) a poem with four characters per line

四野(sìyě) the surrounding country; all around

四则运算(sìzé yùnsuàn) the four fundamental operations of arithmetic (addition, subtraction, multiplication and division)

四诊(sìzhěn)(medicine) the four methods of diagnosis(observation, auscultation and olfaction, interrogation, and pulse feeling and palpation)

寺观(sìguàn) a Buddhist or Taoist temple; a monastery

寺庙(sìmiào) a temple; a monastery

寺院(sìyuàn) a temple

俟河之清，人寿几何（sìhé zhīqīng, rénshòu jǐhé）（lit.）"one cannot live long enough to see the Yellow River flow clear" – what one expects can not be realized

嗣位（sìwèi）to succeed to the throne

松明（sōngmíng）a pine torch

松烟墨（sōngyānmò）Chinese ink or ink stick made from pine soot

嵩山（sōngshān）Songshan Mountain (one of China's five sacred mountains); Mount Song

讼棍（sònggùn）a legal pettifogger

讼师（sòngshī）a legal pettifogger; a legal practitioner

宋朝（sòngcháo）the Song Dynasty (960 – 1279)

宋词（sòngcí）*ci* poetry of the Song Dynasty (960 – 1279)

宋代（sòngdài）the Song Dynasty (960 –1279)

宋江起义（sòngjiāng qǐyì）Song Jiang Rebellion (1119)

宋锦（sòngjǐn）the Song brocade of Hangzhou; Song Dynasty (960 – 1279) brocade

宋诗派（sòngshī pài）the Song Poetry School

《宋四大书》（sòng sìdàshū）*The Four Great Books of the Song* – a book compiled by Li Fang (李昉, 925 – 996) et al. in 977 – 984

宋体字（sòngtǐzì）the Song typeface

宋元话本（sòngyuán huàběn）huaben storytelling scripts from the Song and Yuan dynasties

送殡（sòngbìn）to attend a funeral

送君千里，终须一别（sòngjūn qiānlǐ, zhōngxū yìbié）even though you may escort your friend for a thousand li, yet you must part in the end

送人情（sòng rénqíng）to make a gift in hope of a return favor; to do favors at no great cost to oneself

送丧（sòngsāng）to attend a funeral

送上西天（sòngshàng xītiān）（lit.）"to send somebody to heaven" – to kill

送死（sòngsǐ）to court death

送瘟神（sòng wēnshén）（lit.）"to send away the god of plague" – to get rid of sb or something undesirable

送葬（sòngzàng）to carry a coffin to the cemetery; to hold a funeral procession

送灶（sòngzào）the ceremony of sending off the kitchen god (on his annual trip to Heaven); to send off the kitchen god

送终（sòngzhōng）to attend upon a dying parent or other senior member of one's family

《搜神记》（sōushénjì）*In Search of the*

Supernatural - an anthology by Gan Bao(干宝,? -336) of the Eastern Jin Dynasty, 317 - 420; *Records of Spirits*

馊主意(sōuzhūyi) a stupid suggestion; a lousy idea

苏白(sūbái) ①the Suzhou dialect② the lines in Kunqu or Beijing opera that are spoken in Suzhou Dialect

苏菜(sūcài) Jiangsu cuisine

苏剧(sūjù) Suzhou opera

苏区(sūqū) the revolutionary area

《苏三起解》(sūsān qǐjiè) *Su San under Police Escort* - a Beijing opera

《苏武牧羊》(sūwǔ mùyáng) *Su Wu the Shepherd* - a song and a piece of music about Su Wu(苏武,140 -60 BC); a Beijing opera compiled by Wang Yaoqing(王瑶卿, 1881 - 1954); a poem by Yang Weizhen (杨维桢, 1296 - 1370); *Su Wu Tending Sheep*

苏绣(sūxiù) Suzhou embroidery

苏州码子(sūzhōu mǎzi) the Suzhou numerals(for marking prices)

苏州作家群(sūzhōu zuòjiā qún) the Group of Suzhou Writers(a group of playwrights in the early period of the Qing Dynasty)

酥油(sūyóu) butter

酥油茶(sūyóu chá) buttered tea

酥油花(sūyóu huā) a butter sculpture

俗话(súhuà) a common saying; a proverb

俗家(sújiā) my parents' home

俗名(súmíng) a popular name

俗人(súrén) a layman

俗套(sútào) a conventional pattern; a convention or stereotype

俗体字(sútǐzì) (calligraphy) the popular form of characters; the vulgar style script

俗文学(súwénxué) popular literature

俗语(súyǔ) a common saying; a folk adage

夙敌(sùdí) an old enemy; an arch-rival

夙愿(sùyuàn) a long-cherished wish

素服(sùfú) plain white clothes

素面(sùmiàn) ①vegetarian noodles② simple and natural; to wear no make-up

素面朝天(sùmiàn cháotiān) to wear no make-up in public

素质教育(sùzhì jiàoyù) a quality-oriented education; an education for all-round development

宿逋(sùbū) a long-standing debt

宿将(sùjiàng) a veteran general

宿缘(sùyuán) a predestined relationship

酸溜溜(suānliūliū) sour; envious; pedantic

酸甜苦辣(suāntiánkǔlà) (lit.)

"sour, sweet, bitter, hot" – the joys and sorrows of life

蒜头鼻(suàntóu bí) a pug nose; a snub nose

算卦(suànguà) to tell somebody's fortune; to divine by using the Eight Trigrams

算旧账(suànjiùzhàng) to settle an old account; to settle an old score

算命(suànmìng) fortune-telling; augury; to tell somebody's fortune

算命先生(suànmìng xiānsheng) a fortune teller

算盘(suànpán) an abacus

算学(suànxué) mathematics; arithmetic

算总账(suànzǒngzhàng) to settle the final score with somebody

隋朝(suícháo) the Sui Dynasty (581 – 618)

随笔(suíbǐ) ① an informal essay ② jottings; notes

随波逐流(suíbō zhúliú) to swim with the tide; to go with the flow

随大溜(suídàliù) to drift with the stream; to follow the trend; to follow the herd

随份子(suífènzi) ① to contribute one's share of a group gift ② to present a gift of money (for a wedding, funeral, etc.)

随风倒(suífēngdǎo) (lit.) "to bend with the wind" – to be easily swayed

随喜(suíxǐ) to join in charitable and pious deeds

《随想录》(suíxiǎnglù) *Random Thoughts* – a book by Ba Jin (巴金, 1904 – 2005) in 1978 – 1985

岁差(suìchā) the precession of the equinoxes

岁朝(suìcháo) the first day of the lunar New Year

岁除(suìchú) New Year's Eve

岁寒三友(suìhán sānyǒu) (lit.) "the three friends who thrive in cold weather" (the pine, the bamboo, and the plum) – friendship which outlasts hardship

岁寒知松柏(suìhán zhī sōngbǎi) (lit.) "only when the year grows cold do we see the qualities of the pine and the cypress" – adversity reveals virtue.

岁首(suìshǒu) the beginning of the year; the first month of the lunar year

岁星(suìxīng) (former name for) the planet Jupiter

碎嘴子(suìzuǐzi) ① to chatter ② a chatterbox

燧人氏(suìrénshì) Suiren (the legendary discoverer of fire)

《孙膑兵法》(sūnbìn bīngfǎ) *Sun Bin's Art of War* – a military classic by Sun Bin(孙膑,? －316 BC) of the Warring States Period, 475 －221 BC

孙悟空(sūnwùkōng) the Monkey King

孙中山(sūnzhōngshān) Sun Yat-sen (1866－1925)

《孙子兵法》(sūnzǐ bīngfǎ) *The Art of War* － a military classic by Master Sun(孙武,535 －470 BC) of the Spring and Autumn Period (770 －476 BC)

蓑笠(suōlì) a large straw or palm-bark rain hat

蓑衣(suōyī) a straw or palm-bark rain cape

缩头乌龟(suōtóu wūguī)(lit.)"a turtle with its head in its shell"－a cowardly person

唢呐(suǒnà) a ceremonial horn; a *suona* horn

索子(suǒzi) bamboo tiles; stick tiles (in Mahjong)

T

他山攻错(tāshān gōngcuò)(lit.) "there are other hills whose stones are good for working jade"－other people's advice can be helpful

他乡(tāxiāng) a place far away from home; an alien land

他乡遇故知(tāxiāng yù gùzhī) to meet an old friend in a distant land

趿拉板儿(tālabǎnr) wooden slippers; clogs

趿拉儿(tālar) cloth slippers

塔吉克族(tǎjíkèzú) the Tajik nationality (mainly distributed in Xinjiang Uygur Autonomous Region)

塔林(tǎlín) a forest of stupas; a monastic cemetery

塔塔尔族(tǎtǎ'ěrzú) the Tatar nationality (mainly distributed in Xinjiang Uygur Autonomous Region)

踏歌(tàgē) dancing accompanied by singing; rhythmic dancing

踏青(tàqīng) to go on a spring outing

踏雪(tàxuě) to walk in the snow

踏月(tàyuè) to walk in the moonlight

拓本(tàběn) a book of (eg. stone or bronze) rubbings

拓片(tàpiàn)(stone or bronze) rubbings

胎里富(tāilǐfù) to be born with a silver spoon in one's mouth; to be born rich

台步(táibù) a theatrical style of walking; an actor's gait

台阁体(táigétǐ) the Secretariat Style (a style of poetry)

台柱子(táizhùzi) ①the star or leading member (of a theatrical troupe) ②the cornerstone (of an organization)

抬杠(táigàng)to argue for the sake of arguing;to bicker;to wrangle

抬轿子(táijiàozi)(lit.)"to carry somebody in a sedan chair"- to flatter

抬头纹(táitóuwén)wrinkles on one's forehead

太保(tàibǎo)Great Guardian(one of the three highest officials in feudal China)

太白金星(tàibáijīnxīng)Great White Venus(a Chinese heavenly god)

太傅(tàifù)Great Mentor(one of the three highest officials in imperial China)

太和(tàihé)great harmony;universal harmony

太后(tàihòu)the mother of an emperor;the empress dowager

太湖石(tàihúshí)the Taihu rocks(the boulders found around the Taihu Lake)

太极(tàijí)the Supreme Ultimate(the Absolute in ancient Chinese cosmology)

太极(鱼)图[tàijí(yú)tú]the Diagram of the Supreme Ultimate

太极拳(tàijíquán)Tai Chi Boxing;*Tai-chi*;*taijiquan*;the Supreme Ultimate Boxing

太监(tàijiàn)a eunuch

太康诗人(tàikāng shīrén)the Taikang poets(in 280-289)

太庙(tàimiào)the Imperial Ancestral Temple(in Beijing)

太平鼓(tàipínggǔ)the Taiping Drum(a folk dance, accompanied by drums)

《太平公主》(tàipínggōngzhǔ)*Princess Taiping* - a TV drama directed by Li Hantao(李翰韬)in 2011

《太平广记》(tài píng guǎng jì)*The Extensive Records of the Taiping Era* -an anthology of tales compiled by Li Fang(李昉,925 - 996)et al.;*Taiping Miscellany*

太平门(tàipíngmén)an emergency exit

太平盛世(tàipíng shèngshì)times of peace and prosperity

太平天国(tàipíng tiānguó)the Taiping Heavenly Kingdom(1851 - 1864)

太婆(tàipó)great-grandmother

太上皇(tàishànghuáng)①the emperor's father②an overlord

太上老君(tàishànglǎojūn)(Taoism) the venerable Laozi;Lord Lao the Most High

太师(tàishī)Grand Preceptor

太师椅(tàishīyǐ)an old-fashioned wooden armchair

太守(tàishǒu)Commandery Governor

太岁(tàisuì)①the star god presiding

over the year ② the most powerful man in a locality; a local tyrant

太岁头上动土(tàisuì tóushàng dòng tǔ)(lit.)"to break ground where Taisui presides"– to defy the mighty; to provoke somebody in power

太尉(tàiwèi) Grand Commandant

太虚(tàixū) the great vacuity; the great void; the universe

太学(tàixué) the Imperial College

太阳社(tàiyáng shè) the Sun Society (a literary group in 1927–1929)

《太阳照在桑干河上》(tàiyáng zhào zài sānggānhé shàng) *The Sun Shines upon the Sanggan River* – a novel by Ding Ling(丁玲, 1904–1986) in 1948

太爷(tàiyé) ①(paternal) grandfather ②(paternal) great-grandfather

太医(tàiyī) an imperial physician

太一道(tàiyīdào) the Supreme Unity sect(founded in 1138)

太阴历(tàiyīnlì) the lunar calendar

太宰(tàizǎi) Grand Steward

太子(tàizǐ) a crown prince

泰昌(tàichāng) the reign title(1620–1620) of Emperor Guang Zong(光宗朱常洛, 1582–1620, an emperor of the Ming Dynasty)

泰斗(tàidǒu) the leading authority

泰山(tàishān) ①Mount Tai②of great weight or importance③(maternal) father-in-law

泰山北斗(tàishān běidǒu)(lit.)"Mount Tai and the Big Dipper"– a person of distinction; the leading authority

泰山老母(tàishān lǎomǔ) Goddess of Taishan Mountain

泰山压顶(tàishān yādǐng)(lit.)"to bear down on one with the weight of Mount Taishan"– to apply(or to be under) great pressure

泰水(tàishuǐ) mother-in-law

贪杯(tānbēi) to be excessively fond of drinking; to be too fond of a tipple; to drink like a fish

贪便宜(tān piányi) to be eager to get things on the cheap; to be keen on gaining petty advantages

贪官污吏(tānguān wūlì) corrupt officials; venal officials

贪墨(tānmò) to embezzle; corrupt officials

贪天之功(tāntiānzhīgōng) to arrogate to oneself the merits of others; to claim credit for other people's achievements

贪赃枉法(tānzāng wǎngfǎ) to take bribes and bend the law; to pervert the course of justice by taking a bribe

贪嘴(tānzuǐ) greedy(for food); gluttonous

摊牌(tānpái)to lay one's cards on the table;to show one's hand

坛子(tánzi)an earthenware jar

昙花一现(tánhuā yī xiàn)(lit.)"to flower as briefly as the broad-leaved epiphyllum" - to last briefly;to be a flash in the pan

谈家常(tán jiācháng)to talk about everyday matters;to engage in small talk

《谈艺录》(tányìlù)*On the Art of Poetry* - a book by Qian Zhongshu(钱钟书,1910 - 1998)in 1948

弹拨尔(tánbō'ěr)Tambur(a five-stringed instrument)

弹拨乐器(tánbō yuèqì)a plucked string instrument

弹玻璃球(tán bōliqiú)to play marbles

弹词(táncí)①storytelling to the accompaniment of stringed instruments②the script for this kind of storytelling

弹冠相庆(tánguān xiāngqìng)to congratulate each other on getting a high post or honors

弹劾(tánhé)to impeach

弹花弓(tánhuāgōng)a cotton fluffer

弹棉花(tán miánhuā)to fluff cotton

弹弦乐器(tánxián yuèqì)stringed instruments

弹指之间(tánzhǐ zhījiān)(lit.)"during the snapping of the fingers" - in a flash;in the twinkling of an eye;in an instant

潭府(tánfǔ)your house;your residence

探花(tànhuā)tanhua(the scholar who won the third place in the highest imperial examination)

探骊得珠(tànlí dézhū)to grasp the point of the theme;to expound the essence of the theme;to keep to the point

探马(tànmǎ)a scout cavalryman

探赜索隐(tànzé suǒyǐn)to delve into the abstruse;to unravel mysteries

探子(tànzi)a spy

汤包(tāngbāo)steamed dumplings filled with minced meat and gravy

汤头(tāngtóu)a prescription for a medical decoction

汤团(tāngtuán)stuffed dumplings

汤药(tāngyào)a decoction of medicinal ingredients

汤圆(tāngyuán)sticky rice dumplings;sweet glutinous rice balls

蹚浑水(tāng húnshuǐ)to associate with wicked people

《唐伯虎点秋香》(tángbóhǔ diǎn qiū xiāng)*Flirting Scholar* - a film directed by Li Lichi(李力持)in 1993

唐朝(tángcháo)the Tang Dynasty(618 - 907)

唐初四杰(tángchū sìjié)the Four Literary Geniuses[Wang Bo(王勃,650 – 676), Yang Jiong(杨炯,650 –692), Lu Zhaolin(卢照邻,636 –695)and Luo Binwang(骆宾王,640 – 684) of the early Tang Dynasty(618 –907)]

唐传奇(tángchuánqí)the prose romances of the Tang Dynasty(618 – 907); Tang marvel tales; Tang *chuanqi* fiction

唐传奇小说(tángchuánqí xiǎoshuō)the prose romances of the Tang Dynasty(618 – 907); Tang marvel tales; Tang *chuanqi* fiction

唐代传奇(tángdài chuánqì)the prose romances of the Tang Dynasty (618 –907); Tang marvel tales; Tang *chuanqi* fiction

唐代诗人(tángdài shīrén)the Tang poets; the poets of the Tang Dynasty

《唐宫仕女图》(tánggōng shìnǚ tú)*Maids in the Tang Palace* – a classical painting by Zhang Xuan(张萱,713 – 741)and Zhou Fang(周昉)of the Tang Dynasty

《唐会要》(tánghuìyào)*The Institutional History of Tang* – a historical book compiled by Wang Pu(王溥,922 –982)in 961

唐卡(tángkǎ)Thang-ga(scrolls of Tibetan religious paintings)

《唐明皇》(tángmínghuáng)*Sage Emperor of the Tang Dynasty* – a TV drama directed by Chen Jialin(陈家林)in 1990

唐人街(tángrénjiē)Chinatown; the Chinese quarter

唐三彩(tángsāncǎi)the tri-colored glazed pottery of the Tang Dynasty (618 –907); the Tang tri-color pottery

唐僧(tángsēng)Tripitaka; Xuan Zang(玄奘,602 –664, an eminent monk of the Tang Dynasty)

唐诗(tángshī)Tang poetry; the poetry of the Tang Dynasty(618 –907)

唐宋八大家(tángsòng bādàjiā)The Eight Great Writers of the Tang and Song dynasties [Han Yu(韩愈,768 –824), Liu Zongyuan(柳宗元,773 –819), Ou Yangxiu(欧阳修,1007 – 1072), Wang Anshi(王安石,1021 – 1086), Zeng Gong(曾巩,1019 – 1083), Su Shi(苏轼,1037 – 1101), Su Xun(苏洵,1009 –1066) and Su Zhe(苏辙,1039 –1112)]

唐装(tángzhuāng)Tang costume; Chinese-style suit; traditional Chinese garments

唐宗派(tángzōngpài)the Tang Zong Style [writers as Wang Shenzhong(王慎中,1509 – 1559), Tang

Shunzhi(唐顺之,1507 – 1560) and Gui Youguang (归有光, 1506 – 1571) who object the former and latter seven scholars in the Ming Dynasty]

堂房(tángfáng) the relationship between cousins of the same clan

堂鼓(tánggǔ) a bass drum

堂倌(tángguān) a waiter

堂会(tánghuì) a private celebration at one's home, with hired performers

堂客(tángkè) ①a female guest ②a woman ③one's wife

堂屋(tángwū) the principal room; the central room

堂戏(tángxì) Tang opera (a kind of opera which originated in Sichuan)

堂子(tángzi) an imperial sacrificial temple

糖葫芦(tánghúlu) sugarcoated haws (on a stick); candied fruit sticks

糖衣炮弹(tángyī pàodàn) a sugarcoated bullet

螳臂当车(tángbì dāngchē) (lit.) "a mantis trying to obstruct a chariot" – to overestimate one's strength and try to hold back an overwhelmingly superior force

螳螂捕蝉,黄雀在后(tángláng bǔ chán, huángquè zàihòu) (lit.) "the mantis stalks the cicada, unaware of the oriole behind" – to covet gains ahead, and neglect the danger approaching from behind

螳螂拳(tánglángquán) (martial arts) the Praying Mantis style

倘来之物(tǎngláizhīwù) an unexpected gain; a windfall

趟马(tàngmǎ) a stylized representation of horseriding in opera

叨光(tāoguāng) to be much obliged to somebody

叨教(tāojiào) Thank you for your advice

叨扰(tāorǎo) Thank you for your hospitality

掏心窝(tāo xīnwō) from the bottom of one's heart

掏腰包(tāo yāobāo) ①to pay out of one's own pocket; to foot a bill ②to pick somebody's pocket

韬光养晦(tāoguāngyǎnghuì) to withdraw from society; to conceal one's abilities and bide one's time

韬略(tāolüè) military strategy

饕餮(tāotiè) ①a mythical ferocious animal; a taotie ②a fierce and cruel person

饕餮纹(tāotièwén) a taotie design; an image of a taotie

桃符(táofú) ① peachwood charms used to ward off evil ②Spring Festival couplets

《桃花扇》(táohuāshàn) *The Peach-*

Blossom Fan – a play by Kong Shangren(孔尚任,1648 – 1718)

桃花源(táohuāyuán)the Peach Garden;a lost Utopia;Shangri-la

《桃花源记》(táohuāyuán jì) *Peach-Blossom Spring* – a piece of prose by Tao Yuanming(陶渊明,365 – 427)

桃花运(táohuāyùn)lucky in love;to have luck with the opposite sex

桃李不言,下自成蹊(táolǐbùyán,xià zìchéngxī)(lit.)"the peach and the plum do not speak,yet a path is worn beneath them" – a person of true worth attracts admiration(without asking for it)

《桃李劫》(táolǐ jié) *Plunder of Peaches and Plums* – a film directed by Ying Yunwei(应云卫)in 1934

桃李满天下(táolǐ mǎntiānxià)to have pupils everywhere;with former students all over the world

陶文(táowén)an inscription on pottery

陶俑(táoyǒng)a pottery figurine

讨便宜(tǎo piányi)to seek undue advantage;to try to gain something at the expense of others

讨教(tǎojiào)to ask for advice

讨脸(tǎoliǎn)to ingratiate oneself with

讨巧(tǎoqiǎo)to act artfully to get what one wants;to choose the easy way out

讨生活(tǎo shēnghuó)to seek a living

讨债鬼(tǎozhàiguǐ)①a child dying young②a naughty child

套话(tàohuà)cliché;formulaic convention

套交情(tào jiāoqing)to try to get in with somebody

套近乎(tào jìnhu)to try to be friends with sb;to curry favor with somebody;to cotton up to somebody;to ingratiate oneself with somebody

套路(tàolù)①a series of skills and tricks(in martial arts)②a set pattern

套数(tàoshù)①a cycle of songs in a traditional opera②a series of skills and tricks in martial arts,etc. ③conventional remarks

特别行政区(tèbié xíngzhèngqū)a Special Administrative Region;an SAR

特长生(tèchángshēng)students with specific skills;students with specific areas of expertise

特区(tèqū)a Special Zone;a Special Region(in terms of administration)

腾云驾雾(téngyún jiàwù)①(lit.)"to ride the clouds and mount the mist" – to speed across the sky②to feel giddy

誊录(ténglù) to transcribe (by hand);to copy out

滕王阁(téngwánggé) Tengwang Pavilion;Pavilion of Prince Teng(located in Nanchang, Jiangxi province)

《滕王阁序》(téngwánggé xù) *Preface to the Tengwang Pavilion* - a piece of prose by Wang Bo(王勃,650-676)

剔庄货(tīzhuānghuò) bargains; low-cost goods; shop-soiled or substandard goods;cut-price goods

踢毽子(tī jiànzi) to kick a shuttlecock(a popular game)

踢皮球(tī píqiú) to kick something back and forth like a ball; to pass the buck;to shift responsibility onto each other

《啼笑因缘》(tíxiàoyīnyuán) *Fate in Tears and Laughter* - a novel by Zhang Henshui(张恨水,1897-1967)in 1931

提督(tídū) a provincial commander (in imperial China)

提干(tígàn) ①to make somebody a cadre ②to promote a cadre (to a higher position)

提盒(tíhé) a tiered lunchbox (with several round compartments one above the other and a handle)

提亲(tíqīn) to propose marriage on behalf of a family member

题跋(tíbá) ①preface and postscript ②brief annotations on a painting or piece of calligraphy

题壁(tíbì) ①to write on a wall②inscriptions on a wall

题海(tíhǎi) a sea of questions

题记(tíjì) a preface

醍醐灌顶(tíhúguàn dǐng) ①to be filled with wisdom; be enlightened ②to feel refreshed suddenly

体面(tǐmiàn) ①dignity;face②honorable③good-looking

剃度(tìdù) (Buddhism) tonsure

剃光头(tì guāngtóu) (lit.) "to have one's head shaved" - to score no points(in games)

倜傥(tìtǎng) elegant;free and easy

替死鬼(tìsǐguǐ) a scapegoat; a fall guy

天安门(tiān'ānmén) Tiananmen; the Gate of Heavenly Peace

天安门城楼(tiān'ānmén chénglóu) the Tiananmen Rostrum

天安门广场(tiān'ānmén guǎngchǎng) Tiananmen Square

天宝(tiānbǎo) Tianbao[the reign title (742-756) of Xuanzong(玄宗 李隆基,685-762), an emperor of the Tang Dynasty]

天兵(tiānbīng) (lit.) "troops from heaven"- an invincible army

天不怕,地不怕(tiān bùpà,dì bùpà) to fear neither Heaven nor Earth;to fear nothing on earth

天长地久(tiāncháng dìjiǔ) enduring as the universe;everlasting and unchanging

天从人愿(tiāncóng rényuàn) if heaven grants one's wish; if dreams come true;God willing

天道(tiāndào) the laws of Nature; natural law;heavenly laws

天帝(tiāndì) the Lord of Heaven

天方夜谭(tiānfāng yètán) ①a cock-and-bull story;a most fantastic tale ②*Arabian Nights*

天府之国(tiānfǔ zhī guó) ①Sichuan province ②a land of abundance; a land of plenty

天干(tiāngān) the ten Heavenly Stems

天干地支(tiāngān dìzhī) the Celestial Stems and the Terrestrial Branches;the Ten Heavenly Stems and the Twelve Earthly Branches

天高皇帝远(tiāngāo huángdì yuǎn) ①justice is remote ②one may do whatever one wishes without fear of interference; when the cat's away the mice will play

《天工开物》(tiāngōngkāiwù) *Exploitation of the Works of Nature* – a book by Song Yingxing(宋应星, 1587 – 1666) in 1638 – 1654

天公不作美(tiāngōng bù zuòměi) heaven is not cooperative; the weather is bad; the weather is not conducive to one's plans

天公地道(tiāngōng dìdào) absolutely fair

天宫(tiāngōng) the heavenly palace

天荒地老(tiānhuāngdìlǎo) till the end of the world

天皇(tiānhuáng) the Son of Heaven; the emperor

天机(tiānjī) ①divine mystery; God's design ② a secret; something inexplicable

天机不可泄露(tiānjī bùkě xièlòu) God's design must not be revealed to mortal ears;heaven's secrets must not be divulged; don't say a word about it to a soul

《天机富春山居图》(tiānjī Fùchūn shānjūtú) *Switch* – a film directed by Sun Jianjun(孙健君) in 2013; *The Secret of "Dwelling in the Fuchunshan Mountains"*

天经地义(tiānjīngdìyì) perfectly justified; an unalterable principle; a natural law

天井(tiānjǐng) a patio;a small yard;a courtyard;a dooryard;a parvis

天井院(tiānjǐngyuàn) a silo-cave Courtyard;a patio courtyard

天九牌(tiānjiǔpái)Chinese dominoes

天老爷(tiānlǎoyé)God;Heavens

天理(tiānlǐ)①heavenly principles; the ethical system advocated by the Song NeoConfucianists ②(divine) justice

天良(tiānliáng)conscience

《天龙八部》(tiānlóngbābù) *Demi-Gods and Semi-Devils* - a novel by Jin Yong(金庸,1924 -) in 1963; a TV drama directed by Zhou Xiaowen(周晓文)et al. in 2003 or by Li Tiansheng(李添胜)in 1997

天伦(tiānlún)the natural bonds and ethical relationships between members of a family;family ties

天伦之乐(tiānlún zhīlè)family happiness

《天论》(tiānlùn) *On Heaven* - an essay by Liu Yuxi(刘禹锡,772 - 842)

天罗地网(tiānluó dìwǎng)(lit.) "nets above and snares below" - tight encirclement

天马行空(tiānmǎxíngkōng)(lit.)"a heavenly steed soaring across the skies" - a powerful free style

天命(tiānmìng)God's will; the mandate of heaven;destiny;fate

天年(tiānnián)①a natural span of life;one's allotted span②the year's harvest③times;age

天怒人怨(tiānnù rényuàn)the wrath of God and the anger of men;widespread indignation and discontent

天启(tiānqǐ)Tianqi [the reign title (1621 - 1627) of Xi Zong(熹宗朱由校,1605 - 1627), an emperor of the Ming Dynasty]

天人(tiānrén)①Heaven and man②a genius or a beauty

天人合一(tiānrén héyī)man is an integral part of nature;the unification of man and nature;humanity in harmony with nature

《天山牧歌》(tiānshān mùgē) *The Pastoral Songs from Mount Tianshan* - a collection of poems by Wen Jie(闻捷,1923 - 1971)in 1956

天神(tiānshén)god;deity

天生桥(tiānshēngqiáo)the Natural Bridge(located in Shangrila)

天师(tiānshī)(Taoism) Heavenly Teacher;Celestial Master

天师道(tiānshīdào)(Taosim) the Way of the Celestial Masters

天书(tiānshū)①(lit.)"a book from heaven" - abstruse or illegible writing②an imperial edict

天台宗(tiāntái zōng)(Buddhism)the Tiantai Sect;the Tiantai School

天坛(tiāntán)the Temple of Heaven (in Beijing)

天条(tiāntiáo)the Heavenly Commandments (the prohibition decrees of the Taiping Heavenly Kingdom, 1851 – 1864)

天庭(tiāntíng) the middle of the forehead

天网恢恢,疏而不漏(tiānwǎng huī huī, shū'ér bùlòu) The net of Heaven has large meshes, but it lets nothing through; The mills of God grind slowly, but they grind exceedingly small; Justice has a long arm.

《天问》(tiānwèn) *A Request to God* – an essay by Qu Yuan (屈原, 340 – 278 BC); *Questions to Heaven*

天下大势(tiānxiàdàshì) the momentum of history; a historical trend

天下无不散之宴席(tiānxiàwú bùsàn zhī yànxí) (lit.) "there never was a feast where the guests did not have to depart" – all good things must come to an end

《天下无双》(tiānxiàwúshuāng) *Chinese Odyssey* – a film directed by Liu Zhenwei (刘镇伟) in 2002

《天下无贼》(tiānxiàwú zéi) *A World Without Thieves* – a film directed by Feng Xiaogang (冯小刚) in 2004

《天仙配》(tiānxiānpèi) *Goddess Marriage* – a Huangmei opera; a film directed by Shi Hui (石挥, 1915 – 1957) in 1955; *The Heavenly Maid and the Mortal*

天香国色(tiānxiāng guósè) ethereal beauty and celestial fragrance; a beauty unmatched throughout the land

天涯(tiānyá) skyline; the ends of the earth

《天云山传奇》(tiānyúnshān chuánqí) *Legend of Tianyun Mountain* – a film directed by Xie Jin (谢晋) in 1980

天造地设(tiānzào dìshè) as Nature intended; a heavenly ideal

天之骄子(tiān zhī jiāozǐ) God's favoured one; an unusually lucky person

天诛地灭(tiānzhū dìmiè) to be struck down by Heaven; to stand condemned by God

天姿国色(tiānzī guósè) a reigning beauty; a woman of matchless beauty

天子(tiānzǐ) (lit.) "the Son of Heaven" – the emperor

天尊(tiānzūn) celestial worthy (the title of certain deities in the Taoist pantheon); the Buddha

天作之合(tiānzuò zhī hé) a match made in Heaven

添丁(tiāndīng) to have a baby (esp. a boy) born into the family

田塍(tiánchéng) a low bank of earth between fields; ridge

田父(tiánfù)an aged father

田赋(tiánfù)land tax (in imperial China)

田舍翁(tiánshèwēng)an old farmer

田园诗人(tiányuán shīrén) a pastoral poet

田庄(tiánzhuāng)a country estate

《甜蜜的事业》(tiánmì de shìyè) *A Sweet Life* – a film directed by Xie Tian(谢添)in 1979

《甜蜜蜜》(tiánmìmi) *Almost A Love Story* – a film directed by Gao Xixi(高希希)in 2007

填房(tiánfáng)①to marry a widower ②a second wife

挑刺儿(tiāocìr) to find fault with; to pick holes in

挑夫(tiāofū) a porter (carrying luggage on a shoulder pole)

挑毛拣刺(tiāomáo jiǎncì) to find fault deliberately; to pick holes

挑三拣四(tiāosān jiǎnsì) ①to pick and choose; to be choosy; to be picky②to nitpick

挑字眼儿(tiāozìyǎnr) to find fault with the choice of words; to quibble; to be pedantic about language

条案(tiáo'àn)a long narrow table

条陈(tiáochén)①to state item by item; to list one by one②to present an itemized memorandum (to one's superior)

条条框框(tiáotiáo kuàngkuàng) rules and regulations; regulations and restrictions; conventions and taboos

调词架讼(tiáocí jiàsòng) to incite somebody to take legal proceedings against somebody else

调侃儿(tiáokǎnr) to ridicule; to jeer at

调皮捣蛋(tiáopí dǎodàn) mischievous; troublesome

调三窝四(tiáosān wōsì) to sow discord; to foment dissension

调戏(tiáoxì) to molest; to flirt; to dally with

髫龄(tiáolíng)childhood

髫年(tiáonián)childhood

挑拨离间(tiǎobō líjiàn) to sow discord; to foment dissension

挑大梁(tiǎodàliáng) ①to be a leading actor or actress②to shoulder a heavy responsibility or a demanding task

挑灯(tiǎodēng)①to raise the wick of an oil lamp②to hang a lantern from a pole

挑花(tiǎohuā) cross-stitch work; a piece of cross-stitch; hand-stitching work

跳布扎(tiàobùzhā) the devil's dance (performed by lamas at religious festivals to exorcize evil spirits)

跳槽(tiàocáo) to throw up one job

and take on another; job-hopping

跳房子(tiàofángzi) to play hopscotch; hopscotch

跳梁小丑(tiàoliáng xiǎochǒu) a buffoon; a clown; a clumsy

跳马(tiàomǎ) leapfrog; to jump over; a vaulting horse

跳皮筋儿(tiào píjīnr) skipping over elastic bands (a children's game)

跳棋(tiàoqí) Chinese checkers; Chinese draughts

跳神(tiàoshén) ①a mystic dance (by a sorcerer in a trance-like state) ②the devil's dance (at religious festivals to exorcize evil spirits)

跳绳(tiàoshéng) skipping (using a rope)

跳月(tiàoyuè) the moon dance (a courting custom in the middle and southern part of China)

贴画(tiēhuà) ①a poster ②a matchbox picture

贴金(tiējīn) ①to gild ②to boast about

贴谱(tiēpǔ) proper; appropriate

铁案如山(tiě'àn rúshān) an iron-clad case; an indisputable case

《铁齿铜牙纪晓岚》(tiěchǐtóngyá jìxiǎolán) *Eloquent Ji Xiaolan*; *The Legend of Ji Xiaolan* – a TV drama directed by Liu Jiacheng (刘家成) in 2001

铁窗(tiěchuāng) (lit.) "the iron window" – the prison

《铁道游击队》(tiědào yóujīduì) *Railway Guerrilla* – a novel by Liu Zhixia (刘知侠, 1918 – 1991) in 1954; a film directed by Zhao Ming (赵明) in 1956; a TV drama directed by Huang Xinmin (王新民) in 2005

铁饭碗(tiěfànwǎn) (lit.) "an iron rice bowl" – a secure job

《铁弓缘》(tiěgōngyuán) *Romance of the Iron Bow* – a traditional Beijing opera starring Xun Huisheng (荀慧生) or Guan Sushuang (关肃霜); a film directed by Chen Huaiai (陈怀皑) in 1979

铁公鸡(tiěgōngjī) (lit.) "an iron cockerel" – a stingy person

铁观音(tiěguānyīn) oolong tea; *tieguanyin* tea

铁画银钩(tiěhuàyíngōu) vigorous flourishes (in calligraphy); forceful strokes

铁面无私(tiěmiàn wúsī) impartial and incorruptible; strictly impartial

铁耙(tiěpá) an iron-toothed rake

铁树开花(tiěshù kāihuā) (lit.) "the iron tree in blossom" – something seldom seen or hardly possible

铁算盘(tiěsuànpán) ①careful calculation and strict budgeting ②an astute businessman; a financial wizard

铁腕(tiěwàn) (lit.) "an iron wrist" –

a strong rule;ruling with an iron fist

厅堂(tīngtáng)a hall

听差(tīngchāi)a manservant;an office boy

听风是雨(tīngfēngshìyǔ)(lit.)"to hear the wind and mistake it for the rain"-to believe rumours

听墙根(tīng qiánggēn)to eavesdrop

听事(tīngshì)①to hold court;to administer affairs of state ②the hall (in a government office)

《听松》(tīngsōng) *Listen to the Pine Tree* - an urheen solo by A Bing[阿炳,namely,Hua Yanjun(华彦钧,1893-1950)]

听天由命(tīngtiān yóumìng)to submit to providence;to resign oneself to one's fate

听头儿(tīngtóur)to be worth listening to

听政(tīngzhèng)to hold court;to administer affairs of state

听之任之(tīngzhī rènzhī)to let something(undesirable,evil,etc.)go unchecked;to take a laissez-faire attitude; to let somebody have his own way

亭廊阙榭(tínglángquèxiè)pavilions and colonnades

亭桥(tíngqiáo)a bridge to a pavilion

亭亭如盖(tíngtíng rúgài)to stand erect with a canopy of leaves(description of trees)

亭子(tíngzi)a pavilion

亭子间(tíngzijiān)a garret;a cubbyhole

庭训(tíngxùn)parental instructions and admonitions

停灵(tínglíng)to keep a coffin in a temporary shelter before burial;to rest the coffin temporarily

廷尉(tíngwèi)Commandant of Justice

铤而走险(tǐng'érzǒuxiǎn)to take a risk in desperation;to make a reckless move

通背拳(tōngbèiquán)the Through-the-Back Fist

《通典》(tōngdiǎn) *Comprehensive Institutions* - a book by Du You(杜佑,735-812)of the Tang Dynasty

通都大邑(tōngdūdàyì)a large city;a metropolis

通关节(tōng guānjié)to get round (laws,rules,etc.)by bribery

通婚(tōnghūn)to intermarry;to become related by marriage

通奸(tōngjiān)to commit adultery;to fornicate;adultery

通衢(tōngqú)a thoroughfare

通权达变(tōngquán dábiàn)to act as the occasion requires;to adapt to circumstances;to follow a flexible course of action

通儒(tōngrú) an erudite scholar; a man of prodigious learning

通史(tōngshǐ) a comprehensive history; a general history

通事(tōngshì) an interpreter

通书(tōngshū) an almanac

通俗文学(tōngsú wénxué) popular literature

通俗小说(tōngsú xiǎoshuō) popular fiction

通俗小说家(tōngsú xiǎoshuōjiā) popular fiction writers

通俗艺术(tōngsú yìshù) popular art

通天(tōngtiān) ①exceedingly high or great②to have direct access to the top authorities

通用字(tōngyòngzì) interchangeable characters

同胞(tóngbāo) ①brother and sister ②compatriots

同病相怜(tóngbìng xiānglián) those who have the same illness sympathize with each other; fellow sufferers commiserate with each other

同窗(tóngchuāng) ①to study in the same school ② a schoolmate; a schoolfellow

同床异梦(tóngchuáng yìmèng) (lit.) "to share the same bed but dream different dreams" – to be strange bedfellows; to have different priorities, while appearing to be in agreement

同党(tóngdǎng) ①the fellow member of a political faction or party; cohort ②a pal

同道儿(tóngdàor) ①people having a common goal②people of the same trade or occupation

同恶相济(tóng'èxiāngjì) the wicked help the wicked

同房(tóngfáng) ①to live together②to have sex

同甘共苦(tònggān gòngkǔ) to share good times and bad; to go through thick and thin together

同庚(tónggēng) of the same age

同呼吸,共命运(tóng hūxī, gòng mìngyùn) to share a common fate; to throw in one's lot with sb

同僚(tóngliáo) a colleague; a fellow official

同流合污(tóngliú héwū) to wallow in the mire with sb; to asscociate with an evil person

同盟会(tóngménghuì) the Chinese Revolutionary Alliance [a political party organized and led by Sun Yat-sen(孙中山) in 1905]; the Tongmenghui

同年(tóngnián) ①the same year②a person of the same age

同生死,共患难(tóng shēngsǐ, gòng huànnàn) to share good times and

bad

同室操戈(tóngshì cāogē) the members of one family drawing swords on each other; fratricidal strife; an internal strife; domestic discord

同乡会(tóngxiānghuì) an association of fellow provincials or townsmen

同砚(tóngyàn) a fellow student; a schoolmate

同舟共济(tóngzhōu gòngjì)(lit.)"to cross a river in the same boat" - to pull together in times of trouble

《同桌的你》(tóngzhuō de nǐ) *My Deskmate* - a Chinese song; a comic skit

桐城派(tóngchéngpài) the Tongcheng School (the most influential essay school in the mid-Qing Dynasty)

铜板(tóngbǎn) copper clappers (a kind of drum)

铜鼓(tónggǔ) a copper drum

铜壶滴漏(tónghú dīlòu) a copper clepsydra

铜钱(tóngqián) copper cash; bronze coins; copper coins

童婚(tónghūn) child marriage

童伶(tónglíng) a boy actor (in traditional opera)

童男(tóngnán) a virgin boy

童女(tóngnǚ) a maiden; a virgin

童生(tóngshēng) a candidate for the first level of the imperial exams; a tongsheng

童叟无欺(tóngsǒu wúqī)(lit.)"neither old nor young is cheated" - honest with all customers

童养媳(tóngyǎngxí) a child brought up in the home of her husband-to-be; a child bride

童子(tóngzǐ) a boy; a lad

童子军(tóngzǐjūn) the boy scouts

统带(tǒngdài) ①to command ②a regiment commander

统领(tǒnglǐng) ①to command; to lead ②a commander; a leader

统一战线(tǒngyī zhànxiàn) the united front

统制(tǒngzhì) to control

捅娄子(tǒng lóuzi) to make a blunder

捅马蜂窝(tǒng mǎfēngwō) to stir up a hornet's nest

筒车(tǒngchē) a barrel waterwheel

筒裙(tǒngqún) a sarong; a straight skirt

筒瓦(tǒngwǎ) a cylindrical tile

筒箫(tǒngxiāo) a vertical bamboo flute

筒子楼(tǒngzilóu) a tube-shaped apartment (with a long corridor lined with rooms on both sides)

偷汉子(tōu hànzi) to have illicit relations with a man; to commit adultery

偷鸡摸狗(tōujī mōgǒu) ①(lit.)"to

steal chickens and dogs"－to pilfer ②to have affairs with women

偷老婆(tōu lǎopó) to have an affair with somebody's wife; to commit adultery

偷梁换柱(tōuliáng huànzhù)(lit.) "to steal the beams and change the pillars"－to be fraudulent

偷人(tōurén) to commit adultery

偷香窃玉(tōuxiāng qièyù) to philander; to womanize

头彩(tóucǎi) the first prize (in a lottery)

头伏(tóufú) the first period of the hot season

头功(tóugōng) the greatest service; the highest merit

头角峥嵘(tóujiǎo zhēngróng) brilliant; very promising; outstanding

头脸(tóuliǎn)(lit.) "head and face"－reputation; prestige

头面(tóumiàn) a woman's head-ornaments

头面人物(tóumiàn rénwù) a prominent figure; a big shot

头帕(tóupà) a headscarf

头牌(tóupái) the star actor or actress (in traditional opera)

头条新闻(tóutiáo xīnwén) front-page headline

头童齿豁(tóutóng chǐhuō)(lit.) "hair gone and teeth falling out"－decrepit; senile

头头儿(tóutóur) a head; a chief

投笔从戎(tóubǐ cóngróng)(lit.) "to cast aside the pen and join the army"－to renounce the pen for the sword; to give up intellectual pursuits for a military career

投壶(tóuhú) a pitch-pot drinking game

投缳(tóuhuán) to hang oneself

投机倒把(tóujī dǎobǎ) to engage in speculation and profiteering

投机取巧(tóujī qǔqiǎo) to seize every chance to gain advantage by trickery; to be opportunistic

投鼠忌器(tóushǔ jìqì)(lit.) "to hesitate to pelt a rat for fear of smashing the dishes"－to hold back from taking action against an evil-doer for fear of involving or harming good people

投胎(tóutāi) reincarnation

投桃报李(tóutáo bàolǐ)(lit.) "to give a plum in return for a peach"－to repay a favor; to exchange gifts

骰子(tóuzi) dice

秃笔(tūbǐ)(lit.) "a bald writing brush"－a poor writing ability; to be weak at compositon

秃瓢儿(tūpiáor) a bald head

突厥(tūjué) a Turk

图谶(túchèn) an illustrated book

of prophecy

图腾(túténg)a totem

图腾崇拜(túténg chóngbài) totem worship

图章(túzhāng)a seal

徒子徒孙(túzǐ túsūn)①disciples and followers②hangers-on

涂鸦(túyā) poor handwriting; to scrawl;to doodle

涂脂抹粉(túzhī mǒfěn)(lit.)"to apply powder and paint"- to prettify; to embellish

荼毒生灵(túdú shēnglíng)to plunge the people into the depths of suffering

屠龙之技(túlóng zhī jì)(lit.)"the art of slaying dragons"- an art of a high order but of little value

屠苏(túsū) Toso; Tusu (an ancient wine drunk to drive evil spirits away)

土包子(tǔbāozi) a clodhopper; a (country)bumpkin

土地(tǔdì)the local god of the land;a local deity

土地改革(tǔdì gǎigé)land reform

土地庙(tǔdì miào) the Land Deity Temple;a temple to the Earth God

土地神(tǔdì shén) the local god of the land;a local deity

土风(tǔfēng) ① a folk song ② a local custom

土改(tǔgǎi)the land reform

土棍(tǔgùn)a local rascal

土豪(tǔháo)①local tyrants②an uncouth upstart

土豪劣绅(tǔháo lièshēn)local tyrants and evil gentry

土话(tǔhuà)local, colloquial expressions;local dialect

土皇帝(tǔ huángdì)a local despot;a local tyrant

土家族(tǔjiāzú)the Tujia nationality (distributed mainly Hunan and Hubei provinces)

土老冒儿(tǔlǎomàor)a clodhopper;a (country)bumpkin

土坯房(tǔpīfáng) an adobe house; a mud-brick building

土坯拱窑洞(tǔpī gǒng yáodòng) arched cave dwellings(built of sun-dried mud bricks)

土司(tǔsī)①the system of appointing the hereditary headmen of the national minorities ② headman of the national minority

土圆楼(tǔyuán lóu) a tamped earth circular building

土葬(tǔzàng)a burial

土政策(tǔ zhèngcè)a local policy

土专家(tǔ zhuānjiā)a self-taught expert;a local expert

土族(tǔzú)the Tu nationality(distributed mainly in Qinghai province)

吐蕃(tǔbo)the Tubo Kingdom(the first Tibetan regime established in the 7th–9th centuries)

吐苦水(tǔ kǔshuǐ)to pour out one's grievances

兔儿爷(tùryé)a clay toy rabbit(a toy for children at the Mid-Autumn Festival)

兔起鹘落(tùqǐ húluò)(lit.)"the moment a hare emerges, the falcon swoops"①a rapid action②a rapid, flowing style(of a writer, calligraphy or painter)

兔死狗烹(tùsǐ gǒupēng)(lit.)"to kill the hounds for food once the hares are bagged"–to eliminate trusted aides when they have outlived their usefulness

兔死狐悲(tùsǐ húbēi)(lit.)"the fox mourns the death of the hare"–like feels for like

兔子不吃窝边草(tùzi bùchī wōbiān cǎo)(lit.)"a rabbit doesn't eat the grass near its own hole(for its own protection)"–a villain doesn't harm his nextdoor neighbours

团拜(tuánbài)to gather together to exchange greetings

《团泊洼的秋天》(tuánpówā de qiūtiān)*The Autumn of Tuanpowa*–a poem by Guo Xiaochuan(郭小川, 1919–1976)in 1975

团徽(tuánhuī)a league badge(issued in 1959 for the Communist Youth League of China)

团年(tuánnián)family reunion during the Spring Festival

团扇(tuánshàn)a round fan

团圆(tuányuán)reunion(of family members)

团圆节(tuányuán jié)the Family Reunion Festival; the Mid-Autumn Festival; the Moon Festival

推襟送抱(tuījīn sòngbào)to deal with sb in good faith; to treat sb with sincerity

推拿(tuīná)a massage; to massage

推敲(tuīqiāo)to weigh; to deliberate

推手(tuīshǒu)hand-pushing(in martial arts)

颓垣断壁(tuíyuán duànbì)dilapidated walls; a desolate scene

腿脚功夫(tuǐ jiǎo gōngfu)footwork

腿子(tuǐzi)a henchman; a hired thug

退避三舍(tuìbì sānshè)to give way to avoid a conflict

吞金(tūnjīn)to swallow gold(to commit suicide)

吞云吐雾(tūnyún tǔwù)(lit.)"to swallow clouds and blow out fog"–to smoke(opium or tobacco)

屯田(túntián)to have garrison troops or peasants open up wasteland and grow food grain

囤积(túnjī)to hoard

囤积居奇(túnjī jūqí) to hoard and profiteer

托词(tuōcí)①to make an excuse ②an excuse

托辞(tuōcí)①to make an excuse ②an excuse

托儿(tuōr)a salesperson's decoy

托孤(tuōgū)(of a dying emperor) to entrust his young son to the care of a minister

托门子(tuōménzi)to solicit help from potential backers; to gain one's objective by pulling strings

托梦(tuōmèng) to appear in one's dream and make a request

托人情(tuō rénqíng) to ask an influential person to help arrange something; to gain one's objective by pulling strings

托生(tuōshēng) reincarnation; transmigration

拖尾巴(tuō wěiba)①to hold sb back ②to leave a project, etc. unfinished; to leave loose ends

拖油瓶(tuō yóupíng)①to remarry and take one's children to one's second husband's home②such children

脱口秀(tuōkǒuxiù)a talk show

脱兔(tuōtù)(lit.)"a fleeing hare"– at speed

脱孝(tuōxiào)to take off one's mourning clothes; the mourning period is over

陀螺(tuóluó) a whipping top; a peg-top

沱茶(tuóchá) a bowl-shaped compressed mass of tea leaves

鸵鸟政策(tuóniǎo zhèngcè) an ostrich policy (a policy which refuses to face reality)

唾手可得(tuòshǒu kědé) to be extremely easy to obtain

W

挖墙脚(wāqiángjiǎo)to cut the ground from under sb 's feet; to undermine the foundation of something

娃娃亲(wáwaqīn) infant matrimony; child betrothal

娃娃生(wáwashēng) the role of a child (in Chinese operas); a child

瓦当(wǎdāng)an eaves tile

瓦楞(wǎléng)rows of tiles on a roof; corrugated (iron, paper etc.)

瓦垄(wǎlǒng)rows of tiles on a roof

佤族(wǎzú) the Wa nationality (distributed mainly in Yunnan province)

歪才(wāicái) a devious talent; a perverted genius; a talent for coming up with crooked ideas

歪风(wāifēng) an unhealthy trend; an

evil wind; a noxious influence; a bad tendency

歪理(wāilǐ) false reasoning

歪门邪道(wāimén xiédào) crooked ways; a dishonest practice

外埠(wàibù) other towns or cities

外传(wàizhuàn) an unauthorized biography; an unofficial biography

外公(wàigōng) (maternal) grandfather

外号(wàihào) a nickname

外家(wàijiā) ①the family of one's maternal grandparents ②a married man's second or more families (in old China) ③the women (concubines) in the married man's second or more families ④a married woman's parents' home; a wife's maiden home

外家拳(wàijiāquán) external boxing (Shaolin boxing)

外舅(wàijiù) father-in-law

外快(wàikuài) an extra income; extra gains; a windfall

外来妹(wàiláimèi) a nonlocal female laborer

外来文化(wàilái wénhuà) imported culture; foreign culture; alien culture

外婆(wàipó) (maternal) grandmother

外戚(wàiqī) the relatives of a ruler on his mother's or wife's side

外甥(wàishēng) a nephew (sister's son)

外甥女(wàishēngnǚ) a niece (sister's daughter)

外史(wàishǐ) an external history; an unofficial history; an informal history

外室(wàishì) ①a mistress; a concubine; a kept woman ②the house for a mistress or concubine

外孙(wàisūn) the daughter's son; a grandson

外孙女(wàisūnnǚ) a granddaughter (daughter's daughter)

外孙子(wàisūnzi) a grandson (daughter's son)

外心(wàixīn) ①unfaithful intentions (of husband or wife) ②being unfaithful to one's country

外遇(wàiyù) to have an affair; extramarital affair

外子(wàizǐ) ①husband (in ancient China) ②a nephew (sister's son)

外族(wài zú) ①people of a different clan ②foreigners ③other nationalities

外祖父(wàizǔfù) grandfather (on mother's side)

外祖母(wàizǔmǔ) grandmother (on mother's side)

纨绔(wánkù) ①silk trousers ②son of a rich family; playboy

纨绔子弟(wánkù zǐdì)a dandy

纨扇(wánshàn)a flat,round fan with framed gauze

完璧归赵(wánbìguīzhào)(lit.)"to return the jade intact to the Zhao State"-to return something intact to its owner; to return something in perfect condition

玩儿不转(wánr bùzhuàn)can't handle;can't manage

玩儿得转(wánr de zhuàn)to be capable of;can control

玩儿命(wánrmìng)to bust a gut;to be reckless

玩儿票(wánrpiào)①to perform drama in spare-time;to perform amateur dramatics ② to do something just for fun

玩儿完(wánrwán)①to be done for; to be finished②dead

玩忽(wánhū)negligence;to trifle with

玩家(wánjiā)a(game etc.)player

玩意儿(wányìr)① a plaything; a gadget②a guy

顽主(wánzhǔ)a trouble shooter

挽歌(wǎngē) an elegy; a dirge; a monody

挽联(wǎnlián)an elegiac couplet

挽幛(wǎnzhàng)a large elegiac scroll

晚节(wǎnjié)integrity in one's later years

晚景(wǎnjǐng)(lit.)"the evening scene"-circumstances in old age

晚娘(wǎnniáng)stepmother

晚生(wǎnshēng)I;your pupil

婉言(wǎnyán)gentle words;tactful expressions

婉约(词)派[wǎnyuē(cí)pài] the Graceful and Restrained School of *ci* Poems [with representatives of Zhou Bangyan(周邦彦,1056-1121), Liu Yong(柳永,987-1053), Qin Guan(秦观,1049-1100), Li Qingzhao(李清照,1084-1155?),etc. in the Song Dynasty]

皖南事变(wǎnnán shìbiàn)the Southern Anhui Incident(1941)

碗碗腔(wǎnwǎnqiāng) the Bowl Beating opera(a regional opera from Shaanxi province)

万福(wànfú)to wish somebody every happiness and good fortune

万贯(wànguàn)wealthy;ten million cash;a huge fortune

万户侯(wànhùhóu)a high noble

《万家灯火》(wànjiā dēnghuǒ) *Myriad of Lights* - a film directed by Shen Fu(沈浮)in 1948

万劫不复(wànjiébùfù) beyond redemption; to be doomed eternally;irrecoverable

万金油(wànjīnyóu)① Jack of all trades②essential balm;tiger balm

万里长城(wànlǐ Chángchéng) the Great Wall

万里长征(wànlǐ chángzhēng) the Long March(1934 - 1935)

万历(wànlì) Wanli [the reign title (1573 - 1620) of Shen Zong(神宗朱翊钧,1563 - 1620), an emperor of the Ming Dynasty]

万民伞(wànmínsǎn) a silk parasol (hung with strips signed by many people, and given as a farewell gift to a governor); an autographed silk parasol

万年历(wànniánlì) a perpetual calendar

万事俱备,只欠东风(wànshì jùbèi, zhǐ qiàn dōngfēng) (lit.) "everything is ready, and all that we need is an east wind" - all is ready except what is crucial

万事通(wànshìtōng) a know-all; a jack-of-all-trades

万寿宫(wànshòugōng) the longevity palace

万寿无疆(wànshòuwújiāng) a long life; boundless longevity

《万水千山》(wànshuǐqiānshān) *A Long and Arduous Journey* - a film directed by Hua Chun(华纯) and Cheng Yin(成荫) in 1959; a film directed by Yan Jizhou(严寄洲) in 1977

万岁(wànsuì) ①"Long live …" ② Your Majesty; emperor

亡国奴(wángguónú) a slave of a foreign power; a slave without a country; conquered people; subjugated people

亡魂(wáng hún) the soul of the newly deceased; a ghost

亡灵(wáng líng) the soul of a deceased person; a ghost; a spectre

亡命之徒(wángmìng zhī tú) a desperado

王安石变法(wángānshí biànfǎ) Wang Anshi's Political Reform (1069 - 1076)

王八(wángba) ①a tortoise ②a cuckold

王道(wángdào) ①benevolent government; the way of kings ②unreasonable

王法(wángfǎ) ①the law of the land ②criterion

王府(wángfǔ) a prince's palace or mansion

王宫(wánggōng) ①a royal palace; an imperial palace ②a sacrificial altar

《王贵与李香香》(wáng guìyǔ lǐ xiāngxiāng) *Wang Gui and Li Xiangxiang* - a narrative poem by Li Ji (李季,1922 - 1980) in 1946

王莽改制(wángmǎng gǎizhì) Wang Mang's reform(7 - 20)

王母娘娘(Wángmǔ niángniang)the Queen Mother of the Western Heavens;the Empress of Heaven

王孙(wángsūn)the prince's descen dant

王爷(wáng ye)His(Your)Royal Highness(a respectful title for a person with a noble title)

《王爷与邮差》(wángye yǔ yóuchāi) *Rajah and the Postman* – a skit starring by Chen Peisi(陈佩斯)and Zhu Shimao(朱时茂)in 1998

王族(wángzú)blood royal;imperial kinsmen;royal lineage

王佐之才(wángzuǒ zhī cái)the talent to assist a monarch;an extremely capable man;a man of versatile talent

网虫(wǎngchóng)a webaholic;an Internet addict;a netbug;a cyber addict

网恋(wǎngliàn)cyber romance;cyber love;online love;internet romance

魍魉(wǎngliǎng)demons and monsters

忘本(wàngběn)to forget one's class origin;to forget one's bitter past;to forget one's roots

忘恩负义(wàng'ēn fùyì)to bite the hand that feeds;to turn on one's friend;to be devoid of all gratitude;ingratitude

忘年交(wàngniánjiāo)friendship across generations

望穿秋水(wàngchuān qiūshuǐ)to gaze anxiously till one's eyes are worn out;to look forward eagerly to (seeing a dear one)

望风(wàngfēng)to be on the lookout;to keep watch

《望江亭》(wàngjiāngtíng)*The Riverside Pavilion* – a play by Guan Hanqing(关汉卿,1220 – 1300);a Beijing opera adapted by Wang Yan (王雁)and performed by Zhang Junqiu(张君秋)in 1956

望梅止渴(wàngméi zhǐkě)(lit.)"to stare at plums to quench one's thirst" – to console oneself with vain hopes

望门寡(wàngménguǎ)an unmarried widow;a bereaved fiancée

望闻问切(wàngwénwènqiè)inspection,listening,interrogation and palpation(the four diagnostic methods in traditional Chinese medicine)

望诊(wàngzhěn)inspection;observation

望子成龙(wàngzǐ chénglóng)to have great ambitions for one's child;to hold high hopes for one's child

望族(wàngzú)a distinguished family;a well-established family;a prominent family

微词(wēicí) veiled criticism; complaints

微服私访(wēifú sīfǎng) a secret investigation (conducted by officials in plain clothes); a plain-clothes investigation

微言大义(wēiyán dàyì) to imbue words with deep meaning

为人作嫁(wéirénzuòjià) to busy oneself with helping other people; to work for others without getting any benefit for oneself

韦编三绝(wéibiān sānjué) to be diligent in one's studies

《围城》(wéichéng) *Fortress Besieged* – a novel by Qian Zhongshu (钱钟书,1910 – 1998) in 1947

围魏救赵(wéiwèi jiùzhào) (lit.) "to besiege Wei to rescue Zhao" – to relieve the besieged by besieging the base of the besiegers

闱墨(wéimò) selections from the papers of successful candidates in imperial examinations

唯我独尊(wéi wǒ dúzūn) extremely conceited; to assume airs of self importance

维吾尔族(wéiwú'ěrzú) the Uygur nationality; the Uighur nationality; Uighur

维族(wéizú) the Uygur nationality; the Uighur nationality; Uighur

尾巴工程(wěiba gōngchéng) dragging construction projects; overdue construction projects

未卜先知(wèibǔ xiānzhī) to foresee accurately; to have foresight; to be able to foresee the future

未时(wèishí) the period of the day from 1 p. m. to 3 p. m

未亡人(wèiwángrén) the bereaved (self-appellation for a widow)

尉官(wèiguān) a junior officer; a company officer

《尉缭子》(wèiliáozǐ) *The book of Master Wei Liao* – an ancient military book by Wei Liao (尉缭) in the Warring States Period

慰唁(wèiyàn) to express sympathy for; to condole with sb; to give condolences

魏碑(wèibēi) tablet inscriptions of the Northern Dynasties (386 – 581).

魏阙(wèiquè) the gate of the imperial palace

温故知新(wēngù zhīxīn) to gain new insights through restudying old material; to understand the present by reviewing the past; to learn new things by reviewing old things

温居(wēnjū) housewarming; to have a house-warming party; to visit a relative or friend in his/her new house

温良恭俭让(wēnliánggōngjiǎnràng)

temperate, kind, courteous, restrained and magnanimous

温柔乡(wēnróuxiāng)(lit.)"the land of warmth and tenderness" - a place where a man can find solace in feminine charms

温文尔雅(wēnwéněryǎ) gentle and cultivated; refined and cultivated; gentle and graceful; urbane; mild-mannered

瘟神(wēnshén)①the god of pestilence; the god of plague②a jinx

文昌帝君(wénchāngdìjūn) the Wenchang spirit; the god of literature

文场(wénchǎng) the stringed and wind instruments in Chinese opera

文抄公(wénchāogōng) a plagiarist

《文成公主》(wénchénggōngzhǔ) *Princess Wencheng* - a TV drama directed by Cai Xiaoqing(蔡晓晴) in 2000

文丑(wénchǒu) the comic civilian role(in Chinese opera)

文房四宝(wénfáng sìbǎo) the four treasures of the study(writing brushes, papers, ink sticks and ink stones); the "scholar's four jewels"

文革(wéngé) the Cultural Revolution

文工团(wéngōngtuán) song and dance ensemble; arts troupe

文翰(wénhàn)①essays; articles; literary composition ②official documents and correspondence

文化部(wénhuàbù) the Ministry of Culture

文化大革命(wénhuà dà gémìng) the Cultural Revolution; the Great Cultural Revolution

文化革命(wénhuà gémìng) cultural revolution

文化宫(wénhuàgōng) the Cultural Palace

文化馆(wénhuàguǎn) the Cultural Centre; the community centre I

文化下乡(wénhuà xiàxiāng) the dissemination of culture into the rural areas

文化寻根小说(wénhuà xúngēn xiǎo shuō) Root-Seeking Fiction

文化遗产(wénhuàyíchǎn) a cultural legacy; cultural heritage

文景之治(wénjǐngzhīzhì) the Reign of the Wen and Jing Emperors; the Rule of Wen(180 - 157 BC) and Jing(157 - 141 BC)

文侩(wénkuài) a literary prostitute; a phrase-monger

文联(wénlián) the China Federation of Literary and Art Circles

文庙(wénmiào) a Confucius Temple

文墨(wénmò) writing

文墨人(wénmòrén) an intellectual; the literati; a man of letters

文痞(wénpǐ) a literary prostitute; a

lettered crook; an eloquent trickster

文琴戏(wénqínxì) the Wenqin opera; the Qian opera (accompanied by cymbalo in Guizhou and Sichuan)

文人(wénrén) men of letters; the literati

文人墨客(wénrén mòkè) men of literature; men of letters; the literati

文山会海(wénshān huìhǎi) excessive paperwork and meetings; mountains of red tape and bureaucracy

《文史通义》(wénshǐ tōngyì) *General Argumentation of Literary History* - a book by Zhang Xuecheng (章学诚, 1738 - 1801)

文殊菩萨(wénshūpúsà) (Buddhism) the Bodhisattva Manjusri

文坛(wéntán) the literary scene; the literary world

文韬武略(wéntāo wǔlüè) civil and military skills

文物(wénwù) a cultural relic; a historical relic; a cultural object

文物鉴定(wénwù jiàndìng) cultural relic authentification; evaluation of cultural antiques

《文心雕龙》(wénxīndiāolóng) *The Literary Mind and the Carving of Dragons* - a book by Liu Xie (刘勰, 465 - 520) in 501 - 502

文学大师(wénxué dàshī) a literary maestro, a literary master

文学界(wénxuéjiè) the literary world

文学研究会(wénxué yánjiūhuì) the Literature Research Association

文言(wényán) classical Chinese

文言文(wényánwén) classical Chinese

文言小说(wényán xiǎoshuō) classical Chinese fiction; a novel in classical Chinese

文字狱(wénzìyù) the literary inquisition; imprisonment of writers

纹银(wényín) fine silver; sterling silver; sycee

闻达(wéndá) illustrious and influential; well-known; eminent

闻鸡起舞(wénjīqǐwǔ) (lit.) "to rise up upon hearing the crow of a rooster to practice sword playing" - to throw oneself into a good cause

闻人(wén rén) a well-known figure; a famous man; a celebrity

闻诊(wén zhěn) (Medicine) to diagonose through auscultation and olfaction; auscultation and olfaction

刎颈交(wěnjǐngjiāo) friends who would die for one another

稳婆(wěnpó) a midwife

问安(wèn'ān) to pay one's respects; to wish one's elders good health

问卜(wènbǔ) to divine by the eight trigrams; to consult fortune tellers

问鼎(wèndǐng) ① to aspire to the

throne; to have designs on the throne②to entertain a high ambition to be first-rate or the champion; to compete for a championship in

问津(wènjīn)①to make inquiries②to show interest in

问诊(wènzhěn)inquiry(a diagnostic method used by traditional Chinese doctors,asking for the patient's history, symptoms, medicines taken etc.)

问罪(wènzuì)to denounce; to condemn

翁姑(wēnggū)a woman's parents-in-law

倭寇(wōkòu)Japanese pirates

窝点(wōdiǎn)den

窝里斗(wōlǐdòu)an internecine struggle;in-fighting

窝里反(wōlifǎn)an internal or domestic dispute(within a family, etc.)

窝里横(wōlihèng)a tyrant in the home

窝囊(wōnang)①to feel vexed;to be annoyed ② stupid; cowardly; hopeless;good-for-nothing

窝囊废(wōnangfèi)a good-for-nothing;a worthless wretch;a prat

窝气(wōqì)to choke with resentment; to feel injured and resentful

窝窝头(wōwotóu)a steamed corn bun

窝心(wōxīn)to feel irritated;to feel vexed;to feel resentful

窝赃(wōzāng)to harbor stolen property

《蜗居》(wōjū)*Dwelling Narrowness* - a TV drama directed by Teng Huatao(滕华涛)in 2009

蜗居(wōjū)①a humble abode②to live in a humble abode

《我的团长我的团》(wǒde tuánzhǎng wǒde tuán)*My Chief and My Regiment* - a TV drama directed by Kang Honglei(康洪雷)in 2008

《我的兄弟叫顺溜》(wǒde xīongdì jiào shùnliū)*My Brother's name is Sunliu* - a TV drama directed by Hua Jing(花箐)in 2009

《我们村里的年轻人》(wǒmen cūn lide niánqīngrén)*Young People in Our Village* - a film directed by Lu Li(苏里)in 1959

《我们结婚吧》(wǒmen jiěhūnba)*We Get Married* - a TV drama directed by Liu Jiang(刘江)in 2013

我行我素(wǒxíngwǒsù)to persist in one's old ways;to live by one's own precepts;to do what one pleases

卧底(wòdǐ)an undercover agent; an insider

卧佛(wòfó)the reclining Buddha(a huge statue)

《卧虎藏龙》(wòhǔcánglóng) *Crouching Tiger, Hidden Dragon* - a film directed by Ang Lee(李安) in 2000

卧龙(wòlóng) ①an outstanding person who lives in solitude ② Zhuge Liang - a military counselor in the *Romance of the Three Kingdoms*

卧薪尝胆(wòxīn cháng dǎn)(lit.) "to sleep on firewood and taste gall" - to avenge a national humiliation through personal hardship; to stoop to conquer

斡旋(wòxuán) ①to mediate; to intercede; intervene; to use one's good offices or influence ② good offices; mediation

乌合之众(wūhézhīzhòng) sheep without a shepherd; a disorderly band of people; mob

乌江(wūjiāng) the Wujiang River (in Guizhou province)

乌龙茶(wūlóngchá) oolong tea

《乌龙山剿匪记》(wūlóngshān jiǎofěi jì) *Suppress Bandits in Wulong Mountain* - a TV drama directed by Song Zhao(宋昭) in 1986

乌篷船(wūpéngchuán) a boat with a black awning

乌纱帽(wūshāmào) a black gauze hat; an official post

《乌鸦与麻雀》(wūyā yǔ máquè) *Crows and Sparrows* - a film directed by Zheng Junli(郑君里) in 1949

乌有(wūyǒu) nothing; naught

乌孜别克族(wūzībiékèzú) the Ozbek (Uzbek) nationality

呜呼哀哉(wūhū'āizāi) ①alas ②dead and gone

巫婆(wūpó) a witch

巫术(wūshù) witchcraft; the black arts; sorcery

屋里人(wūlǐrén) wife

无常(wúcháng) ①(Buddhism) anicca; anitya; impermanence ② the name of a ghost ③to pass away

无出其右(wúchūqíyòu) matchless; to be unsurpassed; to be second to none; without equal

无道(wúdào) brutal; cruel; tyrannical

无底洞(wúdǐdòng) ①a bottomless pit ②an abyss

无独有偶(wúdú yǒuǒu) not unique, but with its counterpart; it happens that there is a similar case; to come not singly but in pairs

无法无天(wúfǎwútiān) wild; without law and order; to defy all laws; to become absolutely lawless; to run wild

《无极》(wújí) *The Promise* - a film directed by Chen Kaige(陈凯歌) in 2005

无极(wújí) the great nothingness; the ultimate of non-being

无间道(wújiàndào)①infernal affairs ② *Infernal Affairs* - a film directed by Liu Weiqiang(刘伟强)in 2002

无赖(wúlài)①a rascal; a rapscallion; a ruffian②rascally; scoundrel

无名火(wúmínghuǒ)nameless anger

无事不登三宝殿(wúshì bù dēng sānbǎodiàn)(lit.)"to go to the temple only when one is in trouble"- to only visit when one wants something; never go to somebody's place except on business.

无头公案(wútóugōngàn)an intricate case without any leads; an unsolved mystery

无形拳(wǔxíng quán)Five Animal Boxing(belonging to internal boxing)

吴下阿蒙(wú xià ā'méng)an ignorant person; someone whose knowledge is merely superficial

吴语(wúyǔ)the Wu dialect(in Jiangsu, Shanghai, zhejiang provinces, etc.)

《吴越春秋》(wúyuè chūnqiū) *The Spring and Autumn Annals of Wu and Yue* - an ancient book by Zhao Ye(赵晔)in the Eastern Han Dynasty

《吴子》(wúzǐ) *Wuzi* - an ancient military book by Wu Qi(吴起, 440 - 381 BC)

《梧桐雨》(wútóng yǔ) *Rain on the Paulownia Tree* - a play by Bai Pu (白朴, 1226 -?)

五爱(wǔ'ài)the five objects of"love" (the motherland, the people, working, science and communism)

五霸(wǔbà)the Five Overlords(of the Spring and Autumn Period, 770 - 476 BC)

五保户(wǔbǎohù)the household enjoying the five guarantees(food, clothing, medical care, housing and burial expenses)

五笔字型(wǔbǐzìxíng hànzì)the five-stroke method(for computer inputing Chinese characters)

五大三粗(wǔdàsāncū)big and tall; a stalwart

五代十国(wǔdài shíguó)the Five Dynasties and the Ten Kingdoms (907 - 979)

五帝(wǔdì)①the five virtuous emperors of China[Huang Di(黄帝), Zhuan Xu(颛顼), Di Ku(帝喾), Tang Yao(唐尧)and Yu Shun(虞舜)]②the legendary celestial emperors of the five directions(in Chinese ancient myth: the Green Emperor of the east, the Red Emperor of the south, the Yellow Emperor of the center, the White Emperor of the west and the Black Emperor of the north)

五斗米(wǔdǒumǐ)(lit.)"five *dou* of rice"– a trivial amount

五斗米道(wǔdǒumǐ dào)the Way of the Five Pecks of Rice; the Taoist religion

五毒(wǔdú)①the five poisonous creatures(scorpion, viper, centipede, house lizard and toad)②the "five evils"(bribery, tax evasion, theft of state property, cheating on government contracts and stealing of economic information);③the "five poisons"(a campaign launched in 1952 against the "five evils")④the five vices(gluttony, drunkenness, lechery, gambling and drug abuse)

五毒俱全(wǔdú jùquán)to be totally addicted to the five vices(gluttony, drunkenness, lechery, gambling and drug abuse)

《五朵金花》(wǔduǒ jīnhuā)*Five Golden Flowers* – a film directed by Wang Jiayi(王家乙)in 1959

五反运动(wǔfǎn yùndòng)the Five Antis Movement(1952)

五服(wǔ fú)①five classes of mourning clothing②the five generations(great great grandfather, great-grandfather, grandfather, father and son)

五福娃(wǔfúwá)the five Olympic mascots from the Beijing Olympics(2008)

五谷(wǔgǔ)the five Chinese grains(rice, two kinds of millet, wheat and beans)

五好家庭(wǔhǎojiātíng)the Five-Virtues Family

五湖四海(wǔhú sìhǎi)all the corners of the land; all the parts of the country

五荤(wǔhūn)the five vegetables(some religious believers avoid eating)

五经(wǔjīng)the Five Classics(*The Book of Songs*, *The Book of History*, *The Book of Changes*, *The Book of Rites* and *The Spring and Autumn Annals*)

五绝(wǔjué)a five-syllable quatrain; a pentasyllabic quatrain

五口通商(wǔkǒu tōngshāng)to carry out commercial business in the five treaty ports

五粮液(wǔliángyè)Five-Grain Liquor

五律(wǔlǜ)pentasyllabic(or five-syllable)regulated verse; an eight-line poem with five characters per line

五伦(wǔlún)the five cardinal relationships(between ruler and subject, father and son, husband and wife, between brothers and between friends)

五马分尸(wǔmǎfēnshī) to tear a body limb from limb using five horses – a form of the death penalty (in ancient times)

《五牛图》(wǔniútú) *Five Oxen* – a classical painting by Han Huang (韩滉,723 – 787)

《五女拜寿》(wǔnǚ bàishòu) *Five Daughters Offering Birthday Felicitations* – a traditional Chinese costume drama

五七干校(wǔqī gànxiào) the May 7th cadre school (during the Great Cultural Revolution)

五禽戏(wǔqínxì) the Five-Animal Exercises (imitating tigers, deers, bears, apes and birds for good health)

五卅运动(wǔsà yùndòng) the May 30th Movement (1925)

五四青年节(wǔsì qīngniánjié) Youth Day

五四文学(wǔsì wénxué) May Fourth Literature

五四新文学运动(wǔsì xīnwénxué yùndòng) the May 4th New Literature Movement; the New Literature Movement

五四运动(wǔsì yùndòng) the May 4th Movement (1919); the New Culture Movement

五台山(wǔtáishān) Wutai Mountain; Mount Wutai (in Shanxi province)

五味(wǔwèi) ①the five flavors (sweet, sour, bitter, pungent and salty) ②all sorts of flavors

五刑(wǔxíng) the five chief forms of punishment (in slavery and feudal China)

五行(wǔxíng) the five elements (fire, earth, water, metals and wood)

五行相克(wǔxíng xiāng kè) the inter-inhibition of the five elements; the mutual repulsion of the five elements

五行相生(wǔxíng xiāngshēng) the inter-promotion of the five elements; the mutual reproduction of the five elements

五行学说(wǔxíng xuéshuō) the doctrine of the five elements; the theory of the five elements

五言七律(wǔyán qīlǜ) poems with five or seven characters to one line

五言诗(wǔyánshī) a five-syllable-line poem; pentasyllabic verse; five-character style poetry

五音(wǔyīn) ①the five notes of the ancient Chinese pentatonic musical scale ② the five initial consonants (of Chinese syllables)

五月节(wǔyuèjié) the Dragon Boat Festival

五岳(wǔyuè) the Five Sacred Mountains (Taishan Mountain in Shandong, Hengshan Mountain in Hunan, Huashan Mountain in Shaanxi, Hengshan Mountain in Shanxi and Songshan Mountain in Henan)

五脏(wǔzàng) the five internal organs (heart, liver, spleen, kidney and lungs)

五脏六腑(wǔzàng liùfǔ) viscera; the internal organs of the body; the vital organs of the body; entrails

五中(wǔzhōng) the five internal organs; one's innermost being

五族(wǔ zú) the five ethnic groups (Han, Man, Mongolian, Hui and Tibetan)

仵作(wǔzuò) a coroner

忤逆(wǔnì) disobedient (to one's parents)

武把子(wǔbàzi) a person who is good at acrobatic fighting; a person who is skilled in martial arts

武昌起义(wǔchāng qǐyì) The Wuchang Uprising (1911)

武场(wǔchǎng) ①percussion instruments②a percussionist

武丑(wǔchǒu) the acrobatic-fighting comic role (in Chinese opera)

武旦(wǔdàn) wudan (a female role skilled in martial arts in Chinese opera)

武当山(wǔdāngshān) Wudang Mountains (in Hubei province)

武工队(wǔgōngduì) an armed work-team (during the war of resistance against Japan)

武功(wǔgōng) ①military accomplishments② acrobatic prowess (in Chinese opera)

武官(wǔguān) ①a military attaché② a military officer

武侯祠(wǔhóucí) the Temple of Marquis Wu (in Chendu, Nanyang, Mianxian, Qishan, Fengjie and Baoshan)

武花脸(wǔhuāliǎn) the painted-face character (an acrobatic fighting role in Chinese opera)

武举(wǔjǔ) a successful military candidate in the imperial provincial examination; the recruitment examinations for the military service

武科(wǔ kē) the military examinations

武林(wǔlín) the field of martial arts

《武林外传》(wǔlín wàizhuàn) *Legend of Martial Arts* - a TV drama directed by Shang Jing (尚敬) in 2006; a film directed by Shang Jing (尚敬) in 2009

武庙(wǔmiào) the Guan Yu temple

武生(wǔshēng) wusheng (an actor playing a martial role in Chinese operas); a military man

武士俑(wǔshìyǒng)terra-cotta warriors

武术(wǔshù)martial arts

武侠(wǔxiá)a swordsman;a chivalrous knight errant

武侠小说(wǔxiá xiǎoshuō)martial arts novels;martial arts fiction;tales of chivalry and martial arts;kung-fu novels

武行(wǔháng)wuhang(a minor acrobatic fighting role in Chinese opera)

《武训传》(wǔxùnzhuàn)*The Life of Wuxun* - a film directed by Sun Yu(孙瑜)in 1950

武艺(wǔyì)skill in martial arts

《武则天》(wǔzétiān)*Empress Wu Zetian* - a TV drama directed by Li Zhaohua(李兆华)in 1984,directed by Chen Jialin(陈家林)in 1995

舞灯(wǔdēng)the dragon lantern dance

《舞台姐妹》(wǔtái jiěmèi)*Two Stage Sisters* - a film directed by Xie Jin(谢晋)in 1965

舞文弄墨(wǔwén nòngmò)to amuse oneself with writing; to show off one's literary skill

舞榭歌台(wǔxiè gētái)entertainment venues; a place for dancing and singing;music and dance halls

戊戌变法(wùxū biànfǎ)the Reform Movement of 1898;the Wuxu Reform Movement;the Hundred Days' Reform Movement

戊戌六君子(wùxū lìu jūnzǐ)the six martyrs of 1898

物阜民丰(wùfù mínfēng)people are content and products are plentiful;a rich nation with abundant produce

物华天宝(wùhuá tiānbǎo)(lit.)"good products from the earth are natural treasures" - to be rich in natural resources

悟性(wùxìng)comprehension;perception;the power of understandi-ng;savvy

婺剧(wùjù)Wu opera(popular in Jinhua,zhejiang province)

《雾、雨、电》(wù,yǔ,diàn)*Fog;Rain;Lightning* - a love trilogy by Ba Jin(巴金,1904 - 2005)in 1931,1932 and 1933

X

《夕阳箫鼓》(xīyáng xiāogǔ)*Flute and Drum at Sunset* - a piece of lute music

西安碑林(xī'ān bēilín)the Forest of Steles in Xi'an

西安事变(xī'ān Shìbiàn)Xi'an Incident(occurred on December 12,1936)

西方净土(xīfāng jìngtǔ)(Buddhism) the pure land in the west; the Western Paradise

西方三圣(xīfāng sānshèng) the Three Holinesses of the Western Pure Land

西宫(xīgōng) ①the western palaces ②imperial concubines

西宫娘娘(xīgōng niángniang) the Western-Palace Empress

西汉(xīhàn) the Western Han Dynasty(206 BC - 8 AD)

西河大鼓(xīhé dàgǔ) the Xihe Big Drum Recitative (in Hebei and Henan provinces)

西湖(xīhú) the West Lake (in Hangzhou, Zhejiang)

《西江月》(xījiāngyuè) *The Moon on the Western River* - the name of a tune for ci poems

西晋(xījìn) the Western Jin Dynasty (265 - 316)

西陵(xīlíng) the Western Imperial Mausoleum [in Yixian County (易县), Hebei]

西皮(xīpí) xipi (one of the two chief categories of vocal music in traditional Chinese opera)

西施(xīshī) Xi Shi (a famous beauty)

西王母(xīwángmǔ) the Queen Mother of the West

西魏(xīwèi) the Western Wei Dynasty (535 - 556)

西夏(xīxià) the Western Xia regime (1038 - 1227)

《西线轶事》(xīxiàn yìshì) *The Western Front Anecdotes* - a novelette by Xu Huaizhong(徐怀中,1929 -) in 1980

《西厢记》(xīxiāngjì) *Romance of the West Chamber* - a famous poetic play by Wang Shifu (王实甫, 1260 - 1316); *The West Chamber*

《西厢记诸宫调》(xīxiāngjì zhūgōng diào) *Melody in Multi-modes, Romance of the Western Chamber* - a play by Dong Jieyuan (董解元, 1190 - 1208)

西学(xīxué) Western learning

西洋(xīyáng) the West; the Western World

西洋景(xīyángjǐng) ①a peep show; ②chicanery, trickery

西洋镜(xīyángjìng) ①a thaumatrope ②trickery

《西游记》(xīyóujì) *Journey to the West* - a novel by Wu Cheng'en (吴承恩, 1501 - 1582)

西域(xīyù) the Western Region (the area west of Yumenguan)

西岳(xīyuè) the Western Mountain (Huashan Mountain)

西周(xīzhōu) the Western Zhou Dynasty (11th century - 771 BC)

稀客(xīkè) an infrequent visitor

锡伯族(xībózú)the Xibo nationality (in Xinjiang Uygur Autonomous Region and Liaoning Province)

锡剧(xījù)Wuxi opera

锡杖(xīzhàng)a monk's cane

檄书(xíshū)an official call to arms;a proclamation of war

洗钱(xǐqián)money laundering

喜蛋(xǐdàn)a happy egg;a red egg (distributed to friends and neighbors on weddings or on the birth of babies)

喜房(xǐfáng)a bridal chamber

喜封(xǐfēng)a gift envelope;a red envelope(containing a gift of money)

喜酒(xǐjiǔ)a wedding feast;a wedding toast

喜联(xǐlián)a wedding couplet;a marriage couplet;wedding scrolls

喜娘(xǐniáng)a chaperone(at a wedding)

喜期(xǐqī)the happy occasion;a wedding day

喜钱(xǐqián)money distributed to guests at a wedding;tips(given on a happy occasion)

喜丧(xǐsāng)an honorable funeral (for an old man)

喜堂(xǐtáng)a wedding hall

喜糖(xǐtáng)wedding sweets;wedding candy

喜相(xǐxiàng)an amiable expression;a pleasant appearance

喜新厌旧(xǐxīn yànjiù)to abandon the old for the new;to be fickle in one's affections;to love the new and loathe the old;out with the old and in with the new

《喜盈门》(xǐyíngmén)*In-laws* – a film directed by Zhao Huanzhang (赵焕章)in 1981

戏班(xìbān)a theatrical troupe;a theatrical company

戏报子(xìbàozi)an opera poster

戏词(xìcí)an actor's lines

戏法(xìfǎ)conjuring;juggling;a trick;magic

戏份儿(xìfènr)the scenes an actor can have in a show

戏馆子(xìguǎnzi)a theatre

戏剧(xìjù)a drama;a play

戏剧家(xìjùjiā)a dramatist

戏楼(xìlóu)a theatrical stage;a stage;an opera tower

戏路(xìlù)an acting style;a performing style

戏曲(xìqǔ)the traditional Chinese opera

戏文(xìwén)①an actor's lines②the Southern Opera

戏匣子(xìxiázi)a phonograph;a gramophone

戏言(xìyán)a joke, a humorous remark;to say something for fun

戏眼(xìyǎn) the play's keypoint; the most wonderful part of a play; the key scene(of a play)

戏园子(xìyuánzi) a theatre; an opera house

戏子(xìzi)(derog.) an actor or actress;a player

细软(xìruǎn) jewelry, expensive clothing and other valuables;valuables

细伢子(xìyázi) a child

细腰鼓(xìyāogǔ) a waist drum

细作(xìzuò) a spy;a secret agent

虾兵蟹将(xiābīng xièjiàng)(lit.) "shrimp soldiers and crab generals" – ineffective troops

虾皮(xiāpí) dried small shrimps

瞎掰(xiābāi) to talk irresponsibly; to talk nonsense

瞎吹(xiāchuī) to brag wildly about something;to shoot one's mouth off

瞎话(xiāhuà) lies

侠客(xiákè) a chivalrous swordsman; a knight-errant

侠士(xiáshì) a chivalrous person

侠义(xiáyì) chivalrous

狎妓(xiájì) to visit prostitutes; to go whoring

狎客(xiákè) a frequenter of brothels

下辈子(xiàbèizi) the next life

下不来台(xiàbuláitái) to be unable to get out of an embarrassing situation;to be unable to back down with good grace;to feel embarrassed

下策(xiàcè) a bad plan;a poor strategy

下乘(xiàchéng) ①(Buddhism) Hinayana;the Little Vehicle ②inferior quality

下地(xiàdì) ①to be born ②to go to the fields ③to leave a sickbed

下第(xiàdì) inferior

下凡(xiàfán) to descend to the world; to come down to earth

下放(xiàfàng) ①to transfer to a lower level; to be demoted ②to be transferred to work at the grass-roots level; to be sent down to work in the countryside

下岗(xiàgǎng) ①to be laid off;to be made redundant ②to come off sentry duty

下功夫(xiàgōngfu) to take pains; to devote time and energy; to concentrate one's efforts

下官(xiàguān) ①a low-level official ②I(a modest self-appellation for an official)

下海(xiàhǎi)(lit.) "to go to sea" – to go into business;to plunge into the commercial sea

下脚料(xiàjiǎoliào) leftovers (from industrial processing of materials)

下九流(xiàjiǔliú)the humble professions;lowly occupations

下酒菜(xiàjiǔcài)a dish that goes with alcoholic drinks;food which is a good match for wine

下里巴人(xiàlǐbārén)simple and crude folk songs;popular literature or art

下联(xiàlián)the second line or the lower line of a couplet

下马威(xiàmǎwēi)the severity shown by an official on assuming office;an initial display of force to show one's authority;to be firm at first

下人(xiàrén)a servant

下三烂(xiàsānlàn)①indecent,dirty, lacking self-respect ② an indecent person

下台阶(xiàtáijiē)to get out of a predicament;to emerge gracefully from an embarrassing situation

下堂(xiàtáng)①to descend from the hall②to be abandoned or divorced (by one's husband)

下乡(xiàxiāng)to go to the countryside

下乡知青(xiàxiāng zhīqīng)the educated youths(sent to the countryside during the Cultural Revolution)

下药(xiàyào)①to prescribe medicine ②to plant poison in something

下诏(xiàzhào)to issue an imperial edict

夏朝(xiàcháo)the Xia Dynasty(21st century – 16th century BC)

夏历(xiàlì)the lunar calendar

夏至(xiàzhì)the Summer Solstice

仙丹(xiāndān)the elixir of life

仙方(xiānfāng)a magical prescription;medicine prescribed by an immortal

仙姑(xiān'gū)①a female immortal;a female celestial②a sorceress

仙女(xiānnǚ)a female celestial; a fairy maiden

仙人(xiānrén)a celestial being; an immortal

仙人跳(xiānrén tiào)a beauty trap;a honey trap

仙山琼阁(xiānshān qiónggé)a jewelled palace amid the hills of fairyland

仙逝(xiānshì)(euphemism)to pass away

仙子(xiānzǐ)a female celestial; a fairy maiden

先妣(xiānbǐ)deceased mother;"my late mother"

先干为敬(xiāngānwéijìng)to drink first to show respect; to propose a toast to guests

先君(xiānjūn)deceased father;"my late father"

先考(xiānkǎo) deceased father; "my late father"

先礼后兵(xiānlǐ hòubīng) to take strong measures only after courteous ones fail; to try peaceful means before resorting to force; diplomacy before the use of force

先烈(xiānliè) a martyr

先农坛(xiānnóngtán) Xiannong Temple (where emperors worship the God of Agriculture in Beijing)

先秦(xiānqín) pre-qin(770 - 221BC)

先秦哲学(xiānqín zhéxué) pre-qin philosophy(770 - 221 BC)

先贤(xiānxián) the late sage; a sage of ancient times

鲜卑(xiānbēi) the Xianbei nationality (an ancient Chinese tribe)

闲磕牙(xiánkēyá) to have an idle chat

闲盘儿(xiánpánr) ①an unconnected or irrelevant matter ②other people's business; gossip

《闲情偶寄》(xiánqíng ǒujì) *Sketches of Idle Pleasure* - a book by Li Yu (李渔, 1610 - 1680) in 1671

弦子戏(xiánzixì) the Tri-chord opera (a local opera in Shandong)

贤达(xiándá) a prominent personage

贤内助(xiánnèizhù) ① an understanding wife ②my good wife

贤妻良母(xiánqī liángmǔ) a good wife and loving mother

咸丰帝(xiánfēngdì) Emperor Xianfeng [one of the emperors of the Qing Dynasty(1636 - 1912)]

涎着脸(xiánzheliǎn) to be brazen-faced; to be cheeky

衔冤(xiányuān) to nurse a bitter sense of wrong

显摆(xiǎnbai) to show off

显妣(xiǎnbǐ) honorable deceased mother; "my late mother"

显考(xiǎnkǎo) honorable deceased father; "my late father"

显灵(xiǎnlíng) theophany; (of a supernatural being) to reveal its presence or power

显身手(xiǎnshēnshǒu) to display one's talent or skill

显圣(xiǎnshèng) (of a ghost) to make its presence or power felt

县令(xiànlìng) county magistrate

县太爷(xiàntàiyé) county magistrate

县志(xiànzhì) general records of a county; county annals; local gazetteer

现成饭(xiànchéngfàn) ①ready food ②an unearned gain; a windfall

现大洋(xiàndàyáng) a silver dollar

现代中国文学(xiàndài zhōngguó wénxué) modern Chinese literature

现代中国小说(xiàndài zhōngguó xiǎo shuō) modern Chinese fiction

现世报(xiànshìbào) instant kama; timely retribution

现眼(xiànyǎn) to lose face; to make a fool of oneself

线人(xiànrén) an insider; a spy; an informer; an informant

线装(xiànzhuāng) the traditional thread binding of Chinese books

羡余(xiànyú) additional taxes (collected for the emperor)

献丑(xiànchǒu) to show oneself up; to show one's incompetence

献殷勤(xiànyīnqín) to flatter; to try to please somebody; to fawn over somebody

乡巴佬儿(xiāngbalǎor) a country bumpkin; a rustic; a yokel

《乡村爱情》(xiāngcūn àiqíng) *Love Stories in the Countryside* – a TV drama directed by Zhang Huizhong (张惠中) in 2005; *Village Loves*

乡规民约(xiāngguī mínyuē) a pact (made between and observed by locals); village laws; local rules and regulations

乡宦(xiānghuàn) the village gentry holding official positions

乡试(xiāngshì) the imperial examination at the provincial level; the provincial examination

乡土观念(xiāngtǔ guānniàn) provincialism

乡土文学(xiāngtǔ wénxué) native literature; nativist literature

乡土小说(xiāngtǔ xiǎoshuō) Native Fiction; Nativist Fiction

相风测雨(xiāngfēng cèyǔ) meteorological observation

相门户(xiāng ménhù) to visit the home of one's fiancé

相配(xiāngpèi) to be well matched; to be well suited to each other

相亲(xiāngqīn) the traditional custom of having a arranged blind date with one's future spouse; a blind date

《相亲》(xiāngqīn) *Blind Date* – a skit starring by Zhao Benshan (赵本山) and Huang Xiaojuan (黄晓娟) in 2011

相思(xiāngsī) lovesickness; to be lovesick

相中(xiāngzhòng) to be to one's liking; to take a fancy to something

相左(xiāngzuǒ) to fail to agree; to hold conflicting views; to be at odds with

香案(xiāng'àn) a long altar on which incense burners are placed; incense table

香饽饽(xiāngbōbo) ①a popular person ②something popular

香袋(xiāngdài) a sachet; a scent bag

香干(xiānggān) smoked bean curd

香港脚(xiānggǎngjiǎo) (lit.) "Hong

Kong foot" – athlete's foot

香闺(xiāng guī) a young lady's room; a boudoir

香灰(xiānghuī) the ash from burnt incense

香火(xiānghuǒ) ① joss sticks and candles burning (at a temple); worshippers ② the continuation of a family line

香火钱(xiānghuǒqián) offerings received from pilgrims and visitors

香客(xiāngkè) a Buddhist pilgrim

香炉(xiānglú) an incense burner

香钱(xiāngqián) offerings received from pilgrims and visitors

厢房(xiāngfáng) a wing; a wing-room

湘菜(xiāngcài) Hunan Cuisine

湘妃竹(xiāngfēizhú) mottled bamboo

湘江(xiāngjiāng) the Xiangjiang River (in Hunan Province)

湘剧(xiāngjù) Xiang opera; Hunan opera

湘绣(xiāngxiù) Xiang embroidery (popular in Hunan Province)

襄礼(xiānglǐ) an assistant to a funeral or wedding host

祥瑞(xiángruì) an auspicious sign; a propitious omen

祥云(xiángyún) auspicious clouds

祥兆(xiángzhào) a good omen

享年(xiǎngnián) to die at the age of; to live to

响当当(xiǎngdāngdāng) outstanding; noteworthy

响马(xiǎngmǎ) a robber; a bandit; a mounted highwayman

响头(xiǎngtóu) to kowtow noisily

饷银(xiǎngyín) military supplies; the soldier's pay

想不开(xiǎng bù kāi) to take something too much to heart; to take things too hard

想入非非(xiǎngrùfēifēi) to indulge in fantasy; to let one's fancy to run wild; to build castles in the air; to cry for the moon; to chase (after) the rainbow

向隅(xiàngyú) (lit.) "to face the corner" – to be disappointed because of a lack of

巷陌(xiàngmò) alleys; streets and lanes

巷战(xiàngzhàn) a street battle; street combat; to fight in the streets; house-to-house fighting

项庄舞剑,意在沛公(xiàngzhuāngwǔ jiàn, yìzài pèigōng) (lit.) "Xiang Zhuang (项庄) performed the sword dance as a cover for his attempt on Liu Bang's (刘邦) life" – to act with a hidden motive

相公(xiànggōng) ① husband ② a young man

相国(xiàngguó) prime minister

相国寺(xiàngguósì) the Xiangguo Temple (in Kaifeng, Henan Province)

相面(xiàngmiàn) to practice physiognomy; to tell somebody's fortune from the markings of the face

相声(xiàngshēng) cross-talk; a comic dialogue

相士(xiàngshì) a physiognomist

相手术(xiàngshǒushù) palmistry

相术(xiàngshù) fortune-telling by studying facial features; physiognomy

象棋(xiàngqí) Chinese chess

象形字(xiàngxíngzì) pictographic characters, pictogram

象牙之塔(xiàngyázhī tǎ) an ivory tower; the narrow art world (of the litterateur and artists who are removed from reality)

枭将(xiāojiàng) a very brave general

枭雄(xiāoxióng) a fierce and powerful person

宵小(xiāoxiǎo) a scoundrel; a rascal; a ganef

宵夜(xiāoyè) a late night snack; a night-time snack; a midnight snack

消夜(xiāoyè) a late night snack; a night-time snack; a midnight snack

逍遥派(xiāoyáopài) a carefree person; a happy-go-lucky person

萧规曹随(xiāoguī cáosuí) (lit.) "Cao Can(曹参) followed the rules set by Xiao He(萧何)" - to follow established rules; to follow in somebody's footsteps; to follow somebody exactly

萧墙(xiāoqiáng) a screen wall (facing the gate of a Chinese house)

萧蔷之祸(xiāoqiáng zhī huò) internal strife; trouble from within; a domestic dispute

销魂(xiāohún) to be overwhelmed with joy or sorrow

潇湘(xiāoxiāng) ①the drainage area of Xiaoshui River and Xiangjiang River ②the Xiangjiang River ③Hunan Province

霄汉(xiāohàn) sky; firmament

霄壤(xiāorǎng) heaven and earth

小白脸儿(xiǎobáiliǎnr) (lit.) "a young fair face" - a handsome, effeminate young man

小报告(xiǎobàogào) to tell tales about somebody; to make a secret complaint against somebody to their superior

小本经营(xiǎoběn jīngyíng) a small business; to run a small business; to operate on a shoestring; a low budget enterprise

小便宜(xiǎopiányi) small gain; petty advantage

小辫子(xiǎobiànzi) a mistake or

shortcoming (that may be exploited by others); a vulnerable point; an Achilles' heel

《小兵张嘎》(xiǎobīng zhānggǎ) *Zhang Ga, The Soldier Boy* – a film by Cui Wei (崔嵬, 1912 – 1979) in 1963

小不点儿(xiǎobùdiǎnr) a very little child; a tiny tot

小不忍则乱大谋(xiǎo bùrěn zé luàn dàmóu) a lack of tolerance in minor issues can destroy great plans

小菜(xiǎocài) ①pickled vegetables② an easy job

小产(xiǎochǎn) to have a miscarriage; to miscarry; a miscarriage; an abortion; a termination

小抄儿(xiǎochāor) a secret cheat-sheet; a slip of paper with facts, figures or answers to questions

小炒(xiǎochǎo) a stir-fry (cooked in a small wok)

《小城春秋》(xiǎochéng chūnqiū) *Spring And Autumn In A Small Town* – a novel by Gao Yunlan (高云览, 1910 – 1956) in 1952 – 1956; a film directed by Luo Tai (罗泰) in 1981

《小城之春》(xiǎochéng zhī chūn) *Spring in a Small Town* – a film directed by Fei Mu (费穆) in 1948

小乘(xiǎochéng) (Buddhism) the Little Vehicle; the Small Vehicle; Hinayana

小吃(xiǎochī) ① a snack; refreshments② a prepared dish

小春(xiǎochūn) an Indian summer

小聪明(xiǎo cōngmíng) a petty trick; cleverness in trivial matters

小打小闹(xiǎodǎ xiǎonào) on a small scale; in dribs and drabs

小旦(xiǎodàn) xiaodan (a young female role in traditional opera); an actress

小道儿消息(xiǎodàor xiāoxi) the grapevine; hearsay; rumor

小肚鸡肠(xiǎodùjīcháng) petty-minded; narrow-minded

小儿科(xiǎo'érkē) a piece of cake; as easy as pie; child's play

小二(xiǎo'èr) a young waiter

《小二黑结婚》(xiǎoèrhēi jiéhūn) *Little Erhei's Marriage* – a short story by Zhao Shuli [赵树理, 1906 – 1970) in 1943]; *Litter Erhei Gets Married*

小钢炮(xiǎogāngpào) ① a small-sized gun or cannon ② a frank and outspoken person

小姑子(xiǎogūzi) sister-in-law (husband's younger sister)

小褂(xiǎoguà) a Chinese-style shirt (worn next to the skin)

小鬼(xiǎoguǐ) ①an imp; a goblin②

little devil

小寒(xiǎohán) the Slight Cold (one of the 24 Chinese solar terms)

小红书(xiǎohóngshū) the Little Red Book - *Quotations from Chairman Mao*

《小花》(xiǎohuā) *Little Flower* - a film dierected by Zhang Zheng (张铮) in 1979

小花脸(xiǎohuāliǎn) a buffoon; a clown (in Chinese opera)

小皇帝(xiǎohuángdì) a little emperor; a spoiled boy

小家碧玉(xiǎojiā bìyù) a daughter of a humble family; a beautiful girl from a lower middle-class family; a pretty young lady of a humble birth

小家子气(xiǎojiāziqì) uneasy; small-minded; to appear nervous in public; vulgar and ill-at-ease

小脚(xiǎojiǎo) ①bound feet ②a timid and conservative person

小脚女人(xiǎojiǎo nǚrén) a woman with bound feet

《小街》(xiǎojiē) *Narrow Street* - a film directed by Yang Yanjin (杨延晋) in 1981

小金库(xiǎo jīnkù) a private coffer

小襟(xiǎojīn) the inner piece (on the right side of the front of a Chinese garment)

小九九(xiǎojiǔjiǔ) ①a multiplication table ②a little trick

小舅子(xiǎojiùzi) brother-in-law (wife's younger brother)

小剧场运动(xiǎojùchǎng yùndòng) the Little Theatre Movement (starting from 1919)

小楷(xiǎokǎi) the regular script in small characters (calligraphy)

小康(xiǎokāng) comparatively well-off; well-to-do; comfortably well-off; a relatively comfortable life

小两口儿(xiǎoliǎngkǒur) a young couple

小令(xiǎolìng) a short lyric; a short tune; a ditty

小龙(xiǎolóng) the snake (one of the Chinese Zodiac signs)

小满(xiǎomǎn) the Grain Budding (one of the 24 Chinese solar terms, usually falling on the 21st of May)

小门小户(xiǎomén xiǎohù) a poor humble family; a family of limited means and without powerful connections

小蜜(xiǎomì) the young mistress (of a rich or powerful person)

小名(xiǎomíng) a pet name; an infant name

小年(xiǎonián) (lit.) "the little Year" - the 23rd or 24th of the twelfth month of Chinese lunar year

小年夜(xiǎoniányè) the eve of the

Little Year (the 23rd or 24th of the twelfth month of Chinese lunar year)

小鸟依人(xiǎoniǎo yīrén)(lit.)"an endearing little bird" – to behave in a sweet and helpless way

小品(xiǎopǐn)①a skit; a short, light comedy (in the spoken drama style) ②a vignette; a sketch; an essay

小犬(xiǎoquǎn)(lit.)"a small dog" – my son

小人儿书(xiǎorénrshū) picture-story book; comic; picture book; children's book

小日子(xiǎorìzi) the easy life of a small family; the cozy and happy life of a small family or young couple

小三(xiǎosān) a mistress; the other woman

小生(xiǎoshēng) xiaosheng (a young man's role in the traditional opera)

小叔子(xiǎoshūzi) brother in law (husband's brother)

小暑(xiǎoshǔ) the Slight Heat (one of the 24 Chinese solar terms)

《小说月报》(xiǎoshuō yuèbào) *Fiction Monthly*; *Short Story Monthly*

小厮(xiǎosī)①a young male servant; a page boy; a footboy ② a boy; a young lad

小算盘(xiǎosuànpan) selfish calculations; petty considerations

《小孙屠》(xiǎosūntú) *Butcher Xiao Sun* – a play popular in the Song and Yuan Dynasties

小巫见大巫(xiǎowū jiàn dàwū)(lit.) "like a small sorcerer in the presence of a great one" – to pale into insignificance by comparison; a giant in the presence of a super-giant; to appear insignificant when compared with; to outshine

小媳妇(xiǎoxífu)①a young married woman ② the one who always gets blamed

《小巷深处》(xiǎoxiàng shēnchù) *The Depths of an Alley* – a short story by Lin Li(林莉, 1972 –) in 1994

小鞋(xiǎoxié)(lit.)"tight shoes" – a difficult situation (unfairly and deliberately created for somebody)

小心眼儿(xiǎoxīnyǎn) narrow-minded; full of petty considerations; a narrow mind

小婿(xiǎoxù) ① my son-in-law ② I (self-appellation of a son-in-law)

小雪(xiǎoxuě) the Slight Snow (one of the 24 Chinese solar terms)

小阳春(xiǎoyángchūn) warm weather in late autumn; an Indian summer

小姨子(xiǎoyízi) sister-in-law (wife's younger sister)

小意思(xiǎoyìsi) a mere trifle; a

small gift; a small token of appreciation

小灶(xiǎozào) special treatment; special mess (serving higher quality food for officers etc.)

小篆(xiǎozhuàn) the small seal script (calligraphy); the lesser seal script

小酌(xiǎozhuó) drinks and nibbles; to drink with simple foods or snacks

小字辈(xiǎozìbèi) youngster; younger generation

孝道(xiàodào) filial duty; to be a good son or daughter

孝服(xiàofú) ①mourning apparel ②a conventional period of mourning (for a deceased elder member of one's family)

《孝经》(xiàojīng) *The Classic of Filial Piety* - a Confucian classic

孝廉(xiàolián) filial piety and honesty

孝堂(xiào táng) a mourning hall

孝衣(xiàoyī) mourning dress; mourning apparel

《孝庄秘史》(xiàozhuāng mìshǐ) *Empress Dowager Xiaozhuang* - a TV drama directed by You Xiaogang (尤小刚) in 2002

效死(xiàosǐ) to be ready to give one's life for a course

校花(xiàohuā) a school beauty; the prettiest female student; a campus belle

校训(xiàoxùn) school motto

校园歌曲(xiàoyuán gēqǔ) campus ballads; campus songs

《笑傲江湖》(xiàoào jiānghú) *The Legendary Swordman* - a novel by Jin Yong(金庸, 1924 -) in 1967; a TV drama first released in 1984; a film first directed by Sun Zhong(孙仲) in 1978; *The Smiling Proud Wanderer*

笑柄(xiàobǐng) a laughingstock; a standing joke

笑场(xiàochǎng) to burst into uncontrollable laughter during acting

笑面虎(xiàomiànhǔ) (lit.) "a smiling tiger" - an outwardly kind but inwardly cruel person; a wicked person with a hypocritical smile; a wolf in sheep's clothing

笑星(xiàoxīng) a comic star; a famous comedian

歇后语(xiēhòuyǔ) a two-part allegorical saying

邪道(xiédào) a depraved life; vice; evil ways

邪乎(xiéhu) unusual; extraordinary; fantastic; abnormal

邪门儿(xiéménr) strange; odd; abnormal; irregular

邪魔歪道(xiémó wāidào) (lit.) "evil demons and heretics" - unorthodox ways; crooked ways; dishonest practices; immoral or illegal doings

邪气(xiéqì) an evil emanation; an evil influence; a perverse trend

邪说(xiéshuō) heretical ideas; a fallacy; a heresy

偕老(xiélǎo) to grow old together

谐趣园(xiéqùyuán) the Garden of Harmonious Interests (in the Summer Palace in Beijing)

《鞋钉》(xiédīng) *Shoe Spikes* – a skit starring by Huang Hong(黄宏) and Gong Hanlin(巩汉林) in 1997

写意(xiěyì) freehand brushwork (in traditional Chinese painting)

写意画(xiěyìhuà) a freehand painting

泄底(xiè dǐ) to expose what is at the bottom of something

泄愤(xièfèn) to give vent to spite; to vent one's anger; to vent one's indignation

泄气(xièqì) to lose heart; to be discouraged; to feel disheartened; to feel like giving up

卸包袱(xièbāofu) to unburden

亵渎(xièdú) to profane; to violate; to blaspheme; blasphemy; profanity

亵衣(xièyī) underwear; underclothes

谢表(xièbiǎo) a letter of gratitude to one's sovereign

谢恩(xiè'ēn) to express profound gratitude to; to express thanks for great favors

谢客(xièkè) to refuse to meet visitors or guests; to decline to receive visitors

谢礼(xièlǐ) a gift in token of gratitude; a return present

谢媒(xièméi) to express thanks to the matchmaker

谢世(xièshì) to depart from this world; to pass away; to die

《谢瑶环》(xièyáohuán) *Lady Xie Yaohuan* – a Beijing opera adapted in 1961

谢罪(xièzuì) to apologize for an offence; to offer an apology

解数(xièshù) skills

邂逅(xièhòu) to meet unexpectedly; to meet by chance; to run into somebody

心肠(xīncháng) heart; intention; state of mind; affections; sympathies

心得(xīndé) what one has learnt from work or study; a personal understanding or experience

心扉(xīnfēi) heart; mind; way of thinking

心腹(xīnfù) a trusted subordinate; a henchman; a bosom friend; a confidant

心肝(xīngān) ①conscience②darling

心寒(xīnhán) to be bitterly disappointed

心黑(xīnhēi) to have a heart of gall;evil

心火(xīnhuǒ)①internal heat(traditional medicine)②hidden anger;hidden fury

心机(xīnjī)scheming;calculating

心计(xīnjì) calculation; scheming;guile

心上人(xīnshàngrén)a lover;a sweetheart

心术(xīnshù)①intention;design②calculation;scheming;guile

心田(xīntián)①the heart②the intention

心学(xīnxué)the School of the Mind (a school of Confucianism)

心仪(xīnyí)to admire in one's heart

心意拳(xīnyìquán) imitative boxing (a style of shadow boxing)

辛丑条约(xīnchǒu tiáoyuē)The Xinchou Treaty; The Boxer Protocol (1901)

辛词派(xīncípài) the School of the Xin lyrics - a school led by Xin Qiji (辛弃疾,1140 - 1207)

辛亥革命(xīnhài gémìng)the Revolution of 1911;the 1911 Revolution

《新编五代史平话》(xīnbiān wǔdài shǐ pínghuà) *Newly Compiled Popular Stories of the Five Dynasties* - a story-telling script written in the Song Dynasty

新长征突击手(xīnchángzhēng tūjī shǒu)(lit.)"a Pace-setter in the new Long March"- an honorific title for those who have made a particular contribution to China's modernization program

新房(xīnfáng)a bridal chamber

新妇(xīnfù)a bride

新感觉派小说(xīngǎnjuépài xiǎo shuō)Neo-Sensualist fiction

新官上任三把火(xīnguān shàngrèn sān bǎhuǒ) a new official applies strict measures; a newly appointed official works hard to show his efficiency;a new broom sweeps clean

新贵(xīnguì)a parvenu;an upstart

新华门(xīnhuàmén)Xinhua Gate(at the entrance to Zhongnanhai in Beijing)

《新华字典》(xīnhuá zìdiǎn) *New China Dictionary*; *Xinhua Dictionary*

新欢(xīnhuān)a new sweetheart

《新警察故事》(xīn jǐngchá gùshì) *New Police Story* - a film directed by Chen Musheng(陈木胜)in 2004

《新龙门客栈》(xīn lóngmén kèzhàn) *New Dragon Inn* - a film directed by Li Huimin(李惠民) in 1992

新媒体艺术(xīnméitǐ yìshù) new media art

《新女性》(xīn nǚxìng) *New Women* – a film directed by Cai Chusheng(蔡楚生) in 1935

《新青年》(xīnqīngnián) *New Youth* – a magazine from the 1920s

新儒家(xīnrújiā) Neo-Confucianism; a Neo-Confucianist

《新上海滩》(xīn shànghǎitān) *Once upon A Time in Shanghai* – a film directed by Pan Wenjie(潘文杰) in 1996; a TV drama directed by Gao Xixi(高希希) in 2007

新时期文学(xīnshíqī wénxué) literature of the new epoch; literature of the new age

新四军(xīnsìjūn) the New Fourth Army (an army led by the Chinese Communist Party during the Anti-Japanese, 1937 – 1945)

新文化运动(xīnwénhuà yùndòng) the New Culture Movement (1915 – 1919)

新禧(xīnxǐ) good fortune for the new year

新写实小说(xīnxiěshí xiǎoshuō) New Realist Fiction; a neo-realist novel

新秀 (xīnxiù) an up-and-coming youngster; a promising young person; a rising star

新学(xīnxué) the new learning (the natural science and social science introduced from the west in the late Qing Dynasty)

新月派 (xīnyuèpài) the Crescent Moon school of poetry (starting from 1926)

新月社 (xīnyuèshè) the Crescent Moon Society (founded in 1923 in Beijing)

新乐府运动(xīnyuèfǔ yùndòng) the New Music-Bureau Movement (a poetry movement in the Tang Dynasty, 618 – 907)

信步 (xìnbù) to walk aimlessly; to stroll; to take a leisurely walk

信口雌黄(xìnkǒu cíhuáng) to make irresponsible remarks; to talk nonsense; to sound off randomly; to make a malicious remark carelessly

信史(xìnshǐ) a reliable historical account

信士(xìnshì) ①a believer; a follower of religion②an honest man

信天游(xìntiānyóu) Free As A Bird (a kind of Shaanxi local melody)

信物 (xìnwù) a token; a trophy (as proof of something); a keepsake

兴安岭 (xīng'ānlǐng) the Xing'an Mountains (in the east of Inner Mongolian Autonomous Region and north of Heilongjiang Province)

兴中会 (xīngzhōnghuì) the Revive China Society (established by Sun

Yatsen in 1894, a precursor of the Nationalist Party)

星占学(xīngzhānxué) astrology

刑部(xíngbù) the Ministry of Punishments (in imperial China); the Board of Punishments

刑部大堂(xíngbù dàtáng) the hall of the Board of Punishments

刑部尚书(xíngbù shàngshū) Minister of Justice

刑部侍郎(xíngbù shìláng) Deputy Minister of Justice

刑房(xíngfáng) ①officials in charge of case files②torture chamber

刑房小吏(xíngfáng xiǎo lì) a minor official of the torture chamber

刑具(xíngjù) instruments of torture

刑名师爷(xíngmíng shīyé) a judicial assistant; a yamen secretary (handling criminal cases)

刑事诉讼(xíngshì sùsòng) (law) a criminal lawsuit; a criminal action; a criminal prosecution; criminal procedure

刑杖(xíngzhàng) a bludgeon(used for torture)

行草(xíngcǎo) the running cursive script(calligraphy)

行房(xíngfáng) to have sexual intercourse; to make love

行宫(xínggōng) imperial palace (for short stays away from the capital)

行脚僧(xíngjiǎosēng) an itinerant monk; a wandering monk

行楷(xíngkǎi) (calligraphy) the running regular script

行令(xínglìng) ①to send an order② to play drinking games

行门户(xíng ménhù) to give a gift to (friends or relatives at weddings or funerals, etc.)

行囊(xíngnáng) baggage; luggage; a kitbag; a traveling bag

行人情(xíngrénqíng) to send a gift; to do what is required by social etiquette

行善(xíngshàn) to be charitable; to perform charitable deeds

行书(xíngshū) the running script (calligraphy)

行头(xíngtou) ① actor's costumes, props and paraphernalia ② dress; clothing; apparel; outfit

行文(xíngwén) ①the style or manner of writing②to send an official communication to other organizations

行政村(xíngzhèng cūn) an administrative village(usu. in rural areas)

形拳(xíngquán) Form Boxing(a style of shadow boxing)

形神(xíngshén) body and soul

形声字(xíngshēngzì) pictophonetic character; a character consisting of a radical and a phonetic element

形意拳(xíngyìquán) Imitative Boxing (a style of shadow boxing)

省墓(xǐngmù) to tend a grave; to visit one's parents' or elders' graves

省亲(xǐngqīn) to pay a visit to one's parents or elders

醒酒(xǐngjiǔ) to dispel the effects of alcohol; to sober up

醒脾(xǐngpí) to relieve uneasiness of body and mind

《醒世恒言》(xǐngshì héngyán) *Stories to Awaken the World* - a book written by Feng Menglong(冯梦龙,1574 - 1646) in 1627

《醒世姻缘传》(xǐngshì yīnyuán zhuàn) *The Story of a Marital Fate to Awaken the World*; *Marriage as Retribution* - a novel by Xizhou Sheng (西周生) in the Qing Dynasty

杏眼(xìngyǎn) almond eyes (indicative of beauty)

凶年(xiōngnián) a famine year; a failed harvest; a lean year

凶煞(xiōngshà) a demon; a fiend

凶宅(xiōngzhái) a haunted house; an unlucky abode

凶兆(xiōngzhào) something sinister; an ill omen; a threat

匈奴(xiōngnú) the Xiongnu (an ancient nationality in China)

雄关(xióngguān) an impregnable pass

雄黄酒(xiónghuángjiǔ) the realgar liquor; liquor seasoned with ruby sulphur

雄主(xióngzhǔ) a ruler of great talent and bold vision

熊包(xióngbāo) ①a helpless and impotent man ②a good-for-nothing

熊瞎子(xióngxiāzi) a bear

熊样(xióng yàng) stupid or cowardly appearance

休书(xiūshū) a divorce letter (from husband to wife announcing divorce)

修长城(xiū chángchéng) (lit.) "to build the Great Wall" - to play Mah-jong

修道(xiūdào) to cultivate oneself (according to a religious doctrine)

修地球(xiūdìqiú) (lit.) "to repair the globe" - to engage in farming

修脚师(xiūjiǎoshī) a pedicurist

修身(xiūshēn) to cultivate one's moral character

修仙(xiūxiān) to cultivate oneself to be immortal

修行(xiūxíng) to cultivate oneself (according to a religious doctrine)

秀才(xiùcai) ①a xiucai (a scholar who passed the imperial examination at the county level) ②a scholar

秀才遇见兵,有理说不清(xiùcai yùjiàn bīng, yǒulǐ shuōbùqīng) despite being right, a scholar can never vindicate himself against a military man; eloquent reasoning cannot overcome military force

秀士(xiù shì)a scholar;a man of outstanding talent

绣房(xiùfáng)bedchamber(of a young girl)

绣花鞋(xiùhuāxié)embroidered shoes

绣花枕头(xiùhuāzhěntou)(lit.)"an embroidered pillow"- an outwardly attractive but worthless person

绣球(xiùqiú)an embroidered silk ball

戌时(xūshí)the period between 7 p. m. and 9 p. m.

须生(xūshēng)xusheng(the elderly male character in Chinese opera)

虚火(xūhuǒ)excessive internal heat because of general debility as defined in Chinese Medicine

虚岁(xūsuì)the nominal age(the age of a person, usu. one year old at birth and one year more each lunar new year)

虚症(xūzhèng)asthenic symptoms (Chinese Medicine);symptoms indicating deficiencies

《徐九经升官记》(xújiǔjīng shēngguān jì)*The Story of Xu Jiujing's Promotion* - a Beijing opera directed by Yu Xiaoyu(余笑予)in 1980

《徐霞客游记》(xúxiákè yóujì)*Travel Notes of Xu Xiake*; *Travels of Xu Xiake* - a book by Xu Xiake(徐霞客,1587 - 1641)in 1642

《许茂和他的女儿们》(xǔmào hé tāde nǚ'érmen)*Xu Mao and His Daughters* - a novel by Zhou Keqin (周克芹)in 1978;a film directed by Wang Yan(王炎)in 1981;a TV drama directed by Shu Chongfu(舒崇福)in 2009

许配(xǔpèi)to be betrothed to

序跋(xùbá)preface and postscript

叙旧(xùjiù)to talk about the old days;to talk about the past

续命汤(xùmìngtāng)a life-saving medical decoction

续弦(xùxián)to remarry(after the death of one's wife)

轩辕(xuānyuán)the Yellow Emperor

宣笔(xuānbǐ)a Chinese-ink brush;a writing brush

宣德(xuāndé)Xuande(the reign, 1426 - 1435,the title of Xuanzong, the fifth emperor of the Ming Dynasty,1368 - 1644)

宣和(xuānhé)Xuanhe[the reign (1119 - 1125), the title of Huizong, emperors of the Song Dynasty,960 - 1279]

宣统(xuān tǒng)Xuantong[the reign (1908 - 1912, the title of Emperor Pu Yi, the last emperor of the Qing Dynasty,1636 - 1912)]

宣叙调(xuānxùdiào) recitative (an operatic style)

宣召(xuānzhào) to call to worship; to summon to the imperial court

宣旨(xuānzhǐ) to proclaim an imperial edict

宣纸(xuānzhǐ) *xuan* paper (high quality paper for traditional Chinese painting and calligraphy); a Chinese art paper

玄乎(xuánhu) incredible; unreliable; fantastic

玄机(xuánjī) ①a profound theory ② mysterious principles

玄教(xuánjiào) the Xuan Sect of Taoism

玄女(xuánnǚ) Xuannu (one of the Taoist immortals); Goddess of the Ninth Heaven

玄诗(xuánshī) metaphysical poetry

玄孙(xuánsūn) a great-great-grandson

玄武(xuánwǔ) ①a tortoise ②God of Water ③God of the Northern sky

玄武湖(xuánwǔ hú) Xuanwu lake (in Nanjing, Jiangsu province)

玄学(xuánxué) metaphysics; the Metaphysical School [in the Wei (220 -265) and the Jin (265 -420) Dynasties]

玄奘(xuánzàng) Monk Xuanzang (a Buddhist monk in the Tang Dynasty)

悬棺葬(xuánguān zàng) a cliff-side burial; a cave burial

悬壶(xuánhú) (lit.) "to hang up a gourd or bottle (as the sign for a clinic)" - to practice medicine;

悬空寺(xuánkōngsì) the Suspended Temple; the Hanging Temple (in Shanxi province)

悬梁刺股(xuánliáng cìgǔ) (lit.) "to tie one's hair on the house beam and jab one's side with an awl to keep oneself awake" - to submerge oneself in study; to study assiduously

璇玑(xuánjī) ①the armillary sphere ②the first four stars in the Big Dipper ③the Big Dipper ④a hinge; a crux

渲染(xuànrǎn) ①to apply colors to a drawing ②to exaggerate; to play up

《薛仁贵传奇》(xuērénguì chuánqí) *The Legend of Xue Rengui* - a TV drama dierected by Ding Yangguo (丁仰国) in 2006

削发(xuēfà) tonsure; to be tonsured (for a religious life); to take the tonsure

削籍(xuējí) to depose; to remove from office; to be dismissed

削籍为民(xuējí wèimín) to be deposed and become a commoner

穴位(xuéwèi) an acupoint; an acupuncture point

学部(xuébù)Ministry of Imperial Education

学府(xuéfǔ)a seat of learning;an institute of higher learning

学官(xuéguān) officials in charge of education

学棍(xuégùn)scoundrels in the educational world;academic tyrants

学究(xuéjiū)a pedant;a scholar

学堂(xuétáng)a school

学子(xuézǐ)a student

噱头(xuétóu) a stunt; gimmick; a trick

雪耻(xuěchǐ) to avenge an insult; to avenge oneself

血本(xuèběn) hard-earned capital; original capital

血仇(xuèchóu) a blood feud; a vendetta

血气(xuèqì) vigor; courage and uprightness;vitality

血亲(xuèqīn) blood kin; consanguinity

《血色浪漫》(xuèsè làngmàn) *Romantic Life* – a novel by Du Liang(都梁,1954 –)in 2004;a TV drama directed by Teng Wenji(滕文骥)in 2004

血书(xuèshū) a blood letter; a letter written in blood

血洗(xuèxǐ)to slaughter;a bloodbath

血债(xuèzhài) a blood debt; a debt of blood

血战(xuèzhàn)a bloody battle;a sanguinary battle

熏肉(xūnròu)smoked meat;bacon

寻短见(xún duǎnjiàn)to try to commit suicide;to attempt suicide

寻根文学(xúngēn wénxué)Root-Seeking Literature (starting from the 1980s)

寻开心(xún kāixīn)to make fun of;to seek amusement;to look for distractions

巡捕(xúnbǔ)①to go on a tour of inspection;to track down and arrest② a policeman

巡捕房(xúnbǔfáng) a former police station

巡抚(xúnfǔ)the provincial governor; Grand Coordinator;imperial inspector

巡更(xúngēng)to keep night watch

巡幸(xúnxìng)(of a monarch)to go on an inspection tour

旬日(xúnrì)ten days

荀派演员(xúnpài yǎnyuán)an actor from the Xun School in Peiking Opera[learned from Xun Huisheng(荀慧生,1900 – 1968)]

《荀子》(xúnzǐ) *The Book of Master Xun* – a book by Xunzi(荀子,313 – 238 BC)

循吏(xúnlì)an obedient or upright official

训诂(xùngǔ)exegetical studies of ancient texts;textual exegesis;the explanations of words in ancient books;gloss

训诂学(xùngǔxué)exegetics;textual exegesis;the critical interpretation of ancient texts

徇情(xùnqíng)to act wrongly out of personal considerations;to practice favoritism

徇私(xùnsī)to practice favoritism

逊色(xùnsè)to be inferior to;to be in the shade of

殉国(xùnguó)to die for one's country

殉节(xùnjié)to die to preserve one's chastity

殉情(xùnqíng)to die for love;to commit suicide for love

殉葬(xùnzàng)to be buried alive(with the dead)

殉职(xùnzhí)to die a martyr at one's post;to die in the line of duty

Y

丫环(yāhuan)a servant girl;a waiting maid

丫头(yātou)①a daughter②a servant girl;a slave girl③a girl;a young woman

丫头片子(yātoupiànzi)a girl(jokingly)

压宝(yābǎo)to bet;to stake

压不住台(yābùzhùtái)to be unable to control the audience or the situation

压场(yāchǎng)①to keep the situation and the audience under one's control②to serve as the grand finale

压惊(yājīng)to help somebody get over a shock

压境(yājìng)to press on to the border

压卷之作(yājuàn zhī zuò)the top-ranking work(essay,poem,calligraphy,painting,etc.);masterpiece

压岁钱(yāsuìqián)lucky money(for children in the Spring Festival)

压台(yātái)to present the last theatrical performance

压台戏(yātáixì)the last item on a theatrical programme

压寨夫人(yāzhài fūrén)(lit.)"the mistress of the fort"-the wife of a brigand chief

压阵(yāzhèn)to hold the line;to keep a situation well under one's control

压制茶(yāzhìchá)compressed tea-leaves;pressed tea

压轴戏(yāzhòuxì)the last part in a performance;the climax of a performance;an excellent or attractive ending;a grand finale

压轴子(yāzhòuzi)the grand finale

押宝(yābǎo)to bet;to stake

押差(yāchāi)①to be entrusted to be an escort②an escort for a convict

押解(yājiè)①to send convicts or captives②to escort

押契(yāqì)①a mortgage contract ②mortgage

押头(yātóu)mortgage;guarantees

押韵(yāyùn)rhyme

垭口(yākǒu)a narrow mountain pass; a pass(between hills or mountains)

鸦片战争(yāpiàn zhànzhēng)The Opium War; the Opium Wars[including The First Opium War(1840–1842) and The Second Opium War(1856–1860)]

《鸦片战争》(yāpiàn zhànzhēng)*The Opium War*–a film directed by Xie Jin(谢晋)in 1997

鸭黄(yāhuáng)a face powder for women popular in the Tang Dynasty

鸭绿江(yālùjiāng)the Yalu River(in Jilin province)

牙行(yáháng)①a brokerage firm(in old China)②a middleman;a broker agent

牙慧(yáhuì)remarks or opinions (made by others)

牙祭(yájì)a fine meal

牙轿(yájiào)an ivory sedan chair;a sedan chair decorated with ivory

牙口(yákǒu)①the age of a draught animal(indicated by the number of its teeth)②the condition of an old person's teeth

牙侩(yákuài)a middleman

牙牌(yápái)an eburnean domino; a domino

牙婆(yápó)a woman engaging in female trafficking;a female trafficker

牙商(yáshāng)a middleman;a broker

牙子(yázi)①a middleman;a broker ②a child

崖山之战(yáshān zhī zhàn)the Battle of Yashan(in 1279)

睚眦必报(yázì bìbào)(lit.)"to seek revenge just for an angry look"–to be petty and vengeful

衙门(yámen)yamen; a government office;a magistrate's office

衙门作风(yámen zuòfēng)a bureaucratic working style

衙内(yánèi)①imperial bodyguards② the son of a high official

衙役(yáyì)a yamen runner;a yamen errand boy

哑巴亏(yǎbākuī)an unutterable grievance;suffering in silence

哑场(yǎchǎng)awkward silence(at a meeting)

哑号儿(yǎhàor)a secret signal

哑谜(yǎmí)a riddle

雅号(yǎhào)①an elegant name②

a nickname

雅怀(yǎhuái) elegant feelings or sentiments

雅教(yǎjiào) ①to ask for advice or comments②your esteemed opinion; your excellent advice

雅量(yǎliàng) ①magnanimity; generosity②drinking capacity

雅鲁藏布江(yǎlǔzàngbùjiāng) the Yalung Zangbo (Yalu Tsangpo) River (in the Tibet Autonomous Region)

雅趣(yǎqù) a cultivated or refined taste

雅人(yǎrén) a refined scholar

雅什(yǎshí) refined poetry and prose

雅士(yǎshì) a refined scholar

雅兴(yǎxìng) an aesthetic mood; an inspiration

雅驯(yǎxùn) elegant diction

雅言(yǎyán) the standard language (in ancient China)

雅意(yǎyì) ①noble sentiment②your kindness; your kind offer

雅乐(yǎyuè) ceremonial or court music (in ancient times)

雅贼(yǎzéi) a book thief

雅正(yǎzhèng) ①standard②"please be so kind as to correct my errors"

雅座(yǎzuò) a private room (in a restaurant, hotel, etc); the most comfortable seats in a restaurant

轧马路(yàmǎlù) (colloquial) to roam the streets – to take a walk with one's lover

亚父(yàfù) a revered man (who is second only to one's father); a teacher

亚赛(yàsài) can be compared to

亚圣(yàshèng) the second sage, ie Mencius

亚运村(yàyùncūn) the Asian Games Village

压板(yàbǎn) a seesaw

烟袋(yāndài) a long-stemmed pipe

烟袋锅(yāndàiguō) ①the bowl of a long-stemmed pipe; pipe bowl②a long-stemmed pipe

烟袋荷包(yāndài hébāo) a tobacco pouch

烟灯(yāndēng) an opium lamp

烟斗(yāndǒu) ①a (tobacco) pipe②a cigarette holder

烟膏(yāngāo) opium paste

烟鬼(yānguǐ) ①an opium addict②a heavy smoker; a chain smoker

《烟壶》(yānhú) *Snuff Bottle* – a novelette by Deng Youmei (邓友梅, 1931 –); a TV drama directed by Li Baotian (李保田) in 1995

烟花(yānhuā) a firework

烟火(yānhuǒ) ①fireworks②cooked food③fire beacons

烟火食(yānhuǒshí) cooked food

烟岚(yānlán)mist in the mountains

烟霞癖(yānxiápǐ)①a love of sightseeing②opium addiction;an opium addict

胭脂(yānzhi)rouge

燕山(yānshān) Yan Mountain; Mt. Yan(in Hebei province)

燕许大手笔(yānxǔ dàshǒubǐ) the well-known writers Zhang Shuo(张说,667 -730)and Su Ting(苏颋,670 -727)

阉党(yāndǎng) a faction surrounding court eunuchs

阉割(yāngē)to castrate

阉宦(yānhuàn)a eunuch

阉人(yānrén) a eunuch; a castrated person

阉寺(yānsì)a eunuch

阏氏(yānzhī) the principal wife of a Xiongnu monarch

腌菜(yāncài)salted vegetable;pickle

腌货(yānhuò)salted food

延安精神(yán'ān jīngshén) the Yan'an spirit(the spirit of self-reliance and hard struggle, 1936 - 1948)

延安整风运动(yán'ān zhěngfēng yùn dòng) the Yan'an rectification movement(1942 -1944)

延阁(yángé) library(in the imperial palace)

严师出高徒(yánshī chū gāotú)capable students are trained by strict teachers;a strict teacher produces high-achieving students

妍媸(yánchī)beauty and ugliness

言官(yánguān) a counselor to the emperor

言和(yánhé) to make peace; to become reconciled

言欢(yánhuān)to chat cheerfully

言路(yánlù) opportunities to voice views

言情小说(yánqíng xiǎoshuō) romantic fiction;sentimental novels

炎帝(yándì)Emperor Yan,one of the earlist ancestors of Chinese nation

炎黄(yánhuáng) Emperor Yan and Emperor Huang(ancestors of Chinese nation)

炎黄子孙(yánhuáng zǐsūn)(lit.) "the descendants of Emperor Yan and Emperor Huang" - Chinese people

炎凉世态(yánliáng shìtài)the way of the world;snobbery

炎热地狱(yánrè dìyù)(Buddhism) the Hell of Burning;Inferno

盐票(yánpiào)a salt coupon

盐商(yánshāng)a salt trader

盐枭(yánxiāo)a salt smuggler

阎罗(yánluó)Yama,King of Hell

阎王(yánwang)①Yama;King of Hell ②an extremely cruel and violent person

阎王殿(yánwangdiàn)the Palace of Hell;Yama's palace

阎王爷(yánwangyé)①Yama;King of Hell②an extremely cruel and violent person

阎王账(yánwangzhàng)usury;a usurious loan;a loan from a loan shark

颜李学派(yánlǐ xuépài)the School of Yan Yuan(颜元,1635－1704)and Li Gong(李塨,1659－1733)

《颜氏家训》(yánshì jiāxùn)*The Admonitions of the Yan Family* － a book by Yan Zhitui(颜之推,531－595)

颜体(yántǐ)the Yan style[a calligraphic style created by Yan Zhenqing(颜真卿,709－784)]

颜谢(yánxiè)the two great poets in ancient times named Yan Yanzhi(颜延之,384－456)and Xie Lingyun(谢灵运,385－433)

檐马(yánmǎ)a wind chime hung from the eaves

檐牙(yányá)projecting tiles(at the edge of a roof)

衍文(yǎnwén)redundant characters and sentences(due to misprints or copying errors)

偃蹇(yǎnjiǎn)①to stand tall and erect②arrogant③exhausted

偃旗息鼓(yǎnqí xīgǔ)(lit.)"lower the flags and silence the drums"－to cease or stop all activities

偃师戏(yǎnshīxì)a puppet show

偃武修文(yǎnwǔ xiūwén)to desist from military activities and encourage culture and education

偃月(yǎnyuè)①the crescent moon②a crescent-moon shape;a crescent

偃月刀(yǎnyuèdāo)a crescent-moon-shaped sword;a falchion used by Guan Yu,a charather in *The Three king doms*

眼波(yǎnbō)a glance;a woman's bewitching glance

眼馋(yǎnchán)to covet;to be envious

眼毒(yǎndú)sharp-eyed

眼风(yǎnfēng)a meaningful glance;a meaningful gaze

眼福(yǎnfú)a feast for the eyes;a visual treat;a visual feast

眼观六路,耳听八方(yǎnguān liùlù,ěrtīng bāfāng)to be all eyes and ears;to be on the alert;to be listening and on the look-out

眼红(yǎnhóng)①jealous②furious③green-eyes

眼热(yǎnrè)to cast covetous eyes at something

眼中钉,肉中刺(yǎnzhōng dīng,ròu zhōng cì)a thorn in one's side

眼拙(yǎnzhuō)my bad eyes;my bad memory(often used to apologise for not recalling sombody)

演义(yǎnyì) historical novel; historical romance

砚池(yànchí) an inkstone; an inkslab

砚弟(yàndì) a junior fellow student

砚耕(yàngēng) to make a living by writing

砚石(yànshí) an inkstone

砚台(yàntái) an inkstone; an ink slab

砚兄(yànxiōng) a senior fellow student

砚友(yànyǒu) a fellow student

宴安鸩毒(yàn'ān zhèndú) pleasure-seeking is like drinking poison; succumbing to the desires of the flesh will bring harm

宴尔(yàn'ěr) newly married

晏驾(yànjià) the death of an emperor; to die; to pass away

《晏子春秋》(yànzǐ chūnqiū) *Yanzi's Spring and Autumn Annals* – a book by Yan Ying(晏婴,578 – 500 BC)

艳福(yànfú) to be lucky in love; to be lucky with women

艳诗(yànshī) erotic poetry

《艳阳天》(yànyángtiān) *Bright Spring Day* – a novel by Hao Ran (浩然, 1932 – 2008) in 1964; *Bright Sunny Skies*

艳遇(yànyù) a love affair; an affair

验明正身(yànmíng zhèngshēn) to verify the identity of a convict prior to execution

焰口(yànkǒu) (Buddhism) hungry ghosts(who spit fire)

雁门关(yànménguān) the Yanmen Pass(in Shanxi province)

雁塔提名(yàntǎtímíng) (lit.) "to have one's name inscribed in the Wild Goose Pagoda" – to have a high honor conferred on one

雁杳鱼沉(yànyǎo yúchén) to receive no news or letters

燕尔(yàn'ěr) newly married

燕尔新婚(yàn'ěr xīnhūn) newly married

燕好(yànhǎo) to be very fond of each other; to be happily married

燕京(yānjīng) (a former name for) Beijing

燕乐(yànyuè) music at a banquet

燕乐大曲(yànyuè dàqǔ) the court banquet music

燕乐二十八调(yànyuè èrshíbādiào) a kind of ancient Chinese musical system[popular in the Sui (581 – 618) and the Tang(618 – 907) Dynasties]

《燕乐考原》(yànyuè kǎoyuán) *On the Origin of the Court Banquet Music* – a book by Ling Tingkan(凌廷堪,1755 – 1809)

燕礼(yànlǐ) a feast for the emperor, dukes and ministers

燕雀安知鸿鹄之志(yànquè ānzhī hónghú zhī zhì)(lit.)"how could a sparrow understand the ambitions of a swan?"- common people can never understand the ambitions of the great

燕婉之欢(yànwǎn zhī huān) domestic harmony; the harmonious bond between husband and wife

燕窝(yànwō) edible bird's nest

咽气(yànqì) to die

央中(yāngzhōng) to ask somebody to act as a middleman

殃榜(yāngbǎng) an obituary notice giving details of the deceased person

秧歌(yāngge) yangge or *yangko* (a popular rural folk dance)

秧歌剧(yānggejù) the yangge opera (originated in Yan'an in Shanxi province)

秧歌舞(yānggewǔ) the yangge dance (popular in rural areas)

鞅掌(yāngzhǎng) to be fully occupied with business

扬幡招魂(yángfān zhāohún)(lit.) "to fly a funeral banner to summon a dead person's soul"- try to revive what is obsolete

扬剧(yángjù) Yang opera (popular in Yangzhou, Jiangsu province)

扬马(yángmǎ) two famous Han Dynasty poets named Yang Xiong(扬雄,53 BC-18 AD) and Sima Xiangru(司马相如,179-127 BC)

扬琴(yángqín) a dulcimer

扬州八怪(yángzhōu bāguài) the Eight Eccentrics of Yangzhou; the eight famous painters who broke with traditions of Chinese painting and blazed new, unconventional trails in integrating painting with poetry and calligraphy in Yangzhou during the reign of Emperor Qianlong(乾隆,1711-1799)

《扬州画舫录》(yángzhōu huàfǎnglù) *Reminiscences from the Pleasure-boats of Yangzhou* - a book by Li Dou(李斗) in 1795

扬州十日(yángzhōu shírì) the 1645 massacre in Yangzhou (which lasted ten days)

扬子鳄(yángzǐ'è) a Chinese alligator

羊肠小道(yángcháng xiǎodào) a narrow, winding road; a narrow meandering footpath

羊车(yángchē) ① an imperial carriage ② a small goat-drawn cart (used in the palace) ③ a well-decorated vehicle ④ a small car

羊倌(yángguān) a shepherd

羊毫(yángháo) a writing brush made of goat's hair

羊角风(yángjiǎofēng) epilepsy

羊肉串(yángròuchuàn)shish kebab; mutton shashlik; barbecued mutton skewers

《羊肉串》(yángròuchuàn) *Mutton Shashlik* – a skit starring Chen Peisi (陈佩斯) and Zhu Shimao(朱时茂) in 1986

阳春(yángchūn)springtime

阳春白雪(yángchūn báixuě) ① *The Spring Snow* – a piece of ancient music in the Tang Dynasty ② highbrow art and literature

阳春面(yángchūnmiàn) noodles in a simple sauce; plain boiled noodles in soup

阳刚(yánggāng) masculine; masculinity; virility

阳关(yángguān) Yangguan; the Yang Pass(a pass along the silk road in Gansu Province)

阳关道(yángguāndào) a broad highway

《阳关三叠》(yángguān sāndié) *Departure at the Yang Pass* – a piece of ancient music in the Tang Dynasty

阳湖派(yánghúpài) the Yanghu School(a school of prose-writing in the Qing Dynasty)

阳间(yángjiān) this world; the mortal world

阳历(yánglì) ①the solar calendar ② the Gregorian calendar

阳历年(yánglìnián) solar year; a year in the solar calendar

阳平(yángpíng) the rising tone (the second of the four tones in modern standard Chinese pronunciation)

阳世(yángshì) this world

阳寿(yángshòu) one's life in the mortal world; lifespan

阳燧(yángsuì) a brass mirror(used to get fire from the sun in ancient times)

阳文(yángwén) characters cut in relief; protruded characters (cut in seals and wares)

阳羡词派(yángxiàncípài) the School of Yangxian(a school of *ci* poetry in the Qing Dynasty)

阳虚(yángxū) the deficiency of *yang*; lack of vital energy

阳月(yángyuè) October(in the Gregorian calendar)

阳韵(yángyùn) the yang rhymes (ie. all syllables which end in "m", "n" and "ng")

阳宅(yángzhái) residence

旸谷(yánggǔ) the sun-rising valley(a legendary place from which the sun rose)

杨贵妃(yángguìfēi) Royal Concubine Yang(719 – 756); Yang Yuhuan; Yang Guifei

杨辉三角(yánghuī sānjiǎo)(math) the Yang Hui triangle; a binomial array; Pascal's triangle

《杨家府演义》(yángjiāfǔ yǎnyì) *Romance of the Yang Family* - a novel written in the Ming dynasty

《杨门女将》(yángmén nǚjiàng) *Women Generals of Yang Family* - a TV drama directed by Du Qifeng (杜琪峰) in 1981; a film firstly directed by Cui Wei(崔嵬) in 1960

《杨乃武与小白菜》(yángnǎiwǔ yǔ xiǎobáicài) *Yang Naiwu and Little Cabbage* - a TV drama directed by Li Li(李莉) in 1994; *The Adulteress*

洋八股(yángbāgǔ) foreign stereotyped writing; foreign stereotypes

洋插队(yángchāduì) to settle in a foreign country for further education

洋场(yángchǎng) the metropolis infested with foreign adventurers; preliberation Shanghai

洋车(yángchē) a rickshaw

洋倒儿(yángdàor) a foreign profiteer

洋房(yángfáng) a foreign-style house; a western-style house

洋鬼子(yángguǐzi) a foreign devil (a derogatory term used in preliberation China for foreign invaders)

洋行(yángháng) a foreign company

洋火(yánghuǒ) a match

洋碱(yángjiǎn) soap

洋框框(yángkuàngkuang) restrictive foreign conventions

洋码子(yángmǎzi) Arabic numerals

洋妞(yángniū) a young foreign woman

洋奴(yángnú) ① the foreigners' slaves ② a flunkey of the foreign boss ③ a worshipper of everything foreign

洋盘(yángpán) an inexperienced and easily deceived person (in a metropolis)

洋气(yángqì) ① foreign in style or custom ② trendy; popular

洋枪队(yángqiāngduì) foreign musketeers

洋务(yángwù) foreign affairs

洋务运动(yángwù yùndòng) the Wes-ternization Movement (of the late 19th Century); the Self-Strengthening Movement

洋油(yángyóu) ① oil unported from countaies ② kerosene

洋装(yángzhuāng) ① a western-style suit ② the method of western bookbinding

仰慕(yǎngmù) to admire; to look up to

仰韶文化(yǎngsháo wénhuà) Yangshao culture (painted pottery culture in Yangshao Village, Henan province)

仰仗(yǎngzhàng)to rely on;to depend on

养父(yǎngfù)adoptive father

养老送终(yǎnglǎo sòngzhōng)to look after one's parents in their old age and give them a proper burial after they die

养母(yǎngmǔ)adoptive mother

养女(yǎngnǚ)an adopted daughter

养气(yǎngqì)①to cultivate good character and temperament ②to nourish one's vital spirit

养神(yǎngshén)to rest to attain mental tranquility;rest and relaxation

养生之道(yǎngshēng zhī dào)a way of staying healthy;a healthy lifestyle

养小(yǎngxiǎo)to have a concubine

养心殿(yǎngxīndiàn)Hall of Mental Cultivation(in Forbidden City)

养性殿(yǎngxìngdiàn)Hall of Character Cultivation(in the Palace Museum,Beijing)

养子(yǎngzǐ)an adopted son

痒痒挠儿(yǎngyǎngnáor)a backscratcher

样板戏(yàngbǎnxì)the"model operas"(in the Cultural Revolution, 1966-1976)

幺蛾子(yāo'ézi)a wicked idea;mischief

幺叔(yāoshū)the youngest uncle

夭殇(yāoshāng)to die young

夭亡(yāowáng)to die young

夭折(yāozhé)to die young;to stop prematurely

吆喝(yāohe)to call out;to shout

吆五喝六(yāowǔ hèliù)①to shout at gambling②to be arrogant

妖道(yāodào)a Taoist sorcerer or witch;diabolism

妖魔鬼怪(yāomó guǐguài)demons and evil spirits;all kinds of monsters;all sorts of evildoers and ghosts

妖孽(yāoniè)①an evil person;an evildoer②an evil event

腰缠万贯(yāochán wànguàn)very wealthy;to wallow in money

腰鼓(yāogǔ)①a waist drum ②a waist drum dance

腰舆(yāoyú)a sedan chair

腰斩(yāozhǎn)①to be cut in two at the waist(a form of capital punishment in ancient China)②to cut something in half

尧舜(yáoshùn)Yao and Shun(legendary sage kings in ancient China)

尧天舜日(yáotiān shùnrì)(lit.)"the days of Yao and Shun"-(nostalgia for)a golden age;times of peace and prosperity;the good old days

肴馔(yáozhuàn)sumptuous courses at a meal

窑洞(yáodòng) a cave dwelling

窑姐儿(yáojiěr) a prostitute

窑子(yáozi) a brothel

谣谚(yáoyàn) folk songs and popular sayings

徭役(yáoyì) corvée; unpaid labor

摇鹅毛扇(yáo émáoshàn)(lit.) "to wave a goose-feather fan" – to give advice behind the scenes

摇钱树(yáoqiánshù) a source of easy money; a ready source of money

瑶池(yáochí) Jasper Lake (the dwelling-place of the Queen Mother of the West)

瑶琴(yáoqín) a lute with jade mountings

瑶章(yáozhāng) good poetry

瑶族(yáozú) the Yao nationality (in Guangxi, Yunnan, Guangdong and Guizhou)

杳如黄鹤(yǎorúhuánghè)(lit.) "to leave like the yellow crane" – to leave never to return; to be gone for ever; to be nowhere to be found

咬耳朵(yǎo ěrduo) to whisper

咬文嚼字(yǎowén jiáozì) to speak like a book; to pay excessive attention to wording; to be a verbal pedant; verbalism; playing with words

咬字眼儿(yǎo zìyǎnr) to be pedantic about words

窈窕(yǎotiǎo) gentle and graceful

窈窕淑女(yǎotiǎo shūnǚ) a beautiful fair lady; a gentle and graceful young woman

药草(yàocǎo) medicinal herbs

药罐子(yàoguànzi) ①a pot for decocting herbal medicine ②a chronic invalid

药膳(yàoshàn) medicated food

药师佛(yàoshīfó) Medicine Buddha; Bhaishajyaguru

药石之言(yàoshí zhī yán) unpalatable but salutary advice

药引子(yàoyǐnzi) an ingredient of medicine (added to enhance the efficacy of a dose of medicine)

要隘(yào'ài) a strategic pass

要冲(yàochōng) a communications center; a communications hub

要短儿(yàoduǎnr) to disclose one's faults

要厄(yào'è) a narrow pass; a strategic pass

要面子(yàomiànzi) to be face-conscious; to be concerned with one's reputation

要人(yàorén) a personage; an important person; a VIP

要塞(yàosài) a fort; a fortification

鹞子(yàozi) ①a sparrow hawk ②a child's kite

鹞子翻身(yàozi fānshēn) to do a somersault

爷们儿(yémenr)a man;menfolk

也里可温教(yělǐkěwēnjiào)Christianity(introduced in the Yuan Dynasty)

冶游(yěyóu)to go whoring;to visit prostitutes

《野草》(yěcǎo)*Weeds* – a collection of essays by Lu Xun(鲁迅,1881 – 1936)in 1927;*Wild Grass*

野狐禅(yěhúchán)heresy;heterodoxy(Buddhism)

《野火春风斗古城》(yěhuǒ chūnfēng dòu gǔchéng)*Struggles in An Ancient City* – a novel by Li Yingru(李英儒,1913 – 1989)in 1958;a film directed by Yan Jizhou(严寄洲)in 1963;a TV drama directed by Lian Yiming(连奕名)in 2005

野鸡(yějī)a prostitute

野鸡大学(yějī dàxué)a diploma mill;an unlicensed university

野模(yěmó)an amateur model

野史(yěshǐ)an unofficial history

野台子戏(yětáizixì)a traveling entertainment show(usually in the open air)

《野猪林》(yězhūlín)*The Wild Boar Woods* – a Beijing opera film directed by Cui Wei(崔嵬)in 1962

业海(yèhǎi)(Buddhism)the sea of retribution

业师(yèshī)one's(former)teacher

业务尖子(yèwù jiānzi)a top-notch professional

业障(yèzhàng)①an evil little creature;vile spawn②money

业种(yèzhǒng)①a bastard②a hellish breed

叶公好龙(yègōng hàolóng)(lit.)“Lord Ye's love of dragons” – to profess to love what one really fears

《夜半歌声》(yèbàn gēshēng)*Phantom Lover* – a film firstly directed by Yang Yanjin(杨延晋)in 1985;a TV drama directed by Huang Lei(黄磊)in 2005

夜叉(yèchā)①yaksha(a malevolent spirit in Buddhism)② a hideous and ferocious person

夜壶(yèhú)a chamber pot

夜来香(yèláixiāng)evening primrose

夜阑(yèlán)late at night

夜郎自大(yèláng zìdà)to be foolishly conceited

夜猫子(yèmāozi)a night owl;a night person

夜明珠(yèmíngzhū)a legendary luminous pearl

夜生活(yèshēnghuó)nightlife

《夜谭随录》(yètánsuílù)*The Casual Record of Night Talks* – a collection of short stories by He Bang'e(和邦额,1736? –?)

夜未央(yèwèiyāng)not yet dawn;almost dawn; in the small hours

《夜宴》(yèyàn) *The Banquet* – a film directed by Feng Xiaogang (冯小刚) in 2006

夜游神(yèyóushén)(lit.) "a god on patrol at night" – a night person; a night owl

掖门(yèmén) the two side doors (in an ancient palace)

掖庭(yètíng) the residences of concubines (in the imperial palace)

谒拜(yèbài) to pay a formal visit

谒见(yèjiàn) to have an audience with; to call on (a senior or a superior)

谒陵(yèlíng) to pay homage at a mausoleum

一把好手(yībǎhǎoshǒu) to be good at something

一把手(yībǎshǒu) ①a member ②a good hand; a highly competent person ③the first in command

一把抓(yībǎzhuā) to attend to everything by oneself; to take everything into one's own hands

一板一眼(yībǎn yìyǎn) meticulous; in regular sequence

一报还一报(yībào huán yībào) to return like for like; tit for tat

一本万利(yīběn wànlì) to make big profits with a small amount of capital

一鼻孔出气(yībíkǒng chūqì)(lit.) "to breathe through the same nostrils" – to sing the same tune; to hold identical opinions; to sing from the same hymnsheet

一臂之力(yībì zhī lì)(to lend) a helping hand

一边倒(yībiāndǎo) to lean to one side; to be partial to somebody; to predominate; to be superior

一不做,二不休(yībùzuò, èrbùxiū) to see something through, whatever the consequences

一步一个脚印(yībù yíge jiǎoyìn) to work steadily and make solid progress

一场春梦(yīchǎng chūnmèng)(lit.) "a spring dream" – a fleeting illusion

一朝天子一朝臣(yīcháo tiānzǐ yīcháo chén) every emperor has a cabinet of his own favorites; a new chief brings in new aides

一刀切(yīdāoqiē) to make everything rigidly uniform; a clean cut

一得之功(yīdé zhī gōng) just an occasional and minor success

一得之愚(yīdé zhī yú) my humble opinion

《一地鸡毛》(yīdì jīmáo) *Chicken Feathers Everywhere* – a novelette by Liu Zhenyun (刘震云, 1958 –); a

TV drama directed by Feng Xiaogang(冯小刚)in 1995

一肚子坏水(yīdùzi huàishuǐ)a head full of sinister ideas

一帆风顺(yīfān fēngshùn)good luck and smooth sailing; to proceed smoothly without a hitch

一佛出世,二佛涅槃(yīfó chūshì, èrfó nièpán)to suffer extreme hardship

一夫当关,万夫莫开(yīfū dāngguān, wànfū mòkāi)if one man guards the pass, ten thousand cannot get through;fort

《一个和八个》(yīgè hé bāgè)*One and Eight* – a film directed by Zhang Junzhao(张军钊)in 1983

《一个人的战争》(yīgèrén de zhàn zhēng)*One Person's War* – a novel by Lin Bai(林白,1958 –)in 2009

一根筋(yīgēnjīng)with a one-track mind;obstinate

一贯钱(yīguànqián)a string of coins

一锅端(yīguōduān)to eliminate or wipe out completely

一锅粥(yīguōzhōu)(lit.)"a pot of porridge" – a complete mess

一国三公(yīguó sāngōng)(lit.)"a state with three rulers" – a divided leadership

《一剪梅》(yījiǎnméi)*A Twig of Plum Blossoms* – a verse pattern; a TV drama directed by Lu Lunchang(卢伦常)in 1984

《一江春水向东流》(yījiāng chūn shuǐ xiàngdōng liú)*The Spring River Flows East* – a film directed by Jiang Haiyang(江海洋)in 1947

一孔之见(yīkǒng zhī jiàn)a very narrow view;a very limited outlook

一匡天下(yīkuāng tiānxià)to unite the country;to restore peace to the country

一溜烟(yīliùyān)like a streak of smoke;very quickly

一年之计在于春(yīnián zhī jì zàiyú chūn)the whole year's work depends on a good start in spring

一盘死棋(yīpán sǐqí)(lit.)"dead pieces in a chess game" – a hopeless case

一片冰心(yīpiàn bīngxīn)a pure heart pursuing no fame and fortune; a pure and noble character

一品(yīpǐn)the highest official rank in imperial China

一人得道,鸡犬升天(yīrén dédào, jīquǎn shēngtiān)(lit.)"when a man attains the Tao, even his pets ascend to heaven" – when a man gets to the top, all his friends and relatives are in power, too

一日夫妻百日恩(yīrì fūqī bǎirìēn) one day of true love is worth a hundred days of mere affection

一日为师,终身为父(yīrì wéi shī, zhōngshēn wéifù) a teacher for a day is a father for a lifetime

一手包办(yīshǒu bāobàn) to keep sole control of; to monopolise

一条龙(yītiáolóng) ①one continuous line②a connected sequence; a coordinated process

一言既出,驷马难追(yīyánjìchū, sìmǎnánzhuī) what's said can't be unsaid; words cannot be retracted

一言堂(yīyántáng) to decide everything by one man's say-so; a dictatorial style

一枕黄粱(yīzhěn huángliáng) (lit.) "a Golden Millet Dream" - a brief dream or delusion of grandeur

《一枝花》(yīzhīhuā) *A Spray of Flowers* - a Chinese *suona* solo

一中多,多中一(yī zhōng duō, duō zhōng yī) all in one and one in all (Buddhism)

一柱擎天(yī zhù qíngtiān) (lit.) "one pillar supporting the sky" - to shoulder a heavy responsibility

一字师(yīzìshī) the "one word teacher" - a person who corrects a word in your poem or essay can be considered as your teacher

伊犁河(yīlíhé) the Yili River (in Xinjiang Uygur Autonomous Region)

伊耆氏之乐(yīqíshì zhī yuè) the Music of Yiqishi (a dance music of remote antiquity)

伊人(yīrén) that person (usually a female); she

衣钵(yībō) (Buddhism) a mantle and alms bowl left to a monk's disciple; a legacy

衣冠(yīguān) clothes and hats

衣冠冢(yīguānzhǒng) a tomb that holds the clothing and belongings of the deceased

衣锦还乡(yījǐn huánxiāng) to return to one's hometown in glory (i. e. after acquiring wealth and honour)

衣食父母(yīshí fùmǔ) people on whom one's livelihood depends

医道(yīdào) the art of healing; the physician's skill

医家(yījiā) a doctor of traditional Chinese medicine

《医经》(yījīng) *The Classics of Chinese Medicines*

医圣(yīshèng) medical sage; medical guru

《医宗金鉴》(yīzōngjīnjiàn) *The Golden Book of Medicine* - a book by Wu Qian (吴谦, 1689 - 1748) in 1742

揖让(yīràng) to bow with hands clasped and give precedence to (the other); to bow and make way (for each other)

《仪礼》(yílǐ) *The Book of Etiquette and Ceremony* – a Confucian classic; *Etiquette and Rites*

仪仗(yízhàng) the flags and weapons, etc. carried by an honor guard

仪仗队(yízhàngduì) an honor guard; a guard of honor

《夷坚志》(yíjiānzhì) *Record of the Listener*; *Weird Stories and Anecdotes* – a collection of short stories by Hong Mai(洪迈,1123 – 1202)

夷旷(yíkuàng) affable and sanguine; amiable and optimistic

夷犹(yíyóu) ①to hesitate to go forward②calmly

夷州(yízhōu) (an old name for) Taiwan Province

夷族(yízú) ①the extermination of an entire family②a foreign country

沂蒙山(yíméngshān) the Yi-Meng mountains(in Shandong province)

沂蒙山小调(yíméngshān xiǎodiào) "The Madrigal of the Yi-Meng Mountains"(a Shandong folk song)

宜兴壶(yíxīng hú) an Yixing teapot (in Jiangsu province)

姨表(yíbiǎo) maternal cousins; the relationship between the children of sisters

姨夫(yífu) uncle (maternal aunt's husband); the husband of one's mother's sister

姨父(yífù) uncle (maternal aunt's husband); the husband of one's mother's sister

姨姥姥(yílǎolao) great-aunt (grandmother's sister)

姨妈(yímā) maternal aunt; mother's sister

姨母(yímǔ) maternal aunt; mother's sister

姨奶奶(yínǎinai) ① great-aunt (grandmother's sister)②a concubine

姨娘(yíniáng) ①father's concubine② maternal aunt; mother's sister

姨太太(yítàitai) a concubine

姨丈(yízhàng) uncle (maternal aunt's husband); husband of one's mother's sister

贻笑大方(yíxiào dàfāng) to be laughed at by experts; to become a laughing stock

胰子(yízi) a bar of soap

移樽就教(yízūn jiùjiào) (lit.) "to take one's wine cup and go to somebody's table to ask his advice" – to go to somebody for advice

遗老(yílǎo) a surviving adherent of a former dynasty; an old diehard

遗墨(yímò) extant books, handwriting, calligraphy, etc. by a deceased person

遗篇(yípiān) writings left by a deceased author

遗少(yíshào)the young diehards(who remain loyal to the former dynasty)

遗孀(yíshuāng)a widow

遗诏(yízhào)a testamentary edict(an imperial edict left behind by an emperor upon his death)

遗珠(yízhū)(lit.)"a lost pearl"- a lost treasure or unrecognized talent

颐和园(yíhéyuán)the Summer Palace

疑阵(yízhèn)a deceptive battle array

彝剧(yíjù)Yi opera(popupar in Yunnan, Sichuan and Guizhou provinces)

彝陵之战(yílíngzhīzhàn)the Yiling Campaign(222)

彝族(yízú)the Yi nationality(distributed in Yunnan, Sichuan and Guizhou provinces)

乙榜(yǐbǎng)the list of people who passed the imperial examination

乙科(yǐkē)a successful candidate the imperial examination at the provincial level in the Ming and Qing Dynasties

以蠡测海(yǐ lí cèhǎi)(lit.)"to measure the sea with an oyster shell"- to make an appraisal in the light of limited experience

以邻为壑(yǐ lín wéi hè)(lit.)"to use one's neighbor's field as a drain"- to shift one's troubles onto others

以身相许(yǐ shēn xiāng xǔ)to pledge to marry sombody

以天下为己任(yǐ tiānxiàwéi jǐ rèn)to regard the destiny of one's country as one's own responsibility

以小人之心,度君子之腹(yǐ xiǎorén zhī xīn, duó jūnzǐ zhī fù)to gauge the intentions of a gentleman by one's own petty standards

以正视听(yǐ zhèng shìtīng)(to do something)in order to ensure a correct understanding of the facts

以子之矛,攻子之盾(yǐ zǐ zhī máo, gōng zǐ zhī dùn)(lit.)"to set your own spear against your own shield"- to refute somebody with his own argument; to use somebody's own words against him

蚁鼻钱(yǐbíqián)a copper coin

蚁民(yǐmín)common people

蚁命(yǐmìng)a humble life

蚁族(yǐzú)the"ant tribe"(university graduates with low income and living together

《蚁族》(yǐzú)*The Ant Tribe* - a book by Lian Si(廉思,1980 -)

蚁族男(yǐzú nán)a man of the"ant tribe", living a poor and miserable life

倚酒三分醉(yǐjiǔ sānfēn zuì)to behave with impropriety as if one were drunk; to find an excuse to exaggerate the case

倚老卖老(yǐlǎo màilǎo) to take advantage of one's seniority

倚马可待(yǐmǎkědài)(lit.)"to lean on a horse that is about to set out" - to be able to write very fast

倚马千言(yǐmǎqiānyán)(lit.)"to dash off a thousand words at the side of a horse" - to write with great flourish and skill

倚声(yǐshēng) to compose a *ci* poem to a specific tune

旖旎(yǐnǐ) gentle and nice; charming and gentle

义兵(yìbīng) a righteous army

义仓(yìcāng) a regional public granary

义地(yìdì) a public graveyard for the poor

义和拳(yìhé quán) Righteous Harmony Boxing; Yihe boxing

义和团(yìhétuán) The Boxers; The Righteous Harmony Society

义和团运动(yìhétuán yùndòng) the Boxer Uprising; the Boxer Rebellion

义举(yìjǔ) a magnanimous act undertaken for the public good

义理(yìlǐ) ①good sense and significance②argumentation (of a speech or essay)③a universal truth

义利之辩(yìlì zhī biàn) the argument between morality and utilitarianism

义旗(yìqí) the banner of righteousness; the banner of justice

义气(yìqì) loyalty; the code of brotherhood; loyal

义士(yìshì) a high-minded or chivalrous person

义塾(yìshú) a school with no tuition fee; a free private school

义务教育(yìwù jiàoyù) compulsory education

义侠(yìxiá) ① chivalrous ② a righteous and gallant person

义训(yìxùn) semantic gloss

义演(yìyǎn) a charity gala; a charity performance

义勇军(yìyǒngjūn) an army of volunteers; volunteers

《义勇军进行曲》(yìyǒngjūn jìnxíng qǔ) *March of the Volunteers* - the national anthem of the People's Republic of China

义冢(yìzhǒng) a public burial ground for the destitute

亿万斯年(yìwànsīnián) billions of years; for all time

弋阳腔(yìyángqiāng) the Yiyang style of opera (in Jiangxi province)

艺高人胆大(yìgāo rén dǎndà) superb skills make one bold; from competence comes courage

《艺海拾贝》(yìhǎi shíbèi) *Picking up*

Shellfish from the Sea of Art – a collection of essays by Qin Mu(秦牧, 1919 – 1992)

艺名(yìmíng)a stage name

艺术界(yìshùjiè)the art world;artistic circles;art circles

艺术圈(yìshùquān)the art world;artistic circles;art circles

艺徒(yìtú)tapprentice

《艺文类聚》(yìwénlèijù)*Collection of Books* [compiled by Ouyang Xun (欧阳询,557 – 641)in 624]

艺文志(yìwénzhì)descriptive accounts of books in dynastic histories of China;bibliography

艺苑(yìyuàn)art and literary circles;the realm of art and literature

《艺苑卮言》(yìyuànzhīyán)*Observations on Literature* – a work by Wang Shizhen(王世贞,1526 – 1590)

《忆江南》(yìjiāngnán)*The South Recalled* – a verse pattern popular in the Sui and the Tang Dynasties

议政大臣(yìzhèng dàchén)an imperial advisor

异邦(yìbāng)a foreign country

异体字(yìtǐzì)a variant form of a Chinese character; an alternative-style character

异文(yìwén)different versions(of the same book);different narratives(of an event)

异族(yìzú)an exotic nation;of different races

佚游(yìyóu)to ramble without restraint;to loiter around

呓语(yìyǔ)absurd raving;crazy talk;talking in one's sleep

呓怔(yìzhēng)subconscious talk and behavior(in one's sleep)

译意风(yìyìfēng)a simultaneous interpretation installation(used in cinemas or conference rooms)

佾生(yìshēng)a child dancer(in the sacrificial ceremony in Confucius Temples in the Qing Dynasty)

《易传》(yìzhuàn)*The Annotations of The Book of Changes* – a book by unkown Confucians

《易经》(yìjīng)*The Book of Changes;I-Ching* – a Confucian classic

易箦之际(yìzé zhī jì)(lit.)"the time of changing the bamboo mat"– the moment just befo-re death

驿丞(yìchéng)the official in charge of postal delivery

驿道(yìdào)a courier route;a postal road(to deliver official document in ancient times)

驿官(yìguān)a post official

驿馆(yìguǎn)a posthouse(where couriers change horses or rest in ancient times)

驿吏(yìlì)a posthouse officer

驿马(yìmǎ)a post horse

驿站(yìzhàn)a post station;a posthouse(where couriers change horses or rest in ancient times)

驿卒(yìzú)a posthouse runner

弈具(yìjù)a chessboard and chess pieces

弈林(yìlín)community of chess players;chess-playing circles

弈棋(yìqí)to play chess

轶材(yìcái)above-average talents

轶伦(yìlún)to tower above one's peers

益气生津(yìqì shēngjīn)(medicine) supplementing qi and aiding the production of fluids

益友(yìyǒu)a friend and mentor

逸才(yìcái)an outstanding person;an exceptional talent

逸骥(yìjì)a fine horse

逸乐(yìlè)comfort and pleasure

逸民(yìmín)a hermit;a recluse

逸史(yìshǐ)an unofficial history

逸事(yìshì)an anecdote

逸闻(yìwén)an anecdote

逸豫(yìyù)idleness and pleasure;living an easy and confortable life of pleasure

意表(yìbiǎo)beyond one's expectation;what one does not expect

意匠(yìjiàng)an artistic conception

意气(yìqì)①spirit ②temperament ③emotions

意中人(yìzhōngrén)the object of one's affections;one's beloved

意中事(yìzhōngshì)something that is expected

溢美(yìměi)excessive praise;undeserved praise;fulsome praise

裔孙(yìsūn)remote descendants

劓刑(yìxíng)punishment by cutting off the nose

翼宿(yìxiù)Tasuki

懿亲(yìqīn)a very close relative

懿旨(yìzhǐ)the empress's decree

因果报应(yīnguǒ bàoyìng)karma;retribution for sin

因缘(yīnyuán)karma;principal and subsidiary causes;predestined relationship

因缘观(yīnyuánguān)meditation on nidanas,or chain of causation(Buddhism)

阴曹地府(yīncáodìfǔ)hell;the nether world

阴德(yīndé)good deeds credited to the doer in the after life;hidden acts of merit

阴风(yīnfēng)①a cold wind ②an evil wind

《阴符经》(yīnfújīng)*The Yinfujing*;*The Hidden Talisman Classic* – a Taoist classic;*The Classic of Secret*

Revelation

阴功(yīngōng)good deeds credited to the doer in the after life; hidden acts of merit

阴魂(yīnhún)ghost; soul of the departed

阴间(yīnjiān)the nether world

阴历(yīnlì)the lunar calendar

阴平(yīnpíng)the high and level tone (the first of the four tones in modern standard Chinese pronunciation);the first tone

阴山背后(yīnshān bèihòu)a remote and desolate place

阴声韵(yīnshēngyùn)the rhyme ended with a vowel

阴盛阳衰(yīnshèng yángshuāi)①(medical)yin rises while yang declines②the female is stronger and more powerful than the male

阴事(yīnshì)secret deeds

阴寿(yīnshòu)①the age of ghosts in hell②the ceremony commemorating the birthday of a dead person every ten years

阴司(yīnsī)the nether world

阴私(yīnsì)a shameful secret;privacy

阴燧(yīnsuì)a plate for collecting dew drops(in ancient times)

阴文(yīnwén)(print-making)characters or designs cut in intaglio

阴虚(yīnxū)(medicine)deficiency of yin(insufficiency of body fluid or vital essence)

阴阳(yīnyáng)yin and yang(the two opposing principles in nature); feminine and masculine;negative and positive

阴阳家(yīnyángjiā)the Yin-Yang School - a school popular from the end of the Warring States (475 - 221 BC) to the beginning of the Han Dynasty(202 BC - 263 AD); the School of Naturalists; a geomancer

阴阳历(yīnyánglì)the lunisolar calendar

阴阳人(yīnyángrén)a bisexual person;

阴阳生(yīnyángshēng)a geomancer, an astrologer

阴阳水(yīnyángshuǐ)the Yin Yang water(mixed drink of cold and boiling water in Chinese medicine)

阴阳头(yīnyángtóu)a half-shaved head(a sign of humiliation during the Cultural Revolution)

阴阳五行说(yīnyáng wǔxíng shuō) the theory of *Yin* and *Yang* and the five elements

阴阳先生(yīnyáng xiānsheng)a geomancer

阴韵(yīnyùn)the *yin* rhyme(one of the three classifications of the character pronunciation)

阴宅(yīnzhái)a graveyard;a tomb

阴骘(yīnzhì)good deeds done in secret

姻亲(yīnqīn)in-laws;relation by marriage;affinity

姻娅(yīnyà)relatives by marriage;in-laws

姻缘(yīnyuán)a happy marital destiny;a predestined marriage;a marriage made in heaven

音乐发烧友(yīnyuè fāshāoyǒu)a music fan

音律(yīnlǜ)(music)temperament;tonality;swing

音容(yīnróng)voice and countenance

音声人(yīnshēngrén)musicians (in the Tang Dynasty)

音韵(yīnyùn)phonology;rhyme and rhythm

《音韵阐微》(yīnyùnchǎnwēi) *The Study of Phonology* – an eight-volumed compiled by Li Guangdi(李光地,1642 – 1718)et al. in 1728

殷鉴(yīnjiàn)a warning lesson

殷鉴不远(yīnjiàn bùyuǎn)(lit.)"a lesson from Yin is within reach" – lessons from the past are not hard to find

殷商时期(yīnshāng shíqī)the Yin and Shang period (1600 – 1046 BC)

殷实之家(yīnshí zhī jiā)a well-off family

殷墟(yīnxū)the Yin Dynasty Ruins (in Henan province)

吟风弄月(yínfēng nòngyuè)(lit.)"to sing of the moon and the wind" – to write sentimental verse; to write pastoral poetry

寅吃卯粮(yínchīmǎoliáng)to eat next year's food;to anticipate one's income;to be operating on borrowed money

寅时(yínshí)the period of the day from 3 am to 5 am

银饼(yínbǐng)a silver dollar

银锭(yíndìng)a silver ingot

银汉(yínhàn)the Milky Way; the Galaxy

银号(yínhào)a private bank;a banking house

银河(yínhé)the Milky Way;the Galaxy

银两(yínliǎng)silver currency;a tael of silver

银楼(yínlóu)a silverware shop; a jeweler's shop

银票(yínpiào)a banknote

银洋(yínyáng)a silver dollar

银鹰(yínyīng)(lit.)"a silver eagle" – a plane

银元(yínyuán)a silver dollar

银元券(yínyuánquàn)a silver certificate

银圆(yínyuán)a silver dollar

银子(yínzi)silver;money

寅夜(yínyè)late at night;in the dead of night

寅缘(yínyuán)to make use of one's connections to advance one's career

引商刻羽(yǐn shāng kè yǔ)a most accomplished musical performance; high-brow music

引退(yǐntuì)to retire;to resign from an official post

饮食男女(yǐnshí nánnǚ)food, drink and sex – a human being's primary desires;*Eat*, *Drink*, *Man*, *Woman* – a film directed by Ang Lee(李安) in 1994

隐恶扬善(yǐnè yángshàn)to hide one's evil deeds while extolling one's virtues

隐讳(yǐnhuì)to cover up; to avoid mentioning

隐居(yǐnjū)to live in seclusion

瘾君子(yǐnjūnzǐ)①a recluse;a hermit;a retired scholar②a drug addict;an opium addict

隐身草(yǐnshēncǎo)(lit.)"an invisibility weed"– a cover for an(eg illegal)activity

隐身术(yǐnshēnshù)a disappearing act;a vanishing act;invisibility

隐士(yǐnshì)a recluse;a hermit

隐语(yǐnyǔ)①a riddle②enigmatic language;code words;argot;lingo

隐衷(yǐnzhōng)concealed feelings or troubles;inner feelings

荫庇(yìnbì)to protect; to bless; to shelter

荫监(yìnjiān)an imperial college student granted exemption from exams(because of the achievements of his ancestors)

荫生(yìnshēng)an imperial college student granted exemption from exams(because of the achievements of his ancestors)

印把子(yìnbàzi)a seal of authority; an official seal

印鉴(yìnjiàn)an authorized signature or seal

印契钱(yìnqìqián)the official charge for sealing a property transaction

印绶(yìnshòu)an official seal with a ribbon

印堂(yìntáng)part of the forehead between the eyebrows;the glabella

印堂穴(yìntángxuè)(medicine)the glabella point

印文(yìnwén)the print of a seal

印纹陶文化(yìnwéntáo wénhuà)the Stamped Pottery Culture (in the Neolithic Age,Southern China)

印玺(yìnxǐ)the imperial seal

印子钱(yìnzǐqián)usury;a very high-interest loan

胤嗣(yìnsì)descendants;offspring;heirs;to inherit

英才(yīngcái)a talented person;a person of outstanding ability

英豪(yīngháo)heroes

英华(yīnghuá)an outstanding figure

英魂(yīnghún)the spirit of the brave departed

英烈(yīngliè)①heroic ②a heroic martyr

英灵(yīnglíng)the spirit of the brave departed;the spirit of the martyr

英名(yīngmíng)a heroic name;an illustrious name;a celebrated name

英模(yīngmó)a heroic model

《英雄》(yīngxióng)*Hero* – a film directed by Zhang Yimou(张艺谋,1950 –)in 2002

《英雄本色》(yīngxióng běnsè)*A Better Tomorrow* – a film firstly dierected by Kong Lung(龙刚)in 1967;a film directed by Wu Yusen(吴宇森)in 1986

《英雄儿女》(yīngxióng érnǚ)*Heroic Sons and Daughters* – a film directed byWu Zhaodi(武兆堤)in 1964

《英雄无悔》(yīngxióng wúhuǐ)*The Heroes Never Regret* – a TV drama directed by He Mengfan(贺梦凡)in 1996

莺歌燕舞(yīnggē yànwǔ)(lit.)"orioles sing and swallows dance" – the joys of spring;a scene of prosperity

《莺莺传》(yīngyīngzhuàn)*The Story of Yingying* – a short story by Yuan Zhen(元稹,779 – 831)in 804

缨帽(yīngmào)a red-tasselled official hat(in the Qing Dynasty)

璎珞(yīngluò)a necklace of pearls and jade

膺惩(yīngchéng)to send armed forces to attack and punish

膺赏(yīngshǎng)to be rewarded

膺选(yīngxuǎn)to be elected

鹰犬(yīngquǎn)(lit.)"hawks and hounds" – lackeys

鹰隼(yīngsǔn)(lit.)"hawks and falcons" – savage or fierce people

鹰扬宴(yīngyángyàn)the Eagle's Fight Banquet(for the examiners and the examinees who succeeded in passing the martial arts contest)

鹰爪派(yīngzhǎo pài)the Eagle Claw Boxing(a martial art that was popular in Southern China)

迎客松(yíngkèsōng)the Guest-Welcoming Pine(of Huangshan Mountain in Anhui province)

迎亲(yíngqīn)to fetch the bride;to go to pick up the bride at her home

迎娶(yíngqǔ)to marry a woman

迎新(yíngxīn)①to see the New Year in②to welcome new arrivals

营生(yíngshēng)to make a living

《营造法式》(yíngzàofǎshì)*A Treatise on Architectural Methods* – an ancient book compiled during 1068 – 1077

营寨(yíngzhài)a military camp

萦怀(yínghuái)to occupy one's mind;to linger in one's mind

楹联(yínglián)a pillar couplet

蝇拂(yíngfú)a chowry;a whisk to repel flies

蝇甩儿(yíngshuǎi'er)a horse tail whisk

蝇头小利(yíngtóu xiǎolì)(lit.)"a fly's head of profit"– a petty profit

嬴政(yíngzhèng)Yingzheng – the First Emperor of the Qin Dynasty

瀛海(yínghǎi)a vast sea or ocean

瀛寰(yínghuán)the whole world

瀛洲(yíngzhōu)a fabled abode of immortals

郢书燕说(yǐngshū yānshuō)(lit.)"a letter from Ying(in the state of Chu)being explained by the people of the state of Yan"– a distorted interpretation

影壁(yǐngbì)①a screen wall②a wall with carved murals

影格儿(yǐnggér)a model calligraphy sheet;squared paper for tracing over to practice handwriting

影青瓷(yǐngqīngcí)shadowy-blue porcelain;misty blue porcelain

影印本(yǐngyìnběn)a photocopy;a photostat copy

硬道理(yìngdàolǐ)an established truth;an absolute principle;the top priority

硬功夫(yìnggōngfu)great proficiency;masterly skill

硬骨头(yìnggǔtou)(lit.)"hard bone"– a dauntless,unyielding person;a hard nut

硬汉(yìnghàn)an unyielding man;a man of iron

硬派小生(yìngpài xiǎoshēng)a strong-minded young man;an unyielding youth

硬气(yìngqì)①strong-willed;unyielding②to have no qualms

硬气功(yìngqìgōng)hard *qigong*(a system of traditional breathing exercise)

硬仗(yìngzhàng)a tough battle;a tough fight;a stiff task

硬着头皮(yìngzhe tóupí)(lit.)"to toughen one's scalp"– to force oneself to do something

硬着心肠(yìngzhe xīncháng)to toughen or harden one's heart;to be ruthless

应差(yìngchāi)to accept an assignment

应酬(yìngchóu)①to socialize with②

a social engagement;a dinner party

应景(yìngjǐng) to do something for the sake of some special occasion

应举(yìngjǔ) to take imperial examinations

应考(yìngkǎo) to take or sit for an entrance examination

应卯(yìngmǎo) (lit.) "to answer the roll call between 5 a. m. and 7 a. m." - to put in a routine appearance

应声虫(yìngshēngchóng) a yes-man; an echo; a mouthpiece

应试教育(yìngshì jiàoyù) an examination-oriented education system

应诏(yìngzhào) to do something in response to an imperial decree

拥军优属(yōngjūn yōushǔ) to support the army and give preferential treatment to the families of soldiers and martyrs

拥政爱民(yōngzhèng àimín) to support the government and love the people

邕剧(yōngjù) the Yong opera (popular in Guangxi Autonomous Region)

雍和宫(yōnghégōng) Yonghe Lama Temple in Beijing

雍正(yōngzhèng) Yongzheng, the reign title of the fifth emperor of the Qing Dynasty(1636 - 1912)

雍正通宝(yōngzhèng tōngbǎo) Yongzheng Currency (the copper coin with the reign title of the Yongzheng Emperor)

《雍正王朝》(yōngzhèng wángcháo) *Yongzheng Dynasty* - a TV drama directed by Hu Mei(胡玫) in 1997

《永不消失的电波》(yǒng bù xiāoshī de diànbō) *The Unfailing Radio Wave* - a film directed by Wang Ping(王苹) in 1958; a TV drama directed by Zhi Lei(智磊) in 2010

永定门(yǒngdìngmén) the Gate of Everlasting Stability (in Beijing)

永嘉四灵(yǒngjiāsìlíng) the Four Outstanding Poets of Yongjia (a school of poetry in the Southern Song Dynasty)

永嘉学派 (yǒngjiā xuépài) the Yongjia School (in Zhejiang province in the Southern Song Dynasty, 1127 - 1279)

永乐(yǒnglè) Yongle [the reign (1403 -1424) the title of Zhu Di, the third emperor of the Ming Dynasty, 1368 - 1644]

《永乐大典》(yǒnglè dàdiǎn) *Great Encyclopaedia of Yongle* - a set of reference books compiled in 1408

永明体(yǒngmíngtǐ) the poetic style of Yongming (popular in the Southern Dynasties, 420 - 589)

永通万国(yǒngtōngwànguó) (lit.)

"perpetual circulation in all countries" - a copper coin in circulation during the Northern Zhou Dynasty (557 - 581)

《永州八记》(yǒngzhōu bā jì) *Eight Notes from Yongzhou* - an essay by Liu Zongyuan(柳宗元,773 - 819)

甬剧(yǒngjù) Yong opera(popular in Zhejiang and Shanghai)

咏春拳 (yǒngchūnquán) Eternal Spring Boxing (popular in Guangdong and Fujian provinces)

咏怀(yǒnghuái) to express one's emotion by verse or song

勇冠三军(yǒngguàn sānjūn) the most courageous soldiers in the army

用兵如神(yòngbīng rúshén) to direct military operations with miraculous skill

用典(yòngdiǎn) to cite

用功夫(yònggōngfu) to make every effort; to work hard

用命(yòngmìng) to obey

用事(yòngshì) ①to be in power②to act③to quote classical allusions

用武(yòngwǔ) ①to use military force ②to display one's talents

优抚(yōufǔ) to give special care to; to give preferential compensation or comfort to

优伶(yōulíng) an actor or actress

优徘(yōupái) a farce

优婆塞(yōupósài) a layman

优婆夷(yōupóyí) a laywoman

优生优育(yōushēng yōuyù) to give birth to and raise a healthy child

优哉优哉(yōuzai yōuzai) leisurely and carefree; free from restraint

忧患意识(yōuhuàn yìshi) (lit.) "the consciousness of suffering and tribulation" - to be a worrier; to have a sense of anxiety

幽篁(yōuhuáng) a bamboo grove

幽魂(yōuhún) a ghost; a spirit

幽禁(yōujìn) to imprison; to put under house arrest

幽居(yōujū) ①to live in seclusion②a place of seclusion

幽兰(yōulán) an orchid

幽明(yōumíng) the mortal and immortal worlds; the human and spiritual realms

幽期(yōuqī) a secret tryst

幽情(yōuqíng) deep and unspoken feelings

幽人(yōurén) a hermit; a recluse

幽思(yōusī) ①to ponder; to be lost in reverie ② deep contemplation; hidden sentiments

幽怨(yōuyuàn) a hidden grievance

幽韵(yōuyùn) melodious tunes

悠着点儿(yōuzhediǎnr) to take things easy; to avoid overdoing it

尤物(yóuwù) ①a rare thing②an extraordinary person;a woman of great beauty

由头(yóutóu)a pretext;an excuse

由衷之言(yóuzhōng zhī yán)sincere words

油耗子(yóuhàozi)an illegal dealer in petrol and diesel oil

油水(yóushuǐ)profit

油条(yóutiáo)①a fried bread stick;a fried twisted dough stick ② a sly person

油头粉面(yóutóu fěnmiàn)(lit.) "oily hair and powdered face" - coquettish or effeminate in appearance

游春戏(yóuchūnxì) the Tour-in-Spring opera (polular in northern Fujian province)

游词(yóucí)①unfounded remarks② a joke

游方(yóufāng)①to travel far and wide②a traditional social gathering for young Miao men and women

游方僧(yóufāngsēng) a traveling monk

游舫(yóufǎng) a yacht; a pleasure-boat

游击队(yóujīduì)guerrilla

游击战(yóujīzhàn)guerilla warfare

游街(yóujiē) to parade somebody through the streets

游廊(yóuláng)a roofed corridor;a veranda

游民(yóumín)a vagrant;a vagabond; a drifter

游僧(yóusēng) an itinerant monk; a travelling monk

游士(yóushì) a persuasive talker; a lobbyist;a wandering scholar

游说(yóushuì) to lobby; to go about drumming up support for something

游侠(yóuxiá)an errant knight

游仙诗(yóuxiānshī) poetry about imoortals;a poem about immortals

游乡郎中(yóuxiāng lángzhōng) a roving herbal physician;an itinerant doctor

游学(yóuxué) to study away from home

游艺会(yóuyìhuì) a carnival; a cultural get-together

游园会(yóuyuánhuì) a garden party; a mass celebration in a park

游子(yóuzǐ) a wandering person; a traveler far away from home

有案可稽(yǒu àn kě jī) to be a matter of record; to be documented; to be on record

有板有眼(yǒubǎnyǒuyǎn) measured; orderly

有奔头(yǒu bēntou) to have something to look forward to

有道(yǒudào) to have achieved the Way

《有的人》(yǒu de rén) *Some People* -

a poem by Zang Kejia(臧克家,1905－2004)in 1949

有鬼(yǒuguǐ)to have a guilty conscience;to be a bit suspect;for there to be something fishy about something

有脸(yǒuliǎn)①to have fame②to have dignity or face

有两下子(yǒu liǎngxiàzi)to have real skill;to know one's stuff

有眉目(yǒuméimù)to begin to take shape;to be about to materialize

有门儿(yǒuménr)①to get the hang of something②to be hopeful;to find a clue to a solution

有奶便是娘(yǒunǎi biànshì niáng)(lit.)"whoever suckles me is my mother"－to be ready to serve anyone for material benefit

有谱儿(yǒupǔr)to have something to go on;to have confidence

有其父,必有其子(yǒu qí fù,bì yǒu qí zǐ)like father,like son

有情人终成眷属(yǒuqíngrén zhōng chéng juànshǔ)lovers are bound to get married in the end

有人家儿(yǒurénjiār)to be engaged

有容乃大,无欲则刚(yǒuróngnǎi dà,wúyùzégāng)whoever is tolerant is great, whoever is unselfish is strong;greatness and strength lie in tolerance and selflessness

有身子(yǒushēnzi)to become pregnant

有识之士(yǒushí zhī shì)a person with a broad vision;a man of insight

《有事您说话》(yǒu shì nín shuōhuà) *Please Tell Me What You Need* － a skit starring by Guo Donglin(郭冬临)in 1995

有司(yǒusī)officials

有头有脸(yǒutóu yǒuliǎn)to have respect and prestige;respected

有喜(yǒuxǐ)to be pregnant

有戏(yǒuxì)to look hopeful;to look promising

有心人(yǒuxīnrén)①an observant and conscientious person②a person with high aspirations and determination

有志者事竟成(yǒuzhìzhě shì jìng chéng)where there's a will,there's a way;nothing is impossible if you persevere

有志之士(yǒuzhì zhī shì)a person of noble aspirations;a person of lofty ideals

酉时(yǒushí)the period of the day from 5 p. m. to 7 p. m.

《酉阳杂俎》(yǒuyángzázǔ) *Miscellaneous Morsels from Youyang* － a classical miscellany by Duan Chengshi(段成式,803－863)

又红又专(yòuhóng yòuzhuān)both

red and expert; both politically sound and professionally qualified

又想当婊子,又要立牌坊(yòuxiǎng dāng biǎozi, yòuyào lì páifāng) to lead the life of a whore yet want a monument put up to one's chastity

右榜(yòubǎng) the Right Notice Board(for the successful Mongolian or Semu candidates in the imperial examinations)

右丞相(yòuchéngxiàng) right prime minister

右倾机会主义(yòuqīng jīhuìzhǔyì) rightist opportunism

右文(yòuwén) to patronize culture and learning; the right phonetic indicator (of a morpheme-phonetic character)

幼功(yòugōng) skills obtained during childhood

《幼学琼林》(yòuxué qiónglín) *Old Time Primer for Children* – a book by Cheng Yunsheng(程允升) in the Qing Dynasty

釉陶(yòutáo) glazed pottery

迂夫子(yūfūzi) a pedant

迂回战术(yūhuí zhànshù) outflanking tactics

迂拙之举(yūzhuō zhī jǔ) impractical and foolish behavior

于飞(yúfēi)(lit.)"to fly side by side" – conjugal happiness

于归(yúguī) to get married

余音绕梁(yúyīn ràoliáng)(lit.)"music lingering around the beams" – a song or a piece of music that leaves a lasting and pleasant impression

余勇可贾(yú yǒng kěgǔ) with plenty of fight left in one; to still have strength left and to spare

盂兰盆会(yúlánpénhuì) the Buddhist Ghost Festival

鱼沉雁杳(yúchén yànyǎo) for there to be no further news of someone

鱼米之乡(yú mǐ zhī xiāng)(lit.)"a land of fish and rice" – a well-watered place where fish and rice are abundant; a land of milk and honey

鱼肉乡里(yúròu xiānglǐ) to victimize cruelly the people in the locality

鱼水情(yúshuǐqíng)(lit.)"friendship as close as the fish with water" – a close relationship

鱼雁(yúyàn)(lit.)"fish and wild geese" – letters; epistles

鱼雁往来(yúyàn wǎnglái) incoming and outgoing correspondence

娱老(yúlǎo) to live through one's remaining years happily

谀言邀宠(yúyán yāochǒng) to curry favour with somebody by flattery

渔鼓(yúgǔ) ①a bamboo drum(a percussion instrument) ②Fishing Drum chanting (the chanting of folk tales to the accompaniment of a bamboo drum)

渔鼓道情(yúgǔ dàoqíng) the chanting of folk tales to the accompaniment of a bamboo drum

《渔光曲》(yúguāng qǔ) *Song of the Fishermen* – a film directed by Cai Chusheng(蔡楚生) in 1934

渔猎(yúliè) ①fishing and hunting② to grab③to pursue

渔猎百姓(yúliè bǎixìng) to rob ordinary people

《渔樵问答》(yúqiáo wèndá) *Dialogue between the Fisherman and the Woodcutter* – one of the ten pieces of classical Chinese music

渔色(yúsè) to go looking for sex; to philander

渔色之徒(yúsè zhī tú) a philanderer; a sexual predator

渔舟(yúzhōu) a fishing boat

《渔舟唱晚》(yúzhōu chàngwǎn) *Chant on a Returning Fishing Boat at Dusk* – a traditional piece of music; *Singing on the Return of Fishing Boats*

雩祭(yújì) a sacrifice for rain

雩祈(yúqí) a sacrifice for rain

雩祀(yúsì) a sacrifice for rain

雩祝(yúzhù) a sacrifice for rain

愚公移山(yúgōng yíshān) ①(lit.) "the foolish old man who removed the mountains" – dogged perseverance; a spirit of perseverance ② *The Foolish Old Man Who Removed the Mountains* – an article written by Mao Zedong (毛泽东, 1893 – 1976) in 1945

愚见(yújiàn) my humble opinion

愚民政策(yúmín zhèngcè) an obscurantist policy; obscurantism; deliberately keeping people ignorant

榆荚钱(yújiáqián) an elm pod coin (a light and thin coin) (in ancient China)

榆林石窟(yúlín shíkū) the Yulin Valley Grottoes (in Shaanxi province)

虞候(yúhóu) the imperial patrol guard (in the Sui Dynasty, 581 – 618)

虞姬(yújī) Yu Ji [the favorite concubine of Xiang Yu (项羽, 232 – 202 BC)]

虞美人(yúměirén) Yu Ji (虞姬, ? – 202 BC) [the favorite concubine of Xiang Yu (项羽, 232 – 202 BC)]

《虞美人》(yúměirén) *The Tune of the Beauty of Yu* – a *ci* poem by Li Yu (李煜, 937 – 978)

舆台(yútái) lower-class people

舆图(yútú) a map

与君一席话，胜读十年书(yǔ jūn yīxíhuà, shèng dú shíniánshū) to

talk with you for a while is worth more than ten years of study

《与往事干杯》(yǔ wǎngshì gānbēi) *Let's Pay the Piper for the Past* – a novel by Chen Ran(陈染,1962 –); a film directed by Xia Gang(夏刚) in 1994

羽葆盖车(yǔbǎogàichē) the emperor's carriage

羽盖(yǔgài) ①the feather-decorated cover(of a carriage) ②a carriage

羽化(yǔhuà) ①to become an immortal②to pass away;to die

羽化登仙(yǔhuà dēngxiān) to fly to the land of the immortal; to ascend and become an immortal; to die

羽客(yǔkè) a Taoist priest

羽毛画(yǔmáohuà) feather drawings

羽人(yǔrén) a flying god or goddess; an immortal; a Taoist priest

羽扇纶巾(yǔshàn guānjīn) (lit.) "to take a feather fan and wear a black silk ribbon scarf" – graceful in behavior and calm in style; calm; composed

羽士(yǔshì) a Taoist priest

羽书(yǔshū) an urgent dispatch

羽檄(yǔxí) an urgent military document

羽衣(yǔyī) ①a feathered garment or robe②the robe of a Taoist priest③a Taoist priest

《雨打芭蕉》(yǔdǎbājiāo) *Raindrops Falling on Banana Leaves* – a piece of folk music

雨花石(yǔhuāshí) *yuhua* pebbles; colorful fine-grained pebbles

雨花台(yǔhuātái) the Terrace of Raining Flowers in Nanjing, Jiangsu province

雨前(yǔqián) a kind of green tea picked before Grain Rain(the 6th of the 24 solar terms, usually on the 19th, 20th or 21st of April)

雨师(yǔshī) God of Rain; a rainmaker

雨水(yǔshuǐ) Rain Water(the 2nd of the 24 Chinese solar terms)

《雨巷》(yǔxiàng) *A Lane in the Rain* – a poem by Dai Wangshu[戴望舒(1905 – 1950) in 1927]

《禹贡》(yǔgòng) *Yugong Geography* – an ancient article on geography

禹域(yǔyù) the territories of China

语丝社(yǔsīshè) the Yusi Society (during 1924 – 1930)

玉版宣(yùbǎnxuān) strong, white *xuan* paper, for artwork

玉帛(yùbó) jade objects and silk fabrics

玉螭(yùchī) ①a jade carved dragon ②a gallant horse

玉带(yùdài) a jade belt

玉帝(yùdì) the Jade Emperor(the Supreme Deity of Taoism)

玉佛寺(yùfósì) the Jade Buddha Temple(in Shanghai)

玉钩(yùgōu) ①a jade hook②a new moon;a crescent moon

玉皇大帝(yùhuáng dàdì) the Jade Emperor(the Supreme Deity of Taoism)

玉珂(yùkē) ①jade ornaments on a bridle②horses③high-ranking officials

《玉梨魂》(yù lí hún) *The Jade Pear's Soul* – a novel by Xu Zhenya(徐忱亚,1889 – 1937) in 1912

玉门关(yùménguān) the Yumen Pass (in Gansu province)

玉面花骢(yùmiàn huācōng) a fine white-faced horse

玉辇(yùniǎn) the emperor's carriage; the imperial carriage

玉盘(yùpán) ① a jade plate ② the bright full moon

玉佩(yùpèi) a jade pendant

玉泉山(yùquánshān) Jade Spring Hill(in Hangzhou,Zhejiang)

玉人(yùrén) ①a jade carver②a jade figure③a handsome man or a beautiful woman

玉搔头(yùsāotóu) a jade hairpin

玉碎(yùsuì) (lit.) "broken jade" – to die in glory

玉台体(yùtáitǐ) the style of Yutai(a delicate and flamboyant poetic style)

《玉台新咏》(yùtái xīnyǒng) *Anthology of New Odes to Yutai* a collection of ancient poems compiled by Xu Ling(徐陵,507 – 583)

《玉堂春》(yù táng chūn) *The Story of Su San* – a traditional opera released in 1982

玉体(yùtǐ) ①your health②a smooth and tender body (of a beautiful woman)

玉兔(yùtù) (lit.) "the Jade Rabbit" – the moon

玉玺(yùxǐ) the imperial jade seal; the royal seal

玉逍遥(yùxiāoyáo) a fine snow-white horse

玉叶金枝(yùyè jīnzhī) (lit.) "jade leaves and golden branches" – ①the dependents of royal families; aristocrats②a highborn or delicate lady

玉液(yùyè) (lit.) "jade-like wine" – good wine

玉衣(yùyī) a jade burial suit

玉宇(yùyǔ) ① the residence of the immortals; a beautiful palace ② the universe

玉簪(yùzān) a jade hairpin

《玉簪记》(yùzān jì) *The Story of the Jade Hairpin* – a traditional Chinese play by Gao Lian(高濂,1573 – 1620); *The Jade Hairpin*

玉札(yùzhá)a letter

玉照(yùzhào)your photograph

玉质金相(yùzhì jīnxiàng)①beauty both inside and out②superb in form and content

育婴堂(yùyīngtáng) the Foundling Hospital(founded in 1922)

狱吏(yùlì) a prison officer; a prison warder

狱卒(yùzú)a prison guard

预备党员(yùbèi dǎngyuán)a probationary Party member

预备役(yùbèiyì)reserve forces; army reserve

《域外小说集》(yùwài xiǎoshuō jí)*A Collection of Foreign Stories*[by Lu Xun(鲁迅,1881－1936)in 1909]

欲海(yùhǎi)the ocean of desire

欲加之罪,何患无辞(yù jiāzhī zuì, hé huàn wú cí) if you are out to condemn somebody, you can always trump up a charge

谕旨(yùzhǐ)an imperial edict

寓邸(yùdǐ)the dwelling place(of officials)

寓公(yùgōng) a senior government official residing away from home－①a high-ranking gentleman in exile ②a hermit with high ambition

御宝(yùbǎo)the imperial seal

御笔(yùbǐ)(lit.)"the imperial brush"－handwriting or paintings by the emperor

御赐(yùcì)to be bestowed by the emperor

御花园(yùhuāyuán)the imperial garden

御极(yùjí)to ascend to the throne

御驾(yùjià)the imperial carriage

御林军(yùlínjūn)palace guards

御膳(yùshàn)the food of the imperial household

御膳房(yùshànfáng) the imperial kitchen

御史(yùshǐ)Censor(an ancient official title)

御史大夫(yùshǐdàfū)Censor-in-chief

御史台(yùshǐtái)the Censorate

御书钱(yùshūqián)the coin with the words written by the emperor

御医(yùyī) an imperial physician; an archiater

御用文人(yùyòng wénrén)scholoars or writers working for emperors in ancient times

御苑(yùyuàn)the imperial garden or park

御制(yùzhì)made by the emperor or by imperial order

裕固族(yùgùzú)the Yugur(Yuku) nationality(in Gansu province)

《喻世明言》(yùshì míngyán)*Stories to Enlighten the World*－A collection of vernacular short stories by

Feng Menglong(冯梦龙,1574－1646)in 1621

豫剧(yùjù)Yu opera(popular in Henan and parts of Shaanxi and Shanxi provinces)

豫园(yùyuán)the Yuyuan Garden(in Shanghai)

冤大头(yuāndàtóu)someone who is not good with money; a person fooled because of his generosity

冤魂(yuānhún)a wronged ghost

冤家(yuānjiā)an enemy;an opponent

冤家路窄(yuānjiālùzhǎi)(lit.)"enemies are destined to meet on a narrow road"－one cannot avoid one's enemy;unavoidable conflicts

冤枉(yuānwǎng)①to treat unfairly②a wrongful treatment③in vain

冤枉路(yuānwǎnglù)a roundabout way

冤枉钱(yuānwǎngqián)wasted money;money paid for nothing

冤有头，债有主(yuānyǒutóu, zhàiyǒuzhǔ)every injustice has its perpetrator, every debt has its debtor

冤狱(yuānyù)an unjust verdict; a miscarriage of justice

鸳鸯(yuānyāng)①a mandarin duck ②an affectionate couple

鸳鸯蝴蝶派(yuānyāng húdié pài)the Mandarin Duck and Butterfly School(a literature school originated in Shanghai in the beginning of the 20th century)

鸳鸯名片(yuānyāng míngpiàn)a couple's joint name card

鸳鸯座(yuānyāngzuò)a love seat

渊薮(yuānsǒu)a gathering place; a den

元白(yuánbái)two poets in the Tang Dynasty named Yuan Zhen(元稹,779－831)and Bai Juyi(白居易,772－846)

元宝(yuánbǎo)a shoe-shaped ingot of gold or silver

元本(yuánběn)a block-printed book

元朝(yuáncháo)the Yuan Dynasty(1271－1368)

元大都(yuándàdū)Khanbaliq[the capital of the Yuan Dynasty(1271－1368)]

元丰钱(yuánfēngqián)Yuanfeng money(named by the reign title during the two Song Dynasties)

元和体(yuánhétǐ)the Yuanhe style[a poetic style represented by Yuan Zhen(元稹,779－831)and Bai Juyi(白居易,772－846)]

元嘉体(yuánjiātǐ)the Yuanjia style(a style of poetry from 424 to 453)

元嘉之治(yuánjiā zhī zhì)Golded Years of Yuanjia(during the Northern and Southern Dynasties, 420 - 589)

元老(yuánlǎo) the founding member; the patriarch; a grand old man

元谋人(yuánmóurén) the Yuanmou Man (whose fossil remains were found in Yuanmou, Yunnan province)

元年(yuánnián) the first year (of an era or a reign period)

元配(yuánpèi) the first wife

元气(yuánqì) vitality; vital energy; primordial energy

元轻白俗(yuánqīng báisú) the poetic style of Yuan Zhen (元稹, 779 - 831) and Bai Juyi (白居易, 772 - 846)

元曲(yuánqǔ) Yuan opera (popular in the Yuan Dynasty, 1271 - 1368)

元日(yuánrì) the lunar New Year's Day; the first day of the first lunar month

元戎(yuánróng) ①a big chariot ②a supreme commander

《元史》(yuánshǐ) *A History of the Yuan Dynasty* - a historical book compiled by Song Lian (宋濂, 1310 - 1381) and Wang Lian (王濂, 1321 -1373)

元始天尊(yuánshǐ tiānzūn) Superiorman Primordial Supreme (the first god cherished by Taoists)

元宵(yuánxiāo) ①the Lantern Festival ②sweet dumplings

元宵节(yuánxiāojié) the Lantern Festival

元勋(yuánxūn) the founding father; a man of great merit

元夜(yuányè) the night of the 15th day of the first lunar month

元杂剧(yuánzájù) poetic drama of the Yuan Dynasty; Yuan dramas

元贞通宝(yuánzhēn tōngbǎo) the Yuanzhen copper coin (made from 1295 to 1297)

员司(yuánsī) middle and lower ranking government officials; junior officials

员外(yuánwài) ①a Ministry Councilor ②a rich landlord

员外郎(yuánwàiláng) a Ministry Councilor

园丁(yuándīng) ①a gardener ②a teacher

垣墉(yuányōng) a wall

原刻本(yuánkèběn) the first block-printed edition

原配(yuánpèi) ①the first wife ②to get married for the first time

《原野》(yuányě) *Wilderness* - a stage play by Cao Yu (曹禺, 1910 - 1996)

圆场(yuánchǎng) ①to mediate ②to run around on the stage

圆房(yuánfáng)to consummate marriage;consummation

圆坟(yuánfén)to add fresh soil onto the grave three days after the burial

圆寂(yuánjì)(Buddhism) Parinirvana;to pass away

圆梦(yuánmèng)①to interpret dreams②to realize one's dream

圆明园(yuánmíngyuán) The Old Summer Palace; The Gardens of Perfect Clarity;the Yuanmingyuan

袁大头(yuándàtóu)(lit.)"Big Head Yuan" - a silver coin minted with the head of Yuan Shikai(袁世凯, 1859 - 1916);the Big Head silver coin

缘簿(yuánbù)a donation book(Buddhism)

缘分(yuánfèn)fate;destiny

缘起(yuánqǐ) genesis; origin (Buddhist creed)

缘悭一面(yuán qiān yīmiàn)to have no opportunity to meet with somebody

辕门(yuánmén)the outer gate(of a government office)

远房(yuǎnfáng)distantly related

远亲(yuǎnqīn)a distant relative

《远去的白帆》(yuǎnqù de báifān) *Receding White Sail* - a novelette by Cong Weixi(从维熙,1933 -)

苑囿(yuànyòu)an enclosed ground in the emperor's palace for raising animals

怨府(yuànfǔ)a target of common hatred; an object of general indignation

怨女(yuànnǚ)a grumbling maid; a girl pining for a husband

怨偶(yuàn'ǒu)an unhappy couple; two conflicting parties

院本(yuànběn)①drama script in the Jin and Yuan Dynasties②drama or romance in the Ming and Qing Dynasties

院画(yuànhuà) the imperial-court decorative paintings

院试(yuànshì) the pre-examination before the formal imperial examination

院体画(yuàntǐhuà)the imperial-court decorative paintings

约法三章(yuēfǎ sānzhāng) to establish a set of rules; to make a few simple rules to be observed by all concerned

月饼(yuèbǐng)moon cake

月城(yuèchéng) a barbican; a crescent enclosure between the outer and inner city gates

月房(yuèfáng) the bedroom of a woman who is lying-in(after childbirth)

月宫(yuègōng)① the Lunar Palace

②the moon

月供(yuègòng) monthly payment

月规钱(yuèguìqián) monthly pocket money (for an apprentice); monthly stipend

月桂树(yuèguìshù) a bay tree; a laurel

月季(yuèjì) the Chinese rose

月令(yuèlìng) monthly climate

月婆子(yuèpózi) a lying-in woman; a post-partum woman

月琴(yuèqín) the moon mandolin (a stringed moon-shaped Chinese instrument); the moon lute

月嫂(yuèsǎo) a midwife

月台(yuètái) ① a balcony for watching the moon ② a railway platform

月下老人(yuèxià lǎorén) a matchmaker

月相(yuèxiàng) the phases of the moon

月子(yuèzi) the month of confinement after childbirth; the time of childbirth; confinement

乐府(yuèfǔ) ①the Department of Music (in the Han Dynasty for collecting folk songs and ballads); the Music Bureau ②folk songs and ballads

乐府令(yuèfǔlìng) the officer in charge of music

乐府诗(yuèfǔshī) music-bureau poems; folk-song-style verse

《乐府诗集》(yuèfǔ shījí) *The Anthology of Music-Bureau Poems* – a collection of poems compiled by Guo Maoqian (郭茂倩, 1041 – 1099)

乐户(yuèhù) ① female criminal forced to serve as a musician under go-vernment control ② a brothel

《乐记》(yuèjì) *The Records of Music* – a Confucian classic on music theory in the Western Han Dynasty (202 – 9 BC)

《乐经》(yuèjīng) *The Classic of Music* – one of the Chinese classics

乐律学(yuèlǜxué) the theory of ancient Chinese music temperament

刖刑(yuèxíng) a cruel torture practiced in ancient times, of chopping off somebody's feet

岳飞(yuèfēi) General Yuefei, a patriotic military commander and national hero of the Southern Song Dynasty

岳父(yuèfù) father-in-law (wife's father)

岳家(yuèjiā) the wife's parents' home

岳家军(yuèjiājūn) General Yue's (a patriotic military commander and national hero of the Southern Song Dynasty, 1127 – 1279) Army (in the Southern Song Dynasty, 1127 – 1279)

岳麓山(yuèlùshān) Yuelu Mountain (in Hunan province)

岳麓书院(yuèlù shūyuàn) the Yuelu Academy of Classical Learning (in Changsha, Hunan province)

岳母(yuèmǔ) mother-in-law (wife's mother)

岳母刺字(yuèmǔ cìzì) Yue Fei's mother tattooed characters on his back

岳阳楼(yuèyánglóu) the Yueyang Tower (in Yueyang, Hunan province)

《岳阳楼记》(yuèyánglóu jì) *On the Yueyang Tower* - a poetic essay by Fan Zhongyan (范仲淹, 989 - 1052) in 1046

岳丈(yuèzhàng) father-in-law (wife's father)

阅世(yuèshì) to gain experience of life; to see the world

《阅微草堂笔记》(yuèwēicǎotáng bǐjì) *Jottings from the Thatched Abode of Close Observation* - a collection of ghost stories [by Ji Yun (纪昀, 1724 - 1805)]

粤菜(yuècài) Guangdong cuisine; Cantonese food

粤剧(yuèjù) Cantonese opera

粤绣(yuèxiù) Guangdong embroidery (famous for its complicated patterns)

粤语(yuèyǔ) Cantonese

越轨(yuèguǐ) (lit.) "to go off the rail" - to transgress; to go beyond bounds; aberrance; deviance

越剧(yuèjù) Shaoxing opera

《越洋电话》(yuèyáng diànhuà) *Overseas Call* - a skit starring by Guo Da (郭达) and Cai Ming (蔡明) in 1994

越俎代庖(yuèzǔ dàipáo) to exceed one's authority and meddle in other people's affairs

晕菜(yūncài) dizzy; faint; numbed; dumbfounded

云板(yúnbǎn) the cloud-shaped bell plates (used to report the time or make an announcement in a government office, dignitary household or temple)

云鬓(yúnbìn) (lit.) "cloud-like hair" - a woman's beautiful hair

云冈石窟(yúngāng shíkū) the Yungang Grottoes (in Datong, Shanxi province)

云贵高原(yúnguì gāoyuán) the Yunnan-Guizhou Plateau

云肩(yúnjiān) the decoration on a woman's shoulder

云锦(yúnjǐn) cloud-pattern brocade; figured satin

云谲波诡(yúnjué bōguǐ) unpredictably changeable; ever-changing

云锣(yúnluó) chiming gongs

云起龙骧(yúnqǐ lóngxiāng)(lit.)"dragons rise as clouds gather" - great men come to the fore when opportunity offers

云山雾罩(yúnshān wùzhào)covering the mountain with mist and clouds;confused

《云水谣》(yúnshuǐyáo) *The Knot* - a film directed by Yin Li(尹力) in 2006

云梯(yúntī)a scaling ladder

云雨(yúnyǔ)(lit.)"cloud and rain" - sexual intercourse;love-making

云云(yúnyún)①and so on②numerous

云中白鹤(yúnzhōng báihè)(lit.)"a white crane amid the clouds" - a person with elegant taste and moral integrity

芸芸(yúnyún)numerous

芸芸众生(yúnyún zhòngshēng) all living things

运笔(yùnbǐ)to wield a pen

运筹帷幄(yùnchóu wéiwò)to devise strategies behind the scenes; to work out plans and strategies

运脚(yùnjiǎo)①the transport charge or fee②a porter;a removal man

运斤成风(yùnjīn chéngfēng)(lit.)"to create a gust by wielding a hatchet" - to perform an uncanny feat;to have exceptional skill

运思(yùnsī)to conceive;to design;to put one's thoughts into words

晕场(yùnchǎng)to get stage fright;to feel nervous and dizzy at an examination

韫椟(yùndú)(lit.)"hidden in a case" - unrecognized talents; light hidden under a bushel

韵白(yùnbái)①the rhyming spoken parts in traditional opera②the spoken parts in Beijing opera

韵部(yùnbù) rhyme class; rhyme group

韵腹(yùnfù)the head vowel in a compound vowel

韵律(yùnlǜ)rhythm

韵母(yùnmǔ)the vowel or the terminal(n)or(ng)of a Chinese syllable

韵目(yùnmù)the rhyme classes(in traditional rhyming dictionaries)

韵事(yùnshì)a romantic affair

韵书(yùnshū)a rhyming dictionary;a rhyming book

韵头(yùntóu)the head vowel

韵尾(yùnwěi)the tail vowel or the terminal sound

韵味(yùnwèi)lingering charm;lasting appeal

韵文(yùnwén) a verse; a rhyming composition

Z

扎彩(zācǎi)to hang up festoons or streamers

扎筏子(zāfázi)to vent one's spleen or spite on

扎染(zārǎn)tie-dye(a traditional method of printing and dyeing);bandhnu

匝道(zādào)①a ramp②a ring road

匝地(zādì)all over the ground;everywhere

匝月(zāyuè)a full month

咂舌(zāshé)wondering

杂烩(záhuì)①a dish of various ingredients②a mixture

杂烩汤(záhuìtāng)a hotchpotch;an assorted soup

杂家(zájiā)the Eclectics(an ancient school of thought during the Warring States Period);the Eclectic School

杂剧(zájù)poetic drama;drama

杂牌军(zápáijūn)miscellaneous troops;the non-regular army

杂史(záshǐ)①an unofficial history②a private record of anecdotes

杂耍(záshuǎ)a variety show;a side show

杂文(záwén)a satirical essay

杂院儿(záyuànr)a compound occupied by many households

杂字(ázì)a collection of comm-on words

砸饭碗(záfànwǎn)(lit.)"to smash somebody's rice bowl"– to sack somebody;to be fired

砸锅(záguō)to fail;to fall through

砸锅卖铁(záguō màitiě)to give away one's entire fortune;to surrender one's last resources

砸牌子(zápáizi)to ruin the reputation(of a brand,a person,a firm etc.)

灾梨祸枣(zāilí huòzǎo)the printing of useless or unworthy books;a poorly written worthless book

灾星(zāixīng)a star of ill luck;a walking disaster;misfortune

栽跟头(zāigēntou)①to go head over heels;to tumble②to suffer a setback;to come a cropper

栽培(zāipéi)①to plant and grow②to educate and cultivate to help advance

宰客(zǎikè)to rip off;to swindle money from customers

宰人(zǎirén)to overcharge;to rip off

宰相(zǎixiàng)the prime minister;the chancellor

宰相肚里能撑船(zǎixiàng dùlǐ néng chēngchuán)(lit.)"a prime minister's heart is big enough to pole a boat in"– a great person is sure to be large-hearted or magnanimous

《宰相刘罗锅》(zǎixiàng liúluóguō) *Prime Minister Liu Luoguo* – a TV drama directed by Shi Ling (石零), et al. in 1996

崽子(zǎizi) ①a kid; a son ②young birds and beasts ③a bastard

载舟覆舟(zàizhōu fùzhōu) (lit.) "the water that carries the boat can also overturn it" – the people who support the rulers can also overthrow them

《再别康桥》(zài bié kāngqiáo) *Saying Good-bye to Cambridge Again* – a poem by Xu Zhimo (徐志摩, 1897 – 1931) in 1928

再醮(zàijiào) to marry again; to remarry

再生父母(zài shēng fùmǔ) one's great benefactor; a savior

再世(zàishì) ①in the next life ②to be reincarnated; to come into this world

在行(zàiháng) to be expert at something; in one's own territory

在天之灵(zàitiān zhī líng) the soul in heaven

在位(zàiwèi) ①to be on the throne; to be in power ②to be on the job

在下(zàixià) I (a polite expression)

在野(zàiyě) to be out of office; to be in opposition

糌粑(zānba) *zanba*; *tsamba* (a form of bread made from barley in Tibet)

簪挂(zānguà) to wear flowers

簪缨(zānyīng) the ornamental hairpins and tassels on the hats of the noble and influential people; high-ranking officials

簪子(zānzi) a hair clasp

咱家(zánjiā) I, me (more seen in early vernacular); my family; our family

拶指(zǎnzhǐ) to squeeze a criminal's fingers between sticks (a form of torture)

拶子(zǎnzi) the sticks used for squeezing the criminal's fingers together

赞礼(zànlǐ) ①to read out ceremonial procedures ②the master of a ceremony

錾刀(zàndāo) a graver; a burin (an engraving tool)

錾子(zànzi) a chisel

赃官(zāngguān) a corrupt official

臧否(zāngpǐ) to pass judgment

臧否人物(zāngpǐ rénwù) to pass judgement on a person's good and bad points

脏病(zāngbìng) a venereal disease

驵侩(zǎngkuài) horse broker; broker

脏腑(zàngfǔ) ①viscera; internal organs ②the bottom of one's heart

脏象(zàngxiàng) the state of the internal organs; the state of the viscera

藏传佛教(zàngchuán fójiào) Tibetan Buddhism

藏传密教(zàngchuán mìjiào) Tantrism in Tibetan Buddhism

藏红花(zànghónghuā) saffron crocus (Crocus sativus)

藏剧(zàngjù) Tibetan opera

藏历(zànglì) the lunar calendar of Tibet

藏历新年(zànglì xīnnián) the Tibetan New Year Festival

藏羚(zànglíng) the Tibetan antelope

藏羚羊(zànglíngyáng) the Tibetan antelope

藏密(zàngmì) Tantrism in Tibetan Buddhism

藏戏(zàngxì) Tibetan opera

藏香(zàngxiāng) Tibetan joss sticks

藏药(zàngyào) Tibetan medicine

藏医(zàngyī) ①Tibetan medical science②a doctor or physician practicing traditional Tibetan medicine

藏族(zàngzú) the Zang nationality; the Tibetans

遭年成(zāoniánchéng) to suffer from a year of famine; to have a bad year for crops; to have a poor harvest

糟糠之妻(zāokāng zhī qī) (lit.) "the wife of one's 'chaff and husks' days" – a wife who has shared her husband's times of hardship

糟糠之妻不下堂(zāokāngzhīqī bùxià táng) a wife who has shared her husband's hardships should never be cast aside

糟粕(zāopò) rubbish; dross; dreg; scum

凿空之谈(záokōng zhī tán) irrelevant talk; far-fetched words

凿死理儿(záo sǐlǐr) stubborn; dogged

《早春二月》(zǎochūn èryuè) *Early Spring in February* – a film directed by Xie Tieli (谢铁骊) in 1963; a TV drama directed by Li Dawei (李大为) et al. in 2005; *February in Early Spring*

藻井(zǎojǐng) (architecture) a caisson ceiling

藻井顶棚(zǎojǐng dǐngpéng) (architecture) a caisson ceiling

藻饰(zǎoshì) embellishments in writing

灶君(zàojūn) the kitchen god; the God of the Hearth

灶神(zàoshén) the kitchen god; the God of the Hearth

灶台(zàotái) the top of a kitchen range

灶突(zàotū) a stove chimney

灶王爷(zàowángyé) the kitchen god

皂隶(zàolì) a *yamen* runner; a magistrate's office boy

皂靴(zàoxuē)short black boots

皂(早)衣(zàoyī)①the black robe of a relegated official②a junior official

造反派(zàofǎnpài)the rebel faction; rebels; insurrectionists

造府(zàofǔ)to call at one's house

造化(zàohuà)①to create②good fortune③the Creator

造化小儿(zàohuà xiǎo'ér)destiny

造孽(zàoniè)to do evil; to commit a sin

造诣(zàoyì)achievements; attainments; accomplishments

造纸术(zàozhǐshù)paper-making technology

聒噪(guōzào)to be noisy; to make a din

择吉(zéjí)to select an auspicious day (for a marriage, funeral, etc.)

择期完婚(zéqī wánhūn)to select a lucky day for a wedding ceremony

择善而从(zé shàn ér cóng)to choose and follow what is good

择主而事(zé zhǔ ér shì)to choose a wise master to serve

泽国(zéguó)an inundated area; a submerged area

责任田(zérèntián)a contracted field; contracted farmland

责任制(zérènzhì)the responsibility system(a management system with responsibility identified)

咋舌(zéshé)to be speechless or breathless(with wonder or fear); to bite one's tongue

舴艋(zéměng)a small boat

仄声(zèshēng)the oblique tone(distinct from the level tone, in classical Chinese)

贼船(zéichuán)a pirate ship; a criminal gang

贼骨头(zéigǔtou)a thief

贼寇(zéikòu)aggressors; invaders

贼眉鼠眼(zéiméi shǔyǎn)shifty-eyed; shifty; thievish-looking

贼去关门(zéi qù guānmén)to lock the door after the thief has gone; to lock the stable after the horse has bolted

贼子(zéizǐ)traitors

曾孙(zēngsūn)great-grandson

曾孙女(zēngsūnnǚ)great-granddaughter

曾孙子女(zēngsūn zǐnǚ)great-grandchildren

曾祖(zēngzǔ)great-grandfather

曾祖父(zēngzǔfù)great-grandfather

曾祖母(zēngzǔmǔ)great-grandmother

增上果(zēngshàngguǒ)fruit of dominance(one of the five fruits in Buddhism)

增字解经(zēngzì jiějīng)the additional remarks of the implication of scriptures

甑子(zèngzi)a rice steamer

赠序(zèngxù)words for a departing friend

咋呼(zhāhu)①to bluster and shout; to cry out②to show off

渣滓(zhāzǐ)①dregs;residue;scum②a disorderly person;criminals;dregs of society

扎堆儿(zhāduīr)to get together

扎耳朵(zhāěrduo)to grate on the ear;to be ear-piercing

扎根(zhāgēn)to take root

扎花(zhāhuā)to embroider

扎猛子(zhāměngzi)to dive

扎木聂(zhāmùniè)the six-stringed Tibetan guitar

扎年(zhānián)the six-stringed Tibetan guitar

扎什伦布寺(zhāshílúnbùsì) Tashilhunpo Monastery

扎眼(zhāyǎn)①dazzling②showy

扎针(zhāzhēn)to give or have an acupuncture treatment

札记(zhájì)reading notes;occasional jottings

炸酱面(zhájiàngmiàn)noodles served with fried bean sauce

《铡美案》(zháměiàn)*The Case of Chen Shimei* – an opera about *Chen Shimei* in the Song Danasty

乍暖还寒(zhànuǎnhuánhán)it turns cold again after suddenly feeling warmer for a while;a return to cold weather after a brief warm spell

诈尸(zhàshī)①a corpse that suddenly stands up from the coffin②a sudden howl of abusive words;a sudden hurl of abuse

诈降(zhàxiáng)to pretend to surrender;to feign surrender

奓着胆子(zhàzhe dǎnzi)to pluck up one's courage

炸锅(zhàguō)①oil spattering when food is fried②unrestrained anger

炸窝(zhàwō)①to flee in fright②to flee in terror;to be thrown into disarray

斋饭(zhāifàn)①food for Buddhist monks②a vegetarian meal

斋宫(zhāigōng)the Hall of Abstinence(in the Forbidden City)

斋果(zhāiguǒ)oblations;offerings

斋会(zhāihuì)①the gathering of the emperor and vassals to sacrifice in the ancestral temple②temple gatherings on special dates

斋醮(zhāijiào)a Taoist ceremony to pray to the gods for good fortune

斋戒(zhāijiè)①to fast②a day of fasting

斋七(zhāiqī)every-seventh-day prayer for the dead in the seven weeks

斋期(zhāiqī)days of fasting;fast;a period of fasting

斋日(zhāirì)a day of fasting

斋堂(zhāitáng)①an abstinence room ②the dining hall in a Buddhist temple

斋月(zhāiyuè)Ramadan;a month of fasting

摘帽子(zhāimàozi)(lit.)"to take the hat off"-to be reinstated;to be rehabilitated;to have a political label removed

宅第(zháidì)a large house;a mansion

宅门(zháimén)①the gate of an old-style mansion②a family living in an old-style mansion

宅男(zháinán)an indoorsman

宅女(zháinǚ)an indoorswoman

债台高筑(zhàitái gāozhù)to be heavily in debt;to be debt-ridden;to be up to one's neck in debt

寨子(zhàizi)a stockade;an enclosed village

占卜(zhānbǔ)to divine;to tell somebody's fortune;augury;fortunetelling

占卜杖(zhānbǔzhàng)a divining-rod

占卦(zhānguà)to divine by means of the eight diagrams;divination

占课(zhānkè)to divine by tossing coins

占梦(zhānmèng)to divine by interpreting dreams;prophecy by dreams

沾亲带故(zhānqīn dàigù)to have ties of kinship or friendship

毡房(zhānfáng)a yurt

毡帽(zhānmào)a felt hat

谵妄(zhānwàng)delirium

谵语(zhānyǔ)a delirious speech;ravings

瞻谒(zhānyè)to have an audience with

斩获(zhǎnhuò)to be successful;to gain good results;achievements

斩客(zhǎn kè)to rip off customers

斩首市曹(zhǎnshǒu shìcáo)to execute somebody in a marketplace

搌布(zhǎnbù)a dishcloth;a dish towel

占鳌头(zhàn áotóu)to come out first;to top the list

占便宜(zhàn piányì)①to gain extra advantage by unfair means②to have the advantage;to be favourable

占上风(zhàn shàngfēng)①to get the upper hand;to win an advantage ②better

战表(zhànbiǎo)a written official declaration of war

战斗英雄(zhàndòu yīngxióng)a combat hero;a militant hero

战功(zhàngōng)meritorious military service;outstanding military exploits

战鼓(zhàngǔ)a war drum;a battle drum

战国(zhànguó)the Warring States

Period(475 - 221 BC)

《战国策》(zhànguócè) *The Intrigues of the Warring States* - a historical book by Liu Xiang(刘向, 77 - 6 BC); *The Strategies of the Warring States*

战国策派(zhànguócè pài) the School of Warring States Strategies(a radical nationalist cultural group in the early 1940s)

战国七雄(zhànguó qīxióng) the seven powerful states of the Warring States Period(475 - 221 BC)

战国时期(zhànguó shíqī) the Warring States Period(475 - 221 BC)

《战洪图》(zhàn hóng tú) *Fight Flood* - a film directed by Su li(苏里) et al. in 1973

《战火中的青春》(zhànhuó zhōng de qīngchūn) *Youth in Flames of War* - a film directed by Wang Yan(王炎) in 1959

战袍(zhànpáo) a battle robe; a soldier's garb; battledress

战书(zhànshū) a written challenge to war; a declaration of war

栈道(zhàndào) a plank road(built along the face of a cliff)

栈桥(zhànqiáo) a landing stage(in a port); a loading bridge(at a railway station); a trestle

站住脚(zhànzhùjiǎo) to consolidate one's position; to stand one's ground

蘸火(zhànhuǒ)(metallurgy) to quench

张榜(zhāngbǎng) to put up a notice; to post a notice

张本(zhāngběn) ① an anticipatory action ② an anticipatory remark

张冠李戴(zhāngguān lǐdài)(lit.) "to put Zhang's hat on Li's head" - to confuse things

张果老(zhāngguǒlǎo) Zhang Guolao (the oldest of the eight Taoist immortals)

张家长，李家短(zhāngjiā cháng, lǐjiā duǎn)(lit.) "the virtues of the Zhang's, and the shortcomings of the Li's" - to gossip about others

张罗(zhāngluo) ① to manage ② to raise(funds) ③ to attend to

《张铁匠的罗曼史》(zhāngtiějiàng de luómànshǐ) *The Romance of Blacksmith Zhang* - a film directed by Qi Jiaxing(齐兴家) in 1982

张王乐府(zhāngwáng yuèfǔ) the *yuefu* poems by Zhang Ji(张籍) and Wang Jian(王建)

《张协状元》(zhāngxié zhuàngyuán) *Champion Scholar Zhang Xie* - a play in the Southern Song Dynast; *Top Graduate Zhang Xie*

章草(zhāngcǎo) the cursive script

章法(zhāngfǎ) ① the art of composition②techniques;rules;methods

章服(zhāngfú) an embroidered ceremonial robe

章回(zhānghuí) a chapter(in a full-length novel)

章回体(zhānghuítǐ) the chaptered style(of fiction);serialised

章回小说(zhānghúi xiǎoshuō) serial fiction;a serial novel(a traditional Chinese novel with each chapter headed by a couplet giving the gist of its content)

章句(zhāngjù) ①chapters and sentences(in ancient texts)②a syntactic and semantic analysis of ancient texts

章试(zhāngshì) the preexamination before the formal imperial examination

章奏(zhāngzòu) an official document (submitted to the emperor)

《漳河水》(zhānghé shuǐ) *The Zhanghe River Water* - a long narrative by Ruan Zhangjing(阮章竞, 1914 - 2000) in 1950

漳绒(zhāngróng) the Zhang velvet (originating from Zhangzhou, Fujian province)

长房(zhǎngfáng) the eldest branch (of a family)

长公主(zhǎnggōngzhǔ) the eldest princess

长老(zhǎnglǎo) an venerable monk

长年(zhǎngnián)(dialect) ①a shipowner②a boatman;

长史(zhǎngshǐ) zhangshi(an ancient official title)

长孙(zhǎngsūn) ①the eldest grandson ② Zhangsun(a compound surname)

长行市(zhǎng hángshì) to rise in one's social status, prestige, etc.

长子(zhǎngzǐ) the eldest son

掌案儿的(zhǎng'ànr de) a butcher

掌班(zhǎngbān) the manager of a brothel;the manager of a theatrical troupe

掌灯(zhǎngdēng) ①to hold a lamp in one's hand②to light an oil lamp

掌故(zhǎnggù) an anecdote

掌柜(zhǎngguì) a shopkeeper;a manager

掌门(zhǎngmén) the leader of a school of martial arts, a religious group or in an academic field

掌门人(zhǎngménrén) the leader of a school of martial arts, a religious group or in an academic field

掌上明珠(zhǎngshàng míngzhū)(lit.) "a pearl in the palm" - a beloved daughter;the apple of one's eye

掌勺儿(zhǎngsháor) to be a chef;to prepare a banquet

掌嘴(zhǎngzuǐ) to slap one in the

face; to box one's ears

丈二和尚,摸不着头脑(zhàng èr héshang, mōbùzháo tóunǎo)(lit.) "you can't touch the head of the ten-foot monk" - to be unable to make head nor tail of it; to be utterly at a loss

丈母(zhàngmǔ) mother-in-law (wife's mother)

丈母娘(zhàngmǔniáng) mother-in-law (wife's mother)

丈人(zhàngren) ①an old gentleman ②father-in-law (wife's father)

仗马寒蝉(zhàngmǎ hánchán) dare not say anything; to be scared into silence

杖头木偶(zhàngtóu mù'ǒu) a rod puppet; a stick puppet

杖刑(zhàngxíng) punishment by caning

账房(zhàngfáng) ①an accountant's office ②an accountant

账先儿(zhàngxiānr) an accountant

障眼法(zhàngyǎnfǎ) camouflage; cover-up

幛子(zhàngzi) a scroll of silk or cloth

招安(zhāo'ān) to offer amnesty to rebels, to enlist their support

招兵买马(zhāobīng mǎimǎ)(lit.) "to recruit soldiers and purchase war-horses" - to recruit talented personnel and consolidate forces

招财进宝(zhāocái jìnbǎo) to bring in wealth and treasure (used to wish somebody success in business)

招风(zhāofēng)(lit.) "to catch the wind" - to attract too much attention and invite trouble; to be asking for trouble

招风耳(zhāofēng'ěr) protruding ears; flappy ears

招蜂引蝶(zhāofēng yǐndié)(lit.) "to attract bees and butterflies" - to flirt with men; to be flirtatious

招抚(zhāofǔ) to offer amnesty to rebels, to enlist their support

招供(zhāogòng) to confess; to make a confession; confession

招魂(zhāohún) to call back the spirit of the dead; to resurrect; evocation

招女婿(zhāo nǚxu) to take in a man as a son-in-law

招牌(zhāopai) ①a signboard; a shop sign ②the reputation of a firm ③a deceptive guise

招亲(zhāoqīn) ①to take a man into the family as a son-in-law ② to marry into and live with one's bride's family

招式(zhāoshì) ①movements in martial arts or traditional opera ② a method; a trick

招贴画(zhāotiēhuà) a pictorial poster; a poster

招贤(zhāoxián) to summon virtuous and talented people; to recruit able men or women

招降(zhāoxiáng) to call on somebody to surrender

招赘(zhāozhuì) to take a man into the bride's family as a son-in-law

《昭君出塞》(zhāojūn chūsài) *Lady Zhaojun Came out of the Frontier* – a historical story about Wang Zhaojun(王昭君, 52 – 19 BC); a TV drama directed by Leng Shan(冷杉) in 1996

昭穆(zhāomù) *zhaomu* (a system of arranging emperors' temples)

昭雪(zhāoxuě) to exonerate; to rehabilitate; to redress a wrong or an injustice

昭仪(zhāoyí) *zhaoyi* (the title, first conferred in the Han Dynasty, of the imperial concubine, second only to the empress)

着法(zhāofǎ) ①a move in a chess game; a chess move ②a movement in martial arts

着数(zhāoshù) ①a move in chess; a chess move ② a strategic move ③ a trick

《朝花夕拾》(zhāohuā xīshí) *Dawn Blossoms Plucked at Dusk* – a prose anthology by Lu Xun 鲁迅(1881 – 1936) in 1926

朝令夕改(zhāolìng xīgǎi) to keep chopping and changing; to make frequent changes in policies or measures

朝秦暮楚(zhāoqín mùchǔ) to serve the State of Qin in the morning and the State of Chu in the evening – to be quick to switch sides; be fickle or capricious

朝三暮四(zhāosān mùsì) to chop and change; to keep changing one's mind

爪牙(zhǎoyá) a flunkey; a lackey

找不着北(zhǎobùzháo běi) to lose one's sense of direction

找不自在(zhǎo bùzìzai) to be asking for trouble; to bring trouble upon oneself

找茬儿(zhǎochár) to find fault; fault-finding

找碴儿(zhǎochár) to find fault; fault-finding

找婆家(zhǎo pójia) to look for a husband

找台阶儿(zhǎo táijiēr) to find an excuse

找辙(zhǎozhé) to find an excuse

找主儿(zhǎozhǔr) to look for a husband

诏令(zhàolìng) an imperial edict and order

诏书(zhàoshū) an imperial edict

赵公元帅(zhàogōng yuánshuài)Zhao Gongming; Marshal Zhao, the God of Wealth

《赵氏孤儿》(zhàoshì gū'ér) *Orphan of the Zhao Family* – a play by Ji Junxiang(纪君祥)in the Yuan Dynasty

赵体(zhàotǐ)the Zhao style[the calligraphic style of Zhao Mengfu(赵孟頫,1254 – 1322)in the Yuan Dynasty]

赵州桥(zhàozhōuqiáo)Zhaozhou Bridge(in Hebei)

笊篱(zhàolí)a bamboo, wicker or wire strainer

棹歌(zhàogē)rowing songs

照本宣科(zhàoběn xuānkē)(lit.) "to read the text item by item" – to read drafts or articles mechanically; to echo what the books say

照壁(zhàobì)a screen wall

照拂(zhàofú)to look after; to attend to

照面儿(zhàomiànr)to put in an appearance; to show up; to encounter; to show one's face

照妖镜(zhàoyāojìng)a monster-revealing mirror; a ghost detector

罩袍(zhàopáo)a dust-robe; a dust-gown; an overall

罩衣(zhàoyī)a dustcoat; an overall

肇祸(zhàohuò)to cause trouble

遮丑(zhēchǒu)to gloss over one's blemishes; to hide one's shame

遮羞布(zhēxiūbù)a fig leaf; a loin-cloth

折冲(zhéchōng)to defeat an enemy; to vanquish a foe

折冲将军(zhéchōng jiāngjūn)the fifth-ranking general (beginning in the Eastern Han Dynasty)

折冲御侮(zhéchōng yùwǔ)to repel enemies or foreign aggression

折冲樽俎(zhéchōng zūnzǔ)to conquer the enemy at a banquet by negotiations rather than by force; to win by diplomatic means rather than by military force

折叠扇(zhédiéshàn)a folding fan

折福(zhéfú)to ruin one's good fortune through greed

折桂(zhéguì)①to carry off the first prize②to pass the imperial examinations

折进去(zhéjìnqù)①to be in prison②to be involved in

折柳(zhéliǔ)①to part reluctantly; to see somebody off② "Bending the Willow" (an ancient song)

折杀(zhéshā)to overwhelm (somebody by special favors, excessive courtesy etc.)

折扇(zhéshàn)a folding fan

折寿(zhéshòu)to reduce one's lifespan

折腰(zhéyāo)to bow in obeisance

折子钱(zhéziqián)usury

折子书(zhézishū)a highlighted episode from a long story

折子戏(zhézixì)the highlights from operas

哲蚌寺(zhébàngsì)Drepung Monastery(in the west suburb of Lhasa)

蛰居(zhéjū)to live in seclusion

谪官(zhéguān)a disgraced official

谪居(zhéjū)to live in exile

谪迁(zhéqiān)to be relegated to a junior post in a remote place

谪戍(zhéshù)to be banished to a frontier post

浙菜(zhècài)Zhejiang Cuisine

浙东学派(zhèdōng xuépài)the Eastern Zhejiang School(beginning in the Song Dynasty,960 – 1279)

浙西词派(zhèxī cípài)the Western Zhejiang School of *ci* poetry(in the Qing Dynasty,1636 – 1912)

鹧鸪(zhègū)Chinese francolin;partridge

《鹧鸪飞》(zhègū fēi)*Flying Partridge* – a folk tune in Hunan province

着作郎(zhezuòláng)an official historian

贞操(zhēnchāo)①chastity;virtue ②loyalty

贞观(zhēnguān)Zhenguan[the reign(627 – 649),title of Li Shimin(李世民,the second emperor of the Tang Dynasty)]

《贞观长歌》(zhēnguān chánggē)*A Long Song of the Zhenguan Reign* – a TV drama directed by Wu Ziniu(吴子牛)in 2005

贞观之治(zhēnguān zhī zhì)the rule of the Zhenguan Emperor(627 – 649)

贞节(zhēnjié)chastity;chasteness

贞节牌坊(zhēnjié páifāng)a memorial archway of chastity;a chastity arch

贞洁(zhēnjié)chaste;chastity

贞烈(zhēnliè)to rather die than betray one's chastity;to be ready to die to preserve one's chastity

贞女(zhēnnǚ)①a chaste girl;a virgin ②a nun in a convent

针脚(zhēnjiǎo)①stitch②a line of stitches

针灸(zhēnjiǔ)acupuncture and moxibustion

《针灸甲乙经》(zhēnjiǔ jiǎyǐjīng)*A Classic of Acupuncture and Moxibustion* – a medical work compiled by Huang Puyi(皇甫谧,215 – 282)

针灸铜人(zhēnjiǔ tóngrén)a bronze figure marked with acupunctu-re points

针灸医生(zhēnjiǔ yīshēng) an acupuncturist; an acupuncture practitioner

针头线脑(zhēntóu xiànnǎo) the odds and ends used for sewing; needles and threads

针线包(zhēnxiànbāo) a sewing kit; a sewing box

针线活儿(zhēnxiàn huór) needlework

针黹(zhēnzhǐ) needlework

珍本(zhēnběn) a rare edition; a rare book

珍眉(zhēnméi) Chunmee tea; Zhenmei tea (a famous green tea from Zhejiang province)

桢干(zhēngàn) a core member; the backbone

真传(zhēnchuán) to be handed down directly from; a direct and authentic tradition

真迹(zhēnjì) an authentic work

真空教(zhēnkōngjiào) the Absolute Void Sect (Buddhism)

真命天子(zhēnmìng tiānzǐ) the son of Heaven; the Chosen One; the emperor

真人(zhēnrén) a true man; a pure man (one who has attained enlightenment or immortality especially used in official Taoist titles)

真善美(zhēnshànměi) the true, the good and the beautiful

真书(zhēnshū) (calligraphy) the regular script

真武(zhēnwǔ) Zhenwu the great; the Zhenwu Emperor (a Taoist God)

砧板(zhēnbǎn) a chopping board; a chopping block

甄别(zhēnbié) ①to discriminate ②to reexamine a case ③to screen

甄录(zhēnlù) to recruit by an examination

箴言(zhēnyán) a maxim; a proverb

诊脉(zhěnmài) to feel somebody's pulse

枕边风(zhěnbiānfēng) pillow talk; private conversation (to influence one's spouse)

枕戈待旦(zhěngē dàidàn) (lit.) "to keep a spear under one's pillow, and wait for daybreak" - to be ready for battle

枕头风(zhěntóufēng) pillow talk; private conversation (to influence one's spouse)

《枕中记》(zhěn zhōngjì) *Life Is But A Dream* - a romance by Shen Jiji (沈既济, 750 - 800); *Record within a Pillow*; *The World inside a Pillow*

轸念(zhěnniàn) to cherish one's memory sorrowfully

阵法(zhènfǎ) tactical deployment (of troops)

阵脚(zhènjiǎo) ①the front line (of

the army)②position; situation; circumstances

鸩酒(zhènjiǔ)poisoned wine

振兴中华(zhènxīng zhōnghuá)to rejuvenate the Chinese nation; Revitalise China(a political slogan associated initially with Sun Yatsen and thereafter used widely)

朕(zhèn)I; the sovereign (used by emperors in proclamations)

朕兆(zhènzhào)a sign; an omen

镇尺(zhènchǐ)a ruler-shaped paperweight

镇反运动(zhènfǎn yùndòng) the Movement to Suppress Counterrevolutionaries(between December 1950 and October 1951)

镇星(zhènxīng)Saturn

镇宅(zhènzhái) to drive evil spirits out of the house; to protect the house from evil spirits

镇宅之宝(zhènzhái zhī bǎo)a treasure which will protect the house from evil spirits

镇纸(zhènzhǐ)a paperweight

正旦(zhēngdàn)the lunar New Year's Day

正朔(zhēngshuò) the first day of a year

正月(zhēngyuè) the first month (of the lunar year)

争风吃醋(zhēngfēng chīcù) to fight with somebody for the favor of a man or woman; to be jealous of a love-rival

争衡(zhēnghéng) to compete for supremacy

争斤论两(zhēngjīn lùnliǎng) to fuss about trifles

争面子(zhēng miànzi) to try to win credit or honor; to fight for one's dignity; to fight to save face

争气(zhēngqì) to try determinedly to make a good showing; to work hard for something

争权夺利(zhēngquán duólì)to scramble for power and profit

争闲气(zhēngxiánqì)to fuss over trifles

争雄(zhēngxióng) to contend for hegemony

征鞍(zhēng'ān) a horse used for a long journey; a trekking horse

征尘(zhēngchén) dust which settles on somebody during a journey

征马(zhēngmǎ) a horse used for a long journey; a trekking horse

征南将军(zhēngnán jiāngjūn) South Expedition General; General of the Southern regions(an official military rank in the Three Kingdoms Period., 220－280)

征人(zhēngrén)a man who went out to battle; a traveller on a long journey

征书(zhēngshū)①a book recording the omens of disaster②a document to appoint somebody to an official position

峥嵘岁月(zhēngróng suìyuè)unusual and memorable years; an eventful period

症结(zhēngjié)a crux; a sticking point

睁眼瞎子(zhēngyǎn xiāzi)(lit.)"a blind person with their eyes open"-an illiterate

睁一只眼,闭一只眼(zhēng yīzhī yǎn, bì yīzhīyǎn) to turn a blind eye to something

睁着眼睛说瞎话(zhēngzhe yǎnjing shuō xiāhuà) to tell a bare-faced lie; to tell an outright lie

蒸笼(zhēnglóng)①a food steamer②very hot and sultry weather

蒸人(zhēngrén)①common people②very hot and sultry weather

蒸压茶(zhēngyāchá) brick tea (in ancient China prior to the Ming Dynasty)

蒸蒸日上(zhēngzhēng rìshàng) to become increasingly prosperous day by day; to gain wealth by the day

整党(zhěngdǎng) to consolidate the Party organization; Party consolidation

整顿乾坤(zhěngdùn qiánkūn) to administer a country properly; to create order out of chaos

整风(zhěngfēng) the rectification of incorrect styles of thinking and working

整风运动(zhěngfēng yùndòng) the Rectification Movement (happening in 1941, 1950, 1957)

整脸儿(zhěngliǎnr) to keep one's honor; to maintain dignity

正榜(zhèngbǎng) a formal list of the successful examinees (in the imperial examination)

正本(zhèngběn) the original; the reserved copy; the master copy

正炒(zhèngchǎo) lavish praise delivered by the mass media

正旦(zhèngdàn) the main female role in traditional Chinese opera

正当年(zhèngdāngnián) in one's prime

正殿(zhèngdiàn) the main hall in a palace or temple

正儿八经(zhèngérbājīng) serious; earnest

正房(zhèngfáng)①the principal room②a legal wife (as opposed to a concubine)

正宫(zhènggōng)①the empress's palace②the empress

正宫娘娘(zhènggōng niángniang) the emperor's wife; the empress (as opposed to an imperial concubine)

正骨(zhènggǔ)①bonesetting;to set a bone ② an upright and determined quality

正果(zhèngguǒ) the perfect spiritual state (reached by practicing Buddhism)

正经(zhèngjing) ① decent ② Confucian classics③serious

《正经》(zhèngjīng) *The Right Ways* – a classic by Song Zongyuan(宋宗元)in the Qing Dynasty

正经八百(zhèngjīngbābǎi) serious and earnest

正剧(zhèngjù)a serious drama

正楷(zhèngkǎi)(calligraphy) the regular script

正名(zhèngmíng)①the rectification of names; to rectify the name of somebody or something ② the prologue of a Yuan dynasty drama

《正气歌》(zhèngqì gē) *A Song of the Moral Sense* – a poem by Wen Tianxiang(文天祥,1236 – 1283)

正人君子(zhèngrén jūnzǐ) a man of honor;a gentleman

正身(zhèngshēn)identity

正声(zhèngshēng)pure music

正声雅音(zhèngshēng yǎyīn) pure and refined music

正史(zhèngshǐ)an official history

正始体(zhèngshǐtǐ)the poetic style of the late Cao-Wei period(240 – 265 AD)

正室(zhèngshì)①an ancestor temple ②a legal wife③a legal wife's eldest son

正体(zhèngtǐ) ① the standardized form of Chinese characters ② the regular script(calligraphy)③block letters④orthodox

正体字(zhèngtǐzì) the standardized form of Chinese characters

正统(zhèngtǒng) legitimacy; legitimate

正头香主(zhèngtóu xiāngzhǔ) ① a lineal descendant②a true master

正阳门(zhèngyángmén) Zhengyang Gate;the South-facing Gate(in Beijing)

正一道(zhèngyīdào) the Way of Orthodox Unity(one of the two major sects of Taoism)

正一派(zhèngyīpài) the Way of Orthodox Unity(one of the two major sects of Taoism)

正印(zhèngyìn) fortune-telling(using either the Eight Trigrams or horoscopes)

正字(zhèngzì)①to correct a wrongly written character or a misspelt word ②the regular script(calligraphy)③ the standardized form of Chinese characters

诤谏(zhèngjiàn)to criticize one's faults frankly

诤友(zhèngyǒu)a true friend

郑和下西洋(zhènghé xià xīyáng)the voyage of Zheng He(郑和,1371－1433)

政躬(zhènggōng)①your health(a polite reference to the health of the head of state)②government affairs

政审(zhèngshěn)to examine one's political behaviour or record;to vet one's political background

政声(zhèngshēng)an official's political reputation

政事堂(zhèngshìtáng)the Hall of State Affairs(in the Tang and Song Dynasty)

政通人和(zhèngtōng rénhé)a state of affairs whereby government orders are smoothly implemented and the people are united; a prosperous state and harmonious society

政委(zhèngwěi)a political commissar

政务院(zhèngwùyuàn)the Central People's Government Administrative Council(replaced in 1954 by the State Council)

政治挂帅(zhèngzhì guàshuài)to put politics in command

政治局(zhèngzhìjú)the Political Bureau of the CCP;the Politburo

政治立场(zhèngzhì lìchǎng)a political stance;a political standpoint

政治路线(zhèngzhì lùxiàn)the political line;the party line

政治面貌(zhèngzhì miànmào)political status(standpoint, opinions, background and affiliation)

政治诗(zhèngzhìshī)political poetry

政治小说(zhèngzhì xiǎoshuō)political fiction;a political novel

政治嗅觉(zhèngzhì xiùjué)political acumen or sensitivity

挣命(zhèngmìng)to struggle for one's life

之乎者也(zhīhūzhěyě)Chinese literary jargon;pedantic terms;archaic language

之死靡他(它)(zhīsǐmǐtā)to swear never to remarry(of a widow);to be completely devoted to one's lover

支边(zhībiān)to support the border areas

支部委员(zhībù wěiyuán)a member of a Party or Youth League branch; a Party or League branch member

支书(zhīshū)the Secretary of a Party or League branch;a Party or League branch Secretary

支委(zhīwěi)a member of a Party or Youth League branch committee; a member of a Party or Youth League branch committee

支招儿(zhīzhāor)to give advice or

a suggestion

支子(zhīzi)①a support for something;a stand②a gridiron(used for cooking)③a wife's younger sons (ie. not the eldest son);a concubine's sons

支左(zhīzuǒ)to support the Left(during the Cultural Revolution);Leftist

芝兰(zhīlán)(lit.)"irises and orchids"- noble character;true friendship

芝兰玉树(zhīlán yùshù)(lit.)"irises,orchids and jade trees"- an expression of approval of the good conduct of young people;worthy followers or disciples

芝麻官(zhīmaguān)(lit.)"a sesame official"- a low-rank official

知彼知己,百战不殆(zhībǐ zhījǐ, bǎizhàn bùdài)if you know yourself as well as the enemy,you can fight a hundred battles without defeat;to estimate correctly one's own strength as well as that of one's opponent

知府(zhīfǔ)Magistrate(of a prefecture);a prefectural magistrate

知贡举(zhīgòngjǔ)the minister in charge of the highest imperial examination(in the Tang and Song Dynasty)

知交(zhījiāo)an intimate friend; a bosom friend;a soulmate

知客(zhīkè)①a prefect in charge of the reception of guests at ceremonies②a monk in charge of the reception of guests at a monastery

知命(zhīmìng)①to understand the will of Heaven②fifty years old

知命之年(zhīmìng zhī nián)the age of fifty

知其一,不知其二(zhī qíyī, bùzhī qí'èr)to know only one aspect of a thing,and ignore the other;to see only one side of the picture

知青(zhīqīng)the educated youth (sent down to the countryside during the Cultural Revolution)

知青点(zhīqīng diǎn)an educated youth's placement(in the countryside)

知青文学(zhīqīng wénxué)Educated Youth Literature(referring to the works of the urban youth sent to work in the rural areas during the Cultural Revolution between 1966 and 1976)

知青作家(zhīqīng zuòjiā)the Educated Youth Writers

知识青年(zhīshi qīngnián)①the educated youth(sent down to the countryside during the Cultural Revolution)②the educated urban youth

《知堂回想录》(zhītáng huíxiǎnglù)

Recollections of Zhitang – a reminiscence by Zhou Zuoren (周作人, 1885 – 1967) in 1964; *Zhitang's Reminiscences*

知县(zhīxiàn) a county magistrate

知行(zhīxíng) knowing and doing; theory vs practice

知行观(zhīxíngguān) the theory of knowing and doing

知行合一(zhīxíng héyī) the unity of knowledge and practice

知音(zhīyīn) a close friend; a bosom friend; a soulmate

《知音》(zhīyīn) *Intimate Friends* – a film directed by Xie Tieli(谢铁骊) in 1981

知遇(zhīyù) to get appreciation and recognition; to find a superior who is appreciative of one's ability

知制诰(zhīzhìgào) the official in charge of drafting imperial edicts

知州(zhīzhōu) a prefectural magistrate; a prefect

知子莫若父(zhīzǐ mòruò fù) no one knows a son better than his own father

知足常乐(zhīzú chánglè) contentment brings happiness; a contented mind is a perpetual feast

织锦(zhījǐn) ① brocade ② picture-weaving in silk

织女(zhīnǚ) ① a weaving-girl; the Weaver Maid

脂粉(zhīfěn) ① rouge and powder ②women

脂粉气(zhīfěnqì) femininity; womanly ways; feminine wiles

执棒(zhíbàng) a conductor (of music concerts)

执绋(zhífú) to attend a funeral

执柯作伐(zhíkē zuòfá) to be a matchmaker; to act as a go-between; to arrange a match

执礼(zhílǐ) ①to observe the rules of etiquette②to be polite to somebody

执牛耳(zhíniú'ěr) to be the recognized leader in one's field

侄妇(zhífù) one's nephew's wife; the wife of one's brother's son

侄女(zhínǚ) a niece

侄女婿(zhínǚxu) one's niece's husband

侄孙(zhísūn) one's brother's grandson

侄孙女(zhísūnnǚ) brother's granddaughter

侄媳妇(zhíxífu) nephew's wife; the wife of the brother's son

侄子(zhízi) a nephew; brother's son

直肠子(zhíchángzi) straightforward; forthright

直捣黄龙(zhídǎo huánglóng) (lit.) "to drive straight on to Huanglong" – to destroy the enemy's lair

直裰(zhíduō) ① plain clothes ② the

robe of a Taoist priest or Buddhist monk

直谏(zhíjiàn)to admonish frankly;to offer honest advice

直省(zhíshěng)provinces

直筒子(zhítǒngzi)a straightforward or simple-minded person

直系亲属(zhíxì qīnshǔ)lineal relatives;directly related family members;blood relations

直辖市(zhíxiáshì)a municipality directly under the Central Government;a special municipality;a municipality

止念(zhǐniàn)freedom from all thoughts(Buddhism)

只可意会,不可言传(zhǐkě yìhuì, bùkě yánchuán)something which can only be sensed,not explained in words

只许州官放火,不许百姓点灯(zhǐxǔ zhōuguān fànghuǒ, bùxǔ bǎixìng diǎndēng)"the magistrates are free to burn down houses, while the common people are forbidden even to light lamps"(to be overbearing to common people;despotic)

纸老虎(zhǐlǎohǔ)a paper tiger;all bark and no bite

纸上谈兵(zhǐshàng tánbīng)(lit.) "to fight only on paper" - to be an armchair strategist;all talk and no action

纸鸢(zhǐyuān)a kite

咫尺天涯(zhǐchǐ tiānyá)so near and yet so far

指法谱(zhǐfǎpǔ)musical score;tablature;fingering notation

指腹为婚(zhǐfùwéihūn)a prenatal betrothal

指甲雕塑(zhǐjiǎ diāosù)nail sculpture

指鹿为马(zhǐlùwéimǎ)(lit.)"to call a stag a horse" - to distort the facts deliberately

指南车(zhǐnánchē)a cart functioning as a compass

指南针(zhǐnánzhēn)a compass

指桑骂槐(zhǐsāng màhuái)(lit.)"to point at the mulberry and abuse the locust" - to attack by innuendo;to attack somebody obliquely

指事(zhǐshì)self-explanatory characters(one of the six categories of Chinese characters)

至爱(zhì'ài)favorite;most beloved

至宝(zhìbǎo)most valuable treasure

至道元宝(zhìdào yuánbǎo)the Zhidao Gold Ingot(an ancient copper coin)

至好(zhìhǎo)best friend;most intimate friend

至交(zhìjiāo)best friend

至灵(zhìlíng)zhiling(a civil official

in charge of Taoist affairs)

至圣先师(zhìshèng xiānshī) the Greatest Sage and Teacher; the Supreme Sage and Foremost Teacher

至性(zhìxìng) a natural instinct

至正通宝(zhìzhèng tōngbǎo) the Zhizheng Treasure(an ancient copper coin)

至尊(zhìzūn)(lit.) "the most revered and respected" - the emperor

志怪(zhìguài) to record uncanny or supernatural things; records of the strange

志怪小说(zhìguài xiǎoshuō) *zhiguai* fiction; supernatural fiction; supernatural tales; the tales of the supernatural

志人小说(zhìrén xiǎoshuō) anecdotal fiction; stories of mortals; tales about men

制举(zhìjǔ) an ancient system to select talents

制科(zhìkē) an ancient system to select talents

制钱(zhìqián) the standard copper coin; the official copper coin

制台(zhìtái) a governor; a viceroy

制天命(zhìtiānmìng) the control of fate

制义(zhìyì) the eight-legged essay; stereotyped writing

治本(zhìběn) to effect a permanent cure

治标(zhìbiāo) to provide a temporary solution; to cure the symptoms rather than the root of the illness

治病救人(zhìbìng jiùrén) to cure the sickness and save the patient; to help someone mend his or her ways

治丧(zhìsāng) to make funeral arrangements

治世(zhìshì) times of peace and prosperity

挚爱(zhì'ài) true and deep love; devotion

挚友(zhìyǒu) an intimate friend; a close friend; a bosom friend; a soulmate

桎梏(zhìgù) shackles; fetters

致良知(zhìliángzhī) extension of innate knowledge

贽见(zhìjiàn) to take presents when visiting somebody for the first time

贽敬(zhìjìng) gifts for one's teacher

智多星(zhìduōxīng) a wizard; a resourceful person; a mastermind

智囊(zhìnáng) a brainbox; brainpower; a wise and resourceful person

智囊团(zhìnángtuán) a think tank, a group of thinkers; the shadow cabinet

《智取华山》(zhìqǔ huàshān) *Circumvent Hua Mountain* - a film directed by Guo Wei(郭维) in 1953

《智取威虎山》(zhìqǔ wēihǔshān) *Taking Tiger Mountain by Strategy* – a modern Beijing opera

智圆行方(zhìyuán xíngfāng) to be resourceful and upright; to have a good disposition and an upright character

置喙(zhìhuì) to interfere; to intervene; to cut in

中餐(zhōngcān) Chinese meal; Chinese food

中餐馆(zhōngcānguǎn) a Chinese restaurant

中草药(zhōngcǎoyào) Chinese herbal medicine

中钞(zhōngchāo) a medium-sized bill; a medium-sized banknote

中成药(zhōngchéngyào) a ready made Chinese patented drug

中丹田(zhōngdāntián) the middle elixir field (a term in qigong)

中都(zhōngdū) the capital (of a country)

中伏(zhōngfú) the middle phase of the hottest season

中共中央(zhōnggòng zhōngyāng) the Central Committee of the Communist Party of China

《中国大百科全书》(zhōngguó dà bǎikē quánshū) *Encyclopaedia of China*

中国佛教协会(zhōngguó fójiào xiéhuì) the Buddhist Association of China

中国工农红军(zhōngguó gōngnóng hóngjūn) the Chinese Workers' and Peasants' Red Army

中国工农民主政府(zhōngguó gōng nóng mínzhǔ zhèngfǔ) the Chinese Workers' and Peasants' Democratic Government

中国共产党(zhōngguó gòngchǎndǎng) the Communist Party of China (CPC); the Chinese Communist Party (CCP)

中国国民党(zhōngguó guómíndǎng) the Nationalist Party of China; the Kuomintang (KMT); the Nationalists

中国基督教协会(zhōngguó jīdūjiào xiéhuì) the Christian Council of China

中国人民解放军(zhōngguó rénmín jiěfàngjūn) the Chinese People's Liberation Army (PLA)

中国人民志愿军(zhōngguó rénmín zhìyuànjūn) the Chinese People's Volunteers

中国社会科学院(zhōngguó shèhuì kēxuéyuàn) the Chinese Academy of Social Sciences

中国书法协会(zhōngguó shūfǎ xié huì) the Chinese Calligraphers' Association

中国通(zhōngguótōng) a China expert; a Sinologue

中国同盟会(zhōngguó tóngménghuì) Tongmenghui; the Chinese United League; the Chinese Revolutionary Alliance [a secret society and underground resistance movement organized by Sun Yat-sen(孙中山) et al., in Tokyo, Japan, on August 20th, 1905]

中国文联(zhōngguó wénlián) the China Federation of Literary and Art Circles

中国文人(zhōngguó wénrén) Chinese literati

中国戏剧学院(zhōngguó xìjù xuéyuàn) the National Academy of Chinese Theater Arts

中国象棋(zhōngguó xiàngqí) Chinese chess

《中国小说史略》(zhōngguó xiǎoshuō shǐ lüè) *A Brief History of Chinese Fiction* - a book by Lu Xun(鲁迅, 1881 - 1936) in 1923

中国音乐家协会(zhōngguó yīnyuèjiā xiéhuì) the Chinese Musicians Association

中国字(zhōngguó zì) Chinese characters

中国作家协会(zhōngguó zuòjiā xiéhuì) the China Writers' Association; the Chinese Writers' Association

中国作协(zhōngguó zuòxié) the China Writers' Association, the Chinese Writers' Association

中和殿(zhōnghédiàn) the Hall of Central Harmony (in the Imperial Palace of Beijing)

中和韶乐(zhōnghé sháoyuè) the imperial music (used at the sacrifices, banquets and court meetings of the Ming and Qing Dynasties)

中华(zhōnghuá) China

《中华大字典》(zhōnghuá dàzìdiǎn) *Great Dictionary of China* - a dictionary compiled by Lu Feikui(陆费逵, 1886 - 1941) et al.

中华民国(zhōnghuá mínguó) the Republic of China

中华民族(zhōnghuá mínzú) the Chinese nation; the Chinese

中华人民共和国(zhōnghuá rénmín gònghéguó) the People's Republic of China

中轿(zhōngjiào) a four-bearer sedan chair

中经(zhōngjīng) ① the collected scriptures (in the imperial court) ② the main channels and collaterals (of the human body)

中军(zhōngjūn) ① the middle troops (the dominant one of the three class of ancient troops) ② the chief commander of the middle troops

中军将军(zhōngjūn jiāngjūn) General of the Middle Troops

中郎将(zhōnglángjiàng) *Zhonglang* General(an official in charge of the imperial bodyguards, whose status was second only to the general)

中流砥柱(zhōngliú dǐzhù)(lit.)"a firm rock midstream" - a tower of strength;a mainstay

中路梆子(zhōnglù bāngzi) Shanxi opera

中美合作所(zhōngměi hézuòsuǒ) Sino-American Special Technical Co-operative Or Organization(SACO, established in 1943)

中南海(zhōngnánhǎi) Zhongnanhai [the central headquarters for the Communist Party of China(CPC) and the government of the People's Republic of China]

《中南海保镖》(zhōngnánhǎi bǎo biāo) *The Bodyguard from Beijing* - a film directed by Yuan Kui(元奎) in 1994

中农(zhōngnóng) a middle peasant (between the poor and the rich)

中秋(zhōngqiū) ①mid-Autumn ②the Mid-Autumn Festival

中秋节(zhōngqiūjié) the Mid-autumn Festival

中人(zhōngrén) ①a middleman;a go-between ②an ordinary man ③a eunuch

中山狼(zhōngshānláng)(lit.)"the Zhongshan wolf" - a perfidious person;a treacherous individual

中山陵(zhōngshānlíng) Sun Yat-sen's Mausoleum

中山装(zhōngshānzhuāng) Chinese tunic suit

中书令(zhōngshūlìng) the head of the secretariat(the official in charge of the imperial edict)

中书舍人(zhōngshūshěrén) the official in charge of drafting imperial edicts

中书省(zhōngshūshěng) the Department of Drafting Imperial Edicts

中堂(zhōngtáng) ①the central room ②the central scroll of painting or calligraphy(hung in the middle of the wall of the main room) ③Grand Secretary(the prime minister)

中体西用(zhōngtǐxīyòng) Chinese culture for the basic conduct of life and Western knowledge for dealing with practical affairs;Chinese substance and Western application;taking Chinese learning as the essence and Western learning for its utility

中统钞(zhōngtǒngchāo) the Zhongtong Banknote(issued in 1260)

《中文大辞典》(zhōngwén dàcídiǎn) *Great Dictionary of the Chinese Lan-*

guage - a dictionary compiled in Taiwan in the 1960s

中兴四大诗人(zhōngxīng sìdàshī rén) the Four Famous Poets [You Mao(尤袤,1127 - 1202), Yang Wanli(杨万里,1127 - 1206), Fan Chengda(范成大,1126 - 1193) and Lu You(陆游,1125 - 1210)]

中学(zhōngxué) traditional Chinese learning(a late Qing Dynasty term for Chinese natural and social sciences, compared with Western learning)

中学为体,西学为用(zhōngxué wéi tǐ, xīxué wéi yòng) to consider Chinese learning as the fundamental structure and Western learning as practical use; taking Chinese learning as the essence and Western learning for its utility

中央集权制(zhōngyāng jíquánzhì) a centralized system

中央美术学院(zhōngyāng měishù xuéyuàn) Central Academy of Fine Arts(CAFA)

中央全会(zhōngyāng quánhuì) the plenary session of the Central Committee

中药(zhōngyào) Chinese medicine; Chinese herbal medicine

中衣(zhōngyī) underpants; pants

中医(zhōngyī) ①traditional Chinese medicine②the doctor of traditional Chinese medicine

中医学(zhōngyīxué) traditional Chinese medicine (TCM); Chinese pharmacology

中阴(zhōngyīn) (Buddhism) the intermediate existence between death and reincarnation

《中英北京条约》(zhōngyīng běijīng tiáoyuē) *the Sino-British Convention of Beijing*(1860)

中庸(zhōngyōng) ①the Golden Mean (of the Confucian School) ②mediocre③*The Doctrine of the Mean*(one of the four Confucian Classics)

中庸之道(zhōngyōng zhī dào) the doctrine of the Golden Mean

中元(zhōngyuán) ①Zhongyuan (the second of three reign titles of the Han Dynasty, 202 BC - 220 AD) ② the Festival of Dead Spirits

中元节(zhōngyuánjié) the Festival of Dead Spirits; the Ghost Festival

中原(zhōngyuán) the central Chinese plains

中原逐鹿(zhōngyuán zhúlù) to fight for supremacy; to vie for the throne

中岳(zhōngyuè) the Central Mountain; Mount Song (in Henan province)

中灶(zhōngzào) the second class canteen; the second-ranking cadres' dining mess

中州(zhōngzhōu)central China

中州韵(zhōngzhōuyùn)the intonation of central China(based on dialects spoken in North China)

中轴线(zhōngzhóuxiàn)the central axis

忠臣(zhōngchén)a loyal official; a loyal subject

忠良(zhōngliáng)①loyal and honest ②a faithful and upright person

忠恕(zhōngshù)loyalty and consideration

忠孝(zhōngxiào)loyalty and filial piety

忠信(zhōngxìn)faithful and honest

忠义(zhōngyì)loyal and righteous

忠字舞(zhōngzìwǔ)the loyalty dance; the Red Guard dance(a dance performed by the Red Guards during the Cultural Revolution)

终伏(zhōngfú)the last phase of the hottest season

终老(zhōnglǎo)to spend the last years of ono's life; to live out the remainder of one's life

终南捷径(zhōngnán jiéjìng)a shortcut to high office; a shortcut to success

盅子(zhōngzi)a handleless cup

钟点工(zhōngdiǎngōng)a part-time worker; an hourly-paid worker

《钟点工》(zhōngdiǎngōng) *Hourly Employee* – a skit starring by Zhao Benshan(赵本山) and Song Dandan(宋丹丹) in 2000

钟鼎文(zhōngdǐngwén) bronze inscriptions

钟馗(zhōngkuí)Zhong Kui(a deity who drives away evil spirits)

钟离春(zhōnglíchūn)the wife of King Xuan of the State of Qi(齐国, 391 –221 BC), renowned for her lack of beauty

钟律(zhōnglǜ)tonality

钟楼(zhōng lóu)a bell tower

钟琴(zhōngqín)(music)a carillon

衷肠(zhōngcháng)words spoken from the heart; true words; heartfelt words

踵武(zhǒngwǔ)to follow in one's footsteps; to imitate; to follow suit

中计(zhòngjì)to fall into a trap; to be taken in

中举(zhòngjǔ)to pass the imperial examination

中暑(zhòngshǔ)①to be affected by the heat②heatstroke; sunstroke

中意(zhòngyì)to be ideal; to be to one's taste; to catch the fancy of

仲春(zhòngchūn)the second month of spring; mid-spring

仲冬(zhòngdōng)the second month of winter; mid-winter

仲家(zhòngjiā)the Buyi nationality

(in Yunnan)

仲秋(zhòngqiū) mid-autumn

仲夏(zhòngxià) mid-summer

众生相(zhòngshēngxiàng) a panorama of various types of people; all kinds of people and lifestyles

众子(zhòngzǐ) younger sons; all one's sons except for the eldest

重办(zhòngbàn) to punish severely

重宝(zhòngbǎo) the Heavy Treasure copper coin

重臣(zhòngchén) a high-ranking official with major responsibilities

重典(zhòngdiǎn) ①a severe punishment ② important ancient books and records

重男轻女(zhòngnán qīngnǚ) to regard men as superior to women; to value the male; male chauvinism

重身子(zhòngshēnzi) pregnant

重头戏(zhòngtóuxì) ①the important part; an important task or activity② opera involving much singing and acting

重孝(zhòngxiào) in deep mourning

舟车(zhōuchē) ①vessels and vehicles ②a journey

舟子(zhōuzǐ) a boatman

《周髀算经》(zhōubìsuànjīng) *The Zhou Bi Mathematical Classic* – *an* astronomic book written in the Weste-rn Han Dynasty

周公(zhōugōng) Duke of Zhou

《周公解梦》(zhōugōng jiěmèng) *Duke of Zhou's Interpretation of Dreams* – a book on oneiromancy by Ji Dan, a prince of the Zhou dynasty; *Duke's Oneiromancy*

周公吐哺(zhōugōngtǔbǔ) (lit.) "Duke of Zhou spat out his food" – to be too busy to pause for a meal

周姜(zhōujiāng) Zhou Bangyan(周邦彦, 1056 – 1121) and Jiang Kui(姜夔, 1154 – 1221) (two great *Ci* poets of the Southern Song Dynasty)

周口店(zhōukǒudiàn) Zhoukoudian (the site where the fossils of Beijing Man were discovered)

《周礼》(zhōulǐ) *The Rituals of Zhou* – a Confucian classic; *The Rites of Zhou*

周历(zhōulì) the calendar of the Zhou Dynasty(1046 – 256 BC)

周柳(zhōuliǔ) Liu Yong(柳永, 987 – 1053) and Zhou Bangyan(周邦彦, 1056 – 1121) (two great *Ci* poets of the northern Song Dynasty)

周文王(zhōuwénwáng) King Wen (1152 – 1056 BC) of the Zhou Tribes

周武王(zhōuwǔwáng) King Wu of the Zhou Dynasty(1046 – 256 BC)

《周易》(zhōuyì) *The Book of Changes* – a Confucian classic; *Yi*

Jing(《易经》)

《周渔的火车》(zhōuyú de huǒchē) *Zhou Yu's Train* – a film directed by Sun Zhou(孙周) in 2002

周瑜打黄盖(zhōuyú dǎ huánggài) (lit.)"Zhou Yu flogged Huang Gai with his consent" – something done by mutual consent

妯娌(zhóulǐ) the wives of brothers; sisters-in-law

肘腋之患(zhǒuyè zhī huàn) trouble emanating from close quarters; an imminent disaster

酎金(zhòujīn) a tribute(that vassals offered to the emperor)

籀文(zhòuwén) the large seal script (calligraphy)

朱笔(zhūbǐ) a red-inked writing brush

朱卷(zhūjuàn) the red imperial examination paper

朱楼(zhūlóu) gorgeous pavilions and towers

朱楼碧瓦(zhūlóu bìwǎ) gorgeous buildings

朱轮华毂(zhūlún huágǔ) ornate carriages with wheels painted red(the sign of a noble and distinguished person)

朱门(zhūmén)(lit.)"a vermilion gate" – the rich; a wealthy home

朱门绣户(zhūmén xiùhù)①(lit.)"a vermilion gate and gorgeously ornamented portal" – a rich mansion②a wealthy family

朱墨(zhūmò)①red and black②cinnabar ink

朱批(zhūpī) comments written in red

朱雀(zhūquè)①(astronomy) the Red Bird(the seven southern constellations)②(Taoism) the South God

朱雀门(zhūquèmén) Red Bird Gate; the south-facing city gate(of national capital in the Tang Dynasty, 618 – 907)

朱提银(zhūtíyín) Zhuti silver(produced in Yunnan)

朱文(zhūwén) characters on a seal carved in relief

朱颜(zhūyán)①a beautiful face ②youth

朱衣点头(zhūyī diǎntóu) to pass the imperial examination

朱子(zhūzǐ) Zhu Xi(朱熹, 1130 – 1200)(an honorific name); Master Zhu

《朱子家训》(zhūzǐ jiāxùn) *Zhu Xi's Family Exhortations* – a pocket book by Zhu Bailu(朱柏庐, 1617 – 1688)

朱子理学(zhūzǐ lǐxué) Zhu Xi's Neo-Confucianism; the Neo-Confucian School of Reason

《朱子语类》(zhūzǐ yǔlèi) *The Classi-*

fied Conversations of Zhu Xi – an ancient book compiled by Li Jingde (黎靖德) in 1270

株连(zhūlián) to implicate; to involve in a crime

珠茶(zhūchá) pinhead tea (a kind of green tea in Zhejiang)

珠花(zhūhuā) pearl hair-clip

珠玑(zhūjī) ①a pearl; a gem ②exquisite diction

珠江(zhūjiāng) the Zhujiang River; the Pearl River

珠联璧合(zhūlián bìhé) (lit.) "strings of pearls and pairs of jade" – a perfect match

珠穆朗玛峰(zhūmùlǎngmǎfēng) Mt Qomolangma; Mount Everest

珠算(zhūsuàn) to reckon using an abacus; calculation with a abacus

珠圆玉润(zhūyuán yùrùn) (lit.) "round as pearls and smooth as jade" – sweet singing or polished writing; elegant and polished

诸葛亮(zhūgěliàng) ①Zhuge Liang (181 – 234) ②a mastermind; a very resourceful person

诸葛亮会(zhūgěliàng huì) (lit.) "a meeting of Zhuge Liangs" – a meeting to pool ideas; a brainstorming session

诸宫调(zhūgōngdiào) storytelling in all keys and modes (a style of ballad popular in the Song, Jin and Yuan Dynasties)

诸侯(zhūhóu) dukes or princes

诸子百家(zhūzǐ bǎijiā) the hundred schools of thought; the "hundred philosophers"

猪八戒(zhūbājiè) Pigsy; Zhu Bajie (a character in the 16th century novel *Journey to the West*

猪倌(zhūguān) a swineherd

猪婆龙(zhūpólóng) a Chinese alligator

猪头(zhūtóu) (lit.) "a pig's head" – a stupid person

竹板书(zhúbǎnshū) story-telling with bamboo clappers (a kind of folk art form)

竹箅子(zhúbìzi) a bamboo grid; a bamboo steamer

竹编(zhúbiān) a bamboo-woven article; bamboo weaving

竹帛(zhúbó) ①bamboo slips and silk (for writing in ancient times) ②books

竹简(zhújiǎn) bamboo slips (for writing in ancient times)

竹林七贤(zhúlín qīxián) the Seven Worthies of the Bamboo Groves (from 240 to 249)

竹楼(zhúlóu) a house on bamboo stilts

竹马(zhúmǎ) a bamboo hobbyhorse

竹马灯(zhúmǎdēng) the Bamboo

Hobbyhorse dance (popular in Fujian and Anhui provinces)

竹马戏(zhúmǎxì) the Bamboo Hobbyhorse opera (popular in Fujian and Taiwan provinces)

竹马之交(zhúmǎ zhī jiāo) good friends from childhood days

竹书(zhúshū) inscriptions on bamboo slips; a bamboo-slip book

竹叶青(zhúyèqīng) ①a green bamboo snake ② zhuyeqing (a kind of yellowy green alcohol)

竹枝词(zhúzhīcí) the Bamboo Branch *ci* poetry (ancient folk songs with love as their main theme)

竹纸(zhúzhǐ) bamboo parchment

逐北(zhúběi) to pursue and wipe out a defeated army

逐臭之夫(zhúchòu zhī fū) an eccentric person; an eccentric

逐客令(zhúkèlìng) an order for guests to leave

逐鹿(zhúlù) (lit.) "to chase the deer" - to fight for the throne

逐鹿中原(zhúlù zhōngyuán) (lit.) "to chase the deer on the Central Plains" - to try to seize control of the empire; to vie for the throne

主儿(zhǔr) ①a master; an employer ②husband③bloke

主干家庭(zhǔgàn jiātíng) the main family

主公(zhǔgōng) Your Majesty; my lord

主户(zhǔhù) ①indigenous people② the household of a landlord

主家(zhǔjiā) ①to manage a household②a master; a host③husband

《主角与配角》(zhǔjué yǔ pèijué) *The Leading Role and the Supporting Role* - a skit starring by Chen Peisi(陈佩斯) and Zhu Shimao(朱时茂) in 1990

主考(zhǔkǎo) the chief examiner

主上(zhǔshàng) my lord; your majesty

主司(zhǔsī) the chief examiner (in the imperial examinations)

主心骨(zhǔxīngǔ) ①the backbone; the pillar②a clear idea about something; a mind of one's own

主子(zhǔzi) a master; a boss

煮豆燃萁(zhǔdòu ránqí) (lit.) "to cook beans with beanstalks" - to fight among brothers; fratricidal conflict

煮鹤焚琴(zhǔhè fénqín) (lit.) "to cook the crane for meat and burn a stringed instrument for fuel" - to destroy valuable things

住持(zhùchí) a Buddhist or Taoist abbot

助桀为虐(zhùjié wéinüè) (lit.) "to help the tyrant King Jie in his oppression" - to aid and abet an evil-doer; to hold a candle to the devil

助纣为虐(zhùzhòu wéinüè)(lit.)"to help King Zhou in his tyrannical rule"-to aid and abet an evil-doer; to hold a candle to the devil

杼轴其空(zhùzhóu qí kōng) poor and deficient

杼轴(zhùzhóu)(lit.)"the shuttle and axle"-the conception and organization in an article

驻跸(zhùbì) to stop over somewhere (of a monarch on tour)

驻节(zhùjié) to be stationed in a country; to stay somewhere temporarily on business

驻屯(zhùtún) to be stationed; to be quartered

《祝福》(zhùfú) *The New Year Sacrifice*-a short story by Lu Xun(鲁迅,1881-1936); *Blessings*

祝酒(zhùjiǔ) to toast; to drink a toast

祝寿(zhùshòu) to congratulate (an elderly person) on his or her birthday

疰夏(zhùxià) summer fever

筑长城(zhù chángchéng) to play mah-jong

筑巢引凤(zhùcháo yǐnfèng)(lit.)"to build a nest to attract phoenixes"-to improve the environment to attract people of talent and investment

抓辫子(zhuābiànzi) to capitalize on one's vulnerable point; to seize on one's mistake

抓差(zhuāchāi) to press somebody into service; to draft somebody for a particular task

抓哏(zhuāgén) to throw in impromptu lines to stimulate audiences to roar with laughter

抓官差(zhuāguānchāi) ①to arrest local authorities ② to make someone do something without pay

抓髻(zhuāji) hair worn in two buns

抓髻夫妻(zhuāji fūqī) a couple married for the first time

抓尖儿(zhuājiānr) to show off (by being the first to do something)

抓阄儿(zhuājiūr) to draw lots

抓破脸(zhuāpòliǎn)(lit.)"to scratch each other's face"-to break relations openly; to be overtly offensive to someone

抓瞎(zhuāxiā) to be at a loss as to what to do; to be in a muddle

抓药(zhuāyào) to make up (or fill) a prescription of Chinese herbal medicine

抓周(zhuāzhōu) to draw lots (on the occasion of a baby's first birthday)

抓壮丁(zhuāzhuàngdīng) to press able-bodied men into service

抓总儿(zhuāzǒngr) to be in charge of

the overall situation

转文(zhuǎiwén)to speak in classical Chinese to show one's knowledge;to talk like a book;to speak with literary allusions

专宠(zhuānchǒng)to monopolize the favour of a ruler

专擅(zhuānshàn)①to usurp authority②to act presumptuously

专史(zhuānshǐ)a specialized history

专政(zhuānzhèng)dictatorship

砖茶(zhuānchá)the brick tea(a kind of compressed and fermented tea)

颛民(zhuānmín)kind ordinary folk

转包(zhuǎnbāo)to subcontract

转关系(zhuǎn guānxi)to transfer the registration of Party membership or organization from one unit to another

转圜(zhuǎnhuán)①to save or retrieve a situation②to mediate;to reconcile

转蓬(zhuǎnpéng)①to float about in a shiftless way;to drift

转生(zhuǎnshēng)(Buddhism)reincarnation;transmigration

转世(zhuǎnshì)reincarnation

转世灵童(zhuǎnshì língtóng)(Tibetan Buddhism)a reincarnated soul boy;a snoic

转运使(zhuǎnyùnshǐ)a transportation envoy

转韵(zhuǎnyùn)a change of rhyme

转注(zhuǎnzhù)mutually explanatory or synonymous characters;a derivative character

转筋(zhuànjīn)a muscle convulsion;cramp;a muscle spasm

转经筒(zhuàn jīngtǒng)a prayer wheel

转磨(zhuànmò)to go round in circles;to be at a loss as to what to do

转弯子(zhuànwānzi)①to beat about the bush②to change one's position

转腰子(zhuànyāozi)①to stroll②to pace up and down worrying about something③to beat about the bush;to speak in a roundabout way

传舍(zhuànshè)①a lodge for passers-by

传赞(zhuànzàn)the author's commentary(at the end of each biography in the historical record presented in a series of biographies)

赚头(zhuàntou)profits;gains

赚外快(zhuàn wàikuài)to make extra money;to make extra gains

篆刻(zhuànkè)seal cutting;sealengraving

篆书(zhuànshū)a seal character;the seal script

妆奁(zhuānglián)a trousseau;a dowry

妆台(zhuāngtái)a dressing table

庄客(zhuāngkè)a tenant farmer

庄票(zhuāngpiào)a cashier's cheques

庄屈(zhuāngqū)Zhuang Zhou(庄周, 369 - 286 BC) and Qu Yuan(屈原,340 - 278 BC)

庄子(zhuāngzǐ) Zhuang Zi; Chuang-tzu; Zhuangzi (the great thinker, philosopher and writer)

《庄子》(zhuāngzǐ) *The Book of Master Zhuang*; *The Zhuangzi*; *The Chuang Tzu* - a Chinese classic

装裱(zhuāngbiǎo) to mount a picture, etc.

装殓(zhuāngliàn) to dress and lay a corpse in a coffin

装门面(zhuāngménmiàn) to keep up appearances; to put up a front

装蒜(zhuāngsuàn) to pretend not to know

装孙子(zhuāngsūnzi) ①to pretend to be helpless and miserable②to pretend not to know

《装修》(zhuāngxiū) *Home Renovation* - a Chinese skit starring by Huang Hong(黄宏) and Gong Hanlin(巩汉林) in 2005

装洋蒜(zhuāng yángsuàn) to feign ignorance

壮丁(zhuàngdīng) an able-bodied man

壮歌(zhuànggē) ①a solemn and stirring hymn ② a folk song of the Zhuang ethnic group

壮锦(zhuàngjǐn) Zhuang brocade

壮举(zhuàngjǔ) a great feat

壮士(zhuàngshì) a brave man; a hero

壮戏(zhuàngxì) Zhuang opera

壮行(zhuàngxíng) to give someone a decent send-off; to enable someone to depart in style

壮行酒(zhuàngxíngjiǔ) a farewell dinner with wine; departure wine

壮阳(zhuàngyáng) (medicine) to invigorate one's Yang; to promote the functions of the kidney and increase one's virility

壮志未酬(zhuàngzhì wèichóu) to die with one's lofty aspirations unrealized

壮族(zhuàngzú) the Zhuang nationality (distributed mainly in Guangxi)

壮族土戏(zhuàngzú tǔxì) the local opera of the Zhuang nationality

状头(zhuàngtóu) *zhuangyuan* (the scholar who won first place in the highest imperial examinations)

状元(zhuàngyuán) the Top Scholar; No. 1 Scholar (who won first place in the highest imperial examinations)

状元红(zhuàngyuánhóng) Zhuangyuan Red (a high quality Shaoxing wine)

状纸(zhuàngzhǐ) a written complaint

状子(zhuàngzi)a written complaint

撞大运(zhuàng dàyùn)to try one's luck;to take a chance

撞客(zhuàngkè)to encounter an evil spirit

撞木钟(zhuàng mùzhōng)①to do something useless②to deceive; to swindle③to meet with a rebuff

撞骗(zhuàngpiàn)to look for any chance to swindle somebody

撞枪口上(zhuàng qiāngkǒu shàng) to cause oneself trouble; to be asking for trouble

追福(zhuīfú)to pray for the good fortune of the deceased in the nether world

追星(zhuīxīng)to chase or worship movie stars, singing stars or sports stars

追星族(zhuīxīngzú)a groupie;a fan; fans of a celebrity;an idolater

锥处囊中(zhuīchǔnángzhōng)(lit.) "an awl in a bag" - a talent is bound to reveal itself sooner or later

锥刀之末(zhuīdāo zhī mò)petty profits;small gains

坠地(zhuìdì)(of a child)to be born

坠琴(zhuìqín)zhuiqin(a kind of stringed instrument with a fingerplate)

坠腿(zhuìtuǐ)to hold somebody back;to be a drag on somebody

坠子(zhuìzi)an ear pendant

缀文(zhuìwén)to compose an essay

赘婿(zhuìxù)a son-in-law living in the home of his wife's parents

赘疣(zhuìyóu)①a wart②a superfluous or useless thing

准噶尔盆地(zhǔngé'er péndì)the Junggar Basin

准谱儿(zhǔnpǔr)a sure thing;a definite idea

准绳(zhǔnshéng)a criterion

拙笔(zhuōbǐ)(self-deprecatory)my poor writing or painting

拙见(zhuōjiàn)my humble opinion

拙荆(zhuōjīng)(self-deprecatory) my wife

拙政园(zhuōzhèngyuán)The Garden of the Humble Administrator (in Suzhou)

拙作(zhuōzuò)(self-deprecatory)my poor writing or painting; my poor work

捉刀(zhuōdāo)to write (an article, etc.) for somebody else; to ghostwrite

灼见(zhuójiàn)a penetrating insight; a profound view

卓见(zhuójiàn)an excellent opinion; a brilliant idea

卓荦(zhuóluò)outstanding; extraordinary

浊流(zhuóliú)(lit.)"a turbid current" – the forces of darkness and decadence; a villain

浊世(zhuóshì)①the corrupt world; chaotic times②the mortal world

浊物(zhuówù)an absurd creature; an insensitive creature

着墨(zhuómò)to apply ink to paper; to write or paint

着棋(zhuóqí)to play chess

着手回春(zhuóshǒu huíchūn)to bring about a miraculous recovery from illness

着先鞭(zhuó xiānbiān)to take precedence; to get ahead of

擢发难数(zhuófànánshǔ)too numerous to count; uncountable

擢升(zhuóshēng)to promote; to exalt

斲轮老手(zhuólún lǎoshǒu)an experienced person; an old hand

镯子(zhuózi)a bracelet

仔肩(zījiān)official burdens or responsibilities

咨嗟(zījiē)①to heave a sigh②to praise; to marvel at

咨文(zīwén)an official communication; an official report; a message

赀选(zīxuǎn)the selection of officials by contributing some property to the imperial governments of the Han Dynasty

资产阶级自由化(zīchǎn jiējí zìyóu huà)bourgeois liberalization

资历(zīlì)qualifications and record of service

资政(zīzhèng)①to help to administer a country②the presidential political advisor

《资治通鉴》(zīzhìtōngjiàn)*The Comprehensive Mirror to Aid in Government* – a historical work by Sima Guang(司马光,1019 – 1086); *History as a Mirror for Political Administration*

缁布冠(zībùguān)a black silk hat

缁黄(zīhuáng)(lit.)"black and yellow" – Buddhist monks and Taoist priests

缁素(zīsù)①black and white②clergy and laity

缁衣(zīyī)①a black court dress②black clothes③a Buddhist monk

滋事(zīshì)to cause trouble; to stir up trouble

滋阴(zīyīn)(medical)to treat *yin* deficiency by reinforcing body fluid and nourishing the blood

辎重(zīzhòng)supplies for an army

觜宿(zīxiù)the Turtle Beak(one of the twenty-eight constellations)

趑趄(zījū)①to walk with difficulty②to hesitate; to falter

锱铢(zīzhū)a small amount of money; a mere trifle

《子不语》(zǐbùyǔ)*What the Master*

Would Not Talk about – an essay by Yuan Mei (袁枚, 1716 – 1797) in 1788

子朝之乱 (zǐcháo zhī luàn) the Zichao Riot(520 – 505 BC)

子丑寅卯 (zǐchǒuyínmǎo) the first four of the twelve Earthly Branches (地支); in an orderly way

子弟(zǐdì) children; young generation

子妇(zǐfù) ①son and daughter-in-law ②daughter-in-law

子时(zǐshí) the period of a day from 11 p. m. to 1 a. m.

子书(zǐshū) the works of ancient philosophers(other than those of Confucius); philosophical works

子嗣(zǐsì) sons and heirs; male offspring

子孙娘娘(zǐsūn niángniang) Our Lady of Many Children(an immortal believed to give sons)

子午卯酉(zǐwǔ mǎoyǒu) ①the whole day②the reason; the cause

子息(zǐxí) ①son; male offspring ② loan interest

子弦(zǐxián) fine silk strings (for a Chinese lute, southern fiddle, pipa, etc.)

子虚(zǐxū) fictitious; unreal

子婿(zǐxù) son-in-law

《子夜》(zǐyè) *Midnight* – a novel by Mao Dun(茅盾, 1896 – 1981)

子侄(zǐzhí) a son or nephew

梓宫(zǐgōng) the coffin of the emperor and empress

梓里(zǐlǐ) hometown; a native place

紫光阁(zǐguānggé) Ziguang Pavilion; the Hall of Purple and Light (in Zhongnanhai, Beijing)

紫毫(zǐháo) a writing brush(made of dark purple hair of hares)

紫金山(zǐjīnshān) Mount Zijin; Purple Mountain(in Nanjing)

紫禁城(zǐjìnchéng) the Forbidden City

紫气东来(zǐqì dōnglái) (lit.) "purple air coming from the east" – an auspicious omen

紫砂(zǐshā) a red stoneware

紫砂壶(zǐshāhú) a red stoneware teapot; a boccaro teapot

紫檀(zǐtán) red sandalwood

紫阳派(zǐyángpài) the Ziyang Sect of Taoism

紫芝(zǐzhī) a person of virtue or merit

訾议(zǐyì) to comment on people's weaknesses; to criticize

字调(zìdiào) the tones of Chinese characters

字幅(zìfú) a horizontal or vertical scroll of calligraphy

字号(zìhào) ①the font size; the type size②the title of a shop

字画(zìhuà) calligraphy and painting

字卷(zìjuàn)a calligraphy scroll

《字林》(zìlín)*Collection of Characters* – an ancient book by Lü Chen(吕忱, 420 – 479)

字谜(zìmí)a word riddle;a logogriph

字模(zìmú)(printing)type matrix; typehead

字书(zìshū)a wordbook; a lexicon; a dictionary

字帖(zìtiè)a copybook for calligraphy;a model for calligraphers

字眼(zìyǎn)wording;diction

字正腔圆(zìzhèng qiāngyuán)clear articulation and proficient singing (of opera singers)

自便(zìbiàn)at one's convenience;as one pleases;at one's will

自裁(zìcái)to commit suicide;to take one's own life

自炒(zìchǎo)①to boast②to fire oneself;to sack oneself

自出机杼(zìchū jīzhù)to be original in conception

自给自足(zìjǐ zìzú)to work to support oneself;self-sufficiency

自家人(zìjiārén)people on one's own side;one of us

自尽(zìjìn)to commit suicide;to kill oneself

自掘坟墓(zìjué fénmù)to dig one's own grave;to work for one's own ruin;to invite one's own destruction

自况(zìkuàng)to compare oneself to (someone or something)

自力更生(zìlì gēngshēng)to rely on one's own efforts;self-reliance

自立门户(zìlì ménhù)①to separate from one's family and become independent ② to set up a school of thought or religious schism

自留地(zìliúdì)a private plot

自谦之词(zìqiān zhī cí)self-deprecating remarks; the remarks of being modest

自戕(zìqiāng)to commit suicide

自省(zìxǐng)to examine oneself;self-communion;self-reflection

自我批评(zìwǒ pīpíng)self-criticism

自我作古(zìwǒ zuògǔ)to be original; to be the first(to do something)

自新(zìxīn)to turn over a new leaf;to make a fresh start

自诩(zìxǔ)to praise oneself;to brag

自由职业画家(zìyóu zhíyè huàjiā)a freelance artist

自由主义文学(zìyóuzhǔyì wénxué) the Liberalist Literature(a literary current in the 1920s and 1930s)

自由撰稿人(zìyóu zhuàngǎorén)a freelance writer;a freelancer

自重(zìzhòng)to conduct oneself with dignity;to be self-dignified;to have self-respect

宗伯(zōngbó)①Zongbo(a high official in charge of memorial ceremonies in ancient China) ② an esteemed, learned master

宗臣(zōngchén) ①a minister of the same ancestry as the emperor ②respectable famous ministers

宗祠(zōngcí) an ancestral hall or temple

宗弟(zōngdì) ①the younger brother ②a brother of the same clan

宗藩(zōngfān) the dukes and princes of the imperial clan

宗国(zōngguó) the feudal states of the same surname

宗匠(zōngjiàng) a great master

宗门(zōngmén) the same clan

宗庙(zōngmiào) an ancestral temple or shrine

宗谱(zōngpǔ) a family tree; genealogy

宗亲(zōngqīn) members of the same clan

宗人府(zōngrénfǔ) the government office in charge of affairs of imperial kinsmen

宗社(zōngshè) ①an ancestral temple or shrine ②a country

宗师(zōngshī) a great master; the master of great learning

宗事(zōngshì) ①the affairs of an ancestral temple or imperial clan ②to serve reverently

宗室(zōngshì) ①the imperial clan ② the imperial clansman

宗祧(zōngtiāo) ①an ancestral temple ②the lineage of a family

宗相(zōngxiàng) the prime minister of the same clan with the emperor

宗学(zōngxué) school for children of the imperial clan

宗仰(zōngyǎng) ①to hold in esteem ②to believe in

宗正(zōngzhèng) ① Zongzheng (an high-ranking official in charge of affairs of imperial kinsmen) ② a model; an example

宗支(zōngzhī) descendants of the same clan

宗子(zōngzǐ) ①the eldest son of the principal wife ②the head of a clan ③the children of the imperial clan

宗子试(zōngzǐshì) the imperial examination for children of the imperial clan

宗族(zōngzú) ①a patriarchal clan ② a clansman

总兵(zǒngbīng) ①to lead the army ② Commander (a commanding officer of garrison troops)

总裁(zǒngcái) ①Head Examiner (an official in charge of compiling and editing in the Yuan and Qing Dynasties) ② president; director-general

总管(zǒngguǎn) ①to take overall responsibility for ② a manager ③ a steward; a butler

总角(zǒngjiǎo) childhood

总角之交(zǒngjiǎo zhī jiāo) a childhood friend

纵队(zòngduì) ①a column②an army (a military unit)

纵横家(zònghéngjiā) the Strategists; a political strategist; an elocutionist

纵酒(zòngjiǔ) to drink to excess; to swizzle

纵情(zòngqíng) to one's heart's content

粽子(zòngzi) a glutinous rice dumpling (wrapped in bamboo or reed leaves)

诹访(zōufǎng) to consult; to seek advice from

诹吉(zōují) to choose a happy and auspicious day

走八字(zǒubāzì) to be lucky; to have good luck

走板(zǒubǎn) ①to be off the beat (when singing Chinese opera) ②to stray from the topic

走背运(zǒubèiyùn) to go through an unlucky period; to have bad luck

走背字(zǒubèizì) to be unlucky; to be out of luck

走镖(zǒubiāo) to take people or goods in a convoy with armed escorts

走肚子(zǒudùzi) to have loose bowels

走方郎中(zǒufāng lángzhōng) an itinerant doctor

走钢丝(zǒu gāngsī) ①wire-walking; a tightrope walker②to take risks

走狗(zǒugǒu) a running dog; a lackey; a servile follower

走关节(zǒuguānjié) to evade (laws, rules, etc.) by bribery

走过场(zǒuguòchǎng) ①(theater) to cross the stage without stopping②to muddle through one's work; to go through the motions

走黑道(zǒu hēidào) to go to the underworld; to be not in the good way

走红(zǒuhóng) to have good luck; to be popular

走后门(zǒuhòumén) to get in through the "back door" - to use one's connections to gain advantage; to use influence to aquire what one wants

走江湖(zǒujiānghú) to lead a vagrant life as a juggler, street entertainer, fortune-teller etc.

走马灯(zǒumǎdēng) a trotting horse lantern; a revolving scenic lamp

走马观花(zǒumǎ guānhuā) (lit.) "to ride a horse looking at flowers" - to have a superficial understanding; to do something hurriedly

走马上任(zǒumǎshàngrèn) to go to one's post; to go to take office

走门路(zǒuménlù) to gain one's end by making use of his relationships

走内线(zǒunèixiàn) to use private channels to achieve one's end; to exert private influence to achieve one's end

走娘家(zǒu niángjiā) to visit one's wife's parents; to return to her parents' home

走票(zǒupiào) to act in an amateur production

走亲戚(zǒu qīnqi) to call on relatives; to visit relatives

走弯路(zǒu wānlù) to take a roundabout route; to make detours

《走西口》(zǒu xīkǒu) *Leave for the West Col* – a TV drama directed by Li Sanlin(李三林) in 2009

《走向共和》(zǒuxiàng gònghé) *For the sake of the Republic of China* – a TV drama directed by Zhang Li(张黎) in 2003

走穴(zǒuxué) to go moonlighting; to moonlight; to go out to earn extra money(without permission)

走着瞧(zǒuzheqiáo) to wait and see; to see how it goes

走资派(zǒuzīpài) a capitalist roader

走卒(zǒuzú) a pawn; a dupe; a cat's-paw

走嘴(zǒuzuǐ) to let slip an inadvertent or negligent remark

奏案(zòu'àn) ①a table on which were placed memorials to the throne ② cases approved by the emperor

奏报(zòubào) to submit a memorial to (the emperor)

奏本(zòuběn) ①an official document (presented to the emperor) ② to present a memorial to the emperor

奏捷(zòujié) to win a battle; to achieve success

奏疏(zòushū) a memorial to the emperor

奏议(zòuyì) a memorial to the em peror

奏章(zòuzhāng) a memorial to the emperor

奏折(zòuzhé) a memorial to the emperor

租佃(zūdiàn) to rent out land to tenants; land tenancy

租米(zūmǐ) ①rice paid by peasants as land rent②land tax(paid to feudal officials)

租税(zūshuì) land tax and other levies

租子(zūzi) land rent; ground rent

足本(zúběn) an unabridged version of a book

足炉(zúlú) a foot warmer; a foot stove

足下(zúxià) "you"; "sir" (a polite form of address for friends, used in letters)

足兴(zúxìng) to be enough; to satisfy one's needs

卒岁(zúsuì) to get through the year

卒子(zúzi) ①a rank-and-file soldier ②a pawn(one of the pieces in Chinese chess)

族产(zúchǎn) the property of a clan.

族长(zúzhǎng) the head of a clan

族规(zúguī) the rules and regulations of a clan or a family

族灭(zúmiè) the execution of the whole clan(because of one clansman's crime)

族内婚(zúnèihūn) marriage inside the clan

族谱(zúpǔ) the pedigree of a clan; the clan genealogy

族权(zúquán) the clan authority; clan power

族田(zútián) the common land of a clan

族外婚(zúwàihūn) exogamy; marriage outside the clan

族诛(zúzhū) execution of the offender and members of the same clan

族尊(zúzūn) a clan elder; a senior in a clan

《组织部来了个年轻人》(zǔzhībù láile gè niánqīngrén) *A Young Newcomer in the Organization Department* – a novelette by Wang Meng (王蒙,1934 –) in 1956

俎豆(zǔdòu) ①sacrificial vessels②to offer sacrifice to

俎豆千秋(zǔdòu qiānqiū) to offer sacrifices to ancestors

俎上肉(zǔshàngròu)(lit.)"a piece of meat on the chopping block" – a helpless victim

祖辈(zǔbèi) ancestors; forefathers

祖本(zǔběn) the first edition of a block-printed book; the first stone rubbing of an inscription

祖妣(zǔbǐ) ①one's deceased grandmother②the ancestors

祖传秘方(zǔchuán mìfāng) a secret prescription handed down from one's ancesters; a family recipe

祖道(zǔdào) to give a farewell dinner

祖坟(zǔfén) the ancestral grave

祖饯(zǔjiàn) ①to give a farewell dinner②to hold a memorial service for the souls of the dead

祖居(zǔjū) ①the ancestral home②to have one's ancestral home at; to be a native of

祖考(zǔkǎo) ①one's deceased grandfather②ancestors; forebears

祖龙一炬(zǔlóng yījù) the fire lit(to burn books) by Emperor Qin(秦始皇,259 – 210 BC) in 213 BC

祖庙(zǔmiào) ancestral temple

祖上(zǔshàng) ancestors; forefathers; forbears

祖师(zǔshī)the founder(of a theory, a craft, a school of learning, a religious denomination, etc.)

祖师爷(zǔshīyé)the founder(of a theory, a craft, a school of learning, a religious denomination, etc.)

祖荫(zǔyīn)①to be protected or blessed by one's ancestors②to confer the official posts of ancestors upon descendants

祖茔(zǔyíng)an ancestral grave

祖宗(zǔzong)①ancestors; forefathers ②elders and betters(a polite expression)

钻空子(zuān kòngzi)to exploit loopholes; to avail oneself of loopholes

钻门子(zuānménzi)to manoeuvre for advantage; to fawn on influential officials

钻牛角尖(zuān niújiǎojiān)to take unnecessary pains to study a trivial problem; to split hairs

纂儿(zuǎnr)a chignon hairstyle; a bun

纂修洪业(zuǎnxiū hóngyè)to carry forward a great undertaking

嘴脸(zuǐliǎn)look; features; countenance

嘴皮子(zuǐpízi)eloquence

嘴贫(zuǐpín)loquacious; garrulous

嘴损(zuǐsǔn)sarcastic; sharp-tongued

蕞尔小邦(zuì'ěr xiǎobāng)a small country; a small county

蕞尔小国(zuì'ěr xiǎoguó)a small country

醉酒饱德(zuìjiǔ bǎodé)to be quite well-entertained(used to thank somebody for hospitality)

醉墨(zuìmò)poems and paintings done under the influence of alcohol

《醉拳》(zuìquán)*Drunken Master* – a film directed by Yuan Heping(袁和平)in 1978

醉拳(zuìquán)the Drunken Boxing(a form of boxing suggesting a drunken man reeling along)

醉翁亭(zuìwēngtíng)the Old Tippler's Pavilion(in Langya Hill of Anhui Province)

《醉翁亭记》(zuìwēngtíng jì)*The Record of the Old Tippler's Pavilion* – an essay by Ouyang Xiu(欧阳修, 1007 – 1073)in 1046; *The Roadside Hut of the Old Drunkard*

醉翁椅(zuìwēngyǐ)a rocking deck chair

醉翁之意不在酒(zuìwēngzhīyì bùzài jiǔ)(lit.)"The intention of the old drunken man lies not in wine." – to have an ulterior motive

尊长(zūnzhǎng)elders and betters

尊公(zūngōng)①your father②elders and betters

尊号(zūnhào)①the respectful title of

an emperor or empress②the name of a person or one's business

尊驾(zūnjià)you(an honorific form)

尊亲(zūnqīn)①revered parents or ancestors②elder relatives

尊堂(zūntáng)your mother

尊翁(zūnwēng)your father

樽俎(zūnzǔ)the drinking vessel

作坊(zuōfang)a workshop

作揖(zuōyī)to make a bow(with hands clasped in front of one)

《昨天、今天、明天》(zuótiān,jīntiān,míngtiān)*Yesterday*,*Today*,*Tomorrow* - a skit starring by Zhao Benshan(赵本山)and Song Dandan(宋丹丹)in 1999

左丞相(zuǒchéngxiàng)the left prime minister

《左传》(zuǒzhuàn)*Zuo's Commentaries on the Spring and Autumn Annals* - a historical work by Zuo Qiuming(左丘明,502 - 422 BC);*The Commentaries of Zuo*

左道旁门(zuǒdào pángmén)①a heretical sect;a heterodox school②heresy;heterodoxy

左联(zuǒ lián)the League of Leftist Writers

左券(zuǒquàn)①a duplicate of a contract②self-assurance;self-confidence

左嗓子(zuǒsǎngzi)①an out-of-tune voice②a person who sings in an out-of-tune voice

左师(zuǒshī)deputy to the prime minister

左司马(zuǒsīmǎ)the left minister of war(an official title in ancient China)

左思风力(zuǒsī fēnglì)the vigorous,abundant and copious style of Zuo Si's(左思,250 - 305)poems

左徒(zuǒtú)the official in charge of policy discussion and foreign guests

左翼电影运动(zuǒyì diànyǐng yùndòng)the leftist film movement

左翼文学(zuǒyì wénxué)left-wing literature

左翼作家联盟(zuǒyì zuòjiā liánméng)the League of Leftist Writers

左尹(zuǒyǐn)deputy to the prime minister

左右(zuǒyòu)①left and right②attendants③to control

左右督(zuǒyòudū)the military governor and the military vice-governor

左右拾遗(zuǒyòu shíyí)the admonishing officials

左右手(zuǒyòushǒu)a right-hand man;a capable assistant

左镇人(zuǒzhèn rén)Zuozhen man(homo sapiens found in Zuozhen of southern Taiwan Province)

佐贰(zuǒ'èr)a deputy

佐酒(zuǒjiǔ)①to drink for company ②(of food) to go well with wine

佐领(zuǒlǐng)①zuoling(the name of the basic unit of the Eight Banners of the Manchu nationality) ② the deputy chief (of waterborne forces in the late Qing Dynasty)

佐命(zuǒmìng) a meritorious minister who helped the founder of a Dynasty

作保(zuòbǎo) to be somebody's guarantor; to sponsor somebody; to provide bail for somebody

作壁上观(zuòbìshàngguān)(lit.) "to watch the battle from the ramparts" - to be an onlooker

作法自毙(zuòfǎ zìbì)(lit.) "to make a law only to punish oneself" - to get caught in one's own trap; to be hoist by one's own petard

作梗(zuògěng)①to baffle; to make trouble②to make people vexed

作古(zuògǔ) to die; to pass away

作怪(zuòguài) to make trouble; to do mischief

作脸(zuòliǎn) to bring honor to; win credit for

作美(zuòměi) to help; to make things easy; to cooperate

作孽(zuòniè) to commit a sin

作死(zuòsǐ) to seek death; to look for trouble

作为(zuòwéi)①action; conduct; deed ②achievement; accomplishment

作文章(zuò wénzhāng)①to write an article②to make an issue of

作协(zuòxié) the Writers' Association

作学问(zuò xuéwèn) to engage in scholarship; to do scholarly research

作艺(zuòyì) to give a performance

作俑(zuòyǒng)①to make a tomb figurine ② to originate an immoral practice; to create a bad precedent

坐部伎(zuòbùjì) to sit playing musical instruments (in the imperial court of the Tang Dynasty)

坐禅(zuòchán) to sit in meditation

坐场诗(zuòchǎngshī) the opening poem(in traditional operas or films)

坐大(zuòdà)①to allow something to grow strong freely②to be arrogant

坐地虎(zuòdìhǔ) a local bully; a local villain

坐馆(zuòguǎn) to be a private tutor; to act as an assistant(to a high general or official in old China)

坐红椅子(zuò hóngyǐzi) to be the last of the successful candidates in the imperial examination

坐化(zuòhuà) to pass away while sitting cross legged(Buddhism)

坐家女(zuòjiānǚ) a spinster; a single woman; an unmarried girl

坐江山(zuò jiāngshān) to rule or govern the country

坐具(zuòjù)①something to sit on;a seat ② the cloth by which monks protect the body; clothes; mat (a Buddhist term)

坐蜡(zuòlà) to land in a predicament; to be embarrassed; to be in trouble

坐冷板凳(zuò lěngbǎndèng)(lit.) "to sit on a cold bench" - to be in an insignificant position;to be neglected

坐商(zuòshāng) a tradesman;a shopkeeper

坐堂(zuòtáng)①(of a magistrate) to sit in a court to hear cases②to sit in meditation (Buddhism) ③ to do business in a shop;to practice medicine in a hospital

坐天下(zuò tiānxià) to rule or govern the country

坐忘(zuòwàng)(Taoism) to sit upright with full oblivion

坐月子(zuò yuèzi) pregnant woman with the one-month confinement after childbirth

坐庄(zuòzhuāng)①to be a resident buyer of a business firm②to be the dealer or banker in a gambling game

座山雕(zuòshāndiāo) a cinereous vulture

座上客(zuòshàngkè) a guest of honor;an ho-nored guest

座师(zuòshī) the chief examiner

座主(zuòzhǔ) the chief examiner

做东(zuòdōng) to be host; to host somebody

做工(zuògōng)①to work;to do manual work②workmanship③dramatic performance(in Chinese opera)

做功夫(zuò gōngfu) ① to rehearse one's skill ② to sit in meditation (Buddhism)

做鬼(zuòguǐ) to play tricks;to be up to mischief

做活局子(zuòhuójúzi) to gang up to deceive others;to trap;to swindle

做辣(zuòlà) to put somebody in a tough situation

做满月(zuò mǎnyuè) to celebrate a baby's one-month birthday

做媒(zuòméi) to be a matchmaker;to be a go-between

做亲(zuòqīn)①to become related by marriage②to get married

做人情(zuò rénqíng) to do somebody a favor

做手脚(zuò shǒujiǎo) to use underhand methods; to play a trick; to mess about with

做寿(zuòshòu) to celebrate a birthday (of an elderly person)

做戏(zuòxì)①to put on a show; to

act in a play②to pretend

做秀(zuòxiù) to show; to make a show;to put on a show

做学问(zuò xuéwèn) to engage in scholarship;to do scholarly research

做眼色(zuò yǎnsè) to signal to somebody by winking

参考文献

1. 北京外国语大学英语系词典组编：《汉英词典》，外语教学与研究出版社 1997 年版。

2. 程立、程建华编著：《英汉文化比较词典》，湖南教育出版社 2000 年版。

3. 丁守和：《中华文化词典》，广东人民出版社 1989 年版。

4. 胡世庆等编著：《中国文化史》，中国广播电视出版社 1991 年版。

5. 惠宇主编：《新世纪汉英大词典》，外语教学与研究出版社 2002 年版。

6. 廖华英：《中国文化概况》，外语教学与研究出版社 2007 年版。

7. 沈善洪主编：《中国语言文化背景汉英双解词典》，商务印书馆 1998 年版。

8. 中国社会科学院语言研究所词典编辑室：《现代汉语词典》（汉英双语版），外语教学与研究出版社 2002 年版。

9. 吴光华：《汉英综合大辞典》，大连理工大学出版社 2004 年版。

10. 吴景荣等编著：《新时代汉英大辞典》，商务印书馆 2000 年版。

11. 杨恒达等编著：《汉英中国文化词典》，南京大学出版社 2005 年版。

12. 杨金鼎主编：《中国文化史词典》，浙江古籍出版社

1987 年版。

13. 杨敏：《中国文化通览》，高等教育出版社 2006 年版。

14. 舆水优等编著：《朗文汉英中华文化图解词典》，上海外语教育出版社 2002 年版。

15. 中国社会科学院语言研究所词典编辑室编：《现代汉语词典》，商务印书馆 1992 年版。

16. 朱一飞主编：《英译中国文化寓言故事》，上海外语教育出版社 2007 年版。

17. Patricia Buckley Ebrey, *Chinese Civilization*: *A Sourcebook*, New York: the Free Press, 1993.

18. Patricia Buckley Ebrey, *The Cambridge Illustrated History of China*, Cambridge: Cambridge University Press, 1996

19. Peter Neville, *China*: *People*, *Place*, *Culture*, *History*, New York: DK Publishing, 2007.

20. Wolfram Eberhard, *A History of China*, Kindle Book, 2006.

21. Y. L. Liang & Neville Whymant, *China*, Macdonald & Co. Ltd. , 1946.